OXFORD WORLD'S CLASSICS

LA REINE MARGOT

ALEXANDRE DUMAS was born at Villers-Cotterêts in 1802, the son of an innkeeper's daughter and of one of Napoleon's most remarkable generals. He moved to Paris in 1823 to make his fortune in the theatre. By the time he was 28, he was one of the leading literary figures of his day, a star of the Romantic Revolution, and known for his many mistresses and taste for high living. He threw himself recklessly into the July Revolution of 1830, which he regarded as a great adventure. Quickly wearying of politics, he returned to the theatre and then moved on to fiction. By the early 1840s he was producing vast historical novels at a stupendous rate and in prodigious quantities for the cheap newspapers which paid enormous sums of money to authors who could please the public. A master story-teller, he became the best-known Frenchman of his age. He earned several fortunes which he gave away, or spent on women and travel, or wasted on grandiose follies like the 'Château de Monte Cristo' which he built to symbolize his success. In 1848 he stood unsuccessfully in the elections for the new Assembly. By 1850 his creditors began to catch up with him and, partly to escape them and partly to find new material for his novels, plays, and travel books, he lived abroad for long periods, travelling through Russia, where his fame had preceded him, and Italy, where he ran guns in support of Garibaldi's libertarian cause. Without guile and without enemies, the 'great' Dumas was a man of endless fascination. He died of a stroke at Puys, near Dieppe, in 1870.

DAVID COWARD is Senior Fellow and Emeritus Professor of French Literature at the University of Leeds. He is the author of studies of Marivaux, Marguerite Duras, Marcel Pagnol, and Restif de La Bretonne. For Oxford World's Classics, he has edited eight novels by Alexandre Dumas, including the whole of the Musketeer saga, and translated Dumas *fils*'s *La Dame aux camélias*, two selections of Maupassant short stories, Sade's *Misfortunes of Virtue and Other Early Tales*, and Diderot's *Jacques the Fatalist*. Winner of the 1996 Scott-Moncrieff Prize for translation, he reviews regularly for the *Times Literary Supplement*.

OXFORD WORLD'S CLASSICS

*For almost 100 years Oxford World's Classics have brought
readers closer to the world's great literature. Now with over 700
titles—from the 4,000-year-old myths of Mesopotamia to the
twentieth century's greatest novels—the series makes available
lesser-known as well as celebrated writing.*

*The pocket-sized hardbacks of the early years contained
introductions by Virginia Woolf, T. S. Eliot, Graham Greene,
and other literary figures which enriched the experience of reading.
Today the series is recognized for its fine scholarship and
reliability in texts that span world literature, drama and poetry,
religion, philosophy and politics. Each edition includes perceptive
commentary and essential background information to meet the
changing needs of readers.*

OXFORD WORLD'S CLASSICS

ALEXANDRE DUMAS

La Reine Margot

Edited with an Introduction and Notes by
DAVID COWARD

OXFORD
UNIVERSITY PRESS

OXFORD

UNIVERSITY PRESS

Great Clarendon Street, Oxford OX2 6DP

Oxford University Press is a department of the University of Oxford
and furthers the University's aim of excellence in research, scholarship,
and education by publishing worldwide in

Oxford New York

Athens Auckland Bangkok Bogotá Buenos Aires Calcutta
Cape Town Chennai Dar es Salaam Delhi Florence Hong Kong Istanbul
Karachi Kuala Lumpur Madrid Melbourne Mexico City Mumbai
Nairobi Paris São Paulo Singapore Taipei Tokyo Toronto Warsaw

and associated companies in Berlin Ibadan

Oxford is a registered trade mark of Oxford University Press

Revised translation and editorial matter © David Coward 1997

First published as a World's Classics paperback 1997

Reissued as an Oxford World's Classics paperback 1999

British Library Cataloguing in Publication Data

Data available

Library of Congress Cataloging in Publication Data

Data available

ISBN 0-19-283844-X

1 3 5 7 9 10 8 6 4 2

Typeset by Best-set Typesetter Ltd., Hong Kong
Printed in Great Britain by
Cox and Wyman Ltd.
Reading, Berkshire

CONTENTS

INTRODUCTION

AFTER 1789 France traversed forty stormy years of change. The repressive *ancien régime*, based on landed property, hierarchy, and privilege, gave way to power rooted in political influence and middle-class enterprise which was to bring about an industrial revolution and new institutional structures. But though it killed a king and removed many a noble head, the French Revolution did not quite see off either the monarchy or the aristocracy, both of which returned after the defeat of Napoleon in 1815. It offered tenured promotion to the middle classes and gave both content and form to the notion of the People, who ceased to be subjects, having a duty of obedience, and became citizens with inalienable rights. It was a momentous change which neither Napoleon's empire nor the absolutism of the restored monarchy after 1815 could reverse. Having for centuries lived very local lives, French men and women were increasingly subjected to the attentions of central government. But if politicians, who needed their support, began to notice them, they were also courted by intellectuals, who sought to educate them, and by business, which saw in them a lucrative market for manufactured products.

By the beginning of the nineteenth century playwrights and novelists too began catering for this new and less sophisticated public by ladling out large helpings of violence, passion, and sensation which were to remain the staple fare of popular literature. Theatre audiences demanded highly coloured melodrama and most novels showed, in various forms and settings, Innocence rescued from Wickedness at the eleventh hour. However, readers required more than escapism. They demanded information about the new world into which they had been brutally catapulted, and the growing number of newspapers supplied it. But they also needed a sense of continuity, a means of bridging the gulf which separated the *ancien régime*, which many remembered clearly, and the new social order. If popular literature is a reflection of popular concerns, then the fact that half the novels published between 1815 and 1830 were historical suggests that French people sought to come to terms with the present by examining their collective past, in other words to understand how modern France had grown out of the old.

The way had been shown from overseas. Walter Scott had not only told exciting stories but, in pitting Saxons against Normans, had given the British a sense of national identity. Fenimore Cooper's tales of pioneering life did the same for Americans. The French read them in translation and, catching their mood, fell hopelessly in love with their own history. Historians like Guizot and Michelet were on hand to explain the forces which had shaped their destiny, but readers were drawn less by historiography than by the raw material of history itself. From about 1820 onwards, publishers issued multi-volume collections of journals, memoirs, and letters written by the men and women who had played notable parts in climactic events. It was anecdotal history, the direct reportage of eye-witnesses, and it was strong on drama, gossip, and the clash of personalities. In the preface to his novel *Chronique du règne de Charles IX* (1829), Prosper Mérimée expressed the widespread fascination with this kind of unmediated, strongly narrative history which spilled from the pages of Pierre Lestoile or Agrippa d'Aubigné in the sixteenth century to Saint-Simon and his successors in the eighteenth:

Memoirs are an intimate conversation between author and reader and they alone furnish me with the portraits of human nature which I find both fascinating and amusing. . . . Moreover, the manner of these contemporary authors is as revealing as what they tell. For example, I find the following concise entry in Lestoile's *Journal*: 'Mademoiselle de Châteauneuf, one of the mistresses of the King before he went into Poland, having through a passing infatuation married Antinotti, an Italian of Florence and the superintendent of the galleys at Marseilles, and having caught him out in lewdness, slew him like a man, with her bare hands.' Armed with this anecdote and many others besides . . . I am able to imagine a character and resuscitate a Lady of the Court of Henry III.

Mérimée was one of the new generation of rebellious Romantic writers who, chafing at the conservatism of an increasingly repressive regime, eagerly fished through these 'intimate conversations' for plots, characters, and the 'local colour' they admired in Scott and Cooper. In their nets they caught foul deeds, heroes, heroines, villains, snatches of conversation and enough antiquarian detail to fascinate the most curious reader. Their concern, however, was not simply with the picturesque.

In 1826 Alfred de Vigny published *Cinq-Mars*, which retold the 'tragedy' of two young nobles, Cinq-Mars and de Thou, who had plotted against Richelieu in 1639 and were, for their pains, beheaded in 1642. In a preface he insisted that history was more than a chronicle of recorded fact but, when properly understood, a collection of myths which inform the collective memory and explain the destiny of nations. Alfred the Great may never have burnt the cakes and Archimedes may never have jumped out of his bath shouting 'Eureka!', but the achievements of both are better encapsulated in dramatic fables than in more factual, duller, and infinitely less readable accounts of their contribution to the development of humankind. It is in this sense that Vigny's remark, 'history is a novel written by the People', must be understood. Folk-knowledge, deeper and more instinctive than the analyses of scholars, makes clearer sense of the complexities of history by reducing the past to the simple values by which all deeds, individuals, and regimes are ultimately to be judged.

Victor Hugo, though generous with descriptions of people, manners, and places which gave great comfort to the current Gothic revival, also transcended the facts for similar reasons. *Notre Dame de Paris* (1831), set in the fifteenth century, underlined the structural continuities which, though times and causes change, are endlessly replayed throughout the ages. If Esmeralda symbolizes Love, Frollo the Church, and Phoebus the army, then Quasimodo has all the faults and virtues of the common man and through him Hugo reclaimed history for the People. Yet, by 1831, that battle had already been won, though not in the novel. In 1829 Alexandre Dumas had unleashed a revolution in literature with *Henri III et sa cour*, a drama set in the Renaissance which the Romantics had rescued from two centuries of neglect.

Dumas was born in 1802 at Villers-Cotterêts, 80 km north-east
of Paris. His mother was the daughter of an innkeeper but there
was both blue and negro blood on his father's side. Thomas-
Alexandre Dumas (1762–1806) was the son of a minor French
nobleman, the Marquis Davy de la Pailleterie, who had left
France for San Domingo (Haiti) under a cloud in about 1750,
and a slave, Marie-Cessette Dumas. During the Revolution, he
rose rapidly through the ranks and was a general at 32. A large
man—he was known to his troops as 'the black Hercules'—and
fearless in action, he was naturally insubordinate and during the
Egyptian campaign of 1798, Napoleon more than once threatened to have him shot for seditious talk. In 1799 his request to be
allowed to return to France was granted but, held captive in a
pestilential prison in southern Italy where his ship had unwisely
called, he did not reach home for two years, with both his career
and his health in ruins. When he died in 1806, he left his family
a name, trails of glory, but little else.

Alexandre grew up boisterously happy and largely unimpeded
by education, though his mother ensured that he learned to write
a good hand and acquire the elements of Latin from a local
priest. At 14 he became an office boy, made friends, discovered
girls, and found that making his fortune was not as easy as he had
imagined. By his own account, after several false starts, he took
part in 1823 in a marathon billiards match and won 600 glasses of
absinthe which, converted into 90 francs, financed a serious
assault on Paris. He did the rounds of his father's former col-
leagues, who showed less interest in him than he had hoped.
Eventually he was given work as a copyist by the Duke
d'Orléans, more on the strength of his clear handwriting, he said,
than for any other qualities. Determined to avoid doing anything
which might earn promotion and lead to job-security, he nailed
his colours to the flag of Literature. He haunted the Paris thea-
tres and sampled the artistic life. With a friend, he wrote melo-
dramas which were rejected and he fell in love with Catherine
Labay, a seamstress. In 1824 she gave birth to a son who would
become famous as Alexandre Dumas *fils*, author of *La Dame aux
Camélias*.

Increasingly conscious that his defective schooling placed him
at a disadvantage, Dumas set about educating himself with a

determination of which Samuel Smiles, the champion of Self-Help, would have approved wholeheartedly. He worked up his Latin by reading Juvenal, Tacitus, and Suetonius, and made inroads into the 'two or three hundred' volumes of historical memoirs to which he, like many others, looked for inspiration. It was the beginning, he recalled in an article published in the *Revue des deux mondes* in 1833, of a life of toil.

I was chained for eight hours daily to my desk where my presence was also required each day between 7 and 10 in the evening, and only my nights were my own. It was during those feverish hours that I fell into the habit, which I have never abandoned, of working at night, a circumstance which makes my writing a matter utterly incomprehensible even to my friends; they cannot understand when I find time for it.

He published—at his own expense as many budding authors did—a collection of tales which sold only four copies. However, his heart was in the theatre and his ambition to succeed as a playwright was confirmed by his discovery of Shakespeare, whom he revered as the supreme genius and 'the greatest creator after God'. Now

invention is the work not of Man but of Men. Each arrives on the scene in his turn and in his hour, appropriates to himself those things which were known to his predecessors, shapes them into new combinations and then dies after adding a few particles to the sum of human knowledge which he bequeaths to those who come after him: he becomes another star in the Milky Way. As to whether any man can ever create anything new, I do not believe such a thing possible. Even God, when he created man, either could not or dared not invent: He made him in His own image.

Dumas cheerfully confessed to many faults, but never to modesty.

Ransacking books for plots, characters, and strong situations was another habit he never lost and to which he admitted with utterly disarming frankness. Shrewdly diagnosing the public mood, which called for melodrama and high, 'Shakespearian' colours, he dipped into an odd volume of Anquetil's *Histoire de France depuis les Gaulois* (Paris 1805, 14 vols.) and found the tragic tale of Saint-Mégrin, who in 1578 fell victim to love and political skulduggery. *Henry III and his Court* was performed to ecstatic audiences in 1829. It broke all the rules of dramatic art, pitted youthful heroism against the cynicism of age, and was a short-fused political bomb which articulated the frustrations of a people subject to a reactionary monarchical regime.

Dumas was suddenly famous both as a playwright and as a leader of the literary insurrection which preceded the upheaval of 1830. He played—again by his own account—a somewhat comic-opera role in events during the July Revolution, appearing on barricades with a gun on his arm, overcoming single-handedly the bewildered garrison of a gunpowder depot at Soissons, and spectacularly failing to persuade the royalists of the Vendée to join the National Guard. Quickly wearying of politics, he returned to the theatre with a succession of plays on both historical and contemporary subjects which ran on the high-octane fuel of conflict, emotion, and melodrama. He earned a great deal of money and spent it all on women, clothes, travel, good food (though he drank little) and his many friends whom he treated with amazing liberality. Dumas, always in debt, had little sense of the value of money and could not understand why creditors should be such disagreeable people.

His play *Kean* was a success in 1836, but it was clear that the vogue for Romantic drama was waning and Dumas began to consider other avenues for his talents. Though he would not commit himself finally to the novel until the 1840s, he was favoured by circumstances. In 1836 *La Presse* and *Le Siècle* began accepting advertising which enabled them to halve their cover-price. Other newspapers were forced to follow suit and thus began a battle for circulation in which fiction was to play a crucial role. For the press barons discovered that a gripping serial (the *roman feuilleton*) generated brand loyalty and they were prepared to pay large sums to authors who could supply, at high speed and to strict deadlines, cliff-hanging adventures in instalments which were, in the hallowed phrase, 'to be continued . . .'. Frédéric Soulié was the first of a new breed of popular novelists but he was overtaken in the 1840s by Eugène Sue and Dumas who, in modern terms, were the first media stars. Newspapers outbid each other for their novels, which were then trailed in a blaze of publicity. Thereafter, serial publication became the norm for popular and serious fiction alike and most novels, until the advent of cheap books in the 1880s, were pre-published in newspapers and magazines.

Dumas throve on the pressures which kept him nailed to his chair—at times, he said, for fourteen hours at a stretch—filling blank pages with his clear handwriting, dropping them on the floor for a squad of secretaries who copied them (and added punctuation and corrected his spelling) before rushing them round to waiting printers. In the 1840s he wrote 35 novels, 20 plays, 8 travel books, and 7 works of history. If most of the novels were mortal in length, others—and they rank among his best—now seem supernatural in size and scope. *The Three Musketeers* (1844), *The Count of Monte Cristo* (1844–5), *Twenty Years After* (1845), *La Reine Margot* (1845), *La Dame de Monsoreau* (*Chicot the Jester*) (1846), *Joseph Balsamo* (1846), the three vast parts of *The Vicomte de Bragelonne* (1847–50), *Les Quarante-Cinq* (*The Forty-Five Guardsmen*) (1848), and *Le Collier de la Reine* (*The Queen's Necklace*) (1849) cover four distinct periods (the Renaissance, the seventeenth century, the prelude to the Revolution, and the years between 1815 and the near present), and work out at a rough count at half a million words a year, making a commitment of 10,000 words a week in addition to his other output.

His friends might well have wondered how he managed to produce so much in the gaps left by stormy love-affairs, travels abroad, hob-nobbing with grandees, the opening of his own theatre in 1847, the attention he lavished on the Château de Monte-Cristo—the splendidly garish house he built for himself at Marly—and his unsuccessful attempt to be elected to Parliament in 1848. Those who envied his success, however, believed they had the answer. In 1845, Eugène de Mirecourt, a journalist, published a tract in which he accused him of running a 'fiction factory' staffed by hacks who turned out, to order, all the novels and plays which appeared under his name. Dumas sued and won. He cheerfully admitted that his novels and plays were frequently produced in association with what would now be called 'research assistants', 'story-consultants', and the like. 'I have collaborators,' he said, 'the way Napoleon had generals.' His defence was accepted and, broadly speaking, it is vindicated by what we know of his working methods. It is probably true that there were occasions when, to meet a deadline, he sent whole chapters written by other hands to the printers without even reading them. But the evidence of his books is categorical. While he received prompts for story-lines, the background, and the historical details which he did not have time to research himself, Dumas did indeed write what he gave the public to read. The Dumas touch is unmistakable: unflagging drama, twisting plots, artful suspense, strongly differentiated characters, the injection of horror, violence, and humour, the unfailing wholesomeness, and the clear, though not uncomplicated, victory of Good over Evil. Though he was always comfortable reworking the dramas and base intrigues unearthed by collaborators, his own creative juices flowed strongly, enabling him to invent the characters of Athos, Porthos, and Aramis from the sound of their names, or to turn half a page of the *Memoirs* of La Rochefoucauld into fourteen breathless chapters which tell how d'Artagnan restores a full set of diamond studs to the Queen of France in *The Three Musketeers*. It was also Dumas who changed the plan to start *The Count of Monte Cristo* in Italy, with the story of Edmond Dantès's imprisonment told in flashbacks. The result is one of the most enthralling tales of imprisonment ever written.

He formed an especially close working relationship with Auguste Maquet (1813–88), a former history teacher with literary ambitions. They met in 1838 when Maquet asked Dumas's advice about a play he could not persuade any theatre to accept. Dumas promptly rewrote it and, when it was performed, insisted that Maquet be given sole credit. If only Dumas's name appeared on his extensive reworking of Maquet's novel, *Le Chevalier d'Harmental* (1843), it was on the grounds that anything signed by him was sure to sell. Maquet accepted this commercial argument, though he did receive billing on a number of plays, the practice of collaboration being more acceptable in the theatre. Their arrangement was financial and Maquet never claimed that Dumas had stolen his literary property. He did, however, reluctantly sue him in 1857 for failing to pay him sums which had been contractually agreed, a failure on Dumas's part more attributable to his carelessness with money than to any intention to cheat his erstwhile collaborator. When Maquet then proceeded to write novels on his own, success eluded him. Clearly, Maquet needed Dumas more than Dumas needed him.

By 1844, the year of *The Three Musketeers* and *The Count of Monte Cristo,* their working habits were not only firmly established but capable of responding quickly to any challenge. In the first days of December *La Presse* began serializing Balzac's *Les Paysans.* After three episodes, the plot had not advanced beyond the elaborate scene-setting and descriptions of character which are the hallmark of the Balzacian novel but which proved not to the liking of subscribers who deserted in droves: there were 700 cancellations, complained Dujarrier, the paper's editor. Fearing for his circulation, he turned to Dumas and on 6 December *La Presse* was proud to announce the imminent publication in its columns of *La Reine Margot.*

Dumas's decision to weave a tale of love, intrigue, and murder around Marguerite de Navarre may have been prompted by his familiarity with the 1570s, which he had already exploited in *Henry III and his Court.* He was certainly aware of the highly marketable image of the Italian, Spanish, and French Renaissance which had attracted Romantic dramatists and novelists, and he had himself already exploited it in *Ascanio* (1843), a novel loosely based around the life of the Florentine goldsmith, Benvenuto Cellini, and a history of the Medicis family (1844). He might too have seen possibilities in the name of Marguerite de Valois, who still survived in the popular memory as 'la reine Margot', a wayward royal and ready-made Romantic heroine of love and intrigue. But wherever he got the idea, he made up his mind quickly. He summoned Maquet and began work at once.

In less than a fortnight, eight chapters were written and the first instalment appeared on Christmas Day, 1844. By the end of December, Dumas was up to Chapter 13. By 20 January 1845 he had reached Chapter 31 and, chiding Maquet for being slow, had completed a further five chapters by the end of the month. On 10 February he decided, in view of other commitments, that *La Reine Margot* had to be finished by 1 March: by 20 February, Chapter 53 was written and the remaining fourteen chapters were finished in early March. Despite the interruption of the

Mirecourt affair, which involved a court appearance, Dumas, abetted by Maquet, had written the novel's quarter of a million words in three months. It was a stupendous effort of concentration, and called for extraordinary powers of imagination, a vast fund of historical knowledge, and quantities of stamina. His achievement is even more remarkable when it is remembered that among those 'other commitments' were the completion of *The Count of Monte Cristo* (serialized in *Le Journal des débats*, 28 August 1844–15 January 1846), *La Guerre des femmes* (in *La Patrie*, 2 January–1 June 1845), and the Musketeer sequel, *Twenty Years After* (*Le Siècle*, 21 January–28 June 1845).

The action of *La Reine Margot* spans the twenty-two months between August 1572 and the death of Charles IX on 30 May 1574, with an epilogue set in 1575. It opens with the Massacre of Saint Bartholomew's Day. Since the death of Henry II in 1559, France had been governed by Catherine de Medicis, who ruled as regent during the minority first of François II (who died in 1560) and then of Charles IX (born in 1550). For a decade the country had been bitterly divided by a series of Religious Wars which pitted the majority of the population, who were Catholic, against the million and a half Huguenots who had embraced the reformed religion of Calvin and Luther. A Treaty of Pacification (1570) had paved the way for reconciliation and all parties—the ruling Valois family, the conservative Catholic Guise family, and Admiral Coligny, the Huguenot leader—accepted a policy of coexistence as a means of replacing strife and restoring national unity. As part of the healing process a marriage was celebrated on 18 August 1572 between the King's sister, Marguerite de Valois, and the Protestant Henry of Navarre. Many Huguenot nobles gathered for the festivities, which were abruptly curtailed by an attempt on the life of Coligny. The main instigators of the murder plot were Catherine, who regarded the admiral as a threat to her influence over Charles IX, her son the Duke d'Anjou, and Henry de Guise, leader of the Catholic party. Charles IX was shocked but was persuaded that Coligny's supporters, massed in the capital, now constituted a danger to the throne itself and he ordered a general massacre on 24 August.

The result was a kind of ethnic cleansing from which the Huguenots never recovered. The slaughter lasted three days and spread to the major Protestant strongholds in the south and west, where unrest continued and was to flare at La Rochelle, besieged by Catholic forces between December 1572 and June 1573. These events form the basis of Dumas's first forty chapters which, once the bloodbath is over, focus on a tense game of attack and defence setting Catherine and d'Anjou against Marguerite, Henry of Navarre, and Charles IX, with the wavering François d'Alençon serving and betraying both in pursuit of his own ambition.

Though only weeks seem to pass, the action moves imperceptibly to the summer of 1573, when Henry d'Anjou was elected to the vacant throne of Poland. Charles IX was in poor health and had no male heir, and Catherine realized that the departure of d'Anjou, next in line to the throne, threatened the Valois dynasty with extinction. She became even more suspicious of Henry of Navarre, a Bourbon and a semi-lapsed Huguenot, who was an increasingly plausible candidate for the succession. Charles feared his brother, d'Anjou, who was popular with the army, and forced him into exile in Poland, though he did not leave until November. Dumas collapses the events of many months into the dramatic confrontations and realignments which begin in Chapter 41 and merge seamlessly into a new plot, which fills the rest of the book.

In the winter of 1573, moderate nobles (known as the 'Malcontents') who sought civil and religious peace applied pressure on François d'Alençon, Charles's remaining brother, to join a revolt against the crown. In March 1574, they attempted to force the King's hand by surrounding Saint-Germain-en-Laye where the court was in residence. But they were betrayed. Two minor members of François's retinue—La Mole and Coconnas—were executed (30 April), prominent 'Malcontents' were imprisoned (4 May), and François and Henry of Navarre were placed under house arrest. When Charles IX died on 30 May, word was sent to the King of Poland, who made a leisurely return and was crowned in Paris in February 1575. François escaped from the court in 1574 but Henry of Navarre remained a virtual prisoner until 1576 when he reverted to Protestantism and led the Huguenot forces against the extremist Catholic League formed under François de Guise.

When Dumas's novel is set against the historical record, it is seen to be—in spite of the accuracy of many details to which the Explanatory Notes at the end of this volume bear ample witness—selective and highly partial. He omits a number of crises and dimensions, ignores many significant figures, and builds his narrative around three major events: the Saint Bartholomew's Massacre, the election of d'Anjou to the Polish throne, and the revolt of the Malcontents of 1574. But of course Dumas wrote not as a historian but as a novelist skilled at weaving characters of his own invention into the already colourful tapestry of events which had attracted many before him.

In the immediate aftermath of the Massacre, Huguenot apologists published numerous accounts of the martyrdom of Admiral Coligny, slain by the paid assassin Maurevel, and chronicled the horrors of the slaughter of, they estimated, 30,000 of their co-religionists. They laid most of the blame at the door of the Duke de Guise and Henry d'Anjou, who exerted a baleful influence on Charles IX. But their fiercest criticisms were directed at Catherine de Medicis, whose ambition to protect the Valois dynasty was fed on poison and murder. It was in their writings that the enduring legend of Catherine, the sadistic embodiment of scheming bloodlust, began. The massacre did not, it was said, displease Pope Gregory III, but it horrified Protestant Europe. One near-contemporary reaction was provided by Christopher Marlowe. *The Massacre at Paris* (? 1592) follows events from the butchery of 1572 to the murder of Henry III in 1589, and attributes responsibility to French knavery in general and the villainy of Catherine de Medicis, the Duke de Guise, and the Duke d'Anjou in particular—machiavellians, murderers, and poisoners all.

The story was subsequently retold many times from many different angles, though it was rare for Catherine to appear as anything other than the true villain of the piece, a monster of evil, ambitious, ruthless, and devoid of human feeling except a blind love for her degenerate sons. In Dumas's time, several interpretations were put on events and the people who made them. In his *Chronique du règne de Charles IX*, Mérimée largely

ignored what Vigny called the 'principal actors' of history, devised adventures for an obscure hero, Bernard de Mergy, and
presented the massacre not as a conspiracy by Charles IX against
one section of his subjects but as a kind of improvised, 'popular
insurrection', an instinctive uprising against heretics not unlike
the revolt of the Spaniards against Napoleon in 1809. In 1843
Balzac published a novel, *Catherine de Medicis,* which portrayed
her as a woman of courage and vision, a Robespierre in skirts, a
clinical Marat, who deliberately used a policy of terror to promote national unity. Dumas's approach was to mix 'principal
actors' and obscure heroes, real events with fiction, and to devise
non-stop action which carries the weight of his own engaging
individualism.

For whether Dumas writes of the Renaissance, the seventeenth century, the French Revolution, or the stultifying, bourgeois world of Louis-Philippe, he projects the same heady
defence of freedom and independence through his family of
recurring types. Catherine is a mixture of the Milady of *The
Three Musketeers* and his gallery of callous politicians—Richelieu
and Mazarin, for instance—who symbolize the grim manipula-
tions of the power of the state. La Mole is a sensitive hero, as full
of honour and passion as Athos or Raoul de Bragelonne. There
is, too, more than a hint of Porthos in Cocconas, not only in the
light relief he supplies but also in his fidelity to a very male ideal:
in choosing to remain with La Mole when he might have escaped, he prefers friendship to life itself. Charles IX learns to be
as wise a king as the twin Dumas substitutes for Louis XIV in
The Man in the Iron Mask. Henry of Navarre, as cool a hand as
Aramis, plays a waiting game but emerges as a leader as far-
sighted as William the Stadthouder of *The Black Tulip,* and a
man who knows how to bide his time as well as Monte Cristo
himself.

But it is in Margot that the flame of Dumas's romantic ideal-
ism burns brightest. He makes no attempt to disguise her ambition: she accepts her marriage to Henry of Navarre because she
hopes it will one day set her on the throne of France. Nor is
he afraid to show that she has iron in her soul: when attacked,
she defends herself with skill and determination. Yet she is
much less steely and far more vulnerable than the Marguerite of

history who ordered the murder of her enemies and chose to have many lovers. Margot may be alluring, cultured, and cool in a crisis, but it is as a creature of feeling that she makes her strongest impact. She is engagingly spontaneous—coy with La Mole, skittish with Henriette—but does not find warmth within her family, nor does she expect to in marriage. She may be an adulteress, yet, as the victim of a political match, she is free of blame. And if Henry will not give her love, she is capable of offering friendship, which she understands as well as any man. Margot is a creature of light who knows instinctively that there is more to life than the sordid manœuvrings of the court. Yet when right, honour, and love are at stake, she rises to the challenge, thriving on danger and boundlessly resourceful. Cerebral and passionate, virginal and sexual, a woman in her affections and a man in her actions, Margot is not only a character of considerable complexity but a full-blown Romantic heroine.

The world they inhabit stands on uncomplicated values. The good serve honour and love, while the wicked oppress, betray, and murder. Dumas never wearied of articulating the perennial conflict between freedom and tolerance on the one hand and, on the other, the regimentation, injustice, and oppression of tyrants, not in philosophical or general terms, but through action and the basic emotions which unite and divide his characters: jealousy, love, hate, and ambition. He begins with an ideal of loyalty and comradeship. Marguerite may know that her marriage to Henry of Navarre is an empty sham but she never reneges on the alliance she has sworn with him. La Mole and Cocconas quarrel their way to a friendship so absolute that each would lay down his life for the other. Henry may compromise in public, but there can be no doubt of his long-term commitment to justice and the freeing of the human spirit: unlike d'Artagnan, he cannot skewer Valois despotism and sectarian prejudice with a flashing blade, but we know for sure that he would if he could. Dumas's heroes breathe a liberal spirit which is made all the more convincing because it is so affecting. They are all fulfilled by the deepest, most selfless love which, though eternal in a spiritual sense, cannot survive in a world dominated by private and public evil. There are many couples in *La Reine Margot*, yet happiness is denied them all. Marguerite and La Mole, Henry of Navarre and Mme de Sauve, Cocconas and Henriette de Nevers, Charles IX and Marie Touchet may be no advertisements for marital fidelity, but they all love deeply, sincerely, and tragically. They are all ultimately separated by death made inevitable by the hatred of the self-obsessed and the unloved, from Catherine to René, from d'Anjou to François d'Alençon and Guise. In death, they find a bitter victory. They defeat their enemies but in the din of battle lose the better half of themselves: those who stand up for love and honour will be rewarded, as are Marguerite and Henry of Navarre, with a life of solitude. Such is their destiny.

Like all Dumas's novels, *La Reine Margot* carries a political charge, for its abhorrence for the murderous methods of Catherine, the political opportunism of d'Anjou and d'Alençon, and the religious intolerance which divided France was a stinging commentary on the values of the reign of Louis-Philippe. The Revolutionaries of 1830 believed they had thrown off the yoke of oppression and inaugurated a new age of justice, open government, and freedom. But the July Monarchy freed only capitalism and created a corporate society based on narrow self-interest and new forms of injustice. In this sense, *La Reine Margot* is an act of resistance. In giving the French a sense of their own history, Dumas reminded them that the permanent condition of political life is instability, secrecy, and injustice, that men of goodwill must not sit on their hands, and that sooner or later the air is cleared by revolt, as would happen in 1848. But if Dumas projects this political subtext successfully, it is because he makes us care so much for his heroes and ensures that we detest their enemies. Through a marvellously sustained series of adventures seasoned with gothic horror, violence, and suspense, he creates a world in which we always know where we stand: with love, honour, and courage and against the power of evil, which is real and must never be underestimated. The good may not end happily, but Dumas's constitutional optimism also denied victory to the wicked. Catherine exults but, as she watches Henry ride away, she knows in her heart that he will live to fight another day, for he is as unstoppable as the generous impulses which Dumas

suggests run through history. It is an uplifting ending and
readers close the book knowing that when the challenge comes—
as it invariably will—good men will rise up and thwart the
wicked.

If *La Reine Margot* gives hope to the downtrodden, it does so
against a background of crashing melodrama and strong Romantic types: black-hearted villains, four-square heroes, a heroine
who stakes all for love, and, in Henry of Navarre, a leader
doomed by fate to achieve greatness at the expense of personal
happiness. It was a formula which Dumas repeated many times
and it made him the most famous living Frenchman of his day.
His reputation in Britain and the United States rose dramatically
in 1846 with the appearance of the first translations of *The Three
Musketeers, Monte Cristo,* and *Twenty Years After. La Reine
Margot* was also made available in English, in two versions, one
of which—published by David Bogue in London in 1846—was
so frequently reissued that it became the standard text. It is
an abridged version, shorter by about a quarter than the
French original, and omits passages devoted to the topography
of Paris, the poetry Dumas was fond of quoting, and other
such materials doubtless judged less interesting to Anglo-Saxon
readers than to their French counterparts. Though some scenes
are curtailed, none of the action is cut and, indeed, the novel
gains in pace by the loss of much of the padding with which
Dumas—who was paid by the line—regularly filled out his instalments to satisfy newspaper editors. But whatever the rights
and wrongs of unauthorized abridgement, the fact remains that
the anonymous translation published by Bogue commended itself to generations of English-speaking readers the world over. It
is for this reason that it has been chosen as the basis of the
present edition.

The success of *La Reine Margot* prompted Dumas, in March
1845, to propose two sequels, which would complete a Renaissance trilogy, though they are unconnected save by the period in
which they are set and do not pretend to the continuity of the
Musketeer saga. *La Dame de Monsoreau* (translated as *Chicot the
Jester*), serialized between August 1845 and 1846, begins in 1578
and introduced a new hero, Bussy d'Ambois, who loves and loses
all save honour. *Les Quarante-Cinq (The Forty-Five Guardsmen)*

which appeared in instalments in 1847, opens in 1585 and shows Catherine defeated: the Valois line is fated to end, while Henry of Navarre waits in the wings . . .

But France too was poised for change. Though the Revolution of 1848 ended the bourgeois monarchy of Louis-Philippe, it did not sweep society clean of the spirit of acquisitiveness which Dumas continued to denounce. Nor did it make life easier for writers. Not only did the upheaval disturb reading habits, but a law enacted in 1850 introduced a crippling tax on newspapers which ran serials. Dumas's income fell dramatically. His Théâtre Historique closed, the Château de Monte Cristo, which symbolized his success, was sold off to an American dentist, and in 1851 he was declared bankrupt. He fled to Belgium to escape both his creditors and the stultifying new regime of Louis-Napoleon. But he kept his public; Dumas never went out of fashion. In the 1850s he wrote 43 novels, 11 plays, 8 works of history, his *Mémoires* in 6 volumes, and 2 travel books. He founded newspapers, began new affairs, journeyed through Russia, where his fame had preceded him, and ran guns to Italy for Garibaldi's revolution. His girth swelled but his energy and sparkle continued undimmed. On 14 February 1866 the Goncourt brothers (not the most charitable of observers) wrote in their diary:

We are in the middle of a conversation when Dumas enters, wearing a white tie and a waistcoat, also white, hugely fat, perspiring, puffing and blowing, and in roistering good spirits. He is just back from Austria, Hungary, Bohemia . . . He talks of Budapest where he had a play put on in Hungarian, of Vienna where the Emperor loaned him a room in his palace to give a lecture. He talks of his novels, his contribution to the drama, of plays which the Comédie-Française refuses to stage, of *Le Chevalier de Maison-Rouge* [a novel set in the French Revolution] which has been banned, a performing licence for a play which he cannot obtain, and then of a restaurant he is thinking of opening on the Champs-Élysées. A personality as large as the man, but overflowing with unselfconscious good humour and twinkling with wit.

At last, however, age began to creep up on him, though he still had enough energy in 1869 to stage *Les Blancs et les bleus*, which warned France of the threat represented by Prussia. He survived long enough to witness the defeat of France the following year and to outlive his creativity. In September 1870, he suffered a stroke and moved to Puys, near Dieppe, where his son cared for him until his death on 5 December. Hugo, the most famous writer in France, saluted the 'universal' Dumas, newspapers recycled his novels, publishers issued new editions—nearly 3 million copies sold between his death and 1893, his son claimed—and fresh generations of readers discovered him at home and, in vast numbers, abroad. The Anglo-Saxon world was consumed by Dumasmania between 1890 and the First World War, by which time his immortals—Monte-Cristo and the Musketeers in particular—had migrated to the silver screen, where they still strut and thrill: a spectacular version of *La Reine Margot* was made in 1994. Dumas may have been a lesser artist than Balzac, Flaubert, or Zola, but as a creator, he has a unique place in the literary firmament: his very own niche in the Milky Way.

NOTE ON THE TEXT

La Reine Margot was published in *La Presse* between 25 December 1844 and 5 April 1845. This serialized text was pirated four times by Belgian publishers in 1845. The first French edition, slightly revised, appeared in 6 volumes (Paris: Garnier, February–July 1845). The novel was reserialized in *Le Siècle* (5 October 1845–8 February 1846). An anonymous English translation (*Margaret of Navarre: or the Massacre of St. Bartholemew's Eve*, London: G. Pierce, 2 vols.), based on the text of the serialization, was rushed out immediately. However, the somewhat compressed *Marguerite de Valois: An Historical Romance* (London: David Bogue, 1846) was preferred by English and American publishers who were to reprint it regularly. Though there were unabridged or slightly edited translations (*Marguerite de Valois* (London: Walter Scott, 1901), being the fullest), the present edition is based on the text most frequently reprinted, the 'classic' version through which generations of Anglo-Saxon readers read Dumas's novel. It has been extensively modernized and revised against the standard French text, excellently edited by Claude Schopp (*La Reine Margot, La Dame de Monsoreau, Les Quarante-cinq*, Paris: Laffont, 'Collection Bouquins', 1992, 2 vols.), which also helped to resolve a number of editorial difficulties. *La Reine Margot* was staged as a drama in five acts at Dumas's new Théâtre Historique by Dumas in collaboration with Maquet on 20 February 1847.

SELECT BIBLIOGRAPHY

Readers wishing to follow the complex printing history of Dumas's voluminous writings in French may usefully consult Frank W. Reed's *A Bibliography of Dumas père* (London, 1933) and Douglas Munro's *Dumas: A Bibliography of Works Published in French, 1825–1900* (New York and London, 1981). *Alexandre Dumas père: A Bibliography of Works Translated into English to 1910* (New York and London, 1978), also by Douglas Munro, is the best guide to British and American editions. The text of the stage version of *La Reine Margot* is reproduced by Claude Schopp (op. cit., ii. 647–779). Dumas's early drama set in the same period, *Henri III et sa cour*, may be read in Fernande Bassan's edition (Alexandre Dumas *père*, *Théâtre Complet I* (Paris, 1974–   ), 461–582).

Dumas's autobiography, *Mes Mémoires* (1852–5) (ed. Claude Schopp (Paris, 1989; English trans. London, 1907–9), stops short at 1832 and is as unreliable as it is entertaining. The best French biographies are: Claude Schopp, *Dumas, le génie de la vie* (Paris 1985; English trans. New York, 1988) and Daniel Zimmerman, *Alexandre Dumas le Grand* (Paris, 1993). For a concise, lavishly illustrated introduction, see Christian Biet, Jean-Paul Brighelli, and Jean-Luc Rispail, *Alexandre Dumas, ou les aventures d'un romancier* (Paris, 1986).

Among the many books in English devoted to Dumas, approachable introductions are provided by: Ruthven Todd, *The Laughing Mulatto* (London, 1940); A. Craig Bell, *Alexandre Dumas* (London, 1950); and Richard Stowe, *Dumas* (Boston, 1976). Michael Ross's *Alexandre Dumas* (Newton Abbot, 1981) gives a sympathetic account of Dumas's life. The most balanced and comprehensive guide to the man and his work, however, is F. W. J. Hemmings's excellent *The King of Romance* (London, 1979).

Of the many books written about the years 1572–5, when the action is set, accessible studies include Philippe Erlanger (*La Reine Margot*, Paris 1972), the best biography of Marguerite, Desmond Seward's *The First Bourbon: Henri IV, King of France and Navarre* (London, 1971), and Robert M. Kingdon's *Myths about the Saint Bartholomew's Day Massacres* (Cambridge, Mass., 1988), which illuminates the background in very readable form.

Sources quoted in the notes include: Agrippa d'Aubigné, *Histoire universelle*, ed. André Thierry (Geneva, 1985–); Brantôme, *Œuvres complètes*, ed. Ludovic Lalanne, 11 vols. (Paris, 1864–82), and *Recueil des dames, poésies et tombeaux*, ed. Étienne Vaucheret (Paris, 1991); Pierre Lestoile, *Journal de Henri III*, 5 vols. (The Hague, 1744), *Mémoires-journaux*, ed. Brunot *et al.*, 12 vols. (Paris, 1887–96), and *Registre-journal du règne de Henri III*, ed. Madeleine Lazard and Gilbert Schrenck, vol. i (Geneva, 1992); Marguerite de Valois, *Mémoires et lettres*, ed. F. Guessard (Paris, 1842); François Eudes de Mézeray, *A General Chronological History of France, Beginning before the Reign of King Pharamond, and Ending with the Reign of King Henry the Fourth. Translated by John Bulteel, Gent.* (London, 1683; 1st pub. in French, Paris, 1637–43); Christopher Marlowe, *'Dido Queen of Carthage' and 'The Massacre at Paris'* (?1592), ed. H. J. Oliver, (London, 1960), which also reprints relevant extracts from *A True and Plaine Report of the Furious Outrages of Fraunce, & the Horrible and Shameful Slaughter of Chastillion the Admirall, and Divers Other Nobles and Excellent Men, and of the Wicked and Straunge Murder of Godlie Persons, Committed in Many Cities of Fraunce, without any Respect of Sorte, Kinde, Age or Degree* (1573), attributed to 'Ernest Varamund of Freseland', but translated from the Latin of the leading Huguenot polemicist, François Hotman.

A CHRONOLOGY OF
ALEXANDRE DUMAS

1762 25 March: Birth at Santo Domingo of Thomas-Alexandre, son of the French-born Marquis Davy de la Pailleterie and Marie-Cessette Dumas. After returning to France in 1780, he enlists in 1786 and rises rapidly through the ranks during the Revolution.

1802 24 July: Birth at Villers-Cotterêts of Alexandre Dumas, second child of General Dumas and Marie-Louise-Elizabeth Labouret, an innkeeper's daughter.

1806 26 February: Death of General Dumas. Alexandre is brought up in straitened circumstances by his mother. He attends local schools and has a happy childhood.

1819 Dumas, now a lawyer's office-boy, falls in love with Adèle Dalvin, who rejects him. Meets Adolphe de Leuven, with whom he collaborates in writing unsuccessful plays.

1822 Visits Leuven in Paris, meets Talma, the leading actor of the day, and resolves to become a playwright.

1823 Moves to Paris. Enters the service of the Duke of Orléans. Falls in love with a seamstress, Catherine Labay.

1824 27 July: Birth of Alexandre Dumas *fils*, author of *La Dame aux camélias*.

1825 September: Dumas's first performed play, written in collaboration with Leuven and Rousseau, makes no impact.

1826 Publication of a collection of short stories, Dumas's first solo composition, which sells four copies.

1827 A company of English actors, which includes Kean, Kemble, and Mrs Smithson, performs Shakespeare in English to enthusiastic Paris audiences: Dumas is deeply impressed.

   Liaison with Mélanie Waldor.

1828–9 Dumas enters Parisian literary circles through Charles Nodier.

1829 11 February: First of about fifty performances of *Henry III and his Court*, which makes Dumas famous and thrusts him into the front ranks of the Romantic revolution in literature. Dumas meets Victor Hugo. He consolidates his reputation as a dramatist with *Antony* (1831), *La Tour de Nesle* (1832), and *Kean*

(1836), which are all landmarks in the history of Romantic drama.

1830   May: Start of an affair with the actress Belle Krelsamer. Active in the July Revolution in Paris and Soissons. Sent by Lafayette to promote the National Guard in the Vendée.

1831   5 March: Birth of Marie, his daughter by Belle Krelsamer.
17 March: Dumas acknowledges Alexandre, his son by Catherine Labay.

1832   6 February: Start of his affair with the actress Ida Ferrier.
15 April: Dumas ill with the cholera which kills 20,000 Parisians.
29 May: First performance of *La Tour de Nesle:* Gaillardet unsuccessfully accuses Dumas of plagiarism.
July: Suspected of republican sympathies, Dumas leaves Paris for Switzerland. After the spectacular failure of his next play, he begins to take an interest in the literary possibilities of French history.

1833   Serialization of a book of impressions of Switzerland, the first of his travelogues.

1834–5 October: Dumas travels in the Midi. From the Riviera, he embarks on the first of many journeys to Italy.

1836   31 August: Dumas returns triumphantly to the theatre with *Kean.*

1838   Death of Dumas's mother. Travels along the Rhine with Gérard de Nerval, who introduces him to Auguste Maquet in December.

1840   1 February: Dumas marries Ida Ferrier, travels to Italy, and publishes *Le Capitaine Pamphile*, the best of his children's books.

1840–2 Dividing his time between Paris and Italy, Dumas increasingly abandons the theatre for the novel.

1843   June: Publication of *Le Chevalier d'Harmental*, the first of many romances written in association with Maquet.

1844   March–July: Serialization of *The Three Musketeers* in *Le Siècle.*
August: First episode of *The Count of Monte Cristo* in *Le Journal des débats.*
15 October: Amicable separation from Ida Ferrier.
Summer–Autumn: Publication of *Louis XIV and his Century.*
December 6: Begins writing *La Reine Margot*, the first episode of which appears in *La Presse* on 25 December.

1845   21 January–2 August: Serialization of the second Musketeer
        story, *Twenty Years After*, in *Le Siècle*.
        February: He wins his libel suit against the journalist Eugène
        de Mirecourt, author of *A Fiction Factory: The Firm of Alexan-
        dre Dumas and Company*, in which he was accused of publishing
        other men's work under his own name.
        5 April: Final instalment of *La Reine Margot* in *La Presse*.
        August–February 1846: serialization of *La Dame de Monsoreau*
        (*Chicot the Jester*).
        September: Extracts of *La Reine Margot* published in English
        in *Blackwood's Magazine*.

1846   Final break with Ida Ferrier. Brief liaison with Lola
        Montès.
        Marguerite de Valois: An Historical Romance (London: David
        Bogue).
        November–January 1847: Travels with his son to Spain and
        North Africa.

1847   30 January: Loses a lawsuit brought by newspaper proprietors
        for failure to deliver copy for which he had accepted large
        advances.
        11 February: Questions are asked in the National Assembly
        about Dumas's appropriation of the navy vessel *Le Véloce* dur-
        ing his visit to North Africa.
        20 February: *La Reine Margot*, a drama in five acts, inaugurates
        the Théâtre Historique.
        7 March: Completion of the Château de Monte Cristo at
        Marly-le-Roi.
        May–October: Serialization of *Les Quarante-Cinq* (*The Forty-
        Five Guardsmen*).

1848   Dumas stands unsuccessfully as a parliamentary candidate and
        votes for Louis-Napoleon in the December elections.

1850   20 March: The Théâtre Historique is declared bankrupt. The
        Château de Monte Cristo is sold off for 30,000 francs.

1851   Michel Lévy publishes the first volumes of Dumas's complete
        works.
        7 December: Dumas flees to Belgium to avoid his creditors.

1852   Publication of the first volumes of *My Memoirs*. Dumas de-
        clared bankrupt with debts of 100,000 francs.

1853   November: Returns to Paris and founds a periodical, *Le Mous-
        quetaire* (last issue 7 February 1857), for which he writes most
        of the copy himself.

1857   23 April: Founds a literary weekly, *Le Monte Cristo*, which, with one break, survives until 1862.

1858   15 June: Dumas leaves for a tour of Russia and returns in March 1859.

1859   11 March: Death of Ida Ferrier. Beginning of a liaison with Émilie Cordier which lasts until 1864.

1860   Meets Garibaldi at Turin and just misses the taking of Sicily (June). He returns to Marseilles, where he buys guns for the Italian cause, and is in Naples just after the city falls in September. Garibaldi stands, by proxy, as godfather to Dumas's daughter by Émilie Cordier.

        11 October: Founds *L'Indipendente*, a literary and political periodical published half in French and half in Italian.

        19 November: *La Dame de Monsoreau*, drama in five acts.

1863   The works of Dumas are placed on the Index by the Catholic Church.

1864   April: Dumas returns to Paris.

1865   Further travels through Italy, Germany, and Austria.

1867   Publishes *The Prussian Terror*, a novel intended to warn France against the coming Prussian threat. Begins a last liaison, with Adah Menken, an American actress (d. 1868).

1869   10 March: Dumas's last play, *The Whites and the Blues*.

1870   5 December: Dumas dies at Puys, near Dieppe, after suffering a stroke in September.

1872   Dumas's remains transferred to Villers-Cotterêts.

1883   Unveiling of a statue to Dumas by Gustave Doré in the Place Malesherbes.

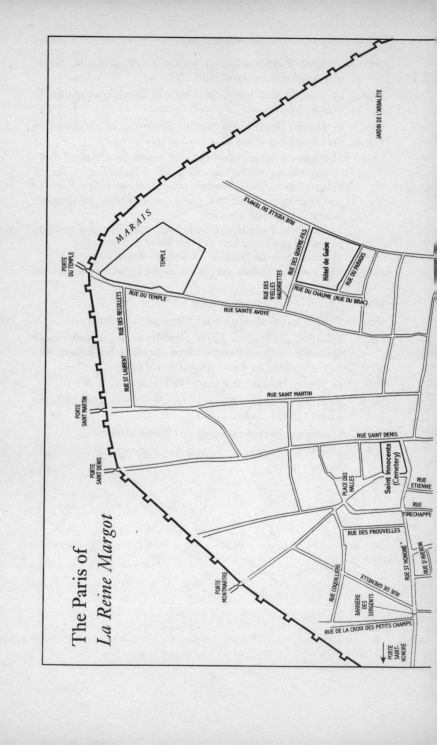

The Paris of
La Reine Margot

JARDIN DE L'ARBALÈTE

MARAIS

TEMPLE

PORTE
DU TEMPLE

RUE VIEILLE DU TEMPLE

RUE DES QUATRE-FILS

Hôtel de Guise

RUE DU PARADIS

RUE DES VIELLES HAUDRIETTES

RUE DU CHAUME (RUE DU BRAC)

RUE DU TEMPLE

RUE DES RECOLLETS

RUE SAINTE AVOYE

RUE ST LAURENT

PORTE
SAINT MARTIN

RUE SAINT MARTIN

RUE SAINT DENIS

PORTE
SAINT DENIS

Saint Innocents
(Cemetery)

RUE
ETIENNE

PLACE DES
HALLES

RUE
TIRECHAPPE

RUE DES PROUVELLES

RUE ST HONORÉ

RUE D'AVERON

PORTE
MONTMARTRE

RUE COQUILLIÈRE

RUE DE GRENELLE

BARRIÈRE
DES
SERGENTS

RUE DE LA CROIX DES PETITS CHAMPS

PORTE
SAINT-
HONORÉ

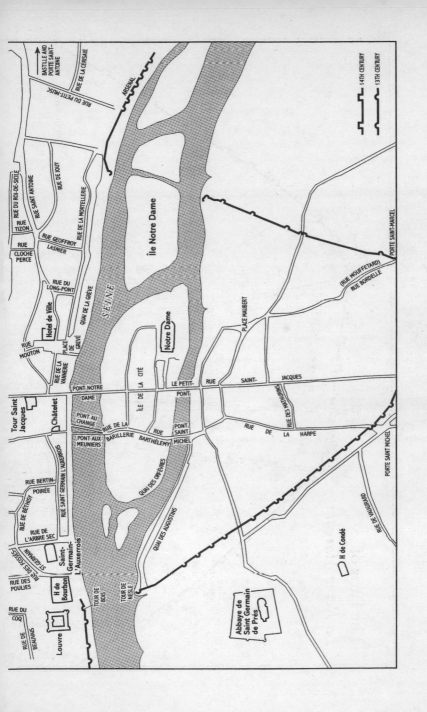

LA REINE MARGOT

CONTENTS

Contents

1

ON Monday, the 18th of August, 1572, there was a splendid fête at the Louvre.*

The windows of the ancient royal residence were brilliantly illuminated, and the squares and streets adjacent, usually deserted after the clock of Saint-Germain-l'Auxerrois* had tolled nine, were now filled with people, although it was past midnight.

In the gloom this surging crowd, threatening, pressing, and turbulent, resembled a dark and rolling sea, with each row of heads a foaming wave. This sea, extending all along the quay, spent its waves at the foot of the walls of the Louvre, on the one hand, and against the Hotel de Bourbon,* which was opposite, on the other. Despite the royal fête, and perhaps even because of it, there was something threatening in the aspect of the people.

The court was celebrating the marriage of Madame Marguerite de Valois, daughter of Henry II and sister of King Charles IX, with Henry de Bourbon, king of Navarre;* and that same morning the Cardinal de Bourbon had united the young couple, with the usual ceremonial observed at the marriages of the royal daughters of France, on a stage erected at the entrance to Notre-Dame.*

This marriage had astonished everybody, and occasioned much surmise to the more discerning. They could not understand the union of two parties who hated each other so thoroughly as did, at this moment, the Protestant party and the Catholic party.* They wondered how the young Prince de Condé could forgive the Duke d'Anjou, the king's brother, for the death of his father, assassinated by Montesquiou, at Jarnac. They asked how the young Duke de Guise could forgive Admiral de Coligny for the death of his father, assassinated at Orleans by Poltrot de Méré.* Moreover, Jeanne de Navarre, the courageous wife of the weak Antoine de Bourbon, who had steered his son Henry towards the royal marriage which awaited him, had died scarcely two months before, and singular reports had been spread abroad as to her sudden death. It was everywhere whispered, and in some places said aloud, that she had discovered some terrible secret; and that Catherine de Medicis, fearing its disclosure, had poisoned her gloves, which had been made by one René, her fellow-countryman, and deeply skilled in such affairs. This report was even more widely spread and believed, when, after the death of this great queen, at her son's request, two celebrated physicians, one of whom was the famous Ambroise Paré, were instructed to open and examine the body, but not the skull. As it was by the smell that Jeanne de Navarre had been poisoned, it was the brain alone that could present any traces of the crime, and that was the sole part excluded from dissection. We say crime, for no one doubted for a moment that a crime had been committed.*

This was not all. The king, Charles, in particular had set his heart on this union, which not only re-established peace in his kingdom, but also attracted to Paris the principal Huguenots of France, and his anxiety almost approached obstinacy.* As the two betrothed belonged one to the Catholic religion and the other to the reformed religion, they were obliged to obtain a dispensation from Gregory XIII, who then filled the papal throne. The dispensation was slow in coming, and the delay causing great uneasiness to the late Queen of Navarre, she had one day expressed to Charles IX her fears lest the dispensation should not arrive; to which the king replied,—

'Be under no alarm, my dear aunt. I honour you more than I do the Pope, and I love my sister more than I fear his Holiness. I am not a Huguenot, but neither am I a fool; and if the Pope makes any difficulties, I will myself take Margot by the hand and unite her to your son for all to see.'*

This speech was soon spread through the Louvre and the city, and, while it greatly rejoiced the Huguenots, had given the Catholics food for thought. They wondered secretly if the king really meant to betray them, or was only playing a role which some fine morning or evening might have an unexpected outcome.

It was particularly with regard to Admiral de Coligny, who for five or six years had been so bitterly opposed to the king, that the conduct of Charles IX appeared inexplicable. After having put on his head a price of a hundred and fifty thousand gold crowns, the king now swore by him, called him his father, and declared openly that he should in future confide the conduct of the war to him alone.* To such a pitch was this carried, that Catherine de Medicis herself, who until then had controlled the actions, will, and even desires of the young prince, seemed beginning to feel uneasy, and not without reason; for, in a moment of confidence, Charles IX had said to the admiral, in reference to the war in Flanders, 'Father, there is one other thing against which we must be on our guard, and this is, that the queen, my mother, who likes to poke her nose everywhere, as you well know, shall learn nothing of this undertaking; we must keep it so quiet that she does not hear a word of it, or, meddler that she is, she will spoil everything.'*

Now, wise and experienced as he was, Coligny had not kept this counsel secret; and although he had come to Paris with great suspicions, and notwithstanding his departure from Châtillon,* a peasant had thrown herself at his feet, crying, 'Ah! sir, good master, do not go to Paris, for if you do you will die—you and all who are with you!'*—these suspicions were lulled and almost destroyed in his mind, and in that of Teligny, his son-in-law, to whom the king was especially kind and attentive, calling him 'brother,' as he called the admiral his 'father,' and behaving to him as he did to his best friends.

The Huguenots, then, excepting some few surly and suspicious spirits, were completely reassured. The death of the Queen of Navarre passed over, as having been caused by a pleurisy, and the spacious apartments of the Louvre were filled with those brave Protestants to whom the marriage of their young leader Henry promised an unexpected return of good fortune. Admiral Coligny, La Rochefoucauld, the young Prince de Condé, Teligny, in short, all the leaders of the party were triumphant when they saw so powerful at the Louvre, and so welcome in Paris, those whom three months before, King Charles and Queen Catherine would have hanged on gibbets higher than those of murderers. The king, the queen, the Duke d'Anjou, and the Duke d'Alençon did the honours of the royal fête with all courtesy and kindness.

The Duke d'Anjou received from the Huguenots themselves

well-merited compliments as to the two battles of Jarnac and
Montcontour,* which he had won before he was eighteen years
of age, more precocious in that than either Cæsar or Alexander,
to whom they compared him, of course placing the conquerors of
Pharsalia and Issus as inferior to the living prince.* The Duke
d'Alençon looked on, with his bland, false smile, while Queen
Catherine, radiant with joy and fulsome in compliment, congratulated Prince Henry de Condé on his recent marriage with Marie
de Clèves, and Messieurs de Guise themselves looked graciously
on the formidable enemies of their house, and the Duke de
Mayenne discoursed with M. de Tavanne and the admiral on the
impending war, which was now more than ever threatened
against Philip II.

In the midst of these groups moved backwards and forwards,
his head a little on one side, his ear open to all that was said, a
young man about nineteen years of age, with a keen eye, black
hair cut very close, thick eyebrows, and a nose curved like an
eagle's,* with a sneering smile and a growing moustache and
beard. This young man, who had first distinguished himself at
the battle of Arnay-le-Duc, for which he had been very highly
complimented, was the dearly beloved pupil of Coligny and the
hero of the day. Three months before—that is to say, when his
mother was living, they called him the Prince of Béarn. Now he
was called the King of Navarre, and later, Henry IV.*

From time to time a gloomy cloud passed suddenly and rapidly over his brow; questionless, he recollected that 'two months,
two little months,'* had scarce elapsed since his mother's death,
and he less than any one doubted that she had been poisoned.
But the cloud was transitory, and disappeared like a fleeting
shadow, for they who spoke to him, they who congratulated him,
they who elbowed him, were the very people who had assassinated the brave Jeanne d'Albret.

Some paces distant from the King of Navarre, almost as pensive and gloomy as the king affected to be joyous and free from
cares, was the young Duke de Guise conversing with Teligny.
More fortunate than the Béarnais, at two-and-twenty he had
almost attained the reputation of his father, François, the great
Duke de Guise. He was an elegant gentleman, very tall, with a
noble and haughty look, and gifted with that natural majesty,

which caused it to be said that by his side other princes seemed to belong to the people. Young as he was, the Catholics looked up to him as the chief of their party, as the Huguenots considered Henry of Navarre, whose portrait we have just drawn, to be their chief. He had hitherto borne the title of Prince de Joinville, and at the siege of Orleans fought his first fight under his father, who died in his arms, denouncing Admiral Coligny as his assassin.* It was then the young duke, like Hannibal,* took a solemn oath to avenge his father's death on the admiral and his family, and to pursue the foes of his religion without truce or respite, promising God to be His exterminating angel on earth until the very last heretic should be eliminated. It was therefore with the deepest astonishment that the people saw this prince, usually so faithful to his word, extend the hand of fellowship to those whom he had sworn to hold as his eternal enemies, and converse familiarly with the son-in-law of the man whose death he had promised to his dying father.

But, as we have said, this was an evening of astonishments.

All continued smilingly within, and a murmur more soft and flattering than ever pervaded the Louvre at the moment when the youthful bride, after having laid aside her ceremonial garb, her long mantle and flowing veil, returned to the ballroom, accompanied by the lovely Duchess de Nevers, her most intimate friend, and led by her brother, Charles IX, who presented her to the principal guests.

The bride was the daughter of Henry II, the pearl of the crown of France, MARGUERITE DE VALOIS, whom, in his familiar tenderness for her, King Charles IX always called *ma sœur Margot.**

Never was there a more flattering reception, never one more deserved than that which awaited the new Queen of Navarre. Marguerite at this period was scarcely twenty, and already she was the object of all the poet's eulogies, some of whom compared her to Aurora, others to Cytherea;* she was truly a beauty without rival in the court in which Catherine de Medicis had assembled the loveliest women of the age and country.

She had black hair and a brilliant complexion; voluptuous eyes, veiled by long lids, delicate coral lips, a graceful neck, a full, enchanting figure, and concealed in satin slippers tiny feet,

scarce larger than a child's.* The French, who possessed her,
were proud to see so lovely a flower flourishing in their soil, and
foreigners who passed through France returned home dazzled
by her beauty, if they had but seen her, and amazed at her
knowledge, if they had talked with her, for not only was Marguerite the loveliest, she was also the most erudite woman of her
time, and on all sides was quoted the remark of an Italian savant
who had been presented to her, and who, after having conversed
with her for an hour in Italian, Spanish, and Latin, had said, on
quitting her presence, 'To see the court without seeing Marguerite de Valois, is to see neither France nor the court.'*

Thus it may be supposed that addresses to King Charles IX
and the Queen of Navarre were not wanting. The Huguenots
were great hands at addresses. Many strong hints about the past,
and stronger hints as to the future, were adroitly slipped into
these harangues; but to all such allusions and speeches he replied, with his pale lips and artificial smile,—

'In giving my sister Margot to Henry of Navarre, I give my
sister to all the Protestants of the kingdom.'*

This phrase reassured some and made others smile, for it had
really a double sense: the one paternal, and with which Charles
IX would not burden his mind; the other injurious to the bride,
her husband, and also to him who said it, for it recalled certain
scandalous rumours with which the chroniclers of the court had
already found means to sully the good name* of Marguerite de
Valois.

However, M. de Guise was conversing, as we have described,
with Teligny; but he did not pay to the conversation such sustained attention but that he turned away from time to time to
cast a glance at the group of ladies, in the centre of whom
glittered the Queen of Navarre. When the princess's eye thus
met that of the young duke, a cloud seemed to spread across that
lovely brow, around which stars of diamonds formed a tremulous circlet, and her restless and impatient manner betrayed an
uneasy mind.

The Princess Claude, the elder sister of Marguerite, who had
been for some years married to the Duke of Lorraine, had observed this uneasiness, and going up to her, was about to inquire
the cause, when all stood aside at the approach of the queen-

mother who advanced, leaning on the arm of the young Prince de
Condé, and the princess was thus suddenly shut out from her
sister. There was then a general movement, of which the Duke
de Guise took advantage to approach Madame de Nevers, his
sister-in-law, and Marguerite.

Madame de Lorraine, who had not lost sight of her sister, then
noticed, instead of the cloud which she had before observed on
her forehead, a burning blush come into her cheeks. The duke
approached still nearer, and when he was within two steps of
Marguerite, she appeared rather to feel than see his presence,
and turned round, making a violent effort to give to her features
an appearance of calmness and indifference. The duke, with a
respectful bow, murmured, in a low voice, '*Ipse attuli*' ('I have
brought it').

Marguerite returned the young duke's bow, and as she bent
forward, replied, in the same tone, '*Noctu pro more*' ('To-night,
as usual').

These words, uttered softly, were so lost in the enormous
collar which the princess wore as to be heard only by the person
to whom they were addressed; but brief as had been the exchange, it doubtless comprised all the young couple had to say,
for after this exchange of two words for three, they separated,
Marguerite more thoughtful, and the duke with his brow less
clouded than when they met. This little scene took place without
the person most interested appearing to remark it, since for his
part, the King of Navarre had eyes but for one individual
amongst those whom Marguerite de Valois had around her, and
that was the lovely Madame de Sauve.

Charlotte de Beaune-Semblançay, grand-daughter of the unfortunate Semblançay,* and wife of Simon de Fizes, Baron de
Sauve, was one of the ladies in waiting to Catherine de Medicis,
and one of the most redoubtable auxiliaries of the Queen who
poured her enemies philtres of love when she dared not pour
them Italian poison. Delicately fair, and by turns sparkling with
vivacity or languishing in melancholy, always ready for love or
intrigue, the two great occupations which for fifty years employed the court of the three succeeding kings:* a woman in
every sense of the word, and in all the charm of the thing, from
the blue eyes, languishing or beaming fire, to the small and

perfectly formed feet, hidden in slippers of velvet, Madame
de Sauve had already for some months seized so completely
on every faculty of the King of Navarre, then making his
debut as lover as well as politician, that Marguerite de Valois,
a magnificent and royal beauty, had not even excited admiration
in the heart of her spouse; and what was more strange, and
astonished all the world, even that soul so full of darkness
and mystery, Catherine de Medicis, while she pursued her
plan for the union of her daughter and the King of Navarre,
had not ceased to favour almost openly his amour with
Madame de Sauve. But despite this powerful aid, and despite
the easy manners of the age, the lovely Charlotte had hitherto
resisted, and this resistance, unheard of, incredible, un-
precedented, even more than the beauty and wit of her
who resisted, had excited in the heart of the Béarnais a passion
which, unable to find satisfaction, had destroyed in the young
king's heart all timidity, pride, and even that nonchalance,
part philosophy, part inertia, which formed the basis of his
character.

Madame de Sauve had been only a few minutes in the
apartment. From spite or grief, she had at first resolved on
not being present at her rival's triumph, and under the pretext
of an indisposition, had allowed her husband, who had been
for five years secretary of state, to go alone to the Louvre. But
when Catherine de Medicis saw the baron without his wife,
and learned the cause that kept her dear Charlotte away, and
that the indisposition was slight, she wrote a few words to
her, which the lady instantly obeyed. Henry, sad as he had
been at first at her absence, had nevertheless breathed
more freely when he saw M. de Sauve enter alone. But at the
moment when, not expecting her appearance, he was about to
pay court to the charming creature whom he was condemned,
if not to love, at least to treat as his wife, he saw Madame de
Sauve arise, as it were, from the farther end of the gallery.
He was nailed to the spot, his eyes drawn to the Circe* who held
him as if by magic chains. Instead of continuing his steps towards his wife, by a movement of hesitation which betrayed
more astonishment than alarm, he advanced to meet Madame
de Sauve.

The courtiers, seeing the King of Navarre, whose inflammable heart they knew, approach the beautiful Charlotte, had not the courage to prevent their meeting but drew aside complaisantly. Thus at the same moment when Marguerite de Valois and M. de Guise exchanged the few words in Latin which we have noted above, Henry, having approached Madame de Sauve, began in very intelligible French, although with a marked Gascon accent,* a much less mysterious conversation.

'Ah *ma mie!*'* he said, 'so you have come at the very moment when they assured me that you were unwell, and I had lost all hope of seeing you?'

'Your Majesty,' replied Madame de Sauve, 'would perhaps have me believe that having your hope dashed was the cause of some pain?'

'*Sang Diou!** I do believe it!' replied the Béarnais; 'surely you know you are my sun by day, and my star by night? By my faith, I was in deepest darkness till you appeared and illumined everything.'

'Then, monseigneur, I serve you a very ill turn.'

'What do you mean, *ma mie?*' inquired Henry.

'I mean that he who is master of the handsomest woman in France should only have one desire—that the light should disappear, and give way to darkness and to happiness.'

'You know that my happiness is in the hands of one woman only, and that she laughs at poor Henry.'

'Oh!' replied the baroness, 'I believed, on the contrary, that it was this person who was the sport and jest of the King of Navarre.'

'By my faith, my dear, you reproach me very unjustly, and I do not understand how so lovely a mouth can be so cruel. Do you suppose for a moment that it was I who arranged my own marriage? No, *ventre-saint-gris*, not I!'

'Perhaps it was me,' said the baroness sharply.

'With your lovely eyes have you not seen farther, baroness? No, no; it is not Henry of Navarre who weds Marguerite de Valois.'

'And what is it, then?'

'Why, *sang Diou!* it is the reformed religion which marries the pope—that's all.'

'No, no; your Majesty loves Madame Marguerite. And can I blame you? Heaven forbid! She is beautiful enough to be adored.'

Henry reflected for a moment, and, as he reflected, a knowing smile curled the corner of his lips.

'Baroness,' said he, 'you have no right to seek a quarrel with me. What have you done to prevent me from marrying Marguerite? Nothing. On the contrary, you have always driven me to despair, and I wed her because you do not love me.'

'If I loved you, sire, I would have been dead an hour from now.'

'In an hour! What do you mean? And of what death would you have died?'

'Of jealousy!—for in another hour the Queen of Navarre will send away her women, and your Majesty your gentlemen.'

'Is that really the thought that occupies your mind, *ma mie?*'

'I have not said so. I only say, that if I loved you it would torment my mind.'

'But suppose,' said Henry, 'that the King of Navarre should not send away his gentlemen this evening?'

'Sire,' replied Madame de Sauve, looking at the king with astonishment which was for once unfeigned, 'you say the most impossible and incredible things.'

'What must I do to make you believe them?'

'Give me proof—but that proof you cannot give me.'

'Yes, baroness, yes! By Saint Henry, I will give it you!' exclaimed the king, gazing amorously on her.

'Oh, your Majesty!' murmured the lovely Charlotte, with downcast eyes, 'I do not understand.'

'There are four Henries in this room, my darling!' replied the king. 'Henry de France, Henry de Condé, Henry de Guise; but there is only one Henry of Navarre.'

'Well?'

'Well; if this Henry of Navarre is with you all night——'

'All night!'

'Yes; then you will be certain that he is not with any one else.'

'Ah! if you do that, sire—' said Madame de Sauve.

'On the honour of a gentleman, I will do it!'

Madame de Sauve raised her beaming and love-promising eyes to the king, whose heart beat with joy.

'And then,' said Henry, 'what will you say?'

'I will say,' replied Charlotte, 'that your Majesty truly loves me.'

'*Ventre-saint-gris!* then you shall say it. Do you not have some waiting-woman whom you can trust?'

'Yes, Dariole* is devoted to me.'

'*Sang Diou!* then tell her that I will make her fortune when I am King of France, as the astrologers prophesy.'

Charlotte smiled, for even at this period the Gascon reputation of the Béarnais* was already established with respect to his promises.

'Well, then, what do you desire of Dariole?'

'Little for her, a great deal for me. Your apartment is above mine?'

'Yes.'

'Let her wait behind the door. I will knock three times quietly, and——'

Madame de Sauve said nothing for several seconds, and then, as if she had looked around her to observe if she were overheard, she fixed her gaze for a moment on the group which surrounded the queen-mother: brief as the moment was, it was sufficient for Catherine and her lady-in-waiting to exchange a look.

'Oh, if I were inclined,' said Madame de Sauve, in a siren's voice that would have melted Ulysses himself*—'if I were inclined to make your Majesty tell a lie——'

'*Ma mie*, try——'

'Ah, *ma foi*! I confess I am tempted to do so.'

'Women are never so strong as in defeat.'

'Sire, I shall hold you to your promise for Dariole, when you are King of France.'

Henry uttered an exclamation of joy.

It was at the precise moment when the cry escaped the lips of the Béarnais that the Queen of Navarre replied to the Duke de Guise,—

'*Noctu pro more.*'

Then Henry left Madame de Sauve as happy as the Duke de Guise when he left Marguerite de Valois.

An hour after the double scene we have just related, King Charles and the queen-mother also retired to their quarters. Almost immediately the apartments began to empty; the base of each marble pillar in the galleries became visible once more. The admiral and the Prince de Condé were escorted home by four hundred Huguenot gentlemen through the middle of the crowd, which murmured as they passed. Then Henry de Guise, with the Lorraine and Catholic gentlemen, left in their turn, greeted by the cries of joy and plaudits of the people.

Marguerite de Valois, Henry of Navarre, and Madame de Sauve did not leave. They lived in the Louvre.

2

THE QUEEN OF NAVARRE'S CHAMBER

THE Duke de Guise escorted his sister-in-law, the Duchess de Nevers, to his house in the Rue du Chaume,* and then proceeded to his own apartment to change his clothes, put on a night cloak, and arm himself with one of those short and sharp poniards which are called '*foi de gentilhomme*' and were worn without swords; but at the moment he took it off the table on which it was placed, he saw a small note between the blade and the scabbard.

He opened it, and read as follows:—

'I hope M. de Guise will not return to the Louvre to-night; or, if he does, that he will at least take the precaution to arm himself with a good coat of mail and a trusty sword.'

'Ah! ah!' said the duke, 'this is a singular warning; but I always take good advice—my steel jacket and my sword.'

The valet-de-chambre, accustomed to these changes of costume, brought both. The duke put on his jacket, which was made of rings of steel so fine that it was scarcely thicker than velvet; he then drew on a coat and doublet of grey and silver, his favourite colours, placed a dagger in his belt, handed his sword to a page, the only attendant he allowed to accompany him, and made his way to the Louvre, which he reached in safety.

In front of the royal château was a deep dry moat overlooking which were the apartments of most of the princes who inhabited the palace. Marguerite's was on the first floor, and, easily accessible but for the moat, was, in consequence of the depth to which the trench was cut, thirty feet below the wall, and therefore out of the reach of robbers or lovers; but nevertheless the Duke de Guise approached it without hesitation.

At the same moment was heard the noise of a window being opened on the ground floor. This window was grated, but a hand appeared, lifted out one of the bars that had been loosened, and dropped from it a silken cord.

'Is that you, Gillonne?' said the duke, in a whisper.

'Yes, monseigneur,' replied a female voice, in a still lower whisper.

'And Marguerite?'

'Awaits you.'

'Good.'

Hereupon the duke made a signal to his page, who, opening his cloak, took out a small rope ladder. The prince fastened one end to the silk cord, and Gillonne drawing it up, fastened it, and the prince, after having buckled his sword to his belt, ascended without accident. When he entered, the bar was replaced and the window closed, while the page, having seen his master quietly enter the Louvre, to the windows of which he had accompanied him twenty times in the same way, laid himself down in his cloak on the grass of the moat in the shadow of the wall.

The night was extremely dark, and several large rain-drops fell from heavy clouds charged with sulphur and electricity.

The Duke de Guise followed his guide, who was no other than the daughter of Jacques de Matignon, maréchal of France. She was the confidante of Marguerite, who kept no secret from her, and it was said that amongst the number of mysteries entrusted to her incorruptible fidelity, there were some so terrible as to compel her to keep the rest.

There was no light remaining either in the lower chamber or in the corridor. But from time to time a livid glare illuminated the dark apartments with a vivid flash, which as instantly disappeared.

The duke, still following his guide who held his hand, reached a staircase formed in the thickness of the wall, and which opened by a secret and invisible door into the antechamber of Marguerite's apartment.

In this antechamber, which was utterly dark, Gillonne stopped.

'Have you brought what the queen requested?' she inquired in a whisper.

'Yes,' replied the Duke de Guise; 'but I will only give it to her Majesty in person.'

'Come, then, and do not waste an instant!' said a voice from the darkness, which made the duke start, for it was Marguerite's.

At the same moment a curtain of violet velvet covered with fleurs-de-lis was raised, and the duke made out the form of the queen, who, in her impatience, had come to meet him.

'I am here, madame,' he said and passed through the curtain, which fell behind him. Gillonne remained in the antechamber.

As if she understood the jealousies of the duke, Marguerite led him to the bedchamber, and then paused.

'Well,' she said, 'are you content, duke?'

'Content, madame?' was the reply—'and with what?'

'Of the proof I give you,' retorted Marguerite, with a slight tone of vexation in her voice, 'that I belong to a man, who, on the very night of his marriage, makes me of such small importance that he does not even come to thank me for the honour I have done him, not in selecting, but in accepting him for my husband.'

'Oh! madame,' said the duke sorrowfully, 'be assured he will come if you desire it.'

'And is it you who say that, Henry?' cried Marguerite; 'you, who better than any know the contrary of what you say. If I did desire it, should I have asked you to come to the Louvre?'

'You have asked me to come to the Louvre, Marguerite, because you are anxious to destroy every vestige of the past, and because that past lives not only in my memory, but in this silver casket which I bring to you.'

'Henry, shall I say one thing to you?' replied Marguerite. 'You are more like a schoolboy than a prince. I deny that I have loved you! I desire to quench a flame which will die, perhaps, but whose reflection will never die! No, no, duke! you may keep the letters of your Marguerite, and the casket she gave you. Among these letters she asks but one, and that only because it is as dangerous for you as for herself.'

'It is yours,' said the duke.

Marguerite searched anxiously in the open casket, and with a tremulous hand took, one after the other, a dozen letters, of which she examined the address only, as if by the inspection alone of these she could recall to her memory what the letters themselves contained. But after a close scrutiny, she looked at the duke, pale and agitated:—

'Sir,' she said, 'what I seek is not here. Have you lost it, by any chance?'

'What letter do you seek, madame?'

'The one in which I told you to marry without delay.'

'As an excuse for your infidelity?'

Marguerite shrugged her shoulders.

'No: to save your life. The one in which I say to you that the king, seeing our love and my exertions to break off your proposed marriage with the Infanta of Portugal,* had sent for his brother, the Bastard of Angoulême, and said to him, pointing to two swords, "With this slay Henry de Guise this night, or with the other I will slay thee in the morning." Where is that letter?'

'Here,' said the duke, drawing it from his breast.

Marguerite snatched it from his hands, opened it anxiously, reassured herself that it was really that which she wanted, uttered an exclamation of joy, and applying the lighted candle to it, the flames instantly consumed the paper. Then, as if Marguerite feared that her imprudent words might be read in the ashes, she trampled them under foot.

During all this, the Duke de Guise had watched his mistress attentively.

'Well, Marguerite,' he said, when she had finished; 'are you satisfied now?'

'Yes, for now you have married the Princess de Porcian, my brother will forgive me your love. He would never have pardoned me for revealing a secret such as that which in my weakness for you I had not the strength to conceal from you.'

'True,' replied de Guise, 'but then, you loved me.'

'And I love you still, Henry, as much—more than ever!'

'You——?'

'I do; for never more than at this moment did I need a sincere and devoted friend. Queen, I have no throne: wife, I have no husband!'

The young prince shook his head sorrowfully.

'I tell you, I repeat to you, Henry, that my husband not only does not love me, but hates—despises me; besides your presence in the chamber in which he ought to be is full proof of his hatred and contempt.'

'It is not yet late, madame, and the King of Navarre requires time to dismiss his gentlemen. If he has not already come, he will not be long.'

'And I tell you,' cried Marguerite, with increasing vexation— 'I tell you that he will not come!'

'Madame!' exclaimed Gillonne, suddenly entering—'the King of Navarre is just leaving his apartment!'

'Oh, I knew he would come!' exclaimed the Duke de Guise.

'Henry,' said Marguerite quickly, seizing the duke's hand, 'Henry, you shall see if I am a woman of my word and if I may be relied on. Henry, enter this closet.'

'Madame, allow me to go while there is yet time, for remember that with the first mark of love you bestow on him, I shall not stay hidden, and then woe to him!'

'Are you mad? go in—go in, I say, and I will be responsible for everything.' And she pushed the duke into the closet.

It was not a moment too soon. The door was scarcely closed behind the prince when the King of Navarre, escorted by two pages who carried eight flambeaux of pink wax in two candelabras, appeared smiling, on the threshold of the chamber.

Marguerite concealed her trouble, and made a very low curtsey.

'You are not yet in bed, madame,' observed the Béarnais, with his frank and joyous look. 'Were you by chance waiting for me?'

'No, sir,' replied Marguerite; 'for yesterday you repeated to me that our marriage was a political alliance, and that you would never thwart my wishes.'

'Assuredly; but that is no reason why we should not talk a little together. Gillonne, close the door, and leave us.'

Marguerite, who was sitting, then rose and extended her hand, as if to desire the pages to remain.

'Must I call your woman?' inquired the king. 'I will do so if such be your desire, although I confess that what I have to say to you would make me prefer our being alone.'

And the King of Navarre advanced towards the closet.

'No!' exclaimed Marguerite, hastily going before him; 'no—there is no occasion for that; I am ready to hear you.'

The Béarnais had learned what he wanted to know—he threw a rapid, penetrating glance towards the closet door, as if, in spite of the thick curtain which hung before it, he would dive into its obscurity. Then turning his looks to his lovely wife, pale with terror, he said, with the utmost composure,—

'In that case, madame, let us talk for a few moments.'

'As your Majesty pleases,' said the lady, falling into, rather than sitting upon, the seat which her husband pointed out to her.

The Béarnais sat beside her.

'Madame,' he continued, 'whatever many persons may have said, I think our marriage is a good marriage. I stand well with you—you stand well with me.'

'But——' said Marguerite, alarmed.

'Consequently, we ought,' observed the King of Navarre, 'to behave towards each other like trusting allies, since we were to-day allied in the presence of God. Don't you agree?'

'Unquestionably, sir.'

'I know, madame, how great your penetration is. I know how the court has many pitfalls for the unwary. Now I am young, and, although I never harmed any person, I have a great many enemies. In which camp, madame, must I range her who bears my name, and who has vowed her affection to me at the foot of the altar?'

'Sir, could you think——'

'I think nothing, madame. I hope, and I am anxious to know that my hope is well founded. It is quite certain that our marriage is merely a pretext or a snare.'

Marguerite started, for the same thought had occurred to her.

'Now, then, which of the two?' continued Henry of Navarre. 'The king hates me, the Duke d'Anjou hates me, the Duke d'Alençon hates me, and Catherine de Medicis hated my mother too much not to hate me.'

'Oh, sir, what are you saying?'

'The truth, madame,' replied the king; 'and I wish, so that it may not be supposed that I am the dupe of the assassination of M. de Mouy* and the poisoning of my mother, that some one were here who could hear me say it.'

'Oh, sir,' replied Marguerite, with an air as calm and smiling as she could assume, 'you know very well that there is no one here but you and myself.'

'It is for that very reason that I thus give vent to my thoughts. It is this that emboldens me to declare that I am not the dupe of the caresses showered on me by the house of France, or the house of Lorraine.'*

'Sire, sire!' exclaimed Marguerite.

'Well, what is it, *ma mie*?' inquired Henry, smiling in his turn.

'Why, sir, such remarks are very dangerous.'

'Not when we are alone,' observed the king. 'I was saying——'

Marguerite was evidently distressed. She would have liked to stop every word the king uttered, but he continued, with apparent indifference,—

'I was telling you that I was threatened on all sides; by the king, by the Duke d'Alençon, by the Duke d'Anjou, by the queen-mother, by the Duke de Guise, by the Duke de Mayenne, by the Cardinal de Lorraine—threatened, in fact, by everybody. One feels that instinctively, as you know, madame. Well, against all these threats, which must soon become attacks, I can defend myself with your help, for you are loved by all the persons who detest me.'

'I?' said Marguerite.

'Yes, you,' replied Henry, with the utmost easiness of manner. 'You are loved by King Charles, you are loved' (he laid strong emphasis on the word) 'by the Duke d'Alençon, you are loved by Queen Catherine, and you are loved by the Duke de Guise.'

'Sir!' murmured Marguerite.

'Yes. And what is there astonishing in the fact that everyone loves you? All I have mentioned are your brothers or relatives.

To love one's brothers and relatives is to live according to the heart of God.'

'But what,' asked Marguerite, greatly overcome—'what do you want?'

'I would say, that if you will—I do not ask you to love me—but if you will be my ally, I could brave everything. But on the other hand, if you become my enemy, I am lost.'

'Your enemy?—never, sir!' exclaimed Marguerite.

'And my love—never either?'

'Perhaps——'

'And my ally?'

'Most decidedly.'

And Marguerite turned round, and presented her hand to the king.

Henry took it, kissed it gallantly, and retaining it in his own, more from a spirit of curiosity than from any sentiment of tenderness, said,—

'Well, madame, I believe you, and accept the alliance. They married us without our knowing each other—without our loving each other; they married us without consulting us—us whom they united. We therefore owe nothing to each other, as man and wife; but we ally ourselves freely and without compulsion. We ally ourselves, as two loyal hearts who owe each other mutual protection should ally themselves; 'tis as such you understand it?'

'Yes, sir,' said Marguerite, trying to withdraw her hand.

'Well, then,' continued the Béarnais, with his eyes fixed on the closet, 'since the first proof of a frank alliance is total confidence, I will now, madame, relate to you, in all its details, the plan I have formed, in order that we may victoriously meet and overcome all these enemies.'

'Sir,' said Marguerite, turning her eyes towards the closet, whilst the Béarnais, seeing his trick succeed, smiled to himself.

'This is what I mean to do,' he continued, without appearing to notice the uneasiness of his young wife, 'I intend——'

'Sir,' said Marguerite, rising hastily, and seizing the king's arm—'allow me a little air; my emotions—the heat—overpowers me.'

And, in truth, Marguerite was as pale and trembling as if she was about to collapse on to the carpet.

Henry went straight to a window some distance off, and opened it. This window looked on the river.

Marguerite followed him. 'Silence, sire—silence, for pity's sake!' she murmured.

'What, madame,' said the Béarnais, with his peculiar smile, 'did you not say we were alone?'

'Yes, sir; but have you not heard me say that by the aid of a tube introduced into the ceiling or the wall everything could be heard?'

'Well, madame,' said the Béarnais earnestly, and in a low voice; 'it is true you do not love me, but you are, at least, honourable.'

'What do you mean, sir?'

'I mean that if you were capable of betraying me, you would have allowed me to continue, for I might have betrayed myself. You stopped me. I now know that someone is concealed here—that you are an unfaithful wife, but a faithful ally; and, at this moment, I have more need of fidelity in politics than in love.'*

'Sire!' replied Marguerite, confused.

'We will talk of this hereafter,' said Henry, 'when we know each other better.'

Then raising his voice—'Well,' he continued, 'can you breathe more freely now, madame?'

'Yes, sire—yes!'

'Well, then,' said the Béarnais, 'I will no longer intrude on you. I owed you my respects, and some advances towards better acquaintance; deign, then, to accept them, as they are offered, with all my heart. Good-night, and sleep well!'

Marguerite raised to her husband her eyes, brilliant with gratitude, and, in her turn, extended her hand.

'It is agreed,' she said.

'Political alliance, frank and loyal?' asked Henry.

'Frank and loyal,' was the reply.

And the Béarnais went towards the door, followed by Marguerite's look. Then, when the curtain had fallen between them and the bedchamber,—

'Thanks, Marguerite,' he said quickly, lowering his voice,

'thanks! You are a true daughter of France. I leave you with an easy mind; lacking your love, your friendship will not fail me. I rely on you, as you, for your part, may rely on me. Adieu, madame.'

And Henry kissed his wife's hand, and pressed it gently. Then with a quick step he returned to his own apartment, saying to himself in the corridor,—

'Who the devil is with her? Is it the king, or the Duke d'Anjou, or the Duke d'Alençon, or the Duke de Guise? is it a brother or a lover—is it both? I' faith, I am almost sorry now I asked the baroness for this rendezvous; but as my word is pledged, and Dariole awaits me, no matter. Yet, *ventre-saint-gris!* this Margot, as my brother-in-law, King Charles, calls her, is an adorable creature.'

And with a step which betrayed a slight hesitation, Henry of Navarre ascended the staircase which led to Madame de Sauve's apartments.

Marguerite had followed him with her eyes until he disappeared. Then she returned to her chamber, and found the duke at the door of the closet. The sight almost touched her with remorse.

The duke was grave, and his knitted brow bespoke bitter reflection.

'Marguerite is neutral to-day,' he said—'Marguerite will be hostile in a week.'

'Ah, you have been listening?' said Marguerite.

'What else could I do in that closet?'

'And did you find that I behaved otherwise than the Queen of Navarre should behave?'

'No. But differently from the way in which the mistress of the Duke de Guise should behave.'

'Sir,' replied the queen, 'I may not love my husband, but no one has the right to require me to betray him. Would you yourself reveal the secrets of the Princess de Porcian, your wife?'

'Come, come, madame,' answered the duke, shaking his head, 'this is all very well. I see that you do not love me as in those days when you disclosed to me the plot laid by the king against me and my party.'*

'The king was strong and you were weak; Henry is weak, and you are strong. You see I am consistent.'

'But you pass from one camp to another.'

'That was a right I acquired, sir, in saving your life.'

'Good, madame; and as when lovers separate, they return all the gifts that have passed between them, I will save your life, in my turn, and we shall be quits.'

And bowing politely, the duke left the room. Marguerite did not attempt to detain him.

In the antechamber he found Gillonne, who guided him to the window on the ground-floor, and in the moat he found his page, with whom he returned to the Hotel de Guise.

Marguerite went to the opened window.

'What a wedding night!' she murmured to herself; 'the husband leaves—the lover forsakes me!'

She shut the window, and called Gillonne to help her to undress and retire to bed.

3

THE POET-KING

THE following days were passed in a succession of balls, tournaments, and banquets. The king seemed to have laid aside his usual melancholy, and the queen-mother was so occupied with embroidery, ornaments, and plumes, that she could not sleep.

The Huguenots, in some measure appeased,* began to don silken doublets, wear the emblems of their faith,* and parade before certain balconies, as if they were Catholics.

On every side the reaction in favour of the Protestants was so great, that it seemed the court was about to become Protestant itself. Even the admiral, in spite of his discernment, was deceived, and was so carried away that one evening he forgot for two whole hours his toothpick,* which he always used from two o'clock, the hour at which he dined, until eight o'clock at night, when he sat down to supper.

The evening on which the admiral thus unaccountably deviated from his usual habits, King Charles IX had invited Henry of Navarre and the Duke de Guise to sup with him. After the repast, he went into his chamber, and was busily explaining to them the mechanism of a wolf-trap he had invented, when, interrupting himself—'The admiral does not come to-night,' said he. 'Who has seen him to-day? Can anyone tell me anything about him?'

'I can,' said the King of Navarre, 'and if your Majesty is anxious about him, I can reassure you, for I saw him this morning at six, and this evening at seven o'clock.'

'Ah!' replied the king, whose eyes were instantly fixed quizzingly on his brother-in-law, 'for a newly married man, Harry, you rise very early.'

'Yes, sire,' answered the King of Navarre, 'I wished to inquire of the admiral, who knows everything, whether some gentlemen I expect are on their way here.'

'More gentlemen! why, you had eight hundred* on the day of your wedding and more join you daily. You are surely not going to invade us?' said Charles IX, smiling.

The Duke de Guise frowned.

'Sire,' returned the Béarnais, 'a war with Flanders* is spoken of, and I am collecting round me all those gentlemen of my country whom I think can be useful to your Majesty.'

The duke, calling to mind the supposed plan Henry had mentioned to Marguerite on the day of their marriage, listened still more attentively.

'Well, well,' replied the king, with a sinister smile, 'the more the better; let them all come. But who are these gentlemen?— brave ones, I trust?'

'I cannot tell, sire, if my gentlemen will ever equal those of your Majesty, of the Duke d'Anjou, or of the Duke de Guise, but I know that they will do their best.'

'Do you expect many?'

'Ten or twelve, perhaps.'

'What are their names?'

'Sire, I cannot at this moment call any of them to mind, with the exception of one, whom Teligny recommended to me as a most accomplished gentleman, and whose name is De la Mole.'

'De la Mole,' said the king, who was perfectly acquainted with the genealogy of all the noble families of France—'is he not a Lérac de la Mole,* a Provençal?'

'Exactly so, sire; you see, I recruit even in Provence.'

'And I,' added the Duke de Guise, with a sarcastic smile, 'go even further than the King of Navarre, for I seek even in Piedmont* all the brave Catholics I can find.'

'Catholic or Huguenot,' interrupted the king, 'it little matters to me, so long as they are brave.'

The expression on the king's face as he uttered these words, which thus united Catholics and Huguenots in his thoughts, was so full of indifference that the duke himself was surprised.

'Your Majesty is occupied with the Flemings,' said the admiral, to whom Charles had some days previously granted the favour of entering without being announced, and who had overheard the king's last words.

'Ah! here is my father, the admiral!' cried Charles, opening his arms. 'We were speaking of battles, of gentlemen, of brave men—and *he* comes. It is like the lodestone which attracts iron. My brother-in-law of Navarre and my cousin of Guise were speaking of reinforcements they expect for your army. That was the subject of our conversation.'

'And these reinforcements have arrived,' said the admiral.

'Have you any intelligence of them, monsieur?' asked the Béarnais.

'Yes, my son, and particularly of M. de la Mole. He was at Orleans yesterday and will be in Paris to-morrow, or the day after.'

'The devil! You must be a sorcerer, admiral,' said the Duke de Guise, 'to know what is passing at thirty or forty leagues' distance. For my part, I should like to know for certain what will happen, or what has already happened, at Orleans.'

Coligny remained unmoved by this speech, which evidently alluded to the death of François de Guise,* the Duke's father, killed at Orleans, by Poltrot de Méré, and not without a suspicion of the admiral's having been concerned in the murder.

'Sir,' replied he coldly, and with dignity, 'I am a sorcerer whenever I wish to know anything that concerns my own affairs or those of the king. My courier arrived an hour ago from

Orleans, having travelled, thanks to the post, thirty-two leagues in a day.* As M. de la Mole only has his own horse, he rides but ten leagues a day, and can only arrive in Paris on the 24th. Here is all my magic.'

'Bravo, father!' cried Charles IX, 'teach these young men that it is wisdom as well as age which has whitened your hair and beard. We will send them away to talk of love and tournaments, and we ourselves will speak of our wars. Good councillors make good kings. Leave us, gentlemen; we would be alone.'

The two young men left the apartment, the King of Navarre first, then the Duke de Guise. But outside the door they separated, after a formal salute.

Coligny followed them with his eyes, not without uneasiness. For he never saw these two men, who cherished so deadly a hate against each other, meet, without a dread that some spark would kindle a conflagration. Charles saw what was passing in his mind, and, laying his hand on his arm, said:

'Fear nothing, my father; I am here to preserve peace and obedience. I am really a king, now that my mother is no longer queen. And she is no longer queen, since Coligny became my father.'

'Oh, sire!' said the admiral, 'Queen Catherine——'

'Is a quarrel-monger. Peace is impossible with her. These Italian Catholics are furious, and will hear of nothing but extermination. Now, for my part, I not only wish to pacify, but to protect those of the reformed religion. The others are too dissolute. They scandalise me with their amours and their quarrels. Shall I speak frankly to you?' continued Charles, redoubling in energy. 'I mistrust every one around me, except my new friends. I suspect the ambition of Tavannes. Vieilleville only cares for good wine, and would betray his king for a cask of Malvoisie.* Montmorency only thinks of hunting and lives amongst his dogs and falcons. Count de Retz is a Spaniard and the Guises are Lorraines.* I think there are no true Frenchmen in France, except myself, my brother-in-law of Navarre, and yourself. But I am chained to the throne, and cannot command the army: it is as much as I can do to hunt at Saint-Germain or Rambouillet.* My brother-in-law of Navarre is too young and too inexperienced; besides, he seems to me exactly like his father Antoine, ruined by women. There is only you, father, who can be called brave as Cæsar and wise as Plato. So I scarcely know what to do—keep you near me, as my adviser, or send you to the army as its general. If you counsel me, who will command? If you command, who will counsel me?'

'Sire,' said Coligny, 'we must conquer first, and then take counsel after the victory.'

'That is your advice—so be it: Monday you shall leave for Flanders, and I for Amboise.'*

'Your Majesty intends to leave Paris, then?'

'Yes; I am weary of this confusion, and of these fêtes. I am not a man of action; I am a dreamer. I was not born to be a king; I was born to be a poet.* You shall form a council—as long as my mother has no influence in it, all will go well. I have already sent word to Ronsard* to meet me, and at this moment I must go and reply to a sonnet which my dear and illustrious poet has sent me. I cannot, therefore, give you now the documents necessary to make you acquainted with the question now debating between Philip II and myself. There is, besides, a plan of the campaign drawn up by my ministers. I will find it all for you, and give it to you to-morrow.'

'At what time, sire?'

'At ten o'clock; and if by chance I am busy writing verses, or in my cabinet, composing—you will find all the papers in this red morocco portfolio. It is a very bright colour. You cannot mistake it. I am now going to write to Ronsard.'

'Adieu, sire!'

'Adieu, father!'

'Your hand——'

'What, my hand? Your place is in my arms, in my heart! Come, my old soldier, come!'

And Charles, drawing Coligny towards him as he inclined himself before him, pressed his lips to his forehead.

As he left the room, the admiral wiped a tear from his eyes.

Charles followed him with his eyes as long as he could see, and listened as long as he could catch a sound. When he could no longer hear or see anything, he turned and entered his small armoury. This armoury was the favourite apartment of the king. It was there he took his fencing lessons with Pompée, and his lessons of poetry with Ronsard. He had assembled there all the most costly arms he had been able to collect. The walls were hung with axes, shields, spears, halberds, pistols, and muskets,* and that day a famous armourer had brought him a magnificent arquebuse, on the barrel of which were encrusted, in silver, these four verses, composed by the royal poet himself,—

> *Pour maintenir la foy,*
> *Je suis belle et fidèle,*
> *Aux ennemis du Roi,*
> *Je suis belle et cruelle.**

Charles entered this room, as we have said, and shutting the door by which he had entered, he raised the tapestry which masked a passage leading into a little chamber where a woman, kneeling, was saying her prayers.

As this movement was executed noiselessly, and the king's footsteps were deadened by the thick carpet, the woman heard no sound, and continued to pray. Charles stood for a moment looking pensively at her.

She was a woman of thirty-four or thirty-five years of age, whose masculine beauty was set off by the costume of the peasants of Caux.* She wore the high cap, so much the fashion at the court of France during the time of Isabeau of Bavaria,* and her bodice was red and embroidered with gold, like those still worn to-day by the contadine of Nettuno and Sora.* The apartment which she had occupied for nearly twenty years was close to the king's bed-chamber, and presented a singular mixture of elegance and rusticity. The palace had encroached upon the cottage, and the cottage upon the palace, so that the chamber stood between the simplicity of the peasant and the luxury of the court lady.

The *prie-dieu* on which she knelt was oak, beautifully carved, covered with velvet, and embroidered with gold, while the Bible (for she was of the reformed religion)* from which she was reading, was very old and torn, like those found in the poorest cottages.

'Eh, Madelon!' said the king.

The kneeling woman lifted her head smilingly at the well-known voice, and rising from her knees,—

'Ah! it is you, my son,' said she.

'Yes, nurse; come here.'

Charles IX let the curtain fall, and sat down on the arm of a large chair. The nurse appeared.

'What do you want with me, Charles?'

'Come near, and answer me quietly.'

The nurse approached him unceremoniously.

'Here I am,' said she; 'speak!'

'Is the person I sent for there?'

'He has been there half an hour.'

Charles rose from his seat, approached the window, looked to reassure himself there were no eavesdroppers, went towards the door, and looked out there also, shook the dust from his trophies, patted a large greyhound, which followed him wherever he went, stopping when he stopped and moving when he moved—then returning to his nurse,—

'Let him come in, nurse,' said he.

The nurse disappeared by the same passage by which she had come, while the king went and leaned against a table on which were scattered arms of every kind. Scarcely had he done so when the tapestry was again raised, and the person he expected entered.

He was a man of about forty, his large grey eyes full of treachery and falsehood, his nose curved like the beak of a screech-owl, his cheek bones prominent. His face sought in vain to assume an expression of respect, but naught but fear appeared on his blanched lips.

Charles gently put his hand behind him, and grasped the butt of a pistol, of a new construction, that was discharged, not by a match, as formerly, but by a flint brought in contact with a wheel of steel.* He fixed his eyes steadily on the new-comer, while he whistled one of his favourite hunting airs.

After a pause of some minutes, during which the expression on the stranger's face grew more and more uneasy,—

'You are the person,' said the king, 'called François de Louviers Maurevel?'

'Yes, sire.'

'Captain of Musketeers?'

'Yes, sire.'

'I wished to see you.'

Maurevel bowed low.

'You know,' continued Charles, laying a stress on each word, 'that I love all my subjects equally?'

'I know,' stammered Maurevel, 'that your Majesty is the father of your people.'

'And that the Huguenots and Catholics are equally my children?'

Maurevel remained silent, but his agitation was manifest to the piercing eyes of the king, although he was almost hidden in the dark.

'This displeases you,' said the king, 'who are so great an enemy to the Huguenots.'

Maurevel fell on his knees.

'Sire,' stammered he, 'believe that——'

'I believe,' continued Charles, whose eye now changed its glassy look for one that seemed of fire—'I believe that you felt a great desire at Montcontour to kill the admiral,* who has just left me; I believe you missed your aim, and that then you entered the army of my brother, the Duke d'Anjou; I believe that you enlisted into the company of M. de Mouy de Saint-Phale.'

'Oh, sire!'

'A brave gentleman from Picardy.'

'Sire, sire!' cried Maurevel, 'you overwhelm me.'

'He was a brave soldier,' continued Charles, whose features assumed an aspect of almost ferocious cruelty, 'who received you as if you had been his son; fed you, lodged you, and clothed you.'

Maurevel uttered a despairing sigh.

'You called him your father, and a tender friendship existed between you and the young de Mouy.'

Maurevel, still on his knees, bent lower and lower. The king stood immovable, like a statue whose lips only are endowed with life.

'By the way,' continued the king, 'M. de Guise was to give you ten thousand crowns if you killed the admiral—was he not?'

The assassin struck his forehead against the floor.

'One day as your father, the Sieur de Mouy, reconnoitred near Cherveux,* he let his whip fall, and dismounted to pick it up. You were then alone with him; you took a pistol from your holster and shot him in the back; then seeing he was dead—for you killed him on the spot—you escaped on the horse he had given you. That is your story, I believe?'

And as Maurevel remained mute under this accusation, every circumstance of which was true, the king began to whistle again, as accurately and tunefully as before, the same hunting air.

'Now then, assassin!' said he, 'do you know I have a great mind to hang you?'

'Oh, sire!' cried Maurevel.

'Young de Mouy entreated me to do so only yesterday, and I scarcely knew what answer to give him, for his demand was very just.'

Maurevel clasped his hands.

'All the more just, since I am, as you say, the father of my people. And since, as I answered you now, I am reconciled to the Huguenots, they are as much my children as the Catholics.'

'Sire,' said Maurevel, in despair, 'my life is in your hands; do with it what you will.'

'You are quite right, and I would not give a halfpenny for it.'

'But, sire,' asked the assassin, 'is there no means of redeeming my crime?'

'None that I know of; only in your place—but thank God I am not——'

'Well, sire, were you in my place?' murmured Maurevel.

'I think I could extricate myself,' said the king.

Maurevel raised himself on one knee and one hand, fixing his eyes upon Charles.

'I am very fond of young de Mouy,' said the king, 'but, I am equally fond of my cousin of Guise. And if my cousin asked me to spare a man the other wanted me to hang, I confess I should be embarrassed. But for policy as well as religion's sake I should comply with Guise's request. For de Mouy, although a brave gentleman, is but a petty personage compared with a Prince of Lorraine.'*

During these words, Maurevel rose slowly, like a man whose life is saved.

'Since in your situation it is very important to gain the duke's favour, listen to what he said to me last night.'

Maurevel drew nearer.

'"Imagine, sire," said he to me, "that every morning, at ten o'clock, my deadliest enemy passes down the Rue Saint Germain l'Auxerrois, on his return from the Louvre. I see him from a barred window in the room of my old tutor, the canon Pierre Pile, and I pray the devil to open the earth and swallow him in its abysses." Now, Maurevel, perhaps if you were the devil, would the duke be pleased?'

'But sire,' stammered Maurevel, 'I cannot make the earth open.'

'You made it open, however, wide enough for de Mouy. It was with a pistol that—have you this famous pistol still?'

'I am a better marksman, sire, with an arquebuse than a pistol,' replied Maurevel, now quite reassured.

'Never mind,' said the king; 'I am sure M. de Guise will not care how it is done, as long as it is done.'

'But,' said Maurevel, 'I must have a weapon I can rely on, as I may have to fire from a long distance.'

'I have ten arquebuses in this chamber,' replied Charles IX, 'with which I hit a crown-piece at a hundred and fifty paces—will you try one?'

'Most willingly, sire!' cried Maurevel, advancing towards one that had been brought to the king that day.

'No, not that one,' said the king; 'I reserve that for myself. Some day I will have a grand hunt, and then I hope to use it. Take any other you like.'

Maurevel detached one from a trophy. 'And who is this enemy, sire?' asked he.

'How should I know,' replied Charles, with a contemptuous look.

'I must ask M. de Guise, then?' faltered Maurevel.

The king shrugged his shoulders.

'Do not ask,' said he; 'for M. de Guise will not answer. People do not generally answer such questions. It is for those who do not wish to be hanged to guess.'

'But how shall I recognize him?'

'I tell you he passes the canon's house every morning at ten o'clock.'

'So many pass. Would your Majesty deign to give me some idea?'

'Oh, to-morrow he will carry a red morocco portfolio under his arm.'

'That is sufficient, sire.'

'You still have the horse M. de Mouy gave you, have you not?'

'Sire, I have a horse that is fleeter than any other in France.'

'Oh, I am not the least anxious about you. But it is as well to let you know there is a back-door.'

'Thanks, sire; pray Heaven for me!'

'Oh, pray to the devil rather, for only by his aid can you escape a noose.'

'Adieu, sire.'

'Adieu! By the way, M. de Maurevel, remember, that if I hear of you before ten to-morrow, or do *not* hear of you afterwards, there is an *oubliette** at the Louvre.'

And Charles began to whistle, with more than usual accuracy, his favourite tune.

4

THE EVENING OF THE 24TH OF AUGUST 1572

OUR readers have not forgotten that in the previous chapter Henry was anxiously expecting the arrival of a gentleman named La Mole.

This young gentleman, as the admiral had anticipated, entered Paris by the gate of Saint Marcel* on the evening of the 24th of August, 1572. Bestowing a contemptuous glance on the numerous hostelries which displayed their picturesque signs on either side of him, he rode on into the heart of the city, and after having crossed the Place Maubert, Le Petit-Pont, the Pont-Notre-Dame, and along the quays, he stopped at the end of the Rue de l'Arbre-Sec.

The name pleased him,* no doubt, for he entered the street, and finding on his left a large iron plate swinging, creaking on its hinges, he stopped, and read these words, '*La Belle Etoile*,' written on a scroll beneath the sign, which was a most attractive one for a traveller, as it represented a fowl roasting against a black sky, while a man in a red cloak held out his hands and his purse towards it.

'Here,' said the gentleman to himself, 'is an inn that promises well, and the landlord must be a most ingenious fellow. I have heard that the Rue de l'Arbre-Sec was near the Louvre; and if the inside lives up to the promise of the outside, I shall be admirably lodged.'

Whilst this monologue was going on, another person entered the other end of the street, and also stopped to admire the sign of *La Belle Etoile*.

The first gentleman, whom we already know, at least, by name, rode a white horse, and wore a black doublet decorated with jet; his cloak was made of violet velvet, his boots of black leather, and the hilts of his sword and dagger of steel beautifully worked. He was twenty-four or twenty-five, his complexion dark, his eyes blue; a small moustache shaded a beautifully-shaped mouth, full of pearly teeth, that seemed, whenever he showed them, to light up his whole face with a smile of melancholy sweetness.

Nothing could form a greater contrast with him than the second traveller. Beneath his felt hat appeared a profusion of hair, more red than brown; large grey eyes that on the slightest occasion sparkled so fiercely that they seemed black; a fair complexion, a light moustache, and splendid teeth, completed his description. He was, with his white skin and fine figure, what is generally termed a handsome cavalier, and during the last hour, which he had employed in staring up at all the windows, the ladies had honoured him with no small share of their attention.

He it was who first addressed the other gentleman, who was with himself looking at the sign of *La Belle Etoile*.

'*Mordi!* monsieur,' said he, with the accent that characterizes the natives of Piedmont. 'We are close to the Louvre, are we not? At all events, I think your choice is the same as mine, and I am highly flattered by it.'

'Monsieur,' replied the other, with a southern accent that rivalled that of his companion, 'I believe this inn is near the Louvre, but I have not yet made up my mind to try it.'

'You are undecided; the house is tempting, nevertheless. You must admit the sign is very inviting.'

'Very! and it is for that very reason I mistrust it, for Paris is full of sharpers, and you may be just as well tricked by a sign as by anything else.'

'*Mordi!*' replied the Piedmontese. 'I don't care a fig for their tricks; and if the host does not serve me a chicken as well roasted as the one on his sign, I will put him on the spit and roast him instead. Come, let us go in.'

'You have made up my mind for me,' said the Provençal, laughing. 'After you.'

'Impossible, monsieur—I could not think of it; for I am only your most obedient servant, Count Annibal de Coconnas.'

'And I, monsieur, but Count Joseph Boniface de Lérac de la Mole, equally at your service.'

'Since that is the case, let us take each other's arm, and go in together.'

The result of this proposition was that the two young men got off their horses, threw the bridles to the ostler, linked arms, adjusted their swords, and advanced towards the door of the inn, where stood mine host, who did not seem to notice them, so busy was he talking with a tall man, enveloped in a large sad-coloured cloak like an owl sunk in its feathers.

The two gentlemen were so near the host and his friend in the sad-coloured cloak that Coconnas, impatient at being thus neglected, touched his sleeve.

He appeared suddenly to see them, and dismissed his friend with an: '*Au revoir!* be sure and let me know the hour appointed.'

'Well, my fine fellow,' said Coconnas, 'do not you see we are customers?'

'I beg pardon, gentlemen,' said the landlord, 'I did not see you.'

'Eh, *mordi!* then you ought to have. And now that you do see us, say, "M. le comte," and not "monsieur."'

La Mole stood by, leaving Coconnas, who seemed to have undertaken the affair, to speak. But it was plain, from the expression of his face, that he was fully prepared to act should the need arise.

'Well, what is your pleasure, M. le comte?' muttered the landlord.

'Ah, that's better, is it not?' said Coconnas, turning to La

Mole, who inclined his head affirmatively. 'Monsieur le comte and myself wish to sup and sleep here to-night.'

'Gentlemen,' said the landlord, 'I am very sorry, but I have only one room, and I am afraid it would not suit you.'

'Very well,' said La Mole, 'we will go and lodge somewhere else.'

'I shall stay here,' said Coconnas; 'my horse is tired. I will have the room, since you will not.'

'Ah! that is quite different,' replied the landlord coolly. 'I cannot lodge you at all, then.'

'*Mordi!*' cried Coconnas, 'here's a pretty fellow! Just now you could not lodge us because we were two, and now you have no room for one. You will not lodge us at all, then?'

'Since you take this high tone, gentlemen, I will answer you frankly.'

'Answer, then; only answer quickly.'

'Well, then, I would rather not have the honour of lodging you at all.'

'For what reason?' asked Coconnas, growing white with rage.

'Because you have no servants, and for one master's room full, I should have two servants' rooms empty; so that if I let you have the master's room, I run the risk of not letting the others.'

'M. de la Mole,' said Coconnas, 'do you not think we ought to thrash this fellow?'

'Decidedly,' said La Mole, preparing himself to join with Coconnas and lay his whip over the landlord's back.

But the landlord, despite this demonstration, contented himself with retreating a step or two.

'It is easy to see,' said he mockingly, 'that these gentlemen are from the provinces. In Paris, it is no longer the fashion to kill innkeepers—only great men are killed nowadays; and if you make any disturbance, I will call my neighbours, and, instead of you beating *me*, *you* shall be beaten yourselves.'

'*Mordi!*' cried Coconnas, in a rage, 'he is laughing at us.'

'Gregoire, my arquebuse,' said the landlord, with the same voice with which he would have said, 'Give these gentlemen a chair.'

'*Trippe del papa!*'* cried Coconnas, drawing his sword, 'rouse yourself, M. de la Mole.'

'No, no; for while we rouse ourselves, our supper will get cold.'

'What, you think——' cried Coconnas.

'That Monsieur de la Belle Etoile is right; only he does not know how to treat his guests, especially when they are gentlemen. For instead of saying, "Gentlemen, I do not want you," he should have said, "Enter, gentlemen"—at the same time reserving to himself the right to charge in his bill—Master's room, so much; servants', so much.' With these words, La Mole pushed aside the innkeeper, who was looking for his arquebuse, and entered with Coconnas.

'Well,' said Coconnas, 'I am sorry to sheathe my sword before I have ascertained that it is as sharp as that rascal's pig-sticker.'

'Patience, my friend,' said La Mole. 'All the inns in Paris are full of gentlemen come to attend the King of Navarre's marriage, and we shall have great difficulty in finding another apartment. Besides, perhaps it is the custom to receive strangers at Paris in this manner.'

'*Mordi!* how reasonable you are, M. de la Mole!' muttered Coconnas, curling his red moustache with rage. 'But let the scoundrel take care; for if his meat be not excellent, if his bed be hard, his wine less than three years in the bottle, and his waiter be not as pliant as a reed——'

'Ah, ah!' said the landlord, whetting his knife on a strap, 'you may make yourself easy; you are in a land of plenty.'

Then, in a whisper, he added, 'These are Huguenots. They have grown so insolent since the marriage of their Béarnais with Mademoiselle Marguerite!' Then with a smile that would have made his guests shudder had they seen it,—

'How strange it would be if I were just to have two Huguenots come to my house, when——'

'Now then,' interrupted Coconnas, 'are we going to have any supper?'

'Yes, as soon as you please, monsieur,' returned the landlord, placated, no doubt, by the last thought that had entered his head.

'Well, then, the sooner the better,' said Coconnas; and turning to La Mole,—

'Pray, M. le comte, while our room is being prepared, tell me, do you think Paris seems a gay city?'

'*Ma foi!* no,' said La Mole. 'All the Parisians I saw had most forbidding faces. Perhaps they are afraid of the storm, for the sky looks very black, and the air feels heavy.'

'Are you not looking for the Louvre, count?'

'Yes! and you also, Monsieur de Coconnas.'

'Well, let us look for it together.'

'It is rather late to go out, is it not?' said La Mole.

'Early or late, I must go out: my orders are clear—"Come instantly to Paris, and communicate with the Duke de Guise, without delay."'

At the name of the Duke de Guise, the landlord drew nearer.

'I think the rascal is listening to us,' said Coconnas, who could not forgive the innkeeper his rude welcome.

'I am listening, gentlemen,' replied he, taking off his cap, 'but it is to serve you. I heard the great Duke's name mentioned, and I came immediately. What can I do for you?'

'Ah! this name is magical, since it makes you so polite. Tell me,—what's your name?'

'La Hurière,'* replied the innkeeper, bowing.

'Well, Master la Hurière, do you think my arm is lighter than the Duke de Guise's, who makes you so civil?'

'No, M. le comte, but it is not so long. Besides, I must tell you that the great Henry is the idol of the Parisians.'

'What Henry?' asked La Mole.

'There is only one.'

'Which?'

'Henry de Guise!'

'You are mistaken. There is another, whom I desire you do not speak ill of, and that is Henry of Navarre, besides Henry de Condé, who has his share of merit.'

'I do not know them,' said the landlord.

'But I do. And since I am directed to the King of Navarre, I desire you not to speak slightingly of him to me.'

The landlord merely replied by touching his cap, and continued speaking to Coconnas,—

'Monsieur is going to see the great Duke de Guise. Monsieur is very fortunate. He has come, no doubt, for——'

'What?' asked Coconnas.

'For the fête,' replied the innkeeper, with a singular smile.

'For all the fêtes,' replied Coconnas, 'for Paris is, I hear, a succession of fêtes. Does not everyone find plenty of amusement?'

'Pretty well: but they will have more soon, I hope.'

'The marriage of the King of Navarre has brought a great many people to Paris, has it not?' said La Mole.

'A great many Huguenots—yes,' replied La Hurière, but suddenly changing his tone,—

'Pardon me, gentlemen,' said he, 'perhaps you are of that religion?'

'I?' cried Coconnas. 'I am as good a Catholic as the pope himself.'

La Hurière looked at La Mole, but La Mole did not, or would not understand him.

'If you do not know the King of Navarre,' said La Mole, 'perhaps you know the admiral? I have heard he has some influence at court, and as I have letters for him, perhaps you will so far sully your mouth as to tell me where he lives?'

'He *did* live in the Rue de Béthisy,'* replied the landlord, with a satisfaction he could not conceal.

'He *did* live?' said La Mole. 'He has left, then?'

'Yes—this world, perhaps.'

'What!' cried both the gentlemen together—'the admiral dead?'

'What, M. de Coconnas, are you a friend of the Duke de Guise, and do not know *that*?'

'Know what?'

'That the day before yesterday, the admiral was passing before the house of the canon Pierre Pile, when he was fired at*——'

'And killed?' said La Mole.

'No; he had his arm broken, and two fingers shot off. But it is hoped the bullets were poisoned.'

'What do you mean, wretch!' cried La Mole—'hoped?'

'Believed, I mean,' said the landlord, winking at Coconnas; 'it was a slip of the tongue.'

'Really!' said Coconnas joyfully.

'Really!' said La Mole sorrowfully.

'It is just as I tell you, gentlemen,' said the landlord.

'In that case,' said La Mole, 'I must go at once to the Louvre. Shall I find the King of Navarre there?'

'Most likely, since he lives there.'

'And I,' said Coconnas, 'must also go to the Louvre. Shall I find the Duke de Guise there?'

'Most likely; for he has just ridden by with two hundred gentlemen.'

'Come, then, M. de Coconnas,' said La Mole.

'I am ready,' returned he.

'But your supper, gentlemen!' cried La Hurière.

'Ah!' said La Mole, 'I shall most likely sup with the King of Navarre.'

'And I,' said Coconnas, 'with the Duke de Guise.'

'And I,' said the innkeeper, after having watched the two gentlemen take the road to the Louvre, 'I will go and burnish my steel helmet, put a match to my arquebuse, and sharpen my partisan,* for no one knows what may happen.'

5

OF THE LOUVRE IN PARTICULAR,
AND OF VIRTUE IN GENERAL

THE two young men, directed by the first person they met, went down the Rue d'Averon, the Rue Saint-Germain-l'Auxerrois, and soon found themselves outside the Louvre, whose towers were beginning to be lost in the darkness of the night.

'What is the matter with you?' Coconnas asked La Mole, who stopped before the old château, and gazed, not without awe, on the drawbridges, the narrow windows, and the pointed belfries, which suddenly met his gaze.

'I scarcely know,' said La Mole, 'my heart beats strangely. I am not timid, but this old palace seems so gloomy and terrible.'

'For my part,' replied Coconnas, 'I feel in excellent spirits. My clothes are rather disordered,' continued he, 'but never mind; it will prove I have obeyed my instructions, and come promptly on my arrival.'

The two young men continued on their way, each influenced by the feelings he had expressed.

The Louvre was guarded with more than usual care, and all the sentinels were doubled. Our travellers were somewhat puzzled as to how they should proceed, but Coconnas, who had remarked that the Duke de Guise's name acted like a talisman on the Parisians, approached the sentinel, and making use of the duke's name, demanded entry. The name seemed to produce its ordinary effect upon the soldier, who, however, asked Coconnas if he had the pass-word.

Coconnas was forced to confess he had not.

'Stand back, then,' said the soldier.

At this moment, a person who was talking with the officer of the guard when Coconnas demanded leave to enter, advanced to him.

'What do you want with M. de Guise?' asked he, with a strong German accent.

'I wish to see him,' said Coconnas.

'Impossible—the duke is with the king.'

'But I have a letter for him.'

'Ah! that is different. What is your name?'

'The Count Annibal de Coconnas.'

'Will Monsieur Annibal give me the letter?'

'On my word,' said La Mole to himself, 'I hope I may find another gentleman, equally polite, to conduct me to the King of Navarre.'

'Give me the letter,' said the German gentleman, holding out his hand to Coconnas.

'*Mordi!*' replied the Piedmontese, 'I scarcely know whether I ought, as I have not the honour of knowing you.'

'It is Monsieur de Besme,' said the sentinel, 'you may safely give him your letter, I'll answer for it.'

'M. de Besme!' cried Coconnas 'I am delighted. Here is the letter. Pardon my hesitation, but when one is entrusted with an important commission, one has to be careful.'

'There is no need of any excuse,' said De Besme.

'Perhaps, sir,' said La Mole, 'you will be so kind as to do the same for my letter that you have done for that of my friend?'

'Who are you, monsieur?'

'The Count Lérac de la Mole.'

'I don't know the name.'

'No doubt, for I am only just arrived in Paris, for the first time.'

'Where do you come from?'

'From Provence.'

'With a letter also?'

'Yes.'

'For the Duke de Guise?'

'No; for the King of Navarre.'

'I am not in the service of the King of Navarre,' said De Besme coldly, 'and therefore I cannot take your letter.'

And turning on his heel, he entered the Louvre, bidding Coconnas follow him.

La Mole was left alone.

At this moment a troop of riders, about a hundred in number, rode out of the Louvre.

'Ah, ah!' said the sentinel to his comrade—'here come de Mouy and his Huguenots! See how joyous they all are. The king has promised them, no doubt, to put the would-be assassin of the admiral to death. And as it was he who murdered de Mouy's father, the son will kill two birds with one stone.'

'Did you say,' interrupted La Mole, 'that this officer is M. de Mouy?'

'Yes, monsieur.'

'Thank you,' said La Mole. 'That was all I wished to know'— and advancing towards the man leading the riders,—

'Sir,' said he, 'I am told you are M. de Mouy.'

'Yes, sir,' returned the officer courteously. 'May I inquire whom I have the honour of addressing?'

'The Count Lérac de La Mole.'

The young men bowed to each other.

'What can I do for you, monsieur?' asked de Mouy.

'Monsieur, I am just arrived from Aix, and I have a letter from M. d'Auriac, governor of Provence, for the King of Navarre. How can I give it to him? How can I enter the Louvre?'

'Nothing is easier than to enter the Louvre,' replied de Mouy; 'but I fear the king will be unable to see you at this hour. But if you wish, I will conduct you to his apartments, and then you must manage for yourself.'

'A thousand thanks!'

'Come, then,' said de Mouy.

De Mouy dismounted, advanced towards the wicket, passed the sentinel, led La Mole into the château, and, opening the door leading to the king's apartments,—

'Enter, and inquire for yourself, monsieur,' said he.

And saluting La Mole, he withdrew.

La Mole, left alone, looked round. The anteroom was vacant. He advanced a few paces, and found himself in a passage.

'I will walk straight on,' thought he, 'I'm bound to meet someone.'

Suddenly the door opposite the one through which he had entered opened, and two pages appeared, lighting a lady of noble bearing and exquisite beauty.

The glare of the torches fell full on La Mole, who stood motionless.

The lady stopped also.

'What do you want, sir?' said she, in a voice of exquisite sweetness.

'Oh, madame,' said La Mole, 'pardon me. I have just left M. de Mouy, who was so good as to conduct me here, and I wish to see the King of Navarre.'

'The king is not here, sir; he is with his brother-in-law. But, in his absence, could you not say to the queen——'

'Oh, yes, madame,' returned La Mole, 'if I could obtain audience of her.'

'You have it already, sir.'

'What!' cried La Mole.

'I am the Queen of Navarre.'

La Mole started with surprise.

'Speak, sir,' said Marguerite, 'but speak quickly, for the queen-mother is waiting for me.'

'If the queen-mother waits for you, madame,' said La Mole, give me leave to withdraw, for I am incapable of collecting my ideas, or of thinking of anything but admiration.'

Marguerite advanced graciously towards the handsome young man, who, without knowing it, had behaved like a finished courtier.

'Recover yourself, sir,' said she, 'I will wait.'

'Pardon me, madame,' said La Mole, 'that I did not salute you with the respect due to you, but——'

'You took me for one of my ladies?' said Marguerite, smiling.

'No. For the ghost of the beautiful Diana of Poitiers, who is said to haunt the Louvre.'

'Come, sir,' said Marguerite, 'I see you will make your fortune at court; your letter was not needed, but, still, give it me: I will take care the King of Navarre has it.'

In an instant La Mole threw open his doublet and drew from his breast a letter enveloped in silk. Marguerite took the letter and glanced at the writing.

'Are you not M. de la Mole?' asked she.

'Yes, madame. Can I hope my name is not unknown to you?'

'I have heard my husband and the Duke d'Alençon, my brother, speak of you. I know they expect you.'

And she placed the letter in her corsage which glittered with gold and diamonds.

'Now, sir,' said she, 'descend to the gallery below and wait until someone comes to you from the King of Navarre. One of my pages will show you the way.'

And Marguerite disappeared, like a dream.

'Are you coming, sir?' cried the page who was to conduct La Mole to the lower gallery.

'Oh, yes—yes!' cried La Mole joyfully, for, as the page led him the same way that Marguerite had gone by, he hoped to see her again.

As he descended the staircase, he saw her below. Whether she heard his step, or it was by chance, she looked round, and La Mole saw her features a second time.

The page preceding La Mole descended a storey lower, opened one door, then another, and stopping—'It is here you are to wait,' said he.

La Mole entered the gallery, the door of which closed after him.

The gallery was empty, with the exception of one gentleman who was sauntering up and down and seemed also waiting for someone.

It was so dark that, though not twenty paces apart, it was impossible for either to recognize the other's face.

La Mole drew nearer.

'By Heaven!' muttered he. 'Here is M. de Coconnas again!'

At the sound of footsteps, Coconnas turned, and recognized La Mole.

'*Mordi!*' cried he. 'The devil take me, but here is M. de la Mole! What am I doing? Swearing in the king's palace! Well, never mind; the king does not much care where he swears. Here we are at last, then, in the Louvre!'

'Yes; I suppose M. de Besme introduced you?'

'Oh, he is the most polite German I ever met with. Who brought you in?'

'M. de Mouy. I told you the Huguenots had some influence at court. Have you seen M. de Guise?'

'No—not yet. Have you obtained an audience with the King of Navarre?'

'No; but I soon shall. I was brought here, and told to wait.'

'Ah! you will see, we shall be invited to some grand supper, and placed side by side. How odd! We seem inseparable. By the way, are you hungry?'

'No.'

'And yet you seemed anxious to taste the good cheer of *La Belle Etoile*.'

At this moment the door communicating with the king's apartments opened, and M. de Besme entered.

He scrutinized both gentlemen, and then motioned Coconnas to follow him.

Coconnas waved his hand to La Mole.

De Besme traversed a gallery, opened a door, and stood at the head of a staircase.

He looked cautiously round, and,—

'M. de Coconnas,' said he, 'where are you staying?'

'At the *Belle Etoile*, Rue de l'Arbre-Sec.'

'Ah! that is close by. Return to your hotel, and to-night——'

'And—to-night?'

'Come here, with a white cross in your hat. The pass-word is "*Guise*." Hush! not a word.'

'What time am I to come?'

'When you hear the tocsin.'

'Good—I shall be here,' said Coconnas.

And saluting de Besme, he took himself off to the hostelry of *La Belle Etoile*.

At this instant the door of the King of Navarre's apartments opened, and a page appeared.

'You are the Count de la Mole,' said he.

'That is my name.'

'Where are your lodgings?'

'At the *Belle Etoile*.'

'That is close to the Louvre. His Majesty the King of Navarre has desired me to inform you that he cannot at present receive you: perhaps he may send for you to-night. But, at all events, come to the Louvre to-morrow.'

'But the sentinel will refuse me admission.'

'True: the pass-word is "*Navarre*". That will secure your entrance.'

'Thanks!'

The first thing La Mole saw on entering the inn was Coconnas seated in front of a large omelette.

'Oh, oh!' cried Coconnas, laughing, 'I see you have no more dined with the King of Navarre than I have supped with the Duke de Guise.'

'*Ma foi!* no.'

'Are you hungry now?'

'Yes, very.'

'Well, then, sit down, and have some of my omelette.'

'I see that fate makes us inseparable. Are you staying here?'

'I don't know.'

'No more do I.'

'Well, then, I know where I shall pass the night.'

'Where?'

'Wherever you do. There's no avoiding it.'

Thus saying, the two gentlemen fell to work on the omelette of Maître la Hurière.

6

THE DEBT PAID

Now, if the reader is curious to know why M. de la Mole had not been received by the King of Navarre, why M. de Coconnas had not seen M. de Guise, and why both, instead of supping at the Louvre, on pheasants, partridges, and kid, supped at the hotel of the *Belle Etoile* on an omelette, he must kindly accompany us to the old palace of kings, and follow the queen, Marguerite of Navarre, of whom La Mole had lost sight at the entrance of the grand gallery.

While Marguerite was descending this staircase, the duke, Henry de Guise, whom she had not seen since the night of her marriage, was in the king's study. To this staircase, which Marguerite was descending, there was a way out. To the study in which M. de Guise was, there was a door, and this door and this way out both led to a corridor. And this corridor led to the apartments of the queen-mother, Catherine de Medicis.

Catherine de Medicis was alone, seated near a table, with her elbow on a half open Prayer-book, and her head leaning on a hand still remarkably beautiful—thanks to the cosmetics with which she was supplied by the Florentine, René, who combined the double duty of perfumer and poisoner to the queen-mother.

The widow of Henry II was dressed in mourning which she had not thrown off since her husband's death. At this period she was about fifty-two or fifty-three years of age, and preserved a figure full of freshness and still of considerable beauty. Her apartment, like her clothes, was all mourning. By her side was a small Italian greyhound, called Phœbe, a present from her son-in-law, Henry of Navarre.

Suddenly, when the queen-mother appeared plunged in some thought which brought a smile to her lips, which were reddened with carmine, a man opened the door, raised the tapestry, and showed his pale face, saying,—

'It is all going badly.'

Catherine raised her head, and recognized the Duke de Guise.

'What do you mean, badly?' she replied. 'What do you mean, Henry?'

'I mean that the king is more than ever taken with the accursed Huguenots. If we await his leave to execute our great enterprise, we shall wait a very long time, and perhaps for ever.'

'What has happened?' inquired Catherine, still preserving the tranquillity of countenance that was habitual to her, and yet to which, when required, she could give so different an expression.

'Why, just now, for the twentieth time, I opened the conversation with his Majesty as to whether he intends to go on permitting these shows of bravado which the gentlemen of the reformed religion indulge in, since the wounding of their admiral.'

'And what did my son reply?' asked Catherine.

'He replied, "*Monsieur le duc*, you must necessarily be suspected by the people as the author of the attempted assassination of my second father, the admiral; defend yourself against the imputation as best you may. As to me, I will defend myself if I am insulted"; and then he turned away, to feed his dogs.'

'And you made no attempt to detain him!'

'Yes; but he replied to me in that tone which you know so well, and looking at me with the gaze peculiar to him, "*M. le duc*, my dogs are hungry. And they are not men, whom I can keep waiting." Whereupon I came straight to you.'

'And you have done right,' said the queen-mother.

'But what is now to be done?'

'Make one last try.'

'And who will try it?'

'I will! Is the king alone?'

'No; M. de Tavannes is with him.'

'Wait here. Or rather follow me at a distance.'

Catherine rose and went to the chamber, where, on Turkey carpets and velvet cushions, lay the favourite greyhounds of the king. On perches ranged along the wall were two or three favourite falcons and a small pied hawk, with which Charles IX amused himself in bringing down the small birds in the garden of the old Louvre, and that of the Tuileries, which they had just commenced building.*

On her way the queen-mother arranged her face so that it

wore a pale, anguished expression, down which rolled a last—or rather a first—tear.

She approached Charles IX noiselessly, as he was feeding his dogs cakes cut into equal portions.

'My son,' said the queen, with such a tremulous voice, so adroitly managed, that the king started.

'What do you want, madame?' said Charles, turning round suddenly.

'I want, my son,' replied Catherine, 'your permission to retire to one of your châteaux, no matter which, provided it is as far as possible from Paris.'

'But why, madame?' inquired Charles IX, fixing on his mother that glassy eye, which, on certain occasions, could be so keen.

'Because every day I receive new insults from persons of the new faith; because to-day I hear that you have been freshly threatened by the Protestants, even in your own Louvre, and I have no wish to be present at such spectacles.'

'But madame,' replied Charles IX, with an expression full of conviction, 'an attempt has been made on the life of their admiral. An infamous murderer has already assassinated the brave M. de Mouy. *Mort de ma vie!* mother, there must be justice in a kingdom!'

'Oh, be easy on that head, my son,' said Catherine. 'Justice will not be wanting to them. For if you should refuse it, they will still have it in their own way: on M. de Guise to-day, on me to-morrow, and yourself hereafter.'

'Oh, madame!' said Charles, allowing a first accent of doubt to break through, 'do you think so?'

'Oh, my son,' replied Catherine, giving way entirely to the violence of her thoughts, 'do you not see that it is no longer a question of the death of François de Guise or the admiral, of Protestant religion or Catholic, but simply of the substitution of the son of Antoine de Bourbon for the son of Henry II?'*

'Come, come, mother, you are falling again into your usual exaggeration,' said the king.

'What is, then, your opinion, my son?'

'To wait, mother—to wait. All human wisdom is in this single word. The greatest, the strongest, the most skilful, is he who knows how to wait.'

'You wait, then: I will not.'

And on this Catherine made a curtsey and, advancing towards the door, was about to return to her apartment.

Charles IX stopped her.

'Well, then, what is best to be done, mother?' he asked, 'for I am just or I am nothing, and I want everyone to be satisfied with me.'

Catherine turned towards him.

'Come, count,' she said to Tavannes, who was stroking the pied hawk, 'and tell the king your opinion as to what should be done.'*

'Will your Majesty permit me?' inquired the count.

'Speak, Tavannes, speak!'

'What does your Majesty do when you are hunting and the wounded boar turns on you?'

'*Mordieu*, sir, I wait for him, with firm foot and hand,' replied Charles, 'and stab him in the throat with my good sword.'

'Just so he may not hurt you,' remarked Catherine.

'And to amuse myself,' said the king, with a smile which indicated courage pushed to ferocity. 'But I will not amuse myself with killing my subjects, for, after all, the Huguenots are my subjects as well as the Catholics.'

'Then, sire,' said Catherine, 'your subjects, the Huguenots, will do like the wild boar who escapes the sword-thrust at his throat: they will bring down the throne.'

'Bah! Do you really think so, madame?' said Charles IX, in a tone which denoted that he did not place great faith in his mother's predictions.

'But have you not seen M. de Mouy and his party to-day?'

'Yes, I have seen them, and indeed just left them. But what does he ask for that is not just? He has requested the death of the murderer of his father and the would-be assassin of the admiral. Did we not punish M. de Montgommery for the death of my father and your husband, although his death was a simple accident?'

'Very well, sire,' said Catherine, piqued, 'let us say no more. Your Majesty is under the protection of God who gives strength, wisdom, and confidence. But I, a poor woman, whom God abandons, no doubt, on account of my sins, fear, and give way.'

And Catherine again curtseyed and left the room, making a

sign to the Duke de Guise, who entered as she was going to remain in her place, and try one more time.

Charles IX watched his mother as she left, but this time did not recall her. He then began to stroke his dogs, whistling a hunting air.

He suddenly paused.

'My mother,' said he, 'is a right royal spirit, and has doubts about nothing. Really, now, is it really a sound proposal to kill off some dozens of Huguenots, because they come to demand justice, as if it were not their right?'

'Dozens!' murmured the Duke de Guise.

'Ah! are you here?' said the king, appearing to see him for the first time. 'Yes, dozens. A tolerable waste of life! Ah! if any one came to me and said, "Sire, you shall be rid of all your enemies at once, and to-morrow there shall not remain one to reproach you with the death of the others," why, then, I do not say——'

'Well, sire?'

'Tavannes,' said the king, 'you will tire Margot;* put her back on her perch. It is no reason, because she bears the name of my sister, the Queen of Navarre, that she should be stroked by all and sundry.'

Tavannes put the hawk on her perch, and amused himself by playing with the ears of a greyhound.

'But, sire, if any one should say to your Majesty, "Sire, your Majesty shall be delivered from all your enemies to-morrow"?'

'And by the intercession of what saint would this great miracle be effected?'

'Sire, we are to-day at the 24th of August, and it will therefore be by the intervention of Saint Bartholomew.'

'A worthy saint,' replied the king, 'who allowed himself to be skinned alive!'*

'So much the better; the more he suffered, the more he should have wanted vengeance on his executioners.'

'And is it you, my cousin,' said the king—'is it you, with your pretty little gold-hilted sword, who will to-morrow slay ten thousand Huguenots? Ah, ah! *mort de ma vie!* you are very amusing, M. de Guise!' And the king burst into loud laughter, but a laughter so forced that the room echoed with its sinister sound.

'Sire, one word—and one only,' continued the duke, shuddering in spite of himself at the sound of this laugh which had nothing human in it—'one sign, and all is ready. I have the Swiss* and eleven hundred gentlemen, I have the light horse and the citizens on my side. Your Majesty has your guards, your friends, the Catholic nobility. We are twenty to one.'

'Well, then, cousin of mine, since you are so strong, why the devil do you come to fill my ears with all this! Act without me—act——'

And the king turned again to his dogs.

Then the tapestry suddenly moved aside, and Catherine reappeared.

'All goes well,' she whispered to the duke. 'Urge him, and he will yield.'

And the tapestry fell on Catherine, without the king seeing, or at least appearing to see her.

'But,' continued de Guise, 'I need to know, if, in acting as I desire, I shall be acting according to your Majesty's views.'

'Really, cousin Henry, you put your knife to my throat! But I shall resist. *Mordieu!* am I not the king?'

'No, not yet, sire. But if you wish, you shall be so to-morrow.'

'Ah!' continued Charles, 'you would kill the King of Navarre and the Prince de Condé, in my Louvre—ah!' Then he added, in a voice scarcely audible, 'Outside the walls, I do not say——'

'Sire,' cried the duke, 'they are going out this evening to join in a revel with your brother, the Duke d'Alençon.'

'Tavannes,' said the king, with well-affected impatience, 'do not you see that you are upsetting Actæon?* Here, boy—here!'

And Charles IX strode out of the apartment, without waiting to hear any more, leaving Tavannes and the Duke de Guise almost as uncertain as before.

Another scene was passing in Catherine's apartments, who, after giving the Duke de Guise her counsel to remain firm, had returned to her rooms, where she found assembled the persons who usually assisted at her going to bed.

Her face was now as full of joy as it had been downcast when she set out. One by one she dismissed her women until there only remained Madame Marguerite, who, seated on a chest near the open window, was looking at the sky, lost in thought.

Two or three times, now that she was alone with her daughter, the queen-mother opened her mouth to speak, but each time a gloomy thought held back the words ready to escape her lips.

Suddenly the tapestry moved, and Henry of Navarre entered.

The little greyhound, which was asleep on a sofa, leaped towards him at a bound.

'You here, my son!' said Catherine, starting. 'Are you to sup in the Louvre to-night?'

'No, madame,' replied Henry; 'we are going into the city with Messieurs d'Alençon and Condé. I almost expected to find them here.'

Catherine smiled.

'Ah! you men are so happy to have such liberty! Are they not, dear daughter?'

'Yes,' replied Marguerite, 'liberty is so glorious, so sweet a thing.'

'Are you suggesting that I limit your freedom, madame?' inquired Henry, bowing to his wife.

'No, sir, it is not for myself that I complain, but for women in general.'*

'Who goes there?' asked Catherine suddenly, and at the same moment the tapestry was raised, and Madame de Sauve showed her lovely head.

'Madame,' she said, 'it is René, the perfumer, whom your Majesty sent for.'

Catherine cast a glance as quick as lightning at Henry of Navarre. The young prince turned red, and then fearfully pale: the name of his mother's assassin had been mentioned in his presence. He felt that his face betrayed his emotion, and he leaned against the bar of the window.

The little greyhound growled.

At the same moment two persons entered; the one announced, and the other having no need to be so.

The first was René, the perfumer, who approached Catherine with all the servile obsequiousness of Florentine servants. He held in his hand a box, which he opened, and all the compartments were seen filled with powders and phials.

The second was Madame de Lorraine, the eldest sister of Marguerite. She entered by a small private door which led from the king's closet, and, all pale and trembling, hoping not to be observed by Catherine, who was examining with Madame de Sauve the contents of the box brought by René, seated herself beside Marguerite, near whom the King of Navarre was standing, with his hand on his brow, like one who tries to rouse himself from some sudden shock.

At this instant Catherine turned round.

'Daughter,' she said to Marguerite, 'you may retire to your rooms. My son, you may go and amuse yourself in the city.'

Marguerite rose, and Henry turned half round.

Madame de Lorraine seized Marguerite's hand.

'Sister,' she whispered, with great urgency, 'in the name of the Duke de Guise, who now saves you as you saved him, do not leave here—do not go to your apartments.'*

'Eh! what did you say, Claude?' inquired Catherine, turning round.

'Nothing, mother.'

'What did you whisper to Marguerite?'

'Only a message from the Duchess de Nevers.'

'And where is the lovely duchess?'

'With her brother-in-law, M. de Guise.'

Catherine looked suspiciously at her two daughters, and frowned.

'Come here, Claude,' said the queen-mother.

Claude obeyed, and the queen seized her hand.

'What have you said to her, indiscreet girl that you are?' she murmured, squeezing her daughter's wrist until she nearly shrieked with pain.

'Madame,' said Henry to his wife, he having missed none of the movements of the queen, Claude, or Marguerite—'Madame, will you allow me the honour of kissing your hand?'

Marguerite held out her trembling hand.

'What did she say to you?' murmured Henry, as he stooped to imprint a kiss on her hand.

'Not to go out. In the name of Heaven, therefore, you must not go out either!'

It was only a glimmer, but by its light, rapid as it was, Henry at once saw through the whole plot.

'That is not all,' added Marguerite. 'Here is a letter, which a country gentleman brought.'

'M. de la Mole?'

'Yes.'

'Thanks,' he said, taking the letter, and putting it in his doublet. Then passing in front of his bewildered wife, he placed his hand on the shoulder of the Florentine.

'Well, Master René!' he said, 'and how is business?'

'Pretty well, monseigneur—pretty well,' replied the Poisoner, with his perfidious smile.

'I should think so,' said Henry, 'with men who, like you, supply all the crowned heads at home and abroad.'

'Except the King of Navarre,' replied the Florentine impudently.

'*Ventre-saint-gris*, Master René,' replied the king, 'you are right. And yet my late mother, who also bought from you, recommended you to me with her dying breath. Come to me to-morrow, or the day after to-morrow, and bring your best perfumes.'

At this moment, the Duchess of Lorraine, who could no longer contain herself, burst into loud sobs.

Henry did not even turn towards her.

'Sister, dear, what is the matter?' cried Marguerite, going towards her.

'Nothing,' said Catherine, passing between the two young women—'nothing; she has these nervous attacks, for which Mazille has prescribed aromatic preparations'. Then again, and with more force than before, she pressed her eldest daughter's arm before turning towards the youngest,—

'Why, Margot,' she said, 'did you not hear me ask you to retire to your room? If that is not sufficient, I command you.'

'Forgive me, madame,' replied Marguerite, trembling and pale. 'I wish your Majesty good-night.'

'I hope your wishes may be heard. Good-night—good-night!'

Marguerite withdrew, staggering with fright, and in vain seeking a glance from her husband, who did not even turn towards her.

There was a moment's silence, during which Catherine remained with her eyes fastened on the Duchess of Lorraine, who said nothing, but looked at her mother, with clasped hands.

Henry's back was still turned, but he was watching the scene in a mirror, while seeming to curl his moustache with a pomade which René had given to him.

'And you, Henry, do you mean to go?' asked Catherine.

'Yes, you are right,' exclaimed the king. '*Ma foi!* I forgot that the Duke d'Alençon and the Prince de Condé were waiting for me! These are admirable perfumes; they quite overpower one, and destroy one's memory. Good-evening, madame.'

'Good-evening! To-morrow you will perhaps bring me tidings of the admiral.'

'Without fail.—Well, Phœbe, what is it?'

'Phœbe!' said the queen-mother impatiently.

'Call her, madame,' said the Béarnais, 'for she will not allow me to leave.'

The queen-mother rose, took the little greyhound by the collar, and held her while Henry left the apartment, with his features as calm and smiling as if he did not feel in his heart that his life was in imminent peril.

Behind him the little dog, set free by Catherine de Medicis, rushed to try and catch him, but the door was closed, and Phœbe could only put her long nose under the tapestry and give a long and mournful howl.

'Now, Charlotte,' said Catherine to Madame de Sauve, 'go and find M. de Guise and Tavannes who are in my oratory, return with them, and stay with the Duchess of Lorraine, who has the vapours.'

7

THE NIGHT OF THE 24TH OF AUGUST 1572

WHEN La Mole and Coconnas had finished their meagre supper, Coconnas stretched his legs, leaned one elbow on the table, and, drinking a last glass of wine, said,—

'Do you mean to go to bed straight away, Monsieur de la Mole?'

'*Ma foi!* I am very much inclined to, for I may be called up in the night.'

'And I, too,' said Coconnas, 'but it appears to me that, in the circumstances, instead of going to bed and making those wait who are to come to us, we should do better to call for cards and play a game. That way they will find us quite ready.'

'I would willingly accept your proposal, sir, but I have very little money to play with. I have scarce a hundred gold crowns in my valise, and that is all the money I have.'

'A hundred gold crowns!' cried Coconnas, 'and you complain? *Mordi!* I have but six!'

'Why,' replied La Mole, 'I saw you take from your pocket a purse which appeared not only full, but I should say, brimful.'

'Ah!' said Coconnas, 'that is to defray an old debt which I am compelled to pay to an old friend of my father, whom I suspect to be like yourself, something of a Huguenot. Yes, there are here a hundred rose nobles,'* he added, patting his pocket, 'but these hundred rose nobles belong to a man named Mercandon.* My personal fortune, as I said, is limited to six crowns.'

'How, then, can you play?'

'Why, it is on that account that I wish to play. Besides, an idea occurs to me.'

'What is it?'

'We both came to Paris on the same errand.'

'Yes.'

'We have each sought a powerful protector.'

'Yes.'

'You rely on yours, as I rely on mine.'

'Yes.'

'Well, then, it occurred to me that we should play at first for our money, and afterwards for the first favour which comes to us, either from the court or from our mistress.'

'Really, a very ingenious idea,' said La Mole, with a smile, 'but I confess I am not such a gambler as to risk my whole life on a card or a turn of the dice; for the first favour which may come either to you or to me will, in all probability, involve our whole life. But, if you wish, let us play until your six crowns be lost or doubled, and if lost, and you desire to continue the game, you are a gentleman, and your word is as good as gold.'

'Done,' replied Coconnas; 'a gentleman's word is gold, especially when he has credit at court. So you see, I did not risk much when I suggested we play for the first favour we might receive at court.'

'Quite. For if you lost, I could not win since, being with the King of Navarre, I could not receive anything from the Duke de Guise.'

'Ah, the heretic!' murmured the innkeeper, while rubbing up his old helmet—'I smelt you out, so I did!' and he crossed himself devoutly.

'Well, then,' continued Coconnas, shuffling the cards which the waiter brought him, 'you are of the——'

'What?'

'New religion.'

'I?'

'Yes, you.'

'Well, say that I am,' said La Mole, with a smile, 'have you anything against us?'

'No, thank God! I hate Huguenotry with all my heart, but I do not hate the Huguenots, for they are in fashion just now.'

'Yes,' replied La Mole, smiling, 'to wit, the shooting of the admiral; but let us play.'

'Yes, let us play, and fear not, for if I lose a hundred crowns of gold against yours, I shall have wherewithal to pay you tomorrow morning.'

'Then your fortune will come while you sleep.'

'No. I shall go and look for it.'

'Where? I'll go with you.'

'At the Louvre.'

'Are you going back there to-night?'

'Yes. I have, to-night, a private audience with the great Duke de Guise.'

Since Coconnas had mentioned the Louvre, La Hurière had left off cleaning his headpiece, and placed himself behind La Mole's chair, so that Coconnas alone could see him, and made signs to him, which the Piedmontese, absorbed in his game and conversation, did not notice.

'Well, it is all very strange,' remarked La Mole. 'You were right to say that we were born under the same star. I have also an appointment at the Louvre to-night, but not with the Duke de Guise. Mine is with the King of Navarre.'

'Have you a pass-word?'

'Yes.'

'A watchword?'

'No.'

'Well, I have one, and my pass-word is——'

At these words of the Piedmontese, La Hurière made so significant a gesture that Coconnas, glancing up, was even more astonished by it than by the game, at which he had lost three crowns.

'What's the matter?' asked La Mole, but seeing nothing, he shuffled the cards again while La Hurière retired, placing his finger on his lips to recommend discretion, and leaving Coconnas so amazed that he again lost almost as rapidly the second time as the first.

'Well,' observed La Mole, 'there go your six crowns. Will you have your revenge on your future fortune?'

'Willingly,' replied Coconnas.

'But before you begin, did you not say you had an appointment with the Duke de Guise?'

Coconnas turned his looks towards the kitchen, and saw the great eyes of La Hurière.

'Yes,' he replied, 'but it is not yet time. But now let us talk a little about yourself, M. de la Mole.'

'We shall do better, I think, by talking of the game, my dear M. de Coconnas, for unless I am very much mistaken, you are in a fair way of losing six more crowns.'

'*Mordi!* you are right! I always heard that the Huguenots had good luck at cards. Devil take me if I haven't a good mind to turn Huguenot!'

'Do, count, do,' said La Mole; 'and you shall be well received amongst us.'

Coconnas scratched his ear.

'If I were sure that your good luck came from that direction,' he said, 'I would, for I really do not hold so entirely with mass, and since the king does not think so much of it either——'

'It is such a simple religion,' said La Mole; 'so pure——'

'And, moreover, it is in fashion,' said Coconnas, 'and it brings good luck at cards, for, devil take me if you do not hold all the aces. Yet I have watched you closely, and you play very fairly; it must be the religion——'

'You owe me another six crowns,' said La Mole quietly.

'Ah, you tempt me!' said Coconnas.

'Hush!' said La Mole, 'you will get into a quarrel with our landlord.'

'Ah, that is true!' said Coconnas, turning his eyes towards the kitchen; 'but—no, he is not listening, he is too busy.'

'What is he doing?' inquired La Mole, who could see nothing from where he was sitting.

'He is talking with—devil take me! it is him!'

'Who?'

'Why, that night-bird with whom he was talking when we arrived. The man in the yellow doublet and sad-coloured cloak. *Mordi!* How earnestly he talks.'

At this moment, La Hurière hurried over to Coconnas, and whispered in his ear, 'Silence, for your life! and get rid of your companion.'

Coconnas, turning to La Mole, said, 'My dear sir, I must beg you to excuse me. I have lost fifty crowns in no time. My luck is out to-night.'

'Well, sir, as you please,' replied La Mole. 'Besides, I shall not be sorry to lie down for a while. Master La Hurière!'

'Sir.'

'If any one comes for me from the King of Navarre, wake me immediately. I shall be dressed, and, consequently ready.'

'So shall I,' said Coconnas, 'and so that I do not keep his Highness waiting, I will prepare the sign. Master La Hurière, some white paper and scissors!'

'Good-night, M. de Coconnas,' said La Mole; 'and you, land-lord, be so good as to light me to my room. Good luck, my friend!' and La Mole disappeared up the staircase, followed by La Hurière.

Then the mysterious personage, taking Coconnas by the arm, said to him with great urgency:

'Sir, you very nearly betrayed a secret on which depends the fate of a kingdom. One word more, and I would have brought you down with my arquebuse. Now we are alone.'

'But who are you?'

'Did you ever hear talk of Maurevel!'

'The assassin of the admiral?'

'And of Captain de Mouy.'

'Yes.'

'Well, I am Maurevel.'

'Ah!' said Coconnas.

'Hush!' said Maurevel, putting his finger on his mouth. Coconnas listened.

At this moment, he heard the landlord close the door of a room, then the door of a corridor, and bolt it. Then he returned hurriedly to Coconnas and Maurevel, offering each a seat, and taking a third for himself.

'All is shut and barred now,' he said. 'You may speak freely, M. Maurevel.'

Eleven o'clock struck by Saint Germain-l'Auxerrois. Maurevel counted each stroke of the clock, which sounded full and dull in the night, and, when the last sound had died away,—

'Sir,' he said, turning to Coconnas, who was amazed at all the precautions taken, 'are you a good Catholic?'

'I believe so,' replied Coconnas.

'Sir, are you devoted to the king?'

'Body and soul! You offend me, sir, by asking such a question.'

'Will you follow us?'

'Where?'

'That is of no consequence—let me guide you; your fortune, and perhaps your life, will hang on the result.'

'I tell you, sir, that at midnight, I have an appointment at the Louvre.'

'That is where we are going.'

'M. de Guise awaits me there.'

'And us also!'

'But I have a private pass-word.'

'And so have we!'

'I have a sign of recognition.'

Maurevel drew from beneath his doublet a handful of crosses

made of white material, gave one to La Hurière, one to Coconnas, and took another for himself. La Hurière fastened his to his helmet, Maurevel attached his to the side of his hat.

'Ah,' said Coconnas, amazed, 'so the appointment, the password, and the rallying mark were for everybody?'

'Yes,—that is to say, for all good Catholics.'

'Then there is a fête at the Louvre—some royal banquet, is there not?' said Coconnas, 'and they wish to exclude those hounds of Huguenots—good—capital—excellent! They have had the best of it for too long.'

'Yes, there is a fête at the Louvre—a royal banquet, and the Huguenots are invited—moreover, they will be the heroes of the fête, for they will foot the bill. If you will be one of us, we will begin by going to invite their principal champion—their Gideon,* as they call him.'

'The admiral!' cried Coconnas.

'Yes, old Gaspard, whom like a fool I missed, although I aimed at him with the king's arquebuse.'

'And this, my gentlemen, is why I was furbishing my helmet, sharpening my sword, and putting an edge on my knives,' said La Hurière, with a loud, bear-like voice.

At these words, Coconnas shuddered and turned very pale, for he began to understand.

'Then,' he exclaimed, 'this fête—this banquet is a——'

'You are a long time guessing, sir,' said Maurevel, 'and it is easy to see that you are not so weary of these insolent heretics as we are.'

'And you take on yourself,' he said, 'to go to the admiral and——'

Maurevel smiled, and, drawing Coconnas to the window, he said,—

'Look there! Do you see, in the small square at the end of the street, behind the church, a troop drawn up quietly in the shadow?'

'Yes.'

'The men who form that troop have, like Master la Hurière, and myself, and yourself, a cross in their hats.'

'Well!'

'Well; these men are a company of Swiss from the smaller cantons, commanded by Tocquenot*—you know they are friends of the king.'

'Ah, ah!' said Coconnas.

'Now, look at that troop of horse passing along the Quay—do you recognize their leader?'

'How can I recognize him,' asked Coconnas, with a shudder, 'when it was only this evening that I arrived in Paris?'

'Well, then, it is with him you have a rendezvous at the Louvre at midnight. See, he is going there to wait for you!'

'The Duke de Guise?'

'Himself! His escorts are, Marcel, the former provost of merchants, and Jean Charron, the present provost.* These two are going to summon their companies, and here comes the district captain. See what he will do!'

'He knocks at each door. But what is there on the doors he knocks on?'

'A white cross, young man, like those we have in our hats.'

'But at each house at which he knocks they open, and from each house there come out armed citizens.'

'He will knock here in turn, and we shall in turn go out.'

'But,' said Coconnas, 'if everyone is on foot to go and kill one old Huguenot—*Mordi!* it is shameful! It is work for cut-throats, and not for soldiers.'

'Young man,' replied Maurevel, 'if the old are objectionable to you, you may choose young ones—you will find plenty for all tastes. If you despise daggers, use your sword, for the Huguenots are not men to allow their throats to be cut without defending themselves, and you know that Huguenots, young or old, are hard-lived.'

'But are they going to kill them all, then?' cried Coconnas.

'All of them!'

'By order of the king?'

'By order of the king and M. de Guise.'

'When?'

'When you hear the clock of Saint Germain-l'Auxerrois strike.'

'So that was why that polite German told me to jump to it at the first sound of the tocsin.'

'You have seen M. de Besme?'

'I have seen and spoken to him.'

'Where?'

'At the Louvre.'

'Look there!'

'*Mordi!*—it is him.'

'Would you like to speak with him?'

'Why, yes, I should like that.'

Maurevel opened the window at once; Besme was passing at that moment with twenty soldiers.

'Guise and Lorraine,' said Maurevel.

Besme turned round, and seeing that it was himself who was hailed, he came to a halt under the window.

'Oh, is it you, Sire de Maurevel?'

'Yes. What are you looking for?'

'The inn of the *Belle Etoile*, to find a Monsieur Coconnas.'

'I am here, M. de Besme,' said the young man.

'Good, good; are you ready?'

'Yes—to do what?'

'Whatever M. de Maurevel may tell you, for he is a good Catholic.'

'Do you hear?' inquired Maurevel.

'Yes,' replied Coconnas, 'but M. de Besme!—where are you going?'

'I am going to say a word to the admiral.'

'Say two, if necessary,' said Maurevel, 'and this time, if he gets up again at the first, do not let him rise at the second.'

'Make yourself easy, M. de Maurevel, and set the young gentleman on the right path.'

'Ah, do not fear for me. The Coconnas have keen noses, and well-bred dogs hunt from instinct.'

'Adieu! start the hunt, for we are on the trail of the deer.'

De Besme strode on, and Maurevel closed the window.

'You hear, young man?' said Maurevel. 'If you have any private enemy, although he may not be a Huguenot, you can put him on your list and he will be seen to with the others.'

Coconnas, more bewildered than ever with what he saw and heard, looked about him, at the innkeeper and Maurevel, who quietly drew a paper from his pocket. 'Here's my list,' said he;

'three hundred. Let each good Catholic do one-tenth part of the business I shall do to-night, and to-morrow there will not be a single heretic left in the kingdom.'

'Hush!' said La Hurière.

'What is it?' inquired Coconnas and Maurevel together.

They heard the first stroke of the bell of Saint-Germain-l'Auxerrois.

'The signal!' exclaimed Maurevel. 'It is time—for it was agreed for midnight. So much the better. When it is the interest of God and the king, it is better that the clock should be fast than slow.' And the sinister sound of the church bell was distinctly heard. Then a shot was fired, and in an instant, the light of several flambeaux blazed like flashes of lightning in the Rue de l'Arbre-Sec.

Coconnas passed his hand over his brow which was damp with perspiration.

'It has begun!' cried Maurevel. 'Now to work—away!'

'One moment!' said the innkeeper. 'Before we begin let us make the house secure. I do not wish to have my wife and children killed in my absence. There is a Huguenot here.'

'M. de la Mole!' said Coconnas, starting.

'Yes, the fowl has thrown himself into the wolf's throat.'

'What!' said Coconnas—'you do not propose to attack your guest?'

'It was for him I gave an extra edge to my rapier.'

'Oh, oh!' said the Piedmontese, frowning.

'I never yet killed anything but rabbits, ducks, and chickens,' replied the worthy innkeeper, 'and I do not know very well how to kill a man; but I can practise on him, and, if I am clumsy, no one will be there to laugh at me.'

'*Mordi!* it is hard,' said Coconnas. 'M. de la Mole is my companion; M. de la Mole has supped with me; M. de la Mole has played cards with me.'

'Yes; but M. de la Mole is a heretic,' said Maurevel. 'M. de la Mole is doomed; and if we do not kill him, others will.'

'Not to say,' added the innkeeper, 'that he has won fifty crowns from you.'

'True,' said Coconnas; 'but fairly, I am sure.'

'Fairly, or not, you will have to pay up. But, if I kill him, you are quits.'

'Come, come!' cried Maurevel, 'make haste, or we shall not be in time with the help we have promised M. de Guise at the admiral's.'

Coconnas sighed.

'I'll make haste!' cried La Hurière; 'wait for me.'

'*Mordi!*' cried Coconnas, 'he will put the poor gentleman to great trouble and, perhaps, rob him. I must be there to finish him, if necessary, and to prevent him from stealing his money.'

And impelled by this happy thought, Coconnas followed La Hurière upstairs, and soon overtook him, for the latter slackened his pace as he approached the intended victim.

When he reached the door, Coconnas still following, several discharges of musquetry in the streets were heard.

'*Diable!*' muttered La Hurière, somewhat disconcerted, 'that has woken him up, I'll wager.'

'I should say so,' observed Coconnas, 'and he will defend himself. I do not know a likelier man. Suppose now, La Hurière, he were to kill you, that would be amusing, eh?'

'Hum, hum' responded the innkeeper, but knowing himself to be armed with a good arquebuse, he dashed the door in with a kick of his foot.

La Mole, without his hat, but dressed, was positioned behind his bed, his sword between his teeth and his pistols in his hands.

'Ah!' said Coconnas, his nostrils expanding like a wild beast who smells blood—'this grows interesting, La Hurière. Forward!'

'Ah, someone intends to murder me, it seems!' cried La Mole, whose eyes glared, 'and it is you, wretch!'

La Hurière's reply to this was to take aim at the young man with his arquebuse. But La Mole was on his guard, and, as he fired, dropped to his knees, and the bullet passed over his head.

'Help!' cried La Mole—'help, M. de Coconnas!'

'Help, M. de Maurevel!—help!' cried La Hurière.

'*Ma foi!* M. de la Mole,' replied Coconnas, 'all I can do in this affair is not to join the attack against you. It seems that all the Huguenots are to be put to death to-night, in the king's name. Get out of it as well as you can.'

'Ah, traitors! assassins!—is it so? Well, then, take this!' And La Mole, aiming in his turn, fired one of his pistols. La Hurière, who had kept his eye on him, moved suddenly to one side. But Coconnas, not anticipating such a reply, had not stirred, and the bullet grazed his shoulder.

'*Mordi!*' he exclaimed, grinding his teeth. 'So that's the way of it. Well, then, let it be us two, since you will have it so!'—and, drawing his rapier, he rushed at La Mole.

Had he been alone, La Mole would certainly have waited for his attack. But Coconnas had La Hurière to aid him, who was reloading his gun, and Maurevel, who was coming rapidly up the stairs. La Mole, therefore, dashed into a small closet, which he bolted behind him.

'Ah, coward!' cried Coconnas, furious, and striking at the door with the pommel of his sword—'wait, wait! and I will make as many holes in your body as you have won crowns off me to-night. Wait there, villain—just you wait!'

La Hurière fired his arquebuse at the lock, and the door flew open.

Coconnas rushed into the closet, but it was empty and the window open.

'He has thrown himself out,' said the innkeeper, 'and as we are on the fourth floor, he must be dead.'

'Or he has escaped by the roof of the next house,' said Coconnas, putting his leg over the sill of the window and preparing to follow him over this narrow and slippery route. But Maurevel and La Hurière pulled him back into the apartment.

'Are you mad?' they both exclaimed at once—'you will kill yourself!'

'Bah!' said Coconnas, 'I am a mountaineer, and used to traverse glaciers. Besides, when a man has once offended me, I will go up to Heaven or descend to Hell with him, by whatever route he pleases. Let me do as I wish.'

'Well,' said Maurevel, 'he is either dead or a long way off by this time. Come with us. If he gets away you'll find a thousand others in his place.'

'You are right,' cried Coconnas. 'Death to the Huguenots! I want revenge, and the sooner the better.'

And the three descended the staircase, like an avalanche.

'To the admiral's!' shouted Maurevel.

'To the admiral's!' shouted La Hurière.

'To the admiral's, then, if it must be so!' shouted Coconnas.

And all three, leaving the *Belle Etoile* in charge of Gregoire and the other waiters, hastened towards the Rue de Béthisy, a bright light and the report of fire-arms guiding them in that direction.

'Who comes here?' cried Coconnas. 'A man without his doublet or scarf!'

'It is someone escaping,' said Maurevel.

'Fire!' said Coconnas, 'you who have arquebuses.'

'*Ma foi!* not I,' replied Maurevel. 'I'll keep my powder for better game.'

'You, then, La Hurière.'

'Wait!' said the innkeeper, taking aim.

'Oh, yes, wait, and he will escape!' replied Coconnas.

And he rushed after the unhappy wretch, whom he soon overtook, as he was wounded. But at the moment when, in order that he might not strike from behind, he exclaimed, 'Turn, turn!' the report of an arquebuse was heard, a bullet whistled by Coconnas's ears, and the fugitive rolled over, like a hare struck by the hunter's bullet.

A cry of triumph was heard behind Coconnas. The Piedmontese turned round, and saw La Hurière brandishing his weapon.

'Ah, now!' he exclaimed, 'I have made my maiden shot!'

'And only just missed making a hole clean through me.'

'Be on your guard!'

Coconnas sprang back. The wounded man had risen on his knee, and, seeking revenge, was about to stab him with his dagger, when the host's warning put the Piedmontese on his guard.

'Ah, viper!' shouted Coconnas, and rushing at the wounded man, he thrust his sword through him three times up to the hilt.

'And now,' cried he, leaving the Huguenot in the throes of death, 'to the admiral's!—to the admiral's!'

'Ah! gentlemen,' said Maurevel, 'you are getting the idea.'

'*Ma foi!* yes,' replied Coconnas. 'I do not know if it is the smell of gunpowder that makes me drunk, or the sight of blood which excites me, but, *mordi!* I have a taste for slaughter. It is like a man-hunt. I have as yet only known hunting bears and wolves, and, on my honour, hunting men seems more amusing.' And the three went on their way.

8

THE VICTIMS

THE admiral's house was, as we have said, situated in the Rue de Béthisy. It was a large building, opening on a court in front, flanked by two wings. One principal and two small gates afforded entrance into this court-yard.

When our three cut-throats entered the Rue de Béthisy, which runs into the Rue des Fossés-Saint-Germain-l'Auxerrois, they saw the house surrounded by Swiss, soldiers and citizens, all armed to the teeth, some holding drawn swords, others arquebuses loaded and matches burning, and some, in their left hand, torches that threw a fitful and lurid glare on this sea of human heads and naked weapons. The work of destruction was proceeding in the Rues Tirechappe, Etienne, and Bertin-Poirée. Agonized cries and the reports of muskets were heard incessantly, and, occasionally, some wretched fugitive rushed wildly through what, seen by the uncertain light, seemed a troop of demons.

In an instant, Coconnas, Maurevel, and La Huriére, vouched for by their white crosses, and received with cries of welcome, were in the midst of the tumult, though they could not have entered the throng, had not Maurevel been recognized. Coconnas and La Hurière followed him, and all three managed to enter the court.

In the centre of this court, the three doors of which had been burst open, a man, around whom a body of Catholics formed a respectful circle, stood leaning on his drawn rapier, eagerly looking up at a balcony about fifteen feet above him, which ran along the front of the principal window of the house.

This man stamped impatiently on the ground, and, from time to time, questioned those around him.

'Nothing yet!' murmured he. 'No one! He has been warned, and has escaped. What do you think, du Gast?'

'Impossible, monseigneur.'

'Why? Did you not tell me, that just before we arrived, a man, bareheaded, a drawn sword in his hand, came running, as if pursued, knocked at the door, and was admitted?'

'Yes, monseigneur. But M. de Besme came up immediately, broke open the doors, and surrounded the house. The man went in, sure enough, but he has not come out.'

'Why,' said Coconnas to La Hurière, 'if my eyes do not deceive me, it is M. de Guise.'

'Himself, monsieur. Yes, the great Henry de Guise has come in person to wait for the admiral to come out, and serve him as he served the duke's father. Every dog has his day, and it is our turn now.'

'Hola, Besme!' cried the duke, with his powerful voice, 'have you not finished yet?'

And he struck his sword so forcibly against the stones that sparks flew.

At this instant cries were heard in the house—then several shots—then a clashing of swords, and then all was again silent.

The duke was about to rush into the house.

'Monseigneur, monseigneur!' said du Gast, detaining him, 'your dignity commands you to wait here.'

'You are right, du Gast. I must stay here. But I am on tenterhooks. What if he were to escape!'

Suddenly the windows of the first floor were lighted up with what seemed the reflection of torches.

The window, on which the duke's eyes were fixed, opened, or, rather, was shattered to pieces, and a man, his face and collar stained with blood, appeared on the balcony.

'Ah! at last! Besme!' cried the duke; 'what news?'

'Here!' replied the German, with the greatest *sang-froid*, as he struggled to lift a heavy body.

'But where are the others?' demanded the duke.

'Finishing off the rest.'

'And what have *you* done?'

'You shall see. Stand back a little!'

The duke retreated a few paces.

The object that Besme was trying to lift was now visible: it was the body of an old man. He raised it above the balcony, held it aloft for a moment, then threw it at his master's feet.

The heavy fall, and the blood that gushed forth from the body, startled even the duke himself. But curiosity soon overpowered fear, and the light of the torches was speedily thrown on the body.

A white beard, a venerable visage, and limbs contracted by death, were then visible. 'The admiral!' cried twenty voices, which fell silent again at once.

'Yes, the admiral!' said the duke, approaching the corpse, and contemplating it with silent ecstasy.

'The admiral! the admiral!' repeated the witnesses of this terrible scene, timidly approaching the old man, majestic even in death.

'Ah, at last, Gaspard!' said the Duke de Guise triumphantly. 'Murderer of my father! Revenge is sweet!'

And the duke dared to plant his foot on the breast of the Protestant hero. But, instantly, the dying warrior opened his eyes, his bleeding and mutilated hand clenched itself, and the admiral, with a sepulchral voice, said to the duke,—

'Henry de Guise, one day the foot of the assassin shall be planted on thy breast! I did not kill thy father, and I curse thee!'*

The duke, pale, and trembling in spite of himself, felt a cold shudder come over him. He passed his hand across his brow, as if to dispel the fearful vision. When he dared again to look at the admiral, his eyes were closed, his hand unclenched, and a stream of black blood had poured over his silvery beard from the mouth which had only moments before uttered that terrible denunciation against his murderer.

The duke lifted his sword, with a gesture of desperate resolution.

'Are you satisfied, monseigneur?' asked Besme.

'Yes,' returned Henry; 'for you have avenged——'

'Duke François!'* said de Besme.

'The Catholic religion,' returned Henry. Then turning to the soldiers and citizens who filled the court and streets, he cried:

'To work, my friends—to work!'

'Good-evening, M. de Besme,' said Coconnas, approaching the German, who stood on the balcony, wiping his sword.

'It was you, then, who settled him!' cried La Hurière; 'how did you manage it?'

'Oh, very easily. He heard a noise, opened his door, and I ran him through the body. But I think they are killing Teligny now, for I hear him yelling.'

At this moment, several cries of distress were heard, and the windows of the long gallery that formed a wing of the house were lighted up with a red glare. Two men were seen fleeing from a body of assassins. An arquebuse-shot killed one. The other sprang boldly, and without stopping to look at the distance from the ground, through an open window into the court below, ignoring the enemies who awaited him there.

'Kill! kill!' cried the assassins, seeing their prey about to escape them.

The fugitive picked up his sword, which in his fall had dropped from his hand, dashed through the soldiers, knocked over three or four, ran one through the body, and, amid the pistol-shots and imprecations of the furious Catholics, darted like lightning past Coconnas, who stood ready for him at the door.

'Got you!' cried the Piedmontese, piercing his arm with his sharp blade.

'Coward!' replied the fugitive, striking him on the face with the handle of his sword, for he lacked room to thrust at him with its point.

'A thousand devils!' cried Coconnas—'it's M. de la Mole!'

'M. de la Mole!' re-echoed La Hurière and Maurevel.

'It was he who warned the admiral!' cried several soldiers.

'Kill him—kill him!' was shouted on all sides.

Coconnas, La Hurière, and half a score of soldiers, rushed in pursuit of La Mole, who, covered with blood, and having reached that state of desperation which is the last resource of human strength, dashed wildly through the streets, with no other guide than instinct. The footsteps and shouts of his pursuers gave him wings. Occasionally a bullet whistled by his ear, and made him dart forward with redoubled speed. He no longer seemed to breathe: it was a hoarse rattle which came from his chest. His doublet seemed to prevent his heart from beating, and he tore it off; soon his sword became too heavy for his hand, and he threw it away. The blood and perspiration matted his hair and trickled in heavy drops down his face. Sometimes it seemed to him that he was gaining on his pursuers, and he heard their steps die away in the distance. But at their cries, fresh slaughterers started up on every side and continued the chase. Suddenly to his left he saw the river rolling silently on and felt, like the stag at bay, an irresistible urge to plunge into it: only the supreme power of reason restrained him. On his right was the Louvre, dark and sinister and full of strange and ominous sounds. Soldiers on the drawbridge came and went, and helmets and breast-plates glittered in the moonlight. La Mole thought of the King of Navarre, as he had thought before of Coligny: they were his only protectors—it was his last hope. He collected all his strength, and inwardly vowing to abjure his faith should he escape massacre, he rushed by the soldiers, on to the drawbridge, received another stab in the side from a dagger, and despite the cries of 'Kill—kill!' that resounded on all sides, and the opposing weapons of the sentinels, darted like an arrow through the court-yard, into the hall, mounted the staircase, then up two floors higher, recognized a door, and leaned against it, knocking on it violently with his hands and feet.

'Who is there?' asked a woman's voice.

'Oh, my God!' murmured La Mole—'they are coming, I hear them; it's me!'

'Who are you?' said the voice.

La Mole remembered the pass-word.

'Navarre—Navarre!' he cried.

The door opened instantly. La Mole, without thanking or even seeing Gillonne, dashed into a hall, then along a corridor, through two or three chambers, until at last he entered a room lighted by a lamp suspended from the ceiling.

Beneath curtains of velvet with gold fleurs-de-lis, in a bed of carved oak, a lady in a dressing-gown raised herself on one elbow, and gazed at him in terror.

La Mole threw himself towards her.

'Madame,' cried he, 'they are killing, they are butchering my brothers—they are trying to kill me too! You are queen—save me!'

And he threw himself at her feet, leaving on the carpet a large pool of blood.

At sight of a man, pale, exhausted, and bleeding at her feet, the Queen of Navarre, who, warned by Madame de Lorraine, had lain down without undressing, clapped her hands over her eyes, and shrieked for help.

'Madame,' cried La Mole, 'for the love of Heaven, do not call! If you do, I am a dead man, for my murderers are at hand. They are on the stairs—listen! I hear them now!'

'Help!' cried the queen—'help!'

'Ah!' said La Mole despairingly, 'you have done for me! I did not think it possible to die by so sweet a voice, so fair a hand!'

At the same time the door flew open, and a troop of men, their faces covered with blood and blackened with gunpowder, their swords drawn, and their pikes and arquebuses levelled, rushed into the apartment.

Coconnas was at their head—his red hair bristling, his eye flashing fire, and his cheek cut open by La Mole's sword. The Piedmontese was terrible to behold.

'*Mordi!*' cried he, 'we have him at last.'

La Mole looked round him for a weapon, but in vain. He glanced at the queen, and saw pity etched on her face: he at once felt that she alone could save him. He threw his arms round her.

Coconnas advanced, and with the point of his long rapier again wounded his enemy's shoulder, and the crimson drops of warm blood stained the white and perfumed sheets of Marguerite's bed.

Marguerite saw the blood flow, and felt the shudder that ran through La Mole's frame. She threw herself with him into the recess between the bed and the wall. It was none too soon, for La Mole was incapable of flight or resistance. His head leaned on Marguerite's shoulder, and his hand seized and tore its thin cambric covering.

'Oh, madame,' he murmured, 'save me!'

He could say no more. A mist came over his eyes, his head sank back, his arms fell at his side, and he collapsed on to the floor, bathed in his blood, and dragging the queen down with him.

At this moment, Coconnas, excited by the sight of blood and heated by the long pursuit, advanced towards the recess. In another instant, his sword would have pierced La Mole's heart, and perhaps Marguerite's too.

At the sight of bare steel, but even more moved by the insolence of the man, this daughter of kings drew herself up to her full height, and sent forth such a cry of fear, indignation, and rage, that Coconnas stood petrified.

Suddenly a door in the wall opened, and a young man of sixteen or seventeen, dressed in black and his hair in disorder, rushed in.

'Stop!' cried he. 'I am here, sister—I am here!'

'François! François!' cried Marguerite—'help! help!'

'The Duke d'Alençon!' murmured La Hurière, grounding his arquebuse.

'*Mordi!* a Son of France!' growled Coconnas, drawing back.

The duke glanced round him. He saw Marguerite, dishevelled, more lovely than ever, leaning against the wall surrounded by men, fury in her eyes, large drops of perspiration on her forehead.

'Wretches!' cried he.

'Save me, brother!' shrieked Marguerite. 'They intend to kill me!'

The duke's pallid face became crimson. He was unarmed, but sustained, no doubt, by the consciousness of his rank, he advanced with hands clenched towards Coconnas and his companions, who fell back, terrified at the lightning darting from his eyes.

'Ha! and will you murder a Son of France, too!' cried the duke. Then, as they recoiled, he called: 'Captain of the guard! Hang me every one of these ruffians!'

More alarmed at the sight of this weaponless young man than he would have been at the aspect of a regiment of lansquenets,* Coconnas had already reached the door. La Hurière sprang after him like a deer, and the soldiers jostled and pushed each other in the passageway, in their endeavours to escape, finding the door far too small for their great desire to be outside it. Meantime

Marguerite had instinctively thrown the damask coverlet of her bed over La Mole, and moved some way off.

No sooner had the last murderer departed, than the duke turned to his sister,—

'Are you hurt?' cried he, seeing Marguerite covered with blood. And he darted towards his sister with a concern which did credit to his brotherly love.

'No,' said she, 'I don't think so. Or if I am, only slightly.'

'But this blood,' said the duke; 'whose is it?'

'I do not know,' replied she. 'One of those wretches seized me, and perhaps he was wounded.'

'What!' cried the duke, 'dare to touch my sister? Oh, had you but shown him to me—if I knew where to find him——'

'Leave me!' said Marguerite.

'Well, Marguerite,' said he, ' I will go. But you cannot remain alone on this dreadful night. Shall I call Gillonne?'

'No, no! leave me, François—leave me!'

The prince obeyed. Hardly had he disappeared than Marguerite, hearing a groan from the recess, hastily bolted the door of the secret passage, and hurrying to the other entrance, closed it just as a troop of archers dashed by in hot pursuit of other Huguenots who lived in the Louvre.

After glancing round to assure herself she was really alone, she lifted the covering that had hidden La Mole from the Duke d'Alençon, and tremblingly drawing the apparently lifeless body, by great exertion, into the middle of the room, and observing that the victim still breathed, sat down, placed his head on her knees, and sprinkled his face with water.

Then it was that as the mask of blood, dust, and gunpowder which had covered his face, was removed, Marguerite recognized the handsome cavalier who, full of life and hope, had only three or four hours before solicited her protection and that of the King of Navarre and who, while dazzled by her own beauty, had attracted her attention by his own.

Marguerite uttered a cry of terror, for now it was more than pity that she felt for the wounded man—it was concern. He was no longer a stranger; he was almost an acquaintance. By her care, La Mole's fine features soon reappeared, free from stain, but pale and distorted by pain. A shudder ran through her whole frame as she tremblingly placed her hand on his heart. It still beat. She then took a smelling-bottle from the table and applied it to his nostrils.

La Mole opened his eyes.

'Oh! *mon Dieu!*' murmured he—'where am I?'

'Safe!' said Marguerite. 'Calm yourself—you are safe.'

La Mole turned his eyes on the queen, gazed earnestly for a moment, and murmuring, 'Oh, fairest of the fair!' closed his lids, as if overpowered, and uttered a long, deep sigh.

Marguerite started. He had become still paler than before, if that were possible, and she feared that sigh was his last.

'O Heaven!' she cried, 'have pity on him!'

At this moment, a violent knocking was heard at the door. Marguerite half raised herself, still supporting La Mole.

'Who is there?' she cried.

'Madame, it is I' replied a female voice, 'the Duchess de Nevers.'

'Henriette!' cried Marguerite. 'There is no danger: it is my friend. Do you hear me, sir?'

La Mole managed to raise himself on one knee.

'Try to support yourself,' said the queen.

La Mole, resting his hand on the ground, managed to keep his balance.

Marguerite advanced towards the door, but stopped suddenly.

'Ah, you are not alone!' she said, hearing the clatter of arms outside.

'No, I have twelve guards which my brother-in-law, M. de Guise, assigned me.'

'M. de Guise!' murmured La Mole. 'The assassin—the murderer!'

'Silence!' said Marguerite. 'Not a word!'

And she looked round, wondering where she could conceal the wounded man.

'A sword! a dagger!' muttered La Mole.

'To defend yourself—useless? Did you not hear? They are twelve, and you are one.'

'Not to defend myself, but so that they shall not take me alive.'

'No, no!' said Marguerite. 'I will save you. Ah! this closet will do! Come! hurry!'

La Mole made an effort, and, supported by Marguerite, dragged himself to the closet. Marguerite locked the door on him, and hid the key in her alms-purse.

'Not a sound, not a movement,' whispered she, through the lattice-work, 'and you will be safe.'

Then hastily throwing a mantle round her, she opened the door for her friend, who embraced her tenderly.

'Ah!' cried Madame Nevers, 'you are unhurt, then?'

'Not hurt at all,' replied Marguerite, wrapping the mantle still more closely round her to conceal the blood on her dress.*

'Good. However, M. de Guise has given me twelve of his guards to escort me to his house. Since I do not need so many, I will leave six with your Majesty. Six of the duke's guards are worth a regiment of the king's to-night.'

Marguerite dared not refuse. She stationed the soldiers in the corridor and embraced the duchess, who then returned to the Hotel de Guise, where she resided in her husband's absence.

9

THE MURDERERS

COCONNAS had not fled, he had simply retreated; La Hurière had not fled, he had flown. The one had disappeared like a tiger, the other like a wolf.

The result was that La Hurière had already reached the Place Saint-Germain-l'Auxerrois, when Coconnas had only just left the Louvre.

La Hurière was prudently thinking of returning home, but as he turned the corner in the Rue de l'Arbre-Sec, he fell in with a troop of Swiss and light horse, led by Maurevel.

'Well!' exclaimed the latter, who had christened himself the King's Assassin,* 'have you finished already? What the devil have you done with our Piedmontese gentleman? Has anything happened to him? It would be a pity, for he went to work like a hero.'

'I hope not,' replied La Hurière. Where are you going?'

'Oh, I have a piece of business of my own to see to.'

'Then let me go with you,' said a voice which made Maurevel start, 'for you know all the good places.'

'It is M. de Coconnas,' said La Hurière.

'Ah! you have come from the Louvre. Did your Huguenot take refuge there?' asked Maurevel.

'*Mon Dieu!* yes.'

'I took a shot at him just as he was picking up his sword in the admiral's court-yard, but somehow or other I missed him.'

'I,' added Coconnas, 'did not miss him: I gave him such a thrust in the back that my sword was wet five inches up the blade. Besides, I saw him fall into the arms of Madame Marguerite, a fine woman, *mordi!* Yet I confess I should not be sorry to hear he was really dead. The rogue is utterly ruthless and capable of bearing me a grudge all his life.'

'Do you mean to go with me?'

'Why, I do not like standing still. *Mordi!* I have only killed three or four up to now, and when I get cold my shoulder pains me. Forward! forward!'

'Captain,' said Maurevel to the commander of the troop, 'give me three men, and go your own way with the rest.'

Three Swiss were ordered to follow Maurevel, who, accompanied by Coconnas and La Hurière, went towards the Rue Sainte Avoye.

'Where the devil are we going?' asked Coconnas.

'To the Rue du Chaume, where we have important business.'

'Tell me,' said Coconnas, 'is not the Rue du Chaume near the Rue des Vieilles Hundriettes, which I believe is near the Temple?'*

'Why?'

'Because an old creditor of our family lives there, one Lambert Mercandon, to whom my father directed me to hand over the hundred rose nobles I have in my pocket for that purpose.'

'Well,' replied Maurevel, 'this is a good opportunity for paying him. This is the day for settling old accounts. Is your Mercandon a Huguenot?'

'Oh, I understand!' said Coconnas. 'He must be——'

'Hush! here we are.'

'What is that large house, with its entrance in the street?'

'The Hotel de Guise.'

'Truly,' returned Coconnas, 'I had to come here sooner or later, as I am under the patronage of the great Henry. But, *mordi!* all is so very quiet in this part of town that it is like being in the country. Devil take it, everybody is asleep!'

And indeed the Hotel de Guise seemed as quiet as in ordinary times. All the windows were closed, and a solitary light burned behind the blind of the main window above the entrance. At the corner of the Rue des Quatre-Fils Maurevel stopped.

'This is the house of the man we are looking for,' he said. 'La Hurière, you look harmless enough: knock at the door. Hand your arquebuse to M. de Coconnas, who has been ogling it this last half-hour. If you are allowed in, you must ask to speak to M. de Mouy.'

'Oh!' said Coconnas, 'now I understand—you have a creditor in the Quarter of the Temple too.'

'Exactly so!' responded Maurevel. 'You will go up to him pretending to be a Huguenot, and inform M. de Mouy of all that has passed: he is brave, and will come down.'

'And once down——?' asked La Hurière.

'Once down, I will request him to cross swords with me.'

La Hurière, without making any reply, knocked at the door, and the sounds echoing in the silence of the night caused the doors of the Hotel de Guise to open, and several heads to appear out of them. It then became evident that the house was quiet after the fashion of citadels—that is to say, in being filled with soldiers. The heads were instantly withdrawn, guessing, no doubt, what was afoot.

'Does your M. de Mouy live here?' inquired Coconnas, pointing to the house at which La Hurière continued to knock.

'No, but his mistress does.'*

'*Mordi!* how gallant you are, to give him an opportunity to draw sword in the presence of his lady-love! We shall be the judges of the field. I should like very well to fight myself—my shoulder burns.'

'And your face,' asked Maurevel, 'is very battered, is it not?'

Coconnas uttered a kind of growl.

'*Mordi!*' he said, 'I hope the man who did it is dead. If I thought not, I would return to the Louvre and finish him.'

La Hurière still kept knocking.

Soon the window on the first floor opened, and a man appeared in the balcony, in a nightcap and shift, and unarmed.

'Who's there?' cried he.

Maurevel made a sign to the Swiss, who retreated into a corner, while Coconnas stood close against the wall.

'Ah! Monsieur de Mouy!' said the innkeeper, in his blandest tones, 'is that you?'

'Yes. What of it?'

'It is he!' said Maurevel joyfully.

'Well, then, sir,' continued La Hurière, 'do you not know what is going on? They are murdering the admiral, and all of our religion. Quick, you must help them!'

'Ah!' exclaimed de Mouy, 'I feared something was afoot for tonight. I ought not to have left my brave comrades. I will come, my friend—wait for me.'

And without closing the window, through which was heard the voice of an alarmed female, uttering tender supplications, M. de Mouy put on his doublet, cloak, and weapons.

'He is coming down; be ready!' murmured Maurevel, pale with joy. Taking the arquebuse from Coconnas, and blowing on the match to ensure it was alight and ready for firing, he returned it to La Hurière.

'*Mordi!*' exclaimed Coconnas, 'the moon is coming out to see this beautiful little fight. I would give a great deal if Lambert Mercandon were here, to serve as M. de Mouy's second.'

'Wait, wait!' said Maurevel. 'M. de Mouy is equal to several men himself, and it is likely that we six shall have enough to do to despatch him. Forward, men!' continued Maurevel, making a sign to the Swiss to stand by the door, so that they could strike de Mouy as he emerged.

'Ah!' said Coconnas, as he watched these arrangements, 'it appears that this will not come off quite as I expected.'

Already they heard the sound of a bolt which de Mouy moved aside. The Swiss were at the door; Maurevel and La Hurière came forward on tiptoe, while, out of a sense of honour, Coconnas remained where he was, when a young female, whom no one had expected, appeared in the balcony, and gave a terrible shriek when she saw the Swiss, Maurevel, and La Hurière.

De Mouy, who had already half-opened the door, paused.

'Come back!' cried the damsel. 'I see swords glitter, and the match of an arquebuse—you are betrayed!'

'Ah!' said the young man, 'let us see, then, what this means.'

And he closed the door, replaced the bolt, and went upstairs again.

Maurevel's order of battle was changed when he saw that de Mouy was not coming out. The Swiss went and posted themselves at the other corner of the street, and La Hurière, with his arquebuse in his hand, waited for his enemy to reappear at the window.

He did not wait long.

De Mouy advanced, holding before him two pistols of such respectable length, that La Hurière, who was taking aim, suddenly reflected that the Huguenot's bullets had no farther to go in reaching him than had his to reach the balcony. 'It is true,' said he, 'I may kill the gentleman; but it is equally true that the gentleman may kill me!' and this reflection persuaded him to retreat into an angle of the Rue de Brac,* so far off as to make any aim of his at de Mouy rather uncertain.

De Mouy cast a glance around him, and advanced like a man preparing to fight a duel. But seeing nothing, he exclaimed,—

'Why, it appears, friend, that you have left your arquebuse at my door! I am here. What do you want with me?'

'Ah, ah!' said Coconnas to himself, 'this is a brave fellow!'

'Well,' continued de Mouy, 'friends or enemies, whichever you are, do you not see I am waiting?'

La Hurière kept silence, Maurevel made no reply, and the three Swiss remained under cover.

Coconnas paused an instant. Then seeing that no one continued the conversation begun by La Hurière and followed by de Mouy, he left his station, and advancing into the middle of the street, took off his hat, and said,—

'Sir, we are not here to murder anyone, as you seem to suppose, but for a duel. Eh, *mordi!* come forward, Monsieur de Maurevel, instead of turning your back. The gentleman accepts.'

'Maurevel!' cried de Mouy; 'Maurevel, the killer of my father! Maurevel, the king's assassin! Ah, *pardieu!* Yes, I accept!'

And taking aim at Maurevel, who was about to knock at the Hotel de Guise to request reinforcements, he sent a bullet through his hat.

At the noise of the shot and Maurevel's cries, the guard who had escorted Madame de Nevers came out, accompanied by three or four gentlemen followed by their pages, and approached the house of young de Mouy's mistress.

A second pistol-shot, fired into the midst of the troop, killed the soldier next to Maurevel, after which de Mouy, having discharged both pistols, took cover behind the parapet.

Meantime, windows began to be opened everywhere, and, according to the respective dispositions of their pacific or bellicose inhabitants, were closed, or bristled with muskets and arquebuses.

'Help! worthy Mercandon,' shouted de Mouy, making a sign to an elderly man, who, from a window which opened in a house opposite the Hotel de Guise, was trying to make out the cause of the confusion.

'Is it you who are calling, Monsieur de Mouy?' cried the old man; 'is it you they are after?'

'Me—you—all the Protestants; and there—there is the proof!'

That moment, de Mouy had seen La Hurière aim his arquebuse at him. There was a shot; but the young man ducked and the bullet broke a window behind him.

'Mercandon!' exclaimed Coconnas, who, in his delight at prospect of battle, had forgotten his creditor, but was reminded of him when de Mouy called his name—'Mercandon, Rue du Chaume—that is it! Ah, he lives here! Good! We shall each settle our affairs with our men!'

And, while the people from the Hotel de Guise broke down the doors of de Mouy's house, and Maurevel, torch in hand, tried to set it on fire—while, once the doors had given way, there was a fearful struggle with one antagonist, who, at each pistol-shot and each rapier-thrust, brought down his foe—Coconnas tried, with the help of a paving-stone, to break down the door of

Mercandon, who, unmoved by his solitary effort, was doing his best with his arquebuse out of his window.

And now, all this deserted and dark quarter was as bright as noon day and peopled like the interior of an ant's nest; for, from the Hotel de Montmorency, six or eight Huguenot gentlemen, with their servants and friends, issuing forth, made a furious charge, and, supported by covering fire from the windows, began to repulse Maurevel's and the de Guises' force, whom at length they drove back to their original position.

Coconnas, who had not yet managed to break down Mercandon's door, though he tried to do so with all his might, was exposed by this sudden retreat. Placing his back to the wall, and grasping his sword firmly, he began, not only to defend himself, but to attack his assailants, with cries so terrible that they were heard above all the uproar. He struck right and left, hitting friend and foe, until a wide space was cleared around him. As his rapier made a hole in some breast, and the warm blood spurted over his hands and face, he, with rolling eye, expanded nostrils, and clenched teeth, regained the ground he had lost, and again approached the beleaguered house.

De Mouy, after a terrible fight in the staircase and hall, had ended by coming out of the burning house like a true hero. In the midst of the struggle, he had not stopped calling, 'Here Maurevel!—Maurevel, where are you?' insulting him with the most opprobrious epithets. He at length appeared in the street, supporting on one arm his mistress, half naked and nearly fainting, and holding a dagger between his teeth. His sword, flaming by the sweeping action he gave it, traced circles of white or red, according as the moon glittered on the blade, or a flambeau glared on its blood-stained brightness. Maurevel had fled. La Hurière, driven back by de Mouy as far as Coconnas, who did not recognize him, and received him at sword's point, begged for mercy from both sides. At this moment, Mercandon saw him, and identified him by his white scarf as one of the murderers. He fired. La Hurière shrieked, threw up his arms, dropped his arquebuse, and, having vainly attempted to reach the wall to support himself, fell with his face flat on the ground.

De Mouy, taking advantage of this circumstance, turned down the Rue de Paradis, and disappeared.

Such had been the resistance of the Huguenots, that the de Guise party, utterly routed, had retired behind their own doors, fearing to be besieged and taken in their own citadel.

Coconnas, drunk with blood and riot, had reached that pitch of excitement when, with the men of the south more especially, courage changes into madness, and had not seen or heard anything. He was going towards a man lying with his face downwards in a pool of blood, whom he recognized as La Hurière, when the door he had in vain tried to break down, opened, and old Mercandon, followed by his son and two nephews, rushed upon him.

'Here he is!' they all cried, with one voice.

Coconnas was in the middle of the street, and, fearing to be surrounded by these four men who attacked him at once, gave one of those chamois bounds which he had so often practised in his native mountains, and in an instant found himself with his back against the wall of the Hotel de Guise. Knowing he could not now be surprised from behind, he put himself in a posture of defence, and said, jestingly, 'Ah! Mercandon, don't you recognize me?'

'Wretch!' cried the old Huguenot, 'I know you well; you have taken sides against me—me, the friend and companion of your father!'

'And his creditor, are you not?'

'Yes, his creditor, as you say.'

'Well, then,' said Coconnas, 'I have come to settle the account.'

'Seize him, bind him!' said Mercandon to the young men who accompanied him, and who at his bidding rushed towards the Piedmontese.

'One moment!' said Coconnas, laughing, 'to seize a man you must have a writ, and you have forgotten that.'

And with these words, he crossed his sword with the young man nearest to him, and at the first blow cut his wrist to the bone.

The wounded man retreated, with a shriek of agony.

'That will do for one!' said Coconnas.

At the same moment, the window under which Coconnas had sought shelter, opened. He sprang on one side, fearing an attack from behind. But instead of an enemy, it was a woman he saw. Instead of the enemy's weapon he was prepared to encounter, it was a nosegay that fell at his feet.

'Ah!' he said, 'a woman!' He saluted the lady with his sword, and stooped to pick up the bouquet.

'Be on your guard, brave Catholic!—be on your guard!' cried the lady.

Coconnas rose, but not before the dagger of the second nephew had pierced his cloak, and wounded his other shoulder.

The lady uttered a piercing shriek.

Coconnas thanked her, reassured her with a gesture, and then made a pass at the nephew, which he parried. But at the second thrust, his foot slipped in the blood, and Coconnas, springing at him like a tiger, drove his sword through his breast.

'Good, brave knight!' exclaimed the lady in the Hotel de Guise—'good! I will send you help.'

'Do not trouble yourself, madame,' was Coconnas's reply, 'but watch to the end, if you will, and see how the Count Annibal de Coconnas deals with Huguenots.'

At this moment, the son of old Mercandon fired almost point-blank at Coconnas. The count fell on one knee. The lady at the window shrieked again; but Coconnas rose instantly: he had only ducked to avoid the bullet, which struck the wall about two feet beneath where the lady was standing.

Almost at the same moment there issued a cry of rage from the window of Mercandon's house, and an old woman who recognized Coconnas as a Catholic by his white scarf and cross threw a flower-pot at him. It struck him above the knee.

'Bravo!' said Coconnas; 'one throws me flowers, and the other flower-pots.'

'Thanks, mother—thanks!' said the young man.

'Don't stop, wife,' said old Mercandon; 'but take care.'

'Ah!' said Coconnas, 'so the women are up in arms, some for me, and others against me! *Mordi!* let us end this.'

The scene, in fact, was much changed, and evidently drew near its close. Coconnas was wounded in the face, it is true, but in all the vigour of his twenty-four years, used to combat, and enraged rather than weakened by the three or four scratches he had received; while on the other side there remained only

Mercandon and his son, an old man of sixty or seventy years, and a stripling of sixteen or eighteen, pale, fair, and weak, and who, having discharged his pistol, which was now useless, was brandishing a sword half the length of that of the Piedmontese. The father, armed only with a dagger and a discharged arquebuse, shouted for help. An old woman, looking out of the window, held a piece of marble in her hand, which she was preparing to hurl down. Coconnas, galvanized on the one hand by threats, and on the other by encouragements, proud of his two-fold victory, drunk with powder and blood, lighted by the reflection of a house in flames, warmed by the idea that he was fighting under the eyes of a female whose beauty was as superior as he felt assured she was of high rank—Coconnas, like the last of the Horatii,* felt his strength redouble, and, seeing the young man falter, rushed on him and crossed his small sword with his terrible and bloody rapier. Two blows sufficed to drive it out of his hands. Then Mercandon tried to drive Coconnas back, so that the projectiles thrown from the window might be sure to strike him. But Coconnas, to counter the double attack of the old man, who tried to stab him with his dagger, and the mother of the young man, who was endeavouring to crush his skull with the stone she was ready to throw, seized his adversary by the body, presenting him against all the blows, like a shield, and wellnigh strangling him in his herculean grasp.

'Help! help!' cried the young man, 'he is breaking my breastbone—help!' and his voice grew faint and turned into a low, choking groan.

Then Mercandon ceased to attack, and began to beg.

'Mercy! Monsieur de Coconnas, mercy!—he is my only child!'

'He is my son, my son!' cried the mother—'the hope of our old age! Do not kill him, sir—do not kill him!'

'Really,' cried Coconnas, bursting into laughter—'not kill him! What did he mean, then, to do to me with his sword and pistol?'

'Sir,' said Mercandon, clasping his hands, 'I have at home your father's pledge, I will return it to you—I have ten thousand gold crowns, I will give them to you—I have the jewels of our family, they shall be yours. But do not kill him!—do not kill him!'

'And I have my love,' said the lady in the Hotel de Guise, speaking low, 'and I promise it you.'

Coconnas reflected a moment, and said suddenly,—

'Are you a Huguenot?'

'Yes,' murmured the youth.

'Then you must die!' replied Coconnas, frowning, and putting his keen and glittering dagger to his adversary's breast.

'Die!' cried the old man—'my poor child die!'

And the wailing of the mother resounded so piercingly and loud, that for a moment it shook the firm resolution of the Piedmontese.

'Oh, madame la duchesse!' cried the father, turning towards the lady in the Hotel de Guise, 'intercede for us, and every morning and evening you shall be remembered in our prayers.'

'Then let him be a convert,' said the lady.

'I am a Protestant,' said the boy.

'Then die!' exclaimed Coconnas, lifting his dagger—'die! since you will not accept the life which those fair lips offer to you.'

Mercandon and his wife saw the blade of his deadly weapon gleam like lightning above the head of their son.

'My son Olivier,' shrieked his mother, 'abjure, abjure!'

'Abjure, my dear boy!' cried Mercandon, falling to his knees to Coconnas, 'do not leave us alone on the earth!'

'Abjure, all together,' said Coconnas. 'For one *Credo*, three souls and one life.'

'I will!' said the youth.

'We will!' cried Mercandon and his wife.

'On your knees, then,' said Coconnas, 'and let your son repeat after me, word for word, the prayer I shall say.'

The father obeyed first.

'I am ready,' said the son, also kneeling.

Coconnas then began to repeat in Latin the words of the *Credo*. But, whether from chance or calculation, young Olivier knelt close to where his sword had fallen. Scarcely did he see this weapon within his reach than, not ceasing to repeat the words which Coconnas dictated, he stretched out his hand for it.

Coconnas watched the movement, although he pretended not to see it. But at the moment when the young man touched the handle of the sword with his fingers, he rushed on him, knocked him over, and plunged his dagger in his throat, exclaiming,—

'Traitor!'

The youth uttered one cry, raised himself convulsively on one knee, then fell dead.

'Ah, ruffian!' shrieked Mercandon, 'you kill us to rob us of the hundred rose nobles you owe us.'

'*Ma foi!* no,' said Coconnas, 'and here's the proof.' And so saying, he threw at the old man's feet the purse which his father had given him before his departure to pay his creditor with.

'And here's your death!' cried the old woman, from the window.

'Take care, M. de Coconnas—watch out!' called out the lady at the Hotel de Guise.

But before Coconnas could turn his head to comply with this advice, or get out of the way of the threat, a heavy mass came hissing through the air, falling on to the hat of the Piedmontese, breaking his sword, and prostrating him on the pavement. He was knocked senseless, crushed, so that he did not hear the double cry of joy and distress which came from right and left.

At once Mercandon rushed, dagger in hand, on the unconscious Coconnas. But at this moment the door of the Hotel de Guise opened, and the old man, seeing swords and partisans gleaming, fled, while the lady he had called the duchess, whose beauty seemed terrible by the light of the flames, dazzling as she was with gems and diamonds, leaned half out of the window, in order to direct the new-comers, her arm extended towards Coconnas.

'There! in front of me—a gentleman in a red doublet. There!—that's the one—yes, that's him!'

10

DEATH, MASS, OR THE BASTILLE

MARGUERITE, as we have said, had shut the door, and returned to her chamber. But as she entered, breathing hard, she saw Gillonne, who, terror-struck, was leaning against the door of the closet, gazing on the traces of blood on the bed, the furniture, and the carpet.

'Oh, madame,' she exclaimed, 'is he dead?'

'Silence, Gillonne!' and Gillonne was silent.

Marguerite then took a small gold key from her purse, opened the door of the cabinet, and pointed to the young man. La Mole had succeeded in raising himself and getting as far as the window; a small dagger, such as females of the period carried, was in his hand.

'Fear nothing, sir,' said Marguerite, 'for, on my soul, you are safe!'

La Mole sank on his knees.

'Oh, madame,' he cried, 'you are more than a queen—you are a divinity!'

'Do not agitate yourself, sir,' said Marguerite, 'your wound is still bleeding. Oh, look, Gillonne, how pale he is! Let us see where you are wounded.'

'Madame,' said La Mole, trying to fix on certain parts of his body the pain which flooded his whole frame, 'I think I have a dagger-thrust in my shoulder, another in my chest—the other wounds are trifles.'

'We will see,' said Marguerite. 'Gillonne, bring me my casket of balms.'

Gillonne obeyed, and returned, holding in one hand a casket, and in the other a silver basin and some fine Holland linen.

'Help me to raise him, Gillonne,' said Queen Marguerite, 'for in his exertions the poor gentleman has lost all his strength.'

'Oh!' cried La Mole, 'I would rather die than see you, the queen, stain your hands with blood as unworthy as mine. Oh, never!'

'Your blood, sir,' replied Gillonne, with a smile, 'has already stained the bed and apartments of her Majesty.'

Marguerite put on her mantle over her cambric dressing-gown, all bespattered with small red spots.

'Madame,' stammered La Mole, 'can you not leave me to the care of the surgeon?'

'Of a Catholic surgeon, perhaps,' said the queen, with an expression which La Mole understood, and made him shudder.

'Come, Gillonne, let us to work!'

La Mole again tried to resist, and repeated that he would rather die than occasion the queen a labour, which, though begun in pity, must end in revulsion; but this exertion completely exhausted his strength, and, falling back, he fainted a second time.

Marguerite, then seizing the dagger which he had dropped, quickly cut the lace of his doublet, while Gillonne, with another blade, ripped open the sleeves.

Next Gillonne, with a cloth dipped in fresh water, staunched the blood which escaped from his shoulder and chest, and Marguerite, with a silver needle with a round point, probed the wounds with all the delicacy and skill that Ambroise Paré could have displayed.

'A dangerous, but not mortal wound, *acerrimum humeri vulnus, non autem lethale*,' murmured the lovely, learned lady-surgeon; 'hand me the salve, Gillonne, and get the lint ready.'

Gillonne had already dried and perfumed the young man's chest and arms. He seemed made on the Greek model. His shoulders sloped gracefully and his neck, shaded by thick hair, seemed rather to belong to a statue of Paros* than the mangled frame of a dying man.

'Poor young man!' murmured Gillonne.

'Is he not handsome?' said Marguerite, with royal frankness.

'Yes, madame. But I think we should lift him on the bed.'

'Yes,' said Marguerite, 'you are right.' The two women, uniting their strength, lifted La Mole and laid him on a kind of large sofa in front of the window, which they partly opened.

This movement aroused La Mole, who heaved a sigh. Opening his eyes, he began to find that delightful sensation which accompanies every healing application to a wounded man when, on his return to consciousness, he finds freshness instead of burning heat, and the perfumes of new salves instead of the acrid stench of blood.

He muttered some unconnected words, to which Marguerite replied with a smile, placing her finger on her mouth.

At this moment several blows were struck at the door.

'Someone is knocking at the secret passage,' said Marguerite. 'I will go and see who it is. You remain here, and do not leave him for a single moment.'

Marguerite went into her room, and closing the door of the closet, opened that of the passage which led to the king's and queen-mother's apartments.

'Madame de Sauve!' she exclaimed, recoiling suddenly with an expression which resembled hatred if not terror: so true it is that a woman never forgives another for stealing from her even a man whom she does not love*—'Madame de Sauve!'

'Yes, your Majesty!' she replied, clasping her hands.

'You here, madame?' exclaimed Marguerite, more and more surprised, and at the same time more and more imperious.

Charlotte fell on her knees.

'Madame,' she said, 'forgive me! I know how guilty I am towards you. But if you knew—the fault is not wholly mine; an express command of the queen-mother——'

'Rise!' said Marguerite, 'and as I do not suppose you have come with the intention of justifying yourself to me, tell me why you have come at all?'

'I have come, madame,' said Charlotte, still on her knees and with a look of wild alarm, 'I came to ask you if he were not here?'

'Here! who?—Who do you mean, madame? for I really do not understand.'

'The king!'

'The king? What, have you come looking for him in my apartments? You know very well that he never comes here.'

'Ah, madame!' continued the Baroness de Sauve, without replying to these attacks, or even seeming to notice them—'ah, would to Heaven he were here!'

'Why is that?'

'Eh, *mon Dieu!* madame, because they are murdering the Huguenots, and the King of Navarre is the chief of the Huguenots.'

'Oh!' cried Marguerite, seizing Madame de Sauve by the hand, and compelling her to rise—'I had forgotten! Besides, I did not think a king could run the same dangers as other men.'

'More, madame—a thousand times more!' cried Charlotte.

'In fact, Madame de Lorraine warned me. I begged him not to leave the Louvre. Has he done so?'

'No, madame, he is in the Louvre; but if he is not here——'

'He is not here!'

'Oh!' cried Madame de Sauve, in a burst of despair, 'then he is a dead man, for the queen-mother has sworn his destruction!'

'His destruction! ah!' said Marguerite, 'you terrify me—impossible!'

'Madame,' replied Madame de Sauve, with that energy which passion alone can give, 'I tell you that no one knows where the King of Navarre is.'

'And where is the queen-mother?'

'The queen-mother sent me to find M. de Guise and M. de Tavannes, who were in her oratory, and then dismissed me.'

'And my husband has not been in your apartment?' inquired Marguerite.

'He has not, madame. I have looked for him everywhere, and asked everybody for him. One soldier told me he thought he had seen him in the midst of the guards who escorted him, with his sword drawn in his hand, some time before the massacre began, and the killing has now begun.'

'Thanks, madame,' said Marguerite, 'and although perhaps the sentiment which impels you is an additional offence towards me—yet, again, thanks!'

'Oh, forgive me, madame!' she said, 'and I shall return to my apartments more fortified by your pardon, for I dare not follow you, even at a distance.'

Marguerite held out her hand to her.

'I will go to Queen Catherine,' she said, 'and return to you. The King of Navarre is under my protection. I have promised him my alliance, and I will be faithful to my promise.'

'But suppose you cannot obtain access to the queen-mother, madame?'

'Then I will go to my brother Charles and speak to him.'

'Go, madame, go,' said Charlotte, 'and may God guide your Majesty!'

Marguerite passed quickly along the passage, and Madame de Sauve followed her.

The Queen of Navarre saw her turn to her own apartment, and then went herself towards the queen's chamber.

Everything was changed there. Instead of the crowd of eager courtiers who usually opened their ranks before the queen and respectfully saluted her, Marguerite met only guards with red partisans* and garments stained with blood, or gentlemen in torn cloaks—their faces blackened with powder, bearing orders and despatches—some going in, others going out, and all these entrances and exits created a terrible and immense confusion in the galleries.

Marguerite, however, went boldly on until she reached the antechamber of the queen-mother, which was guarded by a double line of soldiers who only allowed those to enter who had the pass-word. Marguerite in vain tried to get through this living barrier: several times she saw the door open and shut, and each time she saw Catherine moving and excited, as if she were only twenty years of age, writing, receiving letters, opening them, addressing a word to one, a smile to another. And those on whom she smiled most graciously were those who were the most covered with dust and blood.

Outside were heard, from time to time, the sounds of fire-arms.

'I shall never reach him!' said Marguerite, having made several vain attempts to pass the soldiers.

At this moment, M. de Guise appeared. He had come to inform the queen of the murder of the admiral, and was returning to the butchery.

'Oh, Henry!' cried Marguerite, 'where is the King of Navarre?'*

The duke looked at her with a smile of astonishment, bowed, and, without any reply, passed on.

'Ah, my dear René,' said the queen, recognizing Catherine's perfumer, 'is that you?—you have just left my mother. Do you know what has become of my husband?'

'His Majesty the King of Navarre is no friend of mine,

madame—that you know very well. It is even said,' he added, with a ghastly smile—'it is even said that he dares to accuse me of having been the accomplice, with Queen Catherine, in poisoning his mother.'

'No, no!' cried Marguerite, 'my good René, you must not believe that!'

'Oh, it is of little consequence, madame!' said the perfumer. 'Neither the King of Navarre nor his party are any longer to be feared now!'

And he turned his back on Marguerite.

'Ah, Monsieur de Tavannes!' cried Marguerite, 'one word, I beg you!'

Tavannes stopped.

'Where is Henry of Navarre?'

'*Ma foi!*' he replied, in a loud voice, 'I believe he is somewhere in the city with the Messieurs d'Alençon and de Condé.'

And then he added, in a whisper so low that the queen alone could hear,—

'Your Majesty, if you want to see him—to be in whose place I would give my life—go to the king's armoury.'

'Thanks, Tavannes—thanks!' said Marguerite, 'I will go there.'

And she went on her way, murmuring,—

'Oh, after all I promised him—after the way he behaved to me when that ingrate, Henry de Guise, was concealed in the closet—I cannot let him die!'

And she knocked at the door of the king's apartments. But they were defended by two companies of guards.

'No one is admitted to the king,' said the officer, stepping forward.

'But I——' said Marguerite.

'The order is general.'

'I, the Queen of Navarre!—I, his sister!'

'I dare make no exception, madame.'

And the officer closed the door.

'He is lost!' exclaimed Marguerite, alarmed at the sight of all the sinister faces she had seen. 'Yes, yes! I understand everything. I have been used as a bait. I am the snare which trapped the Huguenots: but I will enter, even if I am killed in the attempt!'

And Marguerite ran like a mad creature through the corridors and galleries, when suddenly, passing a small door, she heard a low chanting, almost as melancholy as it was monotonous. It was a Calvinistic psalm, sung by a trembling voice in an adjacent chamber.

'The nurse of my brother, the king—good Madelon—it is she!' exclaimed Marguerite. 'God of the Christians, help me now!'

And full of hope, Marguerite knocked at the little door.

Now, after the counsel which Marguerite had given him, after his conversation with René, and after leaving the queen-mother's chamber, though poor Phœbe, like a good genius, had tried to prevent his going, Henry of Navarre had met some worthy Catholic gentlemen, who, saying they were doing him honour, had escorted him to his apartments where a score of Huguenots awaited him, who had rallied round the young prince, and, having once rallied, would not leave him—so strongly, for some hours, had the presentiment of that fatal night weighed on the Louvre. They had remained there, without any-one attempting to disturb them. At last, at the first stroke of the bell of Saint-Germain-l'Auxerrois, which resounded through all hearts like a funeral knell, Tavannes entered, and, in the midst of a deathly silence, announced that King Charles IX desired to speak to Henry.

It was useless to attempt resistance, and no one thought of it. They had heard the ceilings, galleries, and corridors crack beneath the feet of the assembled soldiers who were in the court-yards, as well as in the apartments, to the number of two thousand. Henry, after taking leave of his friends whom he might never see again, followed Tavannes who led him to a small gallery adjacent to the king's apartments, where he left him alone, unarmed, and a prey to mistrust.

The King of Navarre counted out alone, minute by minute, two mortal hours; listening with increasing alarm to the sound of the tocsin and the discharge of fire-arms; seeing through a small window, by the light of the flames and flambeaux, the victims and their assassins pass; understanding nothing of the shrieks of murder and cries of distress; not even suspecting, in spite of his knowledge of Charles IX, the queen-mother, and the Duke de Guise, the horrible drama at this moment enacting.

Henry did not possess physical courage,* but he had better than that—he had moral fortitude. Fearing danger, he yet smiled at, and faced it. But if he could face danger in the field of battle—danger in the open air—danger in the eyes of all, and attended by the noisy harmony of trumpets and the loud and vibrating beat of drums—he now stood unarmed, shut up, immured in darkness which was scarcely sufficient to enable him to see the enemy who might glide towards him, and the weapon that might be raised to strike him.

These two hours were, perhaps, the most anguished of his life.

In the hottest of the tumult, just as Henry was beginning to suspect that, in all probability, this was some organized massacre, a captain came to him, desiring the prince to follow him to the king. As they approached, the door opened, then closed behind them. The captain led Henry to the king, who was in his armoury. When they entered, the king was seated in an armchair, his two hands on the two arms of the seat, and his head on his chest. As they entered, Charles looked up, and on his brow Henry saw perspiration dropping like large beads.

'Good evening, Harry,' said the king roughly. 'La Chastre,* leave us.'

The captain retired, and a profound silence ensued. Henry looked around him uneasily, and saw that he was alone with the king.

Charles suddenly stood up.

'*Mordieu!*' said he, passing his hands through his light brown hair, and wiping his brow at the same time, 'you are glad to be with me, are you not, Harry?'

'Certainly, sire,' replied the King of Navarre, 'I am always happy to be with your Majesty.'

'Happier than if you were down there, eh?' continued Charles, following his own thoughts, rather than replying to Henry's compliment.

'I do not understand, sire,' replied Henry.

'Look out, then, and you will.'

And with a quick gesture Charles moved, or rather sprang towards the window, and drawing his brother-in-law towards him, who became more and more alarmed, he pointed out the horrible silhouettes of the assassins, who, on the deck of a boat, were cutting throats or drowning the victims who were brought to them in a constant stream.

'In the name of Heaven!' cried Henry, 'what is going on to-night?'

'To-night, sir,' replied Charles IX, 'they are ridding me of all the Huguenots. Look down there, over the Hotel de Bourbon, at the smoke and flames: they are the smoke and flames of the admiral's house, which has been fired. Do you see that body, which these good Catholics are dragging on a torn mattress—it is the corpse of the admiral's son-in-law—the carcass of your friend, Teligny.'

'What does it mean?' cried the King of Navarre, feeling vainly by his side for the hilt of his dagger, and trembling equally with shame and anger; for he felt that he was, at the same time, mocked and threatened.

'It means,' cried Charles IX, furious, and turning pale with intense rage, 'that I will no longer have any Huguenots about me. Do you hear me, Henry? Am I king? am I master?'

'Your Majesty——'

'My Majesty kills and massacres at this moment all that is not Catholic, at my pleasure. Are you Catholic?' exclaimed Charles, whose anger rose like an excited sea.

'Sire,' replied Henry, 'do you remember your own words, "What matters the religion of those who serve me well!" '*

'Ah! ah! ah!' cried Charles, bursting into a ferocious laugh—'you ask me if I remember my words, Henry! "*Verba volant,*"* as my sister Margot says. Have not they'—and he pointed to the city with his finger—'served me well, also? Were they not brave in battle, wise in council, deeply loyal? They were all useful subjects—but they were Huguenots, and I want none but Catholics.'

Henry remained silent.

'Well! do you understand me now, Harry?' asked Charles.

'I understand, sire.'

'Well?'

'Well, sire! I do not see why the King of Navarre should not do what so many gentleman and poor folk have done. For if they are all dying, poor unfortunates, it is because the same terms were offered to them which your Majesty now proposes to me, and they refused, as I refuse.'

Charles seized the arm of the young prince, and fixed on him a look whose vacancy suddenly changed into a fierce and savage scowl.

'What!' he said, 'do you believe that I have taken the trouble to offer the alternative of the mass to those whose throats are being cut down there?'

'Sire,' said Henry, disengaging his arm, 'do you intend to die in the religion of your fathers?'

'Yes, *Mordieu!* and you?'

'Well, sire, I will do the same!' replied Henry.

Charles uttered a cry of fierce rage, and with trembling hands picked up his arquebuse which was on the table. Henry, who, leaning against the tapestry, with perspiration streaming from his brow, was however, owing to his presence of mind, calm to all appearance, followed every movement of the terrible king with the anxious gaze of a bird fascinated by a serpent.

Charles cocked his arquebuse, and, stamping his foot with blind rage, cried, as he dazzled Henry's eyes with the polished barrel of the brandished weapon, 'Will you accept the mass?'*

Henry remained mute.

Charles IX shook the vaults of the Louvre with the most terrible oath that ever issued from the lips of man, and grew more livid than before.

'Death, mass, or the Bastille!' he cried, taking aim at the King of Navarre.

'Oh, sire!' exclaimed Henry, 'do you intend to kill me—me, your brother-in-law?'

Henry thus, with his incomparable presence of mind, which was one of the strongest faculties of his organization, avoided giving the answer which the king demanded, for doubtless had his reply been in the negative, Henry would have been a dead man.

As immediately after the last paroxysms of rage there is always the commencement of reaction, Charles IX did not repeat the question he had put to the Prince of Navarre. After a moment's hesitation, during which he uttered a hoarse kind of growl, he turned towards the open window, and aimed at a man who was running along the quay below.

'I must kill someone!' cried Charles IX, ghastly as a corpse, his eyes injected with blood. As he spoke, he fired and struck the man who was running.

Henry uttered a groan.

Then, animated by a frightful ardour, Charles loaded and fired his arquebuse without ceasing, uttering cries of joy every time his aim was true.*

'It is all over with me!' said the King of Navarre to himself. 'When he sees no one else to kill, he will kill me!'

'Well!' said a voice behind the princes suddenly, 'is it done?'

It was Catherine de Medicis, who had entered as the king fired his last shot.

'No, thousand thunders!' said the king, throwing his arquebuse on the floor. 'No, the obstinate blockhead will not consent!'

Catherine made no reply. She turned slowly towards the part of the room where Henry stood as motionless as one of the figures in the tapestry against which he was leaning. She then gave a glance at the king, which seemed to say,—

'Then, why is he alive?'

'He lives!' murmured Charles IX who perfectly understood the glance, and replied to it without hesitation—'he lives, because he is my relative.'

Catherine smiled.

Henry saw the smile, and knew that it was with Catherine he must struggle.

'Madame,' he said to her, 'all this comes from you, I see very well, and nothing from my brother-in-law, Charles. You laid the plan for drawing me into a snare. It was you who made your daughter the bait which was to destroy us all. It was you who separated me from my wife, that she might not see me killed before her eyes.'

'Yes, but it shall not be!' cried another voice, breathless and impassioned which Henry recognized at once, and made Charles start with surprise, and Catherine with rage.

'Marguerite!' exclaimed Henry.

'Margot!' said Charles IX.

'My daughter!' muttered Catherine.

'Sir,' said Marguerite to Henry, 'your last words were an accusation against me, and you were both right and wrong. Right, for I am the means by which they attempted to destroy you. Wrong, for I did not know that you were doomed to destruction. I myself, sir, owe my life to chance—to my mother's not thinking of me, perhaps. But as soon as I learned of the danger you were in I remembered my duty, and a wife's duty is to share the fortunes of her husband. If you are exiled, sire, I will be exiled too; if they imprison you, I will be your fellow-captive; if they kill you, I will die too.'

And she extended her hand to her husband, which he eagerly seized, if not with love, at least with gratitude.

'Oh, my poor Margot!' said Charles, 'you would do better to ask him to become a Catholic!'

'Sire,' replied Marguerite, with that lofty dignity which was so natural to her, 'for your own sake, do not ask any prince of your house to commit a base action.'

Catherine darted a significant glance at Charles.

'Brother,' cried Marguerite, who understood the terrible dumb-show of Catherine as well as Charles IX, 'remember you made him my husband!'

Charles, caught between the imperious gaze of Catherine and Marguerite's supplicating look, hesitated momentarily. Then, after a pause, he said in a whisper to Catherine,—

'Faith, madame, Margot is right. Harry is my brother-in-law.'

'Yes,' was Catherine's reply, in a similar whisper to her son— 'but if he were not——!'

11

THE HAWTHORN IN THE CEMETERY
OF THE INNOCENTS

WHEN she returned to her own apartments, Marguerite vainly endeavoured to guess the word Catherine de Medicis had whispered to Charles IX which had cut short the terrible interview on which hung life and death.

A part of the morning was employed by her in attending to La Mole, and the other in trying to guess the enigma, which her mind could not unravel.

The King of Navarre remained a prisoner in the Louvre, while the pursuit of the Huguenots went on hotter than ever. To the terrible night had succeeded a day of massacre still more horrible. It was no longer the tocsin and bells that sounded, but the *Te Deum*, and the echoes of this joyous carillon, resounding in the midst of fire and slaughter, were far sadder by the light of the sun than had been the knell of the previous night sounding in darkness. This was not all. Strange to say, a hawthorn-tree which had blossomed in the spring, and which had lost its odorous flowers in the month of June, had blossomed anew during the night.* The Catholics, seeing in this a miracle and, by making this miracle popular, made the Deity their accomplice, went in procession, cross and banner at their head, to the Cemetery of the Innocents, where this hawthorn bloomed. This endorsement from Heaven had redoubled the efforts of the assassins, and while the city continued to present in each street and thoroughfare a scene of desolation, the Louvre had become the common tomb for all Protestants who had been there when the signal was given. The King of Navarre, the Prince de Condé, and La Mole, were the only survivors.

Reassured as to La Mole, whose wounds were progressing well, Marguerite was occupied now with one sole idea, which was to save her husband's life which was seriously threatened. No doubt, the first sentiment which moved the wife was one of generous pity for a man for whom, as to the Béarnais, she had sworn, if not love, at least alliance. But there was, beside, another less pure sentiment which had penetrated the queen's heart.

Marguerite was ambitious, and had foreseen almost the certainty of royalty in her marriage with Henry de Bourbon. If she lost him, it was not only a husband, but a throne that she would lose.*

While wrapped in her reflections, she heard a knock at the secret door. She started, for only three persons came by that door—the king, the queen-mother, and the Duke d'Alençon. She half opened the door of the cabinet, made a gesture of silence to Gillonne and La Mole, and then opened the door to her visitor.

It was the Duke d'Alençon. The young prince had not been seen since the evening before. For a moment, Marguerite had the idea of claiming his intercession for the King of Navarre, but a terrible thought restrained her. The marriage had taken place contrary to his wishes. François detested Henry, and had only displayed neutrality towards the Béarnais because he was convinced that Henry and his wife had remained strangers to each other. Marguerite therefore shuddered when she saw the young prince more than she had shuddered on seeing the king, or even the queen-mother. D'Alençon was attired with his usual elegance. his clothes and linen exuded those perfumes which Charles IX despised, but of which the Dukes d'Anjou and d'Alençon made liberal use.*

As he came in, he pressed his pale thin lips against the forehead of his sister. Then sitting down, he began to relate to her the bloody particulars of the night: the lingering and terrible death of the admiral, the instantaneous death of Teligny, pierced by a bullet. He paused and emphasized all the more horrid details of this night, with that love of blood peculiar to himself and his two brothers; and Marguerite did not interrupt him until he had finished.

'It was not simply to tell me this,' she said, 'that you came here, brother?'

The Duke d'Alençon smiled.

'You have something else to say to me?'

'No,' replied the duke. 'I am waiting.'

'Waiting! for what?'

'Did you not tell me, dearest Marguerite,' said the duke, drawing his chair close up to that of his sister, 'that this marriage with the King of Navarre was contracted against your will?'

'Yes, no doubt. I did not know the Prince of Béarn when he was proposed to me as a husband.'

'And after you knew him, did you not say that you felt no love for him?'

'I said so, and it is true.'

'Was it not your opinion that this marriage would make you miserable?'

'My dear François,' said Marguerite, 'when a marriage is not extremely happy, it is always excessively miserable.'

'Well, then, my dear Marguerite, as I said to you—I am waiting.'

'But what are you waiting for?'

'For you to display your joy!'

'What have I to be joyful for?'

'The unexpected opportunity you now have to resume your liberty.'

'My liberty?' replied Marguerite, who was resolved on allowing the prince to disclose all his thoughts.

'Yes, your liberty. You will now be separated from the King of Navarre.'

'Separated!' said Marguerite, fixing her eyes on the young prince.

The Duke d'Alençon tried to sustain his sister's look, but his eyes soon sank with embarrassment.

'Separated!' repeated Marguerite—'and how, brother? for I should like to know exactly what you mean, and by what method you propose to separate us?'

'Why,' murmured the duke, 'Henry is a Huguenot.'

'No doubt; but he made no mystery of his religion, and everyone knew that when we were married.'

'Yes, but since your marriage, sister,' asked the duke, allowing, in spite of himself, a ray of joy to illumine his countenance, 'how has Henry behaved?'

'Why, you know better than anyone, François, for he has spent his days almost perpetually in your society, sometimes at the hunt, sometimes at mall, sometimes at tennis.'

'Yes, his days, no doubt,' replied the duke, 'his days—but his nights?'

Marguerite was silent. It was now her turn to cast down her eyes.

'His nights,' repeated the Duke d'Alençon—'his nights?'*

'Well?' inquired Marguerite, feeling that she should say something in reply.

'Well, he passes them with Madame de Sauve!'

'How do you know that?' exclaimed Marguerite.

'I know it, because I had an interest in knowing it,' replied the young prince, picking at the embroidery of his sleeves.

Marguerite began to understand what Catherine had whispered to Charles, but affected to remain in ignorance.

'Why do you tell me this, brother?' she replied, with a well-affected air of melancholy. 'Was it to remind me that no one here loves me or clings to me, not even those whom nature has given to me as protectors, whom the church has given me as my husband?'

'You are unjust,' said the Duke d'Alençon, drawing his chair still nearer to his sister. 'I love you and protect you!'

'Brother,' said Marguerite, looking at him levelly, 'have you anything to say to me from the queen-mother?'

'I! you are mistaken, sister. I swear to you—what can make you think that?'

'What can make me think that?—why, because you break the intimacy that binds you to my husband, you abandon the cause of the King of Navarre—an alliance with whom——'

'Has now become impossible, sister,' interrupted the Duke d'Alençon.

'But why?'

'Because the king has designs on your husband, and our mother has seen through them all. I allied myself to the Huguenots because I believed the Huguenots were in favour. But now they kill the Huguenots, and in another week there will not remain fifty in the whole kingdom. I held out my hand to the King of Navarre because he was your husband; but now he is not your husband. What can you say to that—you, who are not only the loveliest woman in France, but have the clearest head in the kingdom?'

'Why, I have to say,' replied Marguerite, 'that I know our brother Charles. I saw him yesterday in one of those fits of frenzy, every one of which shortens his life ten years. I have to say that these attacks are, unfortunately, very frequent, and that our brother Charles has probably not very long to live;* and finally, I have to say that the King of Poland has just died,* and the question of electing a prince of the house of France in his stead is much discussed. At such junctures it is not the moment to abandon allies, who, in the moment of struggle, might support us with the strength of a nation and the power of a kingdom.'

'And you!' exclaimed the duke, 'do you not act much more treasonably to me in preferring a stranger to your own house?'

'Explain yourself, François! In what way have I acted treasonably to you?'

'Yesterday, you begged King Charles for the life of the King of Navarre.'

'Well?' said Marguerite.

The duke rose hastily, paced round the chamber twice or thrice with a wild look in his eye.

'Adieu, sister!' he said at last. 'You do not wish to understand me. Do not, therefore, complain of whatever may happen to you.'

Marguerite turned pale, but remained where she was. She saw the Duke d'Alençon leave, without making any attempt to detain him. But scarcely had he entered the corridor than he returned.

'Listen Marguerite,' he said, 'I forgot to mention one thing: to-morrow, at this time, the King of Navarre will be dead.'

Marguerite uttered a cry, for the idea that she was the instrument of assassination caused in her a fear she could not subdue.

'And you will not prevent his death,' she said—'you will not save your best and most faithful ally?'

'Since yesterday, the King of Navarre is no longer my ally.'

'Then who is?'

'M. de Guise. By destroying the Huguenots, M. de Guise has become the king of the Catholics.'*

'And is it a son of Henry II who recognizes as his king a duke of Lorraine?'

'You will not see things in their true light, Marguerite.'

'I confess that I seek in vain to read your thoughts.'

'Sister, you are of as good a house as the Princess de Porcian. De Guise is no more immortal than the King of Navarre. Well, Marguerite, suppose that Monsieur is elected King of Poland. That makes me King of France, and you, my sister, shall reign with me, and be Queen of the Catholics.'

Marguerite was overwhelmed at the depths of the views of this youth, whom no one at court even thought possessed common sense.*

'There is only one thing which can prevent this splendid plan from succeeding, brother,' said she, rising as she spoke.

'And what is that?'

'That I do not love the Duke de Guise.'

'And whom, then, do you love?'

'No one.'*

D'Alençon looked at Marguerite with the astonishment of a man who, in his turn, does not understand, and left the apartment, pressing his cold hand to his forehead, which ached to bursting.

Marguerite was alone and thoughtful when Queen Catherine sent to know if she would accompany her in a pilgrimage to the hawthorn at the Cemetery of the Innocents.

She sent word that if they prepared a horse she would most readily accompany their Majesties.

A few minutes later, the page came to tell her that all was ready. After a sign to Gillonne to take care of La Mole, she went forth.

The king, the queen-mother, Tavannes, and the principal Catholics were already mounted. Marguerite cast a rapid glance over the group, which was composed of about twenty persons. The King of Navarre was not of the party.

Madame de Sauve was there, and she exchanged a glance with her, which convinced the Queen of Navarre that her husband's mistress had something to tell her.

As they proceeded, the people shouted and cried, 'God save the King! Long live the Mass! Death to the Huguenots!'

When they reached the top of the Rue des Prouvelles, they met a group of men who were dragging a carcass without a head. It was the admiral. The men were going to hang him by the feet at Montfaucon.*

They entered the Cemetery of The Holy Innocents, and the clergy, forewarned of the visit of the king and the queen-mother, awaited their Majesties to harangue them.

Madame de Sauve took advantage of a moment when Catherine was listening to the speech that was being made to approach the Queen of Navarre and beg leave to kiss her hand. Marguerite extended her arm towards her, and Madame de Sauve, as she kissed the queen's hand, secretly put a small piece of paper up her sleeve.

Quick and well managed as was Madame de Sauve's action, Catherine saw it and turned round at the moment when the maid of honour was kissing Marguerite's hand.

The two women saw that look, which struck them like lightning, but both remained unmoved. But Madame de Sauve left Marguerite, and resumed her place near Catherine.

When the address was finished, Catherine beckoned smilingly to the Queen of Navarre who went towards her.

'Ah, daughter,' said the queen-mother, in her Italian patois, 'so you are on intimate terms with Madame de Sauve?'

Marguerite smiled in turn, but gave her lovely countenance the bitterest expression she could as she said,—

'Yes, mother. The serpent came to bite my hand!'

'Ah, ah!' replied Catherine, with a smile, 'you are jealous, I think!'

'You are mistaken, madame,' replied Marguerite. 'I am no more jealous of the King of Navarre than the King of Navarre is jealous of me. But I know how to distinguish my friends from my enemies. I like those who like me, and detest those who hate me. If not, madame, would I be your daughter?'

Catherine smiled so as to make Marguerite understand that, if she had had any suspicion, it had vanished.

At this moment other pilgrims arrived. The Duke de Guise came with a troop of gentlemen, all warm still from the recent carnage. They escorted a litter, richly covered with tapestry, which stopped in front of the king.

'The Duchess de Nevers!' cried Charles IX, 'let that lovely and pure Catholic come and receive our compliments. Why, they tell me, cousin, that from your window you made war on the Huguenots, and killed one with a stone.'

The Duchess de Nevers blushed bright red.

'Sire,' she said quietly and, kneeling before the king, added, 'on the contrary, I had the good fortune to rescue a wounded Catholic.'

'Good—good, cousin! there are two ways of serving me.'

During this time the people again cried, 'God save the King! Long live Guise! Long live the Mass!'

'Shall you return to the Louvre with us, Henriette?' inquired the queen-mother of the beautiful duchess.

'No, madame, unless your Majesty desire it; for I have business in the city with her Majesty the Queen of Navarre.'

'And what are you going to do together?' inquired Catherine.

'To see some very rare and curious Greek books found at an old Protestant pastor's, and which have been taken to the Tower of Saint Jacques la Boucherie,'* replied Marguerite.

'You would do much better to see the last Huguenot flung from the top of Pont-aux-Meuniers* into the Seine,' said Charles IX, 'that is the place for all good Frenchmen.'

'We will go, if it be your Majesty's desire,' replied the Duchess de Nevers.

Catherine cast a suspicious look on the two young women. Marguerite, who had her eyes wide open, did not miss it, and turning round uneasily, looked about her.

Her unease, assumed or real, did not escape Catherine.

'What are you looking for?'

'I am seeking—I do not see——' she replied.

'Whom are you seeking?'

'La Sauve,' said Marguerite, 'she must have returned to the Louvre.'

'Did I not say you were jealous?' said Catherine, in her daughter's ear. 'Oh, *bestia!** Come—come, Henriette,' she added, 'begone, and take the Queen of Navarre with you.'

Marguerite went on pretending to look around her; then turning towards her friend, she said, in a whisper,—

'Take me away, quickly. I have matters of great importance to discuss with you.'

The duchess saluted the king and queen-mother respectfully, and then, bowing to the Queen of Navarre,—

'Will your Majesty be good enough to ride in my litter?'

'Willingly, only you will have to take me back to the Louvre.'

'My litter, like my servants and myself, are at your Majesty's disposal.'

Queen Marguerite climbed into the litter, while Catherine and her gentlemen returned to the Louvre. On the way, she spoke constantly to the king, pointing several times to Madame de Sauve; and each time the king laughed—as Charles IX did laugh—that is, with a laugh which was more sinister than a threat.

As for Marguerite, as soon as she felt the litter in motion, and had no longer to fear the searching gaze of Catherine, she quickly drew from her sleeve the note from Madame de Sauve, and read as follows:—

'I have received orders to send to–night to the King of Navarre two keys. One is for the chamber in which he is shut up, and the other is the key to my chamber. When I reach my apartment, I am enjoined to keep him there until six o'clock in the morning.

'Let your Majesty reflect—let your Majesty decide. Let your Majesty esteem my life as nothing.'

'There is now no doubt,' murmured Marguerite. 'The poor woman is the tool they wish to use to destroy us all. But we will see if Queen Margot, as my brother Charles calls me, is so easily to be made a nun of.'

'And what is your letter about?' inquired the Duchess de Nevers.

'Ah! duchess, I have so many things to say to you!' replied Marguerite, tearing the note into a thousand pieces, and scattering them to the winds.

12

MUTUAL CONFIDENCE

'BUT, first, where are we going?' asked Marguerite. 'Not to the Pont aux Meuniers, I suppose—I have seen enough slaughter since yesterday.'

'I have taken the liberty to conduct your Majesty——'

'First and foremost, my Majesty requests you to forget my Majesty—you were taking me——'

'To the Hotel de Guise, unless you decide otherwise.'

'No, no, let us go there, Henriette. The duke and your husband are not there.'

'Oh, no!' cried the duchess, her bright eyes sparkling with joy, 'neither my husband, my brother-in-law, nor anyone else. I am free—free as air—free as a bird; free, my queen! Do you understand the happiness there is in that word?—free! I come, I go, I command. Ah, poor queen, you are not free—you sigh.'

'You come, you go, you command. Is that all? Is that all there is to liberty?'

'Your Majesty promised me that you would begin our mutual confidence.'

'Again, "your Majesty!" I shall get cross with you, Henriette. Have you forgotten our agreement?'

'No; your respectful servant in public—in private, your scatter-brained confidante. Is it not so, Marguerite?'

'Yes, yes,' said the queen, smiling.

'No family rivalry, no treachery in love; all fair and open. An offensive and defensive alliance, for the sole purpose of seeking, and, if we can, seizing, that ephemeral thing, called happiness.'

'Just so, duchess. Let us again seal the compact with a kiss.'

And the two beautiful women—the one so glowing, so fair, so animated, the other so pale, so full of melancholy,—united their lips as they had united their thoughts.

'What is the news?' asked the duchess, fixing her eyes upon Marguerite.

'There has been a great deal of news these last two days.'

'Oh, I mean love, not politics. When we are as old as your mother, Catherine, we will think of politics, but at twenty, let us think of something else. Tell me, are you *really* married?'

'To whom?'

'Ah, you reassure me.'

'Well, Henriette, what reassures you, alarms me. Duchess, I must be married.'

'When?'

'To-morrow.'

'Oh, *pauvre* Marguerite! must you really?'

'Absolutely.'

'*Mordi!* as an acquaintance of mine says, that is very sad.'

'You know someone who says "*Mordi*"?' asked Marguerite, with a smile.

'Yes.'

'And who is this acquaintance?'

'You ask questions instead of answering them. Finish your story, and then I will begin mine.'

'In a word, it is this. The King of Navarre is in love, but not with me; I am not in love, and certainly not with him;* yet we must both of us change, or seem to change, before to-morrow.'

'Well, you change, and he will soon do the same.'

'That is quite impossible, for I am less inclined to change than ever.'

'Only with respect to your husband, I hope.'

'Henriette, I have a scruple.'

'A scruple! about what?'

'Of religion. Do you distinguish between Huguenots and Catholics?'

'In politics?'

'Yes.'

'Of course.'

'And in love?'

'*Ma chère!* we women are such heathens that we admit every kind of sect, and recognize many gods.'

'Who are all rolled into one, eh?'

'Yes,' replied the duchess, her eyes sparkling: 'he is called *Eros*, *Cupido*, *Amor*.* He has a quiver on his back, wings on his shoulders, and a bandage over his eyes. *Mordi*, long live devotion!'

'You have a peculiar method of praying; you throw stones at Huguenots.'

'Let them talk. Ah, Marguerite! how the finest ideas, the noblest actions, are spoilt in passing through the mouths of the vulgar.'

'The vulgar! why, it was my brother Charles who congratulated you on your exploits.'

'Your brother Charles is a mighty hunter, who sounds his horn all day, which makes him very thin.* I reject his compliments; besides, I gave him his answer. Did you hear what I said?'

'No; you spoke too quietly.'

'So much the better. I shall have more news to tell you. Now, then, finish your story, Marguerite.'

'Why—'

'Well?'

'Why, in truth,' said the queen, laughing, 'if the stone my brother spoke of is a fact, I don't think I want to tell you my story at all.'

'Ah!' cried Henriette, 'you have chosen a Huguenot. Well, to settle your conscience, I promise you to choose one myself at the first opportunity.'

'Ah, you have chosen a Catholic, then?'

'*Mordi!*' replied the duchess.

'I see.'

'And what is this Huguenot of yours?'

'I have not adopted him. He is nothing, and probably never will be anything to me.'

'But what is he like? You can tell me that; you know how curious I am about such things.'

'A poor young fellow, beautiful as Benvenuto Cellini's "Nisus,"* who took refuge in my apartment.'

'Oh!—of course without any prompting from you?'

'Do not laugh, Henriette. At this very moment, he is between life and death.'

'He is ill, then?'

'He is dangerously wounded.'

'A wounded Huguenot is very disagreeable, especially in these times. And what have you done with this wounded Huguenot, who is not, and never will be, anything to you?'

'He is hiding in my closet: I intend to save him.'

'He is young, handsome, and wounded—you hide him, and wish to save him. He will be very ungrateful if he does not show himself very grateful.'

'He is already, I fear, more grateful than I could wish.'

'And this poor young man interests you?'

'Only for humanity's sake.'

'Ah! humanity is precisely the virtue that undoes all us women.'

'Yes, but the king, the Duke d'Alençon, my mother, or even my husband, may at any moment enter the apartment——'

'Ay, you want me to hide your Huguenot, so long as he is ill, on condition I send him back to you when he is cured?'

'No,' said Marguerite, 'I am not thinking that far ahead. But if you could conceal the poor fellow, if you could preserve the life I have saved, I should be most grateful. You are free at the Hotel de Guise; you have no one watching you. Besides, behind your chamber there is a little room like mine, which no one is allowed to enter. Lend me this cabinet for my Huguenot, and, when he is cured, open the cage, and let the bird fly away.'

'There is only one difficulty, my dear: the cage is already occupied.'

'What, have *you* saved somebody too?'

'That is exactly what I answered your brother with.'

'Ah! that's why you spoke so quietly and why I could not hear you.'

'Listen, Marguerite: my story is no less poetic and amazing than yours. After I left you six of my guards, I returned with the rest to the Hotel de Guise. I was looking at a house across the street that was on fire, when I heard the voices of men swearing, and women crying. I went out on the balcony, and saw, in the thickest of the fight, a complete hero—I like heroes—an Ajax-Telamon;* I stood trembling at every blow aimed at him, and at every thrust he dealt, until, all of a sudden, my hero disappeared.'

'How?'

'Struck down by a stone an old woman threw at him. Then, like the son of Crœsus,* I found my voice, and screamed, "Help! help!" My guards went out, picked him up, and carried him to my apartment.'

'Alas! I can the better understand this story because it is so nearly my own.'

'With this difference, that as I have served the king and the Catholic religion in helping him, I have no reason to send M. Annibal de Coconnas away.'

'His name is Annibal de Coconnas!' said Marguerite, laughing.

'A terrible name, is it not? Well, he who bears it is worthy of it. Put on your mask, for we have arrived.'

'Why put on my mask?'

'Because I wish to show you my hero.'*

'Is he handsome?'

'He seemed so to me during the conflict. This morning, I must confess, he did not look quite as impressive as last night, by the light of the flames. But I do not think you will find great fault with him.'

'So my protégé cannot hide at the Hotel de Guise? I am sorry for it, for that is the last place that they would look for a Huguenot.'

'Oh, no; your Huguenot shall come. He shall have one corner of the closet, and Annibal the other.'

'But when they recognize each other, they will fight.'

'Oh, there is no danger of that. M. de Coconnas has a cut down the face that prevents him from seeing very well and your Huguenot is wounded in the chest. Anyway, you have only to tell him to keep quiet on the subject of religion, and all will go well.'

'So be it.'

'It's a bargain. Now let us go in.'

'Thanks,' said Marguerite, pressing her friend's hand.

'Here, madame,' said the duchess, 'you are again "Your Majesty"; allow me, then, to do the honours of the Hotel de Guise, as befits the Queen of Navarre.'

And the duchess, descending from the litter, bent her knee as she aided Marguerite to alight. Then pointing to the gate guarded by two soldiers, arquebuse in hand, she followed the queen respectfully through it.

On reaching her chamber, the duchess closed the door, and, calling to her waiting-woman, a full-blooded Sicilian, said to her, in Italian,—

'How is M. le Comte?'

'Improving,' replied she.

'What is he doing?'

'At this moment, madame, he is taking some refreshment.'

'It is always a good sign,' said Marguerite, 'when the appetite returns.'

'Ah, I forgot you were a pupil of Ambroise Paré. Leave us, Mica.'

'Why did you send her away?'

'So that she can keep watch.'

'Now,' said the duchess, 'will you go in to see him, or shall I ask him to come here?'

'Neither the one nor the other. I wish to see him without his seeing me.'

'Does it matter? You have your mask.'

'He may recognize me by my hands, my hair, my ring.'

'How cautious we have become, since we've been married!' Marguerite smiled.

'Well,' said the duchess, 'I see only one way.'

'What is that?'

'To look through the keyhole.'

'Take me to the door, then.'

The duchess led Marguerite to a door hung with tapestry. Lifting it, she applied her eye to the keyhole.

'It is as you could wish. He is sitting at table, with his face turned towards us.'

The queen took her friend's place. Coconnas was, as the duchess had said, sitting at a groaning table, and, despite his wounds, was doing ample justice to the good things before him.

'Ah, *mon Dieu!*' cried Marguerite.

'What is the matter?' asked the duchess.

'Impossible!—no!—yes!—it's him!'

'Who?'

'Hush!' said Marguerite, 'the man who pursued my Huguenot into my apartment, and would have killed him in my arms! Oh, Henriette, how fortunate he did not see me.'

'Well, then, you have seen him in battle. Is he not handsome?'

'I do not know,' said Marguerite, 'for I was looking more at the fugitive he was pursuing.'

'What is his name?'

'You will not mention it to the count?'

'No.'

'Lérac de la Mole.'

'And what do you think of him now?'

'Of La Mole?'

'Of Coconnas.'

'*Ma foi!*' said Marguerite, 'I confess I think——'

She stopped.

'Come, come,' said the duchess, 'I see you cannot forgive him for wounding your Huguenot.'

'Why, so far,' said Marguerite, smiling, 'my Huguenot owes him nothing. The cut he gave him on his face——'

'They are quits, then, and we can reconcile them. Send me your wounded man.'

'Not now—by-and-by.'

'When?'

'When you have found yours another hiding place.'

'Where!'

Marguerite looked meaningly at her friend, who, after a moment's silence, laughed.

'So be it,' said the duchess. 'Alliance firmer than ever!'

'True friendship for ever,' replied the Queen.

'And the pass-word, in case we need each other?'

'The triple name of your triple god, "*Eros, Cupido, Amor.*"'

And the two princesses separated after one more embrace, after pressing each other's hand for the twentieth time.

13

HOW THERE ARE KEYS THAT OPEN DOORS THEY ARE NOT MEANT FOR

THE Queen of Navarre, on her return to the Louvre, found Gillonne in a state of great excitement. Madame de Sauve had come in her absence. She had brought a key sent her by the queen-mother. It was the key of the room in which Henry was confined. It was obvious that the queen-mother wished the Béarnais to pass the night in Madame de Sauve's apartment.

Marguerite took the key, and turned it round and round in her hand. She made Gillonne repeat Madame de Sauve's each and every word, weighed them, letter by letter, and at length thought she saw through Catherine's plan.

She took pen and ink, and wrote,—

'Instead of going to Madame de Sauve to-night, come to the Queen of Navarre.—MARGUERITE.'

She rolled up the paper, put it in the hollow shank of the key, and ordered Gillonne to slip the key under the king's door as soon as it was dark.

This done, Marguerite thought of the wounded man, closed all the doors, entered his room, and, to her great surprise, found La Mole dressed in all his clothes, torn and bloodstained as they were.

On seeing her he strove to rise, but could not stand, and fell back upon the sofa which had served for his bed.

'What is the matter, sir?' asked Marguerite; 'and why do you disobey the orders of your physician? I advised rest, and instead of following my advice you do the opposite.'

'Oh, madame,' said Gillonne, 'it is not my fault. I begged M. le comte not to commit this folly, but he declares that nothing shall keep him any longer at the Louvre.'

'Leave the Louvre!' said Marguerite, astonished. 'Why, it is impossible—you can scarcely stand. You are pale and weak. Your knees tremble. Only a few hours ago, the wound in your shoulder still bled.'

'Madame,' said the young man, 'as earnestly as I thanked your Majesty for having saved my life, as earnestly do I pray you to allow me to go.'

'I scarcely know what to call such resolution,' said Marguerite, 'it is worse than ingratitude.'

'Oh,' cried La Mole, clasping his hands, 'do not think I am ungrateful; my gratitude will end only with my life.'

'It will not last long, then,' said Marguerite, moved at these words, the sincerity of which it was impossible to doubt. 'For your wounds will open, and you will die from loss of blood, or you will be recognized as a Huguenot, and killed, before you go fifty yards in the street.'

'But I must leave the Louvre,' murmured La Mole.

'Must?' returned Marguerite, fixing her clear, honest gaze upon him—'ah, yes: forgive me, I understand. No doubt there is someone who is waiting anxiously for news of you. I appreciate the feeling, and blame myself for not having thought of it before; I should have attended to your mind as well as to your body.'

'Madame,' said La Mole, 'you are mistaken—I am wellnigh alone in the world, and absolutely so in Paris. My pursuer is the first man I have spoken to in this city; your Majesty the first lady who has addressed me.'

'Then,' said Marguerite, 'why do you want to go?'

'Because,' replied La Mole, 'last night you had no rest, and because to-night——'

Marguerite blushed.

'Gillonne,' said she, 'it is time to take the key to the King of Navarre.'

Gillonne smiled and left the room.

'But,' continued Marguerite, 'if you are alone, without friends, what will you do?'

'Madame, I soon shall have friends, for while I was pursued, I saw the spirit of my mother guiding me to the Louvre, and I vowed, if I were spared, to abjure. Heaven has done more than save my life—it has sent me one of its angels to make life dear to me.'

'But you cannot walk. You will faint before you go a hundred yards.'

'Madame, I have tried to walk round this room. I do so slowly, it is true, but, once outside the Louvre, I will take my chance.'

Marguerite leaned her head on her hand, and reflected for an instant.

'And the King of Navarre,' said she emphatically—'you do not speak of him? In changing your religion, have you also changed your desire to enter his service?'

'Madame,' returned La Mole, 'I know that his Majesty runs a great risk at present, and that all your influence will scarce be enough to save him.'

'What!' said Marguerite, 'how do you know that?'

'Madame,' returned La Mole, after some hesitation, 'one can hear everything in this room.'

'True,' said Marguerite to herself, 'M. de Guise told me so before.'

'Well,' added she, aloud, 'what did you hear?'

'In the first place, the conversation between your Majesty and your brother.'

'With François?' said Marguerite.

'With the Duke d'Alençon. And after you left, I heard Gillonne and Madame de Sauve.'

'And it is thcsc two conversations———?'

'Yes, madame. Married scarcely a week, you love your husband; to-night he will come, in his turn, in the same way that the Duke d'Alençon, and Madame de Sauve have come; he will talk with you of his affairs. I do not wish to hear; I might be indiscreet—I will give myself no chance of being so.'

At the last words, and their manner, Marguerite understood everything.

'Ah!' said she, 'you heard everything that has been said from this room?'

'Yes, madame.'

These words were uttered with a sigh.

'And you wish to leave to-night, to avoid hearing any more?'

'This very moment, if it please your Majesty.'

'Poor man!' said Marguerite, with an accent of tender pity.

Astonished at so gentle an answer, when he expected an abrupt reply, La Mole raised his head timidly—his eyes met those of the queen and remained caught in her clear, magnetic gaze.

'So you are incapable of keeping a secret, M. de la Mole?' said the queen, who, seated in a large chair, could watch La Mole's face whilst her own remained in the shadow.

'Madame,' said La Mole, 'I do not trust myself, and the happiness of another gives me pain.'

'The happiness of whom? Ah, yes—of the King of Navarre! Poor Henry!'

'You see,' cried La Mole passionately, 'he is happy.'

'Happy?'

'Yes, for your Majesty pities him.'

Marguerite played with the golden tassels of her alms-purse.

'So you will not see the King of Navarre—you are quite resolved?'

'I fear I should be an embarrassment to his Majesty at present.'

'But the Duke d'Alençon, my brother?'

'Oh, no!' cried La Mole, 'the Duke d'Alençon even less than the King of Navarre.'

'Why is that?' asked Marguerite.

'Because, although I am already too bad a Huguenot to be a

faithful servant of the King of Navarre, I am not a sufficiently good Catholic to be friends with the Duke d'Alençon and M. de Guise.'

Marguerite lowered her eyes. What La Mole had said struck to her very heart.

At this juncture Gillonne returned; Marguerite looked at her questioningly, and Gillonne, in the same manner, answered in the affirmative: the King of Navarre had received the key.

Marguerite turned her eyes towards La Mole, who stood, his head drooping on his chest, sad, pale, grief-laden, as one suffering alike in mind and in body.

'M. de la Mole is so proud,' said she, 'that I hesitate to make him an offer I fear he will refuse.'

La Mole rose, and advanced a step towards Marguerite, but a feeling of faintness came over him, and he clutched at a table to save himself from falling.

'You see, monsieur,' cried Marguerite, supporting him in her arms, 'that I am still necessary to you.'

'Oh, yes!' murmured La Mole, 'as necessary as the air I breathe—as the light of heaven.'

At this moment three knocks were heard at the outer door.

'Do you hear, madame?' cried Gillonne, alarmed.

'Already!' exclaimed Marguerite.

'Shall I let them in?'

'Wait! it is the King of Navarre, perhaps.'

'Oh, madame!' cried La Mole, given new strength by these words, which the queen hoped had been heard by Gillonne alone, 'I implore—I beg you, let me depart. Oh! you do not answer. I will tell you everything, and then you will drive me away, I hope.'

'Be silent,' said Marguerite, who found an indescribable charm in the reproaches of the young man—'be silent.'

'Madame,' replied La Mole, who did not find the anger he expected in the voice of the queen—'madame, I tell you again, I can hear everything from this room. Oh, do not condemn me to tortures more cruel than the executioner could inflict——'

'Silence!' said Marguerite.

'Oh, you are merciless! you will not listen. You must understand that I——'

'Silence! I tell you,' said Marguerite, putting over his mouth her white and perfumed hand which he seized and pressed eagerly to his lips.

'But——' murmured he.

'Be silent!—who is this unruly subject that refuses to obey his queen?'

Then hastily leaving the room, she pressed her hand to her heart, as if to quieten it.

'And now, open the door, Gillonne.'

Gillonne left the apartment, and a moment later the fine, intelligent, but at present rather anxious face of the King of Navarre appeared.

'You sent for me, madame?'

'Yes, sir. Your Majesty received my letter?'

'And not without some surprise, I confess,' said Henry, looking round with a distrust, which, however, almost instantly vanished from his mind.

'And not without suspicion?' added Marguerite.

'I admit it! But still surrounded as I am by deadly foes, by friends still more dangerous, perhaps, than my declared enemies, I remembered that one evening I saw noble generosity radiant in your eyes—the night of our marriage: that on another evening I saw courage glance from them—that was yesterday, the day fixed for my death.'

'Well, monsieur!' said Marguerite, smiling, while Henry seemed striving to read her heart.

'Well, madame,' returned the king, 'thinking of these things, I said to myself, when I read your letter: Without friends, for he is a disarmed prisoner, the King of Navarre has only one means of dying nobly, of dying a death that will be recorded in history. It is to die betrayed by his wife; and I have come——'

'Sire,' replied Marguerite, 'you will change your tune when you learn that all this is the work of a woman who loves you, and whom you love.'

Henry started at these words, and his piercing grey eyes were fixed on the queen with earnest curiosity.

'Oh, reassure yourself, sire,' said the queen, smiling, 'I am not that person.'

'But, madame,' said Henry, '*you* sent me this key, and this is *your* writing.'

'It is my writing, I confess; but the key is a different matter: be content with knowing that it passed through the hands of four women before it reached you.'

'Four women?'

'Yes,' said Marguerite; 'Queen Catherine, Madame de Sauve, Gillonne, and myself.'

Henry pondered this enigma.

'Let us speak plainly,' said Marguerite. 'Report says your Majesty has consented to abjure. Is this true?'

'Report is somewhat premature; I have not yet consented.'

'But your mind is made up?'

'That is to say I am deliberating. At twenty, and almost a king, there are many things that are well worth a mass.'*

'Life, for instance?'

Henry smiled.

'You are not telling me everything,' said the queen.

'I have reservations which concern my allies; and you know we are no more than allies as yet. But if you were both my ally and——'

'And your wife, sire?'

'*Ma foi!* yes, and my wife——'

'What then?'

'Why, then, it might be different, and I perhaps might resolve to remain King of the Huguenots, as they call me. But, as it is, I must settle for staying alive.'

Marguerite looked at her husband in so odd a way that it would have awakened suspicion in a mind less acute than his.

'And are you quite sure you can manage that?' asked she.

'Why, almost; but, you know, in this world, nothing is certain.'

'Truly, your Majesty shows such moderation, such disinterestedness, that after having renounced both your crown and your religion, you may confidently be expected to satisfy the hopes of some people and renounce your alliance with a daughter of France!'

There was a meaning in these words that sent a thrill through Henry's whole frame. But containing his emotion, he said,—

'Remember, madame, that at this moment I am not my own master. I shall therefore do what the King of France orders me. As for myself, were I to be consulted on this question, affecting as it does my throne, my honour, and my life, rather than build my future hopes on this forced marriage of ours, I would enter a monastery or turn gamekeeper.'

Such calm resignation, this renunciation of the world, alarmed Marguerite. She thought, perhaps, a dissolution of the marriage had been arranged between Charles IX, Catherine, and her husband, and the young queen felt her ambition attacked.

'Your Majesty,' said Marguerite, with a mixture of mockery and scorn, 'has no confidence in the star that shines over the head of every king!'

'Ah,' said Henry, 'I cannot see mine; it is hidden by the storm that now threatens me!'

'And suppose the breath of a woman were to dispel these looming clouds, and make the star reappear, brilliant as ever?'

'That would be difficult.'

'Do you deny the existence of this woman?'

'No, I deny her power.'

'You mean her will?'

'I said her power, and I repeat, her power. A woman is only powerful when love and interest are combined within her in equal degrees: if either sentiment predominates, she is, like Achilles,* vulnerable. And in the case of the woman in question, if I am not mistaken, I cannot rely on her love.'

Marguerite made no reply.

'Listen,' said Henry. 'At the last stroke of the bell of Saint-Germain-l'Auxerrois, you most likely thought of regaining your liberty which was sacrificed to the interests of your party. For myself, I thought of saving my life: that was the essential point. We lose Navarre in the process, but what is that compared with your being able to speak aloud in your apartment, which you dared not do when you had someone listening to you in the next room?'

Marguerite could not refrain from smiling. The king rose and prepared to return to his own apartment, for it was eleven, and everybody at the Louvre was, or seemed to be, asleep.

Henry advanced towards the door, then, as if suddenly remembering the reason for his visit,—

'By the way, madame!' said he. 'Did you not have something to tell me? or did you wish to give me an opportunity of thanking you for saving my life? You came, I confess, like a goddess of antiquity, just in time to save me.'

'What!' exclaimed Marguerite, seizing her husband's arm—'do you not see that nothing is saved, neither your liberty, your crown, nor your life? Poor, blind Henry! Did you see nothing in my letter but an amorous rendezvous?'

'I confess, madame,' said Henry, surprised—'I confess——'

Marguerite shrugged her shoulders contemptuously.

At this instant a strange sound was heard, like a sharp scratching at the secret door.

Marguerite led the king to it.

'Listen,' said she.

'The queen-mother is leaving her apartments,' said a trembling voice outside, which Henry instantly recognized as that of Madame de Sauve.

'Where is she going?' asked Marguerite.

'She is coming to see your Majesty.'

And then the rustling of silk indicated that Madame de Sauve was hurrying rapidly away.

'Oh!' said Henry.

'I was sure of this,' said Marguerite.

'And I,' replied Henry, 'feared it, as this will prove.'

And half opening his doublet of black velvet, he showed the queen that he had beneath it a shirt of mail, and a long Milan blade, which glittered in his hand.

'They are unnecessary,' cried Marguerite. 'Quick, sire! hide your dagger. It's only the queen-mother.'

'Yet——'

'Silence! I hear her.'

And she whispered something in Henry's ear, who immediately took cover behind the curtains of the bed.

Marguerite sprang into the closet where La Mole was waiting for her, and pressing his hand in the darkness,—'Silence,' said she, approaching her lips so near that he felt her breath—'not a word!'

Then returning to her chamber, she tore off her head-dress, cut the lace of her dress with her dagger, and sprang into bed. She was just in time—the key turned in the lock. Catherine had a key for every door in the Louvre.

'Who is there?' cried Marguerite, as Catherine placed on guard at the door the four gentlemen by whom she was attended.

And, as if frightened by this intrusion into her chamber, Marguerite sprang out of bed in a white dressing-gown, and then, seeming to recognize Catherine, came to kiss her hand with so well-feigned a surprise that the wily Florentine herself was deceived.

14

THE SECOND NIGHT OF THE WEDDING

THE queen-mother surveyed the chamber with eager, curious eyes. But the sight of Marguerite's velvet slippers at the foot of the bed, her clothes thrown carelessly over chairs plus the well-feigned drowsiness with which she endeavoured to open her eyes, convinced Catherine that she had really roused her daughter from her slumbers.

So smiling the complacent smile of one whose plan of attack has been successful, she drew a chair towards her, saying,—

'Let us sit down, my child, and have a little talk together.'

'I am all ears, madame.'

'It is time,' said Catherine, shutting her eyes and speaking with that slowness peculiar to persons of great reflection or dissimulation—'it is time, I say, daughter, that you knew how ardently your brother and myself wish to see you happy.'

This was a somewhat alarming preamble for those who were acquainted with Catherine's real disposition.

'What can she be about to say?' thought Marguerite.

'Certainly,' continued the Florentine, 'in finding you a husband, we fulfilled one of those acts of policy often demanded for the interest of the kingdom and of those who govern it; but I must honestly confess to you, my poor child, that we did not expect that the indifference shown by the King of Navarre for one so young, so lovely and fascinating as yourself, would have been so obstinately persisted in.'

Marguerite stood up, and folding her dressing-gown around her, curtseyed with ceremonious respect to her mother.

'It was not until to-night (otherwise I should have paid you an earlier visit) that I heard that your husband is far from showing you those attentions you have a right to claim, not merely as a beautiful woman, but as a princess of France.'

Marguerite sighed gently, and Catherine, encouraged by this mute appeal, proceeded.

'I am even assured the King of Navarre has a *liaison* with one of my maids-of-honour, and that he openly admits his disgraceful passion for her. Now, that he should despise the affection of the superior woman we have bestowed upon him is unfortunately one of those evils which, powerful as we are, we have no means of remedying, although the meanest gentlemen of our court would quickly demand satisfaction for so great an insult.'

Marguerite lowered her eyes. Her mother continued,—

'For some time past, daughter, I have been informed by your red and swollen eyes, as well as the bitterness of your remarks against Madame de Sauve, that, try as you would, your poor wounded heart is not content to bleed and break in silent sorrow.'

Marguerite started—a slight movement shook the curtains of the bed, but, fortunately, it passed unnoticed by Catherine.

'Knowing all this, my beloved child,' said she, with increased gentleness and affection, 'it follows that a tender parent would seek to apply healing balm to the wound your heart has received. Have not those who, hoping to secure your happiness, dictated your marriage, but who now, to their deep regret, discover that the coarse-minded boor on whom they bestowed your hand, neglects your beauty and despises your charms, and is only waiting for the first favourable chance of separating himself from our family, and expelling you from his house—have not, I ask you, those same kind and watchful friends the right to protect your interests by dividing them from his, so that your future prospects may offer a vista of greatness better suited to your illustrious descent and surpassing merits?'

'I beg you, madame,' replied Marguerite, 'to pardon my

presumption in venturing to remark (after observations so replete with maternal love, and so calculated to fill me with joy and pride, as those you have just uttered), that despite everything your Majesty so rightly says, the King of Navarre is my husband.'

Catherine started with rage—then drawing closer to Marguerite she said, 'He your husband? Do the few words pronounced over you by a priest warrant your calling him husband? Ah, my child! such a state of things is a desecration, not a consecration of the marriage ceremony. Were you Madame de Sauve, you might make that assertion. But, wholly contrary to our expectations, directly we bestowed your hand on Henry of Navarre, he seemed more than indifferent towards you, permitting you to hold the empty title of wife,* while another engrossed his time and affections. Come with me. Even as we speak,' said Catherine, raising her voice—'this key is opening the door of Madame de Sauve's apartment—come with me and you will see——'

'Oh, not so loud, madame!—not so loud, I beseech you!' said Marguerite, 'for not only are you mistaken, but——'

'But, what?'

'I fear you will wake my husband!'

As she said these words, Marguerite rose gracefully, her white gown fluttering loosely around her, while the large open sleeves displayed her matchless hands and arms. Carrying one of the rose-coloured tapers towards the bed, she gently drew back the curtain, and, smiling at her mother, pointed to the King of Navarre, who, stretched in easy negligence upon the couch, seemed buried in profound repose.

Pale and wonder-stricken, her body thrown back as though to avoid some abyss that had opened at her feet, Catherine uttered not a cry, but a kind of savage yell.

'You perceive, madame,' said Marguerite, 'you were misinformed.'

Catherine's gaze went from her daughter to the sleeping king, before settling on the face of Marguerite which bore unflinchingly the searching glances of the queen-mother who bit her thin lips with impotent rage at finding herself outmanœuvred. After permitting Catherine to contemplate a picture as hateful to her as the head of Medusa,* Marguerite let the curtain fall, and walking on tiptoe back to her chair, resumed her place beside Catherine, saying, 'What is your opinion now, madame?'

The Florentine again fixed her piercing looks on Marguerite, as though she would read her thoughts. But, baffled and disconcerted by the calm placidity of her daughter's face, she rose in deep and concentrated fury, and saying, 'I have no further opinion than the one I have already expressed!' hurriedly left the apartment.

No sooner had the sound of her departing footsteps died away in the vast corridor than the bed-curtains opened a second time, and Henry, with sparkling eye, trembling hand, and panting breath, sprang to Marguerite's feet. He had quickly removed his velvet doublet, and appeared merely in his undershirt and his coat of mail. Amid all her alarm and agitation, Marguerite could not restrain a hearty laugh at the singular costume adopted by a bridegroom to visit his bride's boudoir. At the same time, she kindly and warmly pressed the hand of him she had so ably assisted.

'Ah, madame! ah, Marguerite!' exclaimed the king, 'how shall I ever repay your goodness?'

'Sire!' replied Marguerite, gently retreating from the warmth of his gratitude, 'have you forgotten that an individual to whom you owe your life is at this moment worried to death on your account? Madame de Sauve,' added she, lowering her voice, 'has forgotten her jealousy in sending you to me, and to that sacrifice she may probably have to add her life, for no one knows better than yourself how terrible is my mother's anger.'

Henry shuddered; and, rising, was about to leave the room.

'On second thoughts,' said Marguerite, 'I see no cause for alarm. The key was given to you without any directions, and you will be assumed to have given me the preference to-night.'

'And so I do, Marguerite! If only you could forget——'

'Not so loud!—not so loud, sire!' replied the queen, employing the same words she had a few minutes before used to her mother: 'anyone in the adjoining room can hear you. I must beg of you to lower your voice.'

'Oh!' said Henry, half smiling, half sadly, 'that's true! I forgot that I was probably not the person with whom the interesting events of to-day were to close! This room——'

'Let me beg of your Majesty to step inside,' said Marguerite, 'for I would like to present to you a brave gentleman, wounded during the massacre, while endeavouring to make his way to the Louvre for the purpose of apprising your Majesty of the danger with which you were threatened.'

The queen advanced towards the door, followed by Henry. She opened it, and the king was thunderstruck at beholding a man in this little room which seemed fated to yield continued surprises.

But, however great the king's astonishment, that of La Mole, at thus unexpectedly finding himself in the presence of Henry of Navarre, was greater still.

The king cast an ironical glance at Marguerite who bore it without flinching.

'Sire,' said she, 'I dread that this gentleman may be murdered even here, in the sanctuary of my apartments; he is devoted to the service of your Majesty, and for that reason I commend him to your royal protection.'

'Sire,' continued the young man, 'I am the Count Lérac de la Mole, the same your Majesty expected, who was so warmly recommended to you by M. de Teligny, who was killed at my side.'

'Indeed!' replied Henry—'is that so, sir? I remember the queen gave me a letter from that honourable gentleman. But if you are the Count de la Mole, you should also be the bearer of a letter from the governor of Languedoc.'

'Your Majesty is right: such a paper was entrusted to me, with earnest recommendation to deliver it into your royal hands as soon as possible.'

'And why did you delay?'

'Sire, I was at the Louvre yesterday evening for that purpose. But your Majesty was too much occupied to give me audience.'

'True!' answered the king. 'But in that case, why not send the letter to me?'

'Because M. d'Auriac had strictly charged me to give it into no other hands than those of your Majesty, since it contained, he said, information so important that he feared to entrust it to any ordinary messenger.'

'The contents are, indeed, of a serious nature,' said the king, when he had received and perused the letter 'advising my instant withdrawal from the court of France, and retirement to Béarn. M. d'Auriac, although a Catholic, was always a staunch friend of mine, and it is possible, that acting as governor of a province he got scent of what was in the wind here. *Ventre-saint-gris!* monsieur! why was not this letter given to me three days ago, instead of now?'

'Because, as I assured your Majesty before, even by using all the speed and diligence in my power, it was wholly impossible to arrive before yesterday.'

'That is very unfortunate,' murmured the king, 'for had you done so, we should now have been safe either at La Rochelle* or on open ground, surrounded by two or three thousand trusty horsemen.'

'Sire,' said Marguerite, in an undertone, 'what is done is done, and instead of wasting time in useless recrimination, it would be better for you to make the best arrangement you can for the future.'

'Then,' replied Henry, with his usual questioning glance, 'I am to suppose that, in my place, you would not despair?'

'Certainly not. I should consider myself as playing a game of three points, of which I had lost only the first.'

'Ah, madame,' whispered Henry, 'if I dared hope that you would go partners with me in the game I should indeed flatter myself with hopes of success.'

'Had I intended to side with your adversaries,' replied Marguerite, 'I should scarcely have delayed thus long in revealing my intentions.'

'True!' replied Henry, 'and I am very ungrateful. But, as you say, the past may still be repaired. Yet, madame,' continued he, attentively observing La Mole, 'this gentleman cannot remain here without causing you considerable inconvenience and being himself liable to very unpleasant surprises. What are you going to do with him?'

'Does your Majesty consider there will be any difficulty in getting him out of the Louvre?—for I share your opinion, as regards his staying.'

'I fear it will be both difficult and dangerous to attempt such a thing as finding a way out for the young man.'

'Then, could not your Majesty find accommodation for M. de la Mole in your own apartments?'

'Alas, madame! you speak as though I were still king of the Huguenots, and had subjects to command. You are aware that I am half converted to the Catholic faith.'

Anyone but Marguerite would have promptly answered, 'And he also is a Catholic.' But the queen wished Henry himself to ask her to do the very thing she wanted to bring about, while La Mole, seeing the hesitation of his protectress, and not knowing what to say or do in so dangerous a court as was that of France, remained silent.

'But what is this the governor says in his letter?' said Henry, again casting his eyes over the missive he held in his hand. 'He states that your mother was a Catholic, and from that circumstance stemmed the interest he felt in you.'

'And what were you telling me, M. le comte, respecting a vow you had formed to change your religion? I confess my memory of the matter is somewhat hazy. Have the goodness to help me out, M. de la Mole. Did not your conversation refer to something of the kind which His Majesty seems to want?'

'Alas! madame, what I did say was so coldly received by your Majesty that I did not have the courage to repeat it.'

'That was because it in no way concerned me,' answered Marguerite. 'But explain yourself to the king—tell him what you wanted to tell me.'

'What is the vow you referred to?' asked the king. 'Let me hear.'

'Sire,' said La Mole, 'when pursued by assassins, being unarmed and almost expiring with pain from my wounds, I fancied I saw the spirit of my mother, holding a cross in her hands, and guiding me towards the Louvre. Under this impression, I solemnly vowed that, if my life were preserved, I would adopt the religion of my mother who had been permitted to leave her grave to direct me to a place of safety during that horrible night. Heaven conducted me here, where I hold myself doubly secure, under the protection of a princess of France and of the King of Navarre. In deep gratitude for my miraculous preservation, I am ready to fulfil my vow and become a Catholic.'

Henry frowned. Sceptic that he was, he could well understand a change of religion from motives of interest. But as a matter of faith and conscience, it was wholly beyond his comprehension.

'It is all over!' thought Marguerite. 'The king evidently will have nothing to do with my protégé.'

La Mole still remained a mute spectator of the rest of a scene in which he felt, without being able to say why, that he played a ridiculous part. Happily, Marguerite's tact and woman's wit again came to his relief and rescue.

'Sire,' said she, 'we both forget that the poor wounded gentleman has need of rest. For myself, I am half asleep. See! he is growing pale, as though he is about to faint.'

La Mole did, indeed, turn pale, but it was at Marguerite's last words, which he had interpreted according to his own ideas.

'Well, madame,' answered Henry, 'nothing could be easier than for you and I to withdraw and leave M. de la Mole to take the rest he so much needs.'

The young man looked pleadingly at Marguerite, and, in spite of the august presence in which he stood, sank into a chair, overcome with fatigue and pain. Marguerite fully understood the passionate love contained in that glance, the utter despair, in the prostration of strength, which deprived his limbs of the power to support him.

'Sire,' said she, 'your Majesty is in honour bound to confer on this young man, who endangered his life for his king, since it was while coming here to acquaint you with the death of the admiral and Teligny that he received his wounds—is bound, I repeat, to confer on him an honour for which he will be ever grateful.'

'What is it, madame?' asked Henry. 'Command me. I am ready to do whatever you dictate.'

'It is to allow M. de la Mole to rest to-night at your Majesty's feet, while you, sire, can sleep on this couch. With the permission of my august husband,' added Marguerite, smiling, 'I will summon Gillonne, and return to bed, for I can assure you I am not the least wearied of us three.'

Henry had shrewd sense, and a quick perception of things: friends and enemies were subsequently to find fault with him for possessing too much of both. He fully admitted that she who thus banished him from the nuptial bed was well justified in so doing by the indifference he had shown her—and then, too, she had just repaid this indifference by saving his life. He therefore did not allow his wounded self-love to dictate his answer, but merely replied,—

'If, madame, M. de la Mole were capable of coming to my apartments, I would give him my own bed.'

'No,' said Marguerite, 'I scarcely think that either you or he would be safe there to-night, and prudence directs that your Majesty should remain here until the morning.'

Then, without awaiting any further reply from the king, she summoned Gillonne and bade her prepare the necessary cushions for the king and arrange a bed at the king's feet for M. de la Mole, who appeared so happy and contented with the honour done him as almost to forget his wounds.

Then Marguerite, curtseying low to the king, passed into the adjoining chamber, the door of which was well furnished with bolts, and threw herself on the bed.

'One thing is certain,' said Marguerite to herself, 'that, to-morrow, M. de la Mole must have a protector at the Louvre. For he who, to-night, sees and hears nothing, may change his mind to-morrow.'

Then calling Gillonne, she said in a whisper, 'Gillonne, you must arrange to bring my brother d'Alençon here to-morrow morning before eight o'clock.'

The loud peal of the Louvre clock chimed the second hour after midnight.

La Mole, after a short parley with the king on political subjects, was left to his own reflections, for Henry fell asleep in the middle of one of his own speeches, and snored as lustily as though he were asleep on his own leather couch in Béarn.

La Mole might also have sunk into the arms of sleep, but his ideas were continually disturbed and disarranged by his proximity to Marguerite who, a prey to disturbed thoughts, turned restlessly on her pillow, and the sounds of her restlessness troubled the young man's thoughts and slumbers.

'He is very young and shy,' murmured the wakeful queen, 'but his eyes are manly, and his form is one of nobleness and beauty. It would be a pity if he should turn out otherwise than brave and loyal. Well, well, it's no good speculating on uncertainties: the affair has begun well, let us hope it will end the same way; and now to commend myself to the triple deity to whom that madcap Henriette pays homage, and court its aid to procure a visit from the god of sleep.'

And as morning broke, Marguerite fell asleep, murmuring, '*Eros, Cupido, Amor.*'

15

WHAT WOMAN WILLS, HEAVEN WILLS ALSO

MARGUERITE was right. The rage which swelled Catherine's heart at being thwarted by a manœuvre the point of which she saw clearly, although powerless to prevent its effects, required some person on whom she could freely vent it. So instead of retiring to her own apartments, the queen-mother proceeded to those of her lady-in-waiting.

Madame de Sauve was expecting two visits—one she hoped to receive from Henry, and the other she feared was in store for her from the queen-mother. Reclining on her bed only half undressed, while Dariole kept watch in the antechamber, she heard a key turn in the lock, followed by a slow, measured tread, the heaviness of which was muffled by the thickness of the rich carpets over which the new-comer trod. But she felt quite sure it was not the light, eager footstep of Henry. Guessing that Dariole had been prevented from coming to warn her of the visitor who came so late to intrude on her rest, she lay with beating heart and attentive ear, awaiting the nearer approach of friend or foe, as it might turn out.

The curtain which covered the doorway was lifted aside, and Catherine de Medicis appeared. She seemed calm. But Madame de Sauve, accustomed for two years to the study of her crafty and deceitful nature, well knew what fatal designs, as well as bitter thoughts of cruel vengeance, might be concealed beneath that cold, imperturbable tranquillity of look and manner.

On seeing Catherine, Madame de Sauve was about to spring from her bed, but Catherine motioned her to stay where she was. And so her unfortunate victim was compelled to remain as though spellbound, vainly trying to collect all her strength to endure the storm she felt was breaking over her.

'Did you convey the key to the King of Navarre?' inquired Catherine, in a voice not very different from her usual tone; the only change was in her lips, which looked paler and paler each moment.

'I did, madame,' answered Charlotte, in a voice that vainly sought to match the firm, assured manner of Catherine.

'And did you see him?'

'No, madame, but I expect him. When I heard the sound of a key in the lock, I fully thought it was him.'

This reply, which indicated either a blind confidence or profound dissimulation on the part of Madame de Sauve, enraged Catherine beyond all power of concealment. She literally shook with fury, and clenching her small plump hands, she said, with a malignant smile,—

'It seems very strange to me that you should expect the King of Navarre in your apartments, when you know how unlikely it is he should be here!'

'How, madame?'

'Yes, I repeat, you are quite aware that the King of Navarre neither could nor would visit you to-night.'

'I am certain that nothing short of death would keep him away,' replied Charlotte, urged to a still more determined dissimulation by the certainty of how bitterly she should have to pay for her deceit, if it were to be discovered.

'But did you not write to the king, my pretty Carlotta?' inquired Catherine, with the same cruel and unnatural smile.

'No, madame,' answered Charlotte, with well-assumed innocence, 'I cannot recall receiving your Majesty's command to do so.'

A short silence followed, during which Catherine continued to gaze on Madame de Sauve as the serpent regards the bird it wishes to hypnotize.

'You think yourself a beauty and a skilful manœuvrer, do you not?' asked Catherine.

'No, indeed, madame,' answered Charlotte. 'I only remember that there have been times when your Majesty has been graciously pleased to commend both my personal attractions and finesse.'

'Well then,' said Catherine, growing eager and animated, 'whatever I may have said or thought, I now declare that you are a hideous dolt compared to my daughter Margot.'

'Oh, madame,' replied Charlotte, 'that is something I would not try to deny—least of all in your presence.'

'It follows then, naturally enough, that the King of Navarre prefers my daughter to you, a situation, I presume, not to your wishes, and certainly not what we agreed should be the case.'

'Alas! madame,' cried Charlotte, bursting into a torrent of tears, which now flowed from no feigned source—'if that is so, I can only say I am very unhappy!'

'Then take my royal word for its truth,' repeated Catherine, again fixing her reptile-like eye upon her victim, till her words seemed to pierce her heart like a two-edged dagger.

'But what reason has your Majesty for coming to this conclusion?'

'Go to the apartments of the Queen of Navarre, you simpleton! and you will find your lover there. How do you like that? Does it make you jealous?'

'Me jealous?' said Madame de Sauve, summoning her fast-fading strength and courage.

'Yes, you! Tell me how you mean to act. I am curious to observe the symptoms of jealousy in a Frenchwoman.'

'No,' said Madame de Sauve, 'why should your Majesty suppose I am wounded in any other feeling than vanity, since the only interest I feel in the King of Navarre stems from my wish to be of service to your Majesty.'

Catherine stared hard at her.

'You may be speaking the truth,' said she. 'Am I, then, to consider you as wholly loyal to my service?'

'Command me, madame, and judge.'

'Well, then, Carlotta, if you are really sincere in your professions and protestations you must (to serve me, you understand) feign the utmost affection for the King of Navarre, and, above all, violent jealousy. Pretend to be as jealous as an Italian.'

'And in what manner, madame, do Italian females show their jealousy?'

'I will instruct you,' replied Catherine who, after remaining some moments as though striving to keep down some powerful emotion, left the apartment slowly and noiselessly as she had come.

Thankful to be freed from the oppressive gaze of eyes which seemed to expand and dilate like those of a cat or panther, Charlotte let her go without trying to say a word. Nor did she breathe freely till Dariole came to tell her that her terrible visitor had really gone. She then bade the waiting-maid to bring an arm-chair beside her bed and spend the night in it, fearing, as she said, to be left alone. Dariole obeyed. But, despite the company of her faithful attendant, despite the bright light from a lamp lit by her orders, Madame de Sauve remained in trembling expectation of Catherine's return, and did not close her eyes till the dawn of day.

Notwithstanding the late hour at which Marguerite had fallen asleep, she awoke at the first sound of the hunting-horns and dogs, and instantly rising, dressed herself in a negligé too eye-catching to escape observation. She then summoned her maids, and ordered the attendants of the King of Navarre to be shown into an antechamber adjoining that in which he had passed the night. Then opening the door of the room which contained both Henry and La Mole, she cast an affectionate glance on the latter, and said to her husband,—

'It is not enough, sire, to have persuaded my royal mother that matters are different from what they seem, you must also impress upon your whole court the most incontrovertible proof of the good understanding existing between us. But be easy,' added she, laughing, 'and remember my words, which are all the more impressive for the circumstances under which I utter them: to-day is the very last time your Majesty will be subjected to so severe a trial.'

Henry smiled, and ordered that the officers of his suite should be admitted. But at the moment of returning their salute, he feigned suddenly to remember having left his cloak on the queen's bed and begged their pardon for receiving them before he was fully dressed. Then taking his cloak from the hands of Marguerite who stood blushing by his side, he wrapped it round his shoulders. Next, turning to his gentlemen, he carelessly inquired what was stirring abroad.

Marguerite's quick eye caught the expression of utter

astonishment impressed on every countenance at the sight of the excellent terms existing between herself and the King of Navarre. Then, while they were still recovering from the shock, an attendant announced the arrival of the Duke d'Alençon with three or four officers of his suite.

Gillonne had required no other means to make him come than the news that the king had spent the night in the queen's apartments; and so hurried was the manner of François in entering, that he narrowly escaped knocking into every person he met in his way. His first glance was directed at Henry; his next to Marguerite. The former replied to him by a courteous greeting, while the calm, composed features of Marguerite displayed the utmost serenity and happiness.

Again the sharp scrutiny of the duke travelled round the room, and he noted the two pillows at the head of the bed, the disturbed bed-clothes, and the king's plumed hat carelessly thrown on a chair beside it.

At this sight his colour left his cheeks, but, quickly recovering himself, he said,—

'Will my royal brother Henry join this morning with the king in his game of tennis?'*

'Does his Majesty do me the honour to select me as his partner?' inquired Henry, 'or is it only a little attention on your own part, brother-in-law?'

'His Majesty has not so said, certainly,' replied the duke, somewhat embarrassed; 'but as you play with him regularly, I thought——'

Henry smiled, for so many and such serious events had occurred since he last played with the king that he would not have been astonished to learn that the king had changed his usual partners at the game.

'I shall certainly join the king for a game,' said Henry, with a smile.

'Then, come!' cried the duke.

'Are you going too?' inquired Marguerite.

'Yes, sweet sister!'

'Are you in great haste to be gone?'

'Yes!'

'Might I venture to ask you to grant me a few minutes before you go?'

So strange and unusual a request from Marguerite filled d'Alençon with a vague, uneasy feeling of something to be feared, and his colour changed rapidly from a deep flush to the palest hue.

'What can she be going to say to him?' thought Henry, taken as much by surprise as the duke himself.

Marguerite quietly proceeded to the door of the little room, and called forth the wounded man, saying to Henry,—

'It is for your Majesty to explain to my brother the reason for our taking an interest in M. de la Mole.'

And Henry, caught in the snare so cleverly laid by Marguerite, briefly related to M. d'Alençon, half a Protestant for the sake of opposition, as he himself was partly a Catholic from prudence, the arrival of M. de la Mole at Paris, and how the young man had been severely wounded, while bringing to him a letter from M. d'Auriac.

As the duke turned round after listening to this explanation, he saw the hero of the tale standing before him.

At the sight of his pale handsome face made still more attractive by the marks of recent weakness and suffering, a fresh feeling of anger and distrust shot through his heart.

'Brother,' said Marguerite, after she had observed the various changes in d'Alençon's expression, 'I will vouch for this young gentleman, and guarantee that he will loyally serve whoever may employ him. Should you accept his services, he will obtain a powerful protector, and you a faithful, zealous follower. In such times as these, brother,' continued she, 'we cannot have too many devoted friends; more especially,' added she, lowering her voice so as to be heard only by the duke, 'when one is ambitious, and has the misfortune to be only third in the succession to the throne.'

Then placing her finger knowingly on her lip, she intimated to d'Alençon that she had not revealed the whole of her views and ideas on the subject, but had kept the most important part still to herself.

'Perhaps' added she, 'you may differ from Henry, in

considering it neither decorous nor fitting that this young gentleman should remain so close to my apartments.'

'Sister,' replied François, 'if it meet your wishes, M. de la
Mole shall, in half an hour, be installed in my apartments, where
I think he shall have no cause to fear any danger. Let him try to
win my affection, and I promise him he shall obtain it.'

François lied: he already hated La Mole.

'Excellent,' murmured Marguerite to herself, seeing the
frown on the brow of the King of Navarre. 'Ah, I see plainly
enough that to lead you both as I would have you go, I have to
make one lead the other.'

And in half an hour after this, La Mole, having been gravely
lectured by Marguerite, kissed the hem of her robe and descended to the apartments of d'Alençon, with a step miraculous-
ly light and agile for one who had been so recently wounded.

Several days passed which appeared still further to consoli-
date the apparent harmony existing between Henry and his wife.

Henry had obtained permission not to make a public renunciation of his religion.* But he had formally recanted in the
presence of the king's confessor and went openly to mass every
day.

At midnight he would ostensibly take the road to his wife's
apartments, enter by the principal door, and, after remaining
some time in conversation with her, leave by the secret door, and
go up to the chamber of Madame de Sauve, who had informed
him of the visit of the queen-mother as well as of the imminent
danger which threatened him. Thus warned and protected on
both sides, Henry redoubled his mistrust and his caution against
Catherine, a proceeding which was amply justified since the
queen-mother had lately bestowed smiles instead of frowns on
him, and addressed him with words of studied cordiality.

Though the massacres still continued, their extent and violence decreased* and seemed likely to die away. For so great had
been the butchery of the Huguenots that the supply began to fail,
and fresh victims were not easily found. The greater part of
those unfortunate people had already been sacrificed. Many had
found safety in flight, and others in concealment. Occasionally, a
great outcry would arise in some neighbourhood in which a fresh
object of popular fury was discovered; and the execution was

either public or private, according to whether the victim was caught with his back to a wall or could find a means of getting away.

Charles the Ninth had taken great pleasure in hunting down the Huguenots, and when he could no longer continue the chase himself, he took delight in the noise of others hunting.

One day, returning from playing at mall,* which with tennis and hunting were his favourite amusements, he went to his mother's apartments in high spirits, followed by his usual train of courtiers.

'Mother,' he said, embracing the Florentine, who, observing his joy, tried to discover its cause—'Mother, good news! By all the saints! The illustrious corpse of the admiral, which was said to be lost, has been found!'

'Ah!' said Catherine.

'Oh, *mon Dieu!* yes. You thought as I did, mother, that the dogs had eaten a wedding dinner off him, but it was not so. My people, my dear people, my good people, had an ingenious idea, and have hung the admiral up at the gibbet at Montfaucon.'*

'Well!' said Catherine.

'Well, good mother,' replied Charles IX, 'I have a strong desire to see the old man again, now I know he is really dead! It is very fine out, and the flowers seem to smell very sweet to-day. The air is full of life and perfume, and I feel better than I ever did. If you like, mother, we will ride out to Montfaucon.'

'Willingly, my son,' said Catherine, 'if I had not an appointment that I cannot defer. Besides, if we are to pay a visit to a man of such importance as the admiral, we should assemble the whole court. It will be an opportunity for making interesting observations. We shall see who comes and who stays away.'

'*Ma foi!* you are right, mother, and it will be better to-morrow. Send out your invitations, and I will send mine; or, rather, do not let us invite any one. We will only say we are going, and then everyone will be free to do as they please. Adieu, mother! I am going hunting.'

'You will wear yourself out, Charles, as Ambroise Paré is always telling you; and he is right. It is too exhausting an exercise for you.'

'Bah!' said Charles. 'I wish I was sure nothing else would kill me; I would then bury everybody here, including Harry, who will one day succeed us all—as Nostradamus* prophesies.'

Catherine frowned.

'My son,' she said, 'mistrust all things that appear impossible, and meanwhile take care of yourself.'

'Only two or three blasts with my horn to cheer up my dogs who are sick to death with doing nothing, poor things! I ought to have let them loose on the Huguenots; that would have done them good!' And Charles IX left his mother's apartment, went into his armoury, took down a horn, and sounded it with a vigour that would have done honour to Roland himself.* It was difficult to understand how so weak a frame and such pale lips could blow a blast so powerful.

Catherine, in truth, was waiting for someone, as she had told her son. A minute after he had left her, one of her women came and whispered to her. The queen smiled, rose, and saluting the persons who formed her court, followed the messenger.

René the Florentine, to whom the King of Navarre had given so diplomatic a reception on the eve of St. Bartholomew, entered the oratory.

'Ah; there you are, René,' said Catherine. 'Have you done as I asked? Have you checked the horoscope drawn by Ruggieri, which confirms the prophecy of Nostradamus which says that all my three sons shall reign?'*

'Yes, madame,' replied René, 'for it is my duty to obey you in all things.'

'Well—and the result?'

'Still the same, madame.'

'What, the black lamb uttered three cries?'

'Yes, madame.'

'The sign of three cruel deaths in my family,' murmured Catherine.

'Alas!' said René.

'Is there more?'

'Well, madame, there was in the entrails of the third the same curious displacement of the liver which we had already observed in the first two.'

'So there is still to be a change of dynasty!' muttered Catherine. 'This must be changed, René,' she added.

René shook his head.

'I have told your Majesty,' he said, 'that destiny rules everything.'

'Is that your opinion?' asked Catherine.

'Yes, Madame.'

'Do you remember d'Albret's horoscope?'*

'Yes, Madame.'

'Let me hear it again and we shall reconsider. I have forgotten it. Repeat it to me, René.'

'*Vives honorata*,' said René, '*morieris reformidata, regina amplificabere.*'

'Which means, I believe,' said Catherine, '*Thou shalt live honoured*—and poor Jeanne lacked common necessaries; *Thou shalt die feared*—and we laughed at her; *Thou shalt be greater than thou hast been as a queen*—and she is dead, and sleeps in a tomb, on which we have not even engraved her name?'

'Madame, your Majesty does not translate the *vives honorata* rightly. The Queen of Navarre lived honoured. All her life she enjoyed the love of her children, the respect of her followers. The love and respect which she knew were all the more sincere, in that she was poor.'

'Yes,' said Catherine, 'I pass over the *vives honorata*; but *morieris reformidata*: how will you explain that?'

'Nothing easier: Thou shalt die feared.'

'Well—did she die feared?'

'So much so, that she would not have died had not your Majesty feared her. Then—*As a queen, thou shalt be greater*; or, *Thou shalt be greater than thou hast been as a queen*. This is equally true, madame; for, in exchange for a terrestrial crown, she has doubtless, as a queen and martyr, a celestial crown; and, besides, who knows how posterity will treat her?'

Catherine was superstitious to excess; she was more alarmed at René's cool pertinacity than at the pertinacity of the auguries; and she said suddenly to him, without any other transition than the working of her own thoughts,—

'Have any Italian perfumes arrived?'

'Yes, madame.'

'Send me a box full.'

'Of which?'

'Of the last ones, the ones which——'

Catherine stopped.

'The Queen of Navarre was so fond of?' asked René.

'Exactly.'

'I need not prepare them, for your Majesty is now as skilful at making them as I am.'

'You think so?' said Catherine. 'They certainly work.'

'Your Majesty has nothing more to say to me?' asked the perfumer.

'Nothing,' replied Catherine thoughtfully. 'But if there is any change in the sacrifices, let me know at once. Let us leave the lambs, and try the chickens.'

'Alas! madame, I fear that in changing the victim we shall not change the prediction.'

'Do as I tell you.'

The perfumer bowed, and left the apartment.

Catherine mused for a short time, then rose, and returning to her bedchamber where her women were waiting for her, announced the pilgrimage to Montfaucon for the next day.*

The news of this outing threw the palace and city into a considerable bustle. The ladies prepared their most elegant outfits; the gentlemen their finest arms and steeds; the tradesmen closed their shops, and the populace killed a few straggling Huguenots, so that the dead admiral would not want company.

La Mole had passed a miserable day, and this miserable day had followed three or four others equally miserable. M. d'Alençon, to please his sister, had installed him in his apartments, but had not since seen him. He felt like a poor deserted child, deprived of the tender cares, the soothing attentions of two women, the memory of one of whom occupied him constantly. He had heard of her through Ambroise Paré, whom she had sent to him, but Ambroise was an old man to whom he could not talk of his feelings. Gillonne had come once, as if of her own accord, to ask after him, and the visit was to him like a sunbeam darting into a dungeon. But Gillonne had not come again.

So as soon as he heard of the brilliant expedition of the court which was fixed for the following day, La Mole asked M. d'Alençon the favour of being allowed to accompany it. The duke did not even trouble himself to inquire whether La Mole

was sufficiently recovered to bear the fatigue, but merely
answered,—

'Humph! well, let him have one of my horses.'

This was all La Mole wanted. Maître Ambroise Paré came to
dress his wounds, and La Mole explained to him that he was
going to have to sit on a horse, and asked him to dress his wounds
with more than usual care.

The two wounds were closed, both the one to his chest and the
one in the shoulder, and the latter alone pained him. They were
both in a fair way of healing. Maître Ambroise Paré covered
them with gummed taffetas,* a remedy greatly in vogue then,
and promised La Mole that if he did not exert himself too much,
everything would go well. La Mole next employed a part of the
money he had received when he left his family to buy a very
handsome white satin doublet, and one of the richest embroidered cloaks he could find. He also bought a pair of boots of
perfumed leather, as were worn at that period. He dressed himself quickly, looked in his mirror, and found that he was suitably
attired, arranged, and perfumed.

While he was thus occupied in the Louvre, another scene of a
similar kind was going on at the Hotel de Guise. A tall gentleman, with red hair, was examining in a mirror a red mark which
ran across his face very disagreeably; he coloured and perfumed
his moustache, and, as he did so, vainly tried to conceal this weal.
In spite of all the cosmetic applied, it would not disappear. The
gentleman then put on a magnificent suit which a tailor had
brought to his apartment without any commands from him.
Thus attired, perfumed, and armed from head to foot, he descended the staircase, and began to pat a large black horse, whose
beauty would have been incomparable but for a small scar in the
flank, caused by a sword wound.

Nevertheless, as pleased with his mount as he was with himself, the gentleman, whom, no doubt, our readers have recognized, was soon on his back, and for a quarter of an hour showed
off his skill as a horseman in the courtyard of the Hotel de Guise,
amidst the neighings of his courser and a barrage of *Mordis*.
Then the horse, completely subdued, recognized by his obedience and subjection the control of the rider. But the victory had
not been obtained without attracting attention, and this attention

had drawn to the windows a lady, whom the rider saluted respectfully, and who smiled at him in the most agreeable manner. Turning to her first gentleman,—

'M. d'Arguzon,'* she said, 'let us set out for the Louvre. But I wish you to keep an eye on the Comte Annibal de Coconnas, for he is wounded, and consequently still weak. I would not want any accident to happen to him. That would make the Huguenots laugh, for they bear him a grudge since the blessed night of Saint Bartholomew.'

And Madame de Nevers, mounting her horse, went joyfully towards the Louvre, which was the general rendezvous.

16

THE BODY OF A DEAD ENEMY ALWAYS SMELLS SWEET

I T was two o'clock in the afternoon, when a procession of horses and riders, glittering with gold, jewels, and rich garments, appeared in the Rue Saint-Denis.

Nothing can be imagined more splendid than this spectacle. The rich and elegant silks, bequeathed as a gorgeous fashion by François I to his successors, had not yet been changed into the formal, sombre vestments which came into vogue under Henry III. The costume of Charles IX, less rich, but perhaps more elegant than those of preceding reigns,* was the perfect embodiment of this new style. Pages, squires, gentlemen of low degree, dogs, and horses—all were there, and turned the royal *cortège* into an army. Behind this army came the people, or rather the people were everywhere.

That morning, in the presence of Catherine and the Duke de Guise, Charles had casually spoken to Henry of Navarre of going to visit the gibbet of Montfaucon, or rather the mutilated corpse of the admiral, which had been hung there. Henry's first reaction had been not to go with them. This Catherine had expected at the first words he said, which expressed his repugnance, and she exchanged a glance and a smile with the Duke de Guise. Henry caught both and understood. Then suddenly turning round, he said,—

'But why should I not go? I am a Catholic, and have a duty to my new religion.'

Then addressing the king,—

'Your Majesty may count on my company,' he said. 'I shall be always happy to accompany you wherever you go'. And he threw a sweeping glance around him, to see whose brows might be frowning.

And perhaps in all this, the person who was looked at with the greatest curiosity was this son without a mother—this king without a kingdom—this Huguenot turned Catholic. His long, strong face, his rather vulgar figure, his familiarity with his inferiors which he carried to a degree almost unseemly in a king—a familiarity acquired by the mountaineer habits of his youth which he preserved till his death, marked him out to the spectators, some of whom cried,—

'To mass, Harry!—to mass!'

To which Henry replied,—

'I went yesterday, to-day, and I shall go again to-morrow. *Ventre-saint-gris!* surely that is sufficient.'

Marguerite was on horseback—so lovely, so fresh, so elegant, that she was admired above all others, although the Duchess de Nevers shared some portion of the general approval.

'Well, duchess!' said the Queen of Navarre, 'what news?'

'Why, madame,' replied the duchess, aloud, 'I know of none.' Then in a lower tone—'And what has become of the Huguenot?'

'I have found him a safe place to hide,' replied Marguerite. 'And the wholesale murderer, what have you done with him?'

'He wanted to come, and so we mounted him on M. de Nevers's war-horse, a creature as big as an elephant. He is a fearful horseman. I allowed him to be present to-day, since I felt that your Huguenot would be prudent enough to keep his chamber, and that there was no fear of their meeting.'

'Oh, *ma foi!*' replied Marguerite, smiling, 'if he were here, and he is not, I do not think that there would be any unpleasantness. My Huguenot is remarkably handsome, but nothing more—a dove, and not a hawk—he coos, but does not bite. After all,' she added, with a gesture impossible to describe and shrugging her shoulders slightly—'after all, perhaps, our king thought him a Huguenot, whilst he is only a Brahmin* and his religion forbids him to shed blood.'

'But where is the Duke d'Alençon?' inquired Henriette; 'I do not see him.'

'Listen. There are shouts down there. It is he, doubtless, who is passing through the Porte-Montmartre.'

'Yes, it is he, and he seems in good spirits to-day,' said Henriette. 'Perhaps he is in love. How nice it is to be a prince of the blood: he gallops through the crowd, and everybody draws on one side.'

'Yes,' said Marguerite, laughing, 'he will ride over us. But draw your attendants on one side, duchess, for one of them will be killed. He won't give way.'

'There's my hero!' cried the duchess—'look!'

Coconnas had left his place in the procession to approach the Duchess de Nevers, but at the moment when his horse was crossing the exterior boulevard which separates the street from the Faubourg Saint-Denis,* a rider in the suite of the Duke d'Alençon, trying in vain to rein in his excited horse, dashed full against Coconnas, who, shaken by the collision, almost lost his seat. His hat nearly fell off, and as he put it on more firmly, he turned round furiously.

'*Dieu!*' murmured Marguerite to her friend, 'M. de la Mole!'

'That pale, handsome young man?' exclaimed the duchess, unable to master her first impression.

'Yes, the one who nearly upset your Piedmontese.'

'Oh,' said the duchess, 'something terrible will happen! they are staring at each other—they have remembered!'

Coconnas had indeed recognized La Mole and, in his surprise dropped his bridle, for he believed he had killed his former companion, or at least put him *hors de combat* for some time. La Mole had also recognized Coconnas, and the blood rushed to his face. For some seconds, which were enough to express all the sentiments which these two men felt towards each other, they gazed on one another in a way that frightened the two women.

After which, La Mole having looked about him and seeing that the place was ill-suited to explanations, spurred his horse and rejoined the Duke d'Alençon. Coconnas remained stationary for a moment, twisting his moustache until the point almost entered his eye. Then seeing La Mole dash off without a word, he did the same.

'Ah!' said Marguerite, with painful contempt, 'I was not mistaken, then!—it is really too much.' And she bit her lip till it bled.

'He is very handsome,' added the Duchess de Nevers consolingly.

Just at this moment the Duke d'Alençon reached his place behind the king and the queen-mother, so that his suite, in following him, were obliged to pass before Marguerite and the Duchess de Nevers. La Mole, as he passed, raised his hat, saluted the queen, and, bowing over his horse's neck, remained hatless until her Majesty should honour him with a look.

But Marguerite turned her head aside disdainfully.

La Mole, no doubt, understood the contemptuous expression on the queen's face, and from pale he became livid, and, so that he would not fall from his horse, was compelled to hold on by the mane.

'Ah, ah!' said Henriette to the queen, 'look, cruel that you are—he is going to faint!'

'Good,' said the queen, with a smile of disdain. 'that's all we need. Where are your salts?'

Madame de Nevers was mistaken. La Mole, with an effort, recovered himself, and, sitting erect on his horse, took his place in the Duke d'Alençon's suite.

They went forward and at length saw the fearful outline of the gibbet, erected and first used by Enguerrand de Marigny.*

The guards advanced and formed a large ring round the spot. At their approach, the crows which had perched on the gibbet flew away, croaking and angry.

The crowd advanced. The king and Catherine arrived first, then the Duke d'Anjou, the Duke d'Alençon, the King of Navarre, M. de Guise, and their followers. Next came Madame Marguerite, the Duchess de Nevers, and all the women who composed what was called the queen's flying squadron. Finally came the pages, squires, attendants, and people—in all ten thousand persons.

On the principal gibbet was hung a misshapen mass stained with coagulated blood and mud, whitened by layers of dust. The carcass was headless. It had been hung up by the legs, and the people, ingenious as they always are, had replaced the head with a bunch of straw, on which they had put a mask, and in the mouth of this mask some wag, knowing the admiral's habit, had introduced a toothpick.*

It was a sight at once appalling and singular, as all these elegant lords and handsome ladies rode past blackened carcasses and the long and sinister arms of the gibbets.

Many could scarcely bear the horrible spectacle, and by his paleness might be distinguished, in the centre of the rallied Huguenots, Henry, who, however great his power over himself and his amount of dissimulation, could not stand it any longer.

He made as his excuse the strong smell which emanated from those human remains, and going towards Charles, who, with Catherine, had stopped in front of the admiral's dead body, he said,—

'Sire, does not your Majesty find that this poor carcass smells so strongly that it is impossible to remain near it any longer?'

'Do you find it so, Harry?' inquired the king, his eyes sparkling with fierce joy.

'Yes, sire.'

'Well, then, I am not of your opinion. The corpse of a dead enemy always smells sweet.'

'Come, come, sir!' said Catherine, who, in spite of the perfume with which she was protected, began to be overcome by the putrid odour. 'Come, however agreeable company may be, it must be left at last—let us therefore bid adieu to the admiral, and return to Paris.'

She made an ironical gesture with her head, in imitation of a leave-taking from a friend, and, going to the front of the columns, rejoined the road, while the procession filed past the corpse of Coligny.

The sun was fast sinking in the horizon.

The crowd followed so rapidly that in ten minutes after the departure of the king there was no one left near the mutilated carcass of the admiral, which was now blown upon by the first breezes of the evening.

When we say no one, we err. A gentleman, mounted on a black horse who, doubtless, could not see without a feeling of revulsion the misshapen and mutilated trunk when it was honoured by the presence of princes, had remained behind, and was closely examining the bolts, stone pillars, chains, and so on, of the gibbet, which no doubt appeared to him (but lately arrived in Paris, and ignorant of the perfection to which things could be brought in the capital) the height of all the ugliness that man can devise.

We need hardly inform our friends that this individual enthralled by the handiwork of Enguerrand de Marigny, was M. Annibal de Coconnas.

A female eye had sought him in the ranks in vain; but this eye was not the only eye that sought M. de Coconnas; another gentleman, remarkable for his white satin doublet and flowing plume, after gazing all around him, at length caught sight of the tall figure of Coconnas and the vast outline of his horse. The gentleman in the white satin doublet left the road which the main body was taking, and turning to the right, and describing a semicircle, returned towards the gibbet. Almost at the same moment, the lady whom we have recognized as the Duchess de Nevers approached Marguerite, and said to her,—

'We were both wrong, Marguerite; for the Piedmontese has remained behind, and M. de la Mole has followed him.'

'*Mordi!*' replied Marguerite, laughing, 'then something is going to happen. *Ma foi!* I confess I shall not be sorry to have the chance of changing my opinion.'

Marguerite turned round, and saw La Mole execute the manœuvre we have described.

Then the two princesses left the main body at the first opportunity, and turned down a path, lined on both sides by hedges, which led back to within thirty paces of the gibbet. Madame de Nevers said a word in her captain's ear, Marguerite made a sign to Gillonne, and all four went by the crossroads and settled themselves behind the bushes nearest to the spot where the scene they desired to witness was to be enacted.

Marguerite alighted, as did Madame de Nevers and Gillonne, and the captain, in his turn, who took charge of the four horses. A gap in the hedge allowed the three women to see all that passed.

La Mole had reached Coconnas, and, stretching out his hand, tapped him on the shoulder.

The Piedmontese turned round.

'Oh!' said he, 'then it was not a dream! You are still alive!'

'Yes, sir,' replied La Mole—'I am still alive. It is no fault of yours, but I am still alive.'

'*Mordi!* I know you again well enough,' replied Coconnas, 'in spite of your pale face. It was redder the last time we met!'

'And I,' said La Mole—'I also recognize you, in spite of that yellow line across your face. You were paler than that when I made that mark for you!'

Coconnas bit his lips, but, resolved to continue the conversation in a tone of irony, he said,—

'It is curious, is it not, Monsieur de la Mole, particularly for a Huguenot, to be able to look at the admiral dangling from an iron hook? And yet they say that we are guilty of killing even Huguenot children, even babes at their mother's breast!'

'Comte,' said La Mole, bowing, 'I am no longer a Huguenot; I have the happiness to be a Catholic!'

'Bah!' exclaimed Coconnas, bursting into loud laughter—'you are a convert—eh, sir? Well, that's most convenient!'

'Sir,' replied La Mole, with the same seriousness and the same politeness, 'I made a vow to become a convert if I escaped the massacre.'

'Comte,' said the Piedmontese, 'that was a very prudent vow, and I congratulate you. Did you make any others?'

'Yes,' answered La Mole, 'I made a second.' And as he spoke, he patted his horse nonchalantly.

'And what might that be?' inquired Coconnas.

'To hang you up there, by that small nail waiting for you next to M. de Coligny.'

'What, as I am now,' asked Coconnas, 'alive and hearty?'

'No, sir. After I have run my sword through your body!'

Coconnas became purple, and his eyes darted flames.

'You are not big enough to do it, little man!'

'Then I'll get on your horse, assassin,' replied La Mole. 'Ah, you believe, my dear M. Annibal de Coconnas, you can kill and murder without danger to yourself when your victim is chivalrously and honourably outnumbered by a hundred to one! But the day comes when a man finds his match; and I believe that day has come now. I should like to send a bullet through your ugly head; but, bah! I might miss you, for my hand is still trembling from the cowardly wounds you inflicted upon me.'

'My ugly head!' shouted Coconnas, dismounting furiously. 'Down—down from your horse, M. le comte, and draw!'

And he drew his sword.

La Mole alighted as calmly as Coconnas had done so precipitately. He took off his cherry-coloured cloak, laid it coolly on the ground, drew his sword, and put himself on guard.

'Ah!' he said, as he stretched out his arm.

'Oh!' muttered Coconnas, as he did the same—for both, as it will be remembered, had been wounded in the shoulder.

A burst of laughter, ill repressed, came from the clump of bushes, and reached the ears of the two gentlemen, who were ignorant that they had witnesses, and, turning round, they saw their ladies.

La Mole resumed his guard as firm as an automaton, and Coconnas crossed his blade with an emphatic *Mordi!*

'Ah! they will murder each other in earnest, if we do not interfere. There has been enough of this. Hola, gentlemen!— hola!' cried Marguerite.

'Let them be—let them be!' said Henriette, who, having seen Coconnas fight, hoped in her heart that Coconnas would make as short work of La Mole as he had done with the two nephews and the son of Mercandon.

'Oh, they are really handsome!' exclaimed Marguerite. 'Look—they seem to breathe fire!'

And the combat, begun with railleries and mutual provocation, became silent once the champions had crossed their swords. Both distrusted their strength, and each, at every quick pass, was compelled to restrain an expression of pain caused by his old wounds. With his eyes fixed and burning, his mouth half open, and his teeth clenched, La Mole advanced with short, firm steps towards his adversary, who, finding in him a most skilful swordsman, retreated step by step. They both thus reached the edge of the ditch, on the other side of which were the spectators. Then, as if his retreat had been only a simple stratagem to draw nearer to his lady, Coconnas took his stand, and on a mistimed motion of his opponent's blade, thrust in quart* with the quickness of lightning, and in a moment the white satin doublet of La Mole was stained with a patch of blood which kept growing larger.

'Courage!' cried the duchess.

'Ah, poor La Mole!' exclaimed Marguerite, with a cry of distress.

La Mole heard this cry, darted at the queen one of those looks which penetrate the heart even deeper than the sword's point, and taking advantage of an ill-judged feint, thrust vigorously at his adversary.

This time the two women uttered two cries which seemed like one. The point of La Mole's rapier had appeared, all covered with blood, at Coconnas' back.

Yet neither fell. Both remained erect, looking at each other with open mouths, aware that on the slightest movement they must lose their balance. At last the Piedmontese, more dangerously wounded than his adversary, and feeling his senses drain from him with his blood, fell on La Mole, grasping him with one hand, whilst with the other he tried to unsheath his dagger. La Mole, for his part, summoned all his strength, raised his hand, and let fall the pommel of his sword on Coconnas's forehead, who, stupefied by the blow, fell, but in his fall pulled his adversary down with him, and both rolled into the ditch.

Then Marguerite and the Duchess de Nevers, seeing that, dying as they were, they were still struggling to kill each other, hastened towards them, followed by the captain of the guards. But before they could reach them, their hands unloosened their mutual grip, their eyes closed, and the combatants, letting go their grasp of their weapons, stiffened as if in the throes of death.

A stream of blood flowed from each.

'Oh, brave, brave La Mole!' cried Marguerite, unable any longer to repress her admiration. 'Ah! forgive me for having a moment doubted your courage.'

And her eyes filled with tears.

'Alas!' murmured the duchess, 'gallant Annibal. Did you ever see two more intrepid heroes, madame?'

And she sobbed aloud.

'Indeed, they were ugly thrusts,' said the captain, trying to staunch the streams of blood. 'Hola! you there, come here as quickly as you can—here, I say——'

He addressed a man, who, seated on a kind of tumbril, or cart, painted red, was singing a snatch of an old song.

The carter, whose repulsive exterior formed a singular contrast with the sweet and sylvan song he was singing, stopped his horse, came towards the two bodies, and looking at them, said,—

'These be terrible wounds, sure enough, but I have made worse in my time.'

'Who, then, are you?' inquired Marguerite, filled with a certain vague terror which she could not overcome.

'Madame,' replied the man, bowing down to the ground, 'I am Maître Caboche,* headsman to the city of Paris, and I have come to hang up at the gibbet a few companions for Monsieur the Admiral.'

'Well! and I am the Queen of Navarre,' replied Marguerite, 'and I order you to throw your corpses into the ditch, spread the coverings of our horses in your cart and drive these two gentlemen carefully to the Louvre with us.'

17

THE RIVAL OF MAÎTRE AMBROISE PARÉ

THE tumbril carrying La Mole and Coconnas took the road to the Louvre, following at a distance the group that served as a guide. It stopped at the Louvre, and the driver was amply rewarded. The wounded men were carried to the Duke d'Alençon's lodgings, and Maître Ambroise Paré sent for.

When he arrived, they were both unconscious.

La Mole was the least hurt of the two. The sword had pierced him below the right armpit, but without touching any vital part. As for Coconnas, he was run through the lungs, and the air that escaped from his wound made the flame of a candle waver.

Ambroise Paré would not answer for Coconnas.

Madame de Nevers was in despair. She it was who, relying on Coconnas's courage and skill, had prevented Marguerite from intervening.

To conceal the cause of their wounds, Marguerite, in having them transported to her brother's apartments, where one of them was already installed, said that they were two gentlemen who had been thrown from their horses. But the real story became known because the admiring captain who had witnessed the duel related all the particulars, and our two heroes soon had a brilliant reputation at court.

Attended by the same surgeon, they both passed through the different stages of convalescence according to the different degrees of severity of their wounds. La Mole was the first to come round. As for Coconnas, he was in a high fever, and his return to life was marked by all the signs of delirium.

Although in the same room as Coconnas, La Mole had not noticed his companion, or, at least, had given no indication of it. Coconnas, on the contrary, when he opened his eyes, fixed them on La Mole with an expression that proved that the blood he had lost had not modified the passions of his fiery temperament.

Coconnas thought he was dreaming, and in this dream he saw the enemy he imagined he had twice slain. Then, after observing La Mole laid, like himself, on a couch, and his wounds dressed by the surgeon, he saw him rise up in bed, while he himself was still too weak to move, get out of bed, walk, first leaning on the surgeon's arm, and then on a cane, and, in the end, without assistance.

Coconnas, still delirious, viewed these different stages of his companion's recovery, with eyes sometimes fixed, at others wandering, but always threatening.

Then arose in his mind, more wounded than his body, an insatiable thirst for vengeance. He was obsessed with one idea, that of procuring a weapon, and piercing this vision which persecuted him so cruelly. His clothes, stained with blood, had been placed on a chair by his bed, but were afterwards removed, it being thought imprudent to leave them in his sight. But his dagger still remained on the chair, for it was imagined it would be some time before he would want to use it.

Coconnas saw the dagger. For three nights, profiting by La Mole's slumbers, he strove to reach it and for three nights his strength failed him, and he fainted. At length, on the fourth night, he made a despairing lunge for it, and, groaning with the pain of the effort, concealed the weapon beneath his pillow.

The next day he saw a new sight. The shade of La Mole, which every day seemed to gain strength, while he, occupied with his plan, seemed to lose his—the shade of La Mole walked pensively up and down the room three or four times then, after having adjusted his cloak, buckled on his rapier, and put on a large hat, opened the door and went out.

Coconnas breathed again. For two hours his blood circulated more freely in his veins than it had done since the duel. One day's absence of La Mole would have recalled Coconnas's senses: a week's absence would have cured him. Unfortunately, La Mole returned two hours later.

The reappearance of La Mole was like a thrust with a dagger to Coconnas. Although La Mole did not return alone, Coconnas did not give a single look at his companion.

That companion was, nevertheless, worth looking at.

He was a man of forty, short, thick-set, and vigorous, with black hair cut short, and a black beard, which, contrary to the fashion of the period, thickly covered his chin.* But he seemed one who cared little for the fashion.

He wore a leather jerkin, stained and spotted with blood, red hose and leggings, thick shoes that came above the ankle, a cap the same colour as his stockings. A belt, from which hung a large knife in a leather sheath, completed his attire.

This singular personage, whose presence in the Louvre seemed so unaccountable, threw his brown cloak over a chair, and unceremoniously approached Coconnas, whose eyes, as if fascinated, remained fixed upon La Mole who remained at the other end of the room. He looked at the sick man, and shaking his head, said to La Mole,—

'You were in no hurry.'

'I could not get out sooner.'

'Why did you not send for me?'

'I had no one to send.'

'True, I forgot where we are. Ah, if my prescriptions had been followed instead of those of that ass, Ambroise Paré, you would have been by this time in a condition to go in pursuit of adventures together, or exchange another sword-thrust if you liked; but we shall see. Does your friend hear reason?'

'Scarcely.'

'Hold out your tongue, sir. Ah, I see there's no time to be lost. This evening I will send you a potion ready prepared. You must make him take it at three times, once at midnight, once at one o'clock, and once at two.'

'Very well.'

'But who will administer it?'

'I will.'

'You personally?'

'Yes.'

'You promise me?'

'On my honour.'

'And if the doctor tries to obtain any of it to analyse it?'

'I will throw it away to the last drop.'

'On your honour?'

'I swear it!'

'Done. But how shall we get it in here? Oh, faith, I'll send it to you as from Maître René, the perfumer. He poaches on my profession so often, I may surely use his name for once.'

'Then,' said La Mole, 'I rely on you.'

'You may.'

'And as for payment?'

'Oh, we will arrange that when the gentleman is well again.'

'You may rest easy on that score, for I am sure he will pay you nobly.'

'No doubt. Adieu, then, M. de la Mole. In two hours you will have the potion. You understand, it must be given at midnight, in three doses, from hour to hour.'

So saying, he left the room, and La Mole was alone with Coconnas.

Coconnas had heard the whole conversation, but remembered nothing except the word 'Midnight.'

He continued to watch La Mole, who remained in the room, pacing thoughtfully up and down.

The unknown doctor kept his word, and at the appointed time sent the potion, which La Mole placed on a small silver heater, and then lay down.

The clock struck twelve. Coconnas opened his eyes; his breath seemed to scorch his lips, and his throat was parched with fever. The night lamp shed a faint light, and made thousands of phantoms dance before his eyes.

He saw La Mole rise from his couch, walk about a few moments, and then advance towards him, threatening him, as he thought, with his clenched hand. Coconnas seized his dagger, and prepared to plunge it into his enemy.

La Mole approached.

Coconnas murmured,—

'Ah! it's you at last! Ah! you threaten me! you smile! Come closer and I will kill you.'

And suiting the action to the word, as La Mole leaned towards him, Coconnas drew the dagger from under the clothes. But the effort exhausted him, and he fell back upon his pillow.

'Come,' said La Mole, supporting him, 'drink this, poor fellow, for you are burning with fever.'

It was in reality a cup that La Mole held out to Coconnas which he had mistaken for his fist.

But on experiencing the soothing sensation of the healing draught which moistened his lips and cooled his throat, Coconnas recovered his wits, or rather his instinct. A feeling of delight pervaded his frame. He looked hard at La Mole, who was supporting him in his arms, and smiled gratefully on him. From those eyes, so lately glowing with fury, a tear rolled down his burning cheek.

'*Mordi!*' murmured Coconnas, 'If I get over this, M. de la Mole, you shall be my friend.'

'And you will get over it,' said La Mole, 'if you drink the other two cups, and have no more ugly dreams.'

An hour afterwards La Mole, obedient to his instructions, rose again, poured a second dose into the cup, and carried it to Coconnas, who, instead of welcoming him with his dagger, opened his arms, eagerly swallowed the potion, and then fell asleep.

The third cup had a no less marvellous effect. The sick man's breathing became more regular, his limbs supple, a gentle perspiration spread over his skin, and when Ambroise Paré visited him the next morning, he smiled complacently,—

'I answer for M. de Coconnas now; and this will not be one of the least difficult cures I have effected.'

The result of this scene was the friendship of the two gentlemen, which, commencing at *La Belle Etoile*, and violently interrupted by the night of St Bartholomew, now surpassed that of Orestes and Pylades* by five sword-thrusts and one pistol-wound exchanged between them.

Old and new wounds, slight or serious, were at last in a fair way of cure. La Mole, though now fully fit, would not forsake his post of nurse until Coconnas was also recovered. He raised him in bed, and helped him when he began to walk, until by the aid of Count Annibal's naturally vigorous constitution, he was restored to perfect health.

However, one and the same thought occupied both the young men. Each had in his delirium seen the woman he loved approach his couch. Yet since they had recovered their senses, neither Marguerite nor Madame de Nevers had appeared. It is true that the gentleman who had witnessed the combat had come several times, as if of his own accord, to inquire after them. It is also true that Gillonne had done the same. But La Mole had not dared to speak to the one concerning the queen and Coconnas had not dared to speak to the other of Madame de Nevers.

18

THE VISIT

FOR some time the two young men kept their secret to themselves. At last, on a day of warm and mutual feeling, the thought which had so long occupied them escaped their lips, and both cemented their friendship by this final proof, without which there is no friendship—namely, trust.

They were both madly in love—one with a princess, and the other with a queen.

They both, as they recovered from their illness, took great pains with their personal appearance. Every man, even the most indifferent to physical appearances, has, at certain times, mute interviews with his looking-glass, understandings with his mirror, after which he generally quits his confidant, quite satisfied with the conversation. Now our two young friends were not men whose mirrors gave them no encouragement. La Mole, thin, pale, and elegant, had the beauty of distinction. Coconnas, powerful, large-framed, and fresh-coloured, had the beauty of strength. He had more, for his recent illness had been of advantage to him: he had become thinner, grown paler. The famous scar, which had formerly marked his face with the prismatic colours of the rainbow, had disappeared.

The most delicate attentions continued to be lavished on the two wounded men, and on the day when each was well enough to get up, he found a dressing-gown on the arm of his easy-chair: on the day when he was able to dress himself, a complete suit of clothes; moreover, in the pocket of each doublet was a well-filled purse, which they each intended, as a matter of course, to return, in time and place, to the unknown protector who watched over them.

This unknown protector could not be the prince with whom the two young men resided, for not only had the prince never once paid a visit, but he had not even sent to make any inquiry after them.

A vague hope whispered to each heart that this unknown protector was the woman he loved. The two wounded men therefore awaited with intense impatience the moment when they could go out. La Mole, stronger and sooner cured than Coconnas, could have done so long before, but a kind of tacit convention bound him to his friend.

At length, after two months passed in convalescence and confinement, the long-looked-for day arrived, and about two o'clock in the afternoon, on a fine day in autumn, such as Paris sometimes offers to her astonished population who have already made up their minds that winter is on them, the two friends, leaning on each other's arms, left the Louvre.

La Mole undertook to guide Coconnas, and Coconnas allowed himself to be guided without resistance or reflection. He knew that his friend meant to take him to the unknown doctor's, whose potion (not patented) had cured him in a single night, when all the drugs of Master Ambroise Paré were killing him slowly. He had divided the money in his purse into two parts, and intended a hundred rose nobles for the unknown Esculapius,* to whom his recovery was due. Coconnas was not afraid of death, but he was not unhappy to be alive and well.

La Mole directed his steps towards the Place des Halles. Near the ancient fountain was an octagonal stone building, surmounted by a vast lantern of wood, which was again crowned by a pointed roof, on the top of which was a weathercock. This wooden lantern had eight openings, traversed, as that heraldic device which they called the *fess** traverses the field of blazonry, by a kind of wooden wheel, which was divided in the middle, in order to accommodate in the holes cut in it for that purpose the heads and hands of sentenced persons who were exposed at one or other of all these eight openings.

This singular construction, the like of which was not to be found in the surrounding buildings, was called the pillory.

An ill-constructed, irregular, crooked, one-eyed, limping house, its roof covered with moss, like the skin of a leper, had, like a toadstool, sprung up at the foot of this tower.

This house was the executioner's.

A man was exposed and was poking his tongue out at the passers-by. He was a robber who had plied his trade around the gibbet of Montfaucon, and had by ill luck been arrested in the exercise of his functions.

Coconnas believed that his friend had brought him to see this singular spectacle, and mingled in the crowd of onlookers who responded to the thief's grimaces by vociferations and shouts. Coconnas was naturally cruel, and the sight very much amused him; and when the moving lantern was turned on its base, in order to exhibit the man to another part of the crowd which followed it round, Coconnas would have accompanied them, had not La Mole checked him, murmuring,—

'That's not why we are here.' And he led Coconnas to a small window in the house adjacent to the tower, at which a man was leaning.

'Ah! is it you, gentlemen?' said the man, raising his blood-red cap and showing his thick, black hair which almost came down to his eyebrows. 'You are welcome.'

'Who is this man?' inquired Coconnas, trying to remember,

for he believed he had seen his face during one of the crises of his fever.

'Your preserver, my friend,' replied La Mole. 'He brought you that refreshing drink at the Louvre which did you so much good.'

'Oh!' said Coconnas, 'in that case——'

And he held out his hand to him.

But the man, instead of returning the gesture, stood up and retreated a pace from the two friends.

'Sir,' he said to Coconnas, 'thanks for the honour you offer me, but it is most probable that if you knew me, you would withdraw it.'

'*Ma foi!*' said Coconnas. 'I declare that were you the devil himself, I am very greatly obliged to you, for I owe you my life.'

'I am not exactly the devil,' replied the man in the red cap. 'Yet there are many people who would rather see the devil than me.'

'Then, who are you?' asked Coconnas.

'Sir,' replied the man, 'I am Maître Caboche, the executioner of the city of Paris——'

'Ah——' said Coconnas, withdrawing his hand.

'You see!' said Maître Caboche.

'No, no; I will take your hand, or may the devil strike me dead! Hold it out——'

'Really?'

'Most certainly.'

'Here it is!'

'Open it—wider—wider!'

And Coconnas took from his pocket the handful of gold he had prepared for his anonymous physician, and placed it in the executioner's hand.

'I would rather have had just your hand,' said Maître Caboche, shaking his head; 'for I am not in want of money, but of hands to grasp mine. Never mind! God bless you, sir!'

'So, my friend,' said Coconnas, looking at the executioner with curiosity, 'it is you who give men pain, who put them on the wheel, quarter them,* cut off heads, and break bones. I am very glad to have made your acquaintance.'

'Sir,' said Maître Caboche, 'I do not do everything myself.

Just as you have lackeys to do what you do not choose to do yourself, so have I my assistants, who do the coarser work and make preparations. But when, by chance, I have to do with persons of quality, like yourself and this other gentleman, for instance, then it is very different. I take a pride in doing everything myself, from first to last—that is to say, from the first putting of the *question*, to the beheading!'

In spite of himself, Coconnas felt a shudder pervade his veins, as if the wedge was actually being driven beside his legs—as if the edge of the axe was against his neck.

La Mole, without being able to account for it, felt the same sensation. But Coconnas overcame the emotion, of which he was ashamed, and, determined to take leave of Maître Caboche with a jest on his lips, said to him,—

'Well, master headsman, I hold you to your word, and when it is my turn to climb the gallows of Enguerrand de Marigny, or the scaffold of M. de Nemours,* you alone shall lay hands on me.'

'That's a promise.'

'Then, this time here is my hand, as a pledge that I accept your promise,' said Coconnas.

And he gave the headsman his hand, which the headsman took timidly in his own, although it was evident that he would have liked to grasp it warmly.

At this light contact, Coconnas turned rather pale, but a smile still remained on his lips. Then La Mole, ill at ease and seeing the crowd turn with the lantern and come towards them, touched his cloak.

Coconnas, who in reality had as great a desire as La Mole to put an end to this scene, nodded to the executioner, and went his way.

'*Ma foi!*' said La Mole, when he and his companion had reached the Cross du Trahoir*—'we breathe more freely here than in the Place des Halles!'

'Decidedly,' said Coconnas; 'but I am not sorry to have made Maître Caboche's acquaintance. It is no bad thing to have friends everywhere.'

19

THE ABODE OF MAÎTRE RENÉ, PERFUMER
TO THE QUEEN-MOTHER

A T the period in which our story is set, there existed in Paris, for passing from one part of the city to another, but five bridges, some of stone and the others of wood, and they all led to the Cité.* Of these five bridges, each of which has its history, we shall now speak more particularly of the Pont-Saint-Michel.*

In the midst of the houses which lined the bridge, facing a small islet, was a house remarkable for its panels of wood, and for a large overhanging roof, like the lid of an immense eye. At the only window which opened on the first floor, above the window and door at street level, both closely shut, was observed a reddish light which attracted the attention of the passers-by to the low façade, which was wide, painted blue and decorated with rich gold mouldings. A kind of frieze, which separated the ground-floor from the first-floor, represented groups of devils in the most grotesque postures imaginable. A large plain strip, painted blue like the façade, ran between the frieze and the window, with this inscription:

René, Florentine, Perfumer to Her Majesty the
Queen-Mother

The door of this shop* was, as we have said, closely bolted, but it was defended against nocturnal attacks better than by bolts: it was secured by the reputation of its occupier, so fearsome that all those who crossed the bridge usually kept away from contact with the building, as if they feared the very smell of the perfumes that might exhale from the house.

From similar motives, the neighbours right and left of René had abandoned their houses, which were thus entirely empty. Yet, in spite of its isolation, belated passers-by had frequently seen, glittering through the crevices of the shutters of these deserted buildings, certain rays of light, and had heard certain noises like groans, which proved that some beings frequented these premises, although they did not know if they belonged to this world or the next.

It was, doubtless, owing to the privilege which such fears, widely circulated, had procured for him, that Maître René had dared to keep up a light after hours. No patrol or guard, however, would have dared to molest him, a man doubly dear to her Majesty, as her fellow-countryman and perfumer.

The shop of the ground-floor had been dark and deserted since eight o'clock in the evening, which was when it closed, not to open again until next morning, and it was there that there took place the daily sale of perfumery, unguents, cosmetics, and all the articles of a skilful chemist. Two apprentices helped him in the retail business, but did not sleep in the house.

In the evening they went out a few moments before the shop was closed, and in the morning waited at the door until it was opened.

In the shop, which was large and deep, there were two doors, each leading to a staircase. One of these staircases was in the wall itself, and the other was exterior and visible from the Quai des Augustins and from what is now called the Quai des Orfèvres.

Both led to a room on the first-floor, of the same size as the ground-floor, except that it was divided into two compartments by a tapestry suspended in the centre. At the end of the first compartment opened the door which led to the outer stairs. On the side face of the second opened the door of the secret staircase. This door was hidden, being concealed by a large carved cupboard fastened to it by iron cramps which moved with it when pushed open. Only Catherine, besides René, knew the secret of this door, and by it she came and went; and with eye or ear placed against the cupboard, in which were several small holes, she could see and hear all that passed in the room.

Two other doors, visible to all eyes, led out through the side walls of the second compartment. One opened to a small chamber lit from the roof. It was empty but for a large stove, alembics, retorts, and crucibles: it was an alchemist's laboratory. The other opened on to a cell more singular than the rest of the apartment, for it was not lit at all and had neither carpet nor furniture, only a kind of stone altar.

The floor sloped from the centre to the ends, and from the ends to the base of the wall was a kind of gutter ending in a funnel, through which might be seen the sombre waters of the Seine. On nails driven into the walls hung instruments of singular shape, all keen and well-ground, with points as fine as a needle and edges as sharp as a razor: some shone like mirrors; others, on the contrary, were dull grey or murky blue. In a corner were two black fowls, struggling with each other and tied together by the claws. This was the Sanctuary of the Augury.

Let us return to the middle chamber, the one with two compartments.

It was here that the run-of-the-mill clients were introduced: here were Ibises of Egypt, mummies with gilded bands, a crocodile yawning from the ceiling, and death's heads with eyeless sockets and gumless teeth. Old, musty volumes, torn and rat-eaten, met the eye of the visitor in pell-mell confusion. Behind the curtain were phials, singularly shaped boxes, and vases of curious construction and all was lit by two small silver lamps which, supplied with perfumed oil, cast their yellow flame around the sombre ceiling from which each hung by three blackened chains.

René, alone, his arms crossed, was striding around the second compartment, shaking his head. After a lengthy, troubled musing he paused before an hour-glass.

'Ah!' he said, 'I forgot to turn it. Perhaps the sand has all passed a long time ago.'

Then looking at the moon, as it struggled through a heavy black cloud which seemed to hang over Notre-Dame, he said, 'It is nine o'clock. If she comes, she will come, as usual, in an hour or an hour and a half; then there will be time for everything.'

At this moment a noise on the bridge was heard. René applied his ear to a long tube, the end of which reached into the street.

'No,' he said, 'it is neither *she* nor *them*: it is men's footsteps. They have stopped at my door—they are coming to see me.'

And three knocks were heard at the door.

René rapidly descended, and placed his ear against the door without opening it.

The knocks were repeated.

'Who's there?' asked René.

'Do we have to state our names?' inquired a voice.

'Absolutely indispensable,' replied René.

'Then, I am the Comte Annibal de Coconnas,' said the same voice.

'And I am the Count Lérac de la Mole,' said another voice.

'Wait, wait a second, gentlemen, and I am at your service.' And without further ado, René, drawing the bolts and lifting the bars, opened the door to the two young men, locking it after them. Then leading them up the exterior staircase, he showed them into the second compartment.

As he entered, La Mole made the sign of the cross under his cloak. He was pale, and his hand trembled without his being able to master this symptom of weakness.

Coconnas looked at everything in turn and, seeing the door of the cell, tried to open it.

'Allow me to observe, sir,' said René gravely, placing his hand on Coconnas's, 'that those who do me the honour of a visit have access only to this apartment.'

'Oh, very well,' replied Coconnas, 'besides, I must sit down,' and he placed himself on a chair.

There was profound silence for the next minute—Maître René expecting that one or other of the young men would open the conversation.

'Maître René,' said Coconnas at length, 'you are a very skilful man, and I would like you to tell me if I shall always remain a sufferer from my wound—that is, shall I always experience this shortness of breath which prevents me from riding on horseback, practising feats of arms, and eating rich omelettes?'

René put his ear to Coconnas's chest, and listened attentively to the workings of the lungs.

'No, comte,' he replied, 'you will be cured.'

'Really?'

'Yes, I assure you.'

'Well, I am glad to hear it.'

Again no one spoke.

'Is there nothing else you wish to know, M. le comte?'

'I wish to know,' said Coconnas, 'if I am really in love?'

'You are,' replied René.

'How do you know?'

'Because you ask the question.'

'*Mordi!* you are right. But with whom?'

'With the woman who frequently uses the oath you have just uttered.'

'Ah!' said Coconnas, amazed; 'Maître René, you are a wonderful man! Now, La Mole, it is your turn.'

La Mole blushed, and seemed embarrassed.

'I, M. René,' he stammered, then speaking more firmly as he proceeded, 'do not want to ask you if I am in love, for I know that I am, and do not seek to conceal it from myself. But tell me, shall I be loved in return? For everything that at first seemed favourable has turned against me.'

'Perhaps you have not done all you should do.'

'What is there to do, sir, but to testify, by our respect and devotion to the lady of our thoughts, that she is really and profoundly loved?'

'You know,' replied René, 'that such displays are frequently quite unimportant.'

'Then there is no hope?'

'There is always hope: we must have recourse to science. There are in human nature antipathies to be overcome—sympathies which may be forced. Iron is not the lodestone; but by impregnating it, we make it, in its turn, attract iron.'

'Yes, yes!' muttered La Mole, 'but I do not care for spells and sorcery.'

'If you have such objections, you should not come here,' answered René.

'Come, come, you are talking like a child!' interposed Coconnas. 'Maître René, can you show me the devil?'

'No, M. le comte.'

'I'm sorry for it. I had a question or two to put to his dark highness, and it might have encouraged La Mole.'

'Well, let it be so,' said La Mole; 'let us get to the point at once. I have been told of figures modelled in wax after the resemblance of the beloved object. How effective is it as a method?'

'Infallible.'

'And in the experiment there is nothing which can in any way affect the life or health of the person loved?'

'Nothing.'

'Let us try it, then.'

'Shall I go first?' said Coconnas.

'No,' said La Mole, 'since I have begun, I will go through to the end.'

At this moment, some one rapped lightly at the door—so lightly that Maître René alone heard the knock for which he had been waiting.

He immediately put one ear to the tube, while he made several inquiries of La Mole. Then he added, suddenly,—

'Formulate your wish and call the person you love.'

La Mole knelt, as if about to name a divinity while René going into the other compartment, went out noiselessly by the exterior staircase. An instant afterwards light steps were heard in his shop.

La Mole rose, and saw Maître René standing before him. The Florentine held in his hand a small figure in wax, very indifferently modelled, and wearing a crown and cloak.

'Do you wish to be always loved by your royal mistress?' demanded the perfumer.

'Yes, if my life—my soul, should be the sacrifice!' replied La Mole.

'Good,' said the Florentine, and taking with the ends of his fingers some drops of water from a ewer, he sprinkled them over the figure, and muttered certain Latin words.

La Mole shuddered, believing that some sacrilege was being committed.

'What are you doing?' he inquired.

'I am christening this figure with the name of Marguerite.'

'For what purpose?'

'To establish a bond.'

René then traced on a small strip of red paper certain cabalistic characters, put it into the eye of a steel needle, and with the needle pierced the small wax model in the heart.

Strange to say, at the mouth of the wound a small drop of blood appeared. He then burnt the piece of paper.

The warmth of the needle melted the wax, and dried up the spot of blood.

'Thus,' said René, 'by the bond of sympathy, your love shall pierce and burn the heart of the woman you love.'

Coconnas, as the bolder spirit of the two, laughed, and made light of the whole affair. But La Mole, in love and superstitious, felt a cold dew start from the roots of his hair.

'And now,' continued René, press your lips to the lips of the figure, and say,—

'Marguerite, I love you! Come, Marguerite, come!'

La Mole obeyed.

At this moment they heard the door of the second chamber open and light steps approach. Coconnas, curious and sceptical, drew his dagger, and, fearing a rebuke from René if he raised the tapestry, cut a small piece out with it, and, applying his eye to the hole, uttered a cry of astonishment, to which two female voices answered.

'What is it?' exclaimed La Mole, nearly dropping the waxen figure which René caught from his hands.

'Why,' replied Coconnas, 'the Duchess de Nevers and Madame Marguerite are here!'

'Well, then, sceptic!' replied René, with an austere smile, 'do you still doubt the bond of sympathy?'

La Mole was petrified on seeing the queen: Coconnas was amazed at beholding Madame de Nevers. One believed that René's witchcraft had evoked the spectre of Marguerite: the other, seeing the door through which the lovely phantoms had entered was still open, soon found a rational explanation of the mystery in the world of concrete reality.

Whilst La Mole was crossing himself and sighing, Coconnas, who had driven away all ideas of the foul fiend with the aid of his strong scepticism, having observed, through the chink in the curtain, the astonishment of Madame de Nevers and the rather caustic smile of Marguerite, judged it to be a decisive moment, and understanding that a man may say on behalf of a friend what he cannot say for himself, instead of going to Madame de Nevers, went straight to Marguerite, and bending his knee, after the manner in which the great Artaxerxes was portrayed by fairground mummers,* cried, in a voice not deficient in effect,—

'Madame, a moment ago, at the request of my friend the Count de la Mole, Maître René evoked your spirit. And here, to my utter astonishment is your spirit, accompanied by a body most dear to us, and which I recommend to my friend. Shade of

her Majesty the Queen of Navarre, will you desire the body of
your companion to come to the other side of the curtain?'

Marguerite laughed heartily, and made a sign to Henriette,
who went through the curtain.

'La Mole, my friend,' continued Coconnas, 'be as eloquent as
Demosthenes, as Cicero, as the Chancellor de l'Hôpital!* and be
assured that my life will be in mortal danger if you do not
persuade the body of Madame de Nevers that I am her most
devoted, most obedient, and most faithful servant.'

'But——' stammered La Mole.

'Do what I ask! And you, Maître René, see that we are not
interrupted.'

René did as Coconnas commanded.

'*Mordi!* sir,' said Marguerite, 'you are a man of sense. I will
listen to you. What do you have to say?'

'I have to say to you, madame, that the ghost of my friend—
for he is a ghost, and he proves it by not uttering a single
syllable—I say that this ghost has begged me to use the faculty
which material bodies possess, and to say to you: Lovely Spirit,
the gentleman who thus lost his corporeality has been deprived
of it by the rigour of your eyes. If you were yourself, I would ask
Maître René to plunge me in some sulphurous hole rather than
use such language to the daughter of Henry II, the sister of King
Charles IX, and the wife of the King of Navarre. But ghosts are
freed from all terrestrial pride, and are never haughty when they
love. Therefore, entreat your body, madame, to bestow a little
love on poor La Mole—a soul in trouble, if ever there was one;
a soul persecuted by friendship, which three times thrust into
him several inches of cold steel; a soul burnt by the fire of your
eyes—fire a thousand times more consuming than all the flames
of Tartarus!* Have pity, then, on this poor soul! Love a little
what was the handsome La Mole; and if you no longer possess
speech, ah! bestow a gesture, a smile upon him. The soul of my
friend is a very intelligent soul, and will easily understand. Be
kind to him, then; or, *mordi!* I will run my sword through the
body of René, so that, by virtue of the power which he possesses
over spirits, he may force yours, which he has already evoked at
such a timely juncture, to do all a shadow so kindly disposed as
yours appears to be, should do.'

Marguerite could not repress a burst of laughter at this tirade. Yet preserving the silence which on such an occasion may be supposed characteristic of a royal spirit, she presented her hand to Coconnas, who took it tenderly in his own, and, calling to La Mole, said,—

'Shade of my friend, come here at once!'

La Mole, amazed, overcome, silently obeyed.

'Good,' said Coconnas, taking him by the back of the head—'and now bring the shadow of your dark, handsome countenance into contact with the white and vaporous hand before you.'

And Coconnas, suiting the 'action to the word,' placed this most delicate hand to La Mole's lips, and kept them for a moment respectfully united, without the hand seeking to withdraw itself from the gentle pressure.

Then La Mole, summoning his presence of mind, got to his feet, and leaving the hand of Marguerite in that of Coconnas, took that of the Duchess de Nevers, and, bending his knee, said,—

'Loveliest—most adorable of women—I speak of living women, and not of shadows!' and he turned a look and a smile to Marguerite—'allow a soul freed from its mortal trappings to repair the absence of a body fully absorbed by material feelings. M. de Coconnas, whom you see, is but a man—a man of bold and hardy frame, a living man handsome to gaze upon perhaps, but perishable like all flesh. Yet although a stalwart and knightly gentleman, who, as you have seen, distributes blows as heavy as were ever seen in France—this champion, so full of eloquence in presence of a spirit, dares not approach a female body in the flesh. Which is why he has addressed the spirit of the queen, charging me to speak to your lovely body and tell you that he lays at your feet his soul and heart; that he entreats from your divine eyes a look of pity, from your rosy fingers a favourable sign, and from your musical and heavenly voice words which he will never forget; if not, he pleads for another boon—which is, in case he should not soften your heart, that you will run for the second time my sword—which is a real blade, for swords have no shadows but in the sunshine—run my sword right through his body, for he can live no longer if you do not allow him to live exclusively for you.'

Henriette's eyes (she herself had been a little jealous of Coconnas's address to the Queen of Navarre) turned from La Mole, to whom she had listened, towards Coconnas, to see if the expression on that gentleman's face chimed with the declaration of his friend. It seemed that she was satisfied, for blushing, breathless, conquered, she said to Coconnas, with a smile, which revealed a double row of pearls enclosed in coral,—

'Is this true?'

'*Mordi!*' exclaimed Coconnas, fascinated by her look, 'it is true, indeed. Oh, yes, madame, it is true—true on my life—true on my death!'

'There, then,' said Henriette, holding out her hand, while her eyes proclaimed the feelings of her heart.

Coconnas and La Mole each approached his lady-love. Suddenly the connecting door opened, and René appeared.

'Silence!' he exclaimed in a voice which at once damped all the ardour of the lovers—'silence!'

And they heard in the solid wall the sound of a key in a lock, and of a door grating on its hinges.

'But,' said Marguerite haughtily, 'no one has the right to enter while we are here!'

'Not even the queen-mother?' murmured René in her ear.

Marguerite instantly rushed out by the outer staircase, leading La Mole after her. Henriette and Coconnas followed them.

All four took wing, like so many love-birds on a flowering branch when disturbed by a sudden noise.

20

THE BLACK HENS

THE two couples went just in time. Catherine turned the key in the lock, just as Coconnas and Madame de Nevers closed the secret door. Catherine heard their steps on the stairs.

She cast a suspicious glance around, and then fixing her eyes on René, who stood motionless before her, said,—

'Who was that?'

'Only some lovers, who are quite content with the assurance I gave them that they are really in love.'

'Never mind them,' said Catherine, shrugging her shoulders; 'are we alone?'

'There is no one here but your Majesty and myself.'

'Have you done what I ordered you?'

'About the two black hens?'

'Yes!'

'They are ready, madame.'

'Ah,' muttered Catherine, 'if you were a Jew—'

'Why a Jew, madame?'

'Because you could then read the Hebrew treatises concerning sacrifices.* I have had one of them translated, and I found that it was not in the heart or liver that the Hebrews sought for omens, but in the brain and in the letters traced there by the all-powerful hand of Destiny.'

'Yes, madame, so I have heard from an old rabbi.'

'There are,' said Catherine, 'characters marked that reveal all the future. But the Chaldean seers recommend——'

'What?' asked René, seeing the queen hesitate.

'That the experiment shall be tried on the human brain, as being more developed and more sympathetic to the wishes of the consulter.'

'Alas!' said René, 'your Majesty knows that is impossible.'

'Difficult, at least,' said Catherine. 'But if we had known this on St. Bartholomew's Night, what a rich harvest we might have had. But I will think of it the first time anybody is to be hanged. Meantime let us do what we can. Is the sacrificial room prepared?'

'Yes, madame.'

'Let us go there.'

René lighted a taper made of strange substances which gave off strong odours, and preceded Catherine into the cell.

From among the sacrificial instruments Catherine selected a knife of blue steel, whilst René took up one of the fowls which cowered in the corner.

'How shall we proceed?'

'We will examine the liver of one and the brain of the other. If these two experiments lead to the same result as on the previous occasion, we shall have our proof.'

'Which shall we start with?'

'The liver.'

'Very well,' said René, and he tied the bird to two rings attached to the little altar, so that the creature, turned on its back, could only struggle without stirring from the spot.

Catherine cut open its breast with a single stroke of her knife. The fowl uttered three cries, and, after some convulsions, expired.

'Always three cries!' said Catherine—'three signs of death.'

She then cut open the body.

'And the liver inclining to the left—always to the left, a triple death, followed by a downfall. This is a frightening start, René.'

'We must see, madame, whether the presages from the second correspond with those of the first.'

René threw the dead fowl into a corner, and went towards the other. But it tried to escape, and seeing itself pent up in a corner, flew suddenly over René's head, and in its flight, extinguished the magic taper in Catherine's hand.

'Thus shall our race be extinguished,' said the queen. 'Death shall breathe upon it, and remove it from the face of the earth! Yet three sons! three!' she murmured sorrowfully.

René took the extinguished taper and went to re-light it.

On his return, he found the hen huddled in a corner.

'This time,' said Catherine, 'I will prevent the cries, for I will cut off the head at once.'

And so, as soon as the hen was bound, Catherine severed the head at a single blow. But in the throes of death the beak opened three times, and then closed for ever.

'Did you see?' said Catherine, terrified. 'Instead of three cries, three sighs?—they will all three die. Let us now see the brain.'

She severed the comb from the head, and, carefully opening the skull, tried to make out a letter formed in the bloody cavities that divide the brain.

'There it is again!' cried she, clasping her hands, 'and this time clearer than ever. Look!'

René approached.

'What is this letter?' asked Catherine.

'An H,' replied René.

'How many times repeated?'

'Four,' said he.

'Ay, ay! I see it! that is to say, HENRY IV. Oh,' cried she, casting the knife from her, 'I am accursed in my posterity!'

She was terrible: pale as a corpse, lighted by the dismal taper, and clasping her bloody hands together.

'He will reign!' she exclaimed—'he will reign!'

'He will reign!' repeated René, deep in thought.

The gloomy expression on Catherine's face soon disappeared as a sudden thought passed through her mind.

'René,' said she, without lifting her head from her breast— 'René, do you recollect the terrible history of a doctor at Perugia, who killed both his daughter and his daughter's lover by means of a pomade?'

'Yes, madame.'

'And this lover——'

'Was King Ladislas,* madame.'

'Ah, yes!' murmured she. 'Have you any account of that story?'

'I have an old book that mentions it,' replied René.

'Well, let us go into the other room, and you can show it me.'

They left the cell, the door of which René closed after him.

'Has your Majesty any other orders to give me concerning the sacrifices?'

'No, René, none. I am quite satisfied for now; only at the next execution, you must arrange with the executioner to have the head.'

René bowed and approached the shelves which held his books, reached down one of them, opened it, turned over the leaves an instant, and then handed it to the queen-mother.

Catherine sat down at a table. René placed the magic taper close to her, and by its dim and livid glare she read a few lines.

'Good!' said she, 'this is all I wanted to know.'

She rose from her seat, leaving the book on the table, but bearing away the idea which had germinated in her mind, and would ripen there.

René waited respectfully, taper in hand, in case the queen,

who seemed on the point of leaving, should give him fresh orders or ask fresh questions.

Catherine walked up and down several times without speaking. Then suddenly stopping before René, and fixing on him her eyes, round and piercing like those of a bird of prey,—

'Confess you have given her some love-draught,' said she.

'Who?' asked René, starting.

'La Sauve.'

'I, madame?' said René. 'Never!'

'Never?'

'I swear it.'

'But there must be some magic in it. For he is desperately in love with her, though he is not famous for his constancy.'

'Who, madame?'

'He, Henry the accursed, who is to succeed my three sons, who shall one day sit upon the throne of France, and be called Henry IV,* and is still the son of Jeanne d'Albret.'

And Catherine accompanied these words with a sigh that made René shudder, for he thought of the famous gloves he had prepared, by Catherine's order, for the Queen of Navarre.

'He runs after her still, then?' said René.

'More than ever,' replied the queen.

'I thought that the King of Navarre was in love with his wife now.'

'All a pretence, René. I do not know why, but everybody is seeking to deceive me. My daughter Marguerite is leagued against me. Perhaps she, too, is looking forward to her brother's death. Perhaps she, too, hopes to be Queen of France.'

'Perhaps so,' re-echoed René, resuming his own reverie.

'Ha! we shall see,' said Catherine, advancing towards the main door, for she doubtless judged it useless to use the secret staircase, after René's assurance that they were alone.

René preceded her, and in a few minutes they stood in the laboratory of the perfumer.

'You promised me fresh cosmetics for my hands and lips, René. Winter is approaching,* and you know how tender my skin is.'

'I have already thought of that, madame. I intended to bring you some to-morrow.'

'I shall not be visible before nine o'clock to-morrow evening.
I shall be occupied with my devotions during the day.'

'I will be at the Louvre at nine o'clock, then, madame.'

'Madame de Sauve has beautiful hands and lips,' said Catherine, in a careless tone. 'What pomade does she use?'

'Heliotrope.'

'For her hands?'

'Yes.'

'And her lips?'

'She is going to try a new composition of my invention. I
intended to bring your Majesty a box at the same time.'

Catherine mused an instant.

'She is certainly very beautiful,' said she, pursuing her secret
thoughts, 'and the passion of the Béarnais for her is astonishing.'

'And she is so devoted to your Majesty,' said René.

Catherine shrugged her shoulders.

'When a woman loves, is she faithful to anyone but her lover?
You must have given her some love-potion, René.'

' I swear I have not, madame.'

'Well, we'll say no more about it. Show me this opiate you
spoke of which will make her lips still more rosy.'

René approached a drawer, and showed Catherine six small,
round, silver boxes in a row.

'This is the only spell she ever asked me for,' observed René.
'It is true, as your Majesty says. I composed it expressly for
her, for her lips are so tender that both the sun and wind affect
them.'

Catherine opened one of the boxes. It contained a beautiful
carmine paste.

'Give me some paste for my hands, René,' said she. 'I will take
it with me, for I have none.'

René took the taper, and went to seek, in a private drawer,
what the queen asked for. As he turned, he fancied that he saw
the queen conceal a box under her mantle. He was, however, too
familiar with these habits of the queen to show that he had
noticed the movement. Wrapping the cosmetic she had asked for
in a paper bag ornamented with fleurs-de-lis,—

'Here it is, madame,' he said.

'Thanks, René,' returned the queen. Then after a moment's

silence, 'Do not give Madame de Sauve that paste for a few days; I want to try it myself first.'

And she approached the door.

'Shall I have the honour of escorting your Majesty?' asked René.

'Only to the end of the bridge,' replied Catherine. 'My gentlemen and my litter wait for me there.'

They left the house. At the end of the Rue Barillerie four gentlemen on horseback and a plain litter stood waiting.

On his return, René's first care was to count his boxes of opiates. There was one missing.

21

MADAME DE SAUVE'S BOUDOIR

CATHERINE had calculated rightly in supposing that Henry would speedily resume his habit of spending his evenings with Madame de Sauve. The utmost caution was at first observed in making these visits, but by degrees all precaution was laid aside, and so openly did the King of Navarre admit his preference for the society of Madame de Sauve, that Catherine experienced not the smallest difficulty in ascertaining that, although her daughter Marguerite might claim the title of his queen, the real sovereign of his affections was the fair Charlotte.

We have already made some mention of her apartments, but for the reader's better information we will state that they were situated on the second-floor of the palace, almost immediately above those occupied by Henry himself. Like the suites of rooms occupied by such as were officially employed by the royal family, they were small, dark, and inconvenient. The door opened upon a corridor, feebly lit by an arched window at the farther end, but so completely did the cumbrous sashes interfere with the purpose for which the window had been originally intended, that it was only during a few hours of a sunshiny day that a few straggling rays gained admittance. In winter, it was necessary to light the lamp placed at the end by two o'clock in the day, and since this lamp only contained a certain amount of oil, it followed that, by the hour of Henry's usual visit, it had run out, leaving the whole corridor in a state of darkness.

The suite of rooms devoted to the service of Madame de Sauve consisted of a small antechamber, hung with yellow damask; a receiving-room, with hangings of blue velvet; a sleeping-room, with its bed of curiously carved wood, heavy curtains of rose-coloured satin, and a boudoir containing a looking-glass, set in silver, and paintings representing the loves of Venus and Adonis. Such was the residence, or rather nest, of the lovely Charlotte de la Sauve, lady-in-waiting to her Majesty Queen Catherine.

A more careful examination of the apartment we have just been describing revealed a dressing-table abundantly and luxuriously provided with all the accessories of female beauty, and a small door opening into a kind of oratory, where, raised two steps off the floor, stood a carved *prie-dieu*. On the walls hung three or four paintings, representing the most striking passages in the lives of the saints, together with weapons for female use, both offensive and defensive. For in those times of mysterious intrigue, women carried arms as well as men, and very frequently employed them as skilfully.

The evening on which we have introduced the reader to Madame de Sauve's apartments was the one following the scenes in which Maître René had played so conspicuous a part. The fair Charlotte, seated beside Henry in her sleeping chamber, eloquently discoursing of her fears and affection, touched on the devotion she had shown the night succeeding the massacre of St Bartholomew—the only night Henry had passed in Marguerite's apartments.

Henry, meanwhile, though duly grateful for the deep interest expressed for him by the beautiful creature, who looked more than usually captivating in her simple white peignoir, was more grave and thoughtful than exactly suited Madame de Sauve, who had strictly obeyed Catherine's injunction to demonstrate the most extreme affection for Henry. She looked at him long and eagerly, as though to ascertain how far his words and looks agreed.

'Charlotte,' said Henry, at last, roused by her manner from his meditations, 'there is one question I want to ask you, and I trust to you to answer me truly. How is it that I find you suddenly listening so readily to my advances, and lavishing upon so unworthy a creature as myself the rich treasures of that love I so earnestly, though vainly, sought to obtain before my marriage? Something whispers to me that I am indebted to the interference of her Majesty Queen Catherine for your delightful change of attitude.'

Madame blushed, and hastily exclaimed, 'For Heaven's sake, do not speak so loud when you name the queen-mother!'

'Nay,' answered Henry, with such an air of confidence as to deceive even Madame de Sauve herself, 'there was a time when such caution was essential. But now that I am her daughter's husband, the situation has changed.'

'Ah, Henry!' replied Madame de Sauve, 'you have been sporting with my credulity in persuading me you love me. It is only too clear that you have bestowed your affections with your hand—on Madame Marguerite.'

Henry smiled.

'There!' exclaimed Madame de Sauve, 'you smile so provokingly that I feel I could be very cross with you and forbid you ever to see my face again! May I ask to be informed what your Majesty meant by saying that you owed my love to the orders of the queen-mother?'

'Why, I meant this, my love, and nothing more, that, though your heart felt inclined to return my feelings, you did not dare listen to its dictates till authorized by Catherine herself. But be content, and believe that I fully return your affection. For this reason I will not confide to you the secret working of my thoughts, lest you should be a sufferer, for the friendship of the queen is unstable—there is no depending on it—it is the uncertain, changeable regard of a mother-in-law.'

This was not the point at which Charlotte aimed, and it seemed to her as though an impenetrable barrier separated her from her lover directly she attempted to sound the fathomless recesses of his heart. Her eyes filled with tears, but just as she was about to reply, ten o'clock struck.

'Your Majesty will pardon me for reminding you that it is late and that I am required to be early in my attendance on the queen-mother to-morrow morning.'

'In other words, you are tired of my company, and want to get rid of me—eh, pretty one? Is it not so?' said Henry.

'No,' answered Charlotte, 'I am not well to-night. Since I fear I may be led to say what it may displease your Majesty to hear, I would humbly request you to retire, and leave me to my own sad thoughts.'

'Well!' cried Henry, 'be it as you will. But, as a reward for my obedience, will you not allow me to be present while that beautiful hair is arranged for the night?'

'Does not your Majesty fear the displeasure of Queen Marguerite, should you delay your departure?'

'Charlotte,' answered Henry gravely, 'we agreed never to allude to or mention the name of the Queen of Navarre, yet it seems to me as though, to-night, we have talked of nothing else.'

Madame de Sauve rose with a sigh and seated herself at her toilet-table, while Henry, drawing up a chair beside her, placed one knee on the seat, and, leaning on the back, exclaimed,—

'Mercy on us! what a heap of wonderful things you have here, my pretty Charlotte!—scent bottles, powders, pots of perfume, scented pastilles, phials, washes. Who would think so many accessories were needed to improve upon the perfection of beauty?'

'Still,' replied Charlotte, 'it seems that my toilet lacks the one vital embellishment that would enable me to reign exclusively over your Majesty's heart!'

'Come, come, sweetheart,' interrupted Henry, 'do not let us dwell upon past subjects, but tell me—for I am dying to know— what is the use of this very fine pencil? Now, if I were good at guessing, I would venture to ask if it were intended to trace out the arched brow of my beautiful Charlotte?'

'Your Majesty has guessed correctly. As you say, it is designed to emphasize the form of the eyebrow.'

'Then reward my skill by explaining the purpose of this little ivory rake?'

'To form a perfect and accurate division of the roots of the hair.'

'And this charming little silver box, with the lid so elegantly wrought and embossed?'

'That, sire, was sent to me from René. It contains the lip-salve he has been promising to send for some time to embellish the lips your Majesty has been kind enough to admire.'

And, intending to show the cosmetic to Henry, Charlotte took the little box in her hands, but, just as she was about to open it, a sudden knocking at the door made the lovers start.

'Madame,' said Dariole, poking her head through the curtains that hung before the entrance to the chamber, 'there is someone at the door.'

'Go, see who it is and return quickly,' said her mistress.

During the absence of the confidante, Henry and Charlotte exchanged looks of considerable alarm; the former contemplating a hasty retreat to the oratory, which had more than once afforded him a safe hiding-place when similarly surprised.

'Madame!' cried Dariole, 'it is Maître René, the perfumer.'

At this name, a frown darkened the brows of Henry, and his lips were suddenly and involuntarily compressed.

'Shall I send him away?' asked Charlotte.

'By no means,' answered Henry. 'Maître René is one of those people who do nothing without a motive. He is here for some reason or other. So let him in at once.'

'Will your Majesty want to hide?'

'On no account,' replied Henry, 'for Master René, from whom nothing is hidden, knows perfectly well that I am here.'

'But are there not reasons why his presence should be unpleasant to your Majesty?'

'No!' answered Henry, vainly striving to conceal his emotion, 'none whatever. True, there was a coolness between us, but since the night of St Bartholomew, we have made up all our differences.'

'Show Maître René in,' said Madame de Sauve to Dariole.

And the next instant René entered the chamber, casting around him a quick, searching glance which took in the assembled group as well as every trifling circumstance. He found Madame de Sauve sitting at her dressing table, and Henry reclining on the sofa at the opposite end of the room, so that while the full light fell upon Charlotte, Henry remained in shadow.

'Madame,' said René, with a mixture of respect and familiarity, 'I come to offer my apologies to you.'

'What for, René?' asked Madame de Sauve, with that air of eager coquetry with which a pretty woman greets purveyors of products designed to make her prettier.

'For having so long delayed fulfilling my promise of inventing a fresh beautifier for those lovely lips—and——'

'And for deferring the keeping of that promise until today?—that is what you mean, is it not, worthy Maître René?' inquired Charlotte.

'Today?' repeated René.

'Yes, indeed. It was earlier this evening that I received this box from you.'

'Ah, yes. I had forgotten,' said René, gazing with a singular expression on the small box of lip-salve lying on Madame de Sauve's dressing table, which resembled those in his shop exactly; 'and may I inquire whether you have yet tried it?'

'Not yet. I was just about to do so when you entered.'

René's face became thoughtful, a change which did not escape the notice of Henry. Few things escaped Henry.

'What is the matter, René?' inquired the king.

'Nothing, sire,' answered René. 'I was simply waiting till your Majesty should condescend to address me, before I took my leave of madame la baronne.'

'Nay, nay,' answered Henry smilingly, 'you need no words of mine to know that I am always happy to see you. What do you say, René?—did you doubt it?'

René glanced around him, as though searching each nook and corner of the apartment. Then suddenly ceasing his survey, he took up a position which brought both Madame de Sauve and Henry within his gaze.

Warned by that admirable instinct which in Henry was almost a sixth sense, the king felt sure that some strange conflict was going on in the mind of the perfumer, and hastily turning round, so as to throw his own features into shade, while those of the Florentine were fully lit, he said,—

'By the way, what brings you here so late to-night, Maître René?'

'Have I been so unfortunate as to disturb your Majesty by my visit?' replied the perfumer, retreating backwards to the door.

'Not in the least, I promise you. But I should like to know one thing?'

'What is that, sire?'

'Whether you expected to find me here?'

'I was quite sure your Majesty was nowhere else.'

'You were looking for me, then?'

'I am at least very happy to have met your Majesty.'

'You have something to say to me?' persisted Henry. 'Come, come, don't try to deny it.'

'It is possible I have two words to say to your Majesty,' said René.

Charlotte blushed, for she feared that the revelation the perfumer seemed tempted to make might relate to her previous conduct towards Henry. Feigning to be so absorbed at her dressing-table that she had not heard a word that had passed, she suddenly interrupted the conversation, exclaiming as she opened the box of lip-salve,—

'René, you are a dear good man to have made me this beautiful ointment. And come to think of it, it would be an excellent opportunity to try it while you are here, so that you can assist me with your valuable aid and direction as to the right way of using it.'

So saying, she dipped the tip of her finger in the vermilion paste, and was about to raise it to her lips.

René shuddered, and half extended his arm to prevent her. The hand of the baronne had almost touched her lips.

Henry, concealed in deep shadow, marked well the action of the one and the reaction of the other.

René became ghastly pale as the distance between the finger of Charlotte and her lips was reduced to the smallest possible space. Then, suddenly springing forwards, he stopped her arm at the very instant that Henry arose with the same intention. The king immediately fell back on the sofa, without saying a word.

'One moment, madame!' cried René, with a forced smile, 'but this salve must not be used without very particular directions.'

'And who will supply me with these directions?'

'I will.'

'When?'

'Directly I have finished saying what I have to say to his Majesty the King of Navarre.'

Charlotte opened her eyes with amazement by the singular and mysterious conversation which was being carried on without her understanding a word of its import. And she continued in mute astonishment, holding the pot of salve in one hand, staring at the extremity of the finger tinged by the pink ointment she had intended for her lips.

Meanwhile, Henry rose, and moved by an idea which, like all the thoughts of the young king, had two sides, one apparently superficial and the other deep and profound, went straight to Charlotte, and taking her hand, reddened as it was with the ointment, feigned to be on the point of putting it to his lips.

'Wait one minute!' exclaimed René eagerly—'just an instant! Be kind enough, madame, to wash your fair hands with this Naples soap. I quite forgot to send it when I sent the salve, but I now have the honour of presenting it to you in person.'

And taking from its silver envelope a cake of greenish coloured soap, he put it into a gilt basin, poured water upon it, and, bending one knee to the ground, he presented the whole to Madame de Sauve.

'Why, really, Master René,' cried Henry, 'your gallantry quite astonishes me. You put our court beaux to shame!'

'Oh, what a delicious fragrance!' exclaimed Charlotte, rubbing her fair hands with the pearly froth that arose from the soap.

René, unmoved by Henry's jest, continued to fulfil his self-imposed duties with the utmost exactness. Removing the basin he had been holding, he offered Charlotte a towel of the most delicate texture, and when she had thoroughly dried her hands, said,—

'And now, my lord, you are at liberty to follow your royal inclination.'

Charlotte held out her hand to Henry, who kissed it and returned to his seat, more convinced than ever that something very extraordinary was going on in the mind of the Florentine.

'Well?' said Charlotte.

The Florentine seemed as though he were trying to summon all his resolution, and, after a short hesitation, he turned towards Henry.

'SIRE!' said René to Henry, 'I wish to speak to you on a matter which has for a long time occupied my attention.'

'Of perfumes?' asked Henry, with a smile.

'Well, yes, sire—of perfumes,' replied René, with a singular nod of his head.

'Well, then, speak on, for it is a subject which has much interested me.'

René looked at the king, trying to read his thoughts, but they were impenetrable. So he continued:

'One of my friends, sire, has just arrived from Florence. This friend has devoted much of his time to astrology.'

'Yes,' said Henry, 'I know it is a Florentine pursuit.'

'And he has, in association with the leading savants of the world, drawn the horoscopes of the principal personages in Europe.'

'Indeed!' said Henry.

'And as the house of Bourbon is amongst the leading houses, descending, as it does, from the Comte de Clermont, fifth son of Saint Louis,* your Majesty may well suppose that yours has not been forgotten.'

Henry listened still more attentively, adding, with a smile as indifferent as he could make it, 'And do you remember this horoscope?'

'Ah!' answered René, with a shrug, 'your horoscope is one that is not easily forgotten.'

'Really!' said Henry, with an ironical look.

'Yes, sire. According to the indications of this horoscope, your Majesty is called to the most brilliant destiny.'

The eyes of the young prince blazed involuntarily, and then as rapidly reassumed their look of indifference.

'All these Italian oracles are flatterers,' said Henry, 'and he who flatters, lies. Are there not some who say I shall command armies?'

And he burst into loud laughter. But an observer less preoccupied than René would have seen the effort this laugh had cost.

'Sire,' said René coolly, 'the horoscope announces better than that.'

'Does it announce that at the head of one of these armies I shall win battles?'

'Better than that, sire.'

'Well, then,' said Henry, 'at all events, I shall be a conqueror.'

'Sire, *you will be king!*'

'Eh, *ventre-saint-gris!*' said Henry, as his heart beat with sudden violence, 'am I not so already?'

'Sire, my friend knows what he promises. Not only will you be king, but you will reign.'

'And then,' said Henry, in the same mocking strain, 'your friend needs ten golden crowns, does he not, René? For such a prophecy in times like these is indeed an ambitious one. Well, René, I am not rich, so I will give your friend five now, and the other five when the prophecy shall come to pass.'

'Sire,' said René, 'allow me to proceed.'

'What, is there more?' said Henry. 'Well, if I am to be an emperor, I will offer double.'

'Sire, my friend came from Florence with his horoscope, which he has renewed in Paris, and which gives again the same result, and he has confided the secret to me.'

'A secret that concerns his Majesty?' inquired Charlotte eagerly.

'I believe so,' replied the Florentine.

'Then say it,' answered the Baroness de Sauve. 'What is it?'

'It is,' said the Florentine, weighing each of his words well— 'it is in reference to the reports of poisoning which have been circulated for some time at court.'

A slight expansion of the nostrils was the only indication which the King of Navarre showed of his increased attention to the sudden change in the conversation.

'And does your friend, the Florentine,' inquired the king, 'know anything of these poisonings?'

'Yes, sire.'

'How can you confide to me a secret which is not your own, René, particularly when the secret is so important?' inquired Henry in the most natural tone he could assume.

'My friend has some advice to ask of your Majesty.'

'Of me?'

'What is surprising about that, sire? When my friend confided his secret to me, your Majesty was the leader of the Calvinistic party, and M. de Condé the second.'

'So?' observed Henry.

'This friend hoped you would use your all-powerful influence with the Prince de Condé to beg him not to be hostile towards him.'

'Explain yourself, René, if you would have me follow your drift,' replied Henry, without manifesting the least alteration in his features or voice.

'Sire, your Majesty will follow at the first word. This friend knows all the particulars of the attempt to poison monseigneur, the Prince de Condé.'*

'What! did they attempt to poison the Prince de Condé?' exclaimed Henry, with well-feigned surprise. 'Indeed! and when was that?'

René looked steadfastly at the king, and replied in these words only,—

'A week ago, your Majesty.'

'Was it an enemy?' inquired the king.

'Yes,' replied René; 'an enemy whom your Majesty knows, and who knows your Majesty.'

'Yes, now I remember,' said Henry. 'I must have heard about it but I forget the details, which your friend wishes to disclose to me, you say.'

'Well, a scented apple was offered to the Prince de Condé, but fortunately his physician was there when it was brought to him: he took it from the messenger, and smelt it. Two days afterwards a gangrenous humour formed in his face, then a suffusion of blood, and then a cancerous sore which ate into his cheeks, were the price of his devotion or the result of his imprudence.'

'Unfortunately, being already half a Catholic,' answered Henry, 'I have lost all my influence over M. de Condé, and therefore your friend would gain nothing by approaching me.'

'It was not only with M. de Condé that your Majesty might,

through your influence, be useful to my friend, but with the Prince de Porcian, brother of the Porcian who was poisoned.'

'What!' observed the king, 'do you also know the details of the poisoning of the Prince de Porcian?'*

'Yes,' was the reply. 'They knew that every night he burnt a lamp near his bed: they poisoned the oil, and he choked in the fumes.'

Henry clenched his moistened palms together with rage.

'So,' he replied, 'this man you term your friend knows not only the details of this poisoning, but also the perpetrator?'

'Yes, which is why he wished to ascertain from you, if you had sufficient influence with the Prince de Porcian to induce him to pardon the murderer of his brother?'

'Unfortunately,' replied Henry, 'being still half Huguenot, I have no influence over the Prince de Porcian. Your friend was wrong, therefore, to approach me.'

'But what do you make of the leanings of the Prince de Condé and M. de Porcian?'

'How can I tell how they stand, René? God has not, as far as I know, given me the privilege of reading hearts.'

'Your Majesty may ask yourself the question,' said the Florentine calmly, 'has there not been in your Majesty's life some event so gloomy that it may serve as an example of clemency—so painful that it may be a touchstone for generosity?'

These words were pronounced in a tone that made Charlotte shudder. The allusion was so direct, so manifest, that the young woman turned aside to hide her flushed face and avoid Henry's eyes.

Henry made an effort to control himself, smoothed his brow, which, during the Florentine's address, had been heavy with menace, and changing the deep filial grief which weighed upon his heart into an air of vague reflection, said,—

'In my life—a gloomy event!—no, René—no; I can only remember the folly and recklessness of my youth, mixed with those fatalities, more or less cruel, which are inflicted on all mankind by the laws of nature and the tribulations sent by God.'

René mastered himself in his turn, and turning his glance

from Henry to Charlotte, as if to excite the one and restrain the other—for Charlotte, going towards her dressing-table to conceal the feelings aroused by this conversation, again reached out for the box of salve.

'But, what if, sire, you were the brother of the Prince de Porcian, or the brother of the Prince de Condé, and your brother had been poisoned, or your father assassinated?'

Charlotte uttered a cry, and again was about to apply the salve to her lips. René saw this, neither stopped her by word nor gesture, but exclaimed urgently:

'In the name of Heaven! sire, answer. Sire, if you were in their place, what would you do?'

Henry collected himself, wiped, with tremulous hand, his forehead bedewed with drops of cold perspiration, and elevating his figure to its full height, replied, in the midst of the breathless silence of René and Charlotte,—

'If I were in their place, and were sure of being king—that is to say, of representing God on earth—I would do like God, and forgive!'

'Madame,' exclaimed René, snatching the salve from Madame de Sauve's hands—'madame, give me that box! I see my assistant has brought you the wrong one. I will send you another tomorrow.'

23

A NEW CONVERT

ON the following day there was to be a hunt in the forest of Saint-Germain. Henry had ordered that there should be made ready, at eight o'clock in the morning, saddled and bridled, a small horse of the Béarn breed,* which he intended as a present for Madame de Sauve, but which he first wished to try himself. The horse was duly brought, and as the clock struck eight Henry descended.

The horse, full of breed and fire, in spite of its small size, was plunging about in the court-yard. It was cold, and a slight hoar frost covered the ground.*

Henry was about to cross the court-yard on his way to the stables where the horse and his groom were waiting, when passing before a Swiss soldier, who was on guard at the door, the sentinel presented arms to him, saying,—

'God preserve his Majesty the King of Navarre!'

At these words, and particularly the accent and emphasis of the voice that uttered it, the Béarnais started, and retreated a step, muttering the words, 'de Mouy!'

'Yes, sire, de Mouy.'

'And what are you doing here?'

'Looking for you.'

'What do you want?'

'I must speak to your Majesty!'

'Rash man!' said the king, going close to him, 'do you know that you are risking your head?'

'I know it, and I am here.'

Henry turned pale, looked around him, and retreated a second time no less quickly than before.

He saw the Duke d'Alençon at a window.

Then changing his air, Henry took the musket from de Mouy, and appeared to be examining it.

'De Mouy,' he said, 'you must have some very powerful reason that brings you here and prompts you to throw yourself into the wolf's throat.'

'I have, sire, and for a week I have been on the watch. It was only yesterday I learned that your Majesty meant to try this horse this morning, and I took my post, accordingly, at this door of the Louvre.'

'Why in this disguise?'

'The captain of the company is a Protestant, and one of my friends.'

'Take your musket, and continue your guard. We are being watched. When I return, I will try to say a word to you. But if I do not speak to you, do not stop me. Adieu!'

De Mouy resumed his measured tread, and Henry advanced towards the horse.

'What is that pretty creature?' inquired the Duke d'Alençon, from his window.

'A horse I am going to try this morning.'

'But it is not a man's horse.'

'It is intended for a pretty woman.'

'Be careful, Henry, or you will be indiscreet, for we shall see this pretty woman at the chase. If I do not know whose knight you are, I shall at least learn whose squire you may be.'

'Eh, *mon Dieu!* you will not know,' said Henry, with his wonted laugh, 'for this pretty woman is unwell this morning and cannot ride to-day.' And he sprang into the saddle.

'Bah!' said d'Alençon, laughing, 'poor Madame de Sauve!'

'François! François!—it is you who are indiscreet.'

'And what ails the lovely Charlotte?' inquired the duke.

'Why,' answered Henry, 'I hardly know. A kind of heaviness in the head, as Dariole informed me—a weakness in all her limbs, a general feeling of languor.'

'And will that prevent you from accompanying us?' inquired d'Alençon.

'Why should it?' was Henry's reply. 'You know how madly I love a hunt. Nothing would make me miss one.'

'You will miss this one, however, Henry,' replied the Duke, as he turned round. He spoke briefly to someone Henry could not see, then added: 'I learn from his Majesty that the hunt cannot take place.'

'Bah!' said Henry, with the most disappointed air in the world, 'and why not?'

'Very important letters have arrived from M. de Nevers, and there is a council being held by the king, the queen-mother, and my brother the Duke d'Anjou.'

'Ah!' said Henry to himself, 'does this mean there is news from Poland?'* Then he added, aloud, 'In that case, it is useless for me to run any more risk on this slippery ground. *Au revoir!* brother.' And pulling his horse up short by de Mouy, 'My friend,' he said, 'call one of your comrades to finish your guard. Help the groom to take the saddle off my horse, put it on your head, and carry it to the goldsmith in the royal stable: there is some embroidery to do to it, which he did not have time to finish. You can bring me back his answer.'

De Mouy hastily obeyed, for the Duke d'Alençon had disappeared from his window, and it was obvious he had conceived some suspicion. Scarcely, indeed, had the Huguenot chief left his post, than the duke appeared. A real Swiss had taken de Mouy's place.

D'Alençon looked attentively at the fresh sentinel, then turning to Henry,—

'This is not the man with whom you were conversing just now, is it, brother?'

'The other was a young fellow of my household, for whom I obtained a post amongst the Swiss. I gave him an errand, which he has gone about.'

'Ah!' said the duke, as if satisfied with the answer, 'and how is Marguerite?'

'I am just going to inquire, brother.'

'Haven't you seen her since yesterday?'

'No. I went last night at eleven o'clock, but Gillonne told me she was very tired and asleep.'

'You will not find her in her apartment. She has gone out.'

'Yes,' replied Henry, 'most likely. She was going to the Convent of the Annunciation.'*

There was no means of pushing the conversation further, as Henry appeared determined to reply reasonably to all his questions.

The two brothers-in-law then separated—the Duke d'Alençon to go and hear the news, as he said, and the King of Navarre to return to his apartment.

He had not been there five minutes, when there was a knock at his door. He let de Mouy in and closed the door after him.

'Sire,' said de Mouy, 'the time for action has arrived. Fear nothing, sire—we are alone. I will be quick, for time is very precious. Your Majesty may now, by a single word, restore to us everything our holy religion has lost during this disastrous year. Let us be explicit, let us be brief, let us be frank.'

'I listen, gallant de Mouy,' replied the king, seeing that it was impossible any longer to avoid an explanation.

'Is it true that your Majesty has abjured the Protestant religion?'

'It is true,' said Henry.

'Yes, but is it an abjuration of the lips or of the heart?'

'We are always grateful to God when He has saved our life,'

replied Henry, not replying directly to the question, 'and God has visibly spared me in a most cruel strait and danger.'

'But, sire,' continued de Mouy, 'confess that your abjuration is not a matter of conviction but of calculation. You abjured so that the king might let you live, and not because God spared your life.'

'Whatever may be the cause of my conversion, de Mouy,' answered Henry, 'I am not less a Catholic.'

'Yes, but shall you always continue one? Should an occasion present itself, would you not relapse? Well, this occasion presents itself at this moment: La Rochelle has rebelled; Roussillon and Béarn only await the signal to act, and Guyenne is ripe for revolt.* Only admit that you turned Catholic on compulsion, and I will answer for all the rest.'

'My dear de Mouy, a gentleman of my birth is never forced—what I have done, I have done freely.'

'But, sire,' continued the young man, his heart oppressed by this unexpected resistance. 'You do not realize that in thus abandoning us, you betray us.'

Henry remained perfectly unmoved.

'Yes,' de Mouy continued, 'you betray us, sire. For very many of us have come, risking our lives, to save your honour and liberty. We have prepared everything to give you a throne, sire; not only liberty, but power; a throne for your acceptance; for, in two months, you may choose between France and Navarre.'

'De Mouy,' replied Henry, looking downwards for an instant to conceal the joy that sparkled in his eyes; 'de Mouy, I am safe; I am a Catholic; I am the husband of Marguerite; I am the brother of King Charles; I am son-in-law of my good mother Catherine. When I took all these relations upon me, I not only calculated the chances, but also the obligations.'

'But, sire,' replied de Mouy, 'what am I to believe? They say that your marriage is incomplete; they say you are free in your own heart; they say that Catherine's hatred——'

'Lies, lies, all lies!' interrupted the Béarnais quickly. 'You have been impudently misled, my friend. My dearest Marguerite is indeed my wife—Catherine is truly my mother; King Charles IX is really the lord and master of my life and of my heart.'

De Mouy started, and an almost contemptuous smile passed over his lips.

'Then, sire,' said he, trying to see into a mind so full of concealment, 'this is the answer I shall bear to my brothers in arms. I shall say that the King of Navarre extends his hand and gives his heart to those who cut our throats. I shall say that he has become the flatterer of the queen-mother, and the friend of Maurevel.'

'My dear de Mouy,' was Henry's response, 'the king is just breaking up the council. I must go and learn what were the important reasons which postponed the hunt. Adieu! imitate me, my friend: renounce politics, swear allegiance to the king, and take the mass.'

And Henry led, or rather pushed the young man to the door of his antechamber, whilst de Mouy's amazement was fast giving way to fury.

Scarcely was the door closed than, unable to resist his desire of visiting his vengeance on something for want of somebody, de Mouy grabbed his hat, threw it on the ground, and trampling it under foot, as a bull does the cloak of a matador,—

'By God!' he cried. 'He is a cowardly prince. I have a great mind to kill myself on this very spot, that my blood may stain him and his name for ever.'

'Hush! M. de Mouy,' said a voice which came from behind a half-opened door, 'hush! or someone else will hear you besides myself.'

De Mouy turned round suddenly, and saw the Duke d'Alençon wrapped in his cloak, who was thrusting his pale face into the corridor to ascertain if he and de Mouy were really alone.

'The Duke d'Alençon!' cried de Mouy, 'I am lost!'

'On the contrary,' said the prince, in a hushed voice, 'you have perhaps found what you are looking for. Let me say by way of proof that I would prefer you not to kill yourself here as you propose. Believe me, your blood could be better employed than in reddening the floor of the King of Navarre.'

And at these words, the duke opened wide the door of the chamber which had been hitherto ajar.

'This chamber belongs to two of my gentlemen,' said the

duke; 'and no one will come looking for you here. So we may converse at our ease. Come, sir.'

'I am at your Royal Highness's service,' said the amazed conspirator, and he entered the chamber, the duke closing the door after him quickly and securely.

De Mouy entered, furious, enraged, and desperate. But gradually the cold and steady gaze of the young Duke François had the effect on the young Huguenot captain that ice has upon intoxication.

'M. de Mouy,' said François. 'I thought I recognized you in spite of your disguise, as you presented arms to my brother Henry. So, de Mouy, are you not satisfied with the King of Navarre?'

'Monseigneur!'

'Come, come, speak frankly to me, and perhaps you may find I am your friend.'

'You, monseigneur!'

'Yes, I—but speak.'

'I know not what to say to your Highness—what I had to tell the King of Navarre touched on interests impossible to be understood by you. Besides,' added de Mouy, 'we spoke only of trifling matters.'

'Trifles!' exclaimed the duke.

'Yes, monseigneur.'

'Trifles! It was for trifles that you risked your life by returning to the Louvre when you well know your head is worth its weight in gold? For it is well known that you, like the King of Navarre and the Prince de Condé, are one of the principal leaders of the Huguenots.'*

'If you think so, monseigneur, act towards me as the brother of Charles the king, and the son of Catherine the queen-mother, should act.'

'Why would you have me act so, when I tell you I am your friend? Just tell me the truth, and——'

'Monseigneur, I swear to you——'

'Do not swear, sir. The reformed religion forbids oaths, and especially false oaths.'

De Mouy frowned.

'I tell you I know everything,' continued the duke.

De Mouy was still silent.

'Do you doubt it?' proceeded the prince earnestly. 'Well, then, my dear de Mouy, I shall have to convince you, and you will see if I speak the truth or not. Did you or did you not offer my brother-in-law, Henry, there just now'—and the duke pointed towards Henry's apartments—'your aid, and that of your allies, to re-establish him in his kingdom of Navarre?'

De Mouy looked at the duke in amazement.

'Offers which he refused in alarm——'

De Mouy remained stupefied with surprise.

'Did you not, then, invoke your ancient friendship—the remembrance of your common religion? Did you not, then, seek to lure on the King of Navarre by a very brilliant hope and prospect—so brilliant that he was dazzled at it—the hope of acquiring the crown of France itself? Eh! am I, or am I not, well informed? Was it not this you came to propose to the Béarnais?'

'Monseigneur!' exclaimed de Mouy 'This is so accurate a version of all that occurred, that I ask myself at this moment whether I ought not to say to your Highness that you lie, challenge you in this very chamber to combat, and bury this terrible secret under your death and mine.'

'Easy, my brave de Mouy, easy,' replied d'Alençon, without changing the expression on his face or reacting in any way to this threat, 'this secret will be better kept between us two if we both live than if one of us were to die. Listen to me, and relax your grip on your sword. For the third time I tell you, you are with a friend. Reply, then, as to a friend. Tell me, did the King of Navarre refuse your offers?'

'He did, my lord, and I confess it because the admission can compromise no one but myself.'

'And are you still of the same opinion you were when you left my brother Henry's chamber, and said he was a cowardly prince, and unworthy any longer to remain your leader?'

'I am, monsiegneur, and more so than ever.'

'Well, then, M. de Mouy, am I, the third son of Henry II,— I, a son of France—am I good enough to command your soldiers and honourable enough for you to trust my word?'

'You, monseigneur! you, chief of the Huguenots?'

'Why not? This is the age of conversions, as you know, and if Henry has become a Catholic, why may not I turn Protestant?'

'Unquestionably, monseigneur; but perhaps you will explain to me——'

'Nothing more simple. Let me summarize everybody's politics. My brother Charles kills the Huguenots so that he may reign more absolutely. My brother d'Anjou lets him kill them so that he may succeed my brother Charles, and, as you know, my brother Charles is often ill. But I—it is very different with me, who will never reign over France, for I have two elder brothers between me and the crown; I, whom the hatred of my mother and brothers, more even than the law of nature, alienates from the throne—I, who see before me no family affection, no glory, no kingdom—I, who have a heart as noble as my brothers. Which is why, de Mouy, I would dearly love to cut myself out a throne with my sword in this France which they cover with gore! And this is what I want, de Mouy—listen: I want to be King of Navarre, not by right of birth, but by election. Mark well: you can have no objection to this, for I am no usurper. My brother refuses your offers, and, buried in torpor, declares openly that the kingdom of Navarre is a fiction. With Henry of Béarn, you have nothing now in common; with me you may have a sword and a name. François d'Alençon, son of France, can protect all his companions or accomplices, as you may please to call them. Well, then! what say you to this offer,* M. de Mouy?'

'I say it staggers me, monseigneur.'

'De Mouy, we shall have many obstacles to overcome. Do not show yourself so scrupulous and difficult with the son of a king, and the brother of a king, who comes to you.'

'Monseigneur, the thing would be done at once, if I were the one to decide. But we have a council, and, however brilliant the offer, perhaps the leaders will not accede to it unconditionally.'

'That is another matter, and your reply is that of an honest heart and a prudent mind. By the way in which I have acted, de Mouy, you must see that I am frank and honourable. Treat me in turn like a man you respect, not as a prince whom you would flatter. De Mouy, have I any chance?'

'On my word, monseigneur, and since your Highness desires to have my opinion, I say you have every chance, since the King

of Navarre refuses the offer I made him. But I repeat to you,
monseigneur, it is essential that I consult with our leaders.'

'Of course, sir,' was d'Alençon's reply. 'When shall I have the
answer?'

De Mouy considered the prince in silence. Then coming to a
decision, said,—

'Monseigneur, give me your hand. It is vital that the hand of
a son of France should touch mine, so I may be sure I shall not
be betrayed.'

The duke not only extended his hand to de Mouy, but seized
it, and clasped it in his own.

'Now, monseigneur, I am reassured,' said the young Huguenot. 'If we are betrayed, I shall acquit you of all participation.
Without this, monseigneur, however little you were involved in
such treachery, you would be dishonoured.'

'Why do you say that, de Mouy, before you have even brought
me the reply of your chiefs?'

'Because, monseigneur, by wanting to know when the answer
shall be given, you ask me where our leaders are. If I replied,
"this evening," you would know that the chiefs were concealed
in Paris.'

And as he said these words, with a gesture of distrust, de
Mouy fixed his piercing eye on the face of the false and vacillat-
ing young prince.

'So, you remain mistrustful, de Mouy? Still, I cannot expect
to earn your trust at our first conference. You will know me
better by-and-by. You say this evening, then, M. de Mouy?'

'Yes, monseigneur, for time presses. This evening. But
where?'

'Here, in the Louvre: in this apartment, if that suits you.'

'This apartment is occupied.'

'By two of my gentlemen.'

'Monseigneur, I think it would be imprudent for me to return
to the Louvre.'

'Why?'

'Because others may recognize me just as your Highness did.
Yet, if you give me a safe-conduct, I will return to the Louvre.'

'De Mouy,' replied the duke, 'my safe-conduct, if found on
your person, would destroy me and would not save you; I cannot

do what you ask. The least evidence of complicity between us, if revealed to my mother or brothers, would cost me my life. Make, therefore, another call on your courage. I will guarantee your safety: repeat on my word what you tried without my brother's word. Come to the Louvre this evening.'

'But how?'

'I think I see the means before me—here.'

And the duke saw on the bed La Mole's dress spread out—a magnificent cherry-coloured cloak embroidered with gold, a hat with a white plume, its crown decorated with a string of pearls with gold and silver between them, and a grey satin doublet also worked with gold.

'Do you see this cloak, feather and doublet?' said the duke. 'They belong to M. de la Mole, one of my gentlemen, and a fop of the first order. This outfit creates a sensation at court, and M. de la Mole is recognized a hundred yards off when he wears it. I will give you his tailor's address, and, by paying him double the price, he will bring you a similar suit this evening. Remember the name—M. de la Mole.'

The duke had scarcely done speaking when a step was heard of someone approaching, and a key was turned in the lock of the door.

'Who's there?' inquired the duke, hastening towards the door, which he secured with the bolt.

'*Pardieu!*' replied a voice from without, 'that is a very odd question: "Who are you?" It is very strange to come to one's own room and be asked, "Who's there?"'

'Oh! is that you, M. de la Mole?'

'Of course it is. But who are you?'

D'Alençon turned round suddenly and said to de Mouy: 'Do you know M. de la Mole?'

'No, monseigneur.'

'Does he know you?'

'I should say no.'

'Then all will be well. Just pretend to be looking out of the window.'

De Mouy obeyed, and the duke opened the door. La Mole entered hastily, but when he saw the duke he stepped back, surprised, saying,—

'Monseigneur the duke! Your pardon, monseigneur!'

'That is not necessary. I wished to see someone, and made use of your apartment.'

'Quite right, monseigneur. But allow me to take my cloak and hat, for I lost mine last night on the Quai de la Grève.'

'Really! You must have had an encounter with some determined robbers, then?'

The duke handed the young gentleman his clothes, and La Mole retired to dress in the antechamber. On his return in a few moments,—

'Has your Highness heard or seen anything of the Comte de Coconnas?' he asked.

'No, M. le comte. He should have been on duty this morning.'

'Then they have murdered him!' said La Mole to himself, as he bowed and rushed out again.

The duke listened to his retreating footsteps, and then, opening the door, said to de Mouy,—

'Look at him, and try to imitate his easy and distinctive way of walking.'

'I will do my best,' replied De Mouy. 'Unfortunately, I am not a fine gentleman, only a soldier.'

'I shall expect you before midnight here, or in another empty apartment. To-night, before midnight.'

'To-night, before midnight.'

'Ah! by the bye—de Mouy, swing your right arm as you walk; it is a peculiarity of M. de la Mole.'

24

THE RUE TIZON AND THE RUE CLOCHE PERCE

LA MOLE ran out of the Louvre, and went in search of poor Coconnas.

First, he went to the Rue de l'Arbre-Sec, to Maître la Hurière. But he found nothing there except breakfast, to which, despite his anxiety, he did ample justice.

His appetite appeased, La Mole walked along the Seine. Reaching the Quai de la Grève, he recognized the spot where he had been stopped three or four hours before, and found on the field of battle a fragment of his hat-plume. La Mole had ten feathers, each handsomer than the other. But he stopped to pick up this, or rather the only fragment that remained of it, and was looking at it with a sorry air when an authoritative voice bade him stand aside. La Mole looked up, and saw a litter, preceded by two pages and followed by a squire. La Mole thought he recognized the litter and stood to one side.

He was not mistaken.

'M. de la Mole?' said a sweet voice from the litter, while a hand, white and soft as satin, pulled back the curtains.

'Yes, madame,' replied La Mole, bowing.

'M. de la Mole, with a feather in his hand?' said the lady. 'Are you in love? Are you looking for lost traces of your mistress?'

'Yes, madame,' returned La Mole, 'I am in love, and to desperation. As for these relics, they are my own, not the ones I seek. But permit me to inquire after your Majesty's health.'

'Excellent—never better. Probably it is because I spent the night in a convent.'

'Ah, in a convent!' said La Mole, looking at Marguerite with an odd expression.

'Yes. And what is so astonishing in that?'

'May I venture to inquire, in what convent?'

'Certainly; I make no mystery of it: at the Convent of the Annunciation. But what are you doing here, with so wild an air?'

'Madame, I was looking for a friend, and instead of him I find this feather.'

'Which belongs to him? You really alarm me for him. This place has an evil reputation.'

'Your Majesty may be reassured: the feather is mine. I lost it here this morning at about half-past five, in escaping from four bandits who attacked me.'

Marguerite suppressed an exclamation of terror.

'Oh, tell me all about it!'

'A simple matter, madame. It was, as I said, about half-past five——'

'And at half-past five you were already out?'

'No, madame, I had not yet gone home.'

'Ah!' said Marguerite, with a smile that to everyone else would have seemed malicious, but which La Mole thought adorable—'returning home so late! You are rightly served.'

'I do not complain, your Majesty,' said La Mole, 'and had I been killed, I would have thought myself far happier than I deserve. But as I was returning, four scoundrels rushed on me, armed with long knives, and I had to make myself scarce, for I had left my sword in the house where I had spent the night.'

'Oh, I understand,' said Marguerite, with an exquisite air of simplicity—'you are going to fetch your sword.'

La Mole looked at Marguerite uncertainly.

'Madame,' said he, 'I should be glad to return thither, for my sword is an excellent blade; but I do not know where the house is.'

'What!' said Marguerite, 'you do not know where the house is?'

'Devil take it if I have the faintest idea.'

'How very strange! Quite a romance, upon my word.'

'Just so, madame.'

'Relate it to me.'

'It is rather long.'

'No matter, I have plenty of time.'

'And very incredible.'

'Go on, I am excessively credulous.'

'Your Majesty commands me?'

'Yes, if necessary.'

'I obey. Last night we supped at Maître la Hurière's—'

'First,' asked Marguerite, with wide-eyed simplicity, 'who is Maître la Hurière?'

'Maître la Hurière, madame,' answered La Mole, with another uncertain look at the queen, 'is the landlord of the *Belle Etoile*, in the Rue de l'Arbre-Sec.'

'Ah, I understand. And you were supping at La Hurière's, with your friend Coconnas, no doubt?'

'Yes, madame, with my friend Coconnas, when a man entered, and gave each of us a note.'

'And the notes were the same?'

'Exactly.'

'And they contained——'

'But one line,—

' "*You are expected in the Rue Saint Antoine, opposite the Rue de Jouy.*" '

'And no signature?'

'None, but three words, three delicious words, that promised a triple happiness.'

'And what were these three words?'

'EROS, CUPIDO, AMOR.'

'Three soft, pretty names, indeed. And did they deliver what they promised?'

'Oh, yes, madame,' cried La Mole, with enthusiasm, 'a hundred-fold!'

'Continue. I am anxious to know what was waiting for you in the Rue Saint Antoine.'

'Two duennas, who stipulated that our eyes should be bandaged. Your Majesty may imagine we made no great difficulty. My guide led me to the right, my friend's led him to the left.'

'And then?' asked Marguerite.

'I do not know where they took my friend. Perhaps to the infernal regions,' said La Mole. 'But I was taken to Paradise.'

'From which your excessive curiosity no doubt got you expelled.'

'Exactly so: your Majesty has the gift of divination. I had decided to wait for the dawn so that I might know where I was, when the duenna entered, blindfolded me again, and led me away, out of the house, for perhaps a hundred paces, and then made me promise not to take off the bandage till I had counted fifty. I counted fifty, and then, on taking off the handkerchief, found myself in the Rue St Antoine, opposite the Rue de Jouy. On returning here, just now, I perceived a fragment of my feather, which I shall preserve as a precious relic of this glorious night. But amidst my happiness, one thing worries me: what can have become of my friend?'

'He is not at the Louvre, then?'

'Alas, no! and I have sought him at the *Belle Etoile*, at the Tennis Court,* and everywhere, but there is no Annibal to be found.'

As he said this, La Mole accompanied his lamentation by

throwing up his arms. In so doing, he revealed his doublet, which was torn and cut in several places.

'Why, you have been completely riddled!' said Marguerite.

'Riddled—that is the exact word,' said La Mole, not sorry to make the most of the danger he had incurred.

'Why did you not change your doublet at the Louvre, when you got back?'

'Why,' said La Mole, 'because there was someone in my apartment.'

'What do you mean, someone in your apartment?' said Marguerite, whose eyes expressed the greatest astonishment. 'Who?'

'His Highness——'

'Hush!' said Marguerite.

The young man obeyed.

'*Qui ad lecticam meam stant?*' she asked.

'*Duo pueri et unus eques.*'

'*Optime, barbari,*' said she. '*Dic, Moles, quem inveneris in cubiculo tuo?*'

'*Franciscum ducem.*'

'*Agentem?*'

'*Nescio quid.*'

'*Quo cum?*'

'*Cum ignoto.*'[1]

'How very strange,' said Marguerite not thinking of what she was saying. 'So you have not found Coconnas?'

'No, madame, and I am extremely worried.'

'Well,' said Marguerite, 'I will not further delay your search, though I have an idea he will be found before long. But, nevertheless, go and look for him.'

And the queen placed her finger to her lips. Now, as

---

[1] 'Who are with my litter?'
　'Two pages and a groom.'
　'Good; they won't understand us. Tell me, La Mole, whom did you find in your apartment?'
　'Duke Francis.'
　'What was he doing?'
　'I don't know.'
　'Who was with him?'
　'A man I don't know.'

Marguerite had not communicated any secret to La Mole, he guessed that this charming sign must have another meaning.

The litter went on its way, and La Mole proceeded along the quay till he came to the Rue du Long-Pont, which took him into the Rue Saint Antoine.

He stopped opposite the Rue de Jouy.

It was there, the previous evening, that the duennas had blindfolded Coconnas and himself. He remembered clearly that he had turned to the right and counted twenty paces. He did so again, and found himself opposite a house, or rather a wall, with a house in it. In the middle of the wall was a door studded with large nails.

The house was in the Rue Cloche Perce, a narrow little street that commences in the Rue Saint-Antoine and ends in the Rue du Roi-de-Sicile.

'*Sangbleu!*' said La Mole. 'This is it! As I left the house, I touched the nails, then went down the second step. It was then that the man who was killed in the Rue du Roi-de-Sicile passed, crying for help.'

La Mole knocked at the door. A porter with a vast moustache opened it.

'*Was ist dass?*'[1] said he.

'Ah!' said La Mole to himself; 'we are Swiss, it seems. My friend,' he continued, 'I want my sword I left it here last night.'

'*Ich verstehe nicht,*'[2] said the porter.

'My sword——'

'*Ich verstehe nicht.*'

'——That I left——'

'*Ich verstehe nicht.*'

'——In this house, where I passed the night.'

'*Gehe zum Teufel.*'[3]

And he shut the door in his face.

'*Mordieu!*' said La Mole, 'if I had my sword, I would run it through your body.'

He then struck into the Rue du Roi-de-Sicile, turned to the right, counted fifty paces, turned to the right again, and found himself in the Rue Tizon, a little street parallel with the Rue

---

[1] 'What's that?'   [2] 'I don't understand you.'   [3] 'Go to the devil!'

Cloche Perce, and exactly like it. Scarcely had he taken thirty steps when he found the same little door studded with the nails, the narrow loopholes, the two steps and the wall.

La Mole then reflected that he might have mistaken his right for his left, and he knocked at this door. But in spite of his repeated attempts, no one came. He walked round the same way several times, and then arrived at the natural conclusion that the house had two identical entrances—one in the Rue Tizon, the other in the Rue Cloche Perce. But this logical reasoning did not give him back his sword, or his friend.

He had for an instant an idea of purchasing another rapier and making a few holes in the porter. But he was checked by the thought that, if the man served Marguerite, she doubtless had her reasons for selecting him, and would be vexed were she deprived of him.

Now La Mole would not for the world have done anything to vex Marguerite.

To avoid the temptation, he returned to the Louvre.

This time his apartment was empty; and being in no small haste to change his clothes which were considerably the worse for wear, he hastened to the bed to take possession of his fine grey satin doublet, when, to his intense amazement, he saw hanging beside it the identical sword he had left in the Rue Cloche Perce. He took it and examined it: it was indeed the same.

'Ah!' said he, 'there is some magic in this.' Then, with a sigh. 'If only Coconnas would come back, like this sword!'

Two or three hours later, the door in the Rue Tizon opened. It was five o'clock, and consequently dark.

A woman, enveloped in a long fur cloak, accompanied by a servant, came out of the door, glided rapidly into the Rue du Roi-de-Sicile, knocked at a little door in the Rue d'Argenson,* entered, left it again by the great gate that opens into the Vieille Rue du Temple, reached a private door of the Hotel de Guise, opened it with a pass-key, and disappeared.

Half an hour afterwards, a young man, his eyes bandaged, came out of the same door of the same house, led by an old woman, who took him to the corner of the Rue Geoffroy-Lasnier and the Rue de la Mortellerie. There she bade him count fifty paces and then take off the handkerchief.

The young man complied scrupulously with these directions, and at the prescribed number took off the bandage.

'*Mordi!*' cried he, 'I'll be hanged if I know where I am! Six o'clock! Where can La Mole be? I'll run to the Louvre—perhaps I shall have news of him there.'

So saying, Coconnas set off, and arrived at the Louvre in less time than a horse would have performed the distance.

He questioned the Swiss and the sentry. The Swiss thought he had seen M. de la Mole go out, but he had not seen him return. The sentry had only been on guard an hour and a half, and had seen nothing.

Coconnas mounted the stairs, entered La Mole's room, and found nothing but his torn doublet, which increased his anxiety.

He then went to La Hurière's. La Hurière had seen M. de la Mole—M. de la Mole had breakfasted there.

Reassured by these tidings, Coconnas ordered supper, which occupied him until eight o'clock when, fortified by a good meal and two bottles of wine, he again started in search of his friend.

For an hour Coconnas roamed the streets near the Quai de la Grève, the Rue Saint-Antoine, and the Rues Tizon and Cloche Perce.

At last he returned to the Louvre, determined to keep watch at the gate until La Mole's return.

He was not a hundred paces from the Louvre, and was helping a lady to her feet whose husband he had bowled over a moment before, when, by the light of a large lamp, he saw the cherry-velvet cloak and white feather of his friend, disappearing like a phantom through the main gate of the Louvre.

The cherry-coloured cloak was too well known to be mistaken.

'*Mordi!*' cried Coconnas, 'it is he at last! Hey, La Mole! Why does he not answer? Fortunately my legs are as good as my voice.'

He dashed after Cherry Mantle, but only in time to see him, as he entered the court-yard, disappear in the vestibule.

'La Mole!' cried Coconnas—'stop! stop! why are you in such a hurry?'

Cherry Mantle ran up to the second storey as if he had wings.

'Ah, you are angry with me. Well, I give up.'

Coconnas ceased the pursuit, but with his eyes followed the

fugitive who now reached the apartments of the Queen of Navarre. Suddenly a female appeared and took Cherry Mantle by the hand.

'Oh,' said Coconnas, 'that's Queen Marguerite. Now I know why he would not wait!'

After a few whispered words, Cherry Mantle followed the queen into her apartments.

'Good!' said Coconnas. 'There are times when your best friend is in the way: this is one of them, and I'll not poke my nose in.'

So Coconnas sat down on a bench covered with velvet.

'I'll wait here for him. But since he's with the queen, I may be here a long time. It's confounded cold here, and I may just as well wait for him in his room; he must come back some time.'

At this moment he heard a quick step on the stairs above, and a voice singing a tune which La Mole was forever singing. Coconnas looked up. It was La Mole himself, who, seeing the Piedmontese, ran down the stairs four at a time, and threw himself into his arms.

'*Mordi!* here you are!' said Coconnas. 'Which way did you come out?'

'Why, by the Rue Cloche Perce.'

'No, I don't mean there.'

'Where then?'

'From the queen's apartments.'

'The queen!'

'Ay, from the queen.'

'I have not been with her.'

'Come, come!'

'My dear Annibal,' said La Mole, 'I've this instant left my room where I've been waiting for you these two hours.'

'You've just left your room?'

'Yes.'

'It was not you I ran after from the Place du Louvre?'

'When?'

'Just now.'

'No.'

'It wasn't you that disappeared through the gateway ten minutes ago?'

'No.'

'It wasn't you that dashed up the stairs as if the devil was after you?'

'No.'

'*Mordi!*' replied Coconnas. 'The wine of *La Belle Etoile* has not turned my head to that extent. I tell you, I saw your cloak and white feather enter the Louvre. I followed both to the bottom of this staircase, and then saw the said cloak and feather led by a lady into that room, which I believe is Madame Marguerite's.'

'*Mordieu!*' exclaimed La Mole, turning very pale. 'Can there be treachery already!'

'Ah, swear as much as you like,' returned Coconnas, 'but don't tell me I was mistaken.'

La Mole hesitated an instant, and then, carried away by his jealousy, rushed to the queen's door, and knocked furiously.

'You'll get us both arrested,' said Coconnas. '*Mordi!* do you think there are ghosts at the Louvre, La Mole?'

'I do not know,' said the young man. 'But I've always wanted to see one, and would like to find myself face to face with this ghost, if ghost he be.'

'Very good,' said Coconnas, 'but don't knock so loud, or you'll alarm the lady.'

Enraged as La Mole was, he nevertheless saw the justice of this observation. And though he continued to knock, he knocked less violently.

25

CHERRY MANTLE

COCONNAS was not mistaken. The lady who had stopped the man in the cherry-coloured cloak was indeed the Queen of Navarre. The man in the cherry-coloured cloak was, as our readers have doubtless guessed, none other than de Mouy.

On recognizing the Queen of Navarre, the young Huguenot saw there was some mistake, but he feared to say anything lest a cry from the queen should betray him. He therefore allowed himself to be led into the apartment, resolved, once there, to say to his fair guide, 'Silence for silence, madame.'

Marguerite had gently pressed the arm which in the darkness she mistook for La Mole's, and whispered in his ear, in Latin,—

'I am alone; come in, my dear.'

De Mouy entered in silence. But scarcely was he in the ante-chamber, and the door closed, than Marguerite saw that it was not La Mole, and she uttered the cry which the prudent Huguenot had dreaded.

'M. de Mouy!' she exclaimed.

'Yes, madame,' returned the young man. 'I entreat your Majesty to suffer me to go on my way without informing anyone of my presence at the Louvre.'

'Oh, M. de Mouy,' said the queen, 'I was mistaken then.'

'Yes, so I see,' returned de Mouy. 'Your Majesty mistook me for the King of Navarre. The white feather I wear the same as his, and my height and figure, I have been told, are not unlike his.'

Marguerite stared at him.

'Do you know Latin?' asked she.

'I did once, but I have forgotten it,' replied the young man.

Marguerite smiled.

'You may rely upon my discretion, M. de Mouy. And as I think I know the person you seek, I will, if you so please, take you to him.'

'Madame,' replied de Mouy, 'I see that you are mistaken, and that you are completely ignorant who it is I wish to see.'

'What!' cried Marguerite, 'is it not the King of Navarre you seek?'

'Alas! madame, it is with regret I must beg you to conceal my presence in the Louvre from the king, your husband.'

'M. de Mouy,' said Marguerite, 'I have always considered you one of the steadiest supporters of my husband, one of the most zealous Huguenot leaders. Am I, then, mistaken?'

'No, madame, for I was, up to this morning, all that you say.'

'And why have you changed?'

'Madame,' returned de Mouy, 'I ask you to excuse my not replying, and to receive my compliments.'

And de Mouy firmly, but respectfully, proceeded towards the door.

Marguerite stopped him.

'Yet,' said she, 'I would like an explanation.'

'Madame,' returned de Mouy, 'duty bids me be silent. I need hardly say that the duty which prevents my obeying your Majesty can brook no obstacle.'

'Yet, sir——'

'Your Majesty can ruin me, but you cannot make me betray my new friends.'

'Have your old friends no claims on you?'

'Those who have remained faithful, yes. But those who not only have abandoned us, but have abandoned themselves, no.'

Marguerite, feeling very uneasy, was about to pursue her questioning, when Gillonne rushed in.

'The King of Navarre, madame!'

'Which way is he coming?'

'Through the secret passage.'

'Then let this gentleman out by the other door.'

'Impossible, madame, someone is knocking there.'

'Who is it?'

'I do not know.'

'Go and see.'

'Madame,' said de Mouy, 'permit me to observe that I am lost if the King of Navarre sees me in the Louvre at this hour and in these clothes.'

Marguerite seized his hand, and leading him to the famous side-room,——

'Hide here,' said she, 'you will be as safe as in your own house, for you are under my protection.'

De Mouy obeyed, and hardly had he done so when Henry appeared.

He entered with that constitutional suspicion that made him, even when in the least danger, notice the most trifling circumstances. He immediately saw the cloud on Marguerite's brow.

'You were musing, madame,' said he.

'Yes, sire, I was.'

'You are right, madame, thoughtfulness becomes you. I, too, was musing, and came to tell you my thoughts.'

Marguerite bowed her head in welcome, and, pointing to a seat, placed herself in a beautifully carved ebony chair.

There was an instant's pause: Henry broke the silence first.

'I remembered, madame,' said he, 'that my dreams as to the future had this in common with yours, that, though separated as husband and wife, we nevertheless wished to unite our fortunes.'

'That is true, sire.'

'I also conjectured that in all my plans for our common advantage I should find in you not only a faithful but an active ally.'

'Yes, sire, and I only ask to have an early opportunity of proving it to you.'

'I am delighted to find you so well disposed; and I believe you have not doubted for a moment that I have lost sight of the plans I made on the day, thanks to your courage, my life was saved.'

'Sire, I see that your indifference is merely a mask. I have confidence not only in the predictions of astrologers, but also in your genius.'

'What would you say, then, if someone were to come in and thwart our plans and threaten to destroy our hopes?'

'I would reply that I am ready to strive with you, openly or in secret, against him, whoever he may be.'

'Madame,' returned Henry, 'you have the right of entering the Duke d'Alençon's apartments at all times. Might I request of you to go and see if he is not presently engaged with someone.'

'With whom?' asked Marguerite.

'With de Mouy.'

'Why?' replied Marguerite.

'Because if it be so, adieu to our plans.'

'Lower your voice, sire,' said Marguerite, pointing to the side-room.

'Someone there again?' said Henry. 'By my faith, that room is occupied so often that it makes your apartments virtually uninhabitable.'

Marguerite smiled.

'At all events, I hope it is M. de la Mole again?' said Henry.

'No, sire, it is M. de Mouy.'

'De Mouy!' cried Henry joyfully. 'He is not with the Duke d'Alençon? Oh, let me speak to him.'

Marguerite ran to open the door, and without further ceremony presented de Mouy to the king.

'Ah, madame,' said the young Huguenot reproachfully, 'you have not kept your promise. Suppose I were to take my revenge by saying——'

'You will not take any revenge, my dear de Mouy,' said Henry, pressing his hand, 'at least, not before you have heard me. Madame,' he continued, 'have the kindness to see that no one overhears us.'

Scarcely were these words uttered, when Gillonne entered all aghast, and said something to Marguerite that made her leave the room instantly. Meanwhile, not troubling himself as to the cause of her abrupt departure, Henry lifted the tapestry, tapped the walls, and looked into every recess. De Mouy, somewhat alarmed by these precautions, loosened his sword in its scabbard.

Marguerite, on leaving her apartment, found herself in the presence of La Mole, who, in spite of Gillonne, who was trying to stop him, was forcing his way in. Behind him stood Coconnas, ready to advance or retreat with him, as the case might be.

'Ah, it is you, M. de la Mole!' said the queen. 'What is the matter? what makes you look so pale?'

'Madame,' said Gillonne, 'M. de la Mole knocked so loud that, in spite of your Majesty's orders, I was forced to admit him.'

'Ha!' said the queen angrily. 'Is this true, M. de la Mole?'

'Madame, I wished to inform your Majesty that a stranger, a robber perhaps, had entered your apartments, wearing my cloak and hat.'

'You are mad, sir,' returned Marguerite 'for I observe your cloak on your shoulders. Moreover, by my faith, I see your hat on your head, though you are speaking to a queen.'

'Forgive me, madame!' cried La Mole, hastily removing it. 'Heaven knows it is not out of disrespect——'

'No, but want of faith,' said the queen.

'Oh, madame,' said La Mole, 'when a man enters apartments wearing my clothes and perhaps using my name——'

'*A* man!' said Marguerite, taking her lover's hand. 'Very well, M. de la Mole. Look through here, and you will see *two* men.'

And she gently raised the velvet curtains, and revealed to La Mole and Coconnas, who, moved with curiosity, stepped forward, Henry speaking to the man in the cherry-coloured cloak, whom both at once recognized as de Mouy.

'Now that you are satisfied,' said Marguerite, 'stand guard at that door, and let no one enter. If any one even approaches, let me know.'

La Mole, docile as an infant, obeyed, and both he and Coconnas found themselves outside the door before they had well recovered from their amazement.

'De Mouy!' cried Coconnas.

'Henry!' muttered La Mole.

'De Mouy with your cloak and hat.'

'My God!' said La Mole, 'this is a plot.'

'Ah, here we are up to our necks in politics again,' grumbled Coconnas. 'Fortunately, I do not see Madame de Nevers mixed up in this business.'

Marguerite returned to her bedroom. She had been absent scarcely a minute, but she had made good use of her time. Gillonne guarding the secret passage, and the two gentlemen outside the principal entrance, afforded full security.

'Madame,' said Henry, 'do you think anyone can overhear us?'

'Sire,' returned Marguerite, 'the walls are all double panelled and lined with padding.'

'Ay, ay, that will do,' said Henry, smiling.

Then turning to de Mouy. 'Now,' said he, in a whisper, as, notwithstanding Marguerite's assurances, his fears were not entirely dispelled, 'why are you here?'

'Here?' repeated de Mouy.

'Yes, here—in this room?'

'He did not come for anything,' said Marguerite 'it was I who brought him here.'

'You knew, then——'

'I guessed.'

'You see, de Mouy, people can guess.'

'M. de Mouy,' continued Marguerite, 'was with Duke François this morning in the apartment of one of his gentlemen.'

'You see, de Mouy,' repeated Henry, 'we know everything.'

'It is true,' said de Mouy.

'I was sure,' replied the king, 'that d'Alençon had got hold of you.'

'It is your fault, sire. Why did you so obstinately reject what I offered?'

'Ah, you refused!' said Marguerite. 'My presentiments, then, were well founded.'

'Madame,' said Henry, 'and you, my worthy de Mouy, you make me smile. What! a man comes to me, and talks to me of thrones and revolutions, and overthrowing states—to me, Henry, a prince tolerated only because I humble myself, a Huguenot, spared only because I pretend to be a Catholic—and thinks I am going to accept his propositions, made in a chamber without double panels, and not protected by padding. You are children, or mad!'

'But, sire, your Majesty might have given me some sign, to raise our hopes.'

'What did my brother-in-law say to you, de Mouy?' asked Henry.

'Oh, sire, that is not my secret to tell!'

'Oh, *mon Dieu!*' said Henry, impatient at having to deal with a man who did not understand him. 'I do not ask what proposals he made you. I only asked if he had listened, if he had overheard us?'

'He had listened, sire, and he had overheard.'

'He listened and overheard! you admit it! You are a poor conspirator! If I had said one wrong word, you would have been a dead man. I was not absolutely sure he was there, but I suspected as much. And if it had not been him, it would have been someone else—d'Anjou, the king, or the queen-mother. The walls of the Louvre have ears; and, knowing that, do you think I could have spoken freely? I am amazed you offer a crown to the King of Navarre, when you give him credit for so little good sense.'

'But, sire,' said de Mouy, 'had you made me a sign, I should not have lost all hope.'

'Eh, *ventre-saint-gris!*' cried Henry. 'If he was listening, was he not looking too? At this very instant, when I say to you, de Mouy, repeat to me your proposals, I dread we may be overheard.'

'Sire,' said de Mouy mournfully, 'I am now engaged with M. d'Alençon.'

Marguerite clapped her fair hands together angrily.

'It is, then, too late', said she.

'On the contrary,' said Henry, 'the hand of Providence is visible in this, for the duke will save us all. He will be a buckler protecting us, whereas the name of the King of Navarre would ruin you all by degrees. Bind him fast; secure proofs; but, naïve politician that you are, you have doubtless committed yourself already without seeking guarantees.'

'Sire,' cried de Mouy, 'despair made me join his party, and fear also, for he held our secret.'

'Then hold his in your turn. What does he want? the kingdom of Navarre? Promise it him. To leave the court? Supply him with the means. When the time comes for us to fly, he and I will fly together: when it is time to reign, I will reign alone.'

'Do not trust the duke,' said Marguerite; 'he is incapable either of hatred or friendship, always ready to treat his enemies as friends, and his friends as enemies.'

'He is waiting for you?' said Henry, without heeding his wife's remark.

'Yes, sire.'

'At what time?'

'Until midnight.'

'It is not yet eleven,' said Henry, 'you are not too late, de Mouy.'

'We have your word, sir?' said Marguerite.

'Come, come,' said Henry, with that air of confidence he so well knew how to show to certain persons and on certain occasions, 'with M. de Mouy that is entirely unnecessary.'

'You do me justice, sire,' returned the young man. 'But I must have your word so that I may tell our leaders that I have received it. You are not, then, a Catholic?'

Henry shrugged his shoulders.

'You do not renounce the kingdom of Navarre?'

'I do not renounce any kingdom, only I shall select the one which suits you and me the best.'

'And, in the meantime, were your Majesty to be arrested, and they should dare so to violate the regal dignity as to torture you, will you swear to reveal nothing?'

'De Mouy, I swear it.'

'One word more, sire. How shall I see you?'

'From to-morrow you will have a key to my apartment, and

you can come in when you will. The duke must explain your presence at the Louvre. I will now guide you up the private staircase. Meantime, the queen will bring in here the other cherry cloak, who was just now in the antechamber. It must not be suspected that there are two of you, eh, de Mouy? eh, madame?'

Henry laughed as he said this, and looked at Marguerite.

'Yes,' replied she, without any emotion, 'for you know M. de la Mole is one of the gentlemen of the Duke d'Alençon.'

'Try and win him to our side, then,' said Henry, with entire gravity. 'Spare neither gold nor promises; I place all my treasures at his disposal.'

'Well, then,' said Marguerite, with one of those smiles that belong only to Boccaccio's* heroines, 'since such is your desire, I will do my best to promote it.'

'Very good, madame. And now go to the duke, de Mouy, and hook him.'

26

MARGUERITE

DURING this conversation, La Mole and Coconnas remained on guard, the former rather deflated and Coconnas somewhat uneasy. For La Mole had had time for reflection, and Coconnas had most liberally assisted him in it.

'What do you make of all this?' asked La Mole.

'I think,' replied the Piedmontese, 'that it is some intrigue of the court.'

'And are you tempted to play a part in it?'

'My dear fellow!' returned Coconnas, 'pay attention to what I shall say, and learn. In all these royal manœuvrings, we are, and should be, but shadows. Whereas the King of Navarre would only lose the end of his feather, or the Duke d'Alençon the skirt of his cloak, you and I should lose our lives. Go crazy with love, if you want, but do not meddle in politics.'

'But I love the queen, Annibal! I love her with all my soul! It's mad, I know; but you, Coconnas, who are prudent, must not suffer by my folly. Go and find our master, but do not compromise yourself.'

Coconnas reflected an instant, then nodding his head,—

'My dear fellow!' said he, 'what you say is very just. You are in love, and you act like a lover. I am ambitious, and think life worth more than the smile of a woman. When I risk my life, I will make my own terms, and be sure you do likewise.'

So saying, Coconnas shook La Mole's hand, and left him.

About ten minutes later, the door opened cautiously, and Marguerite appeared. Without speaking a word, she led La Mole into her apartment, closing the doors with a care that showed the importance of the conversation she was about to begin.

Once in her apartment, she sat down in her ebony chair, and taking La Mole's hand in hers,—

'Now that we are alone, my friend,' said she, 'we will talk seriously.'

'Seriously, madame?' said La Mole.

'Or confidentially, if you like the word better. There may be serious things in confidential conversations, especially in those with a queen.'

'Let us speak seriously, then, but on condition that your Majesty be not offended with what I shall say.'

'I shall only be offended at one thing, La Mole, and that is, if you call me "madame" or "your Majesty". For you, I am only Marguerite.'

'Yes, Marguerite! yes, Marguerite!' cried the young man, gazing passionately at the queen.

'Good,' said Marguerite. 'So you are jealous, fair sir?'

'Oh, madly!'

'Ah! and of whom?'

'Of everyone.'

'But of whom in particular?'

'First, of the king.'

'I thought, after what you had seen and heard, you were easy on that score.'

'Second, of this M. de Mouy, whom I saw this morning for the first time, and whom I find this evening on such intimate terms with you.'

'And what makes you jealous of de Mouy?'

'I recognized him by his manner, his figure and a natural feeling of hate. He was the man with M. d'Alençon this morning.'

'Well, what has he to do with me?'

'I do not know. But in the absence of any firm acknowledgement, a love like mine is entitled to frankness on your part. See, madame, at your feet I implore you! If what you have felt for me is but a passing fancy, I give you back your word and your promises; I will resign my post with M. d'Alençon and go and seek death at the siege of La Rochelle,* if love does not kill me before I arrive there!'

Marguerite listened with a smile to these tender reproaches, then, leaning her head on his burning hand,—

'You love me?' she said.

'Oh, yes, madame, more than life! But you do not love me.'

'Don't be silly,' she murmured. 'So for you, the most important thing in life is love?'

'It is, indeed, madame.'

'You love me, then, and would like to remain with me?'

'My only prayer is that I may never part from you.'

'Were I to tell you I love you, would you be wholly devoted to me?'

'Am I not so already?'

'Yes; but you still doubt.'

'Oh, I am ungrateful, or, rather, I am mad. But tell me, why was M. de Mouy with the Duke d'Alençon this morning? Why was he here to-night? What was the meaning of the white feather, the cherry-coloured cloak? Why did he imitate my walk and manner?'

'Can you not guess? D'Alençon would kill you with his own hand if he knew you were here at my feet and that, instead of ordering you to leave my presence, I said to you then as I now say, stay where you are, for I love you.'

'*Mon Dieu*, is it possible?' murmured La Mole.

'Listen,' continued the queen; 'it was not for me that M. de Mouy came here in your hat and cloak, it was to see M. d'Alençon. But I mistook him for you; I spoke to him, thinking it was you; I led him hither, thinking it was you. He knows our secret, La Mole, and must be managed cautiously.'

'I would rather kill him,' said La Mole, 'it is the shortest and safest way.'

'And I,' said the queen, 'would rather he stayed alive and that you knew everything. Now answer me truly, La Mole; do you love me enough to rejoice if I really were to become queen?'

'Alas, madame,' said La Mole, 'I love you enough to want whatever you want, though it mean utter misery for me!'

'Will you help me to realize this plan?'

'Oh, I shall lose you!' cried La Mole, burying his face in his hands.

'No. But instead of being the first of my servants, you will become the first of my subjects.'

'Oh, speak not of interest, of ambition! Do not dishonour the sentiment I have for you!—my devotion, my ardent, my un-mixed devotion!'

'Noble nature!' said the queen; 'I will accept your devotion, and, be assured, will repay it.'

And she held out her hands, which La Mole pressed in his own.

'Well?' said she.

'Well, yes,' replied La Mole. 'I now begin to understand the plan spoken of by the Huguenots before Bartholomew's Night, the plan which I and so many others came to Paris to further. De Mouy conspires with you. But what has the Duke d'Alençon to do with all this? Is he sufficiently your friend to help you, with-out asking anything in return?'

'The duke plots for himself. Let him go on his own way; his life answers for ours.'

'But how can I, who am in his service, betray him?'

'Betray him! how so? What has he entrusted to you? Has he not betrayed you by giving de Mouy your cloak and hat, to enable him to come here? Were you not in my service before you were in his? Has he given you a greater proof of his friendship than I have of love?'

La Mole rose, pale and agitated.

'Coconnas was right,' he murmured, 'I am becoming entan-gled in a web of intrigue, and it will destroy me.'

'Well?' said Marguerite.

'This is my answer,' returned La Mole. 'Even in my distant province of France, where the reputation of your beauty reached me and gave me my first desire to visit Paris, that I might see you, I heard it said that you have often loved, and that your love was always fatal to its objects: Death, doubtless jealous of their happiness, took them from you.* Do not interrupt me, Marguerite. I have also heard that you keep the embalmed hearts of your dead lovers, and that now and then you bestow on these sad remains a sigh of pity and perhaps a tear. You sigh, my queen, your eyes are lowered to the ground; it is true, then? Let me be favoured as those men were, only with this difference: swear that if, as a sombre presentiment assures me I shall, I perish beneath the executioner's axe in your service, you will preserve that head which I shall lose and will sometimes look upon it. Swear this, and the prospect of such a reward shall make me do whatever you command me.'

'Oh, my love!' said the queen.

'Swear it!'

'Swear?'

'Yes, on this jewel casket engraved with a holy cross.'

'I swear,' said Marguerite, 'that if your dark presentiment be realized, you shall be near me, living or dead, so long as I myself shall live. If I cannot save you, you shall have the poor consolation you ask, and which you will have so well deserved.'

'One word more, Marguerite and I can die happy. But I may live! we may triumph, and not fail! The King of Navarre may become king, you will then be queen. He will take you away; the vow of separation between you may one day be broken, and lead to my separation from you. Oh! dearest Marguerite, reassure me also on this point.'

'Fear not,' said Marguerite, placing her hand on the cross; 'if I go, you shall go with me. If the king refuses to take you, I will not leave.'

'But you will not dare resist him.'

'Dear Joseph,' said Marguerite, 'you do not know the king. Henry thinks only of one thing, of becoming a king, and to that he is prepared to sacrifice everything. But now farewell! It is late.'

From that evening La Mole was no longer an ordinary favourite, and he could proudly hold up his head for which, living or dead, so high a destiny was reserved. Yet sometimes, his eyes were fixed on the ground, his cheeks grew pale, and deep meditation drew furrows on the brow of the young man, once so carefree and now so happy.

27

THE HAND OF PROVIDENCE

As Henry left Madame de Sauve, he said to her:

'Charlotte, confine yourself to your bed, pretend to be gravely ill, and do not receive any person during the day under any pretext whatsoever.'

Charlotte, knowing that Henry had secrets which he revealed to no one, complied with all his directions, certain that his conduct was based on good, solid grounds.

Accordingly, in the evening, she complained to her attendant Dariole of a heaviness in the head and a feeling of faintness, these being the symptoms Henry had requested her to feign.

The next morning she made as though to get up, but scarcely had she placed her foot on the floor than she complained of general weakness, and returned to her bed.

This indisposition, which Henry had already mentioned when speaking to the Duke d'Alençon, was the first information that Catherine received, when she calmly inquired why de Sauve did not attend her, as usual, when she arose.

'She is ill,' said Madame de Lorraine, who was present.

'Ill?' repeated Catherine, while not a muscle of her face announced the interest she took in the reply. 'Or perhaps a little lazy?'

'No, madame,' replied the princess; 'she complains of a violent pain in the head, and a weakness that prevents her from moving.'

Catherine did not reply, but, to conceal her joy, turned towards the window, and seeing Henry cross the court-yard below, after his conversation with de Mouy, she said, as she looked at him, to her captain of the guards,—

'Do you not think that my son Henry looks paler than usual this morning?'

It is true Henry was considerably disturbed in mind, but perfectly well in body.

Catherine's suite left her, and the instant she was alone she closed the door securely, and, going to a secret cupboard, retrieved from a concealed corner a book whose crumpled leaves proved how frequently it was used.

She placed the volume on a table, opened it, and, after consulting its pages for a minute, exclaimed,—

'Yes, it is so: headache, general weakness, pains in the eyes, swelling of the palate. Thus far they mention only headache and weakness, but the other symptoms will appear by and by. Next will follow inflammation of the throat, which spreads to the stomach, surrounds the heart with a circle of fire, and makes the brain burst like a bolt of lightning.'

She read on in a whisper, and then said,—

'The fever lasts six hours, the general inflammation twelve hours, the gangrene twelve hours, the final agony six hours. In all, thirty-six hours.

'Well, then, let us suppose that absorption is a slower process than swallowing. Instead of thirty-six hours let's say forty, or perhaps forty-eight—yes, forty-eight should do it. But how is it that Henry is able to keep going? Probably because he is a man with a robust constitution, and perhaps drank something after he had kissed her, and wiped his lips after drinking.'

Catherine impatiently awaited the dinner-hour—Henry dined with the king daily. When he came, he complained of giddiness in the head and did not eat, but retired immediately after dinner, saying that, as he had been up nearly all the night before, he felt a great need to sleep.

Catherine listened to Henry's retreating, staggering step, and ordered him to be followed, which was done, and the queen-mother was soon informed that the King of Navarre had gone towards Madame de Sauve's apartment.

'Henry,' she said to herself, 'will there complete the deadly process which some untoward circumstance may have interrupted.'

The King of Navarre had gone to Madame de Sauve's apartment, to request her to go on playing her role.

Next day Henry did not leave his room all morning, nor did he dine at the royal table. Madame de Sauve, it was reported, was worse and worse, and the rumours of Henry's illness, encouraged by Catherine herself, spread like one of those presentiments which no one can explain.

And so Catherine waited with mounting curiosity and expectation for the moment when some attendant, pale and aghast, should enter her apartment, and cry,—

'Your Majesty, the King of Navarre is dying, and Madame de Sauve is dead.'

The clock struck four, and Catherine was feeding crumbs of bread to the rare birds which she herself attended to. Although her features were calm, and even melancholy, her heart beat violently at the least sound.

Suddenly the door opened.

'Madame,' said the captain of the guards, 'the King of Navarre is——'

'Ill?' inquired Catherine suddenly.

'No, madame, thank God! his Majesty seems excellently well.'

'What, then, have you to say?'

'That the King of Navarre is here.'

'What does he want?'

'He brings your Majesty a small monkey of a very rare sort.'

And at this moment Henry entered, holding in his hand a basket, and stroking a marmoset which was in it.

Henry smiled as he entered, with apparently no thought save for the small animal he had brought yet, preoccupied as he was, he gave a glance which was only too revealing under his peculiar circumstances. As for Catherine, she was very pale—deadly pale, as she saw the cheeks of the young man, as he approached her, glowing with colour and health.

The queen-mother was stupefied at this, and mechanically accepting the present he made her, and complimenting him in a troubled voice on his healthy appearance, added,—

'I am the more pleased to see you in such health, my son, after having heard that you had been unwell. I remember you complained of an indisposition in my presence, but I see now,' she continued, trying to force a smile, 'it was only an excuse so that you might have your time more freely to yourself.'

'Why, I really was very unwell, madame,' replied Henry. 'But a medicine used in our mountains, given to me by my mother, cured my indisposition.'

'Ah! you will give me the prescription, won't you, Henry?' said Catherine, with a smile whose irony she could not conceal.

'Either some counter-poison,' she muttered, 'or else he was on his guard: seeing Madame de Sauve ill made him suspicious. Really, it would seem that the hand of Providence is extended permanently over this man.'

Catherine waited for nightfall impatiently. Madame de Sauve did not appear, and it was reported that she was still worse. All the evening the queen-mother was uneasy, and everyone wondered what thoughts could cloud a face so little given to revealing inner states.

Everyone retired. Catherine went to bed, and was undressed by her woman. But, when everything was quiet in the Louvre, she rose, put on a long black dressing-gown, and with a lamp in her hand and taking the key that opened Madame de Sauve's door, went to the apartment of her maid of honour.

Had Henry anticipated this visit? Was he in his own apartment? Was he hidden somewhere? The young lady was alone.

Catherine opened the door quietly, passed through the antechamber, entered the salon, placed the lamp on a table, for there was a night-light burning near the invalid, and like a shadow she glided into the bedroom.

Dariole, slumped in a large arm-chair, was sleeping near her mistress's bed, which was closed in by curtains.

The breathing of the young lady was so light that for an instant Catherine thought she was not breathing at all.

At length she heard a low sigh. With malignant glee, she raised the curtain to witness the effect of the terrible poison, and she shuddered at the anticipated spectacle of the livid paleness or devouring purple of the mortal fever she hoped to see. But instead, her face calm, her eyes gently covered by their ivory lids, her mouth rosy and half-open, her soft cheek reposing on one of her arms, beautifully rounded, whilst the other, fresh and slender, lay on the crimson damask counterpane, the young lady was sleeping with a smile on her lovely features.

Catherine could not repress a cry, which aroused Dariole for an instant.

The queen-mother threw herself behind the bed-curtains. Dariole opened her eyes, but, being drowsy, she did not even try to trace the cause of her awaking, and her heavy eyelids again dropping, she soon slept.

Catherine then coming from behind the curtain, looking all around, saw on a small table a flask of Spanish wine, sweetmeats, and two glasses. Henry had supped with the baroness, who was as well as he was.

Catherine then going to the dressing-table, picked up the small box which was one-third empty. It was the same, or similar to the one she had given. She took from it a morsel of the size of a pearl, at the end of a gold pin, returned to her own apartment, and offered it to the small monkey which Henry had presented to her the same evening. The animal, tempted by the aroma, seized and swallowed it greedily, and curling himself up in his basket went to sleep. Catherine waited a quarter of an hour.

'With half such a piece,' she said, 'my dog Brutus died in a minute. I have been trifled with. Can it be René? No, impossible! So it must be Henry. Cursed fatality, it is clear: since he is fated to reign, he cannot die. Perhaps, it is only poison to which he is immune: left us try cold steel.'

Catherine went to her couch, turning over in her mind this fresh idea which she resolved to try next day. In the morning, summoning the captain of her guards,* she gave him a letter to convey to its address, and to be handed only to the person whose name it bore.

It was addressed to 'Sire de Louviers de Maurevel, Captain of the King's Petardiers,* Rue de la Cerisaie, near the Arsenal.'

28

THE LETTER FROM ROME

SOME days had elapsed since the events we have related, when one morning a litter, escorted by several gentlemen wearing the colours of M. de Guise, entered the Louvre. It was announced to the Queen of Navarre that the Duchess de Nevers desired to pay her respects to her.

Marguerite was receiving a visit from Madame de Sauve. It was the first time the lovely baroness had gone out since her supposed illness.

Marguerite congratulated her on her convalescence, and said,—

'You will come, I hope, to the great hunt which is to take place to-morrow.'

'Why, madame,' replied the baroness, 'I do not know that I shall be well enough.'

'Bah!' replied Marguerite, 'you must make an effort and as I myself am a regular warrior, I have authorized the king to place at your disposal a small Béarn horse, which I was to have ridden. It will carry you famously. So you must join us.'

'Your Majesty is too kind. I will be present, as you desire.'

At this moment the Duchess de Nevers was announced.

'To-morrow, then,' said Marguerite to Madame de Sauve. 'Incidentally, you know, baroness,' continued Marguerite, 'that in public I detest you, for I am horribly jealous of you.'

'But in private?' asked Madame de Sauve.

'Oh! in private I not only forgive you, but even thank you.'

'Then your Majesty will allow me——'

Marguerite held out her hand, which the baroness kissed respectfully, made a low curtsey, and left the apartment.

The Duchess de Nevers entered. Gillonne, at a word from her mistress, closed the door, and the duchess taking a seat without ceremony, Marguerite said to her, with a smile,—

'Well! and our famous swordsman—what do we make of him?'

'My dear queen,' replied the duchess, 'he is really a mythological creature, incomparable in mind and infinite in humour. I am really fond of him. And how is your Apollo?'*

'Alas!' said Marguerite, with a sigh.

'Ah! that *alas!* frightens me, dear queen.'

'The *alas!* only refers to myself,' replied Marguerite.

'And what does it mean?'

'It means, dear duchess, that I have an awful fear that I love him in earnest.'

'Really?'

'On my faith, as a woman!'

'Ah, so much the better!' cried Henriette. 'It is so pleasant, dear and learned queen, to seek rest from one's mind in a good and faithful heart. Ah, Marguerite! I have a presentiment that we shall spend an agreeable year.'

'Do you think so?' said the queen. 'I, on the contrary, do not know why it is, but I seem to see everything through a veil of gauze. All these political turmoils torment me terribly. By the way, try and find out if your Annibal is as much devoted to my brother as he appears to be. It is important that we should know.'

'He devoted to anything? Ah, I see, you do not know him as I do. If he is ever devoted to anything, it will be to ambition, and nothing else. There are really moments when this tiger, whom I have trained, makes me afraid for myself. The other day I said to him, "Annibal, mind you are not false to me, for if you are——"'

'Well?'

'Well, what do you suppose was his reply? He said: "And if you are false to me, you take care, for although you are a princess——"; and as he said so, he threatened me not only with his eyes but with his finger—his finger straight and pointed, and with a nail cut like a spear-point, which he held under my nose. Truly, dear queen, I do not mind admitting that his face was so threatening that I trembled, and you know that ordinarily I am no trembler.'

'Did he really threaten you, Henriette?'

'Yes, *mordi!* but I had threatened him, you see.'

'Have you any news for me?'

'Yes, indeed. I have received news from Rome.'*

'Good! And what of matters in Poland?'

'They progress most favourably. In all probability you will in a few days be freed from your brother d'Anjou.'*

'The pope, then, has ratified the election?'

'Yes, my dear.'

'Why did you not tell me sooner? Come, be quick!—tell me all the details.'

'Oh, *ma foi!* I know no more than what I have told you. But here is my husband de Nevers's letter. No, that is not it; that is a note from me, which I beg you to ask La Mole to give to Annibal. This is the duke's letter.'

Marguerite opened and read it eagerly, but it told no more than she knew before from the lips of her friend.

'And how did you receive this letter?' continued the queen.

'By one of my husband's couriers who had his orders to stop at the Hotel de Guise on his way to the Louvre and hand me this letter, before the king received his. I knew the importance which my queen attached to this news, and wrote to M. de Nevers to see that mine was delivered first. And now in all Paris, none but the king, you and I, know this news, unless the man who followed our courier——'

'What man?'

'Oh, what a horrible business! Imagine the poor messenger arriving tired, dusty, and jaded, after travelling for a whole week, day and night without stopping, constantly followed by a fierce-looking man, who also had relays of horses, and travelled as fast as him for these four hundred leagues, our courier expecting every moment to get a bullet in his back. They both arrived at the Barrière St Marcel at the same time—both descended the Rue Mouffetard at a gallop—both crossed the Ile de la Cité. But, at the end of the bridge of Notre-Dame, our courier turned to the right, while the other turned left by the Place du Châtelet, and sped along the Quais by the Louvre like a bolt from a bow.'

'Thank you! dearest Henriette,' cried Marguerite, 'you are right: your information is indeed interesting. Who this other courier is I will find out. Leave me now. We meet to-night in the Rue Tizon, do we not, and to-morrow at the hunt? I will tell you to-night what I wish you to learn from your Coconnas.'

'Do not forget my letter.'

'Don't worry, he shall have it in due course.'

Madame de Nevers went away, and Marguerite immediately sent for Henry, who hastened to her. She gave him the letter, and told him of the two couriers.

'Yes,' said Henry, 'I saw one enter the Louvre.'

'Perhaps he went to the queen-mother.'

'No, for I stepped out into the corridor, and no one passed.'

'Then,' said Marguerite, looking at her husband, 'he must have gone to——'

'Your brother d'Alençon, eh?' said Henry.

'Yes; but how can we be certain?'

'Can we not,' asked Henry carelessly, 'send for one of the two gentlemen, and learn from him——?'

'You are right, sire,' replied Marguerite, set at ease by her husband's suggestion. 'I will send for M. de la Mole.' And calling Gillonne, she desired her to find that gentleman, and bring him.

Henry seated himself at a table, on which was a German book of Albert Durer's engravings,* which he looked at with so much attention that when La Mole appeared he did not seem to hear him, and did not even look up.

Marguerite went to La Mole, and said,—

'M. de la Mole, can you tell me who is on guard to-day at M. d'Alençon's?'

'Coconnas, madame,' was the reply.

'Try and find out if he has let into his master's a man covered with mud, who seemed to have ridden a long and rapid journey.'

'Madame, I am afraid he will not tell me, for he has been uncommonly taciturn during the last few days.'

'Really? But if you give him this note, I should think he would owe you something in exchange.'

'From the duchess? Ah! madame, let me have it, and you may count on me.' And taking the letter, he left quickly.

'We shall know to-morrow if the Duke d'Alençon is informed of the affair of Poland,' said Marguerite, turning towards her husband.

'This M. de la Mole is really an excellent man,' said the Béarnais, with his own most peculiar smile, 'and, by the mass! I will make his fortune.'

29

THE DEPARTURE

WHEN the red rayless sun rose next morning over Paris, the court had already been up and about for two hours.

A splendid barbary stallion, agile as a deer, the swelling veins of whose neck indicated his high breeding, pawed impatiently in the court-yard, awaiting the king. But his impatience was less than his master's, for he had been detained by his mother who wished to speak of an affair of the greatest importance.

They were both in the great gallery, Catherine pale and cold as ever, Charles IX biting his nails, and chastising the two favourite dogs which stood by him, clothed in the coat of mail which protected them from the boars' tusks. A shield emblazoned with the arms of France was attached to their chests, like that on the breast of the royal pages.

'Listen, Charles,' said Catherine. 'None but you and I are aware of the imminent arrival of the Polish ambassadors.* Yet the King of Navarre acts as if he knew of it. In spite of his pretended abjuration, he keeps up a correspondence with the Huguenots. Have you noticed how frequently he has gone out within the last few days? He has money, though he never had any before. He buys horses and weapons, and, when it rains, he practises fencing.'

'Bah! mother,' cried Charles impatiently, 'do you think he is going to kill d'Anjou or myself? He'll have to take a few more lessons first, for yesterday with my foil I touched the buttons on his doublet eleven times, though there are only six of them. D'Anjou is even more skilful than I, or at least he says so.'

'Listen, Charles,' said Catherine, 'and do not treat your mother's warnings with such levity. These ambassadors will soon arrive. Once here, you will see Henry doing his best to attract their attention. He is very insinuating and cunning, and his wife, who abets him, though I don't understand why, will chatter Latin and Greek, Hungarian, and I know not what else,* with them. I tell you, Charles, and I am never mistaken, there is something afoot.'

At this moment the clock struck. Charles listened.

'*Mort de ma vie!* seven! An hour to get there, an hour more with the beaters—good God! it will be nine before we are at it. Down, Risque-tout!*—down, you rascal!'

And as he spoke, a vigorous lash drew from the poor hound, astonished at receiving chastisement instead of a caress, a yelp of agony.

'Charles,' went on Catherine, 'listen to me, and do not risk your own fortune and that of France. Hunting! you will have time enough for that when you have completed the task before us.'

'Bah! mother,' said Charles, livid with rage—'just tell me what you want.'

And he struck his boot with his whip.

Catherine saw the favourable moment had arrived, and determined not to let it slip.

'My son,' said she, 'we know that M. de Mouy is in Paris again; M. de Maurevel has seen him. He can only be here for the King of Navarre's purposes. Here is good reason for increased suspicion.'

'Ah, here you are again at poor Harry! I suppose you want me to kill him.'

'Oh, no!'

'To banish him? But don't you see he would be more dangerous at a distance than here, in the Louvre, where we know everything he does?'

'No, I don't want you to banish him.'

'What, then? Out with it!'

'I would have him locked up while the Poles are here. In the Bastille,* for instance.'

'Oh, *ma foi!* no,' cried Charles IX. 'We are going after boar this morning! Henry is one of my best hunters. The chase would be nothing without him. *Mordieu!* you do nothing but annoy me.'

'My son, I do not say to-day. To-morrow will be time enough.'

'Ah! that is different; we will speak again of this, after the hunt. Adieu! Come Risque-tout, don't sulk!'

'Charles,' said Catherine, taking hold of his arm in spite of the explosion she knew might follow, 'I think it would be best to sign the warrant at once, although we shall not execute it to-night.'

'Sign! write an order! go and look for the seal, when I am going to hunt? Devil take me if I do!'

'Nay, I love you too much to delay you. I have everything ready.'

And Catherine, agile as a girl, opened the door of her private cabinet, and showed the king an inkstand, a pen, a parchment, and a lighted taper.

The king rapidly ran his eye over the parchment:

'Order, etc., etc., to arrest and conduct to the Bastille our brother Henry of Navarre.'

'There!' said he, hastily putting his name to it.

And he ran out of the cabinet, glad to escape so easily.

Charles was waited for impatiently, and as his punctuality in hunting arrangements was well known, his non-appearance caused no small surprise. The instant he appeared, the hunters saluted him with cheers, the whippers-in with their horns, the horses with neighings, and the hounds with eager barking. Charles for a moment was young and happy amidst all this noise, and the colour rose into his pallid cheeks.

He scarcely gave himself time to return the salutations of the brilliant assembly. He nodded to d'Alençon, waved his hand to Marguerite, passed Henry without seeming to notice him, and sprang upon the horse that was waiting for him. The noble animal bounded impatiently, but sensing with how skilled a rider it had to deal, soon became quiet.

The horns sounded again and the king left the Louvre, followed by the Duke d'Alençon, the King of Navarre, Marguerite, Madame de Nevers, Madame de Sauve, Tavannes, and the chief nobles of the court.

As for the Duke d'Anjou, he had been at the siege of La Rochelle for the last three months.*

While waiting for the king, Henry had approached his wife, who whispered,—

'The courier from Rome was led by M. de Coconnas to the Duke d'Alençon a quarter of an hour before the Duke de Nevers's messenger saw the king.'

'Then he knows everything.'

'He must. Look at him! Try as he might, he cannot conceal his joy.'

'*Ventre-saint-gris!*' said the Béarnais, 'he is hunting three thrones to-day: France, Poland and Navarre, without reckoning the boar.'

Then saluting his wife, Henry returned to his place, and called one of his servants, a Béarnais, whom he was in the habit of using as a go-between in his love affairs.

'Orthon,'* said he, 'take this key to Madame de Sauve's cousin, at his house on the corner of the Rue des Quatre-fils. Tell him his cousin wishes to see him this evening, that he is to go to my chamber, that if I am not there, he is to wait for me. If I am late, he can lie down in my bed.'

'There is no answer, sire?'

'None, except to tell me if you have seen him. The key is for him only, is that clear?'

'Yes, sire.'

'Stop, blockhead, you must not go off now, you would attract attention. Before we leave Paris, I will call you, as if my girth was slackened. That way you can wait behind, discharge your commission, and join us at Bondy.'*

Orthon bowed and drew back.

The cavalcade passed down the Rue Saint-Honoré, the Rue Saint-Denis, then the Faubourg. At the Rue Saint-Laurent, the king's saddle became ungirthed. Orthon galloped up, and everything went off as the king had arranged. The royal procession passed down the Rue des Récollets, and the faithful valet dashed into the Rue du Temple.

When Henry rejoined the king, he was so busy talking to d'Alençon about the expected boar that he either did not notice or affected not to notice that Henry had stayed behind.

Madame Marguerite observed that her brother seemed embarrassed whenever he glanced at Henry. Madame de Nevers was in high glee, for Coconnas was in capital vein with his jests.

At a quarter-past eight, the cavalcade arrived at Bondy.

Charles's first care was to inquire whether the boar had broken cover. The boar, however, the huntsman assured him, was still in his lair.

A collation was prepared. The king drank a glass of Hungarian wine,* then, inviting the ladies to be seated, he went to inspect the kennels and the bird-cages, having first given strict orders that his horse should not be unsaddled meanwhile.

During his absence, the Duke de Guise arrived. He was armed more for war than for the hunt, and was attended by twenty or thirty gentlemen in similar array. He went looking for the king, and returned conversing with him.

At nine o'clock, the king himself sounded the signal for the off, and everyone mounted and hastened to the place of meeting.

During the journey, Henry again approached his wife.

'Well,' said he, 'anything new?'

'Nothing, except that my brother looks at you in the strangest way.

'I have noticed it myself.'

'Have you taken your precautions?'

'I have my shirt of mail on, and an excellent Spanish hunting knife, sharp as a razor, pointed as a needle, with which I can pierce a crown-piece.'

'Well,' said Marguerite, 'may God guard us!'

The huntsman gave a signal: they were at the boar's lair.

30

MAUREVEL

WHILE the glittering cavalcade proceeded towards Bondy, the queen-mother, rolling up the parchment the king had signed, gave orders to send for the man to whom the captain of her guards had delivered a letter some days previously—'to the Rue de la Cérisaie, near the Arsenal.'

A large band of sarsenet* covered one of his eyes and only just left the other visible. His cheek-bones were high, and his nose curved like the beak of a vulture; a grizzled beard covered his chin; he wore a large thick cloak, beneath which could be seen the hilts of a whole arsenal of weapons. He had at his side a heavy broadsword, with a basket hilt, and under his cloak one of his hands grasped a long dagger.

'Ah, you are here!' said the queen, seating herself. 'I promised to reward you for the services you rendered us on Saint Bartholomew's Night, and I have at last found an opportunity of so doing.'

'I humbly thank your Majesty,' replied the man.

'An opportunity, such as may never again present itself, of distinguishing yourself.'

'I am ready, madame. But I fear, from this preamble, that——'

'That the task is a difficult one. It is, indeed, and one which might be coveted by a Guise or a Tavannes.'

'Madame, whatever it be, I am at your command.'

'Read that,' said Catherine, and she gave him the parchment. He read it, and turned pale.

'What!' cried he—'an order to arrest the King of Navarre?'

'And what is so very astonishing in that!'

'But a king, madame! I doubt if I am gentleman enough to arrest a king.'

'The confidence I place in you makes you the first gentleman in my court.'

'I thank your Majesty,' returned the assassin—with some hesitation, however.

'You will obey me, then?'

'If your Majesty commands me, it is my duty to obey.'

'I do command you.'

'Then I obey.'

'How will you proceed?'

'I scarcely know—I would ask to be guided by your Majesty.'

'You would prefer to avoid any public outcry?'

'I confess it.'

'Take twelve men, or even more, if necessary.'

'I understand. Your Majesty allows me to make use of every advantage. But where shall I arrest the King of Navarre?'

'Where would you prefer?'

'I should prefer some place where my responsibility——'

'Ah! I understand—a royal palace: the Louvre, for instance.'

'Oh! if your Majesty would allow this, it would be a great favour.'

'Arrest him in the Louvre, then.'

'In what part?'

'In his apartments.'

Maurevel bowed.

'And when, madame?'

'To-night.'

'It shall be done, madame. But tell me what consideration I am to have for his rank?'

'Consideration!—rank!' said Catherine. 'Are you not aware that the King of France acknowledges no one of a rank equal to his own, in France?'

'One further question, madame. Should the king contest the authenticity of this order—it is not likely—but——'

'On the contrary, it is certain——'

'That he will contest it?'

'Without doubt.'

'And so, he will refuse to obey it?'

'I fear so.'

'And will resist?'

'Most likely.'

'Good God!' said Maurevel, 'and should he——'

'Should he what?' asked Catherine.

'Resist.'

'What do you do when you have the king's warrant, and a simple gentleman resists you?'

'I kill him, madame,' returned the bravo.

'I told you just now that everyone in France is, in the king's eyes, no more than a simple gentleman.'

Maurevel turned pale, for he began to understand.

'Oh, oh!' said he, 'kill the King of Navarre!'

'Who spoke of killing him? This order is only to conduct him to the Bastille. If he allows himself to be arrested quietly, well and good. But if he resists, and tries to kill you——'

Maurevel grew still paler.

'You will, of course, defend yourself! A brave soldier like you cannot be expected to let himself be killed. And if you are forced to defend yourself, no one knows what may happen. Do you understand?'

'Yes, madame.'

'Do you want me to write on the order the words—*Dead or alive?*'

'I confess that would remove my scruples.'

'Well—I must do it, I suppose.'

And unrolling the warrant with one hand, with the other she wrote '*Dead or alive.*'

'Is the order sufficiently formal now?' she asked.

'Yes, madame. But I would ask you let me have the execution of it entirely to myself.'

'Will anything I have said interfere?'

'Your Majesty bade me take twelve men.'

'Well?'

'I request your permission to take only six.'

'Why?'

'Because six guards may be forgiven for losing a prisoner whereas twelve would have no excuse.'

'Do as you will,' said Catherine. 'Meantime, you must not leave the Louvre.'

'But how shall I collect my men?'

'Have you no person you can employ to do it for you?'

'There is my servant, a trusty fellow, who sometimes aids me in such things.'

'Send for him and arrange your plans. You will breakfast in the king's armoury. When he returns from hunting, you can go to my oratory and wait there until it is time.'

'How shall we get into the king's chamber? He, doubtless, has his suspicions, and locks the door on the inside.'

'I have keys that open all the doors in the Louvre, and the bolts have been removed from his door. Adieu, M. de Maurevel. Remember, any failure would compromise the king's honour.'

And Catherine, without leaving Maurevel time to reply, called M. de Nancey, the captain of her guards, and bade him escort Maurevel into the king's armoury.

'*Mordieu!*' said Maurevel. 'I am going up in my profession. First I killed a simple gentleman, then I shot at an admiral, now I have business with a king without a crown: who knows but some day I may rise to a king with a crown!'

THE huntsman was not wrong when he affirmed that the game had not broken cover. Scarcely had the hounds been summoned, when the boar, which was, as the huntsman had said, one of the largest size, appeared.

The animal passed within fifty paces of the king, followed only by the hound which had roused him. But twenty dogs were speedily unleashed and laid on his track.

Hunting was Charles's passion. Scarcely had the animal appeared than he dashed after him, followed by the Duke d'Alençon and Henry, who had received a sign from Marguerite, warning him not to lose sight of the king. The other huntsmen followed.

In a quarter of an hour the chase halted before a dense thicket, and Charles returned to the glade, cursing and swearing as was his wont,—

'Good God! D'Alençon! Damnation, Harry! Here you are, as meek and mild as nuns following the abbess in procession. Do you call this hunting? You, d'Alençon, look as if you had just come out of a box; you are so damned perfumed, that if you get between the boar and the dogs, you will spoil the scent. And you, Harry, where is your boar-spear? where is your arquebuse?'

'Sire,' said Henry, 'what is the use of an arquebuse? I know your Majesty likes to shoot the boar at bay. As for the boar-spear, it is never used in my country, where we hunt bears with a knife.'*

'*Mordieu!*' replied Charles, 'you must send me a cart-load of bears when you get back to the Pyrenees. It must be glorious sport to contend foot to foot with an animal that may strangle you in a minute. Hark! I think I hear them. No!'

The king blew a blast on his horn that was answered by several others. At that moment a huntsman appeared, and sounded another note.

'A sighting!' cried the king, and he dug spurs in his horse, followed by all around him.

The huntsman was right. As the king advanced, the pack, now

composed of more than sixty dogs, could be clearly heard. The king no sooner saw the boar pass a second time, than he pursued him at full speed, blowing his horn with all his might.

The princes followed him for some time. But the king's horse was so strong, and bore him over such difficult terrain and through such thick coverts, that first the ladies, then the Duke de Guise and his gentlemen, and then the two princes, were obliged to draw rein. Tavannes followed him a while longer, but he, in his turn, was forced to give up.

All then, except the king and a few huntsmen, eager for a kill, found themselves near the glade they had started from.

The two princes were side by side in a long, broad forest path, with the Duke de Guise and his attendants a little further on.

'Does it not seem,' said the Duke d'Alençon to Henry, 'that Guise, with his armed retinue, is the real king here? He does not spare a glance at us poor princes.'

'Why should he treat us better than we are treated by our own relations? You and I are no more than hostages of our party at court.'

The duke started and looked at Henry, as if calling for further explanation, but the latter remained silent.

'What do you mean?' asked François, evidently put out because his brother-in-law had left him to pursue the subject.

'I mean,' returned Henry, 'that all these armed men seem like guards stationed to prevent two persons from escaping.'

'From escaping! why? how?' asked the duke with admirably affected surprise.

'You have a magnificent jennet* there, d'Alençon,' said Henry, seeming to change the subject, and yet adroitly pursuing his thoughts. 'I am sure he would do fourteen miles in an hour, and forty between now and midday. Look! you see that pretty little side track there? Does it not make you want to let go the reins? Speaking for myself, I would love a gallop.'

François made no reply, but blushed red and affected to listen for the hunters.

'The news from Poland has taken effect,' thought Henry. 'My dear brother-in-law has a plan of his own. He is willing enough I should be off, but I shan't go alone, he can rely upon it.'

At this moment, several converts from Protestantism, who

had been only a short time at court, came up, and saluted the princes with a knowing smile.

The Duke d'Alençon needed but to say one word, to make but one sign; for it was evident that the thirty or forty cavaliers who had gathered round him, as if by chance, were ready to oppose M. de Guise's troop, and cover his escape. The duke, however, turned his head, and, placing his horn to his lips, blew a recall.

Still, the new-comers, as though they believed the duke's hesitation was caused by the presence of the Guisards, gradually placed themselves between that party and the princes in a manner that showed they were well accustomed to military manœuvres. In order to reach the Duke d'Alençon and the King of Navarre, the Guise party would have to pass through them, while as far as the eye could see, the road ahead was empty.

Suddenly, between the trees, at ten paces from the king, appeared a gentleman whom the two princes had not noticed. While Henry was conjecturing who he could be, he raised his hat, and displayed the features of the Vicomte de Turenne, one of the Protestant leaders, who was believed to be in Poitou.*

The vicomte made a sign that asked,—

'Will you come?'

But Henry, after consulting the stony expression of the Duke d'Alençon, turned his head two or three times, as if something in his collar hurt him.

The vicomte understood him, and instantly disappeared.

Suddenly the hounds were heard again; and at the far end of the forest path where the two princes had halted, the boar passed, then the dogs, and then, looking like the wild huntsman of legend, Charles, bareheaded, and blowing his horn furiously. Three or four huntsmen rode after him. Tavannes was not among them.

'The king!' cried d'Alençon, and he instantly galloped after him.

Reassured by the presence of his friends, whom he motioned not to leave him, Henry advanced towards the ladies.

'Well,' said Marguerite.

'Well, madame,' said Henry, 'we are hunting the boar.'

'Is that all?'

'The wind has changed since the morning, as I predicted to you it would.'

'These changes of the wind are very bad for hunting, are they not, sir?' said Marguerite.

'Yes, sometimes they disturb all our arrangements, and we have to form a new plan altogether.'

The pack was now heard and everyone turned to listen.

Suddenly the boar broke out of the wood, and dashed past the ladies and their gallants.

Behind him, close on his haunches, came forty or fifty hounds, followed by the king, bareheaded, without hat or cloak, his clothes torn by thorns, his hands and face all bloody. Only one or two huntsmen had kept up with him.

'Hallali! hallali!'* cried he, as he passed, placing his horn to his bleeding lips, and boar, dogs, and king disappeared like a vision.

Immediately after them came d'Alençon, and two or three grooms.

Everyone followed, for it was plain the boar would soon be brought to bay.

And so it happened. In less than ten minutes, the boar, coming to an open spot, placed his back against a rock, and prepared for a desperate struggle.

The most interesting moment of the hunt had arrived. The dogs, though wellnigh breathless after a pursuit which had lasted more than three hours, rushed upon the boar.

All the hunters ranged themselves in a circle—the king a little in advance of the rest, the Duke d'Alençon behind him with his arquebuse, and Henry, who had only his hunting-knife.

The Duke d'Alençon lit the match of his arquebuse. Henry loosened his knife in its sheath.

The Duke de Guise, who despised all such sports, remained in the background with his party.

At some distance was a dog-handler, who had difficulty holding back the king's two huge boar-hounds, which, struggling and baying, were eagerly waiting for the moment when they would be let loose upon their prey.

The animal fought most gallantly. Attacked at once by forty

dogs surrounding him like a raging sea, he, at every thrust of his tusks, hurled into the air one of the gallant creatures, torn and dying. In ten minutes, twenty dogs were killed or disabled.

'Let loose the mastiffs,' cried the king.

The dog-handler opened the swivels of the leashes, and the two huge animals, protected by their coats of mail, dashed through the thickest of the fray, and seized the boar each by an ear.

'Bravo, Risque-tout! bravo, Dure-Dent!' cried Charles. 'A boar-spear! a boar-spear!'

'Do you want my arquebuse?' said d'Alençon.

'No, no!' cried the king, 'there is no pleasure in shooting him. But feeling a spear going in is another matter! A spear! Give me a spear!'

One was presented to him.

'Take care, Charles,' said Marguerite.

'At him!'

'Do not miss him, sire. Run the heretic through and through!' cried the Duchess de Nevers.

'Never fear!' replied the king and, levelling his spear, he rushed at the boar. But at the sight of the glittering steel, the animal made so sudden a movement that the spear glanced off his shoulder, and broke against the rock. 'Devil take it, I missed!' cried Charles impatiently. 'Another spear!'

And backing his steed, like the knights of old in a tournament, he threw down the broken weapon.

A groom stepped forward with another.

But as if he foresaw his fate, and sought to avoid it, the boar burst from the dogs with a violent effort, his hair bristling, his mouth foaming with rage, and head lowered, he rushed at Charles.

The king was too good a sportsman not to have anticipated this attack. Pulling hard on the rein, he made his horse rear; but either from the curb being too tightly held or from fear, the animal fell back upon its rider.

A cry burst from everyone—the king's thigh was caught be-tween the saddle and the ground.

'Let the bridle go, sire!' cried Henry.

The king abandoned his hold of the reins, seized the saddle

with his left hand, and with his right tried to draw his hunting-knife, but in vain: the sheath was trapped by his body.

'The boar! the boar!' cried Charles. 'Help, d'Alençon!'

The horse, as if sensing the danger of its master, was getting up on to its front legs, when Henry saw d'Alençon turn ghastly pale as he placed his arquebuse to his shoulder and fired. The bullet, instead of hitting the boar, struck the fore-leg of the king's horse which instantly fell again.

'Oh!' murmured d'Alençon, his lips livid with fear, 'I think that d'Anjou is King of France, and I King of Poland!' The boar's tusk already grazed Charles's thigh when the king felt his arm raised, and saw a bright blade flash before his eyes, and bury itself up to the hilt behind the boar's shoulder, while a hand gloved in iron was dashed against the mouth of the monster.

Charles had by this time freed himself from his struggling horse, and rose with difficulty. When he saw his clothes covered with blood, he grew paler than ever.

'Sire,' said Henry, still on one knee with his knife still in the boar's breast, 'you are not hurt. I turned the tusk aside in time.'

He then rose, leaving the knife in the boar, which rolled over dead, bleeding even more profusely from the mouth than from the wound.

Charles, surrounded by a crowd of courtiers all uttering cries of terror, seemed for a moment about to fall alongside the dead boar. But recovering himself, he turned to the King of Navarre, with his eyes beaming with the first ray of sensibility that had touched his heart for full four-and-twenty years.

'Thanks! Harry,' said he.

'My poor brother,' said d'Alençon coming up to him.

'Ah, is that you, d'Alençon!' cried the king. 'Well, famous marksman that you are, where is your bullet?'

'It must have flattened upon the boar.'

'Eh, *mon Dieu!*' said Henry, with an air of surprise, admirably feigned, 'your bullet has broken the leg of the king's horse. How very odd!'

'Ah! is that so?' said the king.

'It may be,' replied the duke, in dismay, 'my hand was trembling as I aimed.'

'Humph! for a first-rate marksman, you made a most curious

shot, d'Alençon,' said Charles, frowning. 'Once again, Harry, thanks!'

Marguerite advanced to congratulate the king and thank her husband.

'Oh, by my faith, Margot, you are right to thank him heartily,' said Charles. 'Had it not been for him, the king of France would be Henry III.'

'Alas, madame!' returned Henry, 'M. d'Anjou, who is already my enemy, will be more than ever so, now. But it can't be helped. No one can be expected to do more than his best. I am sure that d'Alençon would agree—'

And, stooping down, he pulled his knife from the body of the boar, and plunged it several times into the earth to wipe the blood off.

'And now, ladies and gentlemen,' said the king, 'homeward! I have had enough for one day.'

32

FRATERNITY

IN saving the life of Charles,* Henry had done more than save the life of a man. He had prevented three kingdoms from changing monarchs.

Had Charles IX been killed, the Duke d'Anjou would have been King of France, and the Duke d'Alençon most probably King of Poland. As to Navarre, since the Duke d'Anjou was enamoured of Madame de Condé, that crown would in all probability have paid the husband for the complaisance of his wife.

In all this confusion, Henry would have gained nothing. He would have changed masters, that was all. Instead of Charles IX who tolerated him, he would have seen the Duke d'Anjou on the throne, who, having but one head and one heart with his mother Catherine, had sworn his death, and would have kept his oath.

Such were the ideas that floated through his brain when the wild boar had rushed on King Charles, and we have seen the result of this reflection, rapid as lightning, that the life of Charles IX was bound up with his own existence.

Charles IX, then, was saved by a devotion whose spring and action he could not understand. Marguerite, however, had understood it fully, and had admired the strange courage of Henry which, like lightning, shone only in the dark.

Henry, as he returned from Bondy, pondered his situation, and when he reached the Louvre he had formed a plan of action. Without taking off his boots, but all dusty and covered with blood as he was, he went to the Duke d'Alençon, whom he found greatly agitated, and pacing hastily up and down his apartment.

The prince started when he saw him.

'Yes,' said Henry to him, taking both his hands, 'yes, I understand, my good brother, you are angry with me, because I was the first to call the king's attention to the fact that your bullet struck his horse's leg instead of the boar, as was your aim. But I could not repress an exclamation of surprise. In any case, the king had noticed it.'

'No doubt!' muttered d'Alençon, 'yet I cannot help thinking it was ill-intentioned of you to point out this fact, which you must have seen has made my brother Charles suspicious of my intentions and thrown a cloud between us.'

'We will talk of this anon. As for my good or bad intention, I am here so that you can be a judge of that.'

'Humph!' said d'Alençon.

'Brother, your interests are too dear to me to allow me to keep from you that the Huguenots have made me certain proposals.'

'Proposals? what sort of proposals?'

'One of the leaders, M. de Mouy de Saint-Phale, son of the brave de Mouy who was assassinated by Maurevel, has been to see me at the risk of his life, to prove to me that I am a prisoner.'

'Ah, indeed? And what did you reply?'

'Brother, you know how tenderly I love Charles who saved my life and are aware that the queen-mother has been a mother to me. I therefore refused all the offers he made me.'

'What offers?'

'The Huguenots wished to reconstitute the throne of Navarre; and since this throne belonged to me by inheritance, they offered it to me.'

'Yes, and M. de Mouy, instead of the support he had expected, got a refusal?'

'Most decidedly. But since then——' continued Henry.

'You have repented, brother?' interrupted d'Alençon.

'No. But I have learned that M. de Mouy, enraged by my refusal, has cast his eyes in another direction.'

'Where?' asked François quickly.

'I do not know. At the Prince de Condé, perhaps.'

'Very probably,' was the reply.

'I have, however, ways of finding out who is the chief he has chosen.'

François became very pale.

'But,' continued Henry, 'the Huguenots are divided amongst themselves, and de Mouy, brave and loyal as he is, represents only one half the party. Now, the other half, which is not to be despised, has not lost all hope of seeing on the throne that Henry of Navarre, who, after having hesitated in the first instance, may have thought better of it afterwards.'

'Do you think so?'

'I have daily proofs of this. The troop that joined us at the hunt—did you notice the men who composed it?'

'Yes; they were converted gentlemen.'

'The leader of the troop, who gave me a sign—did you recognize him?'

'Yes; it was the Vicomte de Turenne.'

'Did you understand what they wanted?'

'Yes. They wanted you to flee with them.'

'Then,' said Henry, 'it is evident that there is a second party with different views from M. de Mouy, and that it is very powerful. If the cause is to succeed, then the two parties, Turenne's and de Mouy's, must unite. The conspiracy gathers strength—troops are ready—they but await the signal—and between my two resolutions I hesitate. So I have come to submit them to you as a friend.'

'Say rather as a brother!'

'First, let me explain the state of my mind, dear François. I have no desire, no ambition, no special abilities. I am a good sort of country gentleman—poor, easy-going, and diffident: the thought of plotting suggests to me the possibility of disgrace against which the prospect of a throne is a poor compensation.'

'Ah, brother!' said François, 'you are wrong. Nothing is sorrier than the plight of a prince whose fortune is blocked by an obstacle of birth or by some individual in the career of honour. I cannot, therefore, believe what you say.'

'Yet I speak the truth, brother,'* was Henry's reply. 'And if I could believe that I had a real friend, I would resign in his favour all the power which the party attached to me would confer. But,' he added, with a sigh, 'I have no such friend.'

'Perhaps you are mistaken.'

'No, *ventre-saint-gris!*' cried Henry. 'Except for yourself, brother, I see no one who is attached to me. So I must inform my brother the king of all that is going on. I will name no person—I will not mention titles or dates. But I will prevent the disaster.'

'*Grand Dieu!*' exclaimed d'Alençon, who could not repress his alarm—'what are you saying? You, the sole hope of the party since the admiral's death; you, a converted Huguenot—scarce converted, as it would seem—would you raise the knife against your brothers? Henry, Henry, in doing that, you will subject all the Calvinists of the kingdom to another Saint Bartholomew massacre! You must know that Catherine is only waiting for such an opportunity to exterminate all the survivors.'

And the trembling duke, his face marbled with red and livid spots, pressed Henry's hand in his eagerness to make him promise to reverse a decision which must destroy him.

'What!' said Henry, with an air of great surprise, 'do you think, François, that so many misfortunes would then occur? Yet it seems to me that, with the king's guarantee, I could save these hot-headed partisans.'

'The guarantee of King Charles IX, Henry? Did not the admiral have it? Teligny? yourself? Ah, Henry! I tell you, if you do this, you will destroy them all, and not only them, but also all those who are directly or indirectly connected with them.'

Henry appeared to reflect for a moment,—

'If,' he said, 'I were an important prince at court, I should act otherwise. In your place, for instance, François, a son of France, and probably heir to the throne.'

François shook his head sceptically, and said, 'What would you do in my place?'

'In your place, brother,' replied Henry, 'I should put myself at the head of this movement. My name and credit would answer to my conscience for the lives of the seditious; and I would derive from it something useful first for myself and then for the king. And all this from an enterprise which otherwise may terminate in great mischief for France.'

D'Alençon listened to these words with a joy which expanded all the muscles of his face, and replied,—

'Do you think this a practicable proposition, which would avoid all those evils which you foresee?'

'I do,' said Henry. 'The Huguenots like you. Your modest exterior, your situation elevated and difficult at the same time, and the kindness you have always shown to those of the reformed faith, all prompt them to serve you.'

'But,' said d'Alençon, 'there is a schism in the party. Will those who are for you be for me?'

'I will undertake to win them over, on two grounds.'

'What are they?'

'In the first place, the confidence which the chiefs have in me. Secondly, their fear that your Highness, knowing their names—— But without further persuasion, brother, think about this matter. Reign in Navarre. That way you keep for me a place at your table and a good forest for hunting and I shall be perfectly happy.'

'Reign in Navarre!' said the duke, 'but if——'

'If the Duke d'Anjou is named King of Poland, you mean?'

François cast a look of terror at Henry.

'If the Duke d'Anjou is elected King of Poland, and our brother Charles (whom God preserve!) should die, it is but two hundred leagues from Pau to Paris, while it is four hundred from Paris to Cracow.* You would be here to claim the inheritance when the King of Poland would only have learned of its being vacated. Then, if you are satisfied with me, François, you may give me this kingdom of Navarre, which will then be only one of the offshoots of your crown. In those circumstances, I would accept it. The worst that can happen would be to remain king there, and live *en famille* with me and my wife. For what are you here? A poor persecuted prince, a poor third son of the king, a slave of two elder brothers, whom a caprice may send to the Bastille.'

'Yes,' said François.' 'I know all this so well that I cannot understand why you are giving up all the hopes that you offer me.'

'There are,' said Henry, with a smile, 'burdens too heavy for certain hands. I shall not try to lift this one.'

'Then, Henry, you really renounce your claims?'

'I said so to de Mouy, and I repeat it to you.'

'But in such cases, brother,' said d'Alençon, 'men do not *say*, they prove by deeds.'

'I will prove it this evening,' was the reply. 'At nine o'clock, the list of the chiefs and the plan of the enterprise shall be in your hands.'

François took Henry's hand, and shook it warmly.

At the same moment, Catherine entered the apartment, as usual, without being announced.

'Together,' she said, with a smile, 'like two loving brothers.'

'I hope so, madame,' replied Henry, with the utmost composure, while the Duke d'Alençon turned pale with mortification.

The queen-mother then took from her purse a magnificent jewel, and said to François (from whom Henry had retreated several paces), 'This clasp comes from Florence, and I give it you to fasten your sword.' Then she added, in a whisper: 'if you should hear any noise this evening in the apartment of your good brother Henry, pay no attention.'

François grasped his mother's hand, and said: 'Will you allow me to show him the handsome present you have just given me?'

'Do still better: give it to him in your own and my name, for I ordered a second for that purpose.'

'Do you hear, Henry?' said François. 'My mother brings me this jewel, and redoubles its value by allowing me to offer it to you.'

Henry went into raptures at the beauty of the jewel, and was profuse in his thanks.

'My son,' said Catherine. 'I do not feel well, and am going to bed. Your brother Charles is much shaken by his fall and wishes to do the same. We shall not, therefore, all sup together. Ah,

Henry! I forgot to compliment you on your courage and skill. You saved your king and brother, and you must be recompensed for such high service.'

'I already have my reward,' replied Henry, with a bow.

'By the feeling that you have done your duty?' was Catherine's reply. 'But that is not enough for Charles and myself, and we must devise some means of repaying our obligation towards you.'

'Anything that comes from you and my good brother must be welcome, madame,' was Henry's reply, and, bowing, he left the apartment.

'Ah, my worthy brother François!' thought Henry, as he went out—'now I am sure I shall not leave alone. The conspiracy which had a heart has now found a head, and what is still better, that head is responsible to me for my own. But let us be on our guard. Catherine has given me a present—Catherine promises me a reward; there is some devilry or other brewing, and I must speak this evening with Marguerite.'

33

THE GRATITUDE OF KING CHARLES THE NINTH

MAUREVEL had remained for a part of the day in the king's armoury. When Catherine saw the moment approach for the return from the hunt, she sent for him and his accomplices to come to her oratory.

Charles IX, informed by his nurse on his arrival who the man was, and remembering the order his mother had made him sign that morning, understood everything.

'Ah!' he murmured—'the time is badly chosen, on the very day he saved my life.'

And he was about to go to his mother, but suddenly changed his mind.

'*Mordieu!*' he exclaimed, 'if I mention it to her now, there will be an endless discussion. It will be far better if we each act independently. Nurse,' he continued, 'shut all the doors, and inform Queen Elizabeth' (Charles IX was married to

Elizabeth of Austria, daughter of Maximilian)* 'that, being rather unwell from my fall, I shall sleep in my own apartment to-night.'

The nurse obeyed, and as the hour for his plan had not arrived, Charles began to write verses. It was the occupation in which he most delighted, which is why nine o'clock struck when Charles thought it was only seven. He counted the strokes one after the other, and at the last he rose. '*Nom d'un diable!*' he exclaimed, 'it is time.'

Taking his cloak and hat, he went out by a secret door which he had had made in the panelling, the existence of which was unknown even to Catherine herself.

Charles went straight to Henry's apartment. Henry had only gone there to change after leaving the Duke d'Alençon, and had then left it instantly.

'He must have gone to sup with Marguerite,' said the king to himself. 'He was on the best possible terms with her, at least it appeared so to me,' and he turned towards Marguerite's apartment.

Marguerite had invited to her rooms the Duchess de Nevers, Coconnas, and La Mole, and they were enjoying a feast of pastries and sweetmeats.

Charles knocked at the door. Gillonne went to open it and was so frightened at the sight of the king that she could scarcely curtsey to him. Instead of running to inform her mistress of the august visit which was paid to her, she allowed Charles to pass her without any other signal than the cry she had uttered.

The king walked through the antechamber, and, guided by the shouts of laughter, advanced towards the dining-room.

'Poor Harry!' he ejaculated, 'he is making merry, quite unconscious of his danger.'

'Greetings!' he said aloud, and, raising the tapestry, presented his face which was all smiles.

Marguerite uttered a terrible cry. Though the king's face beamed, it produced on her the effect of a Medusa's head. She had recognized Charles.

The two men had their backs turned to the king.

'Your Majesty!' she exclaimed, in a tone of panic, and she rose from her seat.

Coconnas, while the three others remained utterly stunned, was the only one who preserved his presence of mind. He also rose, but with well-contrived awkwardness upset the table with its glass, plates, and wax lights. At once there was complete darkness, and the silence of death.

'Be off!' said Coconnas to La Mole—'quickly now, and be quiet.'

La Mole did not wait for a second hint, but feeling along the wall with his hands, groped his way into the bedchamber, so that he could hide in the closet which he knew so well.

But as he entered the sleeping-room he came in contact with a man who had entered by the secret passage.

'What can all this mean?' said Charles, in the darkness, with a voice that was beginning to sound very impatient. 'Am I an intruder, that on my appearance such a scene of confusion should take place? Harry—Harry! where are you?—answer me!'

'We are saved!' whispered Marguerite, taking a hand which she assumed to be that of Coconnas, 'the king thinks that my husband is one of the guests.'

'And he shall go on thinking so, madame, be assured,' said Henry himself to the queen, in the same tone.

'*Grand Dieu!*' exclaimed Marguerite, suddenly letting go her grasp of the hand she held.

'Hush!' said Henry.

'In the name of ten thousand devils! what are you all whispering for?' cried Charles. 'Henry, answer—where are you?'

'I am here, sire,' said the voice of the King of Navarre.

'The devil!' said Coconnas, 'the plot thickens.'

'And we are doubly lost,' added the Duchess de Nevers.

Coconnas, brave even to recklessness, had realized that the candles must be lit, and thinking the sooner the better, abandoned the hand of the Duchess de Nevers, which he had been holding in his own, picked up a taper, and, going to the stove, lit it.

The room was again illuminated, and Charles cast an inquiring glance around.

Henry was standing next to his wife; the Duchess de Nevers

was alone in a corner; and Coconnas, in the middle of the chamber with his candle in his hand, lighted up the whole scene.

'Excuse us, brother,' said Marguerite; 'we were not expecting you.'

'And your Majesty, as you may see, frightened us not a little,' said Henriette.

'For my part,' added Henry, who at once understood the situation, 'I was so startled that I upset the table.'

Coconnas gave the King of Navarre a look which implied,—

'I like that!—here's a husband who knows what he is about!'

'What a mess!' said Charles. 'Harry, your supper is utterly spoiled. Come with me, and you shall finish it elsewhere. I mean to carry you off this evening.'

'What, sire!' said Henry, 'your Majesty will do me that honour?'

'Yes, my Majesty will do you the honour to take you out of the Louvre. Lend him to me, Marguerite, and I will bring him back again to-morrow morning.'

'Ah, brother!' replied Marguerite, 'you do not need my permission for that. You are master here as everywhere else.'

'Sire,' said Henry, 'I will just go for another cloak and return immediately.'

'There's no need; the one you have on is quite good enough.'

'But, sire——' said the Béarnais.

'I tell you not to return to your apartment. Good God! don't you hear what I say? Come along!'

'Yes—yes, go!' said Marguerite, pressing her husband's arm, for a strange look in Charles's eye had convinced her that something remarkable was going on.

'I am ready, sire,' said Henry.

But Charles was staring at Coconnas who continued his office of torch-bearer by lighting the other candles.

'Who is this gentleman?' he inquired of Henry, still gazing on the Piedmontese. 'Is it M. de la Mole?'

'Who has mentioned M. de la Mole to him?' thought Marguerite.

'No, sire,' replied Henry. 'M. de la Mole is not here, and I regret it the more, as I cannot have the honour of presenting him to your Majesty as well as his friend, M. de Coconnas. They are inseparable, and both belong to the entourage of M. d'Alençon.'

'Ah! our famous marksman!' said Charles. Then frowning, he added, 'Is not M. de la Mole a Huguenot?'

'Converted, sire,' said Henry 'and I answer for him as for myself.'

'When you answer for anyone, Harry, after what you have done to-day, I have no right to doubt you. But no matter. I should have liked to see M. de la Mole, but some other time will do.' Then, looking again around the chamber, Charles kissed Marguerite, and led away the King of Navarre, holding him by the arm.

At the gate of the Louvre, Henry stopped to speak to someone.

'Come along, Harry,' said Charles. 'When I tell you the air of the Louvre is not good for you this evening, why the devil don't you believe me?'

'*Ventre-saint-gris!*' murmured Henry, 'and de Mouy will be all alone in my room. If the air is not good for me, it will be worse for him.'

As they crossed the drawbridge, the king gave a distinctive whistle. Four gentlemen who were waiting in the Rue de Beauvais joined them, and they all advanced into the city.

The clock struck ten.

'Well!' said Marguerite, when the king and Henry had gone— 'let us sit down again to table.'

'No, *ma foi!*' said the duchess, 'I am too frightened. The little house in the Rue Cloche Perce for ever! No one can get in there without laying siege, and our brave friends could use their swords.'

Coconnas went to the cabinet.

'Well!' said a voice in the darkness, 'what happened?'

'Eh, *Mordi!* we are now at the dessert.'

'And the King of Navarre?'

'Saw nothing.'

'And King Charles?'

'Ah! the king has taken the husband away.'

'No, really?'

'Yes, and the ladies have a pilgrimage to make to the Rue du Roi-de-Sicile, and we must guard the pilgrims.'

'Impossible! you know that——'

'Why impossible?'

'Are we not in the service of his Royal Highness and must be present when he retires?'

The two friends represented their position to their fair companions, and Madame de Nevers said——

'Well, then, we will go without you.'

The two young men made their bows, and proceeded to the Duke d'Alençon, who appeared to be waiting for them.

'You are rather late, gentlemen,' was his remark.

'Scarcely ten o'clock, monseigneur,' replied Coconnas.

The duke looked at his watch.

'True, but yet everybody in the Louvre is asleep.'

'Monseigneur,' said Coconnas, 'your Highness, no doubt, will go to bed or work——'

'No, gentlemen, I can dispense with your services until to-morrow morning.'

The two young men ran upstairs as speedily as possible, took their cloaks and night-swords, and, hurrying out of the Louvre, overtook the two ladies at the corner of the Rue du Coq-Saint-Honoré.

34

MAN PROPOSES, BUT GOD DISPOSES

As the duke said, everything was silent at the Louvre.

Marguerite and Madame de Nevers had gone to the Rue Cloche Perce; Coconnas and La Mole had followed them; the king and Henry were roving about in the city; the Duke d'Alençon was anxiously anticipating the outcome of the events his mother had set in motion, and Catherine was in bed, listening to Madame de Sauve, who was reading to her certain Italian tales,* which made the worthy queen laugh heartily.

'Let me know,' said Catherine, 'if my daughter, the Queen of

Navarre, is in her apartments, and, if she is, ask her to come and keep me company.'

The page to whom this order was addressed left the room. He soon returned, accompanied by Gillonne.

'I sent for the queen,' said Catherine, 'not for her attendant.'

'Madame,' replied Gillonne, 'I thought it my duty to come myself, to inform your Majesty that the Queen of Navarre is gone out with the Duchess de Nevers.'

'Out at this hour!' said Catherine, frowning. 'Where has she gone?'

'To a meeting of alchemists, at the Hotel de Guise, in the apartments of Madame de Nevers.'

'And when will she return?'

'The meeting will not break up until very late,' replied Gillonne, 'so that it is probable her Majesty will sleep at the Hotel de Guise.'

'She is very fortunate,' murmured Catherine. 'She has friends, and is a queen; she wears a crown, and is called your Majesty, and she has no subjects.'

Gillonne made her curtsey, and left the room.

'Go on, Charlotte,' said the queen.

Madame de Sauve obeyed.

Ten minutes later Catherine stopped her.

'Oh, by the way,' said she, 'dismiss the guards in the gallery.'

This was the signal agreed upon with Maurevel.

The order was executed, and Madame de Sauve continued. She had been reading for a quarter of an hour, when a long and piercing cry was heard, that made the hair of everyone in Catherine's apartments stand on end.

A pistol-shot followed.

'Well,' said Catherine, 'why do you not go on reading?'

'Madame,' replied Charlotte, turning deadly pale, 'did your Majesty not hear?'

'Hear what?' asked Catherine.

'That cry!'

'And that pistol-shot?' added the captain of the guards.

'A cry and a pistol-shot?' said Catherine, 'I heard nothing. Besides, a cry and a pistol-shot are nothing so very extraordinary at the Louvre. Read on, Carlotta.'

'But listen, madame,' said Madame de Sauve, while M. de Nancey stood grasping his sword-hilt, not daring to leave the apartment without the queen's permission, 'I hear struggling, shouting——'

'Shall I go and see, madame?' asked de Nancey.

'No, sir,' returned Catherine. 'Who will be here to protect me in case of danger? It is only some drunken Swiss quarrelling.'

The calmness of the queen contrasted so strangely with the alarm of everyone else that Madame de Sauve, timid as she was, fixed her eyes inquiringly on her.

'But, madame,' said she, 'it is as if they were killing someone.'

'Who do you think they are killing?'

'The King of Navarre, madame, for the noise comes from his apartments.'

'Stupid girl!' murmured the queen, whose lips, in spite of the control she had over herself, were strangely agitated, for she was muttering a prayer—'she sees her King of Navarre everywhere.'

'*Mon Dieu! mon Dieu!*' said Madame de Sauve, sinking into her chair.

'It is all over,' said Catherine. 'Captain,' she continued, addressing M. de Nancey, 'I hope that to-morrow you will inquire into this, and punish the culprits severely. Continue, Carlotta.'

And Catherine sank back on her pillow in a state that seemed near to fainting, for her attendants remarked large drops of perspiration on her face.

Madame de Sauve obeyed, but her eyes and her voice alone were mobilized. She fancied she saw the man who was most dear to her surrounded by deadly perils, and after a mental struggle of some moments, her voice failed her, the book fell from her hands, and she fainted.

Suddenly an even more violent noise than before was heard, a hasty step shook the corridor, and two more pistol shots made the window-panes rattle. Catherine, astonished at this renewal of the strife, stood up. She was deadly pale, her eyes were dilated, and at the moment de Nancey was about to rush from the apartment, she seized his arm, saying,—

'Let everyone stay here. I will go myself and see what is the matter.'

This was what had happened. That morning de Mouy had

received the key of Henry's apartments from Orthon. In the key he noticed a small roll of paper, which he took out and found to contain the password at the Louvre for the night.

Orthon had also given him the king's instructions to be at the Louvre at ten o'clock.

At half-past nine, de Mouy put on his armour, buttoned a silken doublet over it, buckled on his sword, placed his pistols in his belt, and covered it all with the famous cherry cloak.

We have seen how Henry thought fit to pay Marguerite a visit before returning to his own apartments, and how he arrived by the secret passage just in time to encounter La Mole in Marguerite's chamber and take his place in the supper-room. At exactly the same moment, de Mouy entered through the gate of the Louvre, and, thanks to the password and the cherry cloak, entered the palace without obstacle.

He went straight to the King of Navarre's apartments, imitating, as well as he could, La Mole's walk and manner. He found Orthon waiting for him in the antechamber.

'Sire de Mouy,' he said, 'the king has gone out, but he has ordered me to conduct you to his chamber, where you are to wait. Should he not return until late, he suggests that you rest on his bed.'

De Mouy entered, without asking further explanation.

To fill up the time, de Mouy took pen and paper, and, approaching an excellent map of France that hung on the wall, set himself to count the posting stages from Paris to Pau.*

This did not occupy him long, and when he had finished he was at a loss what to do.

He walked up and down the room a few times, yawned, and then taking advantage of Henry's invitation, and with the familiarity that then existed between princes and their gentlemen, placed his pistols and the lamp on the table, laid his drawn sword by his side, and secure against surprise, for an attendant was keeping watch in the antechamber, was soon sound asleep.

It was then that six men, sword and dagger in hand, glided noiselessly along the corridor that communicated with Henry's apartments.

One of these men led. Besides his sword and dagger, he had pistols attached to his belt by silver hooks. This man was Maurevel. When he reached Henry's door, he stopped.

'Are you quite sure all the sentries have gone?' he asked.

'There is not one left,' replied his lieutenant.

'Good,' said Maurevel. 'Now let us see whether the man we have come for is here.'

'Poor devil of a king!' said one of the men, 'it was written on high he should not escape.'

'And written here also,' said Maurevel, pointing to the order in his belt.

Maurevel placed the key Catherine had given him in the lock, and, leaving two men at the door, went with the others into the antechamber.

'Ah,' said he, hearing even from that distance, the loud breathing of the sleeper, 'it seems we have got him!'

Orthon, thinking it was his master, stepped forward and found himself in the presence of five armed men. At the sight of their sinister faces, and more particularly at that of Maurevel, he recoiled and planted himself before the second door.

'Who are you?' said Orthon—'and what do you want?'

'In the King's name,' said Maurevel, 'where is your master?'

'He is absent.'

'Not true!' replied Maurevel. 'Stand back!'

Orthon seized the handle of the door.

'You shall not enter!' cried he.

At a sign from Maurevel, the four men grasped the faithful page, tore him from his hold, and, as he was about to cry out, Maurevel placed his hand on his mouth. Orthon bit the hand of the assassin who uttered a stifled cry and struck him on the head with the pommel of his sword. Orthon fell, crying 'Treason! treason!'

His voice failed him, and he fainted.

The assassins walked over his body: two stationed themselves at the second door, and the three others, led by Maurevel, entered the bedchamber.

By the light of the lamp they saw the bed: the curtains were closed.

'Oh,' said the lieutenant, 'he has stopped snoring!'

'Now, then—upon him!' replied Maurevel.

At this voice a hoarse cry was heard, more like the roar of a lion than the voice of a human being, the curtains were violently drawn back, and a man in a breastplate and steel helmet appeared sitting on the bed, a pistol in each hand and his drawn sword on his knees. At this sight, Maurevel's hair stood on end, he turned deadly pale, and recoiled as if he had seen a spectre.

Suddenly, the armed figure rose and advanced towards Maurevel, as he retreated, so that it was he who seemed to flee and de Mouy who seemed to pursue.

'Ah, scoundrel!' said de Mouy—'you have come to murder me, as you murdered my father!'

Only the two guards who were with Maurevel heard these terrible words. But as they were uttered, one of de Mouy's pistols was levelled at Maurevel's head. The ruffian sank on his knees at the instant de Mouy pulled the trigger, and one of the guards whom he exposed by this movement fell with a bullet in his heart. Maurevel fired back immediately, but the bullet glanced off de Mouy's breastplate.

Then measuring the distance and calculating his spring, de Mouy, with a back stroke of his large sword, split the skull of the second guard, and, turning to Maurevel, crossed swords with him.

The combat was terrible, but brief. At the fourth pass, Maurevel felt de Mouy's sword in his throat. He uttered a low groan, and fell, upsetting the lamp, which was extinguished in the fall.

Agile and powerful as one of Homer's heroes, de Mouy sprang boldly forward, favoured by the darkness, into the antechamber, felled one of the guards, sent the other staggering from him, passed like lightning between the two at the outer door, escaped two pistol-shots fired at him, the bullets from which grazed the walls of the corridor, and was then safe, for, besides the sword with which he dealt such fearful blows, he had a loaded pistol.

He hesitated an instant whether he should enter d'Alençon's apartments, the door of which seemed ajar, or escape from the Louvre. Resolving upon the latter course, he sprang down the stairs, arrived at the gate, gave the password, adding, 'Go upstairs! they are killing on the king's orders.'

And making the most of the confusion produced by the report of the pistols and his own words, he disappeared down the Rue du Coq, without having received a scratch.

It was at this moment that Catherine stopped M. de Nancey saying,—

'Stay here; I will go myself and see what is the matter.'

Then taking a lamp, and putting her bare feet into slippers, Catherine advanced, pale as a spectre, along the corridor full of smoke, towards Henry's apartments.

Everything was silent.

She arrived at the door, entered, and found Orthon unconscious on the threshold.

'Oh!' said she, 'here is the servant; we shall soon find the master.' She approached the second door.

There her foot struck against a corpse; she turned the lamp upon it; it was the guard whose skull had been split: he was quite dead.

A little further on lay the lieutenant, who was breathing his last.

Beside the bed was a man who, pale as death, was bleeding copiously from a double wound in his throat, and who, clenching his hands convulsively, was trying to get up.

It was Maurevel.

Catherine shuddered. She saw the empty bed, eagerly looked around the room, and in vain sought amongst the three corpses for the one she so earnestly wanted to see.

Maurevel recognized Catherine, and stretched out his hand towards her with a desperate movement.

'Where is he?' said she. 'Have you let him escape?'

Maurevel strove to speak, but a bloody foam covered his lips, and he could only shake his head weakly.

'Speak!' cried the queen—'speak, if it be but one word!'

Maurevel pointed to his wound, and, after a desperate effort to say something, fainted.

She looked around her: there were none but dead and dying there. Blood flowed in every direction, and silence reigned in the chamber. She spoke again to Maurevel, but in vain; a paper was in his belt—it was the order for Henry's arrest. Catherine seized it, and concealed it beneath her robe.

At this instant she heard a slight noise behind her, and, turning round, she saw d'Alençon, who had been attracted by the noise.

'You here, François?' said she.

'Yes, madame. For God's sake, what does this mean?'

'Go back to your apartments; you will know soon enough.'

D'Alençon, however, was not so ignorant of what had passed as Catherine imagined. Seeing men enter the King of Navarre's apartments, he guessed what was to happen, and was secretly relieved at having so dangerous an enemy disposed of by a hand more powerful than his own.

Then the noise of fire-arms and the steps of a fleeing man had roused his attention, and peering through the crack in the door, he had seen Cherry Mantle disappear.

'De Mouy!' he had exclaimed—'De Mouy with my brother-in-law? Or can it be La Mole?'

He had begun to feel alarmed.

Wishing to reassure himself, he had run up to the apartment where the two young men were supposed to be. No one was there, but the cherry-coloured cloak was hanging against the wall. So it was de Mouy! Pale as death, and trembling lest de Mouy had been arrested and had betrayed the secrets of the conspiracy, he rushed to the gate, where he was informed de Mouy had left, saying that someone was being killed on the king's orders.

'He was mistaken,' muttered d'Alençon, 'it is on the queen-mother's orders.'

And returning to the scene of combat, he found Catherine prowling like a hyena amongst the dead.

Catherine, in despair at the failure of this new attempt, called de Nancey, had the bodies removed and Maurevel conveyed to his own house, and forbade them to wake the king.

'Oh!' she murmured, as she entered her apartment, her head sunk on her bosom—'he has again escaped—the hand of God protects him. He will reign—he will reign!'

Then, as she opened her door, she assumed a smile.

'Oh, madame, what was the matter?' demanded everyone except Madame de Sauve, who was too frightened to ask any questions.

'Oh, nothing!' replied the queen—'only a noise, nothing more.'

'But,' cried Madame de Sauve suddenly, 'every step your Majesty takes leaves a trace of blood on the carpet!'*

35

THE TWO KINGS

CHARLES IX walked arm in arm with Henry, followed by his four gentlemen, and preceded by two torch-bearers. 'Whenever I leave the Louvre,' said the poor king, 'I experience a pleasure similar to what I feel when I enter a fine forest—I breathe, I live, I am free!'

Henry smiled.

'Your Majesty would be happy in my mountains in Béarn, then?' was his reply.

'Yes, and I can understand how eager you must be to return there. But if the desire comes very strong upon you, Harry,' added Charles, laughing, 'be careful, for my mother Catherine is so very fond of you that she really cannot do without you.'

The two kings, followed by their escort, had reached the Hotel de Condé,* when they observed two men, wrapped in long cloaks, emerge from a private door which one of them closed carefully.

'Oh!' said the King to Henry, 'this deserves our attention. You, Harry, are sure of your wife' (Charles smiled as he said this), 'but your cousin de Condé is not so sure of his; or if he is sure, devil fetch me! he is very mistaken.'

'But how do you know, sire, that it is Madame de Condé these gentlemen have come to visit?'

'A presentiment. They have seen us, and try to avoid being noticed. And then there is the peculiar cut of one of their cloaks. *Pardieu!* now that would be strange!'

'What?'

'Nothing, only an idea. Let us go and see what they are about.'

And he went towards the two men, who, seeing that they had been spotted, began to move off in the opposite direction.

'Hola! messieurs,' said the king—'stop!'

'What do you want with us?' said a voice, which made Charles and his companion start.

'Ah, Harry!' said Charles, 'do you recognize that voice now?'

'Sire,' replied Henry, 'if your brother, the Duke d'Anjou, were not at La Rochelle,* I should swear it was he who just spoke.'

'Well, then,' said Charles, 'he is not at La Rochelle.'

'But who is with him?'

'A man whose figure can hardly be mistaken. Hola! I say,' continued the king, 'did you not hear me?'

'Are you the watch, to accost us like this?' asked the taller of the two men, thrusting forth his hand from the folds of his cloak.

'Assume that we are the watch,' said the king, 'and stand when you are ordered.'

Then whispering to Henry, he added, 'Now you will see the volcano spit forth flames.'

'There are eight of you,' replied the taller of the two men, showing not only his arm but his face. 'But were you a hundred, I would still bid you keep your distance.'

'Ah, the Duke de Guise!' said Henry.

'Ah! our cousin of Lorraine,' said the king—'it is you, is it? How well met!'

'The king!' exclaimed the duke.

As to the other personage, he muffled himself up still closer in his cloak, and remained motionless, after having first respectfully removed his hat.

'Sire,' said the Duke de Guise, 'I have just been paying a visit to my sister-in-law, Madame de Condé.'

'Yes, and have brought one of your gentlemen with you. Tell me, who is he?'

'Sire,' replied the duke, 'your Majesty does not know him.'

'Then we will make his acquaintance now,' said the king; and, going towards him, he desired the two men to approach with their torches.

'Forgive me, brother,' said the Duke d'Anjou, opening his cloak, and bowing with ill-concealed vexation.

'Ah! Henry. You here? But no, it cannot be possible. I am deceived. My brother of Anjou would never have gone to see any person without first coming to see me. He is not unaware that for princes of the blood there is only one entrance to Paris, and that is by the gate of the Louvre.'

'Pardon me, sire,' said the Duke d'Anjou. 'I entreat your Majesty to forgive this breach of etiquette.'

'Of course,' replied the king, in a jeering tone. 'And what were you doing, brother, at the Hotel de Condé?'

'Why,' said the King of Navarre, with his peculiar air, 'what your Majesty mentioned only a moment ago.' And he laughed loudly.

'And why,' asked the Duke de Guise icily, for, like the rest of the world, he behaved very rudely to the poor King of Navarre, 'should I not visit my sister-in-law? Does the Duke d'Alençon not visit his?'

Henry's cheek turned red.

'What sister-in-law?' remarked Charles. 'I do not know of any other he has than Queen Elizabeth.'

'Your pardon, sire; it was his sister I should have said— Madame Marguerite, whom we saw as we were arriving half an hour ago, in her litter, accompanied by two fine-looking fellows, one on each side.'

'Really?' said Charles. 'What do you say to that, Henry?'

'That the Queen of Navarre is free to go where she pleases. But I doubt that she has left the Louvre.'

'And I am sure of it,' said the Duke de Guise.

'And I also,' said the Duke d'Anjou. 'The litter stopped in the Rue Cloche Perce.'

'Your sister-in-law, then—not this one, but the other,' and he pointed his finger in the direction of the Hotel de Guise—'must also be of the party, for we left them together, and they are, as you know, inseparable.'

'I do not understand what your Majesty implies,' replied the Duke de Guise.

'Now to my mind,' observed the king, 'nothing could be clearer;* and that is why there was a handsome buck riding on each side of the litter.'

'Well,' said the duke, 'if there is any wrong-doing on the part of the queen and of my sisters-in-law, let us call on the justice of the king to put an end to it.'

'Eh, *par Dieu!*' said Henry, 'let us have done with Mesdames de Condé and de Nevers. The king has no uneasiness about his sister and I have none for my wife.'

'No, no,' interposed Charles. 'I will have the affair cleared up, but let us manage it ourselves. The litter, you say, cousin, stopped in the Rue Cloche Perce?'

'Yes, sire.'

'You know the spot?'

'Yes, sire.'

'Well, then, let us go there, and if we have to burn down the house to know who is in it, why, we will do so.'

It was with this feeling, most alarming to those concerned, that the four principal princes of the Christian world proceeded towards the Rue Saint-Antoine.

When they reached the Rue Cloche Perce, Charles, who wished to confine the affair to his family, dismissed his attendants, ordering them to be near the Bastille at six o'clock in the morning, with two horses.

On reaching the house, they knocked and tried to gain admittance, which the German porter decidedly and doggedly refused. Seeing that they could not succeed that way, the Duke de Guise, pretending to give up, went to the corner of the Rue Saint-Antoine, and there picked up one of those stones such as Ajax, Telamon, and Diomedes* lifted three thousand years before, and dashed it with violence against the door which burst open under the impact, knocking down the German who fell heavily and with a loud cry which roused the garrison, which otherwise would have been taken by surprise.

At this noise, La Mole, Coconnas, Marguerite, and Henriette started. They blew out all the lights instantly, and, opening the windows, went out on to the balcony. Seeing four men in the darkness, they began to shower down upon them all the projectiles within reach, and make a hullabaloo by striking the stone walls with the flat of their swords. Charles, the most eager of the assailants, received a silver ewer on his shoulder, the Duke d'Anjou, a basin containing preserved oranges with cinnamon, and the Duke de Guise, a haunch of venison.

Henry was not hit by anything. He was speaking quietly to the porter, whom M. de Guise had tied to the door, and who replied with his eternal—

'*Ich verstehe nicht.*'

The women ably backed the besieged army, by handing missiles to them which fell like hail.

'By God!' cried Charles, taking a direct hit on his head from a stool which knocked his hat over his eyes and nose, 'if they do not open up at once, I'll hang them all.'

'It is my brother!' said Marguerite to La Mole, in a whisper.

'The king!' said he to Henriette.

'The king! the king!' said she to Coconnas, who was dragging a large chest to the window, intending it especially for the Duke de Guise, whom, without knowing him, he had picked out as his particular foe—'the king, I tell you!'

Coconnas abandoned the chest in amazement.

'The king?' said he.

'Yes, the king!'

'Then sound a retreat.'

'Well, so be it. Marguerite and La Mole are off already.'

'Which way?'

'Through here!' and, taking him by the hand, Henriette led Coconnas by the secret door which led to the adjoining house, and, having closed it after them, they all four fled by the way that led to the Rue Tizon.

'Ah!' said Charles, 'I think the garrison has surrendered. Cousin,' he continued, 'get that stone of yours and break the inner door down as you did with the other.'

The duke burst the other door in with his foot.

'Torches! torches!' said the king, and the lackey, having relighted them, came forward. The king took one and handed the other to the Duke d'Anjou.

The Duke de Guise went first, sword in hand, while Henry brought up the rear.

They reached the first floor, and in the dining-room found the remains of supper, with candelabra upset, furniture overturned, and anything that was not of metal destroyed.

They went into the salon, but there was no better clue to the absconders there than in the other room.

'There must be another way out,' observed the king.

'Most probably,' replied d'Anjou.

They searched everywhere, but found no door.

'Where is the porter?' inquired the king.

'I tied him to the door,' replied the Duke de Guise.

Henry looked out of the window, and observed,—

'He is not there now.'

'By God!' said the king, 'we shall learn nothing now.'

'So,' added Henry, 'you see plainly, sire, that nothing proves that my wife and the Duke de Guise's sister-in-law have been in this house; and so the best thing we can do——'

'Is,' said Charles, 'for me to poultice my bruise, d'Anjou to wipe off the marks of the orange jam, and Guise to rub the grease off his ruff.'

And then they all went away, without so much as closing the door after them.

When they reached the Rue Saint-Antoine, the king said to M. d'Anjou and the Duke de Guise,—

'Which way are you going, gentlemen?'

'Sire, we are going to Nantouillet's.* He is expecting my cousin of Lorraine and myself to supper. Will your Majesty accompany us?'

'No, I thank you. Our way lies in an opposite direction. Will you have one of my torch-bearers?'

'No thank you, sire,' was d'Anjou's reply.

'Good! He is afraid I intend to spy on him,' whispered Charles in Henry's ear. Then taking him by the arm, he said,—

'Come, Harry, I will find you a supper to-night.'

'Then we are not going back to the Louvre?' was Henry's response.

'No, I tell you, blockhead! Come with me when I tell you—come!'

And he led Henry along the Rue Geoffroy-Lasnier.

36

THEY reached the Rue du la Mortellerie, and stopped at a small, solitary house in the middle of a garden enclosed by high walls. Charles took a key from his pocket, and opened the door. Then ordering Henry and the torch-bearer to enter, he closed the door after him. One small window only was lit, to which Charles, with a smile, directed Henry's attention, saying,—

'Harry, I told you that when I leave the Louvre I ascend from hell, and when I come here I enter paradise.'

'And who is the angel that guards the entrance to your Eden, sire?'

'You will see,' replied Charles IX, and making a sign to Henry to follow him without noise, he pushed open a first door, then a second, and paused on the threshold.

'Look!' he said.

Henry did so, and remained with his eyes fixed on as charming a picture as he ever saw. It was a woman of eighteen or nineteen years of age, resting at the foot of a bed, on which was sleeping an infant whose two feet she held in her hands, pressing them to her lips, while her long chestnut hair fell down over them like waves of gold.

It was like a picture of Albano's representing the Virgin and the infant Jesus.*

'Oh, sire,' said the King of Navarre, 'who is this charming creature?'

'The angel of my paradise, Harry, the only being who loves me for myself.'

Henry smiled.

'Yes,' said Charles, 'for myself. She loved me before she knew I was the king.'

'And since——?'

'Since,' said Charles, with a sigh, which proved that his glittering royalty was sometimes a burden to him—'since she knew it, she still loves me. Watch!'

The king approached her gently, and on the lovely cheek of

the young woman impressed a kiss as light as that of the bee on a lily, yet it awoke her.

'Charles!' she murmured, opening her eyes.

'You see,' said the king, 'she calls me Charles. The queen says sire.'

'Oh,' exclaimed the young girl, 'you are not alone!'

'No, dearest Marie; I have brought you another king, happier than myself, for he has no crown, but also unhappier, for he has no Marie Touchet.'

'Sire, is it the King of Navarre?'

'It is, my love.'

Henry went towards her, and Charles took his right hand.

'Look at this hand, Marie,' said he. 'It is the hand of a good brother and a loyal friend, and but for this hand——'

'Well, sire?'

'But for this hand, Marie, our boy would have been fatherless today.'

Marie uttered a cry, seized Henry's hand, and kissed it.

The king went to the bed where the child was still asleep.

'Ah!' said he, 'if this fine boy slept in the Louvre instead of this small house, he would change the complexion of things at present, and perhaps for the future.'[1]

'Sire,' said Marie, 'without offence to your Majesty, I prefer him to sleep here, he sleeps better.'

'You are right, Marie,' said Charles IX. 'Let us sup now.'

The two men passed into the dining-room, while the anxious and careful mother covered little Charles, who slept soundly, with a warm coverlet, and then joined the two kings, between whom she seated herself, and served both.

'Is it not well, Harry,' asked Charles, 'to have a place where you can eat and drink without the need of anyone tasting your viands before you eat them yourself?'

'I believe, sire,' was Henry's rejoinder, 'that I can appreciate that better than anyone.'

'Marie,' said the king, 'I present to you one of the most

---

[1] This natural child was afterwards the famous duke d'Angoulême, who died in 1650; and had he been legitimate, would have taken precedence of Henry III, Henry IV, Louis XIII, Louis XIV, etc. What were we given instead? The mind cannot grasp the implications of such a question.*

intelligent and witty men I know, even by the standard of the court. I think I understand him better than anyone, for I speak of his mind, as well as of his heart.'

'Sire,' said Henry, 'I hope that in exaggerating the one you have no doubt of the other.'

'I do not exaggerate anything, Harry,' replied the king. 'He is, for one thing, a master of anagrams. Ask him to make one of your name, and I will guarantee that he will.'

'Oh, what can you find in the name of a poor girl like me? What pleasing idea could such a name as Marie Touchet produce?

'Sire,' said Henry, 'it is too easy, there is no merit in finding one.'

'What! done already?' said Charles. 'You see——'

Henry took his tablets from the pocket of his doublet, tore out a page of the paper, and beneath the name *Marie Touchet* he wrote *Je charme tout* (I charm all), and then handed the leaf to the young girl.

'Really,' she exclaimed, 'it is impossible!'

'What has he found?' inquired Charles.

'Sire, I dare not repeat it.'

'Sire,' said Henry, 'in the name of Marie Touchet there is letter for letter, only changing the I into J, which is customary, the words *Je charme tout*.'

'So it does,' cried Charles, 'exactly—beautifully! This shall be your motto, Marie, and never was motto better merited. Thanks, Harry! Marie, I will give it to you set in diamonds.'

The supper finished as it struck two o'clock by Notre Dame.

'Now, Marie,' said Charles, 'as a reward for the compliment, give him an arm-chair where he can sleep till daybreak—a long way off from us though, for he snores fearfully. If, Harry, you wake before me, rouse me, for we must be at the Bastille by six o'clock. Good-night; make yourself as comfortable as you can. But,' added the king, placing his hand on Henry's shoulder, 'on your life, Harry, on your life, do not leave this house without me.'

Henry had suspected too much to feel any wish to ignore the warning.

Charles IX went to his room, and Henry, the hardy man of the mountains, soon made himself comfortable in his arm-chair, and soon justified the precaution his brother-in-law had taken in keeping him at a distance. In the morning, Charles roused him, and as he was already dressed, his toilet did not occupy him very long.

They both passed through the bedchamber where the young girl was sleeping in her bed, and the baby in its cradle. They were both smiling as they slept. Charles looked at them very tenderly, and turning to the King of Navarre, said to him,—

'Harry, if you should ever learn what service I have this night rendered you, and any misfortune should happen to me, remember this child in its cradle.' Then kissing them both, he said, 'Adieu, my angels!' and left the apartment. Henry followed, deep in thought.

Two horses, held by his gentlemen, awaited them at the Bastille. Charles made a sign to Henry to mount, and, going by the garden of the Arbalète, they headed towards the outer Boulevards. When they reached the Marais,* where they were sheltered by the palisades, Charles directed Henry's attention, through the thick haze of the morning, to some men in long cloaks and fur caps, who were on horseback beside a heavily laden wagon.

'Ah!' said Charles, smiling, 'I thought so.'

'Ah, sire,' observed Henry, 'is not one of them the Duke d'Anjou?'

'Himself,' said Charles. 'Keep back, Harry! don't let them see us.'

'And who are the other men, and what is in the wagon?'

'The men are the Polish ambassadors, and in the wagon is a crown. But now,' he added, putting his horse to a gallop, 'come, Harry, for I have seen all I wished to see.'

37

THE RETURN TO THE LOUVRE

WHEN Catherine believed all was arranged in the King of Navarre's chamber. When the dead soldiers were removed, Maurevel conveyed away, and the carpets washed, she dismissed her maids, for it was nearly midnight, and attempted to sleep. But the shock had been too severe, the disappointment too great. The detested Henry eternally escaped her plots, well laid and deadly as they were. He seemed protected by some invisible power which Catherine persisted in calling chance, although in the depth of her heart a voice told her that the real name of this power was destiny.* Sleep did not come and, with her brain filled with fresh projects, she rose at break of day, dressed, and went towards Charles's apartments, where she found his nurse in the antechamber.

'Nurse, I wish to see my son.'

'Madame, I will not open the door, except on the formal order of your Majesty.'

'Open, nurse, I command you.'

The nurse at this voice, more respected and more dreaded than that of Charles himself, presented the key to Catherine. But Catherine had no need of it, drawing from her pocket a key of her own which opened her son's door in an instant.

The chamber was unoccupied. Charles's bed was undisturbed, and his two greyhounds, lying on a bearskin, rose, and, coming to Catherine, licked her hands.

'Ah!' said the queen, 'he has gone out. I will wait for him.'

And she seated herself gloomily in the recess of a window which overlooked the principal court-yard of the Louvre. For two hours she remained there, pale and immovable as a marble statue, when at length she saw a troop of riders enter the gate, at the head of whom she beheld Charles and Henry of Navarre.

Then she understood everything. Charles, instead of debating with her as to the arrest of his brother-in-law, had carried him off, and thus saved him.

'Blind, blind, blind!' she murmured, and she waited where she was.

A moment afterwards she heard footsteps, and Charles, lifting the tapestry, found himself in the presence of his mother.

Behind him, and looking over his shoulder, was the pale and uneasy face of the Béarnais.

'Ah! you here, madame?' said Charles IX, frowning.

'Yes, my son. I wish to speak with you.'

'To me?'

'You, and alone.'

'Well, well,' said Charles, turning towards his brother-in-law, 'since it cannot be avoided, the sooner the better.'

'I leave you, sir,' said Henry.

'Yes, yes, do,' replied Charles; 'and since you are a Catholic, Harry, go and hear mass on my behalf. I shall stay here and hear the sermon.'

Henry bowed and left the apartment.

Charles IX, anticipating the questions which his mother would ask him, said, trying to turn the affair into a jest, 'Well, madame, *pardieu!* you are going to scold me, are you not? I scuppered your little plot. Well, by God! I really could not allow the man who had just saved my life to be arrested and conveyed to the Bastille; so forgive me, and confess that my little joke was a good one.'

'Sire,' replied Catherine, 'your Majesty is mistaken: it was not a joke.'

'Yes, yes, and so you will say, or the devil take me!'

'Sire, you have by your own fault caused the failure of a plan which would have led us to a great discovery.'

'Come,' said the king, 'come, let us know all the detail. What have you got against Harry?'

'That he is in a conspiracy.'

'Yes, of course; that is your everlasting accusation.'

'Listen,' said Catherine, 'listen, and you will find a way of proving whether or not I am wrong.'

'How, mother?'

'Ask Henry who was in his rooms last night. If he tells you, I am ready to confess that I was wrong.'

'But suppose it was a woman? We cannot suppose——'

'A woman!'

'Yes, a woman.'

'A woman who killed two of your guards and wounded, perhaps fatally, M. de Maurevel!'

'Ah!' said the king—'this grows serious. There has been blood spilt, then?'

'Three men were left dead on his floor.'

'And he who left them in this condition——?'

'Escaped safe and sound.'

'By Gog and Magog!'* cried Charles, 'he was a gallant fellow, and you are right, mother. I should like to meet him.'

'Well, I tell you beforehand you will not find out who it is, at least from Henry.'

'But I will from you, mother. This man did not flee without leaving some traces—perhaps a glimpse of what he was wearing to identify him by?'

'Nothing was observed save the elegant cherry-coloured cloak which he wore.'

'Ah! a cherry-coloured cloak!' said Charles. 'I know but one at court so remarkable.'

'Precisely,' said Catherine.

'Well?' replied Charles.

'Indulge me,' answered Catherine, 'by waiting here, my son, while I go and see if my orders have been executed.'

Catherine went out, leaving Charles alone. He paced up and down thoughtfully, whistling a hunting air, with one hand in his doublet, and letting the other hang down for his dogs to lick every time he paused.

As to Henry, he had left his brother-in-law's apartments very uneasy, and instead of going along the usual corridor, he had climbed the small private staircase we have before referred to which led to the second storey. But scarcely had he gone up four steps than he saw a shadow. He stopped, and put his hand to his dagger, but immediately recognized a woman, and a charming voice familiar to his ear said,—

'Heaven be praised, sire! you are safe and sound. I was extremely worried about you, but Heaven has heard my prayer.'

'What has happened?' inquired Henry.

'You will know when you reach your apartments. Do not be uneasy about Orthon; I am taking care of him.'

And the young lady descended the stairs rapidly, passing Henry as if she had met him accidentally.

'This is very strange,' said Henry to himself. 'What has been going on?—what has happened to Orthon?'

The question, unfortunately, did not reach Madame de Sauve, for Madame de Sauve was already out of hearing.

At the top of the staircase Henry saw another shadow; it was that of a man.

'Hush!' said this man.

'Ah! is that you, François?'

'Do not mention my name.'

'What has happened?'

'Go into your rooms and you will see. Then go quietly into the corridor, look carefully about so no one sees you, and come to me—my door will be ajar.'

And he disappeared, in his turn, down the staircase, like a ghost down a trap in a theatre.

'*Ventre-saint-gris!*' muttered the Béarnais, 'the mystery grows thicker! But as the solution is to be found in my apartment, let us go there.'

He reached the door, and listened; there was not a sound. Charlotte had told him to go there, so it was evident that there was nothing to fear. He entered, and cast a glance around the antechamber, which was deserted, but nothing indicated that anything had taken place.

'Orthon is not here,' he remarked, and went to the inner chamber.

Here everything was explained. In spite of the water which had been copiously used, large red spots stained the floor. One piece of furniture was broken, the hangings of the bed were hacked with sword-cuts, a Venetian mirror had been shattered by a bullet, and a blood-stained hand had leaned against the wall and left against it a terrible imprint which proclaimed that this chamber had been the mute witness of a mortal struggle. Henry started back, and gazed in alarm at all these different details, and passing his hand over his brow, moist with perspiration, he murmured,—

'Ah! now I understand the service which the king has done me! They came to assassinate me, and—ah!—de Mouy! what have they done with de Mouy? Wretches! they have murdered him!'

Anxious to learn the details, he hastened to the Duke d'Alençon, who was waiting for him, and taking Henry's hand, and placing his finger to his lips, led him to a small room in the tower, which was completely isolated and consequently out of the reach of all eyes and ears.

'Brother!' he said, 'what a horrible night!'

'What has happened?' asked Henry.

'They came to arrest you.'

'Me?'

'Yes, you.'

'But why?'

'I do not know—where were you?'

'The king took me away with him into the city.'

'Then he knew what was afoot,' said d'Alençon. 'But since you were not here, who was in your rooms?'

'Was anyone there?' inquired Henry, as if ignorant of the fact.

'Yes, a man. When I heard the noise, I ran to bring you help, but it was too late.'

'Was the man arrested?' inquired Henry anxiously.

'No, he escaped, after having dangerously wounded Maurevel and killed two guards.'

'Ah, brave de Mouy!' cried Henry.

'Was it then, de Mouy?' said d'Alençon quickly.

Henry saw he had blundered.

'At least, I presume so,' he replied, 'for I had given him an appointment to make arrangements for your flight, and to tell him that I have made over to you all my rights to the throne of Navarre.'

'Then if de Mouy is known,' said d'Alençon, turning pale, 'we are lost.'

'Yes, for Maurevel will talk.'

'Maurevel has been wounded in the throat, and I have learned from the surgeon that he will not speak a word for a week.'

'A week! that is a longer time than de Mouy needs to reach a place of safety.'

'But it may be someone else, and not M. de Mouy.'

'Do you think so?' asked Henry.

'Yes. The man disappeared very swiftly, and nothing was seen but a cherry-coloured cloak.'

'Why, really,' remarked Henry, 'a cherry-coloured cloak is a thing for a fop, not for a soldier. No one would suspect de Mouy of wearing a cherry-coloured cloak.'

'No, and if anyone were suspected,' said d'Alençon, 'it would rather be——'

He paused.

'M. de la Mole,' said Henry.

'Certainly. Even I, who saw him myself, doubted for a moment.'

'You doubted? Well, then, it might be M. de la Mole.'

'Does he know nothing?' inquired d'Alençon.

'Nothing important.'

'Brother,' said the Duke, 'I really believe it was him.'

'*Diable!*' observed Henry, 'if it were him, it will greatly annoy the queen who takes an interest in him.'

'An interest, say you?' said d'Alençon, amazed.

'Unquestionably. Do you not remember, François, that it was your sister who recommended him to you?'

'It was indeed,' said the duke, 'and if I were sure you would support me, I would be tempted to accuse him myself.'

'If you accuse him,' replied Henry, 'understand, brother, I shall not contradict you.'

'But the queen?' said d'Alençon.

'Ah, yes, the queen!'

'We must know what she intends to do.'

'I will undertake to find out.'

'Plague take it, brother! she would be wrong to mislead us, for see what a glorious reputation the young fellow will have, and it will have cost him nothing. Still, he may be called on to pay capital and interest at once.'

'Devil take it! what do you expect?' inquired Henry. 'In this world, you get nothing for nothing.' Then, saluting d'Alençon, he went rapidly down the staircase to Marguerite's apartments.

The Queen of Navarre was hardly more easy in her mind than her husband. The expedition of the night, directed against herself and Madame de Nevers by the king, the Duke d'Anjou, the Duke de Guise, and Henry, whom she had recognized, had greatly disturbed her. She had gone to bed, but she could not sleep and trembled at every sound. At this moment, Henry knocked at her door, and Gillonne admitted him at her mistress's order.

Henry paused at the door. Nothing in his manner announced the injured husband; his habitual smile was on his well-defined lips, and not a muscle in his face betrayed the severe emotions he had undergone. He looked at Marguerite, to inquire if she would allow him to remain alone with her, and Marguerite motioned Gillonne to retire.

'Madame,' said Henry, 'I know how deeply you are attached to your friends, and I fear I bring you unwelcome tidings.'

'What is it?' asked Marguerite.

'One of our best-loved followers is greatly compromised at this moment.'

'Who?'

'Our dear Comte de la Mole.'

'How?'

'As a result of last night's little business.'

Marguerite, in spite of her self-command could not refrain from blushing.

'What business?' she said.

'What!' said Henry—'did you not hear all the noise that was made at the Louvre last night?'

'No, sir.'

'Then I congratulate you, madame,' said Henry with much gravity, 'for you must have slept very soundly.'

'Well, what happened?'

'Why, our good mother had ordered M. de Maurevel and six of her guards to arrest me.'

'You, sir—you?'

'Yes, me.'

'But why?'

'Ah! who can tell the "whys and wherefores" of such a mind as your mother's? I suspect them, but do not know them.'

'And you were not in your room?'

'As it chanced, no: you have guessed rightly, madame. Last

evening, the king invited me to accompany him. But if I was not in my apartments, some other person was.'

'And who was that other person?'

'It appears that it was the Comte de la Mole.'

'The Comte de la Mole!' said Marguerite, amazed.

'*Tudieu!* You would never believe what a stout fellow the Provençal was,' continued Henry. 'Why, he wounded Maurevel and killed two of the guards.'

'Wounded M. de Maurevel and killed two of the guards! Impossible!'

'What, do you doubt his courage, madame?'

No, but I say that M. de la Mole could not have been in your apartments.'

'Why not?'

'Because—because,' answered Marguerite, greatly embarrassed,—'because he was elsewhere.'

'Ah! if he can prove an alibi,' observed Henry, 'that is another matter. He will say where he was, and there's an end to it.'

'Where he was?' said Marguerite quickly.

'Of course. But, unfortunately, as they have proofs——'

'Proofs! What kind of proofs?'

'Why, the man who made this desperate defence wore a cherry cloak.'

'But is M. de la Mole the only man who wears a cherry cloak? I know another person who does too.'

'So do I; but then think what will happen. If it was not M. de la Mole, it was some other man in a cherry cloak like him, and you know who that man is.'

'Heavens!'

'That is the problem we have to face. You have seen him, as I have, madame, and your reaction proves it. Let us, then, talk this matter over like two persons who speak of the most coveted thing in the world—a throne; of a thing most precious—life. If de Mouy is arrested, we are lost!'

'Yes, I understand that.'

'But M. de la Mole can compromise nobody, unless he were capable of inventing some such tale as that he was with a party of ladies—'

'Sir,' said Marguerite, 'if that is all you fear, be perfectly easy. He will not say any such thing.'

'What!' said Henry, 'will he be silent, even if silence will surely cost him his life?'

'He will, sir.'

'You are sure?'

'I will answer for him.'

'Then all is well,' said Henry, rising.

'Then you go, sir——'

'To try to get us out of the danger into which this devil of a man in the cherry cloak has plunged us.'

'Ah, *mon Dieu!* poor young man!' exclaimed Marguerite, in a paroxysm of grief, wringing her hands.

'Really,' said Henry, as he withdrew, 'this dear M. de la Mole is a very loyal and chivalrous gentleman!'

38

INTERROGATIONS

CHARLES entered his apartments smiling and jesting, but after ten minutes' conversation with his mother, it was she who had recovered her good humour, and he who was serious and thoughtful.

'M. de la Mole,' said Charles—'M. de la Mole, we must summon Henry and d'Alençon: Henry, because this young man is a Huguenot—d'Alençon, because he is in his service.'

'Summon them if you will, my son, but you will learn nothing. I fear there exists a better understanding between Henry and François than you imagine.'

Charles walked up and down quickly, biting his lips and pressing his hand to his heart, as if to contain his wrath.

'No,' said he, 'I will not wait! Let someone summon the Duke d'Alençon, then Henry. I will interrogate them separately. As for you, you can stay, if you wish.'

The Duke d'Alençon entered. His conversation with Henry had prepared him for this interview. He was therefore perfectly collected.

His answers were very exact. Warned by his mother not to leave his apartments, he was ignorant of the events of the night. But since those apartments were in the same corridor as the King of Navarre's, he had heard footsteps, then the sound of a door opening, and the report of fire-arms. He had ventured to open his door slightly, and had seen a man in a cherry cloak running away.

Charles and the queen looked at each other.

'In a cherry cloak?' said the king.

'Yes.'

'And did not this cloak give you any idea as to who the person might be?'

D'Alençon collected all his presence of mind, in order to lie more naturally.

'I confess,' said he, 'I thought I recognized the cloak of one of my gentlemen.'

'Which of them?'

'M. de la Mole.'

'Why was he not in attendance on you?'

'I had given him leave of absence.'

'That will do: go.'

The duke advanced towards the door.

'No—this way,' said Charles, pointing to the door which led to his nurse's quarters.

Charles did not wish François and Henry to see each other. He was unaware that they had already met for a few moments, and that this short time had sufficed to arrange their plans.

After d'Alençon, and at a sign from Charles, came Henry.

'Sire,' said he, 'you have done well to send for me, for I was coming to see you, to demand justice.'

Charles frowned.

'Yes, justice!' said Henry. 'I begin by thanking your Majesty for having taken me with you last night, for I now know that by so doing you saved my life. But what did I do to deserve being assassinated?'

'It was not an assassination,' said Catherine, 'it was an arrest.'

'Really!' returned Henry—'what crime have I committed? I

am as guilty to-day as yesterday. What is my crime, I ask again, sire?'

Charles looked at his mother, somewhat embarrassed for an answer.

'My son,' said Catherine, 'you hold communication with suspected persons.'

'And these suspected persons compromise me—is it not so, madame?'

'Yes, Henry.'

'Name them, then—name them—confront me with them!'

'Well now,' said Charles, 'Harry has a right to an explanation.'

'And I demand one,' said Henry, who saw an advantage and resolved to use it—'I demand one from my brother Charles, from my mother-in-law Catherine. Since my marriage, have I not been a good husband?—ask Marguerite. A good Catholic?— ask my confessor. A good brother?—ask all those who were at the hunt yesterday.'

'It is true, Harry,' replied the king. 'But they say you conspire.'

'Against whom?'

'Against me.'

'Sire, were that true, I needed only to have let events take their course when the boar was on you.'

'Devil take it! he is right, mother.'

'But who was last night in your apartments?'

'Madame,' returned Henry, 'I can scarcely answer for myself, much less for others. I left my apartments at a quarter past seven, and the king took me with him at nine; and I did not leave his Majesty all night: I could not be with him and in the Louvre at the same time.'

'But,' said Catherine, 'it is no less true that one of your followers killed two of the king's guards and wounded M. de Maurevel.'

'One of my followers!' cried Henry. 'Name him, then.'

'Everyone accuses M. de la Mole.'

'M. de la Mole is not in my service, but in that of the Duke d'Alençon, to whom Marguerite recommended him.'

'But,' said Charles, 'was it M. de la Mole who was there?'

'How should I know, sire? I do not say yes or no. M. de la Mole is a very gallant gentleman, devoted to the Queen of Navarre. He often brings me messages from Marguerite, to whom he is very grateful for having recommended him to the Duke d'Alençon, or from the duke himself. I could not say if it were he or not.'

'It was he,' said Catherine. 'He was recognized by his cherry cloak.'

'Ah, he had a cherry cloak?' asked Henry.

'Yes.'

'And the man who so maltreated your guards and M. de Maurevel wore a cherry cloak?'

'Exactly so,' replied Charles.

'I have nothing to say to that,' answered the Béarnais. 'But it seems to me that it was not me but M. de la Mole who should have been sent for. Yet there is one thing I would point out.'

'What is that?'

'That if I had resisted the king's order I should now be guilty, and merit severe punishment. But it was not me, it was a stranger whom they sought to arrest; he defended himself, and he had every right to do so.'

'Yet——' murmured Catherine.

'Madame,' demanded Henry, 'was the order to arrest me?'

'Yes, and the king signed it.'

'But was it in the order to arrest anyone found in my apartments?'

'No.'

'Well, then,' continued Henry, 'unless it can be proved I am plotting against the king, and that the man in my chamber is plotting with me, he is innocent. Sire,' continued he, turning to Charles IX, 'I shall not leave the Louvre or, if your Majesty order it, I shall retire to any state prison you may think fit to indicate, but in the meantime I have a right to declare myself the loyal subject and brother of your Majesty.'

And saluting them with an air of dignity Charles had never before seen in him, Henry withdrew.

'Bravo, Harry!' cried Charles.

'Bravo! because he has beaten us?'

'And why not? When he hits me in fencing, don't I cry "Bravo!"? Mother, you are wrong to despise this young man.'

'My son! I do not hate him—I fear him.'

'Well, you're wrong, for if he were really plotting against me, he only need have let the boar alone yesterday.'

'Yes,' said Catherine, 'and in so doing have made d'Anjou, his personal enemy, king of France.'

'Never mind what motive made him save my life. It is enough that he did save it. *Mort de tous les diables!* I will not have him meddled with. As for M. de la Mole, I will speak to d'Alençon about him.'

Catherine took her leave. On re-entering her chamber, she found Marguerite waiting for her.

'Ah!' said she—'it is you, daughter. I sent for you last night.'

'This morning, madame, I have come to tell your Majesty you are about to commit a great injustice: you are going to arrest M. de la Mole.'

'It is likely.'

'He is accused of having killed two of the king's guards, and wounded M. de Maurevel last night, in the King of Navarre's apartments.'

'That is what he is charged with.'

'He is wrongfully accused. M. de la Mole is not guilty.'

'Not guilty!' cried Catherine, joyfully, for she hoped to learn something from what Marguerite was about to tell her.

'No,' returned Marguerite, 'he cannot be guilty, for he was not there.'

'Where was he, then?'

'With me.'

'With you?'

'Yes.'

Catherine, instead of darting a look of indignation at her daughter, quietly folded her hands in her lap.

'If it was not M. de la Mole, who was there, then?' said she.

'I do not know,' returned Marguerite hesitatingly.

'Come, do not tell me the truth by halves.'

'I tell you, madame, I do not know,' said Marguerite, turning pale in spite of herself.

'Well,' said the queen-mother, 'we shall find out. Go, my child; your mother watches over your honour.'

Marguerite withdrew.

'Ah!' murmured Catherine. 'Henry and Marguerite have an understanding together: provided she is silent, he is blind. Ah, my children, you think yourselves strong in your union, but I will crush you. Besides, it will all come out the day when Maurevel can write or pronounce six letters.'

And thereupon Catherine returned to the royal apartments, where she found Charles in conference with d'Alençon.

'You here, mother!' said Charles.

'Why not say *again*, for that was in your thoughts?'

'I keep my thoughts to myself,' returned the king, with that harsh tone he sometimes adopted even to Catherine. 'What have you to say?'

'That you were right, Charles; and you, d'Alençon, wrong.'

'How?' cried both together.

'It was not La Mole who was in the King of Navarre's apartments.'

'Who, then?' asked Charles.

'We shall know that when Maurevel has recovered. But let us speak of La Mole.'

'What do you want with him, since he was not with the King of Navarre?'

'No, but he was with the queen.'

'The queen!' cried Charles, bursting into a loud laugh. 'That cannot be. Guise told us he met her in her litter.'

'Just so,' said Catherine; 'she has a house in Paris.'

'In the Rue Cloche-Perce?'

'Yes, I believe so.'

'Ah!' cried the king suddenly—'it must have been he who threw a dish at my head last night—the scoundrel!'

'Quite likely,' replied Catherine; 'and we must take serious note of the situation at once, for the least indiscretion of this gentleman might cause a great scandal. It would only take a moment of intoxication——'

'Or vanity,' said François.

'True,' returned Charles. 'But we cannot lay the matter before the judges until Henry consents.'

'My son,' said Catherine significantly, 'a crime has been committed, and there may be scandal. Were you ordinary gentlemen, I should need say nothing to you, for you are both brave. But you are princes and cannot cross swords with an inferior in rank. You must consider how you might avenge yourselves as princes.'

'*Mort de tous les diables!*' said Charles, 'I will think of it.'

'I leave you,' said Catherine, 'but I leave you this to represent me.'

As she spoke, she untied a silken cord which was wound around her waist three times, and of which the two tassels fell to her knees, and tossed it at the feet of the two princes.

'Ah!' said Charles, 'I understand.'

'This cord——' said d'Alençon.

'Is punishment and silence,'* replied Catherine. 'But first, it would be as well to mention the matter to Henry.'

And she retired.

'*Pardieu!*' replied d'Alençon, 'a good suggestion. I will send for Henry.'

'No,' said Charles, 'I will see him myself. You go and inform d'Anjou and Guise.'

And leaving his apartments, he mounted the private staircase which led to Henry's chamber.

39

PLANS OF REVENGE

HENRY had taken advantage of the moment's respite from the interrogation he had undergone to rush off to Madame de Sauve. There he found Orthon who, though fully recovered, could tell him nothing, except that armed men had entered the apartment, and that one of them had struck him with the hilt of his sword.

As for Orthon, no one had paid any attention to him: Catherine had seen him unconscious and believed he was dead. On coming to himself, in the interval between her departure and the arrival of the captain of the guard, he had taken refuge with Madame de Sauve.

Henry persuaded Charlotte to let the young man remain with her until he heard from de Mouy, who would certainly write to him. He would then despatch Orthon to him, and, instead of one, have two men on whom to rely in any emergency.

Once this plan was agreed, he had returned to his apartment, and was musing deeply, when the door opened and Charles entered.

'Your Majesty!' cried Henry.

'I myself. Harry, you are an excellent fellow, and I love you more and more.'

'Sire,' said Henry, 'you overwhelm me.'

'You have but one fault.'

'If your Majesty will explain what it is, I will seek to correct it,' said Henry, who saw by the king's face he was in an excellent humour.

'It is that having good eyes, you do not use them.'

'Bah!' said Henry; 'am I, then, near-sighted without knowing it?'

'Worse than that, you are blind.'

'If that be so, will your Majesty aid me to recover my sight?'

'When Guise told you last night that he saw your wife pass with a gallant, you would not believe it.'

'Sire, how could I believe your Majesty's sister would commit such an indiscretion?'

'When he told you your wife had gone to the Rue Cloche Perce, you would not believe that either.'

'I could not suppose a princess of the blood royal would thus publicly risk her reputation.'

'When we besieged the house, and I was hit by a silver dish on my shoulder, d'Anjou a bowl of orange jam on his head, and Guise a haunch of venison in his face, did you not see two men and two women?'

'I saw nothing.'

'Eh, *corbœuf!* I did.'

'Ah, if your Majesty saw something, that puts a different complexion on the matter.'

'I saw two men and two women. One of the women, I am sure, was Margot, and one of the men was La Mole.'

'But,' said Henry, 'if M. de la Mole was in the Rue Cloche Perce, he could not have been here.'

'No, he was not here, but never mind that. We shall know who was here when that blockhead Maurevel can write or speak. The question concerns Margot, who is deceiving you, and her lover, whom we are going to strangle.'

Henry started, and looked with an air of bewilderment at the king.

'You won't be sorry for that, I know, Harry. Margot will cry like a thousand Niobes,* but I won't have you made a fool of. Let d'Anjou deceive Condé, I do not care. Condé is my enemy—but you are my brother, my friend.'

'But, sire——'

'I will not have you cuckolded. You are being duped, but you shall have such a reparation, that to-morrow every one shall say, "*Mille noms d'un diable!* The king loves his brother Harry, for he wrung M. de la Mole's neck for his sake last night."'

'Are you quite resolved, sire?' asked Henry.

'Quite; we are going on an expedition against the rascal; myself, d'Anjou, d'Alençon, and Guise. A king, two princes of the blood, and a sovereign prince, without reckoning yourself.'

'How! without reckoning me?'

'Of course you will be coming with us.'

'But, sire, do you know for certain——?'

'Why, the rascal boasts of it. He goes sometimes to see her at the Louvre, sometimes at the Rue Cloche Perce. Bring a dagger with you.'

'Sire,' said Henry, 'upon reflection, your Majesty will understand that I cannot take part in this expedition. I am too closely involved in it not to have my presence attributed to a desire for vengeance. Your Majesty punishes a man who has slandered your sister, and Marguerite, whom I maintain is innocent, is not dishonoured. But if I am associated with it, my co-operation converts an act of justice into murder—my wife is no longer slandered, she is guilty.'

'*Mordieu!* Harry, as I told my mother just now, you have the quickest wit of all of us.'

And Charles gave his brother-in-law an admiring look. Henry bowed in acknowledgement of the compliment.

'Well, leave everything to me. It shall not be the worse executed.'

'I leave it all in your hands.'

'At what time does he usually go to your wife's apartments?'

'About nine o'clock.'

'And at what hour does he leave?'

'Before I come, for I never see him.'

'What time is that?'

'About eleven.'

'Good; come down this evening at midnight, it will all be over.'

And Charles, after shaking Henry's hand, and renewing his protestations of friendship, left the apartment, whistling a favourite hunting air.

Henry laughed as he could laugh when no one was there to hear him.

'*Ventre-saint-gris!*' said he, 'I will wager anything the queen-mother is at the bottom of all this. She does nothing but try to stir up quarrels between my wife and me.'

At seven o'clock the same evening, a young man bathed, perfumed, and dressed himself, humming a gay air the while. Beside him slept, or rather reclined on the bed, another young man.

The one was La Mole, the other Coconnas.

'Where are you going to-night?' asked the latter.

'Where am I going?' said La Mole. 'I am going to the queen.'

'Ah, true! I forgot. Here is your cloak.'

'No, that is the black, I want the cherry one; the queen prefers me in that.'

'Ah, *ma foi!*' said Coconnas, 'look for it yourself. I cannot see it.'

'Not see it!' replied La Mole. 'Where can it be, then?'

At this moment, just as La Mole, having turned everything upside down, was beginning to abuse the thieves who dared even rob in the Louvre, the door opened, and a page of the Duke d'Alençon appeared with the cloak in question.

'Ah!' said La Mole, 'here it is.'

'Yes, sir, monseigneur sent for it, to decide a wager about its colour.'

The page withdrew, and La Mole fastened on his cloak.

'Well,' said he to Coconnas, 'what are you going to do?'

'I do not know.'

'Bah! well, *au revoir!*'

'This La Mole is a terrible fellow,' thought Coconnas. 'He's always wanting to know where one is going, as if one knew'. And he settled down to go to sleep.

As for La Mole, he went straight to the Queen of Navarre's apartments.

In the corridor he met the Duke d'Alençon.

'Ah, there you are, La Mole!' said he.

'Yes, monseigneur.'

'Are you leaving the Louvre?'

'No, your Highness, I am going to pay my respects to the Queen of Navarre.'

'How long will you be with her?'

'Has monseigneur any orders for me?'

'No, but I shall have this evening.'

'At what time?'

'Between nine and ten.'

'I will not fail to wait on your Highness.'

'Well, I rely upon you.'

La Mole bowed, and went on.

'It is very strange,' thought he, 'the duke is sometimes pale as a corpse.'

And he knocked at the door. Gillonne, who seemed to be watching out for his arrival, opened it, and led him to the queen.

Marguerite was occupied with something that seemed to fatigue her greatly. A paper covered with notes and a volume of Isocrates* lay before her. She motioned to La Mole to let her finish the sentence, then, laying aside her pen, invited him to sit by her.

La Mole had never seemed so handsome and so gay.

'Greek!' cried he, glancing at the volume—'Isocrates! what are you doing? Ah, and on this paper, Latin—*"Ad Sarmatiæ legatos reginæ Margaritæ concio"*—you are going to harangue these barbarians in Latin, then?'

'I must, since they do not understand French. They arrived this morning. You will find,' added Marguerite, in a slightly pedantic tone of voice, 'that what I have written is Ciceronian enough. But let us talk of what happened to you.'

'To me?'

'Yes!'

'What happened to me?'

'Ay, what did happen to you?—you look pale.'

'I confess it, but it is from too much sleep.'

'Come, come, do not boast, I know everything.'

'Tell me what you mean, for I do not follow you.'

'Listen: de Mouy, surprised last night in the apartments of the King of Navarre whom they wished to arrest, killed three men, and escaped without being recognized, except by the cherry cloak he was wearing.'

'Well!'

'This cherry cloak, which fooled me, has fooled others too. You are suspected of this triple murder. This morning you would have been tried and condemned, for I knew that even to save yourself you would not say where you really were.'

'Say where I was?' cried La Mole—'oh, never, never! I would have died joyfully to spare your glorious eyes a single tear.'

'Alas! my poor friend,' replied the queen, 'my glorious eyes would have wept many, many tears!'

'But how was this storm averted?'

'Guess.'

'I cannot.'

'There was only one way of proving you were not in the king's chamber.'

'And that was——'

'To say where you were.'

'And——!'

'And I said it.'

'To whom?'

'To my mother.'

'And Queen Catherine——'

'Knows that I love you.'

'Oh, madame, after having done so much for me, my life belongs to you!'

'I have snatched it from those who wished to take it, but now you are safe.'

'Saved by you!' cried the young man—'by you whom I adore——'

At this moment, a sharp noise made them both start. La Mole recoiled, and Marguerite, uttering a cry, fixed her eyes on a broken pane in the window. By this pane a large stone had entered, and lay on the floor.

La Mole saw the broken window, and, understanding the cause of the noise,—

'Who has dared do this?' cried he.

'One moment,' said Marguerite. 'It seems to me something is tied around the stone.'

'It looks like a note,' replied La Mole.

Marguerite eagerly picked up the stone, round which was wound a slip of paper.

The paper was fastened to a length of string which passed out of the window.

Marguerite opened and read it.

'Oh, Heavens!' cried she, holding out the paper—'La Mole!'

He looked and read,—

'M. de la Mole is expected by long swords in the corridor leading to M. d'Alençon's apartments. Perhaps he would prefer leaving the Louvre by this window, and joining M. de Mouy at Mantes.'*

'But,' said La Mole, 'are these swords longer than mine?'

'No, but there are perhaps ten against one.'

'Who sent this note?' asked La Mole.

Marguerite looked at it attentively.

'The writing of the King of Navarre,' said she. 'If he warns us, the danger is real—you must go!'

'How?'

'Does it not mention the window?'

'Command, and I will leap from the window were it twenty times as high!'

'Wait,' said Marguerite, 'this string supports a weight.'

'Let us see.'

And as they pulled up the string, they saw the top rung of a ladder made of silk.

'Ah, you are saved!' said Marguerite.

'It is a miracle of Heaven!'

'No, it is a gift from the King of Navarre.'

'What if it is a trap for me,' said La Mole. 'What if this ladder were to break beneath me: have you not to-day admitted your love for me, Marguerite?'

Marguerite, to whose cheeks joy had restored the colour, became deadly pale.

'You are right,' said she, 'it is possible.' And she darted towards the door.

'Where are you going?' cried La Mole.

'To see for myself if they are waiting for you in the corridor.'

'Never! They may take their revenge on you!'

'What can they do to me? A queen and a woman, I am doubly inviolable.'

The queen said this with so much dignity that La Mole felt she ran no risk, and that it was best to let her do as she wished. Marguerite entrusted La Mole to Gillonne, leaving it to her judgement to decide, according to circumstances, whether he should make his escape, or await her return. She advanced into the corridor that led to the library and a suite of reception rooms, which opened into the king's and queen-mother's apartments, and to the private staircase leading to d'Alençon's apartments.

Although scarcely nine, all the lights were out, and, except for a faint brightness at the end, the corridor was quite dark. The queen advanced with a firm step, but when she reached half-way she heard a sound of voices whispering, and the pains they took not to be heard gave them a mysterious and hollow sound. But all noise soon ceased, and the light, feeble as it was, seemed to grow fainter.

Marguerite advanced. She seemed calm, but in reality the clenching of her hands showed violent nervous agitation. As she approached the light, the silence seemed to grow more intense, and a shadow like a hand obscured the flickering ray. Suddenly, a man sprang forward, uncovered a taper, and exclaimed,—

'Here he is!'

Marguerite found herself facing Charles. Behind him stood d'Alençon, a cord of silk in his hand. Behind them two shadows were visible, with swords in their hands.

Marguerite saw all this at a glance, and replied smilingly,—

'You mean here *she* is.'

Charles recoiled: the rest stood motionless.

'You here, Margot, at this hour?' said he.

'Is it so very late, then?'

'I ask you where are you going?'

'To fetch one of the volumes of Cicero which I left in our mother's apartments.'

'Without a light?'

'I thought the corridor was lit.'

'And you have come from your own apartments?'

'Yes.'

'What are you doing?'

'Preparing my speech for the Polish ambassadors.'

'Is any one helping you?'

Marguerite made a violent effort.

'M. de la Mole,' replied she. 'He is very learned.'

'So much so,' said d'Alençon, 'that I requested him to help me, for I am not so clever as you are.'

'You are waiting for him?'

'Yes,' returned d'Alençon impatiently.

'Then,' said Marguerite, 'I will send him to you.'

'And your book?' said Charles.

'Gillonne can fetch it.'

The two brothers exchanged a sign.

'Go, then,' said Charles. 'We will continue our round.'

'Your round?' asked Marguerite. 'Who are you looking for, then?'

'The man in the cherry cloak,' returned Charles. 'Have you not heard that he is said to haunt the Louvre? D'Alençon says he has seen him, and we are searching for him.'

'Good hunting!' said Marguerite.

In a second she was at her door.

'Open up, Gillonne!' cried she.

Gillonne obeyed.

Marguerite sprang into the apartment, and found La Mole resolute and calm—his sword drawn.

'Go!' said the queen—'go at once!—there is no time to be lost!'

During her absence, La Mole had secured the ladder, and he now stepped on it, after having tenderly embraced the queen.

'If I perish, remember your promise!' he said.

'It is not a promise, but an oath. Adieu!'

Encouraged by these words, La Mole glided down the ladder.

At this moment there was a knock at the door.

Marguerite did not leave the window until she had seen La Mole reach the ground in safety.

'Madame!' said Gillonne—'madame!'

'Well?'

'The king is knocking at the door.'

'Open it.'

Gillonne did so.

The four princes, seething with impatience, stood at the threshold. Charles entered first.

Marguerite advanced to meet him.

The king cast a rapid glance round the room.

'Who are you looking for?' asked the queen.

'Who am I looking for?' said Charles. '*Corbœuf!* I am looking for M. de la Mole.'

'M. de la Mole?'

'Yes, where is he?'

Marguerite took her brother's hand, and led him to the window.

At this moment, two men from beneath the window started off on horseback, at full speed: one of them removed his white satin scarf and waved it in the air. They were La Mole and Orthon.

Marguerite pointed them out with her finger to Charles.

'What does this mean?' asked he.

'It means,' returned Marguerite, 'that M. d'Alençon may put his cord in his pocket, and MM. d'Anjou and Guise may sheathe their swords, for M. de la Mole will not walk through the corridor to-night.'

40

THE ATRIDES*

SINCE his return to Paris, Henry d'Anjou had not had a confidential interview with his mother Catherine, of whom, as everybody knows, he was the favourite son.

And Catherine really preferred him of all her children for his courage, or even more for his beauty. She alone knew of his return to Paris, of which Charles IX would have remained ignorant, if chance had not directed him to the Hotel de Condé at the moment when his brother was leaving it. Charles had not expected him until the next day, and Henry d'Anjou had hoped to conceal from him the two motives which had hastened his arrival by a day, namely, his visit to the lovely Marie de Cleves, Princess de Condé,* and his conference with the Polish ambassadors.

When the Duke d'Anjou, so long expected, entered his mother's apartment Catherine, usually so cold and unmoved, and who, since the departure of her son, had embraced no one with warmth except Coligny, who was to be murdered next day, opened her arms to the child of her love, and pressed him to her heart with a display of maternal affection astonishing to find in that withered heart.*

'Ah, madame,' said he, 'since Heaven gives me the satisfaction of embracing my mother without witnesses, pray console the most wretched man in the world.'

'Eh, *mon Dieu!* my dearest boy,' cried Catherine, 'what has happened?'

'Nothing that you do not know, mother. I am in love; I am loved. But this very love, which would make any other man sublimely happy, is the cause of my misery.'

'Explain yourself, my son,' said Catherine.

'Ah! mother—the ambassadors—my departure.'

'Yes,' said Catherine, 'the ambassadors have arrived—your departure is nigh at hand.'

'It need not be nigh at hand, but my brother urges it. He hates me. I am in his way, and he would be glad to be rid of me.'

Catherine smiled.

'By giving you a throne? And being a king makes you unhappy?'

'Oh, I do not want to be a king, mother,' replied Henry, in despair, 'I do not wish to go. I! a son of France! brought up in the refinement of polite manners beside a tender mother; loved by one of the most charming women on earth, must I go amidst snows at the furthest extremity of the earth, to die by inches amongst coarse rough people who are intoxicated from morning till night, and gauge the capacities of their king as they do those of a cask, according to the quantity it can hold!* No, no, mother, I will not go—I will die first!'

'Courage, Henry,' said Catherine, taking his hands in her own, 'let us inquire into the real reason.'

Henry lowered his eyes, as if he dared not let his mother read what was in his heart.

'Is there no other reason,' she asked, 'less romantic, more rational, more political?'

'Mother, it is not my fault if this idea lurks in my mind, and perhaps looms larger than it should, but have you not said yourself that the horoscope of my brother Charles prophesies that he will die young?'

'Yes,' replied Catherine, 'but a horoscope may lie, my son. I myself, at this moment, hope that all horoscopes are not true.'

'But did not his horoscope foretell it?'

'His horoscope spoke of a quarter of a century, but did not say if that meant his life or his reign.'

'Well, then, dear mother, arrange matters so that I remain. My brother is nearly four-and-twenty,* and another year must decide.'

Catherine pondered deeply.

'Yes, assuredly,' she said, 'it would be better if it could be so arranged.'

'Oh, just think, mother,' cried Henry, 'what despair I should feel if I were to exchange the crown of France for the crown of Poland! To be tormented there with the idea that I might have reigned at the Louvre, in the midst of this cultured and elegant court, near the best mother in the world, whose counsels would save me half of my fatigue and labours, and who, accustomed to share with my father a part of the burdens of state, would have gladly shared them also with me. Ah, mother, I should have been a great king!'

'Come, come, my dearest boy,' said Catherine, to whom this prospect had always been a very sweet hope, 'come, do not despair. Have you thought of any way by which this could be arranged?'

'Yes, assuredly, and that is the main reason why I returned two or three days before I was expected, making my brother

Charles believe that it was to see Madame de Condé. I have also formed an acquaintance with Lasco,* the principal envoy, doing all I could to make myself unpopular and disliked, and I hope I have succeeded.'

'Ah, my dear son,' said Catherine, 'that is bad; we must always put the interest of France before our petty dislikes.'

'Mother, does the interest of France require, in case anything happens to my brother Charles, that d'Alençon or the King of Navarre should occupy the throne?'

'Oh, the King of Navarre!—never!' murmured Catherine.

'*Ma foi!*' continued Henry, 'my brother d'Alençon is no better and does not love you more.'

'Well,' asked Catherine, 'and what has Lasco been saying?'

'Lasco hesitated when I pressed him to seek an audience. Oh! if only he would write to Poland and annul the election.'

'Folly, my son—madness! What a diet has consecrated is sacred.'

'But then, mother, could not these Poles accept my brother instead of me?'

'That would be difficult, if not impossible.'

'Never mind; try; speak to the king, mother; attribute my motives to my love for Madame de Condé; say I am mad, crazy about her. Besides, he saw me leave the hotel of the prince with Guise, who does me every service in that quarter.'

'Yes, in order to make his League.* You do not see his intentions, but I do.'

'Yes, mother, yes. But, in the meantime, I make use of him. Should we not be glad when a man serves us while serving himself?'

'And what did the king say when he met you?'

'He seemed to believe what I told him, which was, that love had brought me back to Paris.'

'But did he not ask you for any account of the rest of the night?'

'Yes, mother. But I went to sup at Nantouillet's, where I made a great riot, so that the king might hear of it and have no suspicion as to where I was.'*

'Then he knows nothing of your visit to Lasco?'

'Nothing.'

'Good! I will try to speak for you, my poor boy; but you know the intractable disposition of him with whom I have to deal.'

'Charles will not allow me to remain. He detests me.'

'He is jealous of you, my handsome hero! Why are you so brave and well-favoured? Why, at scarcely twenty years of age, have you not won battles as great as those of Alexander and Cæsar?* But do not open your heart to everyone. Pretend to be resigned, and pay your court to the king. Leave the rest to me. Incidentally, how did you fare in your expedition of last night?'

'It failed, mother. The gay gallant was warned, and escaped by the window.'

'Some day,' said Catherine, 'I shall learn who is the evil genius who thwarts all my plans. In the meanwhile, I have my suspicions. Malediction be on him!'

'Then, mother——' said the Duke d'Anjou.

'Leave me to manage everything.' And kissing Henry tenderly, she left the apartment.

The princes of the house then arrived. Charles was in a capital humour, for the relief shown by his sister Marguerite had more pleased than vexed him. He felt no animus against La Mole otherwise, and had lain in wait for him with some ardour in the corridor, simply because it was a kind of hunt.

D'Alençon, on the other hand, was deeply preoccupied. The dislike he had always felt for La Mole had changed into hate from the moment he knew that he was loved by his sister.

Marguerite was, at the same time, thoughtful and alert. She had to remember and to watch. The Polish envoys had sent a copy of the speeches to be pronounced.

Marguerite, to whom no more mention had been made of the occurrences of the previous evening than if they had never taken place, read the speeches. Everyone except Charles discussed what the responses should be. Charles allowed Marguerite to reply as she pleased. He was more difficult in his choice of words for d'Alençon, but as to the discourse of Henry d'Anjou, he attacked it bitterly, and made endless corrections and additions.

This meeting, without having any decisive outcome, tended to poison the feelings of all. Henry d'Anjou, who had to re-write nearly all his speech, went away to perform his task. Marguerite, who had not heard of the King of Navarre since he had broken her window-pane, went to his apartment, in the hope of finding him there. D'Alençon, who had read the hesitation in his brother d'Anjou's eyes, and surprised a knowing look between him and his mother, withdrew to ponder over what this new plot might be. Charles was going to his forge to finish a boar-spear he was making for himself, when Catherine stopped him.

Charles, who expected some opposition to his will from his mother, paused, and gazed sternly on her.

'Well,' said he, 'and what is it now?'

'One more word, sire. We had forgotten it, and yet it is of much importance. What day do you propose to set for the public reception?'

'True!' said the king, seating himself; 'let us talk it over, mother. Well, what day shall it be?'

'I think,' replied Catherine, 'that behind your Majesty's silence, in your apparent forgetfulness, there was some deep calculation.'

'Why so, mother?'

'Because,' added the queen-mother very quietly, 'there is no need, my son, as it appears to me, that the Poles should see us so keen to have their crown.'

'On the contrary, mother,' said Charles, 'they have hastened here, by forced marches, from Warsaw. Honour for honour—politeness for politeness!'

'Your Majesty may be right in one sense, as in another I am not wrong. Your opinion then is, that the public reception should be brought forward?'

'Certainly; and is it not yours also?'

'You know that I have no opinions but such as are connected with your royal name: and I tell you that by hurrying the business like this, I fear that you might be seen to be using this occasion as an opportunity to relieve France of the cost and charges of your brother which he repays by returning it in glory and devotion.'

'Mother,' said Charles, 'when my brother leaves France I will so richly endow him that no one will even dare to think that you fear what people might say——'

'Well,' said Catherine, 'I give up, since you have such good answers to all my objections. But to receive this warlike people, who judge the power of states by outward appearances, you must have a considerable display of troops. And I do not think that there are yet enough assembled in the Ile-de-France.'*

'Excuse me, mother, but I had foreseen this event, and was prepared for it. I have recalled two battalions from Normandy and one from Guyenne. My company of archers arrived yesterday from Brittany. The light horse from Lorraine will be in Paris in the course of the day, and, while it is supposed that I can scarcely command four regiments, I have twenty thousand men* ready to appear.'

'Ah! ah!' said Catherine, surprised, 'then there is only one thing missing. But you will procure that.'

'What is that?'

'Money. I imagine you are not oversupplied.'

'On the contrary, madame, on the contrary,' said Charles IX; 'I have fourteen hundred thousand crowns in the Bastille; my private estates have this week brought me in eight hundred thousand, which I have buried in my cellars in the Louvre; and, in case of need, Nantouillet has put another three hundred thousand at my disposal.'

Catherine trembled. She had seen Charles violent and passionate, but never provident.

'Well, then,' she added, 'your Majesty has thought of everything—admirable! and if the tailors, embroiderers, and jewellers set to with a will, your Majesty will be ready to give this audience in less than six weeks.'

'Six weeks!' exclaimed Charles, 'why, mother, the tailors, embroiderers, and jewellers have been hard at work since the day they learnt of my brother's election,* and everything may be ready to-day, perhaps, but certainly in three or four days.'

'Ah!' murmured Catherine, 'you are in greater haste than I thought, my son.'

'Honour for honour, as I have already said.'

'Good; then it is this honour done to the house of France that flatters you—is it not?'

'Assuredly.'

'And to see a son of France on the throne of Poland is your greatest wish?'

'Precisely so.'

'Then it is the fact, and not the man that affects you, and whoever may reign there——'

'No, mother, *corbœuf!* no. Let us be as we are! The Poles have made a good choice—they are skilful, clever fellows! A military nation, a people of soldiers: they want a captain for their ruler. *Peste!*—d'Anjou is their man. The hero of Jarnac and Montcontour fits them like a glove. Who would you have me send them? D'Alençon—a coward!—he would give them a fine idea of the house of Valois! D'Alençon would run away at the very first bullet that whistled by his ears, while Henry of Anjou is a warrior bold and tried; his sword always in his hand, always on the march, on his war-horse or on foot. Forward—cut down, thrust, crush, slay! Ah! he is a brave and skilful man: a gallant soldier, who'll give them fighting from morning till night—from the first of January to the thirty-first of December! He is not a hard drinker, it is true; but he will do his work in cold blood, you'll see. He will be in his element! On! on! to the field of battle! bravo, trumpets and drums! *Vive le roi!* Long live the conqueror! Long live the general! They will proclaim him emperor three times a year! This will be admirable for the house of France and the honour of Valois! he may be killed perchance, but *ventremahon!** it will be a glorious death!'

Catherine shuddered, but her eyes glanced fire.

'Say,' she cried, 'that you wish to send your brother, Henry d'Anjou, away.* Say you do not love your brother.'

'Ah, ah, ah!' exclaimed Charles laughing nervously—'did you think I wished to send him away? Do you suspect I do not love him? And suppose it were so? Love my brother!—why should I love my brother? Ah! do not make me laugh!' and as he spoke his pale cheeks were animated with feverish red. 'Does he love me? Do you love me? Is there, except my dogs, Marie Touchet, and my nurse, is there one living thing that has ever loved me? No, no, I do not love my brother; I love only myself—do you understand? and I do not prevent my brother from doing as I do.'

'Sire,' said Catherine, becoming animated in her turn, 'since you unfold your heart to me, I shall open mine to you. You act like a weak king—like an ill-advised king. You send away your second brother, the natural support of your throne, who would be in all respects fit to succeed you, if any misfortune happened to you—leaving your crown in jeopardy; for, as you said, d'Alençon is young, incapable, weak—more than weak—cowardly! and the Béarnais is waiting in the wings!'

'Well, *mort de tous les diables!*' cried Charles, 'what will that matter to me when I am dead? The Béarnais is waiting in the wings, you say? *Corbœuf!* so much the better! I said I loved no one—I was wrong: I love Harry—yes, I love good Harry, with his easy manner and his warm hand, while I see around me none but false eyes, and touch none but ice-cold hands. He is incapable of treason towards me, I would swear on it! Besides, I owe him a debt: they poisoned his mother, poor fellow, as well as some persons of my family too, it is said. Besides, I am in good health. But if I fell sick, I would send for him, and he should not leave my side. I would take nothing save from his hand. And if I died, I would make him king of France and Navarre, and, *ventre du pape!* instead of laughing at my death, as my brother would do, he would weep, or at least appear to do so.'

Had a thunderbolt fallen at Catherine's feet, she would have been less alarmed than by these words. She remained aghast, looking at Charles in amazement. Then after a few seconds, she cried,—

'Henry of Navarre! Henry of Navarre, king of France, to the prejudice of my children! Ah, *sainte Madona!* we will see! And this is why you intend to send away my son of Anjou?'

'Your son! and what, then, am I—a son of the wolf, like Romulus?'* cried Charles, trembling with rage, his eyes sparkling as if they were on fire. 'Your son! You are right; and the King of France, then, is not your son? The King of France has no brothers; the King of France has no mother; the King of France has no subjects; the King of France has no need of feelings—he has will. He can do without being loved, but he will be obeyed!'

'Sire, you have misunderstood my words. I called him my son who is about to leave me. I love him better at this moment, because I fear to lose him at this moment. Is it a crime for a mother to wish that her son should not leave her?'

'And I—I tell you he shall leave you. I tell you he shall leave

France, and go to Poland, and that in two days*—and if you add another word, in one day—to-morrow; and if you do not smooth your brow, and repress the menace that glares in your eyes, I will strangle him to-night, as you would have strangled your daughter's lover last night; only I will not miss my aim, as we did with La Mole.'

At this threat, Catherine bent her head, and then raised it immediately.

'Ah, poor child!' she said, 'your brother intends to kill you; but do not be afraid, your mother will defend you.'

'Are you determined to oppose me?' cried Charles. 'Well, then, by all the devils! he shall die—not this evening, but this very moment. A weapon! a weapon! a dagger! a knife!—ah!'

Charles, after having vainly sought all around for what he asked for, saw the small stiletto which his mother wore at her girdle, seized it, drew it from its shagreen and silver case, and rushed out of the chamber, with the determination of killing Henry d'Anjou wherever he found him. But on reaching the vestibule, his over-excited strength gave way suddenly, and, extending his arm, he dropped the sharp blade which stuck in the floor, and uttering a lamentable cry, he swooned and fell on the floor, while the blood flowed abundantly from his nose and mouth.

'Help!' he cried—'they are murdering me! help! help!'

Catherine, who had followed him, saw him fall, looked at him for an instant without moving or calling, and then gathering her wits, not out of maternal instinct but prompted by the difficulty of her situation, she opened a door, and shrieked,—

'The king is taken ill. Help! help!'

At this cry, a crowd of servants, officers, and courtiers hastened to the young king. But foremost of all, a woman rushed in, pushing through the crowd, and raised Charles, who was as pale as a corpse.

'They are killing me, nurse—they are killing me!' murmured the king, bathed in perspiration and blood.

'They are killing my Charles!' cried the good creature, looking every one in the face in a way that made even Catherine recoil— 'and *who* is killing you?'

Charles uttered a sigh, and again fainted.

'Ah, ah!' said Doctor Ambroise Paré, whom they had sent for—'the king is very ill.'

'Now, by choice or compulsion,' said the implacable Catherine to herself, 'he must accept a delay'; and she left the king to go to her second son, who was waiting in the oratory for the result of an interview vitally important to himself.

41

THE HOROSCOPE

ON leaving the oratory, in which her son had been acquainted with what had occurred, Catherine found René in her chamber.

'Well,' asked the queen, 'have you seen him?'

'Yes.'

'How is he?'

'Rather better.'

'Can he speak?'

'No, the sword traversed the larynx.'

'I told you to make him write.'

'I tried, but he could only trace two letters, and then fainted. The jugular vein has been cut into, and the loss of blood has greatly weakened him.'

'Have you got the letters he wrote?'

'Here they are.'

René took a paper from his pocket, and presented it to the queen, who hastily opened it.

'An *m* and an *o*,' said she. 'Can it be, after all, M. de la Mole—and that the confession of Marguerite's was only to divert suspicion?'

'Madame,' returned René, 'if I may venture an opinion, I should say M. de la Mole is too much in love to trouble his head about politics, and far too much in love with Madame Marguerite to serve her husband very devotedly. For there is no deep love without jealousy.'

'You think he is in love, then?'

'Desperately.'

'Has he had recourse to you?'

'Yes; I made him a waxen image.'

'Pierced to the heart?'

'To the heart.'

'Do you still have it?'

'At my house.'

'I wonder,' said Catherine, 'if these cabalistic preparations really have the power attributed to them?'

'Your Majesty knows even better than I what their influence is.'

'Does Marguerite love La Mole?'

'Sufficiently to ruin herself for him. Yesterday she saved him at the risk of her honour and her life. You know all this, and yet you still doubt.'

'Doubt what?'

'Science.'

'I doubt because science has misled me,' looking fixedly at René.

'On what occasion?'

'René, have your perfumes lost their pungency?'

'No, madame; not when I prepare them myself.'

'Well,' said Catherine, 'we will speak of that some other time. Tell me what is necessary to arrive at an idea of the probable length of a person's life?'

'To know, first, the day of his birth, his age, and what constellation he was born under.'

'Next?'

'To have some of his blood and hair.'

'If I bring and tell you everything you need, can you tell me the probable time of his death?'

'Yes, to within a few days.'

'I have his hair, and I will procure some of his blood.'

'Was he born in the day, or during the night?'

'At twenty-three minutes past five in the evening.'

'Be with me to-morrow at five o'clock: the experiment must be made at the exact time of birth.'

'Good!' said Catherine. '*We* will be there.'

René saluted, and retired, without affecting to notice the '*we*', which indicated that, contrary to her usual habits, the queen would not come alone.

The next morning, at daybreak, Catherine entered her son Charles's apartment. She had inquired after him at midnight, and was informed that Maître Ambroise Paré was with him, and intended bleeding him if the same nervous agitation continued.

Shivering even in his sleep, pale from loss of blood, Charles slept, his head resting on his faithful nurse's shoulder, who, leaning against the bed, had not changed her position for three hours, fearing to disturb him.

Catherine asked if her son had been bled. The nurse replied he had, and so abundantly that he had twice fainted.

The blood was in a basin in the adjoining room. Catherine entered, under pretence of examining it, and while so doing, she filled with it a phial she had brought with her for the purpose, then returned, hiding her red fingers which would otherwise have betrayed her, in her pockets.

As she reappeared, Charles opened his eyes and saw his mother. Then recollecting the events of the previous evening,—

'Ah! it is you, madame,' said he. 'Well, you may tell your dear son, Henry d'Anjou, it will be to-morrow.'

'It shall be when you please, my dear Charles. Compose yourself, and go to sleep.'

Charles closed his eyes, and Catherine left the room, but no sooner had she gone than Charles, raising himself, cried,—

'Send for the chancellor—the court—I want them all!'

The nurse replaced his head upon her shoulder, and sought to lull him to sleep.

'No, no, nurse!' said he, 'I shall not sleep any more. Summon my people. I wish to work to-day.'

When Charles spoke in this tone, no one dared disobey, and even the nurse, despite the familiarity she enjoyed, did not venture to dispute his orders. The chancellor was summoned, and the audience fixed, not for the morrow, but for the fifth day from that time.

At five o'clock, the queen and the Duke d'Anjou proceeded to René's, who, in expectation of their visit, had prepared everything for the experiment.

In the chamber on the right—that is, in the sacrificial chamber—a blade of steel covered with mysterious arabesques was heating in a brazier of charcoal. On the altar lay the book of fate, and, as the previous night had been very clear, René had been enabled to consult the stars.

Henry d'Anjou entered first. He was wearing a wig, and his face and figure were concealed beneath a mask and large cloak. His mother followed him, and had she not been aware of his disguise, would not have recognized him. The queen took off her mask. D'Anjou did not follow her example.

'Have you consulted the stars?' asked Catherine.

'I have, madame, and they have already informed me of the past. The person whose fate you desire to know has, like all persons born under *Cancer*, a fiery and ardent disposition. He is powerful, he has lived nearly a quarter of a century, and Heaven has granted him wealth and power—is it not so, madame?'

'Perhaps.'

'Have you his hair and blood?'

'Here they are.'

And Catherine gave the magician a lock of fair hair and a small phial of blood.

René took the phial, shook it, and let fall on the glowing steel blade a large drop of blood that boiled for a second, and then spread itself into a thousand fantastic shapes.

'Oh!' cried René, 'I see him convulsed in agony. Hark! how he groans—see, how everything around him turns to blood—see how around his deathbed struggles and wars arise; and see, here are the lances and swords!'

'Will such things be long delayed?' asked Catherine, seizing the hand of her son, who in his anxiety to see, had leaned over the brazier.

René approached the altar and repeated a cabalistic prayer. Then he rose and, announcing all was ready, took in one hand the phial and in the other the lock of hair. Bidding Catherine to open the book of fate at any page, he poured on the steel blade all the blood and cast the hair in the fire, pronouncing a mystic formula as he did so.

Instantly the Duke d'Anjou and Catherine saw on the blade a figure resembling a corpse wrapped in a winding-sheet.

Another figure, that of a woman, leaned over it.

At the same time, the hair burned, casting out one jet of flame like a fiery tongue.

'A year,' cried René—'scarce a year, and this man shall die! One woman alone shall lament him, and yet, no: at the end of the blade is another female, with an infant in her arms.'

Catherine looked at her son, as if, though herself the mother of the man whose death was announced, she would ask him who these two women could be.

But scarcely had René finished, when the forms disappeared.

Then Catherine opened the book at random, and read with a voice that trembled in spite of herself, the following distich:

> *Ainsi a peri cil que l'on redoutoit,*
> *Plutost, trop tost, si prudence n'etoit.* *

'And for the other man that you know of,' said Catherine, 'what say the signs?'

'Favourable as ever: unless Providence intervenes to thwart his destiny, he is sure to be fortunate, but——'

'But, what?'

'One of the stars composing his constellation was covered by a black cloud during my observations.'

'Ah, a black cloud!—then there is hope!'

'Of whom do you speak, madame?' asked D'Anjou.

Catherine drew her son on one side, and spoke to him in a whisper.

During this interval, René, kneeling by the brazier, poured into the hollow of his hand the last drop of blood.

'Strange,' murmured he. 'It only proves how little can human knowledge compete with ours. To everyone but me, even to Ambroise Paré, this blood so pure, so full of health, promises years of life, and yet all will be useless before a year is out.'

Catherine and Henry turned and listened.

'Ah!' continued René, 'to the uninitiated the present is manifest, but to us the future is also manifest.'

'He will die, then, before the year is out?' said the queen-mother.

'As surely as there are three persons present who must one day rest in the grave.'

'Yet you say the blood indicates a long life?'

'Yes, if things were to follow their natural course. But an accident——'

'Ah, yes,' whispered Catherine to Henry—'an accident.'

'All the more reason for staying.'

'Oh, that is impossible.'

Then turning to René,—

'Thanks,' said the young man, disguising the tone of his voice. 'Take this purse.'

'Come, *count*,' said Catherine, purposely using this title to divert René's suspicions.

And they left the chamber.

'Mother,' cried Henry, 'you hear?—an accident. If such a thing happens, I shall be four hundred leagues away.'

'Four hundred leagues may be covered in a week.'

'Yes; but who knows if they will allow me to return.'

'Who knows,' replied the queen, 'if this illness of the king's may be the accident of which René spoke. Go, Henry, go, and beware of antagonizing your brother, should you see him.'

42

MUTUAL CONFIDENCES

THE first thing the Duke d'Anjou learned on reaching the Louvre was that the solemn entry of the ambassadors was fixed for the fifth day.* The tailors and jewellers waited on the prince with magnificent accoutrements and superb ornaments which the king had ordered for him.

While he was being fitted for them in a state of anger that brought tears to his eyes, Henry of Navarre was amusing himself greatly with a splendid collar of emeralds, a gold-hilted sword, and a very valuable ring, which Charles had sent him that morning.

D'Alençon had just received a letter, and had retired to his apartment, in order to read it at his leisure.

As for Coconnas, he was asking for his friend in every quarter of the Louvre.

At length, rumours of the affair in the corridor began to spread. Coconnas was devastated: for a moment he believed that

all these kings and princes had killed his friend and thrown his
body into some dungeon.

He learned that d'Alençon had been of the party, and, ignoring the dignity attaching to a prince of the blood, he went to him
to demand an explanation with as little ceremony as if he had
been a private gentleman.

D'Alençon, at first, was inclined to show the door to an up-
start who came to ask an account of his actions. But Coconnas
spoke so sternly, his eyes glared with such rage, and his three
duels in less than twenty hours fired the Piedmontese up so high
that he paused, and, instead of giving way to his first impulse,
replied with a charming smile,—

'My dear Coconnas, it is true that the king, furious at having
been hit on his shoulder by a silver ewer, the Duke d'Anjou,
angry at having orange jam poured on his head, and the Duke de
Guise, humiliated at having been assailed by a haunch of venison, joined forces to kill M. de la Mole. But a friend of your
friend's averted the blow, and, I assure you, the enterprise
failed.'

'Ah!' said Coconnas, breathing as loudly at this information as
a smith's bellows—'ah, *mordi!* monseigneur, I am pleased to hear
it. I should like to know who this friend is, to show my gratitude.'

D'Alençon made no reply, but smiled more agreeably still,
which made Coconnas believe that this friend was none other
than the prince himself.

'Well, monseigneur,' he continued, 'since you have done so
much as to tell me the beginning of this story, will you be so
obliging as to relate to me the conclusion?'

D'Alençon shook his head.

'The worst of all,' he said, 'my brave Coconnas, is that your
friend disappeared without anyone knowing where.'

'*Mordi!*' cried the Piedmontese, again turning pale with indignation. 'I shall make it my business to find out!'

'Go to Queen Marguerite,' said d'Alençon, who was as
anxious as Coconnas to learn where La Mole was. 'She will
know what has become of your friend.'

'I had already thought of it,' replied Coconnas.

'Do so,' added the prince, 'only do not say it was by my

advice. For if you are so unwise, you may not obtain any information.'

'Monseigneur,' said Coconnas, 'as your Royal Highness recommends me to secrecy on this point, I will be as mute as a tench, or the queen-mother. Good prince! excellent prince! magnanimous prince!' murmured Coconnas, as he went to call on the Queen of Navarre.

Marguerite was expecting Coconnas. The noise of his despair had reached her, and she almost forgave him his cavalier behaviour towards Madame de Nevers, whom the Piedmontese had not visited as the result of a dispute between them two or three days previously. He was therefore introduced to the queen the moment he was announced.

Coconnas entered, not altogether able to overcome the diffidence which he always felt to a certain extent in the presence of the queen, and which was the greater from her superiority of wit than of rank. But Marguerite greeted him with a smile which reassured him at once.

'Ah, madame!' he exclaimed, 'restore my friend to me, I beg you, or, at least, tell me what has become of him; for I cannot live without him. Imagine Euryalus without Nisus, Damon without Pythias, or Orestes without Pylades,* and have pity on my misfortune at the loss of my dear friend.'

Marguerite smiled, and after binding Coconnas to secrecy, told him all about the escape through the window. As to the place of his concealment, although Coconnas urged her to reveal it, she refused, but added,—

'If you wish to learn something definite about your friend, ask the King of Navarre, who is the only person who has a right to speak. As for me, all I can tell you is that he is alive: trust my word!'

'I trust something even more certain, madame: those lovely eyes have not been weeping.'

Then, thinking he could not add anything to this compliment, he withdrew, fully resolved to seek a reconciliation with Madame de Nevers, just to find out if she knew more than Marguerite was prepared to tell him.

The idea of leaving Marguerite had almost broken La Mole's

heart, and it was more to save the reputation of the queen than to save his own life that he had consented to fly.

Thus the next evening he returned to Paris, to try and see Marguerite at her balcony. Marguerite, for her part, as if a secret voice had informed her that he would be there, had spent the evening at her window, and thus they had seen each other with a happiness that may be readily imagined.

La Mole, anxious to be always near Marguerite, occupied himself in organizing, with all possible despatch, the event which would restore her to him—namely, the escape of the King of Navarre.

Marguerite having thus seen La Mole, and knowing that he was safe, was at ease on his account, but, fearing he might be watched and followed, she refused to give him any other rendezvous than these *à l'Espagnole*,* which took place every evening until the night before the reception of the ambassadors. On this evening, about nine o'clock, when everyone in the Louvre was preoccupied with the preparations for next day, Marguerite opened her window and went out onto the balcony. Almost at once the note she expected, according to La Mole's usual custom, was thrown with his usual skill, and fell at the feet of his royal mistress. Since he normally waited to receive her letter first, Marguerite understood that, by anticipating her, he had some important news to communicate, and read it with all haste. The note was in two parts; the first contained these words,—

'Madame,—I must speak to the King of Navarre: it is on a most urgent matter. I shall wait.'

And on the second page, which could be detached from the other, was written,—

'My lady and queen,—Arrange that I may speak with you. I am waiting.'

Marguerite had scarcely finished the second part of this letter when she heard the voice of Henry of Navarre, who, with his usual discretion, tapped at the door, and asked Gillonne if he might be allowed to enter.

The queen at once separated the two notes, put one of the pages in her pocket, ran to the window, which she shut, and, going quickly to the door, said,—

'Come in, sire.'

Gently, quickly, and cleverly as Marguerite had closed the window, the sound had reached the ears of Henry, whose senses were always on the alert, and who had in the society he so greatly mistrusted acquired that exquisite delicacy of hearing and sight which man acquires in the savage state. But the King of Navarre was not one of those tyrants who wish to prevent their wives from taking the air and gazing on the stars. Henry was smiling and urbane as usual.

'Madame,' he said, 'while our people of the court are trying on their fine apparel, I have come to have a few words with you about my affairs which you still regard as your own, do you not?'

'Most assuredly, sir,' replied Marguerite. 'Are not our interests always identical?'

'Yes, madame. Which was why I wished to ask your opinion of the pains which d'Alençon has taken for several days to avoid me, so much so, that since the day before yesterday he has decamped to Saint-Germain. Do you not think from this that it is his intention either to go away alone, or not to go at all? Let me have your ideas on this point, for it would have great weight with me if your opinion were to coincide with mine.'

'Your Majesty is quite right to feel uneasy about my brother's silence. I have been thinking of it all day. It is my opinion that circumstances having changed he has changed with them.'

'That is to say, that seeing King Charles ill, and the Duke d'Anjou king of Poland, he would not be sorry to remain in Paris and keep an eye on the crown of France.'

'Exactly.'

'I agree with you. This is all as I wish,' continued Henry. 'Let him remain; it will not alter our plan. For if I were to escape alone, I would want three times the guarantees I should have asked for had your brother accompanied me, whose name and presence in the enterprise would have been my safeguards. The only thing that astonishes me is not having any news of de Mouy. Have you heard from him, madame?'

'I, sire!' said Marguerite, astonished. 'How could I possibly——'

'Is it not obvious? You were so kind as to oblige me by saving

young La Mole's life. He was bound to go to Mantes, and from
there, it is no great distance to return here.'

'Ah! that gives me the solution to a riddle I have sought for in
vain,' replied Marguerite. 'I left my window open, and found on
my return a kind of note on the carpet.'

'There, now!' said Henry.

'A note which at first I could not understand, and to which I
attached no importance,' continued Marguerite. 'Perhaps I was
wrong, and it came from that quarter.'

'Very possibly,' said Henry, 'nay, most probably. Might I see
this note?'

'Certainly, sire,' replied Marguerite, handing to the king the
half sheet of paper which she had put in her pocket.

The king looked at it.

'Is not this,' he inquired, 'the hand of M. de la Mole?'

'I do not know,' was Marguerite's reply; 'the writing appears
to me forged.'

'Never mind; let us read.'

And he read,—

'Madame,—I must speak to the King of Navarre. It is on a
most urgent matter. I shall wait.'

'Ah! do you see?' said Henry; 'he says he is waiting.'

'Yes, I see he says so; but what then?'

'Why, *ventre-saint-gris!* I want him to come here.'

'Come here!' exclaimed Marguerite, fixing on her husband
her beautiful eyes full of amazement—'how can you say such a
thing, sire? A man whom the king has sought to kill—who is
marked down, threatened. Let him come, do you say! Is that
possible? Were doors made for those who have been——'

'Obliged to escape by the window, you would say?'

'Exactly.'

'But if they know the way by the window, they may use that
route again, since it is impossible for them to enter through the
door. That is simple enough, surely.'

'Do you think so?' said Marguerite, blushing with pleasure at
the thoughts of again having La Mole near her.

'I am sure of it.'

'But how can he get up?' inquired the queen.

'Did you not keep the rope-ladder I sent you?'

'Yes, sire,' said Marguerite.

'Then the whole thing will be easily managed. Fasten it to your balcony, and let it hang. If it is de Mouy who waits—and I am inclined to believe so—he will climb the ladder.'

And without losing his gravity of manner, Henry took the taper to light Marguerite in her search for the ladder. The search was by no means lengthy: it was found in a cupboard in the celebrated closet.

'Here it is,' said Henry. 'And now, madame, if it is not too much to ask, secure it to the balcony.'

'Why me and not you, sire?' asked Marguerite.

'Because the best conspirators are the most prudent. The sight of a man might alarm your correspondent—you understand?'

Marguerite smiled, and fastened the ladder.

'There,' said Henry, ensconcing himself in one corner of the apartment; 'now show yourself—and now drop the ladder. Capital! I am sure de Mouy will come up.'

And in a few minutes afterwards, a man eagerly placed one leg over the balcony. But, seeing that the queen did not approach him, he remained for some moments hesitating. Then Henry advanced.

'Ah!' said he urbanely, 'it is not de Mouy, it is M. de la Mole. Good-evening, M. de la Mole. Do come in.'

La Mole was for a moment amazed, so much so that, had he still been on the ladder, instead of having his feet firmly in the balcony, he might have fallen backwards.

'You wished to speak to the King of Navarre on an urgent matter,' said Marguerite. 'I have informed him of your request, and here he is.'

Henry crossed to the window and closed it.

'I love you!' whispered Marguerite, pressing the young man's hand ardently.

'Well, sir,' said Henry, handing a chair to La Mole, 'what have we to say?'

'We have to say, sire,' he replied, 'that I have left M. de Mouy at the barrier.* He desires to know if Maurevel has spoken, and if his presence in your Majesty's apartment is public knowledge.'

'Not yet; but it must be before long. We must therefore make haste.'

'His opinion coincides with your Majesty's, sire. And if by to-morrow evening M. d'Alençon is ready to depart, de Mouy will be at the Porte Saint-Marcel with a hundred and fifty men. Five hundred will await you at Fontainebleau, and then you will ride through Blois, Angoulême, and Bordeaux.'*

'Madame,' said Henry, turning to his wife, 'to-morrow, I shall be ready: shall you?'

La Mole's eyes were fixed on Marguerite's with intense anticipation.

'You have my word,' replied the queen. 'Wherever you go, I shall follow. But M. d'Alençon must leave at the same time. There is no middle path for him; he is with us, or he betrays us: if he hesitates, we will not stir.'

'Does he know anything of this proposed plan,* M. de la Mole?' inquired Henry.

'He had a letter from de Mouy several days ago.'

'Ah!' said Henry, 'and never told me a word of it.'

'Be on your guard, sir—be on your guard,' said Marguerite.

'Be easy; I am on my guard. But how can we convey an answer to de Mouy?'

'Do not worry on that score, sire. To-morrow, on the right hand or left hand of your Majesty, visible or invisible, during the reception of the ambassadors, he will be there: one word in the queen's address will let him know whether you consent or not; whether he should flee, or await you. If the Duke d'Alençon refuses, he only requires a fortnight to reorganize everything in your name.'

'Really,' replied Henry, 'de Mouy is an invaluable man. Can you introduce a phrase or two in your speech, madame?'

'Nothing easier,' replied Marguerite.

'Well, then,' said Henry, 'I shall see M. d'Alençon to-morrow. Let de Mouy be at his post and ready for the signal.'

'He will be there, sire.'

'Well, then, M. de la Mole, go and give him my reply. You have, doubtless, a horse and servant somewhere near at hand.'

'Orthon is waiting for me on the quay.'

'Go to him, comte. Oh, not by the window: that is all right for emergencies. But you might be seen, and, as it would not be known that it was for me that you showed yourself, it would compromise the queen.'

'But how then, sire?'

'If you could not enter the Louvre alone, you can at least walk out of it with me, for I have the password. You have your cloak, I have mine. We will wrap ourselves up well, and get past the guard without difficulty. Wait here while I see if the corridors are clear.'

Henry with the most natural air in the world went out to examine if the coast was clear. La Mole remained alone with the queen.

'Oh, when shall we meet again?' said La Mole.

'To-morrow evening, if we flee; in the Rue Cloche Perce, if we do not.'

'M. de la Mole,' said Henry, returning, 'you may come. There is no one there.'

La Mole bowed respectfully to the queen.

'Give him your hand to kiss, madame,' said Henry. 'M. de la Mole is no common server of our cause.'

Marguerite obeyed.

'By the way,' added Henry, 'put the rope-ladder away carefully. It is a very precious instrument for conspirators, and at the moment when we least expect it, it may come in useful. Come, La Mole—come!'

43

THE AMBASSADORS

NEXT morning, the whole population of Paris poured towards the Faubourg Saint-Antoine,* through which it was decided that the Polish ambassadors should enter. A line of soldiers restrained the crowd, and a regiment of horse escorted the nobles and ladies of the court.

Soon appeared, close by the Abbey Saint-Antoine, a troop of riders dressed in red and yellow, with fur cloaks and caps, and bearing long sabres curved like Turkish scimitars.

Behind this troop came a second, dressed with oriental

magnificence. They preceded the ambassadors, who, four in number, gorgeously sustained the reputation of their chivalrous country.

One of the ambassadors was the Bishop of Cracow:* his costume was half ecclesiastical, half military, resplendent with gold and jewels. Next to the bishop rode the Palatine Lasco, a powerful noble, closely related to the royal family, rich as a king, and as proud.

Behind these two principal ambassadors, who were accompanied by two other palatines of high rank, came a number of gentlemen, whose steeds, glittering with gold and precious stones, excited the clamorous admiration of the populace.

Up to the last moment Catherine had hoped the reception would be postponed in deference to the king's illness. But when the day arrived—when she saw Charles, pale as a spectre, don the royal robes, she saw she must, in appearance at least, yield to his iron will, and began to believe that the safest plan for Henry d'Anjou was to depart into the splendid exile to which he was condemned.

The large reception chamber had been prepared, and, as such ceremonies were usually public, the guards and sentinels had received orders to admit as many persons into the apartments and courtyards as they could possibly contain.

As for Paris, it presented the same aspect that every great city presents on similar occasions—that is, confusion and curiosity. Yet, had an observer attentively examined the crowd, he would have noticed a considerable number of men in cloaks, who exchanged glances and signs when at a distance, and, when they met, a few rapid whispered words. They seemed much occupied with the procession, and received their orders from an old man, whose keen black eyes, in spite of his long white beard and eyebrows, indicated a vigorous constitution. This old man, by his own and his followers' assistance, entered the Louvre, and, thanks to the officer of the Swiss guard, obtained a place behind the ambassadors, and opposite Henry and Marguerite.

Henry, informed by La Mole that de Mouy in some disguise would be present, looked for him everywhere. At last his eyes met those of the old man, and a sign from de Mouy ended all doubt as to his identity, for de Mouy was so perfectly disguised that the King of Navarre was doubtful as to whether this old man with a white beard could be the intrepid Huguenot leader, who a few days before had defended his life so valiantly.

A word from Henry fixed Marguerite's attention on de Mouy. Then her eyes wandered round the chamber in search of La Mole. La Mole was not there.

The orations began. The first was to the king: Lasco, in the name of the Diet of Poland,* demanded the royal consent to the Duke d'Anjou becoming their king.

The king's reply was brief and succinct. He presented to them the Duke d'Anjou, of whose courage he made a high eulogy. He spoke in French, and an interpreter translated what he said at the end of each sentence.

Whilst the interpreter was speaking, the king applied his handkerchief continually to his mouth, and as often as he removed it a stain of blood was visible.

When Charles had finished, Lasco turned to d'Anjou, and offered him, in the name of the Diet, the throne of Poland. Lasco's address was in Latin.

The duke replied, in the same language, and in a voice he vainly strove to render firm, that he gratefully accepted the honour offered to him. During all this time, Charles, who remained standing, with lips compressed, kept his eyes on him, like an eagle watching his prey.

When the duke had finished, Lasco took the crown of the Jagellons* from the velvet cushion on which it rested, and while two Polish nobles placed the royal robes on the duke, deposited the crown in Charles's hands.

Charles made a sign to his brother. D'Anjou knelt before him, and, with his own hands, Charles placed the crown on his head, and the two brothers exchanged a kiss full of bitter hate.

A herald then cried, 'Alexander Edward Henry of France, Duke of Anjou, is crowned King of Poland. God save the King of Poland!'

All the assembly repeated, 'God save the King of Poland!'

Then Lasco turned to Marguerite. Her discourse had been kept till the last, and, as we have said, Marguerite had written it herself.

Lasco's address was rather a eulogy than an oration. He had yielded, Sarmatian as he was, to his admiration of Marguerite's beauty. While his language was that of Ovid, his style was that of Ronsard.*

His speech was applauded by everybody: by those who understood Latin, because they shared his admiration; by those who did not understand it, because they wished it to appear as though they did.

Marguerite, having made a gracious curtsey to the ambassador, fixed her eyes on de Mouy, and began thus,—

'*Quod nunc hac in aulâ insperati adestis exultaremus ego et rex conjux, nisi ideo immineret calamitas, scilicet non solum fratris sed etiam amici orbitas,*'—'Your unlooked-for presence in this court would overwhelm my husband and myself with joy, did it not threaten us with a great misfortune—that is, not only the loss of a brother, but also that of a friend.'

These words had a double meaning, and though really intended for de Mouy, were supposed to refer to the Duke d'Anjou. The latter, accordingly, bowed in token of gratitude.

Charles did not recall having read this sentence in Marguerite's speech, when it was submitted to him some days before, but he did not trouble himself much about that; and, besides, he understood Latin very imperfectly.

Marguerite continued—

'*Adeo dolemur a te dividi ut tecum proficisci maluissemus. Sed idem fatum quo nunc sine ulllâ morâ Lutetiâ cedere juberis, hac un urbe detinet. Proficiscere ergo, frater; proficiscere amice; proficiscere sine nobis; proficiscentem sequentur spes et desideria nostra.*'—'We are grieved to be separated from you, for we should have preferred to go with you. But the same fate that compels you to leave Paris without delay, retains us in that city. Go, dear brother; go, then, dear friend—go without us. Our hopes and our wishes will follow you.'

It is easy to understand how attentively de Mouy had listened to these words, which, though addressed to the Duke d'Anjou, were meant for him alone. Whilst listening, Catherine was struck with these black eyes so piercing beneath their grey eyebrows.

'What a strange face!' thought she. 'Who can this man be who watches Marguerite so attentively, and whom Henry and Marguerite are scrutinizing so keenly?'

The Queen of Navarre continued. Catherine was still trying to guess the name of this strange old man, when the master of the ceremonies came up behind her, and gave her a little satin bag. She opened it, and found a paper containing these words: 'Maurevel, by the aid of a cordial I have administered to him, has, in some measure, recovered his strength, and has written the name of the man in the King of Navarre's chamber. This man was M. de Mouy.'

'De Mouy,' thought the queen, 'I suspected as much! But this old man—eh, *cospetto!**—this old man is——'

She leaned towards the captain of her guards.

'Do you see,' whispered she, 'that old man with the white beard, in the black velvet cloak, behind Lasco?'

'The one the King of Navarre nodded to a moment ago?'

'Yes; do not lose sight of him. Post yourself at the door with ten men, and when he comes out, invite him, in the king's name, to dinner. If he accepts, take him to the guard-room, and keep him there; if he resists, seize him, dead or alive.'

Fortunately, Henry had glanced at Catherine, and observing her eyes fixed so earnestly on de Mouy, became uneasy. When he saw her give an order to the captain of the guard, he guessed everything.

It was then he made the sign de Nancey had observed, and which meant, 'Save yourself—you are discovered!'

But Henry was not entirely reassured until de Nancey returned, and he saw by Catherine's face that the officer had been unsuccessful.

The audience was finished. The king rose with difficulty, saluted the ambassadors, and retired, leaning on Ambroise Paré, who, since his illness, had not left him an instant.

The Duke d'Alençon had been an insignificant bystander throughout the ceremony. Charles's eyes, which had been fixed on d'Anjou, had not once been turned towards him.

The new King of Poland felt himself lost. Carried off by those barbarians, far from his mother, he was, so to speak, a second Antæus,* removed from the earth to which he owed his strength.

Instead of following the king, he retired to his mother's apartments.

On seeing her beloved son pale beneath his crown, and bending beneath the royal mantle, Catherine advanced towards him.

'Oh, mother!' cried the king, 'I am condemned to die an exile.'

'My son,' returned Catherine, 'have you so soon forgotten René's prediction? Calm yourself; you will not be there long.'

'Mother, I entreat you,' said the Duke d'Anjou, 'at the least sign that the throne of France may become vacant, inform me.'

'My son,' replied the queen, 'until that day which we both long for a horse shall be kept saddled in my stable, and a courier in my antechamber ready to set out for Poland.'

44

ORESTES AND PYLADES

HENRY D'ANJOU once departed, peace and happiness seemed to have returned to the Louvre. Charles, laying aside his melancholy, resumed his usually fine and vigorous health, either hunting each day with Henry, or, if prevented from following that sport, spending the time in discussing subjects relating to it, and scolding his brother-in-law for the indifference he showed for hawking—declaring that he would be the most accomplished prince of his time, if only he understood the management of falcons, gerfalcons, hawks, and tercelets,* as perfectly as he did pointers and hounds. Catherine had returned to all the duties of a good mother. Kind and gentle towards Charles and d'Alençon—affectionate to Henry and Marguerite—gracious to Madame de Nevers and Madame de Sauve, she even carried her kindliness so far as to visit Maurevel twice during the time he lay ill in his house in the Rue de la Cerisaie—alleging, as a reason for this gesture on her part, that the unfortunate object of her pity had been wounded while in the execution of orders received from herself. Marguerite followed up her love affairs after the Spanish mode of conducting such matters. Each evening she stood at her open window, and, both by notes and gestures, kept up a continual correspondence with La Mole; while, in each of his letters, the impatient young man reminded his lovely mistress of her promise to see him in the Rue Cloche Perce.

In a word, there remained but one lonely and discontented person amidst the various members of the now calm and tranquil Louvre.

It was—to the object of the affections of so charming and capricious a person as Madame de Nevers (we mean Coconnas)—certainly something to know that La Mole was still alive. But the Piedmontese would thankfully have surrendered all the tender meetings granted him by the duchess, as well as all the consoling assurances of Marguerite regarding the safety of their common friend, for one hour's enjoyment of his dear La Mole's company.

Urged by the wishes of her own heart, as well as by the pleading of La Mole, and the deep despair of the woebegone Coconnas, Marguerite had arranged to meet Henriette at the house with the double entrance, and there discuss, fully and uninterruptedly, those subjects all four had so much at heart.

Coconnas received Henriette's summons to be in the Rue Tizon at half-past nine with a very ill grace. Nevertheless, he was punctual at the assignation, where he found Henriette already arrived, and not a little offended at being there first.

'Fie, monsieur!' cried she, as he entered, 'is this right, to make—I will not say a princess, but a lady, wait for you?'

'Wait?' replied Coconnas. 'I like that! I'll wager you what you like that we are both early.'

'I was here certainly before the time fixed.'

'Well, and so was I, or, at least, I should have been but for a circumstance. What time is it now? Scarcely ten, I think.'

'And my letter gave half-past nine as the hour you were to meet me here.'

'For the purpose of being punctual, I left the Louvre at nine o'clock to come here; but when I reached the corner of the Rue de Grenelle, I saw a man I mistook for La Mole.'

'Always something tedious involving that La Mole!'

'Certainly, either with your leave or without it.'

'Brute!'

'Upon my word,' said Coconnas, 'we seem bent upon paying each other compliments to-night.'

'You are really overpoweringly civil, it must be confessed. But go on with your story, if you must, and let me hear what became of your meeting with the man who looked like your dear La Mole. But, what's this? for Heaven's sake, why is there blood on your doublet?'

'Ah, that fellow must have sprinkled me when we were fighting together.'

'Have you been fighting?'

'To be sure I have!'

'And on La Mole's account?'

'Who do you think I should fight for? A woman? No, no; I will tell you all about it. I followed the man who had dared to imitate the walk and manner of my friend, and overtook him in the Rue Coquillière. I eyed him every way by the light from a shop window—and it was not my poor La Mole!'

'So far, so good!'

'Ay, but my unknown gentleman turned angry about my following him, and when I said, "Sir, you are an ass and a fool if you think you can bear a distant resemblance to my friend M. de la Mole, who is an accomplished gentleman, for it only requires a closer look at you to see you are a common oaf!" He drew his sword—I did the same; and at the third pass my angry opponent fell senseless at my feet, sprinkling me with his blood as he did so.'

'And did you not try to help him?'

'Just as I was about to do so, another man, but mounted on horseback, came by. Well, this time, duchess, I thought I had found La Mole, for he resembled him even more than the other man. He was going at a great pace, but that did not stop me running after him as hard as I could. But I was obliged to stop to catch my breath, and, in the meantime, the horseman disappeared. And so, tired and dispirited with having had so unsuccessful a chase, I determined to come here!'

'Upon my word,' said the duchess, 'your conduct is most flattering! It is quite easy to see you no longer love me!'

'On the contrary, duchess, I idolize you. But you do not understand. Is it not possible for me to love and cherish and dote upon you, and yet use my idle moments in eulogizing my friend?'

'You call the time you spend with me idle moments!'

'I can't help it. Poor La Mole is for ever in my thoughts!'

'And you prefer him to me! I see, I know you do! Annibal, I hate and detest you—there!—now I've said it. Why not come straight out with it, and tell me you prefer this friend to me. But I warn you—if you dare to prefer any creature in the world to me, I'll—I'll——'

'Henriette, most lovely duchess! let me advise you, for your own sake, not to ask unwise questions—be satisfied that I love you, who are the best of women. But you must also permit me the privilege of loving La Mole above all other men.'

'Well answered!' said a strange voice suddenly, and a large damask curtain being raised, uncovered a panel, which sliding back into the wall and forming a means of communication between the two apartments, revealed La Mole standing in the doorway, like one of Titian's splendid paintings* set in a gilded frame.

'La Mole!' cried Coconnas, without taking the slightest notice of Marguerite, or in any way thanking her for the delightful surprise she had arranged for him—'La Mole! my friend! my dear, dear friend!'

So saying, he threw himself into his friend's arms, knocking over the table that stood in his way, as well as the arm-chair he had been sitting in.

La Mole returned his greetings with equal warmth; then, addressing the Duchess de Nevers: 'You must pardon me, madame, if the mention of my name has been allowed to disturb your happiness; all I can say,' continued he, looking at Marguerite with ineffable tenderness, 'is, that it was not my fault that we have not seen each other before this.'

'You see, Henriette,' said Marguerite, taking up the conversation, 'I have kept my word; here he is!'

Meanwhile, Coconnas, after embracing his friend, and walking round and round him a dozen times and even holding a candelabra up to his face to make sure it was really him, suddenly turned towards Marguerite, and kneeling down reverently, kissed the hem of her robe.

'Well, well!' said the Duchess de Nevers, 'you seem to forget that I am present. I suppose I have become quite unendurable in your eyes.'

'*Mordi!*' replied Coconnas, 'you are, as you always were, the goddess of my idolatry, the only difference being that I can now tell you so with a lighter heart. Why, were a host of savage nations standing by, I would insist and maintain that all their hyperborean* and barbarous countries together could produce nothing so perfect, so lovely as you, my queen of beauty.'

'Steady on, Coconnas,' interposed La Mole. 'Have you forgotten that Madame Marguerite is here?'

'That makes no difference,' answered Coconnas, with that half-serious, half-comic air and manner so peculiarly his own. 'I still assert that Madame Henriette is the queen of beauty, while Madame Marguerite is a beauty of a queen!'

'Come, then, my beautiful queen!' said Madame de Nevers, seeing that Coconnas had neither eyes nor ears for anyone but La Mole, 'let us leave these tender friends to have an hour's chat together. Perhaps M. Coconnas will be a little more rational after that.'

Marguerite whispered a few words to La Mole, and then, with Madame de Nevers, passed through the open panel to the next room, where supper awaited them.

The two young men were then left alone.

The first questions asked by Coconnas concerned that fatal evening which had wellnigh cost him his life. As La Mole proceeded with his narration, the Piedmontese shook with anger.

'And why?' inquired he, 'instead of running about half wild as you have done and causing me all manner of worry—why did you not seek refuge with our master the duke, who would have received and protected you?'

'Do you mean the Duke d'Alençon?' whispered La Mole, 'when you say *our* master? I owe my life to the King of Navarre.'

'Excellent, noble king! but what part did the Duke d'Alençon play in the affair?'

'Oh, he held the rope which I was to be strangled with.'

'*Mordi!*' exclaimed Coconnas, springing up furiously—'are you sure of that? What! a pale-faced, sickly-looking prince, a currish mongrel, dare to lay his hands on my friend! Strangle him, indeed! ha, ha! *Mordi!* to-morrow he shall hear my opinion of this business.'

'Are you mad, Coconnas? For Heaven's sake, calm down, and

try to remember that it is half-past eleven, and that you are on duty to-night at the Louvre.'

'So what? He will have to wait a long time before he sees me on duty! Do you suppose I will ever again serve a man who has held a rope to murder my friend with? You must be joking! No, no, the hand of Providence has reunited us, and I shall not leave you again. If you stay here, I stay too.'

'For the love of Heaven, Coconnas, mind what you are about. You are sober, I trust?'

'Fortunately I am, or I should most certainly set the Louvre on fire.'

'Come, come, Annibal,' persisted La Mole, 'be sensible. Return to your duties, or inform the duke that you are leaving his service.'

'To be sure, to be sure. That is the proper thing, and I will do it. I'll write him a few lines now.'

'Write, Coconnas! You make light work of writing to a prince of the blood.'

'Ah! but whose blood—that of my friend? Have a care!' exclaimed Coconnas, rolling his large, fierce-looking eyes. 'I may yet be tempted to do more than observe the etiquette of sending him written notice that I am resigning from his service.'

So saying, Coconnas took the pen without further opposition from his friend, and hastily composed the following specimen of epistolary eloquence:—

'MY LORD,—There can be no doubt that a person versed as is your Highness in the writings of all the authors of classical antiquity must be perfectly well acquainted with the touching story of Orestes and Pylades, two heroes celebrated alike for their misfortunes and deep friendship. My friend La Mole is equally unfortunate as was Orestes, while I can boast of the same devoted attachment as that which possessed Pylades. Affairs of the utmost importance to him demand my aid and assistance at this particular moment, and render it quite impossible for me to leave his side. I am therefore compelled (craving your Highness's pardon for the same) to take a spell of leave, for the purpose of remaining with the dear friend I mean to part from no more, but to follow his fortune wherever it may lead me.

'I beg your Highness to believe the deep sorrow it causes me to withdraw from your service, and also the deep respect with which I subscribe myself, my lord,

'Your Highness's
Most humble and obedient servant,
ANNIBAL COMTE DE COCONNAS,
And the inseparable friend of M. de la Mole.'

This *chef-d'œuvre* finished, Coconnas read it aloud to La Mole, who merely shrugged.

'Well, what do you think of it?' inquired Coconnas, who either had not seen his friend's gesture, or feigned not to have done so.

'Why, I say that M. d'Alençon will laugh at us both, as a pair of simpletons.'

'Better that than to strangle us. Now, then, I will speak to our landlord to get my letter despatched to the Louvre.'

At this moment the panel was slid back.

'Well,' inquired both princesses in the same breath, 'and how are Pylades and Orestes now?'

'*Mordi!* madame!' replied Coconnas, 'they are both dying of love and hunger.'

It was Maître la Hurière himself, who, at nine o'clock the following morning, conveyed to the Louvre the respectful missive of Comte Annibal de Coconnas.

45

ORTHON

HENRY OF NAVARRE, after the refusal of the Duke d'Alençon, which left everything uncertain and dangerous, even his very existence, had become, if possible, more intimate with the prince than he had been before. By this, Catherine concluded that not only did the two princes understand each other perfectly, but also that they were engaged in some mutual plot or conspiracy.

She questioned Marguerite on the subject, but Marguerite was worthy of her mother. So skilfully did the Queen of Navarre parry her mother's inquisitorial inquiries, that, although replying with apparent openness and candour to each question, she contrived to throw a still greater mystery over the affair than it was wrapped in before.

The Florentine had thus no guide through the labyrinth of her thoughts except the spirit of intrigue which she had brought with her from Tuscany.* The first conclusion she came to was that since the hated Béarnais derived the principal part of his strength from his alliance with the Duke d'Alençon, it would be expedient to separate them as speedily as possible.

From the instant in which she formed this resolution, Catherine continued to beset her son with a patience and skill worthy of the most indefatigable angler, who, having dropped his bait near the prey he wishes to catch, imperceptibly draws it ashore, till his victim is unconsciously lured into his power.

Duke François was aware of the increased affection shown him by his mother, whose advances he received with evident signs of pleasure. As to Henry, he affected to know nothing of what was going on, but he kept a more watchful eye on his ally than he had previously done.

Everybody seemed to be waiting for some great event by which to shape their course. During this state of things it happened that, one fine summer day, when the sun had risen with even more than usual splendour, and the rich balmy air was filled with the odour of a thousand flowers, a pale and sickly-looking man emerged from a small house situated behind the Arsenal, and feebly made his way, supporting himself by a staff, towards the Rue du Petit-Musc.

Having reached the Porte Saint-Antoine, he diverged from the Boulevard and entered the Archery Garden.* The man at the gate received him with every demonstration of respect.

No one was in the garden (which, as the name suggests, belonged to a regiment of cross-bowmen), but had it been crowded with people, the pale stranger would have fully deserved their commiseration and sympathy. For his long moustache and military air and step, though somewhat weakened by sickness and suffering, were enough to indicate that he was some officer recently wounded, and now seeking to regain his strength by taking exercise in the open air. Yet strange to say, when the cloak which (in spite of the increasing warmth) the apparently harmless visitor was wearing blew open, it displayed a pair of long pistols hanging from the silver clasps of his belt, which also held a dagger and a sword of colossal size which hung heavily at his side, and, with its ponderous sheath, clattered against his shrunken and uncertain legs.

Once in the garden, the man selected for his resting place a small covered arbour looking onto the Boulevards, from which it was only separated by a thick hedge and a small ditch which formed, as it were, a second enclosure. Extending his weary limbs on a turfy bank, within reach of a table, he beckoned the porter, who, in addition to the duties of *concierge*, exercised also the vocation of a vintner, and, saying a few words, was quickly supplied with what appeared to be a kind of cordial.

The invalid had been about ten minutes in his shady retreat, slowly discussing the drink brought to him by the *concierge*, when suddenly his face, in spite of its pallor, assumed a fearful expression. He had just detected the approach of a man, who, turning the corner of a street, advanced enveloped in a large cloak and stopped just a little way off, but in full view. Scarcely had the pale stranger in the arbour (who was none other than Maurevel) recovered from the agitation caused by the unexpected arrival of the man, than he observed that the latter had been joined by a second person dressed as a page.

Concealed beneath his leafy bower, Maurevel could see and hear all that was said in a conversation, the importance of which may be imagined when it is known that the man in the cloak was de Mouy, and the young man Orthon the page.

Both looked carefully around them, while Maurevel held his breath, lest a sound should betray him.

'You may speak now in safety,' said the younger and more confident of the two—'we are quite safe here. No one can either see or hear us.'

'Good!' answered de Mouy. 'Now listen to me! you are to go to Madame de Sauve's, and, if she is at home, give this into her own hands. But if she is not in her apartments, then place the letter where the king usually leaves his—behind the mirror. Wait at the Louvre; and if any reply is sent, bring it, you know where. If you are not given an answer to deliver, meet me to-night, armed with a petronel,* at the spot I told you of, and which I have just left.'

'Enough!' said Orthon—'I understand.'

'I must now leave you,' continued de Mouy, 'I have much to do during the day. It will be pointless for you to go to the Louvre till *he* is there, and I have every reason to believe *he* will be engaged all day studying hawking. So be gone, boy, and carry out your orders. Do not be afraid to show yourself at the Louvre; you can say that, being now quite recovered, you came to thank Madame de Sauve for the kind care she took of you during your illness.'

Maurevel, concentrating hard, continued to listen till the perspiration gathered in large drops on his forehead. His first impulse had been to detach one of the pistols from his belt, and take deadly aim at de Mouy. But at that instant the sudden opening of the latter's cloak displayed a breastplate solid enough to resist all such futile attempts.

Then, again, he reflected that being separated by so flimsy a barrier, one spring would bring de Mouy on him. And what chance could a poor wounded, enfeebled being like himself have against so powerful an assailant? With a sigh, therefore, he drew back the weapon, mentally exclaiming,—

'How unfortunate that I cannot leave him dead on the spot, without any other witness than that young varlet, who would have served as an excellent target for my second pistol!'

Then, on the other hand, it occurred to him that the note sent via the page to Madame de Sauve might probably be better worth taking than the life of the Huguenot chief.

'Well,' said he, 'so be it, then: you escape me this morning, but to-morrow I will settle all scores with you, if I have to pursue you to that hell from which you sprang to ruin *me* unless I destroy *you* first!'

At this instant, de Mouy, wrapping his cloak around him, and concealing his features in its large folds, set off towards the Temple, while Orthon took the road that led to the banks of the Seine.

Then Maurevel, rising with more of energy and vigour than he could have dared to count on, went back to the Rue de la Cerisaie, ordered a horse to be saddled, and, weak as he was and at the risk of opening his newly-closed wounds, he set off at full gallop towards the Rue Saint-Antoine, reached the quays, and darted into the Louvre.

Five minutes after he had entered the gate, Catherine was in full possession of all that had transpired, and Maurevel had received the thousand gold crowns promised him for the arrest of the King of Navarre.

'Yes—yes!' exclaimed Catherine exultingly, 'either I am much deceived, or de Mouy will turn out to be the black spot discovered by René in the horoscope of this detested Béarnais.'

A quarter of an hour after Maurevel, Orthon reached the Louvre, and having boldly made himself known, as directed by de Mouy, proceeded unmolested to the apartments of Madame de Sauve. There he found only Dariole, who informed him that her mistress was occupied, by the queen's orders, in transcribing letters for her Majesty who had summoned her for that purpose within the last five minutes.

'No matter,' replied Orthon; 'I can wait.' Then, taking advantage of the freedom he had always been permitted to observe, he went into the adjoining chamber, which was the bedroom of the baroness, and, after ensuring that he was unobserved, carefully hid the note behind the looking-glass. Just as he was withdrawing his hand from the mirror, Catherine entered the room. Orthon changed colour, for he fancied the quick, searching glance of the queen-mother was first directed to the mirror.

'What are you doing here?' asked Catherine—'looking for Madame de Sauve, I suppose?'

'Yes, indeed, your Majesty. It is a long time since I saw her, and if I am much longer in returning her my sincere thanks, I fear she will think me ungrateful.'

'You love Madame de Sauve very much, do you not?'

'Oh, that I do, with all my heart! I can never forget the kindness Madame de Sauve has always shown to a humble servant like myself.'

'And upon what occasion was it that she showed you such care and attention?' inquired Catherine, feigning to be ignorant of what had happened to the youth.

'When I was wounded, madame, the night they tried to arrest the King of Navarre. I was so terrified at the sight of the soldiers that I called out for help, upon which one of them gave me a blow on the head, and I fell senseless to the ground.'

'Poor boy! and you are now quite recovered?'

'Oh, yes, madame!'

'And that being the case,' continued Catherine, 'I suppose you are trying to get back into the service of the King of Navarre?'

'No, indeed, madame. When the King of Navarre learned that I had dared to resist your Majesty's orders, he was very angry and dismissed me.'

'Really!' said Catherine, with a tone which suggested genuine interest. 'Well, I shall take the arrangement of that matter into my own hands. But if you are looking for Madame de Sauve, you will do so in vain: she is at this moment busily occupied in my apartments, and likely to be detained there for some time.'

Then, thinking that Orthon might not have had time to place his note behind the mirror before she had disturbed him, she returned to the adjoining chamber, to give him the opportunity of doing so.

But just as Orthon, uneasy at the unexpected arrival of the queen-mother, was asking himself whether the circumstance did not in some way forebode evil to his master, he heard three gentle taps on the ceiling, the same signal he was in the habit of using to warn his master of the approach of danger during his visits to Madame de Sauve. He started at the sound: a sudden light seemed to break in upon his mind, and he took it as a warning to himself—danger was near. Hastily springing towards the mirror, he withdrew the paper he had previously placed there.

Through a rent in the tapestried hangings, Catherine watched his every movement. She saw him dart forwards to the mirror, but whether to take away or to conceal the coveted paper, she could not tell. Returning to the apartment, with a smile on her face, she said,—

'What, here still, boy? What can you be waiting for? Did I not promise to take charge of your future prospects? Do you doubt my word?'

'Heaven forbid, madame!' replied Orthon, bowing low; then kneeling before the queen, he kissed the hem of her robe, and hastily left the room. As he went out, he observed the captain of the guards, awaiting the orders of Catherine in the ante-chamber. This did little to calm his fears. On the contrary, it increased the ill-defined but real terror under which he already laboured.

Immediately the folds of the heavy curtain which hung before the door had closed behind Orthon, Catherine darted into the chamber, where she expected to find the note. But vainly did she thrust her eager hand behind the mirror; there was no paper of any kind there. Again, she shook the solid frame, tapped the glass, looked diligently around to see if anything had fallen. Her efforts were unrewarded—no letter could she find. Yet her eyes had not deceived her: she had distinctly seen the youth approach the mirror. But doubtless the action she witnessed was to take back what he had put there—not to leave the note.

'Unhappy boy!' cried she—'what evil destiny urged you to attempt to compete with me? I would have preferred not to be your enemy, as I now must be. Ho there, M. de Nancey!'

The sonorous voice of the queen traversed the salon, and reached the anteroom, where M. de Nancey awaited her orders.

At the sound of his name, imperiously pronounced, the captain of the guards wasted not an instant in obeying the summons.

'What is your Majesty's pleasure?' said he, on entering.

'Did you see a youth—a mere boy—pass this way a moment ago?'

'I did, madame.'

'Call him back.'

'By what name shall I address him?'

'Orthon. If he refuses to return, bring him back by force. But do not alarm him, if he comes willingly. I must speak with him directly.'

The captain of the guards rushed out to obey the queen.

Orthon had scarcely got half-way downstairs, when he heard himself called, and a cold shudder seized him, for he guessed who had sent for him.

His first impulse was to run, but with an accuracy of judgement above his years, he quickly saw that flight would be certain ruin. He therefore stopped, and inquired,—

'Who calls me?'

'I do—M. de Nancey,' replied the captain of the guards, hurriedly descending the stairs.

'But I am in a very great hurry, and cannot stay,' replied Orthon.

'By order of her Majesty the queen-mother, I command you to return with me.'

The terrified boy wiped the perspiration from his brow, and followed M. de Nancey back to the apartments of Madame de Sauve.

As Orthon entered the apartment where the queen-mother was waiting, he trembled and a deathly paleness came over him. The poor boy was as yet too young to exercise a more practised control over himself.

'Your Majesty,' said he, with a palpitating heart, 'has done me the honour to recall me—may I presume to inquire for what purpose?'

'Child!' answered Catherine, with a bright and encouraging smile—'your face pleases me, and, having promised to interest myself in your welfare, I have decided to begin at once. But first tell me, can you ride?'

'Oh, yes, madame!'

'Good. Come with me, and I will give you a message to take to Saint-Germain.'*

'I am at your Majesty's command.'

'Then order a horse to be saddled, M. de Nancey.'

The captain of the guards disappeared on his errand.

'Now then, boy!' said Catherine, leading the way and motioning for Orthon to follow her.

The queen-mother went down one floor, then entered the corridor in which were situated the apartments of the Duke d'Alençon and the king, reached the winding staircase, again descended a flight of stairs, and opened a door leading to a circular gallery, of which none but the king and herself possessed the key. She told Orthon to go first, then entering after him, carefully locked the door. This gallery formed a sort of rampart round a portion of the apartments occupied by the king and queen-mother, and, like the corridor of the Castle of St. Angelo, at Rome, or that of the Pitti Palace at Florence, was intended to serve as a place of refuge in case of danger.*

With the door locked behind them, Catherine and her companion found themselves in a dark corridor. Each had advanced a few steps, the queen leading the way and the page following, when suddenly Catherine turned round, and Orthon saw on her face the same grim expression it had worn a few minutes previously. Her eyes, of the shape and colour of a cat or panther, seemed to dart forth sparks of fire.

'Stop!' she cried.

Poor Orthon felt a cold shiver pervade his frame, while the damp, chill air of that unfrequented spot seemed to hang around him like an icy mantle. The ground he trod upon seemed to re-echo with the voice of the grave. All this, combined with the fierce, probing look of Catherine and his own uneasy fears, proved too much for the page, who clung nearly paralysed to the walls of this fearful place.

'Where,' said the queen-mother, fixing on him a sharp intimidating eye, 'is the note you were ordered to give to the King of Navarre?'

'The note?' stammered Orthon.

'Ay, the note—which, if you did not find the king, you were told to place behind the mirror.'

'Indeed, madame,' said Orthon, 'I do not know what your Majesty means.'

'All I want is the note given you by M. de Mouy, about an hour since, behind the Archery Garden.'

'Your Majesty is mistaken or misinformed,' answered Orthon. 'I have no note of any kind.'

'You lie!' said Catherine. 'Give me the letter, and I will carry out the promise I made you.'

'But, madame, I have no note to give you.'

Catherine began to lose all patience. She ground her teeth with rage, then suddenly checking herself, and assuming a bland smile, she said,—

'Come, come, foolish boy, give me that useless paper, and a thousand gold crowns shall be your reward.'

'But how can I give you what I do not have? Your Majesty must believe me: I have no such note in my keeping.'

'You shall have two thousand crowns!'

'But madame, since I have nothing to give, I cannot give it.'

'*Ten* thousand crowns!'

Orthon, who, young as he was, could plainly see the rising anger of the queen, decided that the only chance remaining of preserving his master's secret was to swallow the note. With this in mind, he attempted to take it from his pocket, but the quick eye of Catherine guessed his intention and forestalled his purpose.

'There—there, child!' said she, laughing—'that will do. Your loyalty, it seems, is above all temptation. When royalty wishes to secure the services of a faithful servant, it is always wise to put his loyalty to the test. I now know what opinion to have of your zeal and faithfulness. Take this purse, as a token of my future bounty, and convey the note to your master, saying that, after to-day, I intend to take you into my service. You may now go: you can let yourself out through the door we came in by—it opens from the inside.'

So saying, Catherine placed a heavily-filled purse in the hands of the astonished youth, and then walked on a few steps, placing her hand against the wall.

'Thanks, gracious Majesty!' murmured Orthon. 'Then you are good enough to pardon me all I have done to displease you?'

'Nay, more: I reward you as a faithful bearer of *billet-doux*— a smiling messenger of love! One fault only I find with you: you are forgetting that your master is waiting for you.'

'True!' said the youth, springing towards the door.

But scarcely had he advanced two or three steps when the ground gave way beneath his feet. He stumbled, threw out his hands with a fearful cry, and disappeared into one of those horrible *oubliettes** in the Louvre of which Catherine had just released the spring.

'Now, then,' said Catherine—'thanks to this fool's obstinacy, I shall have nearly two hundred stairs to walk down!'

The Florentine then returned to her apartments, where she took a dark lantern. Returning to the gallery, she closed the spring and opened the door of a spiral staircase, which seemed as though contrived to plumb the very bowels of the earth. Proceeding down the windings of this descent, she reached a second door, which, revolving on its hinges, admitted her to the depths of the *oubliette*, where—crushed, bleeding, and broken by a fall of more than one hundred feet—lay the still palpitating body of poor Orthon. And all the while on the other side of the outer wall, the waters of the Seine could be heard flowing by, brought by a system of underground channels to lap at the foot of the staircase.

Having reached the damp and unwholesome abyss, which during her reign had witnessed numerous scenes similar to the one now enacted, Catherine proceeded to search the corpse, found the note, ascertained by the lantern that it was the one she was looking for, then, pushing the mangled body from her, she pressed a spring. The bottom of the *oubliette* sank down, and the corpse, borne by its own weight, dropped into the river.

Closing the door after her, she climbed the stairs and, returning to her closet, read the paper poor Orthon had so valiantly defended. It was conceived in these words,—

'This evening at ten o'clock, Rue de l'Arbre-Sec, *Hotel de la Belle Etoile*. If you come, no reply is needed; otherwise, send word back, *No*, by the bearer.

'DE MOUY DE SAINT-PHALE.'

As Catherine read these words, a smile of triumph curled her lip. She thought only of the victory she had won, without once considering the price that had been paid for it.

After all, what was Orthon? Merely a faithful, devoted follower; a young, a handsome, and noble-minded youth. Nothing more!

Catherine immediately returned to the apartments of Madame de Sauve, and placed the note behind the mirror. As she returned, she found the captain of the guards in the corridor, awaiting her further orders.

'Madame,' said M. de Nancey, 'according to your Majesty's orders, the horse has been saddled.'

'Ah, indeed!' said Catherine. 'We shall not need it now. Upon questioning the youth, I find he is not sufficiently intelligent to be entrusted with the message I intended to send by him. I have therefore made him a little present, and dismissed him by the side gate.'

'But,' persisted M. de Nancey, 'your Majesty's errand?'

'What errand?' asked Catherine.

'The one your Majesty proposed entrusting to this youth: will it please you that I go myself, or send one of my men to do your royal bidding?'

'No!' said Catherine, 'both you and your men, M. de Nancey, will have other work to do this evening.'

And Catherine returned to her apartments, in full hope and expectation of holding the detested King of Navarre in her power before the new day's sun had risen.

46

THE INN OF 'LA BELLE ETOILE'

Two hours after the event we have described, Madame de Sauve, having completed her attendance on the queen, entered her apartments. Henry followed her, and Dariole having informed him that Orthon had been, he went to the mirror, and took the note.

It was, as we have seen, couched in these terms,—

'This evening at ten o'clock, Rue de l'Arbre-Sec, *Hotel de la Belle Etoile*. If you come, no reply is needed; otherwise, send word back, *No*, by the bearer.

'DE MOUY DE SAINT-PHALE.'

There was no address.

'Henry is certain to go,' Catherine had thought 'for even if he did not want to, he cannot find the bearer to tell him so.'

Catherine was right: Henry inquired after Orthon. Dariole told him he had left with the queen-mother. But Henry felt no uneasiness, as he knew Orthon was incapable of betraying him.

He dined, as was his custom, at the king's table, who chaffed him upon the mistakes he had made that morning in hawking. Henry excused himself, alleging he lived among mountains, and was not used to plains. But he promised Charles to learn the noble art better.

Catherine was in excellent humour. When she rose from table, she requested Marguerite to pass the evening with her.

At eight o'clock, Henry took two of his gentlemen, went out

by the Porte Saint-Honoré, entered again by the Tour de Bois,* crossed the Seine at the Nesle ferry, rode up the Rue Saint-Jacques, and there dismissed them, as if he were going to an amorous rendezvous. At the corner of the Rue des Mathurins he found a man on horseback, enveloped in a large cloak: he approached him.

'Mantes!' said the man.

'Pau!' replied the king.

The horseman instantly dismounted. Henry donned his splashed cloak, sprang on his steed, rode down the Rue de la Harpe, crossed the Pont St-Michel, along the Rue Barthelemy, crossed the river again on the Pont aux Meuniers, descended the quays, reached the Rue de l'Arbre-Sec, and knocked at Maître la Hurière's door.

La Mole was in a little room, writing a long love-letter: to whom may be easily imagined.

Coconnas was in the kitchen, watching half a dozen partridges roasting, and arguing with La Hurière as to whether they were done or not.

At this moment Henry knocked. Gregoire went to take his horse, and the traveller entered, stamping on the floor as if to warm his feet.

'Eh!' said La Mole, continuing to write—'La Hurière, here is a gentleman for you.'

La Hurière advanced, and looked at Henry; and as his large cloak did not inspire him with much respect,—

'Who are you?' asked he.

'Eh, *sang Dieu!*' returned Henry, pointing to La Mole. 'I am, as this gentleman told you, a Gascon gentleman come to court.'

'What do you want?'

'A room and supper.'

'I do not let a room to anyone, unless he has a lackey.'

'I will pay you a rose noble for your room and supper.'

'You are very generous, worthy sir,' said La Hurière suspiciously.

'No; but expecting to sup here, I invited a friend of mine to meet me. Have you any good Arbois wine?'*

'I have as good as Henry of Navarre drinks.'

'Ah, good! Here is my friend.'

As he spoke, the door opened, and a gentleman somewhat older than the first, with a long rapier at his side, entered.

'Ah!' said he, 'you are on time, my young friend. It is something for a man who has travelled two hundred leagues to be so punctual.'

'Is this your guest?' asked La Hurière.

'Yes,' replied the first, shaking hands with the man with the rapier.

'Landlord,' said La Mole to La Hurière, 'rid us of these Huguenot fellows. Coconnas and I cannot talk properly while they are there.'

'Take the supper into No. 2, on the third floor,' said La Hurière. 'Upstairs, gentlemen.'

The two travellers followed Gregoire, who lighted their way.

Coconnas watched them until they disappeared, and then came up to La Mole.

'Did you see them?'

'I did.'

'And who are they?'

'How should I know?'

'I'd swear they are Henry of Navarre, and the man in the cherry cloak.'

'Ay, perhaps so.'

'Take it from me, there is some plot afoot.'

'Oh, no. Some love intrigue.'

'Not at all. But since I am no longer in the Duke d'Alençon's service, I do not care. Let's have supper.'

Meantime Henry and de Mouy were installed in their room.

'Well, sire,' said de Mouy, 'have you seen Orthon?'

'No; but I found his note. I suppose he was frightened, for the queen saw him. I did fear for him, for Dariole told me the queen had a long talk with him.'

'Oh, there is no danger; he is very quick-witted. I will venture to say the queen did not learn much from him.'

'Have you seen him yourself?'

'No; but he will come this evening to fetch me, armed with a good petronel. He can tell us what happened as we walk along.'

'That is right; besides, La Mole is on guard downstairs; and if anything happens, he will let us know.'

'Well! what says M. d'Alençon?'

'He will not go; he says so categorically. The departure of d'Anjou, and the king's illness, have made him change his mind.'

'Was it he who has spoilt our plan?'

'Yes.'

'Was it he who betrayed us?'

'No; but he is ready to do so at the first opportunity.'

'Coward! traitor!—why did he not answer my letters?'

'So that he would have evidence to incriminate you, and that you should have none against him. Meantime, all is lost, is it not so, de Mouy?'

'On the contrary, won. You know all the party, except de Condé's faction, were for you, and regarded d'Alençon as a second choice. Since the day of the ceremony I have arranged everything. I shall have fifteen hundred horse ready in a week; they will be posted on the road to Pau; they will surely be enough?'

Henry smiled, and laid his hand on his friend's shoulder.

'De Mouy,' said he, 'you, and you alone, know the King of Navarre is not such a coward as men think.'

'I know it, sire, and I trust that soon all France will know it too. When are you due to hunt again?'

'In a week or ten days.'

'Well, everything seems quiet now. No one thinks of the Duke d'Anjou; the king gets better every day; the persecution against us has ceased.* Play along with the queen-mother and M. d'Alençon; tell the duke you cannot leave without him, and try and make him believe you.'

'Oh, he shall believe me!'

'Has he such confidence in you?'

'Not in me, but in the queen.'

'And is the queen loyal to us?'

'I have ample proofs of it. Besides she is ambitious.'

'Well, three days before the hunt, tell me where it will be—at Bondy, Saint-Germain, or Rambouillet.* When you see La Mole spur on—follow him; once out of the forest, they will need to have the fastest horses if they want to catch us.'

'Agreed.'

'Have you any money, sire?'

Henry made the same grimace he made all his life at the same question.

'Not much,' said he, 'but I believe Margot has.'

'Well, bring all you can with you. Orthon tells me he saw that scoundrel Maurevel, whom René has cured, walking about the Arsenal.'

'Ah, I understand.'

'You will be king some day, and will avenge yourself as a king; I am a soldier, and avenge myself as soldiers do. When all my affairs are settled, which will be in five or six days, I will walk round the Arsenal myself, and, after giving him two or three rapier thrusts, I shall leave Paris.'

'Do as you will. Ah! what do you think of La Mole?'

'A charming fellow—brave and loyal.'

'And discreet. He must be with us, and then I must think of his reward.'

As Henry pronounced these words, the door flew open, and La Mole rushed in.

'Quick!' cried he, 'the house is surrounded.'

'Surrounded!' said Henry, 'by whom?'

'By the king's guards.'

'Oh,' said de Mouy, drawing two pistols from his belt, 'to battle then!'

'What can you do against fifty men?' said La Mole.

'He is right,' said the king, 'and if there were any means of retreat——'

'I know one,' said La Mole, 'if your Majesty will follow me.'

'And de Mouy——'

'Can follow us; but you must hurry.'

Steps were heard on the stairs.

'It is too late,' said Henry.

'If you could keep them busy for five minutes,' said La Mole, 'I could save the king.'

'I will do plenty to occupy them,' said de Mouy.

'But what will you do?'

'Oh, do not fear for me!'

And de Mouy rapidly cleared away the king's plate, goblet, and napkin, so that it might seem he had supped alone.

'Come, sire—come!' cried La Mole.

'My brave de Mouy,' said Henry.

De Mouy seized his hand, kissed it, pushed the door shut the instant they were outside, and bolted it behind them.

'Quick—quick, sire!' said La Mole, 'they are on the stairs!'

At this moment torches were visible on the stairs, and the rattling of arms was heard.

La Mole guided the king in the darkness, and, leading him two storeys higher, opened a door, which he then secured, and opening the window,—

'Does your Majesty fear a stroll on the roofs?' said he.

'You are talking to a chamois hunter!'

'Follow me, and I will guide you.'

And, getting out of the window, La Mole clambered along the ridge, then passed along a valley formed by two roofs, at the end of which was the open window of a garret.

'Here we are,' said La Mole.

'So much the better,' returned Henry, wiping the perspiration from his brow.

'Now, then,' continued La Mole, 'this garret communicates with a staircase, and the staircase with the street. I travelled this same route on a more terrible night than this.'

'Go on—go on!'

La Mole sprang into the open window, opened the door, and, putting Henry's hand on the rope that served as a baluster,—

'Come, sire,' said he.

Henry stopped before a window opposite the *Belle Etoile*. The stairs were crowded with armed soldiers, bearing torches. Suddenly, the king saw a group descend the stairs, with de Mouy in its midst; he had surrendered his sword, and was going quietly.

'Brave de Mouy!' said the king.

'*Ma foi!* sire, he seems very composed, and even laughs. He has some plan, for he seldom smiles.'

'All is well, then,' replied Henry. 'Let us go back to the Louvre.'

'Nothing easier. Wrap yourself in your cloak, for the street is full of people, and we shall pass for spectators.'

They had both gained the Rue d'Averon, but in passing by the

Rue des Poulies, they saw de Mouy and his escort cross the Place Saint-Germain-l'Auxerrois.

'Ah!' said Henry, 'they are taking him to the Louvre. *Diable!* the gate will be closed. They will take the name of everyone who enters, and I shall be suspected of having been with him.'

'Well, sire,' replied La Mole, 'there's the Queen of Navarre's window.'

'*Mon Dieu!* I did not think of that. But how shall I attract her attention?'

'Oh!' said La Mole, bowing with an air of respectful gratitude, 'your Majesty throws stones so well.'

47

DE MOUY DE SAINT-PHALE

THIS time Catherine had taken her precautions so well that she believed herself sure of her prey.

Consequently, about ten o'clock, she had sent Marguerite away, quite convinced that the Queen of Navarre was ignorant of the plot against her husband, and went to the king.

Puzzled by the air of triumph which, in spite of her habitual dissimulation, was writ large on his mother's face, Charles questioned Catherine who only said,—

'I can make but one reply to your Majesty, and that is, you will this evening be delivered from two of your bitterest enemies.'

Charles frowned, like a man who says to himself: 'This is well—we shall see,' and whistled to his tall boar-hound, who came to him, dragging his belly along the ground like a snake, and sat with his fine and intelligent head on his master's knee.

After a few minutes, which Catherine passed with her eyes fixed and ear attentive, there came the sudden noise of a pistol-shot in the court-yard of the Louvre.

'What noise is that?' inquired Charles, with a frown, while the hound stood up and pricked his ears.

'Nothing,' Catherine replied, 'it was only a signal.'

'And what is the meaning of that signal?'

'It means that, from this moment, sire, your only, your real enemy is no longer able to injure you.'

'Has someone been killed?' inquired Charles, looking at his mother with that eye of authority which signified that murder and mercy are two inherent attributes of royal power.

'No, sire, they have merely arrested two men.'

'Oh,' murmured Charles, 'always hidden plots and conspiracies against the king. *Mort diable!* mother, I am not a boy, I am big enough to take care of myself, and want neither apron-strings nor swaddling-clothes. Go to Poland with your son Henry, if you want to reign. But here you are wrong, I tell you, to play the game you do.'

'My son,' replied Catherine, 'this is the last time I shall meddle with your affairs. But the enterprise was begun long ago. You have always said I was wrong, while I have laboured to prove I was right.'

At this moment M. de Nancey begged an audience of the king. There was a noise of footsteps in the vestibule, and the butts of muskets clattered on the floor.

'Let M. de Nancey enter,' said the king quickly.

M. de Nancey appeared, saluted the king, and then, turning to the queen-mother, said,—

'Madame, your orders are executed—he has been arrested.'

'What do you mean by *he?*' cried Catherine, much troubled; 'have you only arrested one man?'

'He was alone, madame.'

'Did he defend himself?'

'No, he was supping quietly in a room, and handed over his sword the moment he was asked.'

'Who is he?' asked the king.

'You will see,' said Catherine. 'Bring in the prisoner, M. de Nancey.'

De Mouy was introduced.

'De Mouy!' exclaimed the king. 'What is it now?'

'If, sire,' said de Mouy, with perfect composure, 'your Majesty would allow me that liberty, I would ask the same question.'

'Instead of asking the king questions,' said Catherine, 'be so good, M. de Mouy, to tell my son who was the man in the apartment of the King of Navarre, on a certain night, and who, on that night, resisted the king's orders, like the rebel that he is, killed two of the guards, and wounded M. de Maurevel.'

'Yes,' said Charles, frowning, 'do you know the name of that man, M. de Mouy?'

'I do, sire. Does your Majesty wish to know it?'

'Yes, it would give me pleasure.'

'Well, sire, he is called de Mouy de Saint-Phale.'

'It was you, then?'

'It was, sire.'

Catherine, astonished at this audacity, recoiled before the young man.

'What!' inquired Charles IX, 'you dared resist the orders of the king?'

'In the first place, sire, I was ignorant that there was any order from your Majesty. I saw only one thing, or rather but one man, M. de Maurevel, the assassin of my father, the assailant of the admiral. I remembered that a year and a half ago,* in the very room where we are now, on the evening of the 24th of August, your Majesty promised me to let us have justice against this murderer, and as since that time very grave events have occurred, I thought that perhaps the king had been, in spite of himself, turned away from his desires. Seeing Maurevel within my reach, I believed Heaven had sent him there. Your Majesty knows the rest, sire. I struck him down as a murderer, and fired at his men as robbers.'

Charles made no reply. His friendship for Henry had made him see many things from another point of view than he had at first seen them.*

The queen-mother, at this reference to Saint Bartholomew, had noted certain reactions of her son which very much resembled remorse.*

'But,' observed the queen-mother, 'what were you doing at that hour in the King of Navarre's apartments?'

'Oh,' said de Mouy, 'it is a long story, but if his Majesty has the patience to listen——'

'Yes,' replied Charles, 'I want to hear it.'

'I will obey, sire,' said de Mouy, bowing.

Catherine sat down, fixing an uneasy look on the young chief.

'We will listen,' said Charles. 'Here, Actæon!'

The dog resumed the place he had occupied before the prisoner had come in.

'Sire,' said de Mouy, 'I came to his majesty the King of Navarre as the representative of our brethren, your faithful subjects of the reformed religion——'

Catherine made a sign to Charles IX.

'Be quiet, madame,' he said; 'I do not want to miss a word. Go on, M. de Mouy—go on.'

'To inform the King of Navarre,' continued de Mouy, 'that his abjuration had lost for him the confidence of the Huguenot party, but that, nevertheless, in remembrance of his father, Antony de Bourbon, and especially out of regard for the memory of his mother, the courageous Jeanne d'Albret, whose name is dear amongst us, the leaders of the reformed religion considered it a mark of deference due to him, to beg him to desist in his claims to the crown of Navarre.'

'What did he say?' asked Catherine, unable, in spite of her self-control, to take this unexpected blow without wincing a little.

'Ah!' said Charles, 'but this crown of Navarre which, without my permission, was made thus to jump from head to head, seems to belong in some measure to me.'

'The Huguenots, sire, recognize better than anyone the principle of sovereignty, which your Majesty has just enunciated, and therefore hope to induce your Majesty to place the crown on a head which is dear to you.'

'I!' said Charles; 'on a head which is dear to me!—*mort diable!* of whose head, then, do you speak, sir? I do not understand you.'

'The head of the Duke d'Alençon.'*

Catherine turned as pale as death, and her eyes glared fiercely at de Mouy.

'And did my brother d'Alençon know this?'

'Yes, sire.'

'And accepted the crown?'

'Subject to your Majesty's consent, to which he referred us.'

'Ah!' said Charles, 'it is, indeed, a crown which would suit our brother d'Alençon wonderfully well! And it never occurred to me! Thanks, de Mouy—thanks! when you have such ideas you will always be welcome at the palace.'

'Sire, you would long since have been informed of all this, but for the unfortunate little business in the Louvre, which made me fear that I had fallen into disgrace with your Majesty.'

'Yes; but,' asked Catherine, 'what did the King of Navarre say to this proposal?'

'The king, madame, agreed to the wishes of his brethren, and his renunciation was ready.'

'In this case,' cried Catherine, 'you must have that renunciation.'

'I have, madame,' said de Mouy. 'As it happens I have it with me, signed by him and dated.'

'And dated before your encounter with Maurevel?' inquired Catherine.

'Yes, the previous evening, I think.'

And de Mouy drew from his pocket a renunciation in favour of the Duke d'Alençon, written and signed in Henry's hand, and bearing the date assigned to it.

'*Ma foi!* yes,' said Charles, 'and it is quite in order.'

'And what did Henry ask in return for this renunciation?'

'Nothing, madame. The friendship of King Charles, he said to us, would amply repay him for the loss of a crown.'

Catherine bit her lips in anger, and wrung her beautiful hands.

'This is all entirely above board, de Mouy,' added the king.

'But,' asked the queen-mother, 'if everything was settled between you and the King of Navarre, why did you seek an interview with him this evening?'

'I, madame!—with the King of Navarre?' said de Mouy. 'The officer who arrested me will bear witness that I was alone. Will your Majesty call him?'

'M. de Nancey?' said the king, and the captain of the guards entered.

'M. de Nancey,' said Catherine quickly, 'was M. de Mouy alone at the inn of the *Belle Etoile*?'

'In his room, yes, madame: in the inn, no.'

'Ah!' said Catherine, 'who was his companion?'

'I do not know if he was the companion of M. de Mouy,

madame. But I know he escaped by a back door, after having flattened two of my guards.'

'And you recognized this gentleman, no doubt?'

'I did not, but the guards did.'

'And who was he?' inquired Charles IX.

'Count Annibal de Coconnas.'

'Annibal de Coconnas!' repeated the king, gloomy and reflective. 'The same man who made so terrible a slaughter of the Huguenots on St Bartholomew's Night?'

'M. de Coconnas, a gentleman in the service of the Duke d'Alençon,' replied de Nancey.

'Good! good!' said Charles. 'You may withdraw, M. de Nancey. But next time, remember one thing.'

'What is that, sire?'

'That you are in my service, and will take your orders from no one but myself.'

M. de Nancey retired backwards, bowing most respectfully.

De Mouy smiled ironically at Catherine.

There was a brief silence. The queen played with the tassels of her girdle; Charles stroked his dog.

'But what was your intention, sir?' continued Charles. 'Were you acting violently?'

'Against whom, sire?'

'Against Henry, or François, or myself.'

'Sire, we had the renunciation of your brother-in-law, the consent of your brother, and, as I had the honour to tell you, we were on the point of asking for your Majesty's authority, when there happened the unfortunate affair with M. de Maurevel.'

'Well, mother, I see nothing to object to in all this. You were perfectly right, M. de Mouy, in requiring a king. Yes, Navarre may be, and ought to be, a separate kingdom. Moreover, this kingdom seems made for my brother d'Alençon, who has always had so great a thirst for a crown that when we wear our own, he cannot take his eyes off it. The only thing which opposed his coronation was Harry's rights. But since Harry voluntarily abdicates——'

'Voluntarily, sire.'

'It appears to be the will of God! M. de Mouy, you are free to return to your brethren, whom I have chastised with excessive zeal, perhaps. But that is between God and myself. Tell them that, since they want my brother, the Duke d'Alençon, as King of Navarre, the King of France grants their wishes. From this moment, Navarre is a kingdom, and its sovereign's name is François. I ask only one week for my brother to be ready to leave Paris with the pomp and circumstance which appertain to a king. Go, M. de Mouy—go. M. de Nancey, allow M. de Mouy to leave. He is free.'

'Sire,' said de Mouy, advancing a step, 'will your Majesty allow me——'

'Yes,' replied Charles.

And he extended his hand to the young Huguenot.

De Mouy went on one knee, and respectfully kissed the king's hand.

'By the bye,' said Charles, as de Mouy was about to rise, 'did you not ask me for justice against that ruffian Maurevel?'

'I did, sire.'

'I do not know where he is so that I might oblige you, for he is in hiding. But if you meet him, take justice into your own hands. I authorize you to do so, and with all my heart.'

'Oh, sire!' exclaimed de Mouy, 'this is all I could ask. I do not know where he is, but your Majesty may rest assured that I will find him.'

De Mouy respectfully saluted the king and Catherine, and then withdrew unimpeded. He made all haste to the *Belle Etoile* where he found his horse, by whose aid, three hours after leaving Paris, the young man breathed in safety behind the walls of Mantes.

Catherine, bursting with rage, returned to her quarters and then called on Marguerite in her apartments, where she found Henry in his dressing gown, as if just going to bed.

'Satan!' she muttered, 'help a poor queen, for whom God will do nothing more!'

'ASK M. d'Alençon to come to me,' said Charles, as his mother left him.

M. de Nancey hurried to M. d'Alençon's apartments, and delivered the king's message. The duke started when he heard it. He always trembled in Charles's presence, and the more so when he had reason to be afraid. Still, he went to his brother with all speed.

Charles was standing, and whistling a hunting air.

As he entered, the Duke d'Alençon caught from the glassy eye of Charles one of those looks full of hatred which he so well understood.

'Your Majesty sent for me,' he said. 'I am here, sire. What is your Majesty's desire?'

'I desire to tell you, brother, that, in order to reward you for the great friendship you bear me, I have resolved to do for you to-day the thing you most desire in all the world.'

'For me?'

'Yes, for you. Ask yourself what it is you dream of most but dare not ask for, and that thing I will give you.'

'Sire,' said François, 'I swear to you that there is nothing I want more than the continuance of the king's good health.'

'Then you will be deeply gratified to know, d'Alençon, that the indisposition I experienced at the time when the Poles arrived has quite worn of. Thanks to Harry, I escaped a furious wild boar, who would have ripped me to pieces. In short I am so well as not to envy the healthiest man in my dominions. And so, without being an unkind brother, you may wish for something else besides the continuation of my health, which is perfectly restored.

'I desire nothing else, sire.'

'Yes you do, François,' continued Charles impatiently, 'you want the crown of Navarre, and have had an understanding to that effect with Harry and de Mouy: the first that he would abdicate, and the second, that he would offer it to you. Well, Harry has surrendered his rights, de Mouy has mentioned your wishes to me, and the crown you are ambitious to——'

'Stop!' said d'Alençon, in a trembling voice.

'Well, *mort diable!* it is yours.'

D'Alençon turned ghastly pale, and then his face went red. The favour which the king had granted him threw him into utter despair.

'But, sire,' he replied, quivering with emotion, and in vain trying to recover his self-possession, 'I never wanted, and certainly never sought such a thing.'

'That is possible,' said the king, 'for you are very discreet, brother. But it has been wanted and sought for you.'

'Sire, I swear to you that I never——'

'Do not swear.'

'But, sire, do you intend to exile me?'

'Do you call this exile, François? *Peste!* you are hard to please. What better could you hope for?'

D'Alençon bit his lips in despair.

'*Ma foi!*' continued Charles, affecting a kindlier manner, 'I did not think you were so popular, François, and particularly with the Huguenots. Why, they really petition for you; and what more could I want for them than a person devoted to me: a brother I love who is incapable of betraying me, at the head of a party which for thirty years has been in arms against us. This will bring peace as if by magic, to say nothing of the fact that we shall all be kings in the family. There will only be poor Harry, who will continue to be my friend, but nothing more. But he is not ambitious, and this title of Friend, which no one else covets, he claims.'

'Oh, sire, you are mistaken. I covet that title—a title to which no one has as much right as I have. Henry is only your brother by marriage; I am your brother by blood and in heart, and I beg you, sire, keep me near you.'

'No, no, François,' replied Charles, 'it would be wrong.'

'Why, sire?'

'For a thousand reasons.'

'But, sire, have you a more faithful companion than I? From childhood I have never left your Majesty's side.'

'I know it well—and sometimes I have wished you farther off.'

'What does your Majesty mean?'

'Oh, nothing—nothing. Ah! what glorious hunting you will have there, François—I shall envy you! Do you know they hunt bears in the mountains there as we do boars here. You'll send us all such splendid skins. There they hunt with knives—wait for the animal, excite and anger him: he goes for the hunter, and four paces off he rises on his hind legs; then they plunge the steel into his heart, as Henry did the wild boar at our last hunt. You know it is dangerous work. But you are brave, François, and the danger would be real pleasure to you.'

'Ah! your Majesty increases my misgivings, for I shall not be able to hunt with you any more.'

'*Corbœuf!* so much the better,' said the king, 'it does not suit either of us to hunt together——'

'What does your Majesty mean?'

'To hunt with me gives you such pleasure and stirs in you so much emotion, that you—who are skill personified, who with any arquebuse can bring down a magpie at a hundred paces—with a weapon of which you are such a perfect master, failed at twenty paces to hit a wild boar and broke the leg of my best horse! *Mort diable!* François, that gives a man food for thought, you know!'

'Oh, sire, think of my feelings,' said d'Alençon, livid with agitation.

'Yes,' replied Charles, 'I can guess what they might be, which is why I say, François, it is best for us to hunt at a distance from each other, for fear of such feelings. You might, you know, if you felt differently, kill the horseman instead of the horse—the king instead of the animal! When Montgomery killed our father Henry II by accident—feelings, perhaps—the blow placed our brother François II on the throne, and sent our father Henry to Saint-Denis.* A little of that sort of thing can do so much.'

The duke felt the perspiration pour down his brow at this unexpected attack.

The king had guessed everything, and veiling his anger under a jesting tone, was perhaps more terrible than if he had released his lava of hate in its fullest wrath; his revenge was proportioned to his rancour. As the one was sharpened, the other increased, and, for the first time, d'Alençon felt remorse or rather regret, for having meditated a crime that had not succeeded.*

He had kept up the struggle as long as he could, but at this last blow he bowed his head.

Charles fixed on him his vulture gaze, and watched closely every emotion that flitted across the young duke's face, as if reading an open book.

'Brother,' said the king, 'we have made our decision—that decision is immutable. You will go.'

D'Alençon started, but Charles did not appear to notice, and continued—'I wish Navarre to be proud of having at its head a brother of the king of France. Gold, power, honour—you will have all that belongs to your birth, as your brother Henry had. And, like him,' he added, with a smile, 'you will bless me when you are far away—thank Heaven, blessings know no distance!'

'Sire——'

'Accept, or rather resign yourself. Once you are a king, we shall find for you a wife worthy of a son of France, who may—who knows?—bring you another throne.'

'But,' observed the Duke d'Alençon, 'your Majesty has forgotten your good friend Henry.'

'Henry!—why I told you he does not desire the throne of Navarre; he has given up all claim to it. Henry is a jovial fellow, and not a pale-face like you. He likes to enjoy himself and laugh and not weary himself as we are compelled to do, who wear crowns upon our heads.'

'Your Majesty then would like me to occupy myself——'

'By no means. Do not bother your head with any of this business. I will arrange everything myself. Do not say a word to anyone, I will spread the good news. François, good-day.'

There was no reply. The duke bowed and left the apartment, with rage in his heart.

He was very anxious to find Henry and discuss with him everything that had happened. But he could only find Catherine, for Henry had decided to avoid him.

The duke, seeing Catherine, endeavoured to swallow his griefs and tried to smile.

'Well, madame,' he said, 'have you heard the great news?'

'I know that there is an idea of making a king of you, sir.'

'It is a great kindness on the part of my brother, madame, and I am inclined to think that a portion of my gratitude is due to you. Yet I confess that it gives me pain to usurp the King of Navarre like this.'

'You are very fond of Harry, then, my son, it seems.'

'Why, yes, for some time we have been closely allied.'

'Do you suppose that he loves you as much as you love him?'

'I hope so, madame.'

'Can there be brothers, then, amongst kings?' she asked, with a strange smile.

'Oh, we were neither of us kings when our alliance began.'

'Yes, but things have changed. Who can say that you will not both be kings?'

Catherine saw, by the start and sudden colour of the duke, that the shaft had hit the mark.

'Harry? A king? and of what kingdom?'

'The most glorious in Christendom, my son.'

'Ah!' said d'Alençon, growing very pale, 'what do you mean?'

'What a good mother should say to a son—what you have thought of more than once, François.'

'I?' said the duke, 'I have thought of nothing, madame, I swear it!'

'I believe you, for your friend, your brother Henry, as you call him, is, beneath his straightforward manner, a very clever and wily person, who keeps his secrets better than you do yours, François. For instance, did he ever tell you that de Mouy was his right hand?'

And Catherine looked at François, as though trying to read his very heart. But dissimulation was François's forte, and he bore her gaze unshrinkingly.

'De Mouy!' said he, with surprise, and as if he was saying the name for the first time.

'Yes, the Huguenot de Mouy de Saint-Phale, who nearly killed Maurevel, and is intriguing and raising an army to support your brother Henry against your family.'

Catherine, unaware that François knew as much on this matter as herself, stood up at these words, and would have sailed majestically out of the room, but François detained her.

'Mother,' he said, 'another word, if you please. How can

Henry, with the small resources at his command, carry on any sort of war which would threaten my family?'

'Child,' said the queen, smiling, 'he is supported by more than thirty thousand men* who, the day he says the word, will appear as suddenly as if they sprang forth from the ground. These thirty thousand men are Huguenots, remember, in other words, the bravest soldiers in the world. Moreover, he has a protector you have not been able, or have not chosen, to win over.'

'Who is that?'

'He has the king,—the king, who loves and encourages him, the king, who, from jealousy against your brother of Poland, and from spite against you, seeks a successor outside his family.'*

'The king! Do you think so, mother?'

'Have you not seen how he loves Harry, his dear Harry?'

'Yes, madame—yes.'

'And how he is repaid in return! For this same Harry, forgetting how his brother-in-law would have shot him on Saint Bartholomew's Day, grovels on the ground like a dog, and licks the hand which beat him.'

'Yes,' said François 'Henry is very humble with my brother Charles. And because the king is always chiding him about his ignorance, he has begun to study hawking. Only yesterday he asked me if I had some books on that sport.'

'Well,' said Catherine, 'well, and what did you say?'

'That I would look in my library.'

'Good, good!' answered Catherine. 'He must have that book. I will give him one in your name. Will you, d'Alençon, obey me blindly in all I ask you to do with regard to Henry, who does not love you, whatever you may think?'

D'Alençon smiled, and replied, 'I will, mother.'

'Well, then, on the morning of the next hunt come here for the book. I will give it you, and you shall take it to the detested Henry.'

'And——?'

'Leave the rest to Providence or chance.'

François bowed in acquiescence, and left his mother's chamber.

Meantime, through La Mole, Marguerite received a letter from de Mouy, addressed to the King of Navarre. Since in politics the two illustrious allies had no secrets, she opened the missive, and read it. Then going quickly and silently along the secret passage, she went into the King of Navarre's antechamber which was no longer guarded since Orthon's disappearance. This circumstance had greatly disquieted Henry, who was convinced the poor boy had fallen victim to some machination of the queen-mother.

Anyone else but Henry would have kept silence. But Henry calculated cleverly, and saw that silence would betray him. So he sought and inquired for Orthon everywhere, even in the presence of the king and the queen-mother, and of everyone, down to the sentinel at the main gate of the Louvre. But every inquiry was in vain.

The antechamber was thus empty, for Henry had said he would not replace him until he knew for certain that he had disappeared for ever.

Henry turned round as the queen entered.

'You, madame!' he cried.

'Yes,' replied Marguerite; 'read this!' and she handed the open letter to him.

It contained these lines,—

'SIRE,—The moment has arrived for putting our plan of flight into execution.

'In five or six days there will be hawking on the banks of the Seine, from Saint-Germain to Maisons,* through the forest.

'Go to this meeting, although it is only a hawking party: wear a good coat of mail under your doublet, have your best sword by your side, and ride the fastest horse in your stable.

'About noon, when the sport is at its height, and the king is galloping after his falcon, get away alone, if you come alone: with the queen, if her Majesty is with you.

'Fifty of our party will be concealed in the pavilion of François I.* We have the key. No one will know that they are there, for they will come at night and the shutters will be closed.

'You will approach by the Allée des Violettes, at the end of which I shall be keeping watch for you. On the right will be la Mole and Coconnas, with two horses intended to replace yours in case they are fatigued.

'Farewell, sire! be ready, as we shall be.'

'Now then, sire,' said Marguerite, 'be a hero. All you have to do is follow the route indicated, and create for me a glorious throne,' said the daughter of Henry II.

An imperceptible smile rose to the thin lips of the Béarnais, as he kissed Marguerite's lips, and went out to explore the passage, humming the refrain of an old song,—

> *Cil qui mieux battit la muraille*
> *N'entra point dedans le chasteau.**

It was as well that he did so, for, as he opened his bedroom door, the Duke d'Alençon opened that of his antechamber. Henry motioned to Marguerite with his hand, and then said aloud,—

'Ah, is it you, brother?—welcome!'

The queen understood her husband's meaning, and slipped quickly into a dressing-closet, the door of which was concealed by a thick tapestry.

D'Alençon entered cautiously, looking around him.

'Are we alone, brother?' he asked, in an undertone.

'Quite. But what is the matter with you?—you seem greatly disturbed.'

'We have been betrayed, Henry!'

'Betrayed?'

'De Mouy has been arrested!'

'I know.'

'De Mouy has told the king everything!'

'What did he say?'

'He said I was ambitious for the throne of Navarre, and had conspired to obtain it.'

'The blockhead!' said Henry. 'So, you are compromised, dear brother! But why are you not under arrest?'

'I do not know. The king jested with me and offered me the throne of Navarre, but I said nothing.'

'And you did well, *ventre-saint-gris!*' said the Béarnais. 'Stand firm, for our lives depend on it.'

'Yes,' said François, 'our position is difficult, and that is why I came to ask your advice, brother. Should I get out or stay?'

'You have seen the king, and he has spoken to you?'

'Yes.'

'Well, you must have read his thoughts: act accordingly.'

'I would rather stay,' said François.

Master of himself as he was, Henry allowed a movement of relief to escape him, and François observed it.

'Remain, then,' said Henry.

'And you?'

'Why, if you stay I have no motive for going. I will go if you go, but I shall stay if you stay.'

'So, then,' said d'Alençon, 'there is an end of all our plans, and you give up at the first obstacle.'

'Thanks to my contented disposition,' replied Henry, 'I am happy anywhere and everywhere.'

'Well, then,' observed d'Alençon, 'there's no more to be said. But if you change your mind, let me know.'

'*Corbleu!* I shall be sure to do that,' replied Henry. 'Have we not agreed to have no secrets from one another?'

D'Alençon said no more, and withdrew pensively, for he believed he had seen the tapestry move at one point. Scarcely had d'Alençon gone than Marguerite reappeared.

'What do you think of this visit?' inquired Henry.

'That something new and important has happened. What it is, I will find out.'

'In the meanwhile——?'

'In the meanwhile, do not fail to come to my apartments to-morrow evening.'

'I will not fail, be assured, madame,' Henry replied, and he kissed his wife's hand gallantly.

With the same precaution she had used in coming, Marguerite returned to her own apartments.

49

THE BOOK OF VENERIE*

FIVE days had elapsed since the events we have related. The Louvre clock had just struck four when d'Alençon, who with the rest of the court had risen early to prepare for the hunt, entered his mother's apartment.

The queen was not there, but she had left orders that if her son came he was to wait.

After a few minutes she emerged from a cabinet where she carried on her alchemical studies and where no one else ever set foot.

As she opened the door, a strong odour of some acrid perfume pervaded the room, and looking through the door of the cabinet he perceived a thick white vapour, like that of some aromatic substance, floating in the air.

'Yes,' said Catherine, 'I have been burning some old parchments, and their smell was so offensive that I added some juniper to the brazier.'

D'Alençon bowed.

'Well,' continued the queen, concealing beneath the sleeves of her *robe-de-chambre* her hands which were stained with large reddish spots—'anything new?'

'Nothing.'

'Have you seen Henry?'

'Yes.'

'Will he go?'

'He refuses categorically.'

'The knave!'

'What do you think, madame?'

'That he will go.'

'You think so?'

'I am sure of it.'

'Then he will escape us?'

'Yes,' said Catherine.

'And you will allow him to go?'

'I not only will allow him, but, I tell you, he must leave the court.'

'I do not understand you.'

'Listen. A skilful physician, the same who gave me the book of venerie you are about to present to the King of Navarre, has told me that Henry is on the point of being attacked by consumption—an incurable disease. If he is doomed to die, it is better that he should die away from us than at the court.'

'That would be too painful for us.'

'Especially for Charles. Whereas, if Henry dies after betraying him, the king will look upon his death as a punishment from Heaven.'

'You are right: it is better if he leaves. But are you sure he will go?'

'All my measures are taken. The place of rendezvous is in the forest of Saint-Germain. Fifty Huguenots are to escort him to Fontainebleau, where five hundred others will be waiting for him.'

'And will Margot accompany him?' asked d'Alençon.

'Yes. But upon Henry's death she will return to court.'

'Are you sure that Henry will die?'

'The physician who gave me this book assured me of it.'

'And where is this book?'

Catherine entered her cabinet, and returned instantly with the book in her hand.

'Here it is,' said she.

D'Alençon looked at it, not without a certain feeling of terror.

'What is this book?' asked he, shuddering.

'I have already told you. It is a treatise on the art of rearing and training falcons, goshawks, and gerfalcons, written for the Italian prince Castruccio Castracani, of Lucca.'*

'What am I to do with it?'

'Give it to Henry, who asked you for a book on this subject. As he is going hawking this morning with the king, he will not fail to read it; but be sure to give it to him.'

'Oh, I don't dare!' said d'Alençon, shuddering.

'Why not?' replied the queen. 'It is a book like any other, except it has lain unopened for so long that the leaves stick together. Do not attempt to read it yourself, for it can only be read by wetting the finger and turning over each leaf separately, which is a great waste of time.'*

'So that it will only be read by a man who is anxious to learn the art of hawking?'

'Exactly so, my son—you understand?'

'Oh,' said d'Alençon, 'I hear Henry in the courtyard. Give it to me, and I will go in his absence and leave it in his room.'

'I had rather you gave it to him personally; it is more certain.'

'I have already told you, I dare not.'

'At least put it where it can be easily seen.'

'I will put it where he cannot fail to see it. Would it be better to open it?'

'Yes, open it.'

'Give me it, then.'

D'Alençon took with a trembling hand the book Catherine held out to him.

'Take it,' said she. 'There is no danger. In any case, you have your gloves on.'

D'Alençon, still looking frightened, wrapped the book in his cloak.

'Hurry,' continued the queen, 'I expect Henry will be back any moment.'

'Madame, I am going.'

And the duke left the apartment, trembling with emotion.

We have often introduced our readers into the apartments of the King of Navarre, and have made them witnesses of the events that have passed there, but never did the walls of the room see a face so pale as the Duke d'Alençon's, when he entered the apartment, with the book in his hand.

On the wall hung Henry's sword. Some links of mail were scattered on the floor, a well–filled purse and a dagger lay on the table, and there were smouldering ashes in the grate. These signs showed d'Alençon that Henry had put on a coat of mail, collected what money he could, and burnt all papers that might compromise him.

'My mother was right,' thought d'Alençon. 'He intends to betray me.'*

Doubtless, this conviction gave him strength, for, after having sounded the walls and raised the tapestry, he took the book from under his cloak, placed it on the table, then, with a hesitation that betrayed his fears, opened the book at an engraving.

The instant he had done so, he drew off his glove and cast it into the fire: the leather crackled, burned, and was soon reduced to ashes.

D'Alençon waited until he had seen it consumed, and then hastily returned to his own apartment.

As he entered, he heard steps on the winding stair, and, being convinced that it was Henry, he closed his door.

Then he looked out of his window into the courtyard below. Henry was not there, and this strengthened François's belief that it was he whom he had just heard.

The duke sat down, and picked up a book: it was *The History of France*, a work dedicated to Charles IX.*

But the duke could not fix his attention on it: it seemed to him he could see through the walls. His eyes appeared to see clear into Henry's apartment, in spite of the obstacles that separated them.

In order to drive away the terrible sight before his mind's eye, the duke vainly looked at his weapons, his ornaments, his books; every detail of the engraving that he had seen but for a moment was clear in his mind's eye: it was a gentleman on horseback, recalling his falcon, in a flat landscape.

Then it was not the book he saw, but the King of Navarre reading it, and wetting his thumb in order to turn the pages. At this sight, unreal and imaginary as it was, d'Alençon staggered against a table, and covered his eyes with his hands, as if to hide the horrible vision.

Suddenly d'Alençon saw Henry in the courtyard. He stopped a moment to speak to the men who were loading two mules, ostensibly with his provisions for the hunt, but really with the money and other things he wished to take with him. Then having given his orders, he advanced towards the door.

D'Alençon stood motionless: it was not Henry, then, he had heard mount the stairs. He opened his door and listened; this time there was no mistake—it was Henry. D'Alençon recognized his step, even to the peculiar jingle of his spurs.

Henry's door opened, and then closed.

'*Bon!*' said d'Alençon, 'he has gone through the first apartment, he has entered his bedroom, he has looked to see if his sword, his purse, and his dagger are there. Now he sees the book open on the table. "What is this book?" he asks himself; "where has it come from? who brought it?" Then seeing the engraving, he tries to read it, and turns over the leaves.'

François broke into a cold sweat.

'Will he call for help?' said he. 'Is the poison sudden? No! for my mother said he would die of consumption.'

Ten minutes passed in these horrible reflections. D'Alençon could stand it no longer. He stood up, and passed through into his antechamber which was already filled with gentlemen.

'Good-day, gentlemen,' said he. 'I am going to the king.'

And to distract attention, to prepare an alibi, perhaps, d'Alençon went down to his brother's apartments. Why, he knew not—what had he to say?

Nothing! it was not Charles he wanted to see but Henry he was avoiding.

François walked through the salon and the bedroom, without meeting anyone. He thought Charles might be in his armoury, and he opened the door.

Charles was sitting at a table in an arm-chair of carved oak; his back was turned to the door through which François had entered.

The duke approached silently.

Charles was reading.

'*Pardieu!*' cried the king, 'what an admirable book!—I did not think there was such a work in France.'

D'Alençon listened.

'Devil take these damned pages!' said Charles, wetting his thumb as he turned them.

'It is as if they have been deliberately stuck together, to conceal the marvels they contain.'

D'Alençon bounded forward.

The book Charles was reading was the one that d'Alençon had left in Henry's room.

A cry burst from his lips.

'Ah, it is you, d'Alençon!' said the king, 'you are just in time to see the most admirable work on venerie in the world.'

D'Alençon's first thought was to snatch the book from his brother, but an infernal idea restrained him.

'Sire,' asked he, 'how did this book come into your possession?'

'Oh, I went into Harry's room to see if he was ready, and found this treasure, and brought it down with me to read.'

And the king again moistened his finger, and turned another page.

'Sire,' faltered d'Alençon, whose hair stood on end—'sire, I have come to tell you——'

'Let me finish this chapter, François, and then tell me what you please. I have read or rather devoured fifty pages.'

'My brother has tasted the poison five-and-twenty times,' thought d'Alençon. 'He is a dead man!'

François wiped the cold sweat from his brow, and waited in silence, as the king bade him, until he had finished the chapter.

50

THE HAWKING PARTY

CHARLES read, or literally devoured, the pages, and each page, as we have said, was gummed to the next. D'Alençon gazed wildly on this terrible spectacle.

'Oh,' he murmured, 'what will happen now? Shall I go into exile and try to capture a throne which is beyond my reach, while Henry, the moment he hears of Charles's illness, will return to some fortress near Paris, not more than an hour or two away, so that before d'Anjou even hears of Charles's death the whole dynasty will have been changed?'

Instantly his plan with regard to Henry altered. It was Charles who had read the poisoned book: Henry must stay. He was less to be feared in the Bastille, or a prisoner at Vincennes,* than free, and at the head of thirty thousand men.

The duke waited until Charles finished his chapter, and then,—

'Brother,' said he, 'I waited because you ordered me to. But I have something of the greatest importance to say to you.'

'Ah, the devil take you!' returned Charles, whose pale cheeks glowed with unusual fire. 'If you come bothering me, I'll get rid of you as I have the King of Poland.'

'It is not on that subject I would speak to you. Your Majesty has touched me in my most sensitive point, that of my love for you as a brother, and my devotion as your subject. I am here to prove to you I am no traitor.'

'Well,' said Charles, crossing his legs, and leaning back on his chair, 'I suppose it is some fresh report—some new nightmare.'

'No, sire: a certainty—a plot, of which I know all the details.'

'A plot! let us hear about this wonderful plot.'

'Sire,' said François, 'while your Majesty is hawking in the plain of Vesinet,* the King of Navarre will ride into the forest of Saint-Germain where a troop of his friends will be waiting, and will escape with him.'

'I expected this!' cried Charles. 'A fresh calumny against my poor Harry! When will you leave him alone?'

'Your Majesty will not have long to wait to know whether what I say is true or false.'

'Why not?'

'Because this evening he will be gone.'

Charles stood up.

'Listen,' said he: 'I will give you the benefit of the doubt once more. But, mind, it is for the last time. Guard!—summon the King of Navarre.'

A soldier was about to obey, when François stopped him.

'That is the wrong way to learn the truth,' said he. 'Henry will deny it, give a signal, all his accomplices will conceal themselves, and my mother and myself will be accused of making false accusations.'

Charles opened the window, for the blood was rushing to his head.

Then turning to d'Alençon,—

'What would you do, then?' asked he.

'Sire,' said d'Alençon, 'I would surround the wood with three detachments of light horse, who, at a given moment, should beat the forest and drive everyone in it to the Pavilion of François I, which I would, as if casually, have appointed as the place where refreshments were to be served. Then when Henry leaves, I would follow him to the rendezvous, and capture him and his accomplices.'

'A good idea!' returned Charles. 'Call the captain of my guards.'

From his doublet d'Alençon drew a silver whistle, fastened to a chain of gold, and whistled.

De Nancey appeared.

Charles gave him orders, in an undertone.

Meanwhile Actæon, the boar-hound, had dragged a book off the table and began to tear it.

Charles turned round and swore a terrible oath. The book was the precious *Treatise on Venerie*, of which there existed but three copies in the world.

The chastisement fitted the crime. Charles seized a whip and lashed the dog soundly. Actæon yelled, and disappeared under a table covered with a large green cloth.

The king picked up the book, and saw with joy that only one leaf was missing, and that leaf was not a page of text but an engraving.

He locked it up carefully in a cupboard, to d'Alençon's great regret. Now that it had fulfilled its fearful purpose, he would have preferred it out of Charles's possession.

Six o'clock struck, and the king descended.

He first closed the door of his armoury, locked it, and put the key in his pocket. D'Alençon earnestly watched each movement. On his way downstairs, the King stopped, and passed his hand over his eyes.

'I do not know what is the matter with me,' he observed, 'but I feel very weak.'

'Perhaps,' faltered d'Alençon, 'there is a storm in the air.'

'A storm in January! you are mad,' said Charles. 'No, no, I feel dizzy, my skin is dry, I am over-tired, that's all.'

But then the fresh air, the cries of the huntsmen, and the noise of the horses and hounds produced their ordinary effect upon him: he breathed freely, and felt exhilarated.

His first thought was to look for Henry and Marguerite, who seemed such a loving couple that they could not bear being parted from each other.

On seeing Charles, Henry spurred his horse, and in three bounds was beside him.

'Ah, Harry!' said Charles, 'you are mounted as if you were going to hunt stag, and yet you know we are only going hawking.'

Then without awaiting a reply,—

'Forward, gentlemen!' cried he, frowning. 'We must be at the meet by nine.'

Catherine was watching at a window, but only her pale face was visible: the rest of her was concealed by the curtain.

At Charles's order, the whole cavalcade passed through the gate of the Louvre, and headed out on the road to Saint-Germain amidst the acclamations of the people who cheered their young king as he rode by on his white steed.

'What did he say to you?' asked Marguerite of Henry.

'He made complimentary remarks about my horse.'

'Is that all?'

'Yes.'

'I fear he knows something.'

'I agree.'

'We must be careful.'

Henry's face was lit up, in reply, by one of his cordial smiles, as if to say, 'Be easy, *ma mie*.'

As for Catherine, when she had seen them all depart, she let the curtain fall.

'This time,' murmured she, 'I think I have him.'

Then, to satisfy herself, after having waited for a few minutes, she entered the King of Navarre's apartments, using her pass-key.

But she looked in vain for the book.

'He has locked it away,' thought she, 'and if he has not read it already, he soon will.'

And she descended, convinced her plan had succeeded.

The king arrived at Saint-Germain.

The sun, until then hidden by a cloud, lit up the splendid cavalcade.

Then, as if it had been waiting for this moment, a heron flew up out of the reeds with a mournful cry.

'Haw! haw!' cried Charles, unhooding his falcon.

The falcon, dazzled for a moment by the light, flew one circle, then suddenly seeing the heron, dashed after it.

However, the heron, which had risen a hundred yards in front of the beaters, had used the time taken in unhooding the falcon to make considerable ground. It was therefore at least at a height of five hundred feet, and was still climbing rapidly.

'Haw! haw! Bec-de-Fer!' cried Charles—'haw! haw!'

The noble bird, like an arrow, flew after the heron, which had now wellnigh disappeared.

'Ah, coward!' said Charles, spurring his horse to a gallop and throwing back his head, so as not to lose sight of the pursuit—'courage, Bec-de-Fer!'

The contest was finely balanced. The falcon was closing rapidly on the heron. The only question was: which could rise the highest?

Fear had better wings than courage. The falcon passed underneath, and the heron, using its height advantage, dealt him a blow with his long beak.

The falcon faltered, and seemed as if about to abandon the chase. But, soon recovering himself, he went after the heron. The latter, pursuing its advantage, had changed direction and was now seeking the safety of the forest. But the falcon followed so closely that the heron was forced to climb once more, and in a few seconds the two birds were scarcely distinguishable.

'Bravo, Bec-de-Fer!' cried Charles—'see, he is having the best of it!'

'Faith!' said Henry, 'I confess I can't see either of them.'

'Nor I,' said Marguerite.

'If you can't see them, you can hear them. At least the heron,' replied Charles. 'Listen! he is asking for quarter.'

As he spoke, two or three plaintive cries were heard.

'Look! look!' cried Charles, 'and you will see them come down quicker than they went up.'

As the king spoke, both birds reappeared; the falcon was the higher of the two.

'Bec-de-Fer has him!' shouted Charles.

The heron, outflown by the falcon, no longer sought to defend itself: it folded its wings, and dropped like a stone. But its adversary did the same, and when the fugitive again resumed its flight, it received a stroke that stunned it. It fell to earth, and the falcon, uttering a note of victory, alighted near where it lay.

'Brave falcon!' cried Charles, galloping towards the spot where the heron had landed. But suddenly he stopped, and, uttering a piercing cry, dropped his reins, and pressed his hand to his stomach. All the courtiers hastened up.

'It is nothing,' said he, with inflamed features and haggard eyes. 'But I felt as if a hot iron was passing through me. But it is nothing.'

And he galloped on.

D'Alençon turned pale.

'What is the matter?' asked Henry of Marguerite.

'I do not know,' replied she. 'But did you see Charles?—he was purple!'

'He is not usually like that,' said Henry.

Reaching the scene of combat, Charles sprang off his horse. But on alighting, he was forced to hang on to his saddle to prevent himself from falling.

'Brother!' cried Marguerite—'what is the matter?'

'I feel,' said Charles, 'what Porcia must have felt when she swallowed her burning coals.* It seemed as if my breath was flame.'

Meantime, the falcon was reclaimed, and all the hunt gathered round Charles.

'What is the matter with me?' cried he. '*Corps du Christ!* it is nothing, or at most only the sun that affects me. Unhood all the falcons!—there go a whole flight of herons!'

Five or six falcons were instantly unhooded, and all the hunt galloped along the bank of the river.

'Well, madame, what do you think?' asked Henry.

'That the moment is favourable, and that if the king does not look back, we may easily reach the forest.'

Henry called the attendant who had the fallen heron in his keeping, and while the court swept on, remained behind, as if to examine the bird.

At this moment, and as if to abet his plans, a pheasant rose. Henry slipped the jesses of his falcon:* he had now the excuse of a hunt of his own to assist him.

51

THE PAVILION OF FRANÇOIS I

To the right of the Allée des Violettes is a long clearing, so situated that it cannot be seen from the high road, but yet the high road can be seen from the clearing.

In the middle of this clearing two men were lying on the grass, with a travelling cloak spread beneath them, at their side a long sword, and a musketoon (then called a petronel) with the muzzle turned away from them. One of them was leaning on his knee and on one hand, listening like a hare or deer.

'It appears to me,' said this man, 'that the hunt got very close upon us just now. I heard the cries of the huntsmen as they cheered on the falcon.'

'And now,' said the other, who appeared to wait upon events with much more philosophy than his comrade—'I cannot hear them at all. They must be a long way off.'

'Do not worry, Annibal,' said the other, 'they will come. We must wait quietly. This place hides us and our mules and horses very well: de Mouy chose a good spot, with all the concealments and privacy essential to a conspirator.'

'Ah, good!' said the other gentleman—'that's the word, is it? Well, I expected it. So, then, we are conspiring, are we?'

'We are not conspiring; we are serving the king and queen.'

'Well, it's all very odd!' said Coconnas, yawning. 'It is not yet twelve o'clock, so we have time for a nap'; and so saying, Coconnas stretched himself on his cloak like a man who is about to join practice to precept, but, as his ear touched the ground, he raised one finger and motioned La Mole to be silent.

Then a distant sound was heard, at first scarcely perceptible, and to unpractised ears would only have been the wind, but to two waiting men it was the distant galloping of horses.

La Mole sprang to his feet,—

'Here they are!' said he.

Coconnas rose more quietly, and then a regular and measured sound struck the ear of the two friends. The neighing of a horse made their own horses tethered ten paces away prick up their ears, and along a bridle-path there passed, like a white shadow, a woman, who, turning towards them, made a particular signal and disappeared.

'The queen!' they exclaimed, both at once.

'What did she mean?' said Coconnas.

'And she did *this* with her arm,' said La Mole, 'which means "Presently"——'

'No, she did *this*,' said Coconnas, 'which means "Go at once"——'

'The signal means "Wait for me." '

'It means "Away at once!" '

'Well,' said La Mole, 'let each act on his own conviction. You go—I will remain.'

Coconnas shrugged his shoulders, and lay down on the grass. At the same moment, in the opposite direction from the one the queen had taken, but along the same path, there passed, at top speed, a troop of horsemen, whom the two friends recognized as Protestants. They disappeared rapidly.

'Damn! this is getting serious,' said Coconnas, standing up. 'Let us go to the Pavilion of François I.'

'No,' replied La Mole, 'by no means. If we are seen, the attention of the king will be drawn to the pavilion, since that is the general rendezvous.'

'Well, perhaps you are right,' grumbled Coconnas.

Hardly had these words been uttered when a horseman approached like a flash of lightning amidst the trees, and, leaping over ditches, bushes, briers, and all obstacles, reached the young men. He had a pistol in each hand, and guided his horse with his knees only.

'M. de Mouy!' exclaimed Coconnas, uneasy, and now more on the alert than La Mole—'M. de Mouy running away! Then it is every man for himself!'

'Quick—quick!' cried the Huguenot—'away with you!—all is lost!—I came to tell you so. Now, to horse and away!'

'And the queen?' cried La Mole.

But the voice of the young man was lost in the distance, and de Mouy neither heard nor replied.

Coconnas had soon made up his mind, while La Mole remained motionless, following de Mouy with his eyes as he disappeared amongst the branches. He hastened to the horses, and, leaping on his own, threw the bridle of the other to La Mole, and prepared to gallop away.

'Come, come!' he exclaimed—'let us be off, as de Mouy advises, for de Mouy is a sensible man. Away, away, La Mole!'

'One moment,' said La Mole; 'we came here for something.'

'Unless it is to get hanged,' replied Coconnas, 'I would advise you to waste no more time. I would only observe that when M. de Mouy de Saint-Phale retreats, all the world may retreat too.'

'M. de Mouy de Saint-Phale,' said La Mole, 'was not charged with spiriting away Queen Marguerite! M. de Mouy de Saint-Phale is not in love with Queen Marguerite!'

'*Mordi!* and he is quite right too! "*Corne de bœuf!*" as King Charles says,* we are conspiring, my dear fellow. And when men conspire, they should know when to cut and run. Mount, mount, La Mole!'

'Well, let us then to horse and away!'

'That's right.'

La Mole turned round to lay his hand on the pommel of his saddle. But just as he was putting his foot in the stirrup, a loud voice cried,—

'Halt there—surrender!'

And, at the same moment, the figure of a man was seen behind an oak—then another—then thirty: they were the light dragoons who had dismounted and, advancing quietly, were searching the forest.

'What did I tell you?' muttered Coconnas.

The light dragoons were within thirty paces of the two friends.

'Well, gentlemen,' said the Piedmontese, 'what is your pleasure?'

The lieutenant ordered his men to take aim at the two friends.

'Gentlemen,' said Coconnas, drawing his sword, and raising it in the air, 'we surrender; but allow me to ask why we are called on to do so?'

'That you must ask of the King of Navarre.'

'What crime have we committed?'

'M. d'Alençon will inform you.'

Coconnas and La Mole looked at each other. The name of their enemy at such a moment did little to reassure them.

Yet neither of them put up any resistance. Coconnas was ordered to alight from his horse, a manœuvre which he executed without a word, then both were placed in the centre of the light dragoons who rode off in the direction of the Pavilion of François I.

'You wished to see the Pavilion of François,' said Coconnas to La Mole, when they saw the walls of a pretty Gothic building through the trees—'well, there it is.'

La Mole made no reply, but only extended his hand to Coconnas.

By the side of this beautiful pavilion, dating from the time of Louis XII,* and called after François who used it as a favourite hunting lodge was a low building used by the huntsmen and kennel men, which was now almost completely hidden by the muskets, halberds and swords in front of it.

The prisoners were led to this building.

We will now throw a little light on the gloomy position of the two friends, by stating a few details.

The Protestant gentlemen had assembled, as was agreed, in the Pavilion of François I, of which we know de Mouy had the key.

Masters of the forest, as they believed, they had placed sentinels here and there, whom the light dragoons, having exchanged their white scarves for red ones (a precaution due to the ingenious zeal of M. de Nancey), had overpowered without striking a blow.

The light dragoons continued their search, keeping a good watch over the pavilion. But de Mouy, who, as we have seen, was waiting for the king at the end of the Allée des Violettes, had seen these red scarves stealing along, and became suspicious. He hastily hid himself, and observed the vast circle they made in order to beat the forest and hem in the place of rendezvous. At the same moment, at the end of the main avenue, he had glimpsed the white aigrettes* and gleaming arquebuses of the king's bodyguard, and then the king himself, while coming from the opposite direction he saw the King of Navarre.

Then he had made a sign of a cross with his hat, which was the signal agreed upon when all was lost.

At this signal, the king turned back, and rapidly disappeared.

Then de Mouy, digging the two large rowels of his spurs into the sides of his horse, fled like the wind, and as he fled gave those words of advice to La Mole and Coconnas which we have mentioned.

Then the king, escorted by d'Alençon, noticing the absence of Henry and Marguerite, reached the building next to the pavilion where he ordered all those who were found, not only in the pavilion, but in the forest, to be detained.

D'Alençon, full of confidence, galloped close by the king, whose excessive pain did not improve his temper. Two or three times he had nearly fainted, and once had vomited blood.

'Quick, quick!' he said, when he arrived. 'Make haste; I want to return to the Louvre. Winkle these rebels out of their lair. This is Saint Blaise's day,* and he was cousin to Saint Bartholomew.'

At these words of the king, all the pikes and arquebuses were mobilized, and they forced the Huguenots, arrested in the forest or the pavilion, to come out one after the other.

But the King of Navarre, Marguerite, and de Mouy were not among them.

'Well,' said the king, 'where is Henry—where is Margot? You promised them to me, d'Alençon, and, *corbœuf!* I must have them found.'

'We have not seen the King and Queen of Navarre, sire,' said M. de Nancey.

'Here they are,' observed Madame de Nevers.

And at the same moment, at the farther extremity of an avenue, which led down to the river, appeared Henry and Marguerite, both as calm as if nothing had happened; both with their falcons on their wrist, and lovingly side by side on their horses as they galloped along, while their steeds, like themselves, seemed to be caressing each other.

It was then that d'Alençon, furious, ordered the forest to be searched, and that La Mole and Coconnas were apprehended.

They had reached the circle which the guards closed in. But since they were not sovereigns, they could not assume so cool an appearance as Henry and Marguerite. La Mole was too pale, and Coconnas was too red.

52

QUESTIONS

THE spectacle which presented itself to the friends, as they entered, was one of those which, once seen, are never forgotten.

As we have already said, Charles had anxiously observed

each prisoner, as one by one they left the beaters' hut, watching, no less keenly than d'Alençon, to see the King of Navarre emerge.

Both were doomed to disappointment. But, though mistaken in their calculation, there still remained something to be done: to find out why those they believed would be inside were absent.

When, therefore, Henry and Marguerite were seen approaching from the end of an avenue, a mortal pallor seized d'Alençon, while Charles felt relieved of a heavy burden, and his heart beat with a hope that his friend Harry might yet disprove the accusations that had been made against him.

'He will escape again!' murmured François.

But just then the king was seized with such excruciating pains, such spasmodic agony throughout his frame—that, pressing a hand on each side, he shrieked aloud like a delirious man.

Henry hurried towards him, but by the time he had covered the short space that separated them, the paroxysm had passed.

'Where have you been?' inquired the king, with a sternness of manner that frightened Marguerite.

'Why, brother,' replied she, as though the question had been applied to herself, 'we have been following the hunt.'

'Had it been so, you would have stayed near the bank of the river, instead of riding into the depths of the forest.'

'Sire,' said Henry, 'my falcon suddenly struck down a pheasant, at the very time we had stopped to see to your heron.'

'Did you catch it?'

'Here it is, sire—as fine a bird as I have seen!' replied Henry, with the most perfect air of well-assumed innocence, as he held up his beautiful prize.

'Ah, ah!' exclaimed Charles, 'but why did you not rejoin me when you had bagged the pheasant?'

'Because the bird flew towards the park, sire, so that when we returned to the river bank, we saw you more than a mile off proceeding towards the forest. Having been invited to join your Majesty's hunt, we did not like being left out, and proceeded to gallop after you as fast as we could.'

'And were all these gentlemen invited too?' inquired Charles.

'What gentlemen?' replied Henry, casting a look of inquiry around him.

'*Pardieu!*' exclaimed Charles, 'why, your Huguenot friends. All I can say is, that they certainly cannot claim that I invited them to join our sport.'

'Probably, sire,' answered Henry, 'they came because M. d'Alençon asked them.'

'I?' said the Duke d'Alençon.

'Why, yes, brother!' returned Henry. 'Did you not proclaim yourself yesterday King of Navarre! What could be more natural than that the grateful people assembled here to thank you for accepting the crown, and the king for giving it—is that not so, gentlemen?'

'Yes, yes!' shouted forth a number of voices. 'Long live the Duke d'Alençon! long live King Charles!'

'I am not king of the Huguenots!' said François, white with rage, and looking stealthily at Charles, he added, 'and trust I never shall be!'

'No matter,' interposed Charles. 'But you must realize, Henry, that I look upon all this as very strange.'

'Sire,' cried the King of Navarre firmly, 'Heaven pardon me for saying such a thing! But most persons would say I was being interrogated.'

'And if it were so, how would you answer?'

'That I am a king like yourself,' replied Henry proudly, 'for it is not the crown but birth that confers royalty; and that though I would cheerfully answer any questions asked by my friend and brother, I should refuse to reply to my judge.'

'I only wish,' muttered Charles, 'that for once in my life I knew what it was right to do.'

'M. de Mouy is doubtless among those persons detained,' cried the Duke d'Alençon. 'Let him be brought before your Majesty, we shall then know all we need.'

'Is M. de Mouy among the prisoners?' inquired the king.

Henry felt a momentary uneasiness, and exchanged glances with Marguerite. But the moment passed.

No voice answered to the inquiry after de Mouy.

'He is not among the parties arrested,' said M. de Nancey. 'Some of my men fancy they saw him, but no one is certain on the subject.'

An oath escaped from the lips of d'Alençon.

'Ha!' cried Marguerite, pointing to La Mole and Coconnas who had heard everything that had transpired, and on whose wit and intelligence she felt sure she could count—'here, sire, are two gentlemen in the service of M. d'Alençon. Question them—they will give you answers.'

The duke felt the blow.

'I had them arrested deliberately, so that I could prove that neither of them belonged to me,' answered the duke.

The king turned to look at the two friends, and started at seeing La Mole again.

'What! that Provençal here?' said he, frowning.

Coconnas bowed most respectfully.

'What were you doing when you were arrested?' asked Charles.

'Sire, I and my friend were busily engaged in planning deeds of love and war.'

'What, with horses ready saddled, armed to the teeth, and with every preparation made for flight?'

'Not so, sire!' replied Coconnas, 'your Majesty is misinformed. We were lying beneath a sheltering beech, *sub tegmine fagi*,* and might easily have galloped off had we suspected that we had been so unfortunate as to offend your Majesty. Now, gentlemen,' continued he, turning towards the light horse—'say, candidly and fairly, on your honour as soldiers, could we, or could we not have escaped, had we wanted to?'

'Truth compels me to declare,' answered the lieutenant, 'that neither of these cavaliers made the slightest attempt to get away.'

'Because in all probability their horses were too far off,' chimed in the Duke d'Alençon.

'Your pardon, my lord duke,' responded Coconnas, 'but our horses could scarcely be nearer than they were, I being upon mine, and M. de la Mole holding his, in the very act of mounting.'

'Is this correct?' inquired the king.

'Quite correct,' replied the lieutenant, 'and there is more. On seeing us approach, M. de Coconnas got off his horse.'

Coconnas looked at the king with a sort of grim smile that seemed to say—'There, you see!'

'But what were the other horses and mules laden with cases and packages for then?' demanded François.

'How can we tell you,' replied Coconnas, 'we are neither grooms nor squires. Ask the varlet who was in charge of them.'

'He is not to be found!' exclaimed the duke, almost frantic with rage.

'Most likely he was frightened, and ran away,' retorted Coconnas; 'one cannot expect a common oaf to have the notions or manners of a gentleman.'

'Always the same story,' said d'Alençon, gnashing his teeth. 'Fortunately, sire, I told you that neither of these men has been in my service for some days past.'

'Is it possible,' cried Coconnas, 'that I have the misfortune no longer to be part of your Highness's retinue?'

'*Morbleu!* monsieur, why pretend you don't know, when you yourself gave in your resignation in a letter so impertinent that I have thought proper to preserve it, and happily have it with me.'

'I confess,' said Coconnas, 'I flattered myself with the hope of being forgiven for writing that letter, which was prompted by my vexation at learning that your Highness had tried to strangle my friend La Mole in one of the corridors of the Louvre.'

'What does he say?' interrupted the king.

'At first I thought your Highness was alone in the affair. But subsequently I learned that three other persons——'

'Silence!' exclaimed Charles, 'we have heard enough.' Then turning to the King of Navarre, he said, 'Henry, do I have your word not to escape?'

'I give it to your Majesty.'

'Return to Paris with M. de Nancey, where you will remain under house-arrest. As for you, messieurs,' continued he, speaking to the two friends, 'give up your swords.'

La Mole looked at Marguerite, who smiled. The young man immediately delivered his sword to the nearest officer. Coconnas followed his friend's example.

'Has M. de Mouy been found?' inquired the king.

'No, sire,' answered M. de Nancey. 'Either he was not in the forest, or he has escaped.'

'It can't be helped,' rejoined Charles. 'But let us return to Paris. I am cold, and my head feels dizzy.'

'It is anger that excites you, sire,' observed François.

'It may be; but my eyes seem dim. Where are the prisoners? I cannot see anything. Is it dark already? Oh, mercy! help— help!—I am dying!'

So saying, the unfortunate king let go the reins of his horse, and fell backwards, wildly stretching forth his hands, while his terrified courtiers, alarmed at this sudden seizure, prevented him from falling.

Standing apart from the clustering nobles, François wiped the cold drops from his brow, for he alone of all the company knew the cause of Charles's violent attack.

The king was now unconscious. A litter was brought, and he was laid on it, covered with a cloak taken from the shoulders of one of his attendants.

The melancholy procession then proceeded towards Paris, in a very different frame of mind to that in which it had left that morning. Then, a merry party had set out, consisting of conspirators whose hearts beat high with hope, and a joyous monarch, promising himself many such days of princely enjoyment: their return revealed a dying king surrounded by rebel prisoners.

Marguerite, who throughout had not for an instant lost her self-possession, gave her husband a look of complicity, then passing so close to La Mole that he could catch the two brief words of Greek she uttered, she said,—

'*Mé deidê.*' (Fear nothing.)

'Now, gentlemen,' exclaimed the captain of light horse, 'we are ready to start.'

'Would it be a liberty,' inquired Coconnas, 'to ask where we are going?'

'I believe to Vincennes,' replied the lieutenant.

'I would rather be going anywhere else,' answered Coconnas, 'but people are sometimes obliged to do things against their will.'

The king recovered his senses during the journey, and even a part of his strength: he declared himself well enough to remount his horse, but that was not permitted.

'Let Maître Ambroise Paré be summoned immediately,' said Charles, as he reached the Louvre. Then getting out of his litter, he walked slowly towards his apartments, leaning on the arm of Tavannes, and strictly forbidding anyone to follow him.

Everyone had noticed his extreme gravity of look and manner.
During the journey homewards, he had appeared lost in reflection, not addressing a word to those around him. Still it was
evident, that the recently-discovered conspiracy formed no part
of his thoughts, but that he was solely occupied with his own
illness—a malady so strange, so sudden and severe, which displayed symptoms which reminded the spectators of those visible
in the last illness of François II.*

When he reached his apartments, Charles seated himself on a
kind of *chaise-longue*, and supported his head on the cushions.
Then reflecting that there might be some little delay before the
arrival of Maître Ambroise Paré, he determined to employ the
interval as well as he could. He clapped his hands—a guard
appeared.

'Let the King of Navarre be informed I wish to speak with
him,' said Charles.

The man bowed and left.

Again the king was visited by a repetition of the distressing
sufferings he had previously undergone; his head fell back; his
ideas seemed so crowded and confused that he could not separate
one from the other; a sort of blood-coloured vapour seemed to
float before his eyes; his mouth was parched, and he vainly
sought to slake the burning thirst by which he was consumed by
swallowing the contents of a carafe of water.

During the almost lethargic state into which Charles had
sunk, a sudden noise was heard of approaching footsteps. The
door swung back on its hinges, and Henry stood before him.

'You sent for me, sire,' said he. 'I am here.'

The sound of the well-known voice had the effect of rousing
Charles, who, raising his languid head mechanically, held out his
hand to Henry.

'Sire,' observed Henry, whose arms remained at his side,
without making any attempt to imitate the offered cordiality on
the part of the king, 'your Majesty has forgotten that I am no
longer your brother, but your prisoner.'

'True, true,' answered Charles, 'and I thank you for having
reminded me of it. But was there not also some promise on your
part, when we last spoke together, to answer me candidly whatever questions I might put to you?'

'I did so pledge myself to your Majesty, and I am ready to keep my word.'

The king poured some water into the palm of his hand, and then applied it to his temples.

'First, then,' said he, 'tell me truly, Henry, how much of the charge brought against you by the Duke d'Alençon is accurate?'

'Half of it. It was M. d'Alençon who was to have fled, and I who was to have accompanied him.'

'And why should you have done that, Henry? Are you dissatisfied with the way I have treated you?'

'Far from it, sire. Your Majesty is all goodness. And God, to whom the secrets of all men's hearts are known, knows well how truly and affectionately I love and honour my king and brother.'

'Yet,' said Charles, 'it seems to me that it is not usual to run from those we love, and who love us.'

'Your Majesty is right. But it was not from those I loved I sought to escape, but from those who hate me, and plot my ruin. May I speak openly?'

'Of course—proceed.'

'The persons whose hatred I dreaded and wished to escape from were M. d'Alençon and the queen-mother.'

'As for M. d'Alençon, I will not say you are wrong. But the queen-mother has shown you every consideration.'

'It is precisely for that reason I mistrust her, and a very good thing it was that I was on my guard.'

'Against the queen-mother?'

'Ay, the queen-mother, or those who advise her. Now, will your Majesty tell me, as candidly as I have answered the questions put to me, whether my life is of any value in your eyes?'

'I should be very miserable if any harm were to happen to you.'

'Well, then, I can assure your Majesty you have twice very narrowly escaped being made miserable on my account. Twice Providence has intervened on my behalf. On one occasion, it thought fit to assume the features of your Majesty.'

'And who saved you on the other occasion?'

'A very unlikely person to be selected as an agent of Providence: none other than René.'

'And what did he do for you?'

'He saved me from poison.'

'You have all the luck, Harry!' murmured poor Charles, smiling faintly. But this feeble attempt at good humour was quickly dispelled by the sharp spasmodic contraction of another attack.

The king wiped his brow, and indicated to Henry to proceed.

'Well, sire,' said Henry, 'have I spoken as boldly as you wanted? Is there anything else you would like to know?'

'Harry, you are a good and a loyal fellow. Tell me this—do you fear any further attempts by your enemies on your life or honour?'

'I can but assure you, that when evening comes, I am always surprised to find I am still alive.'

'It is because they see I love you that they are so full of hate. But fear not. They shall get their just desserts. Meanwhile you are free.'

'To leave Paris?' asked Henry.

'No, no! You are well aware I cannot possibly do without you. *Mille noms d'un diable!* I must have someone to love me!'

'Then if your Majesty prefers to keep me with you, at least grant me one favour.'

'What is that?'

'Not to have me as a friend, but to detain me as a prisoner.'

'A prisoner, Harry?'

'Yes. Does not your Majesty see plainly enough that it is your friendship that brings all these troubles and disasters on me?'

'And you would prefer my hatred?'

'All I want is that you pretend to dislike me, sire. An outward show of displeasure from you would save me from any further persecution from those who would consider me of too little consequence to be worth their hostility the moment they believe you have disgraced and dismissed me from favour. But your Majesty is still suffering from your recent attack. I can see the efforts your are making to conceal it. Let me summon help.'

'I have sent for Maître Ambroise Paré.'

'Then I shall retire more satisfied.'

'Upon my soul,' said the king, 'I truly believe you are the only person in the world who really loves me!'

'Is such your opinion, sire?'

'It is, on the word of a gentleman.'

'Then I ask you to commend me to the strict keeping of M. de Nancey, as a man your extreme anger may doom to death before a month is out. That way you will have me to love you for many years.'

'M. de Nancey!' cried Charles. The captain of the guards entered. 'M. de Nancey,' said Charles, 'I here commit to your keeping the guiltiest man in my kingdom. You will answer for him with your life.'

The officer bowed low, and with a well-feigned air of consternation, Henry followed his self-solicited keeper from the apartment.*

53

ACTÆON

CHARLES was alone, and much astonished not to have seen one or other of his faithful attendants—his nurse Madeleine and his greyhound Actæon.

'Nurse has gone to sing her psalms with some Huguenot of her acquaintance,' he said to himself, 'and Actæon is still angry with me for the beating I gave him with my whip this morning.'

Charles took a wax candle, and went into the nurse's apartment. She was not there, and he went on into his armoury. But as he went, one of those terrible attacks he had already experienced which came on him suddenly, seized him. He suffered as if his entrails were being perforated with a hot iron; an unquenchable thirst consumed him, and seeing a cup of milk on the table, he swallowed it at a draught, and then felt somewhat easier, and entered the armoury.

To his great astonishment, Actæon did not come to meet him—had he been shut up? If so, he would have known that his master had returned from hunting, and howled to rejoin him.

Charles called—whistled—the animal did not appear.

He advanced four steps, and as the light of the wax candle lit the recesses of the armoury, he saw, in one corner, a large mass on the floor.

'Hallo! Actæon, hallo!' said Charles, whistling again.

The dog did not stir. Charles hastened forward, and touched him: the poor brute was stiff and cold. From his throat, contracted by pain, several drops of watery matter had fallen, mingled with a foamy and bloody slaver. In the armoury, the dog had found an old cap of his master's, and had died with his head resting on something that smelt of a friend.

At this sight, which made him forget his own sufferings, and restored him to all his energy, rage boiled in Charles's veins. He would have cried out, but encompassed in their greatness as they are, kings are not free to yield to the first impulse which every man turns to the profit of his passion or his defence: Charles reflected that there might be some treason here, and was silent.

Then he knelt before his dog, and examined the dead carcass with an experienced eye. The eyes were glassy, the tongue red and covered with pustules. These were strange symptoms and they made Charles shudder.

The king put on his gloves, opened the livid lips of the dog to examine the teeth, and noticed, in the interstices, some whitish fragments clinging about the points of his sharp fangs.

He took these fragments out, and at once saw that they were paper. Near where the paper was, the inflammation was more violent, the gums more swollen, and the skin looked as though it had been attacked by vitriol.

Charles looked around him carefully. On the carpet were several pieces of paper similar to that which he had already recognized in the dog's mouth. One of these fragments, larger than the other, presented the marks of a woodcut.

Charles's hair stood on end. He recognized a fragment of the engraving which represented a gentleman hawking, the one which Actæon had torn out of the book.

'Ah,' said he, turning pale, 'the book was poisoned!' Then suddenly remembering—'Good God! I touched every page with my finger, and as I turned each page I raised my finger to my lips to moisten it. The fainting fits—the pain—the vomiting!—I am a dead man!'

Charles stood for a moment motionless under the weight of this horrible idea, then rousing himself with a groan, he went hastily towards the door.

'Let someone go instantly, and with all despatch,' he cried, 'to Maître René, and bring him here in ten minutes. If Maître Ambroise Paré arrives, tell him to wait.'

A guard went instantly to obey the king's commands.

'Ah,' muttered Charles, 'if I have to put everybody to the torture, I will learn who gave this book to Harry!' And with the perspiration on his brow, his hands clenched, his breast heaving, Charles remained with his eyes fixed on the body of his dead dog.

Ten minutes afterwards, the Florentine knocked timidly at the door.

'Enter!' said Charles.

The perfumer appeared, and Charles went up to him, imperious and tight-lipped.

'Your Majesty wished to see me,' said René, trembling.

'You are a skilful chemist, are you not?'

'Sire——'

'And know everything that the most skilful doctors know?'

'Your Majesty flatters me.'

'No, my mother tells me so. Besides, I have confidence in you, and had rather consult you than anyone else. Look!' he continued, pointing to the carcass of the dead dog; 'I want you to look at that animal's mouth, and tell me what was the cause of death.'

While René, with a wax candle in his hand, bent down to the ground, as much to hide his emotion as to obey the king, Charles, standing up, with his eyes fixed on him, waited with a feverish expectation easily to be imagined, for the reply which would be his sentence of death or his reprieve.

René drew a kind of scalpel from his pocket, opened it, and, with the point, detached from the dog's throat the fragments of paper sticking to the gums, looking long and attentively at the watery matter and blood which oozed from each wound.

'Sire,' he said, in a tremulous voice, 'these are very terrible symptoms.'

Charles felt an icy shudder run through his veins and to his very heart.

'Yes,' he exclaimed, 'the dog has been poisoned, has he not?'

'I fear so, sire.'

'And with what sort of poison?'

'I think a mineral poison.'

'Can you be absolutely certain whether or not he has been poisoned?'

'Yes, by opening and examining the stomach.'

'Open it, then, as I wish to be clear on the point.'

'I must call someone to assist me.'

'I will assist you,' said Charles. 'If he has been poisoned, what symptoms shall we find?'

'Red blotches and herborizations in the stomach.'

'Come then—to work!'

René, with one stroke of the scalpel, opened the hound's body, while Charles, with one knee on the ground, held a light in one clenched and trembling hand.

'See, sire,' said René—'look at these marks. Here are the red blotches I mentioned, and these veins, turgid with blood, like the roots of certain plants, are what I meant by herborizations. I find here every symptom I anticipated.'

'And the dog was undoubtedly poisoned?'

'Unquestionably, sire.'

'With a mineral poison?'

'All the evidence points to it.'

'And what would be a man's symptoms, who had swallowed such a poison accidentally?'

'Severe pains in the head, a feeling of burning in the stomach, as if he had swallowed hot coals, pains in the bowels, and vomiting.'

'Would he be thirsty?' asked Charles.

'Parchingly thirsty.'

'So I was right,' muttered the king. Then aloud he asked— 'What is the antidote you would give a man who had swallowed the same substance as my dog?'

René reflected an instant.

'There are many mineral poisons,' he replied, 'and I would need to know precisely which your Majesty means. Has your Majesty any idea of the mode in which the poison was administered to the dog?'

'Yes,' said Charles, 'he ate the page of a book.'

'The page of a book?'

'Yes.'

'And has your Majesty got that book?'

'Here it is,' was Charles's answer, taking the hunting-book from the shelf where he had left it, and handing it to René who gave a start of surprise which did not escape the king.

'He ate a page of this book?' stammered René.

'Yes, this one,' and Charles pointed out the torn leaf.

'Allow me to tear out another, sire.'

'Do so.'

René tore out a page, held it in the wax candle, and when it caught light, a strong smell of garlic spread through the apartment.

'He has been poisoned with a preparation of arsenic,' he said.

'You are sure?'

'As if I had prepared it myself.'

'And the antidote?'

René shook his head.

'What!' said Charles, in a hoarse voice, 'do you know of no remedy?'

'The best and most efficacious is white of eggs beaten in milk. But——'

'But what?'

'It must be administered immediately; if not——'

'If not——?'

'It is a subtle poison, sire,' replied René.

'Yet it does not kill at once,' said Charles.

'No, but it is deadly. There is no knowing the length of time the person takes to die, though sometimes it may be reduced to a calculation.'

Charles leaned on the marble table.

'Now,' said he, touching René on the shoulder—'have you seen this book before?'

'I, sire!' replied René, turning pale.

'Yes, you. You gave yourself away when you saw it.'

'Sire, I swear to you——'

'Listen to me, René, and listen attentively. You poisoned the Queen of Navarre with gloves. You poisoned the Prince de Porcian with the smoke of a lamp. You tried to poison M. de Condé with a scented apple.* René, I will have your flesh torn off your bones, shred by shred with red hot pincers, if you do not tell me to whom this book belongs.'

The Florentine saw that he must not trifle with Charles's anger, and resolved to reply boldly.

'And if I tell the truth, sire, who will guarantee that I shall not be more cruelly tortured than if I hold my tongue?'

'I will.'

'Will you give me your royal word?'

'On my honour as a gentleman, your life shall be spared,' said the king.

'Then this book belongs to me.'

'To you?' replied Charles, starting, and looking at him in amazement.

'Yes, to me.'

'And how did it leave your possession?'

'Her Majesty the queen-mother took it from my house.'

'The queen-mother?' exclaimed Charles.

'Yes.'

'And with what intention?'

'With the intention, as I believe, of having it sent to the King of Navarre, who had asked the Duke d'Alençon for a book of this description to study hawking from.'

'Ah!' said Charles, 'and is that it? I see it all now. This book was indeed in Harry's chamber. There is a destiny, and I submit to it.'

At this moment, Charles was seized with a cough so dry and violent as to double him up and bring on a fresh attack of pain in the stomach. He uttered two or three stifled groans, and collapsed into a chair.

'What is the matter, sire?' asked René, alarmed.

'Nothing,' said Charles, 'except a raging thirst. Give me something to drink.'

René poured out a glass of water and gave it to Charles, who swallowed it at a draught.

'Now,' said he, taking a pen, and dipping it into the ink— 'write in this book.'

'What shall I write?'

'What I dictate:—

'"This book on hawking was given by me to the queen-mother, Catherine de Medicis.—RENÉ."'

The Florentine wrote and signed as he was ordered.

'You promised my life should be saved,' said René.

'And I will keep my word.'

'But,' said René, 'what about the queen-mother?'

'Oh,' replied Charles, 'that I have nothing to do with. If you are attacked, defend yourself.'

'Sire, may I leave France when I find my life threatened?'

'I will give you my answer in two weeks from now. In the meantime——'

And Charles frowningly placed his finger on his livid lips.

'Rely on me, sire,' said René, who, only too happy to get off so lightly, bowed and left the room.

Behind him the nurse appeared at her chamber door.

'What is the matter, Charlot?' she inquired.

'Nurse, I have been walking in the dew, and it has given me a cold.'

'You look very pale, Charlot.'

'And feel very weak. Give me your arm, nurse, and help me to bed,' and leaning on her, Charles went to his bedroom.

'Now,' said Charles, 'I will put myself to bed.'

'And if Maître Ambroise Paré comes?'

'You must tell him I am better, and do not need him.'

'But, meanwhile, what will you take?'

'Oh, a very simple medicine,—whites of eggs beaten in milk. By the way, nurse, poor Actæon is dead. To-morrow morning have him buried in a corner of the garden of the Louvre. He was one of my best friends, and I will raise a tomb over him, if I have time.'

54

VINCENNES

IN accordance with the order given by Charles IX, Henry was the same evening led to Vincennes,* that famous fortress of which only a fragment now remains, but colossal enough to give an idea of its past grandeur.

At the postern of the prison they halted. M. de Nancey alighted from his horse, opened the gate closed with a padlock, and respectfully invited the king to follow him. Henry obeyed without a word of reply. Anywhere seemed to him more safe than the Louvre, and he was relieved to know that ten doors closing behind him in rapid succession now stood between him and Catherine de Medicis.

The royal prisoner crossed the drawbridge between two soldiers, passed the three doors on the ground floor and the three doors at the foot of the staircase, and then, still preceded by M. de Nancey, went up one flight of stairs. Captain de Nancey requested the king to follow him along a kind of corridor, at the end of which was a very large and gloomy chamber.

Henry looked around him with dismay.

'Where are we?' he inquired.

'In the torture chamber, monseigneur.'

'Ah!' replied the king, looking attentively around him.

There was something of everything in this apartment: pitchers and trestles for the torture by water; wedges and mallets for the question of the boot; and stone benches for the unhappy wretches who were due for the question, most of the way round the chamber. Above, on, and under these seats were iron rings, morticed into the walls with no symmetry but that of the torturing art.

'Ah!' said Henry, 'is this the way to my apartment?'

'Yes, monseigneur, and here it is,' said a figure in the dark, who approached and then became visible.

Henry thought he recognized the voice, and advancing towards the individual said—

'Ah, is it you, Beaulieu?* And what the devil are you doing here?'

'Sire, I have been appointed governor of the fortress of Vincennes.'

'Well, my dear fellow, you have made an excellent start. A king for a prisoner is no bad beginning.'

'Pardon me, sire, but before I received you I had already received two other gentlemen.'

'Who may they be? Ah, your pardon! Perhaps I am being indiscreet?'

'Monseigneur, I have not been bound to secrecy. They are M. de la Mole and M. de Coconnas.'

'Poor gentlemen! And where are they?'

'High up, on the fourth floor.'

Henry gave a sigh. It was there he wished to be.

'Now then, M. de Beaulieu,' said Henry, 'be so good as to show me my room. I am desirous of reaching it, for I am very much fatigued with my day's toil.'

'Here, monseigneur,' said Beaulieu, showing Henry an open door.

'No. 2!' said Henry—'and why not No. 1?'

'Because it is reserved, monseigneur.'

'Ah,' said Henry, and he became even more pensive. He wondered who was to occupy No. 1.

The governor, with profuse apologies, installed Henry in his apartment, made many excuses for its deficiencies, and placing two soldiers at the door, withdrew.

'Now,' said the governor, addressing the turnkey, 'let us visit the others.'

The turnkey preceded him, and walking through the *Salle de la Question*, they went back through the corridor and, reaching the staircase, M. de Beaulieu followed his guide up three flights of stairs.

On reaching the fourth floor, the turnkey opened successively three doors, each equipped with two locks and three enormous bolts.

He had scarcely touched the third door when they heard a cheerful voice, which exclaimed:—

'Eh, *mordi!* open, if it be only to give us a little air! Your stove is so warm, that I cannot breathe in here.'

'One moment, sir,' said the turnkey, 'I have not come to let you out, but to come in to you with the governor.'

'The governor does me great honour,' replied Coconnas, 'and is most welcome.'

M. de Beaulieu then entered, and returned Coconnas's cordial smile with the icy politeness which is the speciality of governors of fortresses, jailers, and executioners.

'Do you have any money, sir?' he inquired of his prisoner.

'I?' replied Coconnas. 'Not a sou.'

'Jewels?'

'I have a ring.'

'Allow me to search you.'

'*Mordi!*' cried Coconnas, reddening with anger.

'We must endure everything for the service of the king!'

'Humph!' replied the Piedmontese, 'the men who rob passers-by on the Pont-Neuf* are also in the service of the king just like you. *Mordi!* I have been very unjust, sir, for until now I mistook them for thieves.'

'Sir, good-day!' said Beaulieu. 'Jailer, lock the door!'

The governor went away, taking with him the ring, a beautiful sapphire which Madame de Nevers had given to Coconnas to remind him of the colour of her eyes.

'Now for the other one,' he said, as he left.

They went through an empty apartment, and the game of three doors, six locks, and nine bolts was played all over again.

The last door being opened, a sigh was the first sound that greeted the visitors.

This cell was even more gloomy than the one which M. de Beaulieu had just left.

La Mole was seated in a corner, his head resting on one hand, and in spite of the visit and the visitors, was as motionless as if he was unaware of their presence.

'Good-evening, M. de la Mole,' said Beaulieu.

The young man raised his head slowly.

'Good-evening,' he replied.

'Sir,' continued Beaulieu, 'I have come to search you.'

'No point,' replied La Mole. 'I will give you all I have.'

'What do you have?'

'About three hundred crowns, these jewels, and these rings.'

La Mole turned out his pockets, stripped his fingers, and took the clasp out of his hat.

'Have you nothing more?'

'Not that I know of.'

'And that silk cord round your neck, what may that be?' asked the governor.

'Sir, it is not a jewel; it is a relic.'

'You must give it to me.'

'Do you really want it?—Well, then, sir, here it is.'

Then turning away, as if to approach the light, he unfastened the pretended relic which was in fact a medallion containing a portrait. The latter he took out of its case, pressed it to his lips, and having kissed it many times pretended to drop it accidentally and, placing the heel of his boot upon it, crushed it to atoms.

'Sir,' said Beaulieu, when he saw the miniature ground to dust, 'I shall report this to the king.'

And without taking leave of his prisoner with a single word, he withdrew so angry that he left the turnkey to secure the doors.

The jailer advanced a few paces, and observing that M. de Beaulieu had already descended several stairs, he said, turning to La Mole,—

'*Ma foi!* sir, it was fortunate you gave me the hundred crowns at once, for which I am to give you leave to see and talk with your companion. For if you had not, the governor would have taken them with the other three hundred, and my conscience would then not have allowed me to do anything for you. But I have been paid in advance, and promised you shall see your comrade, and an honest man always keeps his word. But, if you can avoid it, for your own sake as well as mine, do not talk politics.'

La Mole came out of his apartment and found himself face to face with Coconnas, who was pacing up and down in the intervening apartment.

The two friends threw themselves into each other's arms. The jailer pretended to wipe the corner of his eye, and then withdrew, to watch that the prisoners were not surprised, or rather, himself not suspected.

'Ah, it is good to see you!' said Coconnas. 'Has that brute of a governor been to see you?'

'Yes, and you too, I presume?'

'And taken everything from you?'

'And from you too, eh?'

'Oh, I did not have much—only a ring Henriette gave me.'

'Have you any idea what has happened?'

'Yes: we have been betrayed.'

'By whom?'

'By that scoundrelly Duke d'Alençon. I should have been well advised to break his neck.'

'And do you think our position is serious?'

'I am afraid so.'

'Then we may be tortured?'

'I have already faced the fact.'

'And what shall you do in that case?'

'And you?'

'I shall be silent,' replied La Mole, with a fevered blush, 'if I can.'

'And I,' said Coconnas, 'will tell them a few things they do not expect.'

'What things?' asked La Mole eagerly.

'Oh, don't worry—things that will prevent M. d'Alençon from sleeping quietly for some time.'

La Mole was about to reply, when the jailer, who no doubt had heard some noise, suddenly entered the chamber, and pushing each into his respective cell, locked them in again.

55

THE FIGURE OF WAX

FOR a week Charles was confined to his bed by a slow fever, interrupted by fits like epilepsy. During these attacks his cries were terrible. When they were over, he sank back exhausted into the arms of his nurse.

Henry was kept shut up in his cell at the prison, and, at his own request to Charles, no one was allowed to see him, not even Marguerite. Catherine and d'Alençon thought him lost. Henry himself ate and drank well and felt more at his ease, hoping he was forgotten.

At court no one suspected the real cause of the king's illness. Maître Ambroise Paré and Mazille, his colleague, believed it to be inflammation of the lining of the stomach, and ordered a regimen which aided the operation of the drink prescribed by René, and which Charles took three times a day from the hands of his nurse: it was the only nourishment he took.

La Mole and Coconnas were at Vincennes in close confinement. Marguerite and Madame de Nevers made several attempts to see them or to send them a letter, but in vain.

One morning Charles felt rather better, and ordered the court should be admitted. The doors were accordingly opened, and it was easy to see, by his pale cheeks and the feverish glare of his eyes, what great ravages his illness had made on the young king.

Catherine, d'Alençon, and Marguerite were informed that the king gave audience.

They all three entered at short intervals one after the other: Catherine calm, d'Alençon smiling, Marguerite dejected. Catherine sat down by the side of the bed without noticing the look Charles gave her; d'Alençon stood at the foot; Marguerite leaned against a table. On seeing her brother thus worn down by illness, she could not hold back a sigh and a tear.

Charles, whom nothing escaped, saw the tear and heard the sigh, and made a motion of his head to Marguerite, unseen by all but her.

This sign, slight as it was, gave courage to the poor queen, to whom Henry had not had time, or perhaps had not chosen to say anything. She feared for her husband. She trembled for her lover.

For herself she had no fear. She knew La Mole too well not to know that she could rely upon him utterly.

'Well, my dear son,' said Catherine, 'how are you now?'

'Better, madame, better.'

'And what say the physicians?'

'Oh, my physicians, they are very clever fellows,' cried Charles, bursting into a hollow laugh. 'I take great amusement in listening to their discussions about my illness.'

'What my brother needs,' observed François, 'is fresh air. A day's hunting, which he is so fond of, would do him good.'

'And yet,' replied Charles, with a singular smile, 'the last did me a great deal of harm.'

Then, with an inclination of his head, he signified to the courtiers that the audience was at an end.

D'Alençon bowed and withdrew.

Marguerite seized Charles's wasted hand and kissed it tenderly, then left the apartment.

'Dear Margot!' murmured Charles.

Catherine remained. Charles, seeing her alone with him, recoiled as if from a serpent.

He knew to whom and to what his agony was attributable.

'Why have you stayed, madame?' asked he, with a shudder.

'I wish to speak to you of important matters, my son,' returned Catherine.

'Speak, madame,' said Charles.

'Sire, you said just now your doctors were very skilful.'

'I say so still.'

'Well—I suspect that, clever as they are, they know nothing at all about your disorder.'

'Really, madame?'

'And that they are treating the symptoms instead of treating the cause.'

'On my soul,' replied Charles, astonished, 'I think you are right!'

'Well, my son,' continued Catherine, 'since it is essential for my happiness and for the welfare of the kingdom you should be cured as speedily as possible, I have assembled all the men skilled, not only in curing the diseases of the body, but those of the mind.'

'What was the result?'

'What I expected. I have the remedy that will cure not only your body, but your mind.'

Charles trembled. He thought that his mother intended to give him a fresh poison, finding the first too slow.

'Where is this remedy?' asked he.

'In the disease itself.'

'Where is that situated?'

'Listen, my son,' said the queen. 'Did you never hear of secret enemies, who assassinate their victim from a distance?'

'By steel or poison?' demanded Charles, without changing his expression.

'My son,' asked the Florentine, 'do you believe in magic?'

'Absolutely,' returned Charles, repressing a smile of incredulity.

'Well, then,' continued Catherine, 'all your sufferings have been caused by magic. An enemy, who did not dare attack you openly, has done so in secret. A terrible conspiracy, the more terrible that it was without accomplices, has been directed against your Majesty.'

'Oh?' said Charles.

'You may doubt it, but I know for a certainty.'

'I never doubt what you tell me,' replied the king sarcastically. 'I am curious to know exactly how they tried to kill me.'

'By magic.'

'Explain yourself.'

'If the conspirator I mean, and whom your Majesty suspects already in your mind, had succeeded, there would have been no trace, but fortunately your brother watched over you.'

'What brother?'

'D'Alençon.'

'Ah! true,' said Charles, with a bitter laugh, 'I forgot I had a brother. Well, continue, madame.'

'He discovered a clue to the conspirator's identity.'

'Ah! I suppose you mean the King of Navarre, mother?' replied Charles, curious to see how far her dissimulation would go.

Catherine lowered her eyes hypocritically.

'I have had him arrested and sent to Vincennes for his escapade,' continued the king. 'Is he guiltier than I suspected, then?'

'Do you feel the fever that consumes you?' asked Catherine.

'Yes,' replied Charles, his brow darkening.

'Do you feel the fire that burns your stomach?'

'Ay, madame.'

'Do you feel the shooting pains in your head?'

'Yes. How well you understand the symptoms.'

'Well, look at this.'

And she drew a little figure from the folds of her dress.

The figure was made of yellow wax, about ten inches high, clothed in a robe covered with golden stars, also moulded in wax, and over this a royal mantle of the same material.

'What is this figure?' asked Charles.

'See what it has on the head,' said Catherine.

'A crown,' replied Charles.

'And in the heart——'

'A needle.'

'Well——'

'Well, do you not see that it is you?'

'Me?'

'Yes, in your royal robes, with the crown on your head.'

'And who made this figure?' asked the king, weary of this miserable farce. 'The King of Navarre, of course.'

'No, sire.'

'No? Then I do not understand you.'

'I say *no*,' replied Catherine, 'because you asked the question literally. But if you had put it in a different way, I should have answered, Yes.'

Charles made no answer.

'Sire,' continued she, 'this figure was found by the attorney-general, Laguesle,* in the apartment of the man who led a horse for the King of Navarre on the day of the hawking party.'

'M. de la Mole?'

'Yes. Now look at the needle in the heart, and the name written on the label attached to it.'

'I see an M,' returned Charles.

'That means "*mort*"; it is the magic formula.'

'So, then, the person who wants to kill me is M. de la Mole?' said Charles.

'Yes, he is the dagger; but behind the dagger is the hand that directs it.'

'And this is the cause of my illness? What must be done now? for you know that, unlike you, I know nothing of charms and spells.'

'The death of the conspirator destroys the charm. Its power ceases with his life.'

'Really?'

'Did you not know that?'

'I am no sorcerer.'

'But now you are convinced, are you not, of the cause of your illness?'

'Completely.'

'You do not say so to humour me?'

'Oh, no! from the bottom of my heart.'

'Heaven be praised!' said Catherine.

'Yes, Heaven be praised!' repeated Charles ironically. 'I know the cause of my illness, and whom to punish.'

'And you will punish——'

'M. de la Mole: you say he is the guilty party.'

'I say he is the instrument.'

'Well, we will begin with him, and if he has an accomplice he will confess.'

'If he does not,' muttered Catherine, 'I have infallible means of making him. You will, then, sire, allow the process to be set in motion?'

'Yes, madame, and the sooner the better.'

Catherine pressed her son's hand, not understanding the nervous pressure with which he responded, and left the apartment without hearing his sardonic laugh, or the terrible imprecation which followed that laugh. At this moment he heard a rustling noise, and, turning round, saw Marguerite lifting the tapestry of the door of the nurse's apartments.

'Oh, sire, sire!' cried Marguerite, 'you know what *she* says is not true.'

'*She!* Who?' said Charles.

'Oh, Charles! it is terrible to accuse one's own mother. I knew the only reason she stayed behind was to persecute him. I swear to you, by all I hold sacred, that what she says is false.'

'Who is she trying to persecute?'

'Henry, your own Henry, who loves you, and is devoted to you.'

'You think so, Margot?'

'I am sure of it.'

'And so am I.'

'Why, then, did you arrest him, and send him to Vincennes?' said Marguerite.

'Oh, he has odd ideas. Perhaps he is wrong, perhaps he is right, but he thought he would be safer in disgrace than in favour, at Vincennes than in the Louvre, and so he asked me to arrest him.'

'Is he safe?'

'As safe as a man can be, for Beaulieu answers for his life with his own.'

'Oh, thanks! but——'

'But what?'

'There is another person in whose welfare I am interested.'

'Who is this person?'

'Sire, spare me; I hardly dare name him to my brother, much less to my king.'

'M. de la Mole, is it not?'

'Alas! sire, you tried once before to kill him, and he only escaped by a miracle.'

'He had committed only one crime then, now he has committed two.'

'But he is not guilty of the second.'

'But do you not know what our mother says?'

'I have already told you what she says is false.'

'Do you not know that a figure dressed in royal robes and pierced to the heart was found in De la Mole's apartment?'

'Yes, but it was the figure of a woman, not of a man.'

'And the needle——'

'Was a charm to make a woman love him, not to kill a man.'

'What was the name of this woman?'

'MARGUERITE!' cried the queen, throwing herself at Charles's bedside, and bathing his hand with tears.

'Silence, Margot,' said Charles, 'you too may be overheard.'

'Oh, no matter!' cried the queen. 'If all the world were present to hear me, I would declare it infamous to abuse the love of a gentleman, by staining his reputation with a charge of murder.'

'What if I knew the real perpetrator of this crime?'

'Brother——'

'It was not La Mole.'

'You know then——'

'The real author of the crime.'

'A crime has been committed, then?'

'Yes.'

'Impossible!'

'Look at me.'

Marguerite obeyed, and shuddered as she saw him so pale.

'I have not three months to live!'

'*You*, brother!'

'Margot, I have been poisoned!'

Marguerite screamed.

'Silence!' said Charles. 'It must be thought I was murdered by magic!'

'You know who is guilty?'

'Yes.'

'Who is it? D'Alençon?'

'Perhaps.'

'Or——' Marguerite whispered as if alarmed at what she was going to say—'our mother?'

Charles remained silent. Marguerite, however, read the answer in his eye, and sank into a chair.

'My God!' murmured she. 'It is impossible!'

'Impossible?' said Charles. 'It is a pity René is not here.'

'René?'

'Yes, he could tell you all about it. A book he lent to his mistress was poisoned, and that book has poisoned me. But this must be hidden from the world, and that it may be so, it must be believed I die of magic, and by the hand of the man they accuse.'

'But it is monstrous!' exclaimed Marguerite. 'Forgive me, but you know he is innocent!'

'I know it, but everyone must believe him guilty. Let your lover die; his death alone can save the honour of our family. I myself die that the secret may be preserved.'

Marguerite saw her only hope lay in her own resources, and withdrew, weeping.

Meantime, Catherine had not wasted a moment, but had written to Laguesle the following historical letter, which we give word for word,* and which throws a considerable light on this bloody drama:—

'M. LE PROCUREUR,—I have this evening been informed for certain that La Mole has committed sacrilege. Many wicked books and papers have been found in his apartments in Paris. Call upon the president of the court, and inform him of the whole affair and of the waxen figure meant for the king which was pierced to the heart.

'CATHERINE.'

56

THE INVISIBLE SHIELDS

THE day after Catherine wrote this letter, the governor entered Coconnas's cell with an imposing escort of two halberdiers and four black-gowned men.

Coconnas was ordered to the room where Laguesle and two

judges waited to interrogate him, according to Catherine's instructions.

During the week he had spent in prison, Coconnas had reflected deeply; besides that, he and La Mole, seeing each other daily, had agreed on the conduct they were to pursue, which was to persist in an absolute denial. They were convinced that with a little thought the affair would take a more favourable turn. Coconnas did not know that Henry was in the same prison as themselves, and the complaisance of his jailer suggested to him that over his head considerable powers of protection were at work, which he called *invisible shields*.

Thus far, the interrogations had been confined to the intentions of the King of Navarre, his plans for flight, and the part the two friends had played in those plans. Coconnas had consistently given vague and carefully calculated answers and was ready to go on doing so, having prepared beforehand all his little repartees, when he suddenly found the object of the interrogation had been altered.

It was now directed at several visits made to René, and at one or more waxen figures made at La Mole's instigation. Prepared as he was, Coconnas believed that the accusation had lost much of its intensity, since it no longer concerned the betrayal of a king but the making of a figure of a queen, and that queen not more than eight or ten inches high at most. He therefore replied, with much vivacity, that neither he nor his friend had played with dolls for many years, and he saw, with much satisfaction, that his replies more than once made the judges laugh. His interrogation concluded, he went up to his chamber singing so merrily that La Mole, for whose benefit he made all this noise, drew from it the brightest auguries.

La Mole was brought down from his tower, as Coconnas had been, and noted with equal astonishment the fresh turn which the investigation took. He was questioned about his visits to René. He replied that he had only once visited the Florentine. Had he not ordered a waxen figure? He replied that René had showed him such a figure, ready-made. Then he was asked if this figure did not represent a man? He replied that it represented a woman. Was not the purpose of the charm to cause the death of this man? He replied that the purpose of the charm was to make the woman love him.

These questions, put in a hundred different ways, were always answered by La Mole in the same manner.

The judges were glancing at each other with indecision, not knowing very well what to say or do, when a note brought to the attorney-general solved the difficulty. It was thus couched,—

'If the accused denies, put him to the torture.—C.'

The attorney put the note in his pocket, smiled at La Mole, and politely dismissed him. La Mole returned to his cell almost as reassured, if not as cheerful, as Coconnas.

'I think everything will go well now,' he said.

An hour afterwards, he heard footsteps, and saw a note which was slipped under his door, without seeing the hand that did it. He took it up with a trembling hand, and almost cried out with joy when he recognized the writing. 'Courage!' said the note. 'I am watching over you.'

'Ah! if she is watching,' cried La Mole, kissing the note which had touched the hand he loved—'if she is watching, I am saved!'

It is necessary, in order that La Mole should understand the purport of the note, and rely, with Coconnas, on what the Piedmontese called his *invisible shields*, that we should guide the reader to that small house, to the room in that house, where so many tender memories, so many bitter feelings, were twisting the heart of a woman who lay on a divan covered with velvet cushions.

'To be a queen—powerful, young, rich, beautiful—and suffer what I suffer!' she exclaimed—'oh, it is horrible!'

Then, in her agitation, she got up, paced up and down, suddenly paused, pressed her burning forehead against the ice-cold marble, straightened, pale, with her face covered with tears, wrung her hands in despair, and fell back, fainting, into the nearest chair.

Suddenly the tapestry which separated the apartment in the Rue Cloche Perce from the apartment in the Rue Tizon was raised, and the Duchess de Nevers appeared.

'Ah!' exclaimed Marguerite—'is it you? With what impatience I have awaited you. Well, what news?'

'Bad news—bad news, my dear! Catherine herself is hurrying the trial on, and is at this moment at Vincennes.'

'And René?'

'Has been arrested.'*

'And our prisoners?'

'The jailer informs me that they see each other daily. The day before yesterday they were searched, and La Mole broke your miniature to smithereens rather than let them have it.'

'Dear La Mole!'

'Annibal laughed in the teeth of the inquisitors.'

'Worthy Annibal!—Anything else?'

'They were interrogated this morning about the flight of the king, his plans for rebellion in Navarre, but they said nothing.'

'Oh, I knew they would keep silent. But silence will kill them just as much as if they spoke.'

'Yes, but we must save them.'

'You have thought over our plan?'

'I have been working on it since yesterday.'

'Well?'

'I have come to terms with Beaulieu. Ah, my dear queen, what a hard and greedy man! It will cost a man's life and three hundred thousand crowns.'

'Only the life of a man and three hundred thousand crowns! Why, it is a trifle!'

'A trifle? Why, it will cost us all our jewels at least.'

'Oh, that's nothing. The King of Navarre will pay something, the Duke d'Alençon shall pay something, my brother Charles must pay something, or if not——'

'Oh, do not trouble yourself on that score. I have the money, or at least three diamonds that will raise it, and the man.'

'The man!—what man?'

'The man who must be killed. Have you forgotten that there is a man to be killed?'

'And you have found the man you wanted?'

'Yes.'

'At the same price?' asked Marguerite, with a smile.

'At that price I could have found ten,' replied Henriette. 'No, no, for five hundred crowns.'

'Really?'

'Now listen: this is the plan. The chapel is the only place in the fortress where women (not being prisoners) are admitted. We shall hide behind the altar. Under the cloth will be laid two daggers. The door of the sacristy will have been unlocked beforehand. Coconnas will strike the jailer, who will fall down as if dead; we shall then appear, and each cast a cloak over the shoulders of our friend. We shall then escape with them through the small door of the sacristy, and, since we shall have the password, we shall get out without difficulty.'

'And once out?'

'Two horses will be waiting at the gate. They will mount, ride off, leave France, and reach Lorraine, occasionally returning incognito.'

'Oh, you restore me to life,' said Marguerite. 'In this way we shall save them.'

'I feel pretty confident.'

'And will it be soon?'

'In three or four days—Beaulieu is to let us know.'

'But if you were recognized in the vicinity of Vincennes, all our plans might be ruined.'

'How could anyone recognize me? I go dressed as a nun, with a large hood over my face. No one would ever recognize the end of my nose.'

'We cannot be too careful.'

'I know that well enough, *Mordi!* as my poor dear Annibal says.'

'Have you any news of the King of Navarre?'

'Yes, he was never happier, it seems. He laughs, sings, and eats, drinks, and sleeps well—all he asks is to be well guarded.'

'He is right.'

'Farewell, Marguerite! I am going to take the field again.'

'Are you sure of Beaulieu?'

'I think so.'

'Of the jailer?'

'He has promised.'

'Horses?'

'The best in the Duke de Nevers's stables.'

'Henriette, I adore you;' and Marguerite threw her arms

around her friend's neck. Then the two women separated, promising to see each other again next day and every day, at the same
place and the same time. They were the two charming and
devoted creatures whom Coconnas, with so much justification,
called the *invisible shields*.

<h2 style="text-align:center">57</h2>

THE TRIAL

'WELL, my brave friend,' said Coconnas to La Mole, when left
together at the end of their interrogations,* 'everything seems to
be going as well as we could possibly wish, and we shall soon be
free.'

'No doubt,' answered La Mole. 'Moreover the friendliness
with which our jailers treat us clearly proves that our noble
friends are at work for us.'

'To be sure they are!' rejoined Coconnas, 'and how could
a queen or a princess better employ their riches than in
obtaining our freedom. Now let us go over our lesson. We
are to be taken to the chapel, where we shall be left in the
keeping of our turnkey; we each of us find a dagger hidden
in a place described to us. Well, then I manage to inflict a
severe-looking but superficial wound on our guard, to make
it appear that we, being two, overpowered him. The next thing,
we barricade the door of the chapel by piling the benches
up against it, while our two princesses emerge from their
hiding-places behind the altar, and Henriette opens the small
side door!'

'And then,' exclaimed La Mole delightedly, 'we walk out and
exchange our gloomy prison for good fresh air. A couple of
vigorous horses are waiting for us; a hasty embrace with our fair
rescuers, and away we go to Lorraine. True, I could have wished
to be banished to Navarre, for that is her home. But, as things
are, we must settle for Nancy, which is only fifty leagues from
Paris.'*

'But what is the matter, my friend?'

'Nothing. Just an idea that struck me.'

'I should think not a very agreeable one: you have turned quite pale.'

'I was wondering to myself why we are to be taken to the chapel.'

'Why,' said Coconnas, 'to pray, of course—what else?'

'But,' answered La Mole, 'it is customary for only those who have undergone the torture or are sentenced to death to spend the night in the chapel.'

'Truly,' replied Coconnas, becoming pale in his turn; 'this needs thinking about. Let us speak to the worthy fellow I am to carve my name on with my dagger. Here, I say, turnkey!'

'Did you call?' said the man, who had been keeping watch at the top of the stairs.

'We want to know if it is all arranged for us to escape from the chapel?'

'Hush!' said the turnkey, looking round him with terror.

'Don't be frightened, no one can hear you—speak out.'

'Yes. You will be taken to the chapel, according to the custom that all persons sentenced to death pass the night before their execution in prayer.'

Coconnas and La Mole exchanged looks of surprise and alarm.

'You expect that we shall be sentenced to death?'

'Why, you think so yourselves, don't you? Otherwise why take the trouble to make these arrangements to escape?'

'There is sense in what he says,' said Coconnas.

'We are playing a dangerous game, it seems,' replied La Mole.

'And what about me?' said the jailer. 'Suppose, in the excitement of the moment, you were to wound me in the wrong place, strike your dagger an inch or two deeper than you intended!'

'*Mordi!*' exclaimed Coconnas, 'I only wish we could change places, and I had nothing more to fear than you have. But listen! I fancy someone is coming.'

'Gentlemen, get into your cells—make haste!'

'And when will our trial take place?'

'To-morrow at latest. But don't worry. The friends who are working on your behalf shall be duly informed.'

'Then let us say farewell to each other for the present, and to these detested walls forever!'

The friends exchanged an affectionate embrace, and each retired to his place of confinement—La Mole sighing, Coconnas humming a tune.

Nothing unusual occurred until seven o'clock in the evening. Night descended, dark and rainy, on the fortress of Vincennes: it was perfect weather for an escape. Coconnas's supper was brought and eaten with his ordinary appetite. He was almost ready for sleep, while listening to the loud murmurs of the wind and the splashing rain as it drove heavily against the walls, when he was roused by a sound of footsteps passing to and fro from La Mole's cell.

In vain did Coconnas strain his ears—he could make out nothing. The time passed—no one came near him.

'Strange,' murmured he, 'that La Mole should receive so many visits, while I am quite forgotten. Perhaps La Mole was suddenly taken ill and called out for assistance. What can it mean?'

An hour and a half was thus spent in vainly watching for some explanation of this mystery, and Coconnas was beginning to feel both angry and sleepy, when the sudden turning of the key in the lock made him spring to his feet.

'It's all right,' he said mentally, 'they are coming to take us to the chapel, without going through the motions of sentencing. *Mordi!* the night favours us—dark as a pit. I only hope the horses they give us will be able to find their way.'

He was just about to ask some jocular question of the turnkey, who had by that time entered, when he observed the man put his finger to his lips and roll his great eyes in the most portentous manner.

Coconnas then perceived a dim outline of persons following the jailer, and made out two figures wearing helmets on which the candle, smoking and flickering in the strong current of air rushing up the staircase, cast a reflection.

'Hallo!' exclaimed he. 'What is the meaning of all this? Where are we going?'

The jailer replied only with a sigh, which resembled a groan.

'Follow the halberdiers, sir,' said a voice, which at once informed Coconnas that the soldiers were accompanied by an officer of some kind.

'And where is M. de la Mole?' inquired the Piedmontese. 'What has become of him?'

'Follow the halberdiers!' repeated the same voice that had given the command.

Further protest was useless. Without another word, therefore, Coconnas began to descend the spiral staircase. At the first floor the guards stopped, a door was opened, and he saw a number of men dressed as judges seated in judicial order, while in the background Coconnas made out the dim outline of a man with naked arms and a look that made his forehead break into a cold sweat.

Still concealing his alarm, he entered the chamber with an easy, nonchalant air, his head a little on one side, and his hand on his hip, after the approved manner of court gallants.

As Coconnas advanced, he perceived La Mole sitting on a bench near the judges and officials.

The guards led Coconnas to the front of the tribunal. There he stopped, turned round, and smilingly nodded to La Mole, then paid close attention to the proceedings of the court.

'What is your name?' inquired the president.

'Marc Annibal de Coconnas,' replied the Piedmontese, with gentlemanly grace, 'Count of Montpantier, Chenaux, and other places. But I imagine you don't wish to know all that.'

'Where were you born?'

'At Saint Colomban, near Suza.'*

'How old are you?'

'Twenty-seven years and three months.'

'Good!' answered the president.

'He seems to be pleased with my account of myself,' murmured Coconnas.

'Now, then,' continued the president, 'what was your motive in leaving the service of the Duke d'Alençon?'

'To rejoin my friend, M. de la Mole, who, when I left M. d'Alençon, had done likewise some days before.'

'And what were you doing when you were arrested, the day of the hunt at Saint-Germain?'

'Why, hunting, of course!' replied Coconnas.

'The king was also present at the hunt, and it was there that he was first seized with violent illness.'

'I know nothing about that. I was not near the king myself, and I did not even know he had been taken ill.'

The judges regarded each other with an air of incredulity.

'Oh! you were ignorant of his Majesty's illness, were you?'

'Yes, completely, and I regret to hear of it. For though the King of France is not my king, I still pity him, and feel very sorry for him.'

'Really?'

'On my honour I do. I wouldn't say as much for his brother, the Duke d'Alençon, for there, I must confess——'

'We have nothing to do with the Duke d'Alençon, our business is with his Majesty——'

'Whose very humble servant I have already told you I am,' answered Coconnas.

'Then being his servant, as you say, please tell us what you know about a certain wax figure.'

'Oh! what, we are going over that story again, are we?'

'If you have no objection.'

'*Pardi!* on the contrary, I prefer it—go on.'

'How was it that this figure was found in M. de la Mole's possession?'

'M. de la Mole's! No, no, you mean in René's possession.'

'Then you acknowledge the existence of such an image?'

'I don't know whether it exists or not—I could tell you better if I saw it.'

'Here it is. Is it the one you have previously seen?'

'It is.'

'Write down,' said the judge, 'that the accused recognizes the figure as the one he saw in the possession of M. de la Mole.'

'No, no, no!' interposed Coconnas, 'do not let us mislead one another. Write that I say it is the same figure I saw at René's.'

'Well, so be it—at René's and on what day?'

'The only day La Mole and myself were ever at René's.'

'So you admit that you were there with M. de la Mole?'

'I never denied it, did I?'

'Write down that the accused admits having gone to Rene's to work certain charms and spells——'

'Hold hard, M. le President, and moderate your enthusiasm a little—I said no such thing.'

'You deny having gone to René's house for the sake of charms and magical purposes?'

'I do. The conjuration that took place occurred by chance, and was wholly unpremeditated.'

'But still it took place?'

'Certainly. I cannot deny that something resembling the working of a charm did occur.'

'Write down that the accused admits having gone to René's for the sake of obtaining a charm against the king's life.'

'The king's life?' exclaimed Coconnas—'That's a base lie. No such charm was ever made or asked for.'

'There, gentlemen!' said La Mole, 'you hear!'

'Silence!' vociferated the president, then turning towards the clerk he said, 'Against the king's life. Have you written it?'

'No, no!' cried Coconnas, 'I said no such thing. Besides the figure is not of a man, but of a woman.'

'What did I tell you, gentlemen?' inquired La Mole.

'M. de la Mole,' said the president, 'reply when you are questioned, but do not interrupt the interrogation of others.'

'You say that the figure is that of a female?' resumed the judge.

'Of course I do.'

'Why, then, does it wear a royal crown and mantle?'

'*Pardieu!* for a very simple reason—because the figure was meant to represent——'

Here La Mole stood up, and placed a finger on his lips.

'True!' said Coconnas, 'I was beginning to relate matters with which these gentlemen have nothing at all to do.'

'You persist, then, in your assertion, that this waxen image was intended to represent a woman?'

'I certainly persist in stating the truth.'

'And you refuse to say who the woman was?'

'A female in my own country,' said La Mole, 'whom I loved, and by whom I wanted to be loved.'

'You are not the person being interrogated, M. de la Mole,' exclaimed the president. 'Either be silent, or I shall be obliged to have you gagged.'

'Gag a gentleman who is my friend merely for speaking—can it be possible that I hear aright? For shame! for shame!'

'Bring in René!' said the attorney-general.

'Yes, by all means fetch René,' said Coconnas. 'We shall soon see who is right.'

René entered, pale, shrunken, and so altered that the two young men seemed scarce to recognize him. The wretched old man appeared more conscience-stricken and crushed by the weight of the crime he was about to commit, than by those he had already perpetrated.

'Maître René!' said the judge, 'do you recognize the two accused persons here present?'

'I do,' answered René, in a voice which trembled with emotion.

'As having seen them where?'

'In various places, but more especially at my own house.'

'How frequently at your house?'

'Only once.'

As René proceeded, Coconnas's face grew brighter. La Mole, on the contrary, as though warned by some presentiment of evil, looked graver than before.

'And on what occasion did they pay you a visit?'

René seemed to hesitate a moment, then said,—

'To order me to make a small waxen figure.'*

'Maître René,' interrupted Coconnas, 'permit me to tell you, you are mistaken.'

'Silence!' cried the president. Then turning towards René, he said, 'And was this figure to represent a man or a woman?'

'A man!' answered René.

Coconnas sprang up as though he had received an electric shock.

'A man, do you say?' asked he.

'A man!' responded René, but in so faint a voice that the president could scarcely hear him.

'And why was this figure dressed in a royal mantle, with a crown on its head?'

'Because,' replied René, 'it represented a king.'

'Infamous liar!' cried Coconnas, beside himself with rage.

'Hold your peace, Coconnas,' interposed La Mole, 'every man

has a right to sell his soul his own way. Let the wretched man say what he chooses.'

'Ay, but he has no right to destroy the bodies of others while he barters his own soul!' answered Coconnas.

'And what is the meaning of the needle found sticking in the heart of the image, with a small banner bearing the letter *m* at the end?'

'The needle represents the sword or dagger, and the letter *m* stands for *mort*.'

Coconnas sprang forward, as though to strangle René, but was held back by the guards.

'That will do!' said the officer. 'The court is in possession of all it wants to know. Let the prisoners be returned to the antechamber.'

'But,' exclaimed Coconnas, 'it is impossible to hear oneself accused of such crimes without protesting against them.'

'Protest as much as you like, gentlemen, no one is preventing you. Guards, take the prisoners away.'

The officials seized La Mole and Coconnas, and led them away, each by a separate door.

The attorney-general then beckoned to the man with bare arms whom Coconnas had observed on entering, and said,—

'Do not go away, my good fellow, there will be work for you before the night is over.'

'Which shall I begin with?' said the man, respectfully raising his cap.

'With that one!' answered the president, pointing to La Mole, whose shadow could just be made out between his two guards. Then turning to René, who stood in trembling expectation of being ordered back to his place of confinement in the Châtelet*—

'You have done well, my friend. Do not be alarmed. Both the king and queen shall be informed that it is to you they will be indebted for coming at the real truth of this affair.'

But this promise, instead of inspiring René with fresh hope, seemed to increase his alarm, and he replied only with a deep sigh which was not unlike the groan of one in pain.

58

THE TORTURE OF THE BOOT

IT was only when back in his cell with the door secured on him, that Coconnas, no longer sustained by the altercation with the judges, began to think about their predicament.

'It seems to me,' thought he, 'things are going against us. They really intend to cut off our heads. I think it is time to go to the chapel.'

These words, spoken in a whisper, were cut short by a cry so shrill, so piercing, that it seemed impossible it could come from a human being, for it penetrated through the thick wall, and reverberated against the iron bars.

Coconnas shuddered with terror, although he was so brave that his courage was nearly the equal to that of wild beasts.

He stood motionless, doubting whether what he had heard was not the wind, when he heard it again. This time he was convinced not only that the voice was human, but that it was the voice of La Mole.

At this voice, the Piedmontese forgot he was a prisoner confined by two doors, three portcullises, and a wall twelve feet thick. He hurled himself forward, crying,—

'A man is being murdered!'

But he collided so violently with the wall that the shock threw him back on a stone bench.

'Oh, they have killed him!' repeated he. 'This is abominable! He is unarmed!'

He looked about on every side for a weapon.

At this moment the door opened, and the same voice that had been before so disagreeable to him said,—

'Come, sir, the court is waiting for you.'

'Good!' said Coconnas, 'to read me my sentence, I suppose?'

'Yes, sir.'

'I breathe again—lead on.'

And he followed the officer who led the way, his black wand in his hand.

Despite his show of confidence, Coconnas glanced anxiously on either side.

'Oh,' murmured he, 'I do not see my worthy jailer. I wish he was here.'

On entering the chamber, Coconnas saw the attorney-general, who had conducted the prosecution with such palpable animosity, for Catherine had ordered him to carry on the affair with the utmost zeal.

A curtain was drawn back, and revealed the recesses of this chamber which, now being fully visible, were so hideous that Coconnas felt his knees tremble, and he exclaimed,—

'Oh, *mon Dieu!*'

The sight before him was indeed alarming. The section of the apartment which had been concealed during the interrogation by a curtain, now raised, seemed like the vestibule of Hell.

'Oh!' said Coconnas, 'the torture chamber has been prepared, and only awaits a victim. What does this mean?'

'Kneel, M. Annibal de Coconnas!' thundered a voice, 'kneel, and hear your sentence.'

And before he had time even to collect his thoughts, two strong hands laid hold of him, and forced him to his knees.

The voice continued,—

'Sentence of the court sitting at Vincennes on Marc Annibal de Coconnas, accused and convicted of the crime of high treason, of an attempt to poison, of sacrilege and magic against the person of the king, of conspiracy against the state, and of having driven a prince of the blood into rebellion by his pernicious counsels.'

At each fresh charge, Coconnas shook his head defiantly.

The judge continued,—

'In consequence of which, the aforesaid Marc Annibal de Coconnas will be taken from his prison to the Place Saint-Jean-en-Grève,* to be there decapitated, his property confiscated, his woods cut down, his châteaux destroyed, and a post, with a copperplate bearing an inscription recording his crime and punishment, planted there.'

'As for my head,' said Coconnas, 'that I know is in jeopardy. But, as for my woods and châteaux, I do not fear for them in the least, and I defy all your axes and saws to harm them.'

'Silence!' said the judge, and he continued,—

'And moreover, the aforesaid Coconnas——'

'What!' interrupted Coconnas, 'do you intend to do anything more to me after cutting my head off?—that is very cruel!'

'No, monsieur,' replied the judge—'*before.*'

He continued,—

'And prior to the execution of this sentence, the aforesaid Coconnas will undergo the extraordinary question, consisting of ten wedges.'

Coconnas sprang to his feet, and fixing his eyes with a withering expression on his judges,—

'For what?' cried he.

This torture spelled ruin to Coconnas's hopes. He would not be taken to the chapel until after the torture, and the torture often led to death. For it was held to be a proof of cowardice to confess, and the torture became more severe in proportion to the patient's obstinacy.

The judge made no reply, but continued,—

'In order to compel the aforesaid Coconnas to confess who were his accomplices.'

'*Mordi!*' cried Coconnas, 'this is infamous—this is cowardice!'

The judge, accustomed to the indignant protestations of the victims, gave a sign.

Coconnas, seized by the legs and arms, was overpowered and bound to the rack, before he could even see who were the perpetrators of this violence.

'Wretches!' shouted Coconnas, straining the ropes that bound him so violently that his tormentors retreated in alarm.

'Cowards! do your worst; I defy you to extract one word from me. No torture can make one of my race speak.'

'Clerk, prepare to write,' said the judge.

'Yes, prepare to write,' cried Coconnas; 'and if you write down everything I tell you, you scoundrel, you will have your work cut out.'

'Will you confess?' said the judge.

'Never!'

'You would be well-advised to reflect whilst it is yet time. Executioner, make ready.'

At these words, a man holding a rope in his hand advanced towards him.

It was Maître Caboche.

Caboche, without moving a muscle of his face, or indicating that he recognized Coconnas, placed two planks between his legs, then two more outside, and bound them together with the rope.

This formed what was called the *Boot*.

In the *ordinary* question, six wedges were used, which crushed the flesh. In the *extraordinary* question, ten were employed, which not only crushed the flesh, but also broke the bones.

Maître Caboche inserted a wedge between the planks, and then, with his mallet in his hand, looked at the judge.

'Will you confess?' asked the latter.

'Never!' returned Coconnas, although he felt a damp chill spread over his brow.

'Proceed,' said the judge.

Caboche raised his heavy mallet, and gave the wedge a tremendous blow.

Coconnas did not make a sound as this first wedge was driven home, though it usually extorted a groan from the most resolute.

On the contrary, his face expressed the greatest wonder, and he gazed in astonishment at Caboche, who, his arm raised, stood ready to repeat the blow.

'What was your intention in concealing yourself in the forest?' demanded the judge.

'To enjoy the fresh air.'

'Proceed,' said the judge.

Caboche struck again.

Coconnas did not flinch, but kept his eyes fixed on the executioner with the same expression of surprise.

The judge frowned.

'He is very determined!' he muttered. 'Has the wedge entered, executioner?'

Caboche stooped, as if to examine it, and whispered to Coconnas,—

'Cry out! cry out!' Then rising,—

'To the head, sir,' said he to the judge.

'Second wedge!' was the reply.

The words of Caboche explained everything to Coconnas. The worthy executioner was rendering him the greatest service in his power: he was sparing him not only pain, but, moreover, the shame of a confession, by driving, in place of oak wedges, wedges of leather with only the top made of wood. Moreover, he thus left him all his strength to mount the scaffold with dignity.

'Oh, excellent Caboche!' muttered Coconnas, 'fear nothing; I will shout loud enough.'

Caboche had inserted a second wedge, larger than the first, and, at a sign from the judge, struck as if he intended to demolish the fortress of Vincennes with one blow.

'Ah! ah!—hou! hou!' roared Coconnas, 'you are breaking my bones!'

'Ah!' said the judge, 'the second seems to be having some effect. What were you doing in the forest?'

'I have already told you.'

'Proceed.'

'Confess,' whispered Caboche.

'What?'

'Anything—only confess.'

And he struck the wedge again.

'Oh, oh!' cried Coconnas. 'You wish to know by whose order I was in the forest?'

'Yes.'

'By the order of M. d'Alençon.'

'Write that down,' said the judge.

'If I laid a snare for the King of Navarre,' continued Coconnas, 'I was only obeying my master's orders.'

'You denounced me, tallow-face!' thought Coconnas, 'I will be even with you.'

And he related all the visits of François to the King of Navarre, the interviews between de Mouy and d'Alençon, and the story of the cherry-coloured cloak. He gave precise, terrible, incontrovertible evidence against d'Alençon, making it seem all the while as though his statements were extorted from him by the pain. He yelled, screamed, and foamed so naturally that the judge at last became terrified himself at having to record details which so fearfully compromised a prince of the blood.*

'Ah!' said Caboche to himself, 'this gentleman gives the clerk enough to do. What would he have said if the wedges had been of wood?'

The judge withdrew, excusing Coconnas the other wedges in

consequence of his confession, and Caboche was left alone with Coconnas.

'Well,' said he, 'how are you, sir?'

'Ah, excellent Caboche, I will never forget what you have done for me!'

'You are right, for if they knew what I have done for you, I should soon take your place, and they would not use leather wedges.'

'But what made you——?'

'I will tell you,' said Caboche, twisting, for the sake of appearances, bandages of bloody linen about Coconnas's legs; 'I knew you had been arrested and that Queen Catherine wanted you dead. I guessed you would be put to the question, and took my measures accordingly.'

'Ignoring the risk of what might happen to you?'

'Sir,' replied Caboche, 'you are the only gentleman who ever gave me his hand, and I wished to prove to you that, executioner though I may be, I have a heart. Moreover, you shall see how I will perform my office to-morrow.'

'To-morrow?'

'Yes.'

'What office?'

Caboche stared.

'Have you forgotten the sentence?'

'Ah! true, I had forgotten all about it.'

He had not forgotten it, but he was thinking of the chapel, the knife concealed beneath the altar-cloth, of Henriette and the queen, of the door of the sacristy, the two horses waiting for them, of liberty, of fresh air, and happiness and safety beyond the frontiers of France.

'Now,' said Caboche, 'I must get you from the rack to the litter. Do not forget both your legs are broken, and that the least movement is agony.'

'Ah! oh!' cried Coconnas, as the two assistants stepped forward.

'Take courage,' said Caboche. 'If you cry so now, what will you do later?'

'Maître Caboche,' replied Coconnas, 'I would prefer you to lift me yourself, for I do not wish your two estimable acolytes to touch me.'

'Bring the litter near the rack,' said Caboche.

The two assistants obeyed.

Caboche then lifted Coconnas in his arms, as if he had been a child, and laid him on the litter.

The jailer then appeared with a lantern.

'To the chapel,' said he.

The bearers and Coconnas moved off, but only after Coconnas had again given his hand to Caboche.

He had shaken the man's hand once before with such useful results that he was easily persuaded to do so again.

59

THE CHAPEL

THE grim procession silently crossed the two drawbridges of the fortress and the court-yard which led to the chapel, through the windows of which a pale light coloured the figures of the men in red robes.

Coconnas eagerly breathed the night air, although it was heavy with rain. He looked at the darkness, and rejoiced to see that everything conspired to favour the flight of himself and his companion. On entering the chapel he saw in the choir, and at three paces from the altar, a mass of something wrapped in a large white cloak. It was La Mole.

'Since we are once more reunited,' said Coconnas, in a voice of affected languor, 'place me next to my friend.'

La Mole was gloomy and pale. His head was propped against the marble wall, and his black hair, dank with perspiration which gave his face the pallor of ivory, seemed to have set in the form it had assumed after having been stiffened on his head with the pain.

On a signal from the turnkey, the two lackeys went to fetch the priest Coconnas had asked for.

This was the signal agreed upon.

Coconnas followed them with anxious eyes. But his was not the only ardent look fixed on them. Scarcely had they disappeared than two women rushed from behind the altar, and hastened rapidly towards the choir.

Marguerite hurried to La Mole and took him in her arms. La Mole uttered a piercing shriek—one of those cries which Coconnas had heard in his dungeon.

'*Mon Dieu!* what is the matter?' inquired Marguerite. 'Oh, Heaven! you are covered in blood!'

Coconnas, who had rushed towards the altar, found the dagger, and now had his arm round Henriette's waist, turned suddenly.

'Get up,' said Marguerite—'get up, I beg you! There is not a moment to lose.'

A terrible smile of regret passed over La Mole's pale lips, which seemed as though they would never smile again.

'Queen of my heart!' said the young man, 'you reckoned without Catherine. I have been put to the torture; my bones are broken, all my body is one wound, and the effort I make at this moment to press my lips upon your forehead causes me agony worse than death.'

And as he spoke, with great exertion, and ghastly pale, La Mole pressed his lips on the queen's brow.

'Torture?' cried Coconnas—'but I was tortured too. But the executioner did not do for you what he did for me?' And Coconnas told everything.

'Ah!' replied La Mole, 'that is easily explained. You gave him your hand on the day of our visit;* I forgot that all men were brothers, and was arrogant. God punishes me for my pride. God be praised!'

La Mole clasped his hands. Coconnas and the two ladies exchanged a look of indescribable horror.

'Come, come,' said the jailer, who had been to the door to listen, and had returned—'come along! Do not waste time, M. de Coconnas. Give me my blow with the dagger, and do it like a good and worthy gentleman, for they will soon be here.'

Marguerite was kneeling beside La Mole, like one of the reclining figures on a monument.

'Come, my friend,' said Coconnas—'courage! I am strong and will carry you. I can sit you on your horse, or hold you on my own, if you are not able to stay upright in the saddle. Come, let us go—let us go! You understand what the good fellow says: our lives are at stake.'

La Mole made a superhuman, a sublime effort.

'True,' he said, '*your* life is at stake,' and he tried to stand.

Annibal put his arms under him, and lifted him. La Mole, during this time, had only uttered a low moaning; but at the moment when Coconnas let him go to speak to the turnkey, and he was supported only by the arms of two women, his legs bent under him, and in spite of Marguerite's efforts, the tears gushing from her, he fell in a heap, and the piercing shriek he could no longer hold back made the chapel echo through all its gloomy vaults.

'You see,' said La Mole, in an agony of distress—'you see how it is with me my beloved. Go, but leave me with one last adieu. I have not revealed one word, Marguerite. Your secret is wrapped in my love and will die with me. Goodbye, my love!'

Marguerite, almost lifeless herself, threw her arms round that dear and beautiful head, and imprinted on his brow a kiss that was almost holy.

'You, Annibal,' said La Mole—'you who have been spared these agonies, who are young and may escape, go quickly! my dearest friend, and give me the consolation, as I die, of knowing that you are safe.'

'The time is passing,' exclaimed the jailer. 'Come, gentlemen, make haste!'

Henriette tried to lead Annibal gently away, while Marguerite was on her knees in front of La Mole, her hair dishevelled, and eyes overflowing with tears.

'Go, Annibal!' repeated La Mole—'go! Do not give our enemies the pleasure of seeing the death of two innocent men.'

Coconnas quietly disengaged himself from Henriette, who was leading him to the door, and with a gesture so solemn that it was regal, said,—

'Madame, first give the five hundred crowns we promised this man.'

'Here they are,' said Henriette.

Then, turning towards La Mole and shaking his head sorrowfully, he said,—

'As for you, La Mole, you have offended me by thinking for one moment that I would leave you. Did I not swear to live and die with you? But you are in such pain that I forgive you.'

And he seated himself with a resolute air near his friend, towards whom he leaned his head, and whose forehead he touched with his lips.

Then he drew gently—gently as a mother would a child—the head of his dear friend towards him, until it slipped off the wall, and rested calmly on his chest.

Marguerite was in despair: she picked up the dagger which Coconnas had dropped.

'Oh, my love!' cried La Mole, reaching out with his hands as he understood her purpose, 'do not forget that I die in order to destroy the slightest suspicion of our love.'

'What can I do,' exclaimed Marguerite despairingly, 'if I cannot die with you?'

'You can,' replied La Mole, 'make my death sweet so that I may meet it with a smile.'

Marguerite clasped her hands, and looked inquiringly at him.

'Do you remember the evening, Marguerite, when in exchange for the life I offered you then and to-day lay down for you, you made me a sacred promise?'

Marguerite started.

'Ah, you do remember!' said La Mole, 'for you shudder.'

'Yes, yes, I remember,' said Marguerite, 'and on my soul, Joseph, I will keep that promise.'

Marguerite held out her hand towards the altar, as if to call on God to witness her oath afresh.

La Mole's face lit up as if the vaulted roof of the chapel had opened.

'They are coming!' exclaimed the jailer.

Marguerite uttered a cry, and hastened towards La Mole, but for fear of increasing his agony, she paused trembling before him.

Henriette pressed her lips to Coconnas's brow, and said to him,—

'Dearest Annibal, I understand you, and I am proud of you. I know the heroism that makes you die, and I love you for that heroism. Before God, I will always love you more than anything that lives. And what Marguerite has sworn to do for La Mole (although I do not know what it is) I will also do for you.'

And she held out her hand to Marguerite.

'Well said! Now Heaven be with you!' replied Coconnas.

'Before you leave me, dearest,' said La Mole, 'one last favour: give me some last souvenir, so that I may kiss it as I climb the scaffold.'

'Ah, yes,' cried Marguerite, 'here, take this!'—and she untied from her neck a small reliquary of gold fastened to a chain of the same metal.

'Here,' she said, 'is a holy relic which I have worn since childhood: my mother put it round my neck when I was very little and she still loved me. It was given by our uncle, Pope Clement,* and has never left me. Take it!'

La Mole took it and kissed it eagerly.

'They are opening the door,' said the jailer. 'Go, ladies, begone!'

The two women ran behind the altar and disappeared at the moment the priest entered.*

60

THE PLACE SAINT-JEAN-EN-GRÈVE

IT was seven o'clock in the morning,* and the crowd was waiting, dense and riotous, in the squares, the streets, and along the quays.

At six o'clock in the morning a tumbril, the same in which the two friends after their duel had been conveyed half dead to the Louvre, had left Vincennes, and crossed the Rue Saint-Antoine slowly, and on its route, the spectators, so huddled together that they crushed one another, seemed like statues, with their eyes fixed and their mouths open in wonderment.

For today, a heart-rending spectacle was being offered by the queen-mother to all the people of Paris.

In the tumbril we have said was making its slow way from Vincennes, were lying on some straw two young men, bareheaded and entirely clothed in black, leaning against each other. Coconnas supported on his knees La Mole, whose head hung over the side of the tumbril, and whose eyes wandered vaguely around him.

The crowd, intent on feasting their greedy eyes, pressed, drove, heaved, perched on stones, clung to the angles of the walls, and appeared satisfied when they managed a glimpse of the two bodies which were going from suffering to destruction.

It was rumoured that La Mole would die without having confessed one of the charges imputed to him. On the other hand, Coconnas, it was asserted, could not endure the torture, and had revealed everything.

So there were cries on all sides,—

'Look at the red-haired one! He was the one who confessed! It was he who gave everything away! He is the coward who caused the death of the other one, who is brave and refused to confess anything!'

The two young men understood this—the one the praises, and the other the reproaches, which accompanied their funeral march. While La Mole pressed the hands of his friend, a sublime expression of contempt spread across the face of the Piedmontese, who from the foul tumbril gazed on the stupid mob as if he were looking down from a triumphal car.

Misfortune had done its heavenly work: it had ennobled the face of Coconnas, just as death was about to make his soul divine.

'Are we nearly there?' asked La Mole; 'for I can bear this no longer, my dear friend, and I feel as if I am about to faint.'

'Rouse yourself, La Mole! We are passing by the Rue Tizon and the Rue Cloche-Perce. Look, look!'

'Oh, lift me up, so that I may see that place one last time!'

Coconnas tapped the executioner on the shoulder, as he sat on the tumbril and drove the horse.

'Executioner,' he said, 'do us the kindness to pause a moment in front of the Rue Tizon.'

Caboche bowed his head in assent, and stopped.

La Mole raised himself with a vast effort, aided by Coconnas, and gazed, with tearful eyes, at the small house, now closed and silent as the tomb: a groan burst from his overcharged soul, and he said, in a whisper,—

'Farewell, youth, love, life!'*

And his head fell on his chest.

'Courage,' said Coconnas—'perhaps we shall find all these things in the hereafter!'

'Do you believe we will?' murmured La Mole.

'I think so, because the priest told me so, but more especially because I hope so. But do not faint, my dear friend, or these fools will laugh at us.'

Caboche heard these last words, and whipping his horse with one hand, he gave the other (unseen by anyone) to Coconnas. It contained a small sponge saturated with a powerful stimulant. After inhaling and rubbing it over his brow, La Mole felt himself revived and re-animated, and he kissed the reliquary suspended from his neck.

When they reached the quay they saw the scaffold, which was raised high above the ground.

'My friend,' said La Mole, 'I would prefer to die first.'

Coconnas again touched the headsman's shoulder.

'Executioner,' said Coconnas, 'my friend has suffered more than I have, and he says he should suffer all the more to see me die first. Besides, if I were to die before him, he would have no one to support him on the scaffold.'

'Very well!' said Caboche, wiping away a tear with the back of his hand—'be easy, it shall be as you wish.'

'And with one blow, eh?' said the Piedmontese, in a whisper.

'Yes, with one blow!'

'Good!'

The tumbril stopped. They had arrived. Coconnas put on his hat.

A murmur like that of the waves of the sea reached the ears of La Mole. He tried to rise, but his strength failed him, and Caboche and Coconnas were forced to support him by his arms.

The place was paved with heads, and the steps of the Hotel de Ville* was like an amphitheatre peopled with spectators. Each window was filled with eager faces.

When they saw the handsome young man, who could no

longer support himself on his bruised and broken legs, make an effort to reach the scaffold, a vast sound was heard, like a cry of universal pity: the men groaned, and the women uttered plaintive sighs.

'He was one of the grandest dons at the court,' said one.

'How handsome he is! How pale he looks!' said the women. 'He is the one who would not confess!'

'My dearest friend,' said La Mole—'I cannot stand. Carry me!'

'Stay a moment,' replied Coconnas.

He made a sign to the executioner, who moved aside: then stooping, he lifted La Mole in his arms, as if he were a child, and went up the steps to the scaffold with unfaltering foot, bore his burden firmly on to the platform, and set him down amidst the shoutings and applause of the vast multitude.

Coconnas returned the greeting by raising his hat from his head, and then threw it down on the scaffold beside him.

'Look round,' said La Mole, 'do you see *them* anywhere?'

Coconnas glanced slowly around him, and when his eyes reached a certain spot, paused. Then, without moving his eyes, he touched his friend on the shoulder, saying,—

'Look, look, at the window of that little tower!'

With his other hand he pointed out to La Mole the small building which still exists at the corner of the Rue de la Vannerie and the Rue Mouton—a remnant of past ages. Two women, clothed in black, were leaning on each other, half-hidden by the window frame.

'Ah!' said La Mole, 'I had but one fear, and that was to die without again seeing her. I have beheld her again, and now I can die.'

And with his eyes fixed on the small window, he lifted the reliquary to his lips, and covered it with kisses.

Coconnas saluted the two women with as much grace as if he were in a drawing-room, and they replied to the two devoted men by shaking handkerchiefs wet with tears.

Caboche then touched Coconnas on his shoulder, and gave him a meaningful look. The Piedmontese replied,—

'Yes, yes!'

Then turning to La Mole, he said to him,—

'One last embrace, dear friend, and then die like a man! It will be no hardship for you, who are so brave.'

'Ah,' replied La Mole, 'there will be no merit for me in dying well, suffering the torments I do.'

The priest approached, and offered a crucifix to La Mole, who smiled, and pointed to the reliquary he held in his hand.

'No matter,' replied the priest—'but pray for strength from Him who suffered what you are about to suffer.'

La Mole kissed the feet of the crucifix.

'I am ready,' said La Mole.

'Can you hold your head upright?' asked Caboche, coming with his drawn sword behind La Mole, who was now on his knees.

'I hope so,' was the reply.

'Then all will go well.'

'But you,' said La Mole, 'will not forget what I asked of you: this reliquary will open doors for you.'

'Make yourself easy; and now try and hold your head perfectly straight.'

La Mole held his neck erect, and looking towards the little tower said,—

'Adieu, Marguerite! bless——'

He could not finish; with one stroke of his keen and flashing sword, Caboche severed from the body the head of La Mole, which rolled at Coconnas's feet.

The body fell gently back, as if going to rest.

'Thanks, good friend, thanks,' said Coconnas, giving his hand for the third time to the executioner.

A single shout arose from the lips of a thousand human beings, and amongst them, Coconnas fancied he heard one cry more piercing than all the rest.

'My son,' said the priest to Coconnas, 'have you nothing you would confess to God?'

'*Ma foi!* no, father,' replied the Piedmontese, 'all I had to say, I said yesterday to you.'

Then turning to Caboche, he said,—

'Now then, headsman, my last friend, one final service!'

Before he knelt, he turned on the multitude a look so calm, so full of resignation, that a murmur of admiration came to soothe his ear and flatter his pride. Then taking in his hands the head of his dear friend, and impressing a last kiss on the purple lips, he gave one more glance towards the little tower, and kneeling down, still holding the beloved head in his hands, he cried,—

'Now!'

He had scarcely uttered the word when Caboche with a sweep of his arm had cut his head from his body.*

'It is time it was all over,' said the worthy headsman, trembling all over—'poor, poor fellow!'

With some difficulty he took from the clenched fingers of La Mole the reliquary of gold, and threw his cloak over the sad remains, which the tumbril had yet to convey to his sinister abode.

The spectacle was over: the crowd dispersed.

61

THE HEADSMAN'S TOWER

NIGHT spread her mantle over the city which still shuddered under the recollection of this spectacle, the details of which passed from mouth to mouth and cast a pall of gloom over each family gathering.

In contrast to the city, which was silent and mournful, the Louvre was joyous, noisy, and illuminated. There was a grand fête at the palace—a fête commanded by Charles IX, a fête which he had ordered for that evening at the same time he had ordered the execution for the morning.

The previous evening, the Queen of Navarre had received the king's orders to be present, and in the hope that La Mole and Coconnas would escape in the night as a result of all measures being taken for their safety, she had promised her brother to comply with his wishes.

But once she had lost all hope, after the terrible scene in the chapel—after she had, from a last impulse of that deep love, which was the most real and enduring of her life, been present at the execution, she had made up her mind that neither prayers nor threats would force her to go to a boisterous celebration at the Louvre the same day she had witnessed so terrible a scene at the Grève.

The king on this day gave further evidence of that will-power which no one, perhaps, ever displayed more energetically than Charles IX.

He had been in bed for a fortnight, weak as a dying man, ghastly as a corpse. Yet he got up at five o'clock and put on his gayest clothes, although during his preparations he had fainted three times.

About eight o'clock he inquired after his sister, if any one had seen her, and if they knew where she was. No one could answer satisfactorily, for the queen had gone to her apartments about eleven o'clock, and refused admittance to everybody.

But there was no refusal for Charles. Leaning on the arm of M. de Nancey, he proceeded to the Queen of Navarre's apartments, and entered suddenly by the secret door.

Although he expected a melancholy sight, and was prepared for it, the spectacle which met his sight was even more distressing than he had anticipated.

Marguerite, half dead, was lying on a sofa, her head buried in the cushions, neither weeping nor praying. Ever since her return she had been moaning in bitterest anguish.

At the other end of the chamber, Henriette de Nevers, that bold and daring woman, lay stretched out on the carpet, unconscious.

Charles told Nancey to await him in the corridor, and entered, pale and trembling.

Neither of the women saw him. But Gillonne, who was at that moment trying to revive Henriette, rose on one knee and looked in panic at the king, who made a sign with his hand, whereupon she rose, curtseyed respectfully and withdrew.

Charles then approached Marguerite, looked at her for a moment in silence, and then in a gentle tone of which his harsh voice might have been thought incapable, said,—

'Margot, my sister!'

The queen started, and turned round.

'Your Majesty!' she said.

'Come, come, sister dear, stir yourself.'

Marguerite raised her eyes to heaven.

'Yes,' said Charles, 'I know everything—but listen to me.'

The queen made a sign that she was listening.

'You promised me that you would come to the ball,' said Charles.

'I did?' exclaimed Marguerite.

'Yes, and, since you promised, you are expected. If you do not come, everybody will be surprised at not seeing you.'

'I ask you to excuse me, brother,' replied Marguerite. 'You see how very ill I am.'

'Make an effort.'

Marguerite tried for a moment to summon her courage, and then suddenly giving way again, sank on her sofa.

'No, no, I cannot go,' she said.

Charles took her hand, sat beside her on the sofa, and said,—

'You have just lost a dear friend, Margot, I know full well. But look at me—have not I lost all my friends, and my mother too? You have time to grieve as you now do; but I, at the moment of my deepest sorrows, am always forced to smile—you suffer, but look at me! I am dying! Well, then, Margot, take heart; courage, girl! I beg you, sister, for our name's honour. It is a sacrifice that we bear for the sake of our house: let us bear it, then, let us bear it, sister, courageously and stoically.'

'Oh, *mon Dieu, mon Dieu!*' exclaimed Marguerite.

'Yes,' said Charles, following the train of his thought—'yes, the sacrifice is great, my dear sister, but everyone has his trials—some, of their honour; others, of their life. Do you suppose that, at twenty-five, and occupying the most splendid throne in the world, I do not regret dying? Well, then, look at me! My eyes, my complexion, my lips are those of a dying man; yet my smile—do I not smile such a smile as would make the whole world believe that I still hope? Yet in a week, a fortnight, a month at most, you will weep for me, my sister dear, as you do for him who died to-day.'

'Dearest brother!' cried Marguerite, throwing her arms round Charles's neck.

'Come, get dressed, dear Marguerite,' said the king. 'Hide your pallor, and appear at the ball. I have ordered for you new jewels and ornaments worthy of your beauty.'

'Oh, what are jewels and ornaments to me now!' exclaimed Marguerite.

'Life is long, Marguerite!' said Charles, with a smile, 'at least, for you.'

'No! no!'

'Sister, remember one thing: it is sometimes by holding back, or rather disguising our suffering, that we show most honour to the dead.'

'Very well, sire,' said Marguerite, 'I will come to the ball.'

A tear, which quickly dried upon his parched eyelid, moistened Charles's eye for a moment. He kissed his sister's brow, paused a moment by Henriette, who had not seen or heard him, and then left, saying, as he did so,—

'Poor girl!'

'Get everything ready to dress me, Gillonne,' said Marguerite.

The lady-in-waiting looked at her mistress in astonishment.

'Yes,' said Marguerite, in a tone the bitterness of which is indescribable—'yes, I shall dress: I am going to the ball—I am expected. So be quick about it and the day will then be complete: a fête at the Grève in the morning—a fête at the Louvre in the evening.'

'And the duchess?' asked Gillonne.

'Ah, she is quite happy as she is! She can stay here—she may weep—suffer at her ease. She is not a king's daughter, a king's wife, a king's sister: she is not a queen. Help me to dress, Gillonne.'

The young lady obeyed. The new ornaments sent by the king were splendid, and the dresses gorgeous. Marguerite had never looked so magnificently beautiful.

She looked at herself in a mirror, and said: 'My brother is right—a human being is a miserable creature.'

Gillonne entered at this moment.

'Madame,' she said, 'a man is here who wishes to see you.'

'Who is he?'

'I do not know, but he is horribly ugly. Just looking at him made me tremble.'

'Go and ask his name,' said Marguerite, turning very pale.

Gillonne went out, and returning after a few moments, said,—

'He would not tell his name, madame, but he asked me to give you this.'

And Gillonne handed to Marguerite the reliquary which she had given to La Mole the night before.

'Oh, show him in!' said the queen, eagerly, becoming even paler and her features more rigid.

A heavy step was heard outside, and then a man appeared on the threshold.

'You are——' said the queen.

'The same man you saw one day near Montfaucon, madame, who conveyed in his tumbril two wounded gentlemen to the Louvre.'*

'Yes, yes, I recognize you—you are Maître Caboche.'

'Executioner to the city of Paris, madame.'

These were the only words which Henriette took in of all those that had been spoken around her for the last hour. She raised her pale face from her two hands, and looked at the headsman with her piercing eyes, which seemed to dart flames.

'And you come——?' said Marguerite tremulously.

'To remind you of the promise made to the younger of the two gentlemen, the one who charged me to return this reliquary to you. Do you remember, madame?'

'Yes, yes!' cried the queen, 'and never shall more noble shade have nobler satisfaction—but where is *it*?'

'It is at my house, with the body.'

'Why did you not bring it?'

'I might have been stopped at the gate of the Louvre, and required to open my cloak. What would have been said, if a head had been discovered beneath it?'

'True, true. Keep it at your house, and I will come for it to-morrow.'

'To-morrow, madame?' said Maître Caboche, 'to-morrow may be too late!'

'Why?'

'Because the queen-mother asked me to keep for her magic experiments the heads of the first two criminals I should execute.'

'Oh, profanation! the heads of the men we loved!—Henriette,' exclaimed Marguerite, running to her friend, whom she found standing up as if a spring had propelled her to her feet—'Henriette, my darling friend, do you hear what this man says?'

'Yes, and what are we to do?'

'We must go with him'; and Marguerite threw a velvet cloak over her shoulders. 'Come,' she said, 'we shall see them once more.'

Marguerite took Henriette by the arm, and, going down the secret staircase, made a sign to Caboche to follow. At the door was her litter, and at the gate they found Caboche's servant with a lantern.

Marguerite's bearers were trustworthy men, deaf and dumb, and worthier of confidence than beasts of burden.

They climbed into the litter, and were conveyed onwards, until suddenly they stopped, and the headsman opened the door.

Marguerite alighted, and handed down the Duchess de Nevers.

In their excessive grief, which took its toll on them both, nervous energy overcame the physical weakness of their bodies.

'You may enter, ladies,' said Caboche, 'everybody is asleep in the tower.'

At the same moment the light in the two windows went out, and the two ladies, clinging to each other, passed through the Gothic door, and went along in darkness over a rough-hewn slippery floor.

Caboche, with a torch in his hand, led them into a room which was low, and blackened with smoke.

In a conspicuous place was nailed to the wall a parchment with the king's seal; it was the headsman's patent.

In a corner was a large sword, with a long handle: it was the flaming sword of justice.

Here and there were seen several large images, representing saints undergoing different kinds of martyrdom.

Having arrived here, Caboche bowed low.

'Your Majesty will pardon me,' he said, 'if I dared come to the Louvre and bring you here. But it was the last wish of the gentlemen; so——'

'You have done well, sir,' said Marguerite, 'and this will recompense your loyal service.'

Caboche looked sadly at the purse well filled with gold which Marguerite placed on the table.

'Gold! gold! always gold!' he muttered. 'Alas, madame, I would willingly redeem at the price of this gold the blood I have been compelled to shed to-day!'

'But,' replied Marguerite, hardly daring to speak, 'I do not see——'

Caboche took the torch and opened an outer door which, opening on to the staircase, led down into a cellar. At the same moment a current of air passed, which blew several sparks out of the torch, and brought up with it the nauseous smell of damp and blood.

Henriette, white as a marble statue, leaned on the arm of her friend who advanced with a more assured step. But at the first step she faltered.

'I shall never be able——' she exclaimed.

'When we love truly, Henriette,' replied the queen, 'we love beyond death itself.'

It was a horrid and touching sight to see those two women, resplendent in youth and beauty, bending under this sordid, chalky vault, the weaker leaning on the stronger, and the stronger clinging to the headsman's arm.

They reached the bottom step.

On the floor of this cellar lay two human forms, covered with a large cloth of black serge.

Caboche raised a corner of this shroud, and lowering his torch, said,—

'Look, your Majesty!'

Dressed in black, the two young men lay side by side, in the fearful symmetry of death. Their heads, placed on their bodies, seemed only divided from them by a red circle round the neck. Death had not separated their hands, for either by accident or the pious attention of the headsman, the right hand of La Mole held the left hand of Coconnas.

There was a look of love on the face of La Mole; there was a smile of disdain on the features of Coconnas.

Marguerite knelt down beside her lover, and with her hands glittering with jewels, gently raised the head of the man she had loved so well.

The Duchess de Nevers, leaning against the wall, could not take her eyes off the pale face she had so often gazed upon with joy and love.

'La Mole! dearest La Mole!' murmured Marguerite.

'Annibal! Annibal!' cried the duchess. 'So handsome, so proud, so brave, why do you not speak to me?' and a torrent of tears gushed from her eyes.

Marguerite then put into a bag, embroidered with pearls and perfumed with the finest essences, the head of La Mole, which looked even more striking against the velvet and gold, and whose beauty a special preparation, used at the period in royal embalmings, would not fail to preserve.

Henriette wrapped the head of Coconnas in the folds of her cloak. And both, bending beneath the weight of their sorrow, ascended the stairs, after one last lingering look at the loved remains they left to the mercy of the executioner in this gloomy den of common criminals.

'Fear nothing, madame,' said Caboche, who understood the look. 'The gentlemen shall be buried in holy ground: this I swear to you.'*

'And have masses said for their souls, which this will pay for,' said Henriette, taking from her neck a magnificent necklace of rubies, which she gave to the headsman.

They returned to the Louvre, and the queen, going to her own apartments, deposited the melancholy relic in the cabinet of her bedroom, which would from that moment become an oratory.* Then, leaving Henriette in her room, the queen, paler and lovelier than ever, about ten o'clock, entered the magnificent ballroom—in which we commenced the first chapter of this our history, two years and a half previously.*

All eyes were turned towards her, and she bore the universal gaze with a proud and almost joyous look, for she had scrupulously carried out the dying wish of the beloved of her heart.

Charles, when he saw her, passed through the gilded throng, and said aloud,—

'Thanks, my dear sister!' and then, in a lower tone—'Mind! There is blood on your sleeve.'

'What consequence is that, sire, if I have a smile upon my lips?'*

62

THE SWEAT OF BLOOD

SOME days after the terrible scene we have related, that is, on the 30th of May, 1574, the court was at Vincennes, when suddenly a great noise was heard in the antechamber of the king, who had fallen ill during the grand ball he had given the very day of the young men's execution, and who, by advice of his physicians, had come to Vincennes for a change of air.*

It was eight o'clock in the morning. A small group of courtiers had assembled in the antechamber, when the nurse appeared* at the door of the royal apartment, crying,—

'Help! help! the king is dying!'

'The king is worse, then?' said de Nancey, whom, as we have seen, Charles had attached to his own person.*

'Oh, summon the doctors! summon the doctors!' cried the nurse.

Mazille and Ambroise Paré attended the king by turns, and Paré, having seen Charles fall asleep, had made the most of this opportunity to retire for a few moments.

Meantime, Charles had broken into a heavy sweat, and as he suffered from a relaxation of the capillary vessels, which causes hæmorrhaging of the skin,* this strange appearance had alarmed the nurse, who, being a Protestant, declared it was a judgment for the blood shed in the massacre of St. Bartholomew. Everyone hurried away in search of the doctor, so as to be seen displaying zeal and activity.

A door suddenly opened, and Catherine appeared. She crossed the antechamber, and entered the king's apartment.

Charles was lying across the bed, his eyes closed, and his chest heaving. His body was covered with reddish perspiration, and from the end of each finger hung a drop of blood.

At the sound of footsteps Charles looked up, and saw his mother.

'Excuse me, madame,' said he, 'I wish to die in peace.'

'Die?' replied Catherine. 'Do not lose heart: this is a passing attack.'

'I tell you, *mort de touts les diables!* I am dying—I know it and I feel it!'

'Sire,' said the queen, 'your mind is sick. Since the death of those two assassins, La Mole and Coconnas, your bodily sufferings should have abated, and as for your mental anguish, if I had ten minutes' conversation with you, I could prove——'

'Nurse,' interrupted Charles, 'let no one enter: Queen Catherine de Medicis wishes to speak with her beloved son, Charles the Ninth.'

The nurse obeyed.

'This interview had to take place,' continued he, 'sooner or later, and perhaps to-morrow it may be too late. But a third person must be present.'

'Why?'

'Because, I repeat,' said Charles, with terrible solemnity, 'Death is at the door of this chamber, and may enter at any moment. It is time to put my affairs in order.'

'And who is this third person?'

'My brother.'

'Sire,' said the queen, 'I see with pleasure that the accusations you made, dictated by pain rather than hate, have not left any prejudice in your mind. Nurse—nurse!'

The nurse appeared.

'Nurse,' said Catherine, 'when M. de Nancey comes, order him in the king's name to summon M. d'Alençon.'

Charles made a sign to the nurse to stay.

'I said, my brother,' he repeated.

Catherine's eyes glistened with rage, but an imperious gesture from Charles stopped her.

'I wish to speak with my brother, Henry of Navarre,' continued he. 'I have no other brother.'*

'And do you think,' cried the queen, daring (so great was her hatred of Henry) to brave Charles's anger—'do you think, that if you are really dying, as you say, I will suffer a stranger to usurp my right as a queen and as a mother, to be present at your last moments?'

'Madame,' said Charles, 'I am still king—I still command. If you will not summon Henry, I still have enough strength left to fetch him myself.'

And Charles half rose from the bed.

'Sire,' cried Catherine, restraining him, 'consider what you are doing. For my part I shall stay, as both the law of nature and the requirements of etiquette entitle me to.'

'By which of those titles do you stay?'

'As your mother.'

'You are no more my mother than d'Alençon is my brother.'

'You are mad! when did I forfeit that title?'

'When you took away with one hand what you gave with the other.'

'What do you mean, Charles? I do not understand you,' murmured Catherine in amazement.

Charles felt under his pillow, and drew forth a small silver key.

'Take this key, open my travelling-casket there, and you will find papers that will speak for me.'

Charles pointed to a casket of carved oak, fastened with a silver lock, which stood in the centre of the apartment.

Catherine, controlled, in spite of herself, by Charles's terrible look, opened the casket. But no sooner had she done so, than she recoiled, as if she had seen a serpent inside it.

'What do you see that alarms you, madame?' asked Charles.

'Nothing,' said Catherine.

'Then put your hand in, and give me a book. For there is a book there—is there not?'

'Yes,' faltered Catherine.

'A book of Venerie?'

'Yes.'

'Bring it to me.'

Catherine, trembling in every limb, did as he bade her.

'Fatality!'* murmured she.

'Listen,' continued Charles. 'This book—I was foolish—I loved hunting above everything else—I read this book too much. Do you understand?'

Catherine uttered a muted groan.

'It was a folly!' said Charles. 'Burn it, madame. The world must not know the weaknesses of kings.'

Catherine advanced to the fire, cast the fatal book in, and stood, motionless and haggard, watching as blue flames devoured the poisoned pages of the volume.

As it burnt, a strong odour like garlic filled the apartment.

It was soon entirely consumed.

'And now, madame,' said the king, with irresistible majesty, 'summon my brother Henry.'

Catherine, overwhelmed, crushed by the weight of a complicated emotion she could not analyse, left the room.

'Curse him!' cried she, as she crossed the threshold—'he is irresistible! He draws nearer his goal! Curse him!—curse him!'

'Henry!—my brother Henry!' cried Charles, following his mother with his voice—'I wish to see him instantly, to speak about the regency.'*

At this moment, Ambroise Paré entered by the opposite door.

'Who has been burning arsenic here?' said he.

'I have,' replied Charles.

63

THE TERRACE OF THE FORTRESS OF VINCENNES

HENRY of Navarre was walking alone on the terrace of the fortress of Vincennes. He knew the court was at the château, and it seemed to him he could see, through the walls, Charles on his deathbed. It was a summer's eve. A broad patch of sunlight bathed the distant plains and gilded the stems of the old oaks in the forest.

But it was not on those objects that Henry fixed his attention: he was gazing, in thought, on the capital of France.

'Paris!' murmured he—'Paris! where is the Louvre!—the Louvre, where is the throne! These ramparts keep me from you and confine me with my mortal enemy!'

As his thoughts wandered from Paris back to Vincennes, he saw on the left, in a valley, a man wearing a breastplate which sparkled in the sunbeams. This man was mounted on a splendid charger, and led another.

The king fixed his eyes on this horseman, and saw him draw his sword, place his handkerchief on it, and wave it in the air. Instantly the signal was repeated from the next hill; and continued until the king saw it extend all round the château.

It was de Mouy and his Huguenots who, knowing the king was dying, and fearing lest Henry's life should be in danger, had gathered, and were ready to defend him.

Henry shaded his eyes with his hand, and recognizing the rider,—

'De Mouy!' cried he, as though his friend could hear him.

And he hastily undid his scarf, and waved it in return.

All the handkerchiefs were again waved.

'Ah, they are waiting for me!' said he. 'I cannot join them. Why did I not do so when it was in my power!'

And he made a despairing gesture which de Mouy returned with another, which meant, 'I will wait.'

At that moment Henry heard steps on the stairs. He stepped back out of sight and as if by magic de Mouy and his men disappeared also.

Henry saw, not without a secret dread, his mortal foe, Catherine de Medicis, appear on the terrace.

'Oh,' thought he, 'it must indeed be something important that makes her come looking for me on the terrace of the fortress of Vincennes.'

Catherine sat down on a stone bench, to recover her breath.

Henry approached her.

'Are you looking for me, madame?' he asked.

'Yes,' replied Catherine; 'I wished to give you a proof of my attachment—the king wishes to see you.'

'Me?'

'Yes. He thinks that not content with wanting the kingdom of Navarre, you covet the throne of France too.'

'Oh, madame!'

'I know it is not true, but he believes it, and has laid a snare for you.'

'What does he intend to offer me?'

'How do I know?—things impossible, perhaps.'

'But have you no idea?'

'No, but suppose, for instance——'

'What?'

'Suppose, Henry, he were to offer you a temptation—the regency?'

Henry felt a thrill of joy, but he saw the trap, and avoided it.

'Oh,' said he, 'that would be too obvious. Offer me the regency, when he has both you and d'Alençon!'

'You will refuse it, then?' replied Catherine.

'The king is dead,' thought Henry. 'She has laid a trap for me——'

'I must hear what the king says, madame, for all this is mere supposition.'

'No doubt. But you can tell me your intentions.'

'*Mon Dieu!*' said Henry, 'I have no pretensions, and so can have no intentions.'

'That is no answer,' replied Catherine. 'But let me be blunt with you—for there is no time to lose—if you accept the regency, you are a dead man.'

'The king is still alive' thought Henry.—'Madame,' said he firmly, 'God will inspire me, for the hearts of kings are in His hands. I am ready to see his Majesty.'

'Reflect, monsieur!'

'During the two years that I have been persecuted, and a month that I have been a prisoner,* I have had time for reflection, and I have reflected. Oblige me, therefore, by informing the king of my coming. These two guards would prevent my escaping, even if I were thinking of escape, which I am not.'

Catherine saw she could do nothing more, and hastily descended.

No sooner had she disappeared than Henry made a sign to de Mouy that meant 'Come nearer.'

De Mouy sprang into the saddle, and advanced within a musket-shot of the château.

Henry waved his hand, and hurried after the queen.

On the first landing he found the two sentinels awaiting him.

A double troop of Swiss and light horse guarded the court-yard, and to enter or leave the château it was necessary to pass through a double rank of halberds. Catherine was waiting there for him.

'Look!' said she, laying her hand on his arm. 'This court-yard has two gates. On the other side of this gate, a good horse and freedom await you—if you refuse the regency. But if you follow the dictates of ambition—Come now. Which is it to be?'

'I say that if the king makes me regent, I, and not you, shall command these soldiers.'

'Madman!' murmured Catherine—'be warned, and do not play at life and death with me!'

'Why not?' said Henry, 'since up to now, I have been on the winning side.'

'Go to the king's apartments, sir, since you will not listen to me,' said Catherine, pointing to the stairs with one hand, while the other sought the handle of one of the poisoned daggers she wore at her girdle in the shagreen case of which history speaks.*

'Pass before me, madame,' said Henry. 'Until I am regent, you take precedence.'

Catherine, foiled at every point, made no resistance, but climbed the stairs while Henry followed.

64

THE REGENCY

THE king had become impatient, and was on the point of sending de Nancey in search of Henry, when the latter appeared.

On seeing him, Charles uttered a cry of joy. The two doctors and the priest, who were with the king, instantly rose and left the chamber.

Charles was not greatly loved,* and yet all the courtiers in the antechambers were weeping. At the death of every king, good or bad, there are always some persons who fear they shall lose by it.

Charles smiled sadly.

'Come here, Harry,' said he, holding out his hand to him— 'come here. I was unhappy at not seeing you, for, believe me, I have often reproached myself with making life difficult for you. But a king cannot control events, and, besides my mother and d'Anjou and d'Alençon, something else which now that I am dying does not influence me, influenced me then—state policy.'

'Sire,' replied Henry, 'I recall only the love I bear you, as my brother.'

'Ah, you are right to think so, and I am grateful to you for it,' said Charles. 'But let us not think of the past, but of the future, for it is the future which concerns me.'

And the poor king buried his face in his hands.

After a moment's silence, he continued,—

'We must save the state—we must not let it fall into the hands of fanatics or women.'

Charles spoke these words in a whisper, and yet Henry fancied he heard a suppressed exclamation of rage.

'Of women?' said he, anxious to provoke an explanation.

'Yes, for my mother would like to be regent until d'Anjou's return. But, I tell you, he will not return.'

'How, not return?' cried Henry, his heart beating joyfully.

'His subjects will not let him.'

'But do you not think the queen-mother has already written to him?'

'Yes, but Nancey stopped the courier at Château Thierry and brought me the letter in which she said I was dying. I wrote to Warsaw myself, and d'Anjou will be carefully watched, so that in all probability the throne will become vacant.'

Another angry sound was heard behind the tapestry.

'She is there,' thought Henry, 'and is listening.'

Charles heard nothing.

'I die without male heirs,' continued he.

Then stopping suddenly, he looked intently at the King of Navarre.

'Do you recollect, Harry,' said he, 'the little boy I showed you one night, sleeping peacefully in his cradle and watched over by an angel? Alas, they will kill him too!'

'Oh, no, no!' cried Henry, with tears in his eyes. 'I swear to you that I will watch over him and protect him with my life.'

'Thanks, Harry, thanks!' said the king gratefully. 'I accept your promise: do not make him a king (fortunately, he is not born to a throne), but make him happy. I shall leave him an ample fortune, and I am now more resigned to dying, since you have promised to protect him.'

Henry thought for a moment.

'I have made you a promise,' said he, 'but can I keep it?'

'What do you mean?'

'Shall I not be persecuted, and in more danger than he is, since I am a man, and he is a mere infant?'

'You are mistaken,' said Charles. 'After my death you shall be great and powerful.'

At these words he drew a parchment from under his pillow.

'Here!' said he.

Henry glanced quickly over the document.

'The regency for me?'

'Yes, until d'Anjou's return; and, as he will not return, in all probability, I am giving you the throne.'

'The throne!'

'You alone are worthy of it—you alone are capable of governing. D'Alençon is a traitor—leave him in the prison I have consigned him to. My mother will try to kill you—banish her. D'Anjou will leave Poland in three months, perhaps in a year: reply to him with a papal bull. I have already arranged that matter, and you will receive the document shortly.'

'Oh, my king!'

'You have only one thing to fear—civil war. But, by remaining converted, you will avoid that. The Protestants can do nothing unless you are at their head, for Condé has no real authority.* They say I feel remorse for the Bartholomew massacre: doubts, yes!—remorse, no! They say I bleed through every pore the blood I then shed: what flows from me is arsenic, and not blood.'

'Oh, what do you mean, sire?'

'Nothing. God will, if he thinks fit, avenge my death. I leave you a faithful parliament and a trusty army. They will protect you against your only enemies: my mother and d'Alençon.'

At this moment the sound of arms was heard in the vestibule.

'I am lost!' murmured Henry.

'You fear—you hesitate!' said Charles.

'No, I accept!'

Charles pressed his hand.

'Nurse,' cried he—'nurse, summon my mother and M. d'Alençon.'

65

CATHERINE and d'Alençon entered together. As Henry had conjectured, the queen had overheard everything and briefly acquainted d'Alençon with what had passed.

Henry stood by the head of the king's bed.

The king began thus,—

'Madame,' said he, to his mother, 'if I had a son, he would be king, and you would be regent; in your stead, if you declined, the King of Poland; in his stead, if he declined, d'Alençon. But I have no son, and the throne belongs to d'Anjou, who is absent. I do not choose, therefore, to place a person almost his equal on the throne, at the risk of exciting a civil war; I do not, therefore, make you regent, because it would be painful for you to choose between your two sons; I do not, therefore, make d'Alençon regent, because he might say to d'Anjou, "You had a throne, why did you give it up?" No; I have, therefore, chosen the fittest person for regent. Salute him, madame—salute him, d'Alençon: it is the King of Navarre!'

And with a gesture of supreme authority, he himself saluted Henry: Catherine and d'Alençon made a gesture that was half-way between a shudder and a salute.

'Here, my lord regent,' said Charles, 'is the parchment which, until the return of d'Anjou, gives you the command of the kingdom.'

Catherine devoured Henry with her eyes; d'Alençon turned deadly pale and could hardly stand.

Henry, making a violent effort, took the warrant from Charles, and drawing himself up to his full height, fixed his eyes on the queen, as if to say, 'I am master now!'

'No, never!' said Catherine—'never shall my race yield to a foreign one! Never shall a Bourbon reign while a Valois remains alive!'

'Mother!' cried Charles, sitting up, 'I am still king, and have strength enough to give an order. It does not take much time to punish murderers and poisoners.'

'Give the order, if you dare—I will give mine!'

And she left the room, followed by d'Alençon.

'Nancey!' cried Charles—'Nancey! arrest my mother and brother!'

A stream of blood choked his words.

De Nancey entered. He had heard only his name: the rest of the order had not reached him.

'Guard the door,' said Henry, 'and let no one enter!'

Nancey bowed, and left the apartment. Henry looked at the dying king.

'The fatal moment has come!' said he. 'Shall I reign? Shall I live?'

'Live, sire!' said a voice.

The tapestry of the alcove was lifted, and René's pale face appeared.

'René?' cried Henry.

'Yes, sire.'

'Your prediction was false, then—I shall not be king?'

'You shall be. But the time has not yet come.'

'How do you know? Speak!'

'Listen!'

'I listen.'

'Closer!'

Henry leaned over the bed, and René did the same. Between them lay the body of the dying king.

'Listen!' said René. 'Placed here by the queen-mother to undo you, I prefer to serve you; for I have faith in your horoscope.'

'Is it the queen-mother who ordered you tell me that?'

'No,' said René. 'I will tell you a secret: the King of Poland will soon be here!'

'No, for the king stopped the courier at Château Thierry.'

'The queen sent three, by different routes.'

'Oh, I am lost!' said Henry.

'A messenger arrived this morning from Warsaw. No one knows of Charles's illness there. D'Anjou rode out of the city without opposition, and the courier preceded him by only a few hours.'

'Oh, if I had one week!' muttered Henry.

'You do not have a day! You heard the rattle of weapons in the antechamber, did you not? The soldiers will not hesitate to come into this room and kill you.'

'The king is not dead yet.'

'No,' said René, 'but he will be in ten minutes. You have ten minutes to live.'

'What shall I do?'

'Leave immediately.'

'How? If I cross the vestibule they will kill me there.'

'Listen! I am risking everything for you; do not forget it.'

'I will not forget.'

'Follow me through this passage; it will take you to the postern. To gain time, I will tell the queen you are coming. They will assume afterwards you have discovered the secret door, and escaped.'

Henry stooped, and kissed Charles's forehead.

'Adieu, brother!' he said. 'I will not forget your last wish was to see me king. Die in peace! In the name of my brethren, I forgive you their blood you have spilt.'

Henry seized Charles's sword, put the precious parchment safely in his doublet, pressed his lips again to Charles's forehead, and disappeared through the secret passage.

'Nurse!' murmured the king—'nurse!'

'What do you want, Charlot?' cried she.

'Nurse, while I have been sleeping, something strange has happened, for I see a great light, and saints interceding with God for me. Pardon me, my God! Pardon the crimes of the king, in compassion for the sufferings of the man! I come! I come!'*

And Charles, who had risen nearly to his feet, fell back dead into his nurse's arms.

Meantime, Henry, guided by René, negotiated the passage, passed through the postern, and, springing on his horse, galloped towards de Mouy.

The sentinels, hearing the horse, moved forward and cried,—

'He has escaped!'

'Who has escaped?' said the queen.

'The King of Navarre.'

'Fire on him—fire!' said the queen.

The sentinels levelled their pieces, but the king was out of range.

'He has gone!' said Catherine—'he is beaten, then!'

'He has gone!' muttered d'Alençon—'I am king, then!'

But at this moment the drawbridge was hastily lowered, and a young man galloped into the court, followed by four gentlemen crying, '*France! France!*'

'My son!' cried Catherine joyfully.

'Mother!' replied the young man, springing to the ground.

'D'Anjou!' exclaimed François, thunderstruck.

'Am I too late?' said Henry d'Anjou.

'No, you are just in time—listen!'

At this moment de Nancey appeared at the balcony of the king's apartment: all eyes were fixed on him.

He broke a wand he held in two pieces, and holding one fragment in each hand,—

'King Charles the Ninth is dead! King Charles the Ninth is dead! King Charles the Ninth is dead!' he cried three times.

And he dropped the fragments of the wand on to the ground.

'Charles the Ninth is dead!' said Catherine, crossing herself— 'God Save Henry the Third!'*

All repeated the cry, with the exception of d'Alençon.

'She has betrayed me,' said he.

'I have won,' cried Catherine. 'The odious Béarnais will not reign!'

66

EPILOGUE

A YEAR had elapsed since the death of Charles IX and the accession of his successor.

King Henry III, happily reigning by the grace of God and his mother Catherine, had ordered a grand procession in honour of Notre-Dame de Cléry.*

He had gone on foot with the queen, his wife, and all the court.

King Henry III was able to allow himself this little indulgence, for no serious business occupied him at the moment. The King of Navarre was in Navarre, where he had so long wished to be and where, it was said, he was very much taken up with a beautiful girl of the blood of the Montmorencies, whom he called *la Fosseuse*.* Marguerite was with him,* sad and gloomy, finding only in her beautiful mountains, not amusement but a balm for the two great griefs of human life—absence and death.

Paris was very quiet, and the queen-mother, in effect regent since her dear son Henry was king, resided sometimes at the Louvre, sometimes at the Hotel de Soissons.*

One evening, when she was deeply occupied in studying the stars with René, whose treason she had never discovered, and who had been reinstated in her favour after the false testimony he had so usefully laid against La Mole and Coconnas, she was informed that a man was asking to see her who had a matter of the utmost importance to communicate.

She went immediately to her oratory, and found the Sire de Maurevel.

'HE is here!' exclaimed the former captain of the Petardiers, not giving Catherine time to address him according to royal etiquette.

'Who do you mean?' she asked.

'Who else, madame, but the King of Navarre?'

'Here?' cried Catherine. 'Henry?—and what is that madman doing here?'

'If appearances may be trusted, he has come to see Madame de Sauve.* If probabilities are considered, to conspire against the king.'

'How did you know he was here?'

'Because I saw him enter a house yesterday, and, very soon afterwards, I observed Madame de Sauve join him there.'

'Are you sure it was him?'

'I waited for him to come out. At three o'clock, the two lovers appeared. The king escorted Madame de Sauve to the gate of the Louvre. There the guard, who is no doubt in her pay, let her in, and she entered without difficulty. The king returned humming a tune, and with a step as free and unconcerned as if he were amongst his mountains in Béarn.'

'And where did he go then?'

'To the Rue de l'Arbre-Sec, to an inn called the *Belle Etoile*, the same where the two sorcerers lodged whom your Majesty executed last year.'

'Why did you not come and inform me the moment you saw him?'

'Because I was not quite sure of my man.'

'And now——?'

'I am perfectly certain.'

'You have seen him again?'

'Yes. I hid in the wine-shop opposite the house, and saw him enter the same place as last night. Then, as Madame de Sauve was late, he imprudently put his face against the window on the first floor, and I had no further doubt. Besides, a few moments afterwards, Madame de Sauve came and joined him again.'

'And do you think they will stay, as they did last night, until three o'clock in the morning?'

'It is probable.'

'Where is the house you mention?'

'Near the Croix-des-Petits-Champs, off the Rue Saint-Honoré.'

'Very good!' replied Catherine. 'Does Monsieur de Sauve know your handwriting?'

'No,' said Maurevel.

'Sit down there and write.'

Maurevel obeyed.

'I am ready, madame,' said he.

Catherine dictated,—

'While the Baron de Sauve is on duty at the Louvre, his wife is with her lover in a house near the Croix-des-Petits-Champs, Rue Saint-Honoré. The baron will recognize the house by a red cross on the wall.'

'Well?'

'Now, make a copy of this letter.'

Maurevel did so.

'Now,' continued the queen, 'let this note be given discreetly to the baron, and leave the copy in the corridor of the Louvre.'

'I do not understand.'

Catherine shrugged her shoulders.

'You do not see that a husband who receives such a letter is bound to be angry?'

'In the King of Navarre's time, he was not offended.'

'Do you not know there is a great difference between a king and an exile? Besides, if he is not offended, you will be offended for him.'

'I?'

'Yes; take four or six men, masked. You burst open the door—you surprise the lovers—you strike, in the baron's name, and the next day the letter found in the Louvre proves that it is the husband who revenged himself. Alas, it happened the lover was the King of Navarre. But who would have thought he was there, when everyone believed he was at Pau?'

Maurevel bowed, and withdrew.

At the moment he left the Hotel de Soissons, Madame de Sauve entered the house in the Rue Croix-des-Petits-Champs.

Henry was waiting for her.

'Were you followed?' said he.

'No,' said Charlotte, 'not that I know of.'

'I think I was, not only to-night, but last evening too.'

'Oh, sire, you terrify me. I should be inconsolable if anything were to happen to you.'

'Fear nothing, my love,' said the Béarnais, 'three faithful followers watch over me.'

'Only three?'

'Three are sufficient, when they are called de Mouy, Saucourt, and Barthélemy.'

'De Mouy is in Paris? Has he, like you, some poor lady in love with him?'

'No; but a mortal enemy, whose death he has sworn. Only hate can make men commit such follies as they commit in love.'

'Thank you, sire!'

'Oh, I do not speak of our present follies, but those past and to come: but let us leave off this conversation, for my time is short.'

'You are leaving Paris, then?'

'To-night.'

'Your affairs in Paris are finished?'

'My only business was to see you.'

'Wretch!'

'*Ma mie!* it is true. We have a few hours more together, and then we must separate for ever.'

'Oh, Henry,' said Charlotte, 'nothing but my love is for ever!'

It had been arranged that Henry should leave the house at twelve o'clock, that he and his companions should escort Madame de Sauve to the Louvre, and that they would then go to the Rue de la Cérisaie, where Maurevel lived.

But before this could happen, the three Huguenots guarding Henry had been at their post for about an hour when they saw a man, followed at some distance by five others, approach the door of the house, and try a number of keys in the lock.

At this, de Mouy sprang from his hiding-place, and catching the man by the arm,—

'Stay!' said he—'you cannot enter there!'

The man started, and his hat fell off.

'De Mouy de Saint-Phale!' cried he.

'Maurevel!' thundered the Huguenot, brandishing his sword—'I have been looking for you, and you come to find me!'

But he did not forget Henry, and, turning to the window, he whistled as the Béarnais shepherds do.

'That is enough,' said he to Saucourt.

'Now then, murderer!'

Maurevel had time to draw a pistol from his belt, and levelling it at the young man,—

'This time,' said the king's assassin, 'you are dead.'

But de Mouy sprang to one side, and the bullet missed him.

'It is my turn now!' cried he, and he dealt Maurevel so terrible a thrust with his rapier that it pierced his thick leather belt and inflicted a severe wound.

Maurevel uttered so terrible a cry that his followers thought he had been killed, and ran off down the Rue Saint-Honoré.

Maurevel, seeing himself abandoned, took to his heels crying, 'Help! help!'

De Mouy, Saucourt, and Barthélemy pursued him hotly.

As they reached the Rue de Grenelle, a man jumped out of a window on the first floor.

It was Henry.

Warned by de Mouy's signal and the report of the pistol that something had happened, he rushed to the assistance of his friends.

Active and vigorous, he dashed after them sword in hand.

A cry guided him. It came from the Barrière des Sergents;* it was Maurevel, who, hard pressed by de Mouy, called again for help.

He was forced to turn, or else be run through the back. So he turned, and thrust fiercely at de Mouy, and pierced his scarf. De Mouy lunged, and wounded him a second time.

'At him—at him!' cried Henry.

De Mouy needed no exhortation: he charged Maurevel again, who, pressing his hand over his wound, took to flight once more.

'Finish him quickly!' cried the king. 'Here come the soldiers!'

Maurevel, breathless and exhausted, could go no further. He dropped to one knee, and presented his sword's point to de Mouy.

'There are only two of them!' cried he. 'Fire—fire!'

Saucourt and Barthélemy had gone in pursuit of the other soldiers, so that de Mouy and the king found themselves facing four men.

'Fire!' cried Maurevel, as one of the soldiers prepared his arquebuse.

'Yes; but first die—assassin, murderer, traitor—die!'

So saying, de Mouy seized Maurevel's sword with one hand, and plunged his own so violently into his breast that he pinned him to the earth.

'Take care—take care!' cried Henry.

De Mouy sprang back, leaving his sword in the body of Maurevel, for a soldier was in the act of firing at him.

Henry instantly ran his sword through the soldier's body, who fell, uttering a cry.

The two others fled.

'Come, de Mouy, come!' said Henry. 'We have not a moment to lose; if we are recognized, we are lost!'

'One moment, sire, whilst I recover my sword. You do not think I would leave it sticking in the body of that wretch!'

He went towards Maurevel, who lay, to all appearance, deprived of life. But the moment de Mouy laid his hand on the hilt of the sword which had remained in his body, he raised himself, holding the petronel which the soldier had dropped as he fell, and, placing the muzzle full against de Mouy's breast, pulled the trigger.

De Mouy fell, without a cry. He died instantly.*

Henry rushed towards Maurevel, but he had fallen again, and the king's sword pierced only a dead carcass.

He had to get away. The noise had attracted a number of people, and the guard might arrive at any moment. Henry looked about him, to see if there was a face he knew, and gave a cry of joy on recognizing Maître la Hurière.

'My dear La Hurière, look after de Mouy, though I fear that he is past hope. Have him taken to your house, and, if he still lives, spare no expense—here is my purse. As to the other man, leave the scoundrel to rot in the gutter like a dog!'

'But yourself?' said La Hurière.

'I have a farewell to make. I will hurry, and be back with you in ten minutes. Have my horses ready.'

Henry then hastened away in the direction of the little house in the Croix-des-Petits-Champs. But as he turned the corner, he stopped in dismay.

There was a great crowd outside the door.

'What has happened in this house?' inquired Henry.

'Oh,' replied a bystander, 'a terrible business, sir! A beautiful lady has been stabbed by her husband, to whom someone had sent a note, informing him that she was there with her lover.'

'And the husband?' cried Henry.

'Has gone.'

'The wife?'

'Is still inside.'

'Dead?'

'Not yet, but there is no hope.'

'Oh,' exclaimed Henry, 'cursed fate!' and he rushed into the house.

The room was filled with people, all surrounding the bed on which lay poor Charlotte who had been stabbed twice. Her husband, who had for two years concealed his jealousy of Henry, had seized this chance to take his revenge.

'Charlotte, Charlotte!' cried Henry, falling on his knees at her bedside.

Charlotte opened her beautiful eyes, already veiled by death, and gave a cry which made the blood flow from her two wounds. Making an effort to rise, she said—

'Oh, I was sure I would not die without seeing you once more!'

And, as if she had awaited the moment of Henry's coming to die, she pressed her lips on the King of Navarre's forehead, and murmuring for the last time, 'I love you!' fell back lifeless.*

Henry could not remain a moment longer without placing his own life in jeopardy. He drew his dagger, cut off one of those long, fair tresses he had so often admired and pressed to his lips and, sobbing bitterly amidst the sobs of the lookers-on who had no idea that their pity had been stirred by persons of such high estate, left the room.

'Friend, mistress,' cried Henry, in despair—'all forsake me, all leave me, all fail me at the same time!'

'Yes, sire,' said a man who had stepped out of the crowd outside the house, and followed Henry, 'but the throne is still left to you.'

'René!' cried Henry.

'Yes, sire, René—who still watches over you. The wretch Maurevel named you as he died. They know you are in Paris— the watch are looking for you—Go! Get away!'

'And yet you say, René, that I, a fugitive, shall be king?'

'Look, sire,' said the Florentine, pointing out to the king a star which appeared alone, brilliant amongst the folds of a golden cloud—'it is not I who say so, but *that* which proclaims it!'

Henry heaved a sigh, and disappeared into the darkness.*

LIST OF HISTORICAL CHARACTERS

D'ALBRET: Jeanne d'Albret (1528–72) married Antoine de Bourbon in 1548 and became Queen of Navarre when her husband inherited the throne in 1555. After his death in 1562 she ruled alone, fiercely protecting the independence of her small kingdom and admitting the reformed religion, which she had adopted in 1560 and to whose defence she committed her son, Henry, in 1567. She died of natural causes in Paris on 9 June 1572. Rumours that she had been poisoned by Catherine de Medicis were eagerly seized upon by Huguenot apologists after 1574.

D'ALENÇON: see François, Duke d'Alençon.

ANGOULÊME: see Bastard d'Angoulême.

D'ANJOU: see Henry d'Anjou.

AURIAC: named by Dumas both as governor of Provence and governor of Languedoc. Perhaps a vague memory of the Catholic Étienne de Bonne d'Auriac (1550–1635), Governor of Tallard in 1577, a Catholic fanatic who tried to murder the Bishop of Gap in 1574. Subsequently, he became a leader of the Catholic League in Provence and spent most of his life fighting Calvinists.

BASTARD D'ANGOULÊME: Henry (1551–86), Chevalier d'Angoulême, appointed Governor of Provence in 1579. Illegitimate son of Henry II and Lady Mary Fleming, lady-in-waiting to Mary Stuart, he took an active part in the murder of Coligny and the massacre which followed. Though he figured prominently in Charles IX's Guisard circle, Dumas allows him only a walk-on role.

BESME: Charles Yanowitz (?–1575), known as Besme (after Bohemia, where he claimed to have been born). Said to be the son of the Duke of Württemberg's artillery commander, he entered the service of François de Guise as a page and became squire to Henry de Guise. To avenge François he struck the first blow at Coligny and threw him through the window of his house in the Rue de Béthisy on 22 August 1572. He fought against the Protestants at the siege of La Rochelle in 1573 and died of wounds sustained when ambushed by Calvinist troops outside Barbézieux near Angoulême in September 1575.

BOURBON: the Bourbons had achieved prominence in the tenth century and were one of the oldest aristocratic families of France. Antoine de Bourbon, King of Navarre, founded the senior branch. His son, Henry IV, became first of the Bourbon kings in 1589. The last was deposed in 1830 and the line died out with the Comte de Chambord in

1883. The younger (Orléanist) branch began with Philippe, younger brother of Louis XIV.

BOURBON: Antoine de Bourbon (1518–62) became King of Navarre in 1555. Husband of Jeanne d'Albret and father of Henry of Navarre, he died of wounds received at the siege of Rouen.

BOURBON: Charles (1523–90), Cardinal de Bourbon, brother of Antoine, was named cardinal in 1548 and held various bishoprics. He was politically very active and in 1576 emerged as one of the leaders of the Catholic League in its struggle against the Huguenots.

CATHERINE DE MEDICIS: (1519–89), born in Florence, niece and cousin of popes, she married Henry, the second son of François I in 1533, who neglected her for his mistress, Diane de Poitiers, though she bore him ten children. Though Queen of France on the accession of Henry II in 1547, she played no public role. But after his death in 1559 she became regent during the minority of both her sons François II and Charles IX, her policy being to defend the Valois monarchy by resisting the growing power of the Guise family and keeping the peace between Catholics and Huguenots: to this end she actively promoted the marriage of Marguerite and Henry of Navarre in 1572. But fearing the growing influence of Coligny over Charles IX, she conspired with the Guises to murder him, thus sparking off the Saint Bartholomew's Day Massacre, responsibility for which history has laid mainly at her door. In 1573, she agreed reluctantly to the election of her favourite son, d'Anjou, to the throne of Poland, for she judged the death of Charles IX imminent. When Charles died in 1574 she sent urgent messages to d'Anjou in Warsaw and resumed the regency until his return in January 1575. Thereafter, she continued, though on a reduced scale, to pursue her policies. She was well read and cultivated: she began building the Tuileries and added to the Louvre. But her methods included duplicity and murder, and she placed great faith in astrology. She was hated by Protestants and mistrusted by Catholics, who despised her 'Italian' practices. Dumas does nothing to correct the popular view of Catherine as one of the great monsters of history.

CHARLES IX: Charles (1550–74), second surviving son of Henry II and Catherine de Medicis, became King of France in 1560. During his minority, France was ruled by his mother, who acted as regent and presided over three religious wars. He drew close to Coligny in 1571 and favoured the Admiral's plan to fight Spain in the Netherlands. In 1571 he married Elizabeth of Austria, by whom he had one daughter, Marie-Élizabeth (1572–8). He had no advance knowledge of Coligny's murder on 22 August 1572, which was arranged by Catherine and the Guise family, who proceeded to convince him of the need to take action against the assembled Huguenots on Saint Bartholomew's Day. Wary of d'Anjou, who had the support of the military, suspicious of the unpredictable d'Alençon, and mistrustful of Henry of Navarre, he was opposed by Protestants, papalist Catholics, and the moderate Malcontents. He had literary aspirations, was kind to poets but cruel to animals, which he strangled with his bare hands, and merciless to his enemies. He was unstable and much given to hunting, tennis, and forms of physical exertion which were believed to have contributed to his early death. He failed to achieve domestic peace: another war grew out of the Massacres which he had unleashed and which filled his dreams with horrors, and a fifth had just begun when he died on 30 May 1574.

CHARON: Jean Le Charron (*sic*), a printer-bookseller who was elected Provost of Merchants on 16 August 1572. As Provost he had many of the functions of a mayor, and was responsible for public order in the city. He subsequently accompanied Henry d'Anjou to Poland in 1574. Lestoile (February 1576) records that he was detested by the populace.

CLAUDE DE FRANCE: see Lorraine, Claude de.

CLÈVES: Catherine de Clèves (1548–1633), sister of Marie and Henriette, widow of Antoine de Croy, Prince de Porcian, and wife of Henry de Guise in 1570.

CLÈVES: Marie de Clèves (1553–74), daughter of the Duke de Nevers. Known for her many affairs, she was praised by poets as 'la belle Marie'. When she appeared at court, Henry d'Anjou fell in love with her, though she was already engaged to Henry de Bourbon. On her marriage to the latter in 1572, she became the Princess de Condé but remained d'Anjou's mistress until his departure for Poland in November 1573.

CLÈVES, HENRIETTE DE: see Nevers, Duchess de.

COCONNAS: Dumas's engaging hero asserts that he was born at Saint-Colomban, near Suza, then in Piedmont, in 1537 and lays claim to grandiose titles (p. 421). The much less glamorous historical Annibal de Coconas (or Coconat) (?–1574) also claimed to be descended from an illustrious Piedmontese family, though he was probably born in Italy. He began as a mercenary and came to France in 1569, where he served as Henry d'Anjou's Captain of Guards. He was the lover of the Maréchale de Retz and Henriette de Clèves. For money, he spied both for Spain and Catherine de Medicis. He was prominent in the Saint Bartholomew's Day Massacre, and boasted than he had bought thirty Huguenots, promised them their lives if they would convert, and then stabbed them to death, 'slowly and very cruelly'. In 1573 he accompanied Henry d'Anjou on his journey to Poland as far as the Rhine. In February 1574, he was introduced to d'Alençon by La Mole and helped plan the flight of Henry of Navarre and d'Alençon to Sedan. On 10 April 1574 he was arrested in a cell of the Couvent de Saint Augustin where he had taken refuge. He was sent to Vincennes on 12 April where, under torture, he revealed the plans made to enable François d'Alençon to escape and laid the blame on La Mole and others. He was beheaded and quartered on 30 April 1574. Charles IX, sickened by his boastful account of his part in the Saint Bartholomew's Day Massacre, said that he reckoned him 'a wicked man worthy of the end which he met' (Lestoile, *Registre-journal*, i. 257).

COLIGNY: Gaspard Coligny (1519–72), *seigneur* de Châtillon and Admiral de France. A long-serving political and military Protestant stalwart, he was believed to have ordered the murder of François de Guise in 1563. After the death of Condé in 1569, he emerged as the main Huguenot leader and helped shape the Treaty of Pacification of 1570, which ended the third War of Religion. A committed opponent of both the Guise clan and of Catherine, he captured the imagination of Charles IX (who called him 'father') with a plan to wage war against Spain in the Low Countries in the spring of 1572. Unknown to Charles, Catherine, fearing his influence over the King, and Henry de Guise, who wanted revenge for the death of his father, employed Maurevel to assassinate him on 22 August 1572. Charles was horrified but, convinced that the attempt on Coligny's life put himself and the throne at risk, ordered the massacre of Coligny's supporters on Saint Bartholomew's Day.

CONDÉ: Henry de Bourbon (1552–88) became Prince de Condé on the death of his father Louis. Regarded by some Huguenots as capable of succeeding his father as Protestant leader, he arrived in Paris in July 1572 with Henry for his wedding. He escaped the massacre but was presented with the choice of abjuring his faith or death. He refused to convert and denounced the massacre as shameful. He was present with Henry of Navarre on the royalist side at the siege of La Rochelle but was kept a virtual prisoner until 1574 when he fled to Heidelberg, where he set about raising an army to defend his religion. His intransigence was not to the taste of Henry who also returned to the reformed religion in 1576. Thereafter, Condé became the leader of the uncompromising Huguenots against the Catholic League. He died in 1588, rumoured to have been poisoned by his second wife, whom he married in 1586.

CONDÉ: Louis de Bourbon (1530–69), Prince de Condé, father of the preceding. Leader of the Protestant forces since the beginning of the religious wars which he initiated with a massacre of Catholics at Wassy in 1562. He was assassinated by Montesquiou after having surrendered at the battle of Jarnac (13 October 1569).

CONDÉ, PRINCESS DE: see Marie de Clèves.

DIANE DE POITIERS: Diane (1499–1566), mistress to Henry II, was a woman of great beauty and culture. Her ghost was said to haunt the Louvre.

DU GUAST: Louis Bérenger du Guast (1545–75), one of the *mignons* of Henry d'Anjou, from whom he received numerous honours and favours. He accompanied d'Anjou to Poland in 1573 as colonel of his escort and, when d'Anjou became Henry III, became his Captain of Guards. It was du Guast who, in 1570, showed the King a compromising letter from Guise to Marguerite, thereby provoking a crisis which led to the prompt marriage of Guise. She later accused him of using Madame de Sauves to drive a wedge between Henry of Navarre and d'Alençon. He was murdered on 31 October 1575 in his house by masked men led by the Baron de Viteaux, an agent of d'Anjou, though probably on Marguerite's orders, for having made her affair with Charles de Balzac ('le Bel Entraguet') public knowledge. Brantôme described him as cultured, courageous, and liberal, but Marguerite, who loathed him, called him 'a Machiavelist' (*Mémoires*, 17) who exerted a powerful and 'pernicious' influence over d'Anjou.

FRANÇOIS I: The reign of François I (1494–1547) was marked by bitter conflicts with Spain, but internally he provided France with sound administration and a cultivated court.

FRANÇOIS II: François (1544–60), eldest surviving son of Henry II, acceded to the throne in 1559. He was the sickly husband of Mary Stuart and, though he died of natural causes, it was widely believed he had been poisoned.

FRANÇOIS, DUKE D'ALENÇON: François (1554–84), fourth surviving son of Henry II and Catherine de Medicis and brother to François II, Charles IX, and Henry III. He was tubercular, versatile, and ruthlessly ambitious. Marriage to Elizabeth I of England was mooted several times but came to nothing. Plans for him to promote French interests in the Calvinist Netherlands which rose against Catholic Spain in the spring of 1572 were halted by the Saint Bartholomew's Day Massacre. Thereafter he and Henry de Navarre drew politically close, though both were watched by Catherine. He took part in the siege of La Rochelle (1573), where he became prominent among the moderate 'Malcontents' who sought religious tolerance and civil peace. He hated both the King and Henry d'Anjou, against whom he forged an alliance with Marguerite with the help of La Mole, Cocconas, and others. Implicated in the plot of March 1574, he was, despite the evidence of Cocconas against him, treated leniently, being imprisoned at Vincennes on 8 March 1574 with his co-suspect, Henry of Navarre, unlike La Mole and Cocconas, who were executed (30 April), and leading Malcontents, like Montmorency and Cussey, who were sent to the Bastille. After the death of Charles IX, Catherine and Henry III kept him a virtual prisoner in the Louvre. Wooed by the Huguenots yet dominated by Catherine, and unable to choose between them, he remained in contact with his coterie who included Marguerite and Bussy d'Amboise (the hero of *La Dame de Monsoreau* (1846)). Like many at the court, he was bisexual, and was the lover of La Mole and Madame de Sauves. He escaped to Sedan in September 1575. Thereafter, he wavered between the crown and the Huguenots, his only loyalty being to his permanently frustrated ambition.

GILLONNE: Gillonne de Goyon, Mademoiselle de Thorigny, was the daughter of Jacques de Goyon (1525–97), Comte de Matignon, lieutenant-governor first of Normandy then of Guyenne before becoming Maréchal de France in 1579. Confidante of Margot.

GREGORY XIII: pope between May 1572 and 1585. The calendar was reformed during his pontificate.

GUISE: François de Lorraine (1519–63), Duke de Guise, one of Henry II's most successful military commanders. He wrested Calais from the English in 1558, took part in the massacre at Wassy in 1562, and became commander-in-chief of the Catholic troops. Father of Henry de Guise. He was assassinated by Poltrot de Méré at Orléans.

GUISE: Henry de Lorraine (1550–88), Prince de Joinville, who became Duke de Guise on the death of his father François. He was brought up with Henry of Navarre and, like him, fought at Jarnac and Montcontour in 1569. Leader of the Catholic party, he posed a threat to the monarchy, though at different periods he allied himself with crown policy. He was one of the main architects of the Saint Bartholomew's Day Massacre. Subsequently, he attempted to establish the fortunes of his family on the basis of his popularity with the Paris populace. Disfigured in battle in 1575, he was known as 'Le Balafré' after the scar which marked his face. In 1576, he set up the hard-line Catholic League and, exploiting the unpopularity of Henry III, finally attempted to seize the throne. He was assassinated in 1588 at Blois by the Forty-Five Guardsmen on the orders of the King. The event is chronicled by Dumas in *Les Quarante-Cinq* (1847).

HENRY II: Henry (1519–59), second son of François I, became king on the death of his father in 1547. He maintained the French policy of opposing Charles V, King of Spain and Holy Roman Emperor, who fought for recognition of his claim to be universal monarch. After

Charles abdicated in 1556, he maintained the struggle against his successor, Philip II and his ally Henry VIII of England. He recovered lost territory, including Calais, taken by François de Guise in 1558, but was forced to abandon French interests in Italy. He died in a joust, wounded in the eye by the lance of Montgomery. In 1533, he married Catherine de Medicis, by whom he had ten children, three of whom would be kings of France.

HENRY D'ANJOU: Henry (1551–89), third surviving son of Henry II, brother of François II, Charles IX, and François d'Alençon. The title of Duke d'Anjou was given to the king's immediately younger brother, who was also known at court as Monsieur. Among his mistresses were Madame de Condé and Marie de Clèves, though he was known to be homosexual. His coterie of *mignons* was notorious: 'His mind, you see, runs on his minions, | And all his heaven is to delight himself' (Marlowe, *The Massacre at Paris*, sc. xiv). He won a reputation for bravery in battle at 18, and was an ally of Guise, with whom he plotted—with Catherine—the murder of Coligny on 22 August 1572. In September his name was proposed to fill the vacant throne of Poland. He took part in the siege of La Rochelle in 1573. He was elected King of Poland in June but, aware that Charles IX was unlikely to live long, was reluctant to leave France. In November, the King, aware of d'Anjou's popularity with the army, ordered him to leave. He was crowned King of Poland in February 1574 but sat on the throne for only five months. On 18 June, informed by Catherine of the death of Charles IX, he fled Poland but, after a leisurely progress by way of Italy, did not return to Paris until January 1575, where he was crowned Henry III a month later. He was an unpopular monarch and his reign was characterized by bitter sectarian feuding. The death of François d'Alençon in 1584 left Henry of Navarre heir to the throne. To disqualify him, the king signed the Treaty of Nemours (1585) outlawing Protestantism, though in the event the main challenge to his authority came from the Catholic Henry de Guise, whose ambition finally turned to open revolt. Henry III ordered his murder at Blois in 1588, a year before he himself was assassinated by the fanatical priest Jacques Clément.

HENRY OF NAVARRE: Henry de Bourbon (1553–1610), son of Antoine de Bourbon and Jeanne d'Albret. Prince of Béarn, became King of Navarre on the death of his father. He married Marguerite de Valois on 18 August and narrowly escaped the Saint Bartholomew's Day massacre of the Huguenot nobles who had gathered for his wedding. He was forced to abjure the reformed religion in September but remained suspect to Catherine and Charles IX, who subjected him to long periods of house arrest and, at times, to imprisonment. His sincerity was doubted by Catholics, and sections of the Huguenot faction placed greater trust in Condé. But he survived, partly through his skill at reading situations and partly through his loveless but politically useful marriage to Marguerite, to whom he was regularly unfaithful. He escaped the court in 1576, returned to his faith, and became undisputed commander of moderate Huguenots. An astute politician and a considerable military leader, he succeeded Henry III in 1589 and went on to pacify the country and reconcile Catholic and Protestant. The Edict of Nantes (1598) allowed both religions to live in harmony and remained in force until revoked by Louis XIV in 1685. He divorced Marguerite in 1599. He was assassinated by the Catholic Ravaillac in 1610.

LA CHASTRE: see Nancey.

LA MOLE: Joseph de Boniface, *seigneur* de La Mole, a Provençal gentleman. Dumas makes him a Huguenot and the Romantic lead of his drama. In reality, he was a fervent womanizer and a fundamentalist Catholic who took mass each day (five or six times, some said) to expiate his sexual adventures with both sexes. He took part in the Massacre of August 1572—it was not him whom Marguerite saved but Lérac—and in early September was sent to the Midi to spread the slaughter to the provinces. He was wounded at the siege of La Rochelle in February 1573, by which time he was one of d'Alençon's male lovers. Catherine believed that he soured relations between d'Alençon and d'Anjou. Charles IX disliked him intensely, twice ordered him to be strangled during the siege, and personally held a candle while six men lay in wait for him at the Louvre. In January 1574 he became the lover of Marguerite. He played no very noble role in the plan to enable Henry of Navarre and d'Alençon to escape to Sedan in March. When La Mole sensed that d'Alençon was wavering, he tried to redeem the situation by revealing the plot to Catherine and then to the King. The leaders were arrested. Henry of Navarre and d'Alençon were required to justify themselves; the Malcontents Montmorency and Cussé were sent to the Bastille, and La Mole and Cocconas (whom he had only recently introduced into the service of d'Alençon) were tried in April. La Mole denied all charges, refusing to implicate d'Alençon, but was found guilty of treason by witchcraft. A wax figure, made for him by Ruggieri, was held to be a model of the King. He was tortured, decapitated, and quartered on 30 April. By several accounts, Marguerite kept his embalmed head in her collection of gruesome love relics.

LA ROCHEFOUCAULD: François, Comte de La Rochefoucauld, a very experienced soldier and an intimate of Coligny. He escorted Henry of Navarre to Paris for his wedding in July 1572 and died in the massacre a month later.

LÉRAC: a Protestant gentleman from Gascony, Philippe de Lévis, Vicomte de Lérac (or Léran or Leyran), stumbled bleeding into Marguerite's apartment on Saint Bartholomew's Night. She saved him from his pursuers, persuaded the King to spare his life, and tended his wounds. For Lérac, Dumas substitutes La Mole, and uses the event as the start of his romantic affair with the Queen of Navarre.

LORRAINE: Charles (1524–74), Cardinal de Lorraine, an ambitious, skilful politician opposed to any accommodation with the Calvinists.

LORRAINE: Charles (1543–1606), Duke de Lorraine, husband of Claude de France.

LORRAINE: Claude (1547–74), Margot's eldest sister, became Duchess de Lorraine by her marriage to Charles de Lorraine, by whom she had nine children. She died giving birth to twins shortly after the coronation of Henry III.

MADELEINE, MADELON: nurse to Charles IX, 'a very sensible and honest woman', according to Brantôme, to whom Charles remained devoted. She was a Protestant and he begged her to convert. She did so after the Saint Bartholomew's Day Massacre, 'more to please him than out of zeal' (Brantôme, *Œuvres complètes*, v. 256).

MARCEL, CLAUDE: a goldsmith, with premises on the Pont-au-Change, and Prévot des Marchands between 1570, when his election was ordered by Charles IX, and 16 August 1572, when he was replaced by Le Charron. A favourite of Catherine, who stood as godmother to one of his children, he addressed a meeting at the Hôtel de Ville on the night of 24 August rousing Parisians to support the King by taking up arms against the Huguenots.

MARGUERITE DE VALOIS ('LA REINE MARGOT'): Marguerite (1552–1615), third daughter of Henry II and Catherine de Medicis and sister to François II, Charles IX, Henry d'Anjou, and François d'Alençon. Various husbands were proposed for her, including the King of Portugal in 1570. But she became Queen of Navarre on her marriage to Henry of Navarre in August 1572, a union designed to heal the rift between Catholics and Protestants. It was a loveless marriage. Henry was unfaithful but Marguerite too worked through a stream of lovers—the Vicomte de Martigues, Entraguet, Henry de Guise, La Mole, Jean de Souvray, and many more—and a number of illegitimate children. Her amorousness earned her the popular name of 'La Reine Margot' after 1574. Even into old age she kept a reputation for dissolute behaviour: when she was over 60 she loved a musician named Villars, who was known as 'le roi Margot'. It was said that she kept the hearts of dead lovers in gold boxes and numerous contemporaries reported that she stored the embalmed head of La Mole. She was prepared to dirty her hands when necessary: it was said that she was responsible for the murder of du Guast. But, looking to her own ambition, she protected her husband against her mother Catherine and Charles IX. She was fond of d'Alençon though she was much irritated by his indecisiveness. When her husband was crowned Henry IV, she realized many ambitions. But her reign as Queen of France ended in divorce in 1599. She was praised by poets for her beauty and her learning which enabled her to deliver a speech of welcome in Latin to the Polish envoys in August 1573. Her *Mémoires* (which Dumas or Maquet probably saw in the edition of 1842) are extremely well written but do not give an impartial or truthful account of her role in events.

MATIGNON: Jacques de Matignon, father of Gillonne, an experienced soldier, who commanded the Catholic forces which captured Montgomery in May 1574. He was made Maréchal de France in 1579.

MAUREVEL: Charles de Louviers, *seigneur* de Maurevel (or Maurevert), ran away from home after killing his tutor and became a page in the house of the Catholic Guises. Resenting being punished for a serious misdemeanour, he went over to the Huguenots and fought for them in the first wars of religion. However, he succeeded in re-ingratiating himself with Henry de Guise and d'Alençon, who paid him 12,000 crowns to murder Coligny in 1569. Unable to get near the Admiral, he shot his Protestant protector, Mouy de Saint-Phalle, in the back instead. For his action he was decorated by Charles IX. He was employed by Catherine and Guise to assassinate Coligny on 22 August 1572, an act which sparked off the massacre of Saint Bartholomew's Day. Maurevel was pursued and apprehended at Villeneuve-Saint-Georges but escaped. With royal protection, he fled to Rome in October but returned to France, where he took part in the siege of La Rochelle in 1573. He accompanied the new French ambassador, Retz, to London in September. The following year he was sent to Poitou with orders to assassinate La Noue, the Protestant commander, and, it was said, he attempted to kill the Prince de Condé in 1575. In 1576, he was given title to two profitable abbeys and retired. In 1579, in a quarrel with his cousin, he had one arm shot away, and in 1580 an attempt on his life was made as he crossed the Pont Notre-Dame. Mouy's son, who had sworn vengeance, tracked him down and killed him in April 1583.

MAYENNE: Charles de Lorraine (1554–1611), Duke de Mayenne, younger brother of Henry de Guise.

MAZILLE: the doctor (d. 1578) who attended Charles in his last illness.

MONTESQUIOU: Joseph-François, Baron de Montesquiou, a native of the Béarn, murdered François de Guise in 1563.

MONTGOMERY: Gabriel de Lorges (1530–74), Comte de Montgomery, captain of the Scottish Guard of Henry II, whom he wounded fatally in the eye during a jousting tournament on 30 June 1559 to mark the marriage of the King's daughter and the King of Spain. He retired to his estates until 1562 when he supported the Protestant cause and subsequently became one of its leaders. He escaped the Saint Bartholomew's Day Massacre and fled to England, from which he unsuccessfully attempted a landing at La Rochelle in 1573 and, the following year, led an invasion of Normandy. Captured by Matignon at the château of Domfront on 27 May, he was taken to Paris, tortured, and beheaded on 26 June 1574.

MONTMORENCY: François (1530–79), Duke de Montmorency, was made Maréchal de France in 1559. He fought in many campaigns and sieges and became French ambassador in London in 1572. The following year he joined forces with the Malcontents and was implicated in the plot to free Henry of Navarre and d'Alençon in March 1574, for which he was sent to the Bastille for a year.

MOUY: Louis de Vaudrey, *seigneur* de Mouy de Saint-Phalle, a Protestant commander, assassinated at Niort in 1569 by Maurevel.

MOUY: Claude Vaudrey (d. 1583), *seigneur* de Mouy de Saint-Phalle, son of Louis. A minor Huguenot captain whom Dumas promotes to the front ranks of the Huguenot party on the strength of his pursuit and killing of Maurevel.

NANCEY: Gaspard de La Chastre, *seigneur* de Nancey, Captain of Guards from 1568. He had fought on the Catholic side in many engagements, including Jarnac and Moncontour (1569). He died in 1576 of old wounds received at the battle of Dreux in 1562.

NANTOUILLET: Antoine Duprat, *seigneur* de Nantouillet, baron de Thiers et Vitteaux, was Provost of Paris between 1554 and 1588. His functions were primarily concerned with criminal justice in the capital.

NEVERS: Louis de Gonzague (1539–95) became Duke de Nevers on his marriage to Henriette de Clèves, daughter of the first Duke de Nevers. In September 1572 he was sent as special ambassador to Rome, where he remained during the entire action of the novel. After giving fervent support to the Catholic League after 1576 he later transferred his allegiance to Henry IV. He is Henriette's conveniently absent husband.

NEVERS: Henriette de Clèves (1542–1601), elder sister of Marie, Duchess de Nevers, married Louis de Gonzague in 1565. She was

Lady-in-waiting to Catherine de Medicis, sister-in-law to Henry de Guise, friend and confidante of Marguerite, and mistress of—among others—Guise, du Guast, d'Alençon, and Coconnas.

NOSTRADAMUS: Michel de Nostradamus (1503–66), doctor and physician, and author of a collection of rhymed predictions, in groups of a hundred, known as *Les Centuries*.

PARÉ, AMBROISE (1517–90): Protestant surgeon to four French kings, Henry II, François II, Charles IX, and Henry III. During the Italian campaigns of the late 1530s he substituted the ligature of arteries for the conventional practice of cauterizing gunshot wounds with boiling oil and red-hot irons. His *Cinq Livres de Chirurgie* (1562) influenced treatment in many countries and earned him the title of Father of Modern Surgery. He said that he merely bound wounds: it was God who cured them.

PHILIP II: Philip (1527–98), King of Spain and the Low Countries, who succeeded Charles V in 1556. He campaigned against the French in the hope of seeing a Spaniard on the French throne. He sent an armada against the English in 1588. He left Spain weakened and considerably diminished.

PILE: Pierre Piles (*sic*) de Villemur, former tutor to Henry de Guise, a priest at Sens, was made canon of the church of Saint-Germain-l'Auxerrois by the Cardinal de Guise, whose patronage he enjoyed.

POLTROT DE MÉRÉ: Jean Poltrot de Méré (1537–63), a Protestant gentleman who assassinated François de Guise in 1563. He was sentenced to be decapitated and quartered.

POMPÉE: a Milanese who taught Charles IX to dance and acted as his fencing-master.

PORCIAN: Antoine de Croy (1541–67), Prince de Château-Porcian. Though still a Catholic on his marriage to Catherine de Clèves, he was a bitter enemy of François de Guise and fought alongside the Huguenots. On his deathbed he made his wife promise never to marry Henry de Guise, whom he hated. Catherine married Guise in 1570.

PORCIAN, PRINCESS DE: see Catherine de Clèves.

RENÉ: René Bianchi (or Bianco or Bianque), a Florentine, perfumer to Catherine de Medicis. He worked from premises on the Pont Saint-Michel and was believed to have supplied the poison with which Catherine is said to have murdered Jeanne d'Albret. According to Lestoile, he toured the prisons during the Saint Bartholomew's Day Massacre with a knife, murdering Huguenots. It is said that he gave shelter to a Protestant jeweller, forced him to hand over his goods, cut his throat, and dropped him into the Seine.

RETZ: Albert de Gondi (1522–1602), Count, later Duke de Retz (1581), one of the main instigators of the Saint Bartholomew's Day Massacre. He was wounded at La Rochelle. When the siege was over he was appointed Maréchal de France (July 1573). Though a skilled negotiator, his Italian origins made him suspect to many.

RONSARD: Pierre de Ronsard (1524–85), leader of the Pléiade school of poets who renewed French poetry by breaking with the traditions of the Middle Ages. A Humanist who greatly admired the classical writers of antiquity, he wrote poetry of great lyric power and personal inspiration.

RUGGIERI: Cosmo Ruggieri, born in Florence, was astrologer to Catherine de Medicis. For making a wax figurine of Marguerite for La Mole, he was interrogated at the trial of April 1574. He was sent to the galleys at Marseilles, though Catherine quickly ordered his release, having need of his services.

SAUVE: Charlotte de Beaune-Semblançay (1551–1617) became Comtesse de Sauves (*sic*) on her marriage to Simon de Fizes (d. 1579), Baron de Sauves. She took a second husband, François de La Trémoïlle, Marquis de Noirmoutier. Her numerous lovers included Henry of Navarre, d'Alençon, Souvré, and du Guast. Marguerite called her a 'Circe'. Henry of Navarre said that she was responsible for the hostility which alienated him from d'Alençon. Of her many lovers, she remained most attached to Henry de Guise.

SEMBLANÇAY: Jacques de Semblançay (b. 1497) was executed in 1527 for plotting with Spain against Louise de Savoie, mother of François I.

TAVANNES: Gaspard de Saulx (1509–73), *seigneur* de Tavannes, a member of Guise's circle and one of the instigators of the St Bartholomew's Day Massacre. Author of *Mémoires* reprinted three times between 1822 and 1838.

TELIGNY: Charles de Théligny (*sic*), one of the leading Huguenot commanders and negotiators, son-in-law of Coligny, whose daughter he had married in 1571, and in 1572 a member of Charles IX's intimate circle. On 23 August 1572, 'he produced a dagger and threatened to kill any man who dared suspect the King' of ordering the murder of Coligny. But the following night, 'having escaped from three or four houses, he was killed at a window by the Duke d'Anjou's Guards' (d'Aubigné, *Histoire universelle*, Bk VI, p. 336).

TOUCHET, MARIE: Dame de Belleville (1549–1638), born at Orléans, mistress to Charles IX, by whom she had a son, also Charles, born 28 April 1573.

TURENNE: Henri de La Tour d'Auvergne (b. 1555), Vicomte de Turenne and later Duke de Bouillon. At first a prominent Protestant, he subsequently joined the Malcontents, who valued his qualities of military leadership.

VIEILLEVILLE: François de Scépeaux, *seigneur* de Vieilleville, Maréchal de France. A veteran Catholic commander, he fought in many battles and in 1568 was sent to establish a garrison at Protestant La Rochelle, which he also besieged in 1573.

EXPLANATORY NOTES

(For details of the many real persons who figure in the text, see the List of Historical Characters. Their movements through the streets of Paris may be followed on the map on pp. xxxii–xxxiii).

5 *Louvre*: the Louvre was begun by Philippe-Auguste in 1204 as a fortress on the right bank of the Seine. In the fourteenth century Charles V turned it into a royal residence, though his successors preferred other royal palaces. In 1527, François I declared his intention to live there, but work on a new royal residence did not begin until 1546. The Louvre was subsequently enlarged by numerous monarchs, notably Louis XIII and Louis XIV, and was finally completed in Dumas's day by Napoleon III. When *La Reine Margot* opens, the Tuileries did not exist and the Louvre was a few minutes' walk from the then Porte Saint-Honoré in the city's west wall. The Tuileries is one of a number of landmarks absent from the later landscape of the city: the Luxembourg Palace was begun in 1615, the Palais Royal in 1632, and the Place Vendôme in 1670, while the Île Saint-Louis had still to be reclaimed from the Seine.

Saint-Germain-l'Auxerrois: situated just east of the Louvre. Occupying the site of a sixth-century sanctuary and later destroyed by the Normans, it was rebuilt between the twelfth and sixteenth centuries. It was sacked by rioters in 1831 but was subsequently restored. A peal of its bells was the signal—as we shall see—for the start of the Saint Bartholomew's Day Massacre.

Hotel de Bourbon: sited immediately east of the Louvre and, like the other Paris Hôtels, half town-house, half château. Begun in 1303, it was confiscated by the crown and partly demolished after the treason in 1527 of the 'Constable' Jean de Bourbon, the ninth Duke. It disappeared in 1663 to make way for Louis XIV's Colonnade.

Navarre: the kingdom of Navarre straddled the Pyrenees and had Pamplona as its capital. The southern part became Spanish in 1511 and the rest (now covered by the *département* of the Basses-Pyrénées) was joined to France when its king became Henry IV of France in 1589.

Notre-Dame: at a time when royal marriages were an instrument of international politics, several possible husbands for Marguerite had been considered: Sebastian, King of Portugal, Rudolf, King of Hungary, and Carlos, son of Philip II of Spain. Her marriage to

Henry of Navarre, celebrated by Cardinal de Bourbon on 18 August 1572, was the result of lengthy negotiations and formed part of royal policy which aimed at ending the religious conflict between Catholics and Protestants. For the ceremony, 'a certaine forme of wordes so framed, as disagreed with the Religion of neither side' (Varamund/Hotman, pp. 167–8) was used and a dais was built outside Notre-Dame, so that the mixed marriage, which did not have papal approval, would not be held inside the cathedral: afterwards, Henry did not take mass. The celebrations included plays, tournaments, concerts, balls, and fireworks and drew large numbers of nobles of both factions to Paris.

5 *and the Catholic party*: in the wake of the Reformation, France was split into three bitterly divided factions. Protestants followed Calvin, enjoyed support in the south and the west, and were led by Coligny and the Bourbon family: Henry of Navarre, then 18, and his cousin, Henry de Condé, one year older. Catholics loyal to the Pope took their lead from the faculty of theology of the University of Paris, which accepted the authority of Rome, evangelized Paris, and had the support of the rural majority: military and political leadership was supplied by the Guise family, notably by the Cardinal de Lorraine and the young Henry de Guise. Gallican Catholics, led by the Valois royal family and backed by a new generation of humanist jurists, rejected the canon law of the Church of Rome (which justified certain papal claims on France) in favour of a newly interpreted form of Roman civil law as the necessary basis of an autonomous state. Protestants and Catholics clashed in a series of eight religious wars, the first ending in 1563 and the last in 1588. The royal edict of Pacification (1570) which ended the third of these wars influenced policy in a number of areas. Abroad, the crown opted to back Huguenot unrest in the Spanish Netherlands (thus placating Protestants at home and furthering its own opposition to Spain) while at home, the marriage of Marguerite and Henry was intended as a gesture of reconciliation. However, the policy failed and religious toleration was not established until 1598 when the Edict of Nantes allowed Protestants to live in harmony with Catholics for a century until it was revoked by Louis XIV. French Protestants were commonly known as Huguenots, a borrowing of the Genevese nickname *Eiguenots* (from the German *Eidgenossen*, 'confederates bound by oath') which was given to supporters of the Reformation.

Poltrot de Méré: Louis, Prince de Condé, was murdered in 1569 by Montesquiou, Captain of Guards to Henry d'Anjou, at the battle of

Jarnac (30 km west of Angoulême), a decisive Catholic victory. Duke François de Guise had ordered a massacre of Protestants at Wassy in 1562 which signalled the beginning of the wars of religion. After being taken prisoner at Orléans, he was assassinated in February 1563 by Poltrot de Méré, who had acted (as Henry de Guise and others believed) on the orders of Coligny, the Protestant leader. Méré was publicly quartered with such cruelty that, Brantôme reports, one lady spectator fell down dead with horror.

6 *crime had been committed*: Protestant suspicions that Jeanne d'Albret had been poisoned to remove her from the scene as a preliminary to a general massacre were widespread but unfounded. An autopsy was performed and historians accept her doctors' view that she died (as Dumas reports on p. 7) of pleurisy. Catherine's reputation as a poisoner was already well established (it was part of her 'Italian' origins) but the accusation that she had murdered Jeanne was established by Protestant pamphleteers after 1574.

obstinacy: the policy of Pacification was welcomed by both Protestants, led by Coligny and Jeanne d'Albret, and the Catholic parties. Charles IX favoured his sister's marriage as a means of uniting the country behind his plans for renewed conflict with Spain.

for all to see: Pope Pius V was succeeded in May 1572 by Gregory III. Both were reluctant to give a dispensation for a mixed marriage in which neither partner was expected to change religion. Charles was as good as this statement (taken verbatim from Pierre Lestoile's *Journal de Henri III*, i. 468) suggests: the marriage took place before the dispensation was granted.

7 *to him alone*: Coligny, the most respected of the Protestant commanders, had captured Charles's imagination with his plan to renew hostilities against Spain by actively supporting the Dutch Huguenots against the Catholic regime of the Spanish Netherlands. Charles grew close to Coligny and, as d'Aubigné (*Histoire universelle*, Bk VI, p. 299) records, called him 'mon père' and put the Flanders enterprise in his hands.

will spoil everything: Catherine de Medicis had ruled France as regent during Charles's minority and still saw herself as the power behind the throne. Seeing the erosion of her influence with alarm but also believing that France was too exhausted to wage a foreign war, she could not allow the situation to continue, as Charles was aware. His words are reproduced from Pierre Lestoile (*Journal de Henri III*, i. 473).

7 *Châtillon*: Coligny was born at Châtillon-sur-Loire (Loiret), 50 km south-east of Montargis, where his family's estate was situated.

are with you!: reproduced from Pierre Lestoile (*Journal de Henri III*, i. 473).

8 *battles of Jarnac and Montcontour*: the Catholic army commanded by Henry d'Anjou overcame a Protestant force led by Condé at Jarnac (Charente) in 1569. The same year, he defeated Coligny at Montcontour, near Châtellerault.

the living prince: Caesar vanquished Pompey at Pharsalia in Thessaly in 48 BC, and Alexander overwhelmed Darius III at Issus in Asia Minor in 333 BC.

like an eagle's: an unattributed drawing of Henry at 18 (reproduced in David Buisseret, *Henry IV* (London, 1984)) shows him bushy-haired and broad-browed, with alert eyes and a prominent nose. He was already known for his charm and wit. In Dumas's largely imageless prose, similes involving hawks, falcons, lions, wolves, serpents, and eagles enable him to evoke the strong character types with which he was happiest.

Henry IV: Henry de Bourbon, Prince de Béarn, became King of Navarre on the death of his mother, Jeanne d'Albret, on 9 June 1572. He won his spurs at Arnay-le-Duc (30 km north-west of Beaune in Burgundy) when a Protestant army under Coligny overcame Catholic forces.

two little months: this echo of Hamlet (I. ii), absent in the original, was added by the translator.

9 *his assassin*: see note to p 5.

like Hannibal: it is said that when Hannibal, the Carthaginian general (247–c.183 BC), was 9, his father, Hamilcar Barca, made him swear an oath of eternal enmity to Rome.

Ma sœur Margot: according to d'Aubigné (*Histoire universelle*, Bk. VI, p. 316), Charles IX frequently referred dismissively to his sister as 'ma grosse sœur Margot'.

others to Cytherea: a surname of Venus. Ronsard was prominent among her poetic admirers who compared her regularly to such classical models of beauty and virtue. Brantôme claims (*Recueil*, 126–7) that at his suggestion the poet composed a sonnet (which has not survived) linking Marguerite to Aurora, for she was as beautiful as the dawn.

10 *than a child's*: no portrait exists of Marguerite at the time of her marriage, though a sketch dating from 1571 shows an oval face,

high brow, wide mouth, and full lips. Brantôme thought her excep-
tionally beautiful and recalled her regular features, 'candid, pleasing' eyes and regal walk. Jeanne d'Albret admitted she was handsome but complained that she wore her stays too tight and painted
her face excessively, after the modern fashion. Ronsard sang of this
'unique pearl of France', commending her dark hair, strongly
arched eyebrows, delicate ears, and her small hands and feet. She
was extremely cultured and left a volume of memoirs, and poems.

nor the court: Brantôme (*Recueil*, 128–30) records a number of such
remarks including the words of a provincial noble newly arrived in
Paris: 'I am not surprised that you gentlemen are so attached to the
court. For were you to enjoy no pleasure other than seeing such a
beautiful princess every day, you would know no greater delight if
you lived in a paradise on earth.'

of the kingdom: Charles IX promoted the marriage as a means of
reconciling the warring sects.

sully the good name: Charles's words might be crude, but they were
not without foundation and court gossip not without substance.
Marguerite's lover, the Vicomte de Martigues, was killed in battle
in 1569 and she had been the mistress of Henry de Guise since 1570.

11 *the unfortunate Semblançay*: Jacques de Semblançay was executed
in 1527.

three succeeding kings: François I, Henry II, and François II—not to
mention the dissolute reigns of Charles IX and Henry III.

12 *Circe*: Homer tells (*Odyssey*, X and XII) how, returning from the
Trojan wars, Ulysses called at the island of Æea, home of Circe, a
nymph skilled in magic. She turned his companions into swine but
Ulysses, sword in hand, demanded that she restore them to their
human state. She complied and so bewitched Ulysses that he remained with her for a whole year.

13 *Gascon accent*: as a boy, Henry spoke patois. His southern accent is
well attested and Dumas exploits it to suggest the traditional fire
and swagger of the Gascons, as he does throughout the Musketeer
cycle in the person of d'Artagnan, another Béarnais.

ma mie: a contraction of 'mon amie', used affectionately by both
men and women.

'Sang Diou!': 'Sang Dieu!' (God's blood) in Henry's brogue. Henry was celebrated for a certain roughness of language which Dumas
duly reflects: 'Ventre-saint-gris' was a particular favourite. Dumas
regularly puts religious oaths in various mouths. While 'Mon
Dieu!', 'Ma foi!' or 'Pardieu!' are neutral, some are distortions

intended to avoid offending the Divinity. 'Mordi!' (Mort de Dieu), 'Tudieu!' (Vertu de Dieu), and 'Corbeuf!' (Corps de Dieu), are examples of the same process which, in England, gave 'Zounds!' (God's wounds).

15 *Dariole*: Dumas invents a name for Charlotte de Sauve's faithful maid, though Marguerite's confidante Gillonne de Goyon was real, as Dumas explains on p. 17.

Gascon reputation of the Béarnais: Gascons were thought quick-tempered, belligerent, and boastful, but also gregarious and companionable: Henry already had a reputation for 'southern' warmth, generosity, and charm. Though he had a 'Gascon' accent, he was born at Pau, capital of the Béarn, part of Navarre, which became French in 1607. Gascony, an ancient French province, was joined to Aquitaine in 1052 and covered a vast area extending from Bordeaux to Bayonne and eastwards to Montauban. Most Béarnais reacted with hostility to any suggestions that they were Gascons.

melted Ulysses himself: in Homer's *Odyssey* (Bk. XII), Ulysses binds himself to the mast and fills his men's ears with wax to escape the voices of the Sirens.

16 *Rue du Chaume*: skirted the southern side of the Hotel de Guise. For this and other streets mentioned in the text, see map on pp. xxxii–xxxiii.

19 *Infanta of Portugal*: Dumas reverses the roles. A Portuguese marriage was proposed, in 1570, but for Marguerite, not Henry de Guise: see note to p. 5. Charles IX saw considerable advantages for France in the union. When Du Guast showed him a letter from Marguerite to Guise which put their liaison beyond doubt, he sent for his half-brother, Henry (the Bastard d'Angoulême): 'Of these two swords you see here, one is for you if, by the time I go hunting tomorrow, you have not killed the Duke de Guise with the other' (Antoine Mongez, *Histoire de Marguerite de Valois* (Paris, 1777), 31). According to Mongez, Marguerite warned Guise, who, fearing for his life, promptly and unceremoniously married Catherine de Clèves, widow of the Prince de Porcian. Marguerite (*Mémoires*, 22–3) explained the collapse of the marriage by the opposition of Philip II of Spain, adding that her brother d'Anjou (who had also threatened to kill Guise) made pointed remarks linking her with Guise which had the effect of antagonizing both Catherine and Charles IX.

22 *de Mouy*: Mouy de Saint-Phalle, a prominent Huguenot leader, was murdered near Niort in 1569.

or the house of Lorraine: Henry, now titular head of French Huguenots, was a Bourbon and related by blood to the Condés. He is aware of being wooed by Catholic interests: Charles IX and Catherine (representing the Valois royal 'house of France') and by the Guise family (the 'house of Lorraine'), represented by Henry de Guise and his uncle the Cardinal of Lorraine.

24 *politics than in love*: both Henry and Marguerite accepted that theirs was a political marriage. Though neither invested much affection in it, both kept the bargain until political considerations led to divorce in 1599. Shortly before her death, Marguerite wrote (*Mémoires*, 470): 'All the unhappiness I have known came to me through my marriage: I consider it to be the scourge of my life.' Dumas makes them equal partners and more loyal allies than they in fact were.

25 *and my party*: in the matter of Marguerite's Portuguese marriage. See note to p. 19.

26 *appeased*: Huguenots welcomed the marriage, and their suspicions of the Catholic enemy were lulled. As Dumas remarks, they were well received in Paris and at the court. There is no evidence to support the view of Huguenot propagandists who later suggested that the wedding was a deliberate trap devised by Catherine, Charles IX, and the Guises.

emblems of their faith: while Catholics wore white kerchiefs and sported white cockades in their hats.

his toothpick: Coligny was famous for his toothpicks.

27 *eight hundred*: the figure is confirmed by Marguerite (*Mémoires*, 25).

a war with Flanders: see note to p. 6.

28 *Lérac de La Mole*: see List of Historical Characters.

even in Piedmont: Piedmont had recently been returned to the dukes of Savoy. Guise refers obliquely to the 'Piedmontese gentleman' we shall meet in the next chapter.

death of François de Guise: see note to p. 5.

29 *thirty-two leagues in a day*: a league was the equivalent of about 4 km. Orléans is 130 km from Paris.

Malvoisie: i.e. Malmsey, a strong, sweet wine, originally made in Greece but later associated with the Canary and Madeira islands.

Guises are Lorraines: as Claude Schopp (*La Reine Margot*, 30–1 n.) observes, Charles's comment is taken from Lestoile's *Journal de Henri III*, i. 473–4.

29 *Saint-Germain or Rambouillet*: the forests of Saint-Germain-en-Laye and Rambouillet (20 km west and 50 km south-west of Paris respectively) were two of the favourite hunting grounds of the French kings. Charles IX was a keen hunter.

30 *Amboise*: on the Loire, 220 km from Paris. It was there, in 1560, that Louis de Condé attempted with his fellow Huguenots to rescue François II from the clutches of the Guises. The plot was discovered and conspirators were thrown from the parapets of the château.

born to be a poet: though Dumas later remarks that writing verses 'was the occupation in which he most delighted' (p. 259), Charles left only a few sonnets and other verses which were published in 1575. 'He made Poems which were well enough for those times, and often held Academy with five or six Poets. He composed a Book of Hunting and Venery' (Mézeray, *Chronological History*, 730).

Ronsard: Ronsard received generous patronage from the King. Forgotten for two centuries, his fortunes revived when the Romantics discovered the Pléiade poets.

31 *and muskets*: a halberd consisted of a broad blade with sharp edges, ending in a point and mounted on a handle 5 to 7 feet long. It was still a military weapon in the sixteenth century, though, decorated and engraved, it would soon be used only for ceremonial purposes by palace guards. The (h)arquebuse was a hand gun fitted with a match-holder which struck the priming-pan when the trigger was pulled. After the musket was introduced as an army weapon in 1572, the arquebuse, considered both more versatile and accurate, remained in private hands only. The musket, which weighed 8 kg and was fired from a forked rest, was a cumbersome matchlock. Flintlocks were introduced towards the end of the seventeenth century.

belle et cruelle: 'To maintain the faith | I am fair and faithful | To the King's foes | I am fair and cruel.'

Caux: a part of Normandy (broadly the Seine inférieure), a chalky plateau with deep valleys ending in cliffs and stretching from Le Havre to Dieppe.

Isabeau of Bavaria: Queen of France (1371–1435), wife of Charles VI.

Nettuno and Sora: i.e. by the peasant women of Nettuno (a coastal town 50 km south of Rome) and Sora (80 km to the east) on the Liris, at the entrance to the Abruzzi. A memory of Dumas's travels in Italy.

reformed religion: whereas Holy Writ was interpreted to Catholics by the Church, Huguenots were urged to read the Bible for themselves. Though Charles was Catholic, he remained close to his nurse until the very end of his life.

32 *wheel of steel*: Dumas anticipates; see note to p. 31.

33 *kill the admiral*: Charles is right; see the following note.

Cherveux: 30 km north of Niort. In October 1569, Catholic troops under d'Anjou marched on Niort, which Mouy, hard pressed, was intent on defending. 'Having despatched scouts in the direction of Cherveux, he had dismounted in a garden to supply a need of nature, when Maurevel, with whom he shared his roof, his table and his purse and stood in every manner as a father to him (as he himself said), shot his benefactor in the back and leaping onto a horse he had got from Mouy, made off . . . He was an assassin, sent to kill the Admiral, but not finding an opportunity to do so in safety, let go a shot to repay those who had employed him.' (D'Aubigné, *Histoire universelle*, Bk. V, p. 143.) Charles IX decorated Maurevel and ordered him to be given 'some honest present in accordance with his merit'. Maurevel was paid 10,000 crowns by d'Alençon.

34 *Prince of Lorraine*: Henry de Guise was a member of the house of Lorraine.

36 *oubliette*: a deep, windowless dungeon, often situated below moat-level, which opened from the top. It was used for persons committed to perpetual imprisonment.

the gate of Saint Marcel: Paris was a walled city approached by 16 gates. The Porte Saint-Marcel was the main entry on its southeastern side. In addition, strategically placed 'barrières' controlled street and river traffic. La Mole's route may be followed on the map, pp. xxxii–xxxiii.

pleased him: it means 'dry-tree' and was so named after the gallows which stood at its intersection with the Rue Saint-Honoré.

39 *Trippe del papa*: 'By the Pope's guts!' A suitable Italian oath for the 'Piedmontese gentleman'.

41 *La Hurière*: the name of the innkeeper, like that of his inn, is an invention of Dumas's.

42 *Rue de Béthisy*: Coligny had lived there, in the Hôtel de Silly-Rochefort, since 1568.

fired at: the attack took place on 22 August but not, as Dumas relates (pp. 35–6) on the King's orders. Fearing Coligny's growing influence over Charles IX, Catherine, with the connivance of d'Anjou and the Guises, paid Maurevel to kill the Admiral. 'He posted himself . . . at the Cloister S. Germain de l'Auxerrois in a chamber of the House belonging to Peter Pile of Villemur . . . He takes his stand and fits his gears at a low Window that was barr'd with Iron and faced the street called des Fossés-S. Germain; and as the Admiral came from the Louvre on Foot, and was going to his own house in the Street de Betizy, walking slowly, because he was reading some Papers, he made a Shot at him with an Arquebuse, one Bullet breaking a Finger on his Right Hand, and another grievously wounding him in the left Arm. The execution done, he flies by a Door from the Cloister, upon a Horse lent to him by one of the Duke of Guise's men. The King who was playing at Tenis in the Louvre, falls into a rage, throws down his Racket and leaves off his Play' (Mézeray, *Chronological History*, pp. 717–18). There were rumours that the bullets were poisoned. Charles IX called on Coligny and accepted his view that the attempt on his life had been ordered by Catherine and d'Anjou, though Catherine laid the blame on the Duke d'Albe. Huguenot nobles also accused Guise, manhandled anyone wearing his livery and even uttered threats against the King who, informed by Catherine that the Protestants were raising an army and threatening an insurrection, accepted during a stormy meeting of the Privy Council on 24 August—Saint Bartholomew's Day—that a massacre of Huguenots was necessary.

43 *partisan*: a variant of the halberd. Cf. note to p. 31.

51 *just commenced building*: in 1563 Catherine de Medici ordered the construction of a new palace with Italian gardens on land outside the city limits which was to become the Tuileries. But in 1572, an astrologer informed her that she would die on the site and she immediately halted work which was resumed in 1594.

52 *for the son of Henry II*: Catherine was a skilled politician with wider aims than this obsession with maintaining the Valois line to which Dumas the novelist restricts her, nor were her methods limited to the deceit, treachery, and murder which he ascribes to her Italian origins.

53 *what should be done*: Tavannes's arguments are developed from the *Mémoires* of Marguerite (pp. 29–31), where, however, they are put in the mouth of the Maréchal de Retz.

54 *tire Margot*: Charles's comment may be barbed but Dumas intends it as a reminder that Marguerite has hawkish qualities.

skinned alive: Bartholomew, a first-century saint, is said to have been flayed alive before being beheaded at Derbend, on the Caspian Sea. His most usual emblem is a flaying knife and he became the patron saint of tanners and those who work with skins.

55 *the Swiss*: Swiss mercenaries had served since the Middle Ages in the King's bodyguard and now fought for the Catholics.

Actæon: a hunter who surprised Diana while bathing and was changed by her into a stag. A suitable name for the dog of a king so devoted to hunting, just as Catherine's Phoebe (p. 59)—the moon—echoes its mistress's superstitious beliefs.

56 *women in general*: women's rights were more an issue in the 1840s than in 1572.

57 *to your apartments*: Marguerite (*Mémoires*, 32–3) knew nothing of the imminent massacre: 'The Huguenots suspected me because I was Catholic, and Catholics because I had married the King of Navarre.' On the evening of 24 August, as she was about to leave Catherine and retire, 'my sister [Claude, Duchess of Lorraine] seized my arm, detained me tearfully and said: "For God's sake, sister, do not go!" This frightened me exceedingly. My mother the Queen overheard, called my sister to her and spoke to her angrily, saying she was to speak no more to me. My sister said it was inconceivable I should be sacrificed thus, for if news of what was afoot got out *they* would surely take revenge on me. My mother the Queen replied that, if it pleased God, I should come to no harm but that, however that might be, go I must, for fear they should suspect, which would ruin the plan . . . My sister, bursting into tears, wished me good night, not daring to say more. And so I went, shaking and bewildered, not knowing what it was I should fear. Once in my room, I began to pray God to take me under His protection and keep me safe, though from what or whom I knew not. Thereupon, my husband the King, already abed, sent word that I should do likewise, which I did, and found his bed surrounded by 30 or 40 Huguenot gentlemen whom I did not know, for I had been married a few days only. All night long, they spoke of nothing but what had happened to the Admiral, resolving at first light to ask the King for justice against Monsieur de Guise and that, if this was refused, to take it themselves.'

60 *rose nobles*: the noble was an old English gold coin, worth 6s. 8d., first minted in the reign of Edward III. During the reign of Edward IV, one variety was known as the ryal (i.e. royal) or rose noble because it featured a rose (of either York or Lancaster) in its design

which was much imitated in the Low Countries: it had also been struck at Calais since 1360.

60 *Mercandon*: an invented character.

65 *Gideon*: the greatest of all the judges of Israel, but also conqueror of the Midianites, whom he routed with great slaughter. Thereafter Israel 'was in quietness forty years in the days of Gideon' (Judges 8: 28), who refused the crown which was offered him.

66 *Tocquenot*: Guillaume Tuggener, lieutenant of the Cent-Suisses (the King's Swiss Guard) and one of Charles IX's favourites. The name is spelled thus by Brantôme (*Œuvres complètes*, v. 270).

present provost: Jean Le Charron had replaced the goldsmith Claude Marcel on 16 August as Prévôt des Marchands. On the evening of 23 August he was summoned to the Louvre and officially informed of the Protestant 'conspiracy'. He was ordered to keep the gates of Paris locked, to chain all boats, and arm all citizens capable of using weapons. Claude Marcel informed a meeting at the Hôtel de Ville that Charles IX wanted Coligny dead and authorized the people to take up arms. A peal of bells would be the signal to Catholics who should wear white emblems for identification.

74 *I curse thee!*: Coligny's last words, like much of Dumas's account of the slaughter, are as much an invention as the pious sentiments attributed to him by Huguenot apologists who turned him into a martyr. Marguerite was not present but reported that 'Monsieur de Guise made his way to the house of the Admiral. Besme, a German gentleman, went up to the bedroom and, after stabbing him, threw his body through the window to his master' (*Mémoires*, 31). Most accounts agree that Coligny was killed by Besme, who threw the body down so that Guise could identify it. D'Aubigné adds that Guise placed his foot on the corpse, a detail picked up by Marlowe: 'The Duke de Guise stamps on thy lifeless bulk!' (*Massacre at Paris*, sc. v). The historical Coconnas played a much more bloodthirsty role than he does here and Dumas omits a number of other 'massacrers', such as the Bastard d'Angoulême.

Duke François: i.e. François de Guise, father of Henry, murdered in 1563.

78 *a regiment of lansquenets*: mercenary German foot-soldiers in the service of French Huguenots, who also employed German cavalry (the Reiters).

81 *the blood on her dress*: Dumas follows the *Mémoires* (pp. 33–4) of Marguerite, who had barely got to sleep after her night of fear (see

note to p. 57) when she heard 'a man knocking with hands and feet on my door, crying "Navarre! Navarre!" My nurse, thinking it was my husband the King, rushed to let him in. It was a gentleman, named Monsieur de Léran, who had received a sword-thrust in the elbow and a wound from a halberd in his arm. He was hotly pursued by four archers who all followed him into the room. To escape them, he flung himself on to my bed. Held fast by him, I threw myself, dragging him with me, into the space between the bed and the wall, with my body shielding his. I did not know the man nor whether he had come to do me injury nor if the archers wanted him or me. We were both screaming and equally frightened. But God decreed that Monsieur de Nancey, the Captain of Guards, should come and find me in that state; although he showed compassion, he could not help laughing at the spectacle. He scolded the archers for their insolence, ordered them out and granted me the life of the poor man who still held me close. I had him put to bed and arranged for his wounds to be treated until he was quite well again.' Leaving her rooms to seek refuge with her sister Claude, she saw another man cut down, and two of her husband's most senior servants begged her to save them. She pleaded with Charles IX and Catherine and they were spared. Brantôme asserts that she also begged for her husband's life—an idea later echoed by d'Alençon (p. 109), though this was not the case. The man who entered her room was Philippe de Lérac or Léran: see List of Historical Characters.

King's Assassin: Maurevel had been known as such since his murder of Mouy in 1569.

82 *Temple*: a fortified monastery built by the Templars in the twelfth century and demolished in 1811. It gave its name to the *quartier* du Temple, in north-east Paris.

83 *his mistress does*: there is no evidence that Mouy, of whom little is known (see List of Historical Characters), ever caught the roving eye of Henriette de Nevers (whom we shall soon meet).

85 *Rue de Brac*: also called the Rue de la Chappelle-de-Braque. An alternative name for the Rue de Chaume.

90 *last of the Horatii*: three Roman brothers fought the three Curiatii, representing the rival city of Alba, watched by opposing armies, to determine which city should rule. Two Horatii fell and the third, pretending to flee, separated his opponents and killed them one by one, thus ensuring the victory of Rome.

94 *Paros*: one of the Cyclades islands, once famous for its brilliant white marble.

95 *does not love*: a reflection of the view, promoted by most popular novelists of the nineteenth century and shared by Henriette ('we women are such heathens', p. 115), that a woman's life is dominated by love.

97 *red partisans*: i.e. blood-stained halberds: see note to p. 31.

where is the King of Navarre?: once Marguerite had given orders for Léran to be looked after (see note to p. 81), 'Monsieur de Nancey told me what was happening and assured me that my husband the king was in the King's room and that no harm would come to him' (*Mémoires*, 34–5).

100 *physical courage*: Henry was a courageous soldier, but Dumas stresses his cool, clear mind, his survival skills, and the 'presence of mind' (p. 102) which served him better than futile heroic gestures.

La Chastre: i.e. the family name of Charles IX's Captain of Guards, Gaspard de La Chastre, *sieur* de Nancey.

101 *serve me well*: the words reflect the royal policy of pacification, abruptly terminated by the massacre.

Verba volant: first half of the Latin adage, 'verba volant, scripta manent' ('what is said vanishes; what is written remains').

102 *accept the mass?*: in a stormy confrontation, Charles IX asked this question of both Henry and Condé. Condé denounced the massacre but reluctantly accepted. Henry, skilfully evasive, obtained time to think but a month later was readmitted to the Catholic Church (26 September 1572).

103 *aim was true*: 'when the game was well afoot and it was morning and he put his head out of the window and saw anyone [across the river] in the Faubourg Saint-Germain who was moving or running away, [Charles IX] took a long hunting arquebuse which he had and fired many shots at them, though in vain, for the arquebuse did not carry so far, and all the time shouting: "Kill! Kill!"' (Brantôme, *Œuvres complètes*, v. 255–6).

105 *blossomed anew during the night*: 'About noon on the Sunday the Massacre first began, a white-thorn growing in the Church-Yard called Holy Innocents, half-withered and stript of all its leaves, put forth great store of Blossomes. This wonder much heightned the phrensie of the People: the Fraternities [i.e. Guilds and Corporations] marched along with Drums beating, and strove who should massacre most Huguenots in a Day; the King himself would needs

see that Prodigy. Most people would have it to be a Miracle, and those of either Religion interpreted it to their advantage. The less credulous attributed it to the nature of the Tree, which does many times Blossom when ready to die.' (Mézeray, *Chronological History*, 720.)

106 *would lose*: Marguerite's part in the political struggles of the reigns of Charles IX and Henry III was rooted in the expectations which Dumas attributes to her.

liberal use: an indirect reference to the homosexuality which was a feature of successive royal courts. As Henry III, d'Anjou surrounded himself by *mignons*, a term which had acquired popular currency by 1576, and lavished such attention on his face, hands, and clothes that it was difficult, said d'Aubigné, to tell 'if he were a woman King or a man Queen'.

108 *his nights?*: it was d'Anjou and Guise, rather than d'Alençon, who, realizing that Henry was safe as long as he remained Marguerite's husband, attempted to end the marriage. See note to p. 131.

109 *not very long to live*: Charles IX was noted for rages, which made him unpredictable, and for a taste for strangling animals, including his pets. He was also tubercular and was haunted by memories of the massacre which he had unleashed: they were held to be a contributory factor to his early death in 1574. To dispel his visions, he played tennis and hunted obsessively, sometimes for fifteen hours at a stretch.

has just died: Sigismund II (1520–72), elected king in 1548, died on 7 July, leaving no heir. The Polish Diet (see note to p. 329) proceeded to the election of a successor. A French delegation, headed by the Bishop of Valence, left for Warsaw in September to promote the candidature of Henry d'Anjou.

king of the Catholics: Guise was considered by both Huguenots and Catholics to have plotted the murder of Coligny and inspired the massacre which followed. Paris was predominantly Catholic and hailed him as a hero.

110 *common sense*: if Charles IX died, as was expected, and if Henry d'Anjou ('Monsieur') were to be elected King of Poland, then François d'Alençon, as next in line, would become King of France. Few, including Catherine, would have welcomed such an outcome, since d'Alençon's loyalties were notoriously shifting and his judgement erratic to an extreme.

No one: though Marguerite remained Guise's mistress, despite the alarm of 1570 (see note to p. 19), Dumas here ends their *liaison* in favour of a new and fictitious affair, more suited to his purposes as a novelist in search of a heroine.

110 *Montfaucon*: the site of a gibbet since the thirteenth century. It stood outside the city walls between what is now La Villette and the Buttes-Chaumont. The Admiral's body, severely mutilated, had been dragged around Paris in triumph for three days before being displayed at Montfaucon, where the corpses of criminals were regularly hung as a reminder of the wages of sin. 'A few days later, a servant of the Duke de Montmorency, named Antoine, went alone at night to Montfaucon, with pincers and hammers to break the chains which held the body. He cut it down, conveyed it to Chantilly and there placed it in quicklime where it was consumed.' (D'Aubigné, *Histoire universelle*, Bk. VI, p. 333.) Coligny's bones were kept by the family and were finally laid to rest in 1851.

112 *Saint Jacques la Boucherie*: the old steeple of the church of Saint-Jacques-de-la-Boucherie had been replaced by a tower (built between 1508 and 1522) which became one of the most familiar city landmarks.

Pont-aux-Meuniers: in 1572, the Seine was crossed by five bridges (see map), each 'a narrow thoroughfare lined by a multitude of shops and stores which rose like two parallel walls and completely hid the river from the eyes of passers-by' (P. Mérimée, *Chronique du règne de Charles IX* (1829), ch. 3). The Pont-aux-Meuniers, immediately downstream from the Pont-au-Change, housed mills driven by the river. It was semi-private, being used mainly by the millers ('meuniers') who worked there. It was swept away in 1592.

bestia!: 'fool!'. Dumas reminds us of Catherine's Italian origins.

115 *not with him*: though there was no love in the marriage, it was stoutly defended by both partners: it gave Henry protection against his Catholic enemies and the antagonism of the royal family, and gave Marguerite a power base. Dumas portrays the couple as good friends and allies, thus minimizing their coolness and permitting both to show themselves capable of romantic love.

Eros, Cupido, Amor: Eros and Cupid were the Greek and Roman gods of love (*amor* in Latin).

very thin: Charles IX often hunted to the point of exhaustion: see note to p. 109.

116 *Cellini's "Nisus"*: Benvenuto Cellini (1500–71), Italian engraver, sculptor, and goldsmith, hero of Dumas's novel *Ascanio* (1843). He left no work of this name. Nisus was a handsome youth whose friendship for Euryalus is celebrated by Virgil (*Aeneid*, Bk. X).

117 *Ajax-Telamon*: son of Telamon, also called the Telemonian Ajax (to distinguish him from Ajax, son of Oileus, King of Locris). He was, after Achilles, the bravest of the Greeks who fought in the Trojan war.

son of Crœsus: on seeing a soldier raise a sword against Croesus, King of Lydia, his son Cyrus shouted a warning, though until that moment he had been thought dumb.

118 *my hero*: Henriette, Duchess de Nevers, became the mistress of Coconnas some eighteen months after their fanciful meeting as recounted by Dumas.

126 *worth a mass*: Henry formally renounced Protestantism on 26 September 1572, thus spiking the guns of his Catholic enemies: see note to p. 102. Dumas anticipates the famous remark attributed to him when, as Henry IV, he abjured the Huguenot faith on 25 July 1593: 'Paris is well worth a mass.'

127 *Achilles*: in Homer's view, the bravest of the Greeks who fought at Troy. As a baby, he was dipped in the Styx by his mother and thereafter was invulnerable to all wounds except in the heel, by which he had been held.

131 *empty title of wife*: Marguerite (*Mémoires*, 36) tells how, 'five or six days' after the massacre, Catherine tried to make her admit that the marriage was unconsummated, which would have provided ecclesiastical grounds for ending it. 'She asked me to swear truthfully that my husband was a man, saying that if he was not, then she would have a means of unmarrying me. I begged her to believe that I did not know what she meant.' In reality, Madame de Sauve did not become Henry's mistress for another year.

Medusa: one of the three Gorgons. Her hair was turned into serpents by Minerva, who also gave her eyes the power to transform anyone she looked at into stone. Perseus slew her by cutting off her head.

134 *La Rochelle*: the staunchest Huguenot stronghold on the Atlantic coast. It would be besieged once again in the winter and spring of 1573.

142 *tennis*: originally a medieval handball game (the *jeu de paume*) which by the fourteenth century existed in two forms: *courte paume* (played with rackets in an enclosed space) and *longue paume*, the open-air version. Charles IX was a keen tennis-player and Henry was known for his skill at the game. Marguerite recalls that on the morning that followed the terrible night of 24 August (see note to p. 57), 'at first light, my husband the King announced that he

intended to go and play tennis ('à la paume') until King Charles was awake, when he would demand justice' (*Mémoires*, 33).

144 *of his religion*: on the contrary, Henry's abjuration on 26 September, a triumph for the Catholic parties, was a very public affair. Furthermore, he was required to write a letter to the Pope begging forgiveness (3 October) and on 16 October signed an order reinstating Catholicism in the Béarn.

decreased: the massacres had run their course by late September, but at great cost. After the slaughter of perhaps 1,500 Huguenot nobles who had gathered for the wedding, the violence spread through Paris, where Catholic mobs killed possibly thousands of Protestants, and to the provinces, where supporters of the reformed religion in about fifteen towns were dispatched summarily or, if they were fortunate, given a choice between death and the mass. A broad estimate sets at 30,000 the number of Huguenots massacred in the weeks that followed Saint Bartholomew's Night.

145 *mall*: a game played in an alley, boarded on each side and with an iron hoop at one end, a wooden ball and a mall(et). Points were scored when the ball was struck through the hoop.

gibbet at Montfaucon: 'The Parisians went thither by heapes to see it. And the Queene mother to feede hir eyes with that spectacle, had a mynde also to goe thither, and she caryed with hir the King and both hir sonnes' (Varamund/Hotman, 179). However, the chronology of the novel here begins to part company with history. Henry had abjured (26 September), but the Admiral's body was hung at Montfaucon on 25 August, three days after his death: see note to p. 110.

146 *Nostradamus*: Lestoile (*Mémoires-Journaux*, v. 245–6) relates that in 1564, at Salon de Crau in Provence, Nostradamus entered the bedroom of the young Henry and told his tutor that the boy 'would have all the inheritance' and that if the tutor lived long enough he would have for a master 'a king of France and Navarre'. The power of such pronouncements in an age of superstition was very great: Lestoile estimates that there were 30,000 astrologers in France in 1572 (*Mémoires-Journaux*, iii. 11).

Roland himself: the hero of the twelfth-century epic, *La Chanson de Roland*, sounds his horn to summon help.

sons shall reign?: Ruggieri was Catherine's astrologer. According to Brantôme (*Œuvres complètes*, v. 291–2), 'Nostradamus predicted to the Queen that she would see her four sons become king'. François II, Charles IX, and Henry III were duly crowned. After the massacre, Catherine renewed her efforts to arrange a marriage between Elizabeth I and François d'Alençon, who would sit on the throne of England and thus complete the prophecy.

147 *d'Albret's horoscope?*: Dumas may have found the prediction in one of the many tracts written in praise of Jeanne d'Albret, who, especially after 1574, was considered a Huguenot martyr.

148 *the next day*: Catherine, eager to see the last of Coligny at Montfaucon, 'went to see him one evening, and with her took her sons, her daughter and her son-in-law' (Pierre Lestoile, *Journal des choses mémorables advenues durant le règne de Henri III* (Cologne, 1720), i. 403).

149 *gummed taffetas*: strips of gauze impregnated with gum arabic designed to protect wounds from infection.

150 *d'Arguzon*: the name does not figure in any of Dumas's usual sources.

preceding reigns: French court dress in the first half of the century was influenced first by the Italian and then German styles: bright colours, flowing lines, with male clothes gaudier than women's. From about 1550, flair and individuality were replaced by the soberer Spanish style: Henry II always wore black. The new formality of men's clothes (padded and stiffened doublets topped by a ruff which was the badge of aristocratic privilege) was even more pronounced in female dress: the stomacher (a stiffened bodice), the farthingale (an early hooped skirt), and elaborate ruffs. Though clothes could still be richly ornamented, restraint was to be further encouraged by the religiosity of Henry III.

152 *a Brahmin*: member of the highest Hindu caste.

from the Faubourg Saint-Denis: outside the Porte Saint-Denis.

153 *Enguerrand de Marigny*: superintendent of finances to Philippe le Bel, who installed the first gallows at Montfaucon: he was himself hanged there in 1315.

154 *toothpick*: on 26 August the case against him was heard. The court found him guilty *in absentia* of treason and 'ordained that his body, if it could be found, if not, his Effigie, should be drawn upon a Hurdle, and hanged upon a gallows at Greve and thence carried to a gibbet at Monfaucon.' Sentence was carried out on 'his Fantosme made of Straw, in the mouth of which they did not forget a Toothpicker. The King and Queen Mother stood at a Window in the Town Hall and beheld the execution through a Tiffany Vail' (Mézeray, *Chronological History*, 721). See note to p. 26.

158 *in quart*: in fencing, a thrust at the opponent's upper chest.

159 *Maître Caboche*: the executioner was employed by the Provost of Paris, who had responsibility for the administration of criminal and civil justice. For his headsman, Dumas borrows the name of a private secretary to Henry of Navarre who died on 24 August 1572.

161 *his chin*: beards had been usual among the French gentry between the tenth and twelfth centuries but were not fashionable during the later Middle Ages. In the sixteenth century, full beards were the norm and remained so until the time of Louis XIII.

164 *Orestes and Pylades*: Orestes was aided by his cousin (and later brother-in-law) Pylades, with whom he had formed the strongest of friendships, to avenge the murder of his father Agamemnon by killing Clytemnestra and Aegisthus.

166 *Esculapius*: son of Apollo and god of medicine in Greek mythology. He was said to bring the dead to life, to the point where Pluto, king of the Underworld, fearing that his domain would become empty, complained to Jupiter who struck him dead with a thunderbolt.

fess: in heraldry, a horizontal bearing laid across the field, dividing it into three equal parts.

167 *quarter them*: criminals sentenced to *la roue* (the wheel) were laid on a horizontal cartwheel and beaten with an iron bar until dead. In cases where clemency was recommended by the court, they were first strangled. Men sentenced to be quartered were—before or after death, according to the degree of mercy shown—tied to four horses which were then lashed until the limbs parted company from the trunk. The *question* of a few lines later is fully explained in Ch. 58.

168 *scaffold of M. de Nemours*: Jacques d'Armagnac, Duke de Nemours, was decapitated for treason at Monfaucon in 1477.

Cross du Trahoir: a raised cross, erected during the reign of François I, which stood in the middle of the Rue Saint-Honoré at its junction with the Rue de l'Arbre-sec, named after the gallows which stood on the corner. On the steps of the Cross vegetables were displayed for sale and close by were butchers' stalls.

169 *to the Cité*: the Île de la Cité. Between the Palais de Justice and Notre-Dame lay a maze of small streets from which the nobility had emigrated, leaving a population of clerics, merchants, and lawyers.

Pont-Saint-Michel: the French text continues, with Dumas's customary topographical accuracy: 'The Pont Saint-Michel was built of stone in 1373. Despite its apparent solidity, a part was swept away by flood on 13 January 1408. In 1416, it was replaced by a wooden construction, but during the night of 16 December 1547, it was again swept away. In about 1550 . . . it was rebuilt again of wood and, though it stood in need of repair, it was considered solid enough.'

this shop: Varamund/Hotman (p. 168) confirms that 'one *Renat*, the Kings Apothicarie, an Italian, . . . hath a shop at Paris vpon S. Michaels bridge, neare vnto the *Pallace* (of the Louvre)'. Lestoile (*Mémoires-Journaux*, ii. 322–3) records that in 1586, two of René's sons were broken on the wheel for murder and describes René as 'a murderer, thief and poisoner who after killing and robbing during the Saint Bartholomew's Massacre, died on a dung-heap, 'consumed by fleas and vermine'.

175 *fairground mummers:* Artaxerxes was the name of several kings of Persia between 465 BC and AD 242. Such figures from antiquity figured both in popular chapbooks and in the crude theatrical entertainments which were a feature of the fairs of Saint-Germain (on the left bank) and Saint-Laurent (near the Temple), along with other popular amusements such as jugglers and dancing bears.

176 *Chancellor de l'Hôpital*: to the Greek and Roman orators (Demosthenes (384–322 BC) and Cicero (106–43 BC)), Coconnas adds a French champion of eloquence. Michel de l'Hôpital (1505–73) became chancellor in 1560 and used his gifts to promote religious tolerance. Discredited in 1568, he left the court and retired to his estates.

Tartarus: one of the darkest regions of hell in Greek mythology.

179 *concerning sacrifices*: Catherine de Medicis was well read in the literature of divination. René's reference to Hebraic treatises reflects the widespread belief that Jews (who since the thirteenth century had been expelled from many European countries) were adept at stealing Christian babies, poisoning wells, and other terrible crimes.

181 *King Ladislas*: Ladislas or Lancelot (1375–1414) was king of Naples and Rome between 1386 and 1414. Taken ill at Perugia (poisoned, it was said, by a doctor whose daughter he had seduced), he returned to Rome to die.

182 *Henry IV*: Henry of Navarre would become Henry IV, king of France and Navarre, in 1589.

Winter is approaching: although time has passed barely noticed in the text (where only days seem to have elapsed since the massacre), Dumas moves his tale forward to keep pace with the historical events to come.

192 *fifth son of Saint Louis*: Robert, Comte de Clermont, sixth (*sic*) son of Saint Louis (1214–70). By his marriage to the only daughter of Agnès de Bourbon, he founded the dynasty which was to rule France for more than two centuries.

194 *Condé*: after the death of Coligny and the abjuration of Henry of Navarre, many Huguenots preferred the leadership of Condé, though he too had abjured and, like Henry, fought on the Catholic side at the siege of Protestant La Rochelle in 1573. His movements were watched and his freedom restricted until he escaped on 13 March 1574. Reports of attempts to poison him (with doctored apples and the like) were spread by Huguenot apologists. He died in 1588 of a stomach ulcer, though his second wife was found guilty of poisoning him: she was declared innocent in 1596 by Henry IV.

195 *poisoning of the Prince de Porcian*: Antoine de Croy died in 1567 of a virulent fever after over-exerting himself at tennis, though many—including d'Aubigné—believed that he had been poisoned.

196 *Béarn breed*: a small, sturdy horse used for riding as opposed to larger breeds—such as the Norman Percheron—which hauled carriages and artillery pieces.

covered the ground: it is now winter and the 'disastrous year' of 1572 is nearly over.

198 *news from Poland*: a delegation led by the Bishop of Valence had left in September to set out the case for the election of Henry d'Anjou as king of Poland. Among his rivals were the brother of the Emperor Maximilian, the 8-year-old son of the King of Sweden and various internal candidates. Ivan the Terrible and the King of Transylvania also took an active interest in the election. The Polish nobility met in January 1573 and summoned a diet for April, when the outcome would be settled.

199 *Convent of the Annunciation*: while Paris was a city of steeples and religious houses, there was no such convent in 1573.

200 *ripe for revolt*: in the wake of the Saint Bartholomew's Day Massacre, unrest in these Huguenot strongholds in the west and southwest was high. La Rochelle had rebelled in December and was besieged throughout the first half of 1573.

202 *principal leaders of the Huguenots*: Dumas promotes Mouy—who calls himself 'only a soldier' (p. 207)—above his place in history.

204 *to this offer*: d'Alençon was ambitious and subsequently switched sides in the religious wars several times, always to serve his ambition. An attempt to woo him to the Huguenot cause led, as we shall

see, to the crisis of March 1574 which Dumas initiates here. But it was not d'Alençon who sought an alliance, but the Protestants who tried to win his support.

210 *Tennis Court*: i.e. one of the two tennis courts (*jeu de paume*) situated in the Louvre.

213 *Rue d'Argenson*: there was no such street, though the house with the two gates is clearly situated at the angle formed by the Rue du Roi-de-Sicile and the Rue Vieille du Temple.

224 *Boccaccio's heroines*: born in Paris, Giovanni Boccaccio (1313–75), author of the *Decameron* (1358), a collection of 100 tales, some licentious, others melancholy and poetic. Dumas may be thinking of Fiammetta, the name Boccaccio gave to a Neapolitan lady whom he loved and who is one of the story-tellers of the *Decameron*.

226 *siege of La Rochelle*: La Mole took part in the siege of La Rochelle and was wounded in February 1573.

228 *from you*: the French text continues: 'I have also heard it said that you keep the hearts of your faithful lovers in gold boxes and that sometimes you look piously on these sombre relics'. And a note quotes the seventeenth-century memorialist Tallemant des Réaux (*Historiettes* (Paris 1960), i. 60): 'She wore a farthingale which boasted many pockets, and in each of these pockets she kept a box containing the heart of one of her dead lovers. For as they died, she took the trouble of having their hearts embalmed. At night, she hung this farthingale on a hook, secured by a padlock, behind the head of her bed.' Though Dumas consistently modifies the legend of Marguerite in her favour, he could not resist this detail which consolidated the Romantic myth of the Renaissance.

233 *captain of her guards*: Gaspard de La Chastre, *seigneur* de Nancey. Dumas refers to him by both names at different points in the story, and makes him captain of guards both to Catherine and to Charles IX.

King's Petardiers: a regiment equipped with petards, a kind of mortar of iron or bronze which was used to burst down doors or make a breach in a wall. It was attached directly to the surface to be blown and was lit by a fuse. Elsewhere, Dumas makes Maurevel Captain of Arquebusiers and Captain of Musketeers.

235 *Apollo*: Greek god of light and life-giving influence, but here a byword for male beauty.

from Rome: the French text adds, 'from my husband'. The Duke de Nevers had been ambassador extraordinary to Rome since

September 1572. The news gave the outcome of the Polish election of which the Pope was kept informed.

236 *your brother d'Anjou*: again Dumas moves his tale forward to catch up with history. The Polish Diet elected d'Anjou in May 1573. The decision was made official on 7 July which seems now the time of the action.

237 *Albert Durer's engravings*: Albrecht Dürer (1471–1528), one of the great German masters, remembered principally as an engraver on metal and a designer of woodcuts.

238 *Polish ambassadors*: again Dumas moves the action on. The Polish envoys made a sensational entry to Paris on 19 August 1573.

what else: Marguerite was known for her learning and spoke Latin. But Catherine is being sarcastic in attributing to her fluency in Hungarian.

239 *Risque-tout*: while Catherine, who believes in occult forces, gives mythological names to her dogs, Charles the Hunter opts for more expressive names for his pets (Actaeon, for his favourite dog, and Margot, for his parrot) and his working animals and falcons: 'Risk-All' here, 'Dure-Dent' ('Hard-Fang', p. 250) and 'Bec-de-Fer' ('Iron-Beak', p. 379).

the Bastille: a fortified prison built in the fourteenth century in the east wall of the city, at the Porte Saint-Antoine. It was designed mainly for prisoners of state and by the end of the eighteenth century had become a symbol of the injustice and oppression of the *ancien régime*.

240 *three months*: d'Anjou arrived at La Rochelle in early February, which situates the action in April or May, though the reference to the Polish ambassadors who will 'soon arrive' (p. 238) suggests a date in early August.

241 *Orthon*: the page is an invention of Dumas.

Bondy: the forest of Bondy, east of Paris, was a royal hunting ground but also the haunt of robbers and highwaymen. It largely disappeared under an outburst of building during the 1860s.

242 *Hungarian wine*: probably Tokaï, the best known.

sarsenet: 'Saracen cloth', a fine silk material, plain or twilled, valued for its softness, used until the early nineteenth century especially as linings for women's clothes.

246 *bears with a knife*: bears are still to be found in the Pyrenees.

247 *jennet*: a small Spanish horse bred from Arab stock. It was on a 'Spanish jennet' that Maurevel made his escape after shooting the Admiral on 22 August 1572.

248 *Poitou*: one of the ancient French provinces which now comprise the *départements* of Deux-Sèvres, the Vendée, and the Vienne. It was strong Huguenot territory.

249 *hallali*: 'sonner l'hallali' was to sound the 'mort', i.e. signal the kill.

252 *saving the life of Charles*: there is no historical basis for this episode which was invented by Dumas.

255 *brother*: François d'Alençon was Henry's brother-in-law.

256 *Paris to Cracow*: Paris is 770 km (or 200 leagues) from Pau and just over 1,600 km (400 leagues) from Cracow. D'Aubigné (*Histoire universelle*, Bk. VII, p. 225) reports that in May 1574, the courier dispatched by Catherine reached Cracow in 13 days.

259 *Maximilian*: Charles IX married Elizabeth of Austria (1554–92), daughter of Emperor Maximilian II, on 26 November 1570. A daughter was born in October 1572 but died at the age of 8.

263 *certain Italian tales*: probably those of Boccaccio.

266 *from Paris to Pau*: horses were changed at staging posts, first introduced on the main routes in the thirteenth century. The average distance between posts was about 9 leagues (35 km).

271 *on the carpet*: the fight between Mouy and Maurevel, like Catherine's plot to assassinate Henry of Navarre, is wholly invented by Dumas. However, Maurevel was not idle. According to d'Aubigné (*Histoire universelle*, Bk. VII, p. 205), he was unsuccessful in an attempt in April 1574 to assassinate La Noue, the most effective of the Huguenot generals.

Hotel de Condé: did not yet exist. A large house in a street running north from the Rue de Vaugirard built by the banker Salviati (in the 'Italian' district of Saint-Germain) was rebuilt in 1547 and was further extended as the Hôtel de Gondi and later still the Hôtel de Condé. The Faubourg Saint-Germain, across the river from the Louvre, was the *quartier* favoured by the Protestant nobility.

272 *at La Rochelle*: the time of the novel and historical time continue unsynchronized (see note to p. 240). The truce ending the siege of La Rochelle was agreed on 26 June.

273 *could be clearer*: though Charles IX is known to have had only one mistress (whom we shall meet in the next chapter), the same could not be said for his court where women were notorious predators. 'Before this Reign, it was wont to be the Man's part both by Example and Courtship, to persuade and tempt the Women into Gallantries: but now since amorous intrigues were joined with the greatest Mysteries of State, the Women ran after the Men' (Mézeray, *Chronological History*, 730).

274 *Ajax, Telamon, and Diomedes*: Dumas is ironic at Guise's expense. Though mythology does not link heavy stones to any of these Greek heroes, they were all well endowed with muscles. Ajax fought at Troy (see note to p. 117). His father Telamon, king of Salamis, was a companion of Jason and armour-bearer to Hercules. Diomedes, king of Aetolia, was one of the bravest of the Greeks who besieged Troy.

276 *going to Nantouillet's*: Dumas's account of the farcical confrontation in the Rue Cloche-Perce is an echo of the scandalous conduct of 'three Kings' which began in the Hôtel d'Hercule in the Rue des Augustins in September 1573, which Lestoile describes as a 'stinking' orgy. From there the merriment continued at the house of the Prévôt de Paris, Nantouillet, 'which was one of the most respectable in the city'. Nantouillet was ordered to marry 'a young woman of good family [Mademoiselle de Châteauneuf, mistress of d'Anjou, now King-elect of Poland]. When her hand was refused in no uncertain terms, she demanded to be avenged by the Kings of France and Poland, abetted by the King of Navarre, the Chevalier [d'Angoulême] and the Duke de Guise, the vengeance to take the form of a masked assault. They entered Nantouillet's house and caused much damage, to the extent that coffers were broken open, plate pillaged and money given into the eager hands of those who were with them' (D'Aubigné, *Histoire universelle*, Bk. VII, pp. 157–8). When Nantouillet demanded justice, Charles IX warned him against taking action.

277 *Infant Jesus*: Francesco Albani (1578–1660) painted some forty-five altarpieces. By his second wife, he had twelve extraordinarily beautiful children whom he used as models for the religious and mythological subjects in which he specialized.

278 *such a question*: Charles, Comte d'Auvergne and Duke d'Angoulême in 1619, was born on 28 April 1573. He served in many campaigns, including the siege of La Rochelle in 1628. As Dumas remarks, had he not been illegitimate, he would have taken precedence, by Salic law, over the daughter born to Charles IX and Elizabeth of Austria on 26 October 1572. Dumas's reservation about the kings of France is as evident here as it is in *The Man in the Iron Mask*, where he removes the 'true' Louis XIV, who is selfish and cruel, and replaces him with his twin, who is a liberal statesman of the kind Dumas approved of.

280 *the Marais*: the Chevaliers de l'Arbalète (=cross-bow) were quartered north of the Porte Saint-Antoine, but not for another century. Dumas's Archery Garden (p. 339) was as yet unnamed. The

outer boulevards ran round the city limits. The *quartier* du Marais was home to numerous members of the Parliament and the old nobility: the Hôtels de Guise and de Montmorency were located there. The part of the Marais immediately inside the city wall erected by Charles V was cultivated.

281 *destiny*: if Henry leads a charmed life, it is not simply because he is nimble footed: he has history on his side. Dumas's regular references to Destiny reflect the Romantics' fascination with fate as much as Catherine's superstitious belief in astrology.

283 *By Gog and Magog!*: invoked in the French text from the Bible, where they are named as giants from Genesis (10: 2) to Revelations (20: 8). Contemporary English readers, however, would have remembered a different incarnation. According to Caxton, the thirty-three infamous daughters of Diocletian were shipwrecked on the shores of Albion (Britain) where they consorted with demons and produced a race of giants which was overcome by Brute of Troy. Two survivors, Gog and Magog, were brought to London and kept as porters on the site of the later Guildhall. Wicker effigies of both were raised on Guildhall in the reign of Henry V and stood until they were destroyed in the fire of London. New ones were erected in 1708.

295 *punishment and silence*: Catherine might mean that the cord symbolizes the chastisement and silence imposed by monkish rule, or else holds it as a whip to beat them and a rope to hang them. Either way, her gesture is ominous.

297 *a thousand Niobes*: Niobe, mother of seven sons and seven daughters, made mock of Latona, mother of one son, Apollo, and one daughter, Diana, who, to avenge the insult, killed all of the children of Niobe, who was changed into stone. In Greek mythology Niobe symbolizes maternal grief.

299 *Isocrates*: Athenian orator (436–338 BC) who opposed the destruction of Greek freedom by Philip of Macedon.

Ad Sarmatiæ . . . Margaritæ concio: 'Address by Queen Marguerite to the Sarmathian Ambassadors'. Sarmathia was the name used by the Romans to designate the homeland of the barbarian peoples of south-east Russia.

301 *Mantes*: 60 km from Paris on the road to Rouen. This episode is an amalgam of three distinct events. 1. D'Aubigné (*Histoire universelle*, Bk. VII, p. 194) records that in March 1574 (by Dumas's chronology it is now early August 1573) La Mole left Mantes (then held by an advance guard of Montgomery's invading regiments)

and rode to Paris, not to see Marguerite, but to warn Catherine that a force of 200 men was heading for the court then in residence at Saint-Germain-en-Laye. 2. Lestoile confirms that late in 1573 Charles IX wanted to be rid of La Mole, who was in the service of the actively plotting François d'Alençon, and with six men tried to ambush him in the Louvre: while he held a candle, La Mole was to be strangled. They waited on the route La Mole normally took to d'Alençon's apartments, but in vain: instead, he went to the room of Henriette de Nevers, his mistress, for he did not become the lover of Marguerite until January 1574. 3. The escape by rope through a window of the Louvre is indeed recounted in Marguerite's *Mémoires* (pp. 149–50, 152–3) where, however, it is situated in January 1577, and the fleeing prisoner is d'Alençon.

304 *The Atrides*: the descendants of Atreus, most famously Agamemnon and Menelaus. The house of the Atrides was celebrated for the many crimes which mark its history.

305 *Princess de Condé*: Marguerite (*Mémoires*, 83) confirms d'Anjou's infatuation with Mme de Condé as the major reason for his reluctance to leave France, though he also had a real hope of succeeding the ailing Charles IX.

withered heart: Henry d'Anjou was widely known to be Catherine's favourite son. He had been absent since February (at the siege of La Rochelle) not, as the text suggests, since before the Saint Bartholomew's Day Massacre in which he played an enthusiastic role.

306 *it can hold*: this view of the Poles was not shared by the Romantics who showed great sympathy for the down-trodden, 'people of soldiers' of 'chivalrous' Poland (below, pp. 311, 328).

four-and-twenty: Charles was born on 27 June 1550, under the star-sign Cancer, as Dumas notes on p. 317.

307 *Lasco*: Albert Laski, Count Palatine of Sieradz, a leading Polish Catholic, who supported Henry's claim to the Polish throne. The ambassadors arrived in Paris on 19 August 1573 and were ceremonially welcomed four days later.

his League: Guise would not form his Catholic League until 1576.

where I was: the scandal took place in September and Charles IX was present. See note to p. 276.

308 *Alexander and Cæsar*: Henry d'Anjou was 16 when he fought at Jarnac and Moncontour in 1569. Alexander was 22 when he overcame Darius at Granique in 334 BC, while the conquests of Caesar (100–44 BC) were achieved at an older age.

310 *Ile-de-France*: since the fifteenth century, a province with Paris as its centre, which comprised an area covered since the French Revolution by the *départements* of the Aisne, the Oise, the Seine, Seine-et-Oise, Seine-et-Marne, and a part of the Somme.

twenty thousand men: the details are largely Dumas's invention, like the 20,000 soldiers. But though d'Anjou was more popular with the army, he was powerless to resist Charles IX, who not only saw him as a rival and wanted him far away from Paris, but also saw political advantage in his departure. On the European stage, France would be able to count on Poland as Spain presently counted on the Spanish Netherlands.

my brother's election: d'Anjou had been nominated the previous autumm but was not officially elected until 7 July (see notes to pp. 198, 235).

311 *ventre-mahon*: Mahon is intended as a diminutive of Mahomet.

Henry d'Anjou, away: Henry not only had the support of his mother but was more popular with the army than Charles, who thus had good cause to fear him. Henry took advantage of the King's illness to delay his departure. 'When the King (neglecting affairs of state and seeking the pleasures of the hunt) recovered, he gave orders that all communications should come into his hands. Then, with the oaths which he spoke often, told his brother in the presence of the Queen, that one or other of them would have to leave the Kingdom. Seeing the King's firm resolve, the Queen Mother said to the King of Poland: "Go, but you will not remain there long"' (D'Aubigné, *Histoire universelle*, Bk. VII, pp. 160–1).

312 *Romulus*: with his brother Remus, legendary founder of Rome and its first king (753–715 BC). According to myth, the brothers were raised by a she-wolf.

313 *in two days*: Charles IX was not as good as his word. The new King of Poland did not leave until November, reluctant, it was said, to leave his mistress, but also to abandon France at a juncture when Charles had fallen gravely ill. The King was well enough to escort him but succumbed to smallpox at Vitry. Catherine and a large retinue accompanied him to Blamont, east of Nancy, where they said their farewells on 2 December. Henry arrived in Cracow on 18 February 1574 and was crowned king three days later.

318 *Ainsi . . . prudence n'etoit*: 'Thus perished he who was feared, Sooner, too soon, had caution not been used.' Though this couplet is as baffling as any, it does not figure in Nostradamus' *Centuries*.

319 *fifth day*: 23 August.

321 *without Pylades*: see note to p. 164. Nisus, a Trojan youth who
followed Aeneas into Italy, died attempting to save Euralys: their
friendship is recorded by Virgil (*Aeneid*, Bk. IX). When Pythias,
condemned to death by Dionysius of Sicily, was allowed to travel
to his family estate to settle his affairs, promising to return on the
day appointed for his execution, his friend Damon offered his own
life as surety. Pythias' prompt return led Dionysius, much impressed by their friendship, to pardon him.

322 *à l'Espagnole*: a nod in the direction of the Romantics' discovery of
Spain. Dumas explains on p. 232.

325 *the barrier*: i.e. a *barrière* (or control-point) close by the Porte Saint-
Honoré, through which travellers from Rouen and Mantes entered
Paris.

326 *and Bordeaux*: Fontainebleau, 65 km south-east of Paris, formerly a
royal hunting lodge, had been turned into a royal residence for
François I. The road to Blois followed the Loire valley before
turning south through Protestant country to Angoulême and
thence to Bordeaux and the Huguenot strongholds of the south-
west.

proposed plan: Dumas uses the novelist's licence to reorder events.
Henry of Navarre and d'Alençon had been suspect since the massa-
cre of 24 August 1572 and their movements subject to periodic
restraint as leading sympathizers with the 'Malcontents' (or 'Poli-
tiques'), a moderate party committed to civil peace at home and a
Flanders war which would restore unity. However, in the run-up
to the ceremony described in Ch. 43 (which took place on 23
August 1573), they enjoyed relative freedom: the fourth War of
Religion had ended in July and the fifth would not begin until
March 1574. It was then that Henry and d'Alençon were drawn by
Huguenots, Flemings, and the 'Malcontents' into a plan to join
forces with the Protestant Prince Louis de Nassau (brother of
William of Orange) at Sedan, with a view to sharing the Nether-
lands between France and the House of Nassau. Henry would
become head of the Malcontents and d'Alençon would lead the
Huguenots in the south. The veteran Protestant commander La
Noue would hold the west, Turenne would establish himself in the
east, backed by Louis de Nassau, while Montgomery would invade
Normandy from his base in England. The plot failed because Guit-
ry arrived with 200 cavalry ten days early at Saint-Germain at the
start of March. D'Alençon considered this an insufficient force for
the purpose and, through La Mole, revealed the plot, which was
taken as an attempt on the life of the King. Dumas brings forward

the dramatic events of March and April 1574 as a background to the welcome given to the Poles.

327 *Faubourg Saint-Antoine*: a contingent of 150 richly dressed nobles, with their heads shaven at the back and scimitars at their waists, some mounted on horses with jewelled harness, others riding in magnificent coaches drawn by four or even six horses, caused a sensation. They entered by the Porte Saint-Martin on 19 August and were met by crowds near the convent of the Abbaye de Saint-Antoine-des-Champs in the Rue Saint-Antoine. Four days later they were received at the Louvre. 'The King was there upon a Scaffold Array'd in his Royal Robes, and accompanied by all the Princes and Grandees of his Court.' The Bishop of Posnam read a speech in Latin to which Marguerite replied. 'The King having given them very many civil thanks rose from his Seat and went to embrace the King of Poland his brother . . . ; He kissed the Duke of Alençon and the King of Navarre, and treated the others with more or less ceremony according to their quality.' (Mézeray, *Chronological History*, 725.)

328 *Bishop of Cracow*: Adam Konarski was Bishop of Posnam and leader of the delegation. On Lasco, see note to p. 307.

329 *the Diet of Poland*: the first Polish diet, or legislative assembly, met at Checiny in 1331. By the middle of the fifteenth century its power had grown to the point that Poland had turned from a monarchy into an oligarchy. The nobles continued to assert their rights, though Sigismund II (king 1548–72) succeeded in resisting aristocratic demands that he should divorce his wife and make a political marriage with a foreign nation. The Reformation spread rapidly and led to considerable religious strife. The Diet of Warsaw of 1573 concluded in favour of tolerance of all religious opinions, though nobles retained power over their serfs in spiritual matters. It was the same diet which elected Henry d'Anjou king of Poland, a condition of his election being that all anti-Huguenot action in France—which included the siege of La Rochelle—should cease.

crown of the Jagellons: the name given to the dynasty of Jagello, last of a line of Lithuanian dukes, who became king of Poland in 1386. His line provided Poland with six kings, the last of whom was Sigismund II (d. 1572), though the dynasty continued on the Polish throne until 1668 through his sister.

330 *that of Ronsard*: Dumas seems to suggest that while Lasco drew on the 'classical' manner of Ovid (43 BC–AD 17), he expressed emotion more simply in the 'new' style of Ronsard, a leader of the Pléiade school of poets.

331 *cospetto!*: an Italian interjection of surprise, roughly the equivalent here of 'great heavens!'

Antæus: a giant, son of Poseidon, who received fresh strength each time he touched ground. Hercules overcame him by lifting him and crushing him to death.

332 *gerfalcons . . . tercelets*: a gerfalcon is a large falcon and a tercelet a male falcon.

335 *Titian's splendid paintings*: Titian (1477–1576) painted many mythological, historical, and religious subjects, but was known to his contemporaries mainly as a portraitist for studies such as *The Young Englishman* (1540).

336 *hyperborean*: in Greek mythology, the hyperboreans inhabited a region 'beyond the north wind' where there was perpetual sunshine. But Dumas uses the word as a synonym for 'outlandish'.

339 *from Tuscany*: Catherine was born in Florence, ancient capital of Tuscany.

Archery Garden: the 'Boulevard' ran inside the city wall. On the Garden, see note to p. 280.

341 *petronel*: a matchlock handgun, shorter than the ordinary arquebus but longer than a pistol. Dumas calls it a musketoon on p. 381.

345 *Saint-Germain*: that is, the royal palace at Saint-Germain-en-Laye, 20 km west of Paris.

in case of danger: the citadel of Saint Angelo, completed in AD 139, was successively a burial place for Roman emperors until the time of Caracalla, a place of papal refuge, and finally a state prison. The palace of the Pitti family (rivals of the Medicis) was built in 1440. More recollections from Dumas's Italian journeys.

347 *oubliettes*: see note to p. 36.

350 *Tour de Bois*: originally a crenellated defensive tower four storeys high, built of wood, but in 1572 a stone gate in the city wall built by Charles V. The ferry crossed from the right bank to the Tour de Nesle (built in the thirteenth century and demolished in 1663), which gave access to the city through the Porte de Nesles (on the site now occupied by the Institut de France). Henry's route may be followed on the map.

Arbois wine: Arbois, in the Jura, noted for its wine.

352 *has ceased*: see note to p. 326.

or Rambouillet: all royal hunting grounds. On Saint-Germain and Rambouillet, see note to p. 29. For the Forest of Bondy, note to p. 241.

357 *year and a half ago*: though d'Anjou's departure for Poland (November 1573) seems very recent, it is now, by this reckoning, about January 1574, a date confirmed on p. 378.

seen them: there is no historical basis for this secret understanding between Charles IX and Henry of Navarre though Dumas makes it central to his plot.

resembled remorse: see note to p. 109.

358 *Duke d'Alençon*: though Huguenots remained puzzled by Henry's public stance, there was no general wish that he should abdicate, nor that they wanted d'Alençon on the throne of Navarre, though they continued to court him. It is true, however, that Charles IX, having dispatched Henry d'Anjou to Poland (see note to p. 311), was anxious to give the ambitious d'Alençon something to occupy him. He did not offer him the crown of Navarre (Ch. 48), but he unsuccessfully reopened negotiations for the hand of Elizabeth I of England and, after d'Anjou's departure left the lieutenant-generalship of France vacant, thought of offering it to d'Alençon. However, Catherine persuaded him to give the post to the Duke de Lorraine (husband of Claude, Marguerite's sister) whom, she believed, she could control after the death of Charles. D'Alençon was offended and agreed to join Henry d'Anjou in the designs which Louis de Nassau had on the Spanish Netherlands: see note to p. 326.

364 *Saint-Denis*: the shrine of French kings, then a village outside the city's northern wall, named after the third-century saint who was buried there. An abbey was built over the tomb in 626 by Dagobert I, who was interred in its church. Dead kings were honoured with grandiose memorials, a practice discontinued in the seventeenth century by the Bourbons, who were buried more simply in the crypt.

365 *had not succeeded*: during the boar hunt in Ch. 31.

367 *thirty thousand men*: while it is true that Huguenots remained faithful to Henry, military leadership had passed to the Prince de Condé, who figures only on the edges of Dumas's narrative. At an assembly at Milhaud in July 1574, Condé would be elected chief, governor-general, and protector of the Protestants of Languedoc and therefore of all France.

outside his family: though Catherine feared this outcome, this was not the policy of Charles IX.

368 *Maisons*: now Maisons-Lafitte, 8 km from Saint-Germain-en-Laye through the Forest of Saint-Germain.

368 *pavilion of François I*: a hunting lodge situated near Le Mesnil le Roi, half-way between Saint-Germain-en-Laye and Maisons-Lafitte. The Allée des Violettes was one of the many fine drives and avenues through the forest.

369 *Cil qui . . . le chasteau*: 'he who beat loudest on the walls never entered the castle'.

370 *Venerie*: i.e. hunting.

372 *of Lucca*: Castruccio Castracani (1281–1328), born at Lucca, soldier and adventurer, who became leader of the Ghibelline faction. The book is the same as the one examined by Catherine on p. 181 where the French text names it as: *De la manière d'élever et de nourrir les tiercelets, les faucons et les gerfauts pour qu'ils soient braves, vaillants et toujours prêts au vol* (*On the manner of raising and breeding tercelets, falcons and gerfalcons, that they may be resolute, valiant and always prepared for flight*). In the play *La Reine Margot* (III, Tableau 8, sc. v–vi), the book is given a shorter title and is attributed to 'Pietramonte', of whom there appears to be no trace.

waste of time: though the sixteenth century was an age of poisoners, the use of poisoned gloves, candles, and fruit was less widespread—and ingenious—than the methods reported in legend and adopted by novelists. The device of the poisoned pages was reused by Umberto Eco in *The Name of the Rose* (1980). There is no evidence that Catherine tried to poison Henry.

373 *to betray me*: in reality, d'Alençon and Henry, though each followed his personal ambition, were political allies who faced the same enemies: Charles IX and Catherine.

374 *dedicated to Charles IX*: the French text makes it clear that Dumas has in mind Mézeray's *Histoire de France depuis Faramond jusqu'à maintenant* (1643–51), which he probably saw in a new edition published in 1830. It was not dedicated to Charles IX.

376 *Vincennes*: on the Bastille, see note to p. 239. The fort of Vincennes was built between 1337 and 1370 in the Bois de Vincennes outside the city's eastern wall, on the site of a thirteenth-century château. It was a royal residence (Charles IX died there as did Mazarin in 1660) but it also housed part of the royal administration and served as a secure jail which held prisoners of state until the time of the French Revolution.

377 *Vesinet*: Le Vésinet (Seine et Oise), 3 km on the Paris side of Saint-Germain-en-Laye.

381 *burning coals*: according to Plutarch, Junius Brutus' wife, on hearing of the death of her husband in 42 BC, placed burning coals in her mouth and kept them there until she suffocated.

the jesses of his falcon: a jess is a short leather strap attached to the leg of the falcon, the other end having a ring through which the leash is inserted.

384 *as King Charles says*: 'Those that governed him had imprinted a most wicked custom of Swearing in him, which he turned into his ordinary Language' (Mézeray, *Chronological History*, 730). D'Aubigné also commented on Charles IX's fondness for oaths: see note to p. 311.

385 *time of Louis XII*: it was built not by Louis XII (1462–1515) but by his cousin, François I, who succeeded him, as kennels for his hunting dogs.

white aigrettes: plumes and flashes worn on hats. White was the colour of Catholics.

386 *Saint Blaise's day*: Bishop of Sebaste in Armenia, martyred in the fourth century: he was grated with wool-combs before being beheaded. He is unconnected with St Bartholomew, who died three centuries before. His feast day is 3 February.

389 *sub tegmini fagi*: the first line of the first of Virgil's *Bucolics*.

392 *of François II*: François II (1544–60), eldest son of Henry II and short-lived husband of Mary Stuart, acceded to the throne in 1559. He died of a chronic inflammation of the middle ear which formed an abscess in the brain. It was believed in some quarters that he was poisoned.

395 *from the apartment*: having transferred the real-life betrayal by La Mole (see note to p. 401) to d'Alençon (Ch. 50), Dumas now makes Henry's imprisonment an act of royal friendship. In reality, Charles IX regarded him as a threat. The interrogation of d'Alençon and Henry took place at Saint-Germain-en-Laye and was followed by the arrest of La Mole and Coconnas and of the leading Malcontents, Montmorency and Cossé, who were sent to the Bastille on 4 May.

399 *scented apple*: see note to p. 194. But Condé was almost certainly poisoned by his wife in 1588.

401 *to Vincennes*: in March 1574, Protestant forces, masters of a number of southern towns, were also gathering in Normandy. Weary of d'Alençon's vacillations, Huguenot leaders tried to force his hand by ordering several hundred cavalry to converge on Saint-Germain-en-Laye where the court was in residence. But they arrived ten days early. D'Alençon considered it too small a force for the task and panicked. According to d'Aubigné (*Histoire universelle*, Bk. VII, pp. 194–5), his agent La Mole 'informed the Queen Mother of what was happening. She raised the alarm as loudly as

she could, ordered the château to be searched, and urged the King to leave, reminding him that her astrologers (by which she always set great store) had said that he should be wary of Saint-Germain.' The whole court decamped at once and 'took up residence [6 March] for a few days at the Hôtel de Retz in the Faubourg Saint-Honoré and from there removed [on 8 March] to Vincennes, where the air was better [Charles was ill], where they were safe and where they took good care of the Duke d'Alençon, the King of Navarre and the Prince de Condé, who were kept openly as prisoners.' Both d'Alençon and Henry feared for their lives and published statements (Henry's was written by Marguerite: see her *Mémoires*, 185–94) proclaiming their innocence of any involvement in a treasonable plot to murder Charles and Catherine and set d'Alençon on the throne. Many moderate nobles took fright and left Paris. Catherine did not dare to move against Henry and d'Alençon but instead ordered the trial of La Mole, Coconnas, and the astrologer, Ruggieri (11 April), hoping that it would unveil the plot. She communicated secretly with the judges, insisting that they concentrate on a certain wax figure which will loom large in Dumas's version of events.

402 *Beaulieu*: Lestoile (*Mémoires-Journaux*, vi. 337) records in May 1594 that the governor of the Château de Vincennes was at that time Baulieu (*sic*), a captain.

404 *Pont-Neuf*: an anachronism. Building of the Pont-Neuf began on 31 May 1578 and continued until 1603.

410 *Laguesle*: Jean de La Guesle, *sieur* de La Chaux (d. 1589), a long-serving *procureur* (prosecutor), was one of the judges in the case.

413 *word for word*: Claude Schopp (*La Reine Margot*, 473 n.) identifies the source of this letter in the *Mémoires* of the Duke de Nevers, where it is dated 29 April. The text has been heavily doctored. In particular, the involvement of Ruggieri has been removed: his role in events is played by René.

416 *arrested*: the chief witness against La Mole and Coconnas was Cosmo Ruggieri. For his part in the affair, he was sent to the galleys. 'The Queen Mother, very credulous in Matters of Divination and Sorcerers, released him some time after to make use of him in his Art' (Mézeray, *Chronological History*, 729).

418 *end of their interrogations*: La Mole and Coconnas were not, of course, allowed to communicate. Dumas, who never missed an opportunity for a good prison scene, was not a man to be halted by technicalities of this sort.

from Paris: Nancy is 300 km (75 leagues) from Paris.

421 *near Suza*: now just inside the French border, 40 km east of Turin. San Colombano lies 20 km to the south-east. Coconnas's birth and origins are an invention: see List of Historical Characters.

424 *a small waxen figure*: 'At La Mole's was found an image of Wax, which one Cosmo Ruggieri, a Florentine and famous Quack, had made for him to charm a young Damsel with whom he was in love. The Queen Mother would have it be believed that it was made on purpose to bewitch the King: he denied it stiffly' (Mézeray, *Chronological History*, 728–9). The model was of Marguerite. It was made by Ruggieri (*pace* p. 315) for the superstitious La Mole to win her heart, though he had been her lover since January.

425 *Châtelet*: both a prison and the capital's main centre for the administration of criminal justice. It was situated on the right bank of the Seine near the Pont-au-Change. It began as a fortress in 1130 and was demolished in 1802.

427 *Saint-Jean-en-Grève*: the place de Grève, named after the church of Saint-Jean close by, had been a place of execution since 1310 and remained so throughout the *ancien régime*. The first guillotine was erected there in April 1792. It was renamed the Place de l'Hôtel de Ville in 1806.

430 *prince of the blood*: 'La Mole, a Favourite to the Duke of Alençon, and the Count de Coconnas an Italian, whom he had lately introduced to the Acquaintance and Confidence of that Prince, were arrested. The first denied All, the other, flatter'd with the vain hopes of getting his Pardon, and a great Reward besides, told a great deal more than indeed he knew' (Mézeray, *Chronological History*, 728). Coconnas revealed not a plot to assassinate the King, as Catherine had expected, but the plan to enable Henry and d'Alençon to escape to join Louis de Nassau at Sedan. He also implicated the Malcontents, Montmorency and Cossé, who were not executed but kept prisoners in the Bastille.

433 *our visit*: see pp. 167–8.

436 *Pope Clement*: Jules de Medicis (1478–1534), a rather distant uncle, became Pope in 1523.

priest entered: in her *Mémoires* (pp. 40–1), Marguerite conceals her genuine love for La Mole and tells a different story. 'Realizing that, if La Mole and the Comte de Coconnas were to die, [Henry and d'Alençon] would be accused of crimes which would put their lives in jeopardy, I resolved . . . to save their lives at the expense of my fortune. Since I came and went freely in my coach without the sentries once looking inside it or asking for the masks worn by my women to be removed, I thought I might disguise one of the prisoners as a woman and drive him out in my coach: because they could not both escape, being too closely watched by their jailers, and because it would be enough for one of them to be outside to ensure that the life of the other would be saved. Yet they could not agree which of them should go, each wishing to be that one and neither wishing to remain. Thus it proved impossible to implement the plan.' The masks Marguerite mentions were then in fashion with ladies of quality.

436 *in the morning*: both torture and execution took place on 30 April 1574.

438 *Farewell, youth, love, life!*: a sentiment less resonant of 1574 than of 1845, when doomed Romantic heroes (which is how Dumas presents La Mole) played the game of love and (invariably) lost with style.

441 *from his body*: 'La Mole was taken to the Place de Grève where, with much weeping and screaming, he had his head cut off and was quartered. Coconnas likewise, still warning the King of the traps set beneath his feet' (d'Aubigné, *Histoire universelle*, Bk. VII, p. 202). Lestoile (*Registre-journal*, i. 257) recalled that La Mole was too weak to kiss the cross and reported his last words: 'God and the blessed Virgin have mercy on my soul! Recommend me to the good graces of the Queen of Navarre and her ladies.' Coconnas died well, saying that 'great Captains should always die bravely in the service of greater men who, at the last, would triumph'.

445 *to the Louvre*: see Ch. 16.

448 *I swear to you*: the connivance of Caboche is a Dumas touch. As René informed Catherine on p. 181, an 'arrangement' with the axeman was more than possible: cf. p. 445.

an oratory: cf. *Le Divorce satirique* (published in the *Recueil de pièces servant à l'histoire de Henri III* (1666, p. 191): 'La Mole left his head at Saint-Jean-en-Grève, together with that of Coconnas: neither head was left to moulder or remain exposed to the gaze of the people for long. For as night fell, my noble lady the Queen Marguerite and Madame de Nevers, her companion and faithful lover of Coconnas, having ordered them to be gathered up, carried them off in their carriages and buried them with their own hands in the Chapel of Saint-Martin.' Though Marguerite's action is well documented, Dumas could not resist adding her to the number of similarly inclined Romantic heroines: like Mathilde in Stendhal's

Le Rouge et le Noir or Keats's Isabella, who stored her lover's head in a pot of basil.

two years and a half previously: Dumas has at last caught up with history, though the date given on the next page is a slip for 30 April.

smile upon my lips: Brantôme (*Recueil*, 314) recalls that 'on the day a noble Lord her suitor died, she appeared in the Queen's apartment with a face as gay and smiling as the day before.' However, Marguerite's public grief so touched the popular imagination that she was henceforth known to Parisians as 'La Reine Margot'. La Mole was neither the first nor last of her lovers who met violent deaths. She had been the mistress of Martigues, who was killed at the siege of Saint-Jean-d'Angely in 1569, and would love Bussy d'Amboise, murdered in 1579.

449 *change of air*: Charles IX arrived at Vincennes on 8 March: see note to p. 401. Dumas omits all reference to the continuing political struggle which saw Catholics win another triumph. The Protestant commander, Montgomery, captured when Domfront fell on 27 May, was given a well-publicized trial and execution on 26 June.

the nurse appeared: Charles IX remained attached to his plain-speaking nurse. According to Lestoile (*Registre-journal*, i. 252), she stayed at his bedside and, when Charles wept for the blood shed during his reign, she gave him a handkerchief, saying: 'for the honour of God, your Majesty must stop all this weeping and fretting lest it make you more ill, which is the greatest misfortune which could befall your people and us all.'

his own person: see p. 360.

of the skin: 'Nature did struggle most wonderfully during the two last Weeks of this King's life, he started and stretched himself with extream violence, he tossed and tumbled incessantly, the Blood burst out of every Pore, and from every channel of his Body. After he had suffered thus a long time, he sunk into a weak and fainting condition, and gave up his Soul between the third and fourth hour Afternoon, on the Thirtieth day of May, being the Pentecost.' (Mézeray, *Chronological History*, 729.) Charles's brother, François II, had also been disfigured by red blotches which were probably caused by eczema. But the cutaneous haemorrhaging mentioned here (a form of purpura) was probably a symptom of consumption. An autopsy performed the following day concluded that he had died of natural causes, though rumours that he had been poisoned circulated widely.

450 *no other brother*: 'one of the strongest indications of the [imminent] death of this King was that when the Queen Mother entered his chamber with a glee and a joy which had never been remarked in her before, to announce the capture of Montgomery, he turned his head the other way . . . Just before he died, he commended the Queen his wife and his daughter [Marie-Elizabeth], and of everything he said this was the last: "That he rejoiced that he left no heir, knowing that France needed a man and that when governed by a child both King and Kingdom are unhappy". He desired to embrace and speak to the Duke d'Alençon and the King of Navarre, but when they were brought it was seen that he was unable to speak' (D'Aubigné, *Histoire universelle*, Bk. VII, p. 221).

451 *Fatality!*: Dumas signals Catherine's defeat and, in so doing, defines the real drama as human, not political.

452 *about the regency*: Salic law debarred the young Marie-Elizabeth from the throne. Before he died, Charles IX named the King of Poland as his successor and Catherine as regent until his return.

454 *been a prisoner*: Henry and d'Alençon had been at Vincennes for nearer three months, since early March.

455 *of which history speaks*: or rather legend, which has perpetuated many of the accusations (that she used poison and other foul deeds as political weapons) levelled against her during her lifetime. Louis XIII, her grandson, was convinced that she had poisoned Charles IX.

not greatly loved: Charles was sincerely mourned by his devout wife and by Marguerite. But most shared Hume's (*History of England* (1789), vii. 81) judgement of 'a prince, whose character, containing that unusual mixture of dissimulation and ferocity, of quick resentment and unrelenting vengeance, executed the greatest mischief'.

457 *no real authority*: the wars of religion were set to continue. Condé escaped to Germany in 1574, where he publicly announced his return to the Huguenot faith (as did Henry of Navarre in 1576, despite Charles's advice on p. 457) and set about raising an army to defend it. Guise emerged as head of the Catholic League in 1576 while Henry III defended his throne against both sectarian factions. Civil strife and religious intolerance were not ended until Henry of Navarre, as Henry IV, enacted the Edict of Nantes in 1598.

460 *I come!*: d'Aubigné, an eye-witness, recalls no such last words: see note to p. 450.

461 *Henry the Third!*: Dumas's denouement, like the Epilogue which follows, is exciting but entirely fictitious. Catherine did not dispatch couriers to Poland by three different routes. Immediately the King was dead, she sent a delegation with the news. On 3 June she sent a second, which arrived on 17 June, asking him to return at once. Henry did not ride off to join his Huguenot supporters but remained a virtual prisoner at court with d'Alençon: he escaped in February 1576, d'Alençon having got away in September 1575. D'Anjou left Warsaw on 18 June, the day after receiving Catherine's letter, having been King of Poland for five months. Though eager to flee the Poles, who were incensed, he relaxed once across the border. Reaching Vienna on 24 June, he progressed slowly, reaching Venice on 18 July, Cremona in August, Lyons in September, Avignon in November, and did not make his entry to Paris until 10 January 1575. He was crowned on 13 February. In his absence, Catherine followed the wishes of Charles IX and ruled the country as regent.

Notre-Dame de Cléry: but not in 1575. Henry III (when still d'Anjou) had made the pilgrimage to Notre-Dame de Cléry (14 km south-west of Orléans) in July 1573 to fulfil a vow to give thanks for the protection of the Virgin, who had saved him from an arquebuse bullet during the siege of La Rochelle.

462 *la Fosseuse*: Françoise de Montmorency, fifth daughter of the Baron de Fosseux, one of many women who, remarked Brantôme (*Recueil*, 64), while they could use 'their free will to be as loving as Venus or as chaste as Diana, had common sense, skill and knowledge enough to enable them to avoid any swelling of the belly'. La Fosseuse was part of Marguerite's entourage at Pau and Nérac in 1579–80: only then did she become Henry's mistress. She was 'beautiful, very child-like and good-natured', wrote Marguerite (*Mémoires*, 162).

was with him: shortly after the execution of La Mole, Marguerite left the court, travelled in the south, and did not see Henry again until Catherine reunited them in 1578.

Hotel de Soissons: Catherine's grand town house, on the east side of the Rue de Grenelle (see map). Begun in 1574, it was bought by the Comte de Soissons in 1606 when it began to be known as the Hôtel de Soissons.

to see Madame de Sauve: Henry's romantic love for Charlotte de Sauve is another fiction. In 1574, she was the mistress at court simultaneously of Henry of Navarre, d'Alençon, the Duke de Guise, and du Guast.

466 *Barrière des Sergents*: a guard-house standing in the middle of the Rue Saint-Honoré just opposite the Rue du Coq.

467 *died instantly*: but not in 1575. The episode is based on Lestoile's *Registre-journal*, at 14 April 1583: 'The Seigneur de Mouy, who had sought every means possible to come upon Maurevel with advantage, so that he might avenge the death of his father, treacherously killed at Niort in 1569, encountered him at the Croix-des-Petits-Champs, near the Church of Saint-Honoré, and faced him, sword in hand. Maurevel, firing a shot at him and missing, retreated towards the Barrière des Sergents. Because he had only one arm, he was unable to draw his weapon, so hotly was he pursued by Mouy, and took two or three sword thrusts, by one of which he was pierced from the lower belly to his left nipple. . . . Thinking he must die of the wounds he had inflicted on him, though he was still on his feet, retreating and parrying as he went, [Mouy] chased him [along] the Rue Saint-Honoré and had come so close upon him that he had his blade at his throat and was about to cut it for him, when one of Maurevel's men (for in this business they were nine or ten on each side), taking aim at Mouy with a musketoon, shot him fatally. For the bullet entered his mouth, shattering his lower jaw and severing his tongue, then traversed his brain and emerged at the back of his head. He fell down dead. The young *seigneur* de Saucourt, who fought for Mouy, his relation and good friend, took a shot in the thigh which broke the bone and cut the vein, and died soon after. Maurevel died the following night, mourned by none and loathed by all. Even the Royal Princes, who as long as he lived had shown him favour and given him money, were mightily relieved that such an assassin had been expelled from this world.'

468 *fell back lifeless*: Charlotte de Sauve, who is not known to have had an avenging husband, outlived Henry and died in 1617.

into the darkness: Henry ends as a Romantic stereotype: the great leader who, heroically alone like Moses in Vigny's poem, is doomed to face a destiny of greatness.

The Oxford World's Classics Website

www.worldsclassics.co.uk

- Information about new titles
- Explore the full range of Oxford World's Classics
- Links to other literary sites and the main OUP webpage
- Imaginative competitions, with bookish prizes
- Peruse *Compass*, the Oxford World's Classics magazine
- Articles by editors
- Extracts from Introductions
- A forum for discussion and feedback on the series
- Special information for teachers and lecturers

www.worldsclassics.co.uk

American Literature

British and Irish Literature

Children's Literature

Classics and Ancient Literature

Colonial Literature

Eastern Literature

European Literature

History

Medieval Literature

Oxford English Drama

Poetry

Philosophy

Politics

Religion

The Oxford Shakespeare

A complete list of Oxford Paperbacks, including Oxford World's Classics, OPUS, Past Masters, Oxford Authors, Oxford Shakespeare, Oxford Drama, and Oxford Paperback Reference, is available in the UK from the Academic Division Publicity Department, Oxford University Press, Great Clarendon Street, Oxford OX2 6DP.

In the USA, complete lists are available from the Paperbacks Marketing Manager, Oxford University Press, 198 Madison Avenue, New York, NY 10016.

Oxford Paperbacks are available from all good bookshops. In case of difficulty, customers in the UK can order direct from Oxford University Press Bookshop, Freepost, 116 High Street, Oxford OX1 4BR, enclosing full payment. Please add 10 per cent of published price for postage and packing.